出版说明

人类历史的发展过程也是思想文化不断积累和沉淀的过程。在几千年的人类历史发展长河中，先贤们或在人文社科领域，或在科学技术领域创作出了无数经典名著。这些著作所蕴藏的思想财富和学术价值，早已为世人所熟知，它们无不体现了作者所处的特定时代的思想和文化。通过这些经典名著，读者不仅可以欣赏到流畅的文笔、生动的描述和详细的刻画、深邃的思想，更可以领悟它们各自独特的历史与文化内涵。可以说，这些作品深深地影响了世世代代的读者，也引导着当今的学人以此来充实和丰富自己的头脑。有鉴于此，我们邀请了专门研究世界历史文化的专家学者，精心挑选代表世界历史文化不同领域的经典作品，采取英汉双语对照的形式出版，一方面为读者提供原汁原味的世界经典名著，让读者自由地阅读，在此过程中逐渐提升自己的英语水平；另一方面通过这种阅读，以达到对世界历史文化的整体了解，开阔自己的视野，打开通往世界的心灵之窗，同时又获得思想文化、个人修养、伦理道德等多方面的提升。

我们衷心期待这套书成为大家学习道路上不可或缺的好伙伴！如果您在阅读中发现有疑问或错误之处，请不吝指正，以便我们更加完善这套书。

希利尔讲艺术史

（英汉双语）

［美］希利尔⊙著　欧阳瑾⊙译

A CHILD'S HISTORY OF ART

北京工业大学出版社

图书在版编目（CIP）数据

希利尔讲艺术史：英汉对照 /（美）希利尔著；欧阳瑾译. — 北京：北京工业大学出版社，2017.7

ISBN 978-7-5639-5254-0

Ⅰ. ①希…　Ⅱ. ①希… ②欧…　Ⅲ. ①英语 – 汉语 – 对照读物 ②艺术史 – 世界 – 通俗读物　Ⅳ. ①H319.4：J

中国版本图书馆CIP数据核字（2017）第060432号

希利尔讲艺术史（英汉双语）

著　　者：［美］希利尔
译　　者：欧阳瑾
责任编辑：石嫣飞　曹　媛
封面设计：同人阁文化传媒 · 书装设计
出版发行：北京工业大学出版社
（北京市朝阳区平乐园100号　邮编：100124）
010–67391722（传真）bgdcbs@sina.com
出 版 人：郝　勇
经销单位：全国各地新华书店
承印单位：大厂回族自治县正兴印务有限公司
开　　本：787毫米 × 1092毫米　1/16
印　　张：30
字　　数：684千字
版　　次：2017年7月第1版
印　　次：2017年7月第1次印刷
标准书号：ISBN 978-7-5639-5254-0
定　　价：49.80元

FOREWORD
前 言

The Child's History of Art books were developed by Virgil M. Hillyer and completed by Edward G. Huey. Baltimore's Calvert School and its students constituted Hillyer's life work. Hillyer grew up in Weymouth, Massachusetts. Two years after graduating from Harvard in 1897, he took on what would become the defining challenge of his professional life. As a young man of only twenty- four years, he became Head Master of seventy-one students at Calvert School and embarked on a career filled with innovation and forward thinking.

Within the first few years of Hillyer's leadership, the student body had grown so large that a new building was built. It was a model of educational planning designed to suit the needs of students, with an assembly room for plays and ceremonies, an art room, and a roof garden for fresh air and exercise. It was also during the early years of Calvert School's history, in 1906, that Hillyer envisioned and began the Home Instruction program, which is still educating thousands of children around the world.

Hillyer was a visionary in many ways. Always a teacher at heart, he was responsible for establishing the educational principles and practices still in place today at Calvert School. By the time classes began to be held in the third and present building in 1924, he was a respected author of educational philosophy and children's histories, including the Child's History of Art series. He was also a world traveler, a mentor for his teachers, and a

《少儿艺术史》系列图书，系维吉尔·希利尔开发出来，并由爱德华·休伊最终完成的。巴尔的摩的卡尔弗特学校，以及该校的学生，构成了希利尔毕生为之奋斗的事业。希利尔是在马萨诸塞州的韦茅斯长大的。1897年，他毕业于哈佛大学；两年后，他便开始从事这种后来成了他职业生涯中的一种决定性挑战的职业了。当时，虽说还是个年仅二十四岁的小伙子，他却成了卡尔弗特学校那七十一名学生的校长，开始了一种充满了创新性和前瞻性思维的职业。

在希利尔担任校长的最初几年里，由于学生人数规模激增，所以卡尔弗特学校还修建了一栋新的教学楼。这栋大楼是一种典范，体现了旨在满足学生需要的教学规划：里面有一座用于演出和庆典的礼堂，有一间美术教室，还有一个用于呼吸新鲜空气、进行体育锻炼的屋顶花园。也正是在卡尔弗特学校历史的初期，即1906年，希利尔构想出并开始实施其“家庭教育”大纲；而直到如今，世界各地仍有成千上万的孩子，在根据这一大纲接受教育呢。

从许多方面来看，希利尔都是一个非常有远见的人。虽说本质上始终都是一位教师，但他需要负责制定教学方针和课程；而这些方针和课程，如今在卡尔弗特学校里依然能够看到。到了1924年，学校开始在第三栋，也就是目前这栋教学楼内上课的时候，他已经是一位令人敬重的作者，写出了许多关于教育理念和少儿历史的书籍，其中就包括这套《少儿艺术史》系列。他还是一位环球旅行家，是手下教师们的良师益友，并且成了教育理论界的一位领军人物。在长达三十二年的校长生涯

leader in educational theory. During his thirty-two years as Head Master, Virgil Hillyer led Calvert School with enthusiasm and principles that continue to inspire students today.

Edward G. Huey held the positions of teacher and Assistant Head Master from 1924 until 1959. Considered to be one of Calvert School's most unforgettable teachers, Huey taught science and art and ran the assembly programs. He often drew pictures for students at lunch and recess. Huey, a teacher with much imagination and talent, had worked with Hillyer for seven years, and upon the death of Hillyer, he completed the Child's History of Art books in Hillyer's own style.

While carrying out the most recent revision of the Child's History of Art series, Calvert was fortunate to have the Walters Art Museum as a wonderful resource. William Thompson Walters amassed an extensive collection of French art of the nineteenth century and Asian decorative arts that became the foundation for the development of the Walters Art Museum.

Walters was born in a small town in Pennsylvania in 1819. With no formal education, he was trained as a metallurgist but moved to Baltimore as a young man in search of fortune. In the booming business world of mid-nineteenth century Baltimore, Walters prospered as a businessman through railroad investments. Walters opened his house several times a year to visitors for a fee, bringing his art to the public. The fees were donated to charity, and these annual openings became quite popular.

When William Walters died in 1894, his son, Henry, carried on his interest in art and expanded the scope of the collection. During the time Hillyer was bringing innovative

里，维吉尔·希利尔一直富有激情、满怀信念地领导着卡尔弗特学校；而这些激情和信念，如今仍然在继续激励着该校的学生们。

从1924年到1959年，爱德华·休伊先后担任过卡尔弗特学校的老师和校长助理等职务。他被人们认为是卡尔弗特学校最令人难忘的教师之一，既教授过科学和艺术课程，也负责学校的课程汇编工作。他经常在午餐时间和课后给学生们画画。休伊是个富有想象力和天才的人，他与希利尔共事了七年的时间；而希利尔去世之后，他又用希利尔本人的风格，完成了《少儿艺术史》系列教材的编纂。

在最近对《少儿艺术史》系列教材进行改版的过程中，卡尔弗特学校有幸得到了沃尔特斯艺术博物馆的鼎力支持；这座博物馆，是一种令人觉得不可思议的资源。威廉·汤普森·沃尔特斯收集了大量的十九世纪法国艺术品和亚洲的装饰艺术品；这些藏品，为他后来成立沃尔特斯艺术博物馆打下了基础。

1819年，沃尔特斯出生于宾夕法尼亚州的一个小镇上。他没有受过正规的教育，只是通过培训成了一名冶金学家；不过，他在年轻的时候便移居到了巴尔的摩，去寻找发迹的机会了。在十九世纪中叶百业正兴的巴尔的摩，他通过投资铁路而发迹，成了一名业务兴隆的生意人。沃尔特斯每年都会敞开家门几次，让人们前来付费参观，向公众介绍自己收藏的那些艺术品。由此获得的门票收入，他都捐赠给了慈善机构；而每年进行的这种开放，也受到了公众的热烈欢迎。

1894年威廉·沃尔特斯去世后，他的儿子继承了父亲在艺术方面的兴趣，并将藏品的范围扩大了。就在希利尔将那些新颖的教育理念引入卡尔弗特学校的同时，

ideas to education at Calvert School, Henry Walters was beginning a three-decade period of purchasing art representing Old Kingdom Egypt to Art Nouveau. In 1931, the Walters' home and contents were bequeathed to the city of Baltimore, and the Walters Art Gallery, now the Walters Art Museum, opened to the public in 1934.

For those of you who are planning to visit Calvert School — the school that developed through the vision of Virgil Hillyer — we recommend that you also visit the Walters Art Museum, whose founders believed that a museum was a place of learning for people of all ages and that a great community needed — along with great schools, libraries, symphonies, and theaters — great museums.

Calvert School was assisted in the revision of the Child's History of Art series by two experienced teachers. John Patterson first began his career as a teacher at Calvert School. He credits Calvert with providing the framework and foundation for his vocation as an educator. With a lifelong love of art, he has traveled extensively with his students to see works of art firsthand. Elana Vikan is a high school teacher of art history at a local private school. She has studied and traveled abroad on academic programs that helped expand her knowledge of art, languages, and culture.

Together John Patterson and Elana Vikan have drawn upon their experience as they edited and updated the text first written by Hillyer and Huey. We are grateful for their expertise and that of the Walters Art Museum and its staff, particularly of Gary Vikan, its director.

亨利·沃尔特斯则开始了一段长达三十年的收购活动，并且得到了许多代表着古埃及王国到新艺术派风格的艺术品。1931年，沃尔特斯家族的房子和藏品全都遗赠给了巴尔的摩市；到了1934年，原来的沃尔特斯美术馆，即如今的沃尔特斯艺术博物馆，便向公众开放了。

对于你们当中那些正准备前去参观卡尔弗特学校，准备前去参观这所通过维吉尔·希利尔的远见而创立起来的学校的人来说，我们的建议是，你们不妨也去参观参观沃尔特斯艺术博物馆。这座博物馆的创始人认为，博物馆是男女老少都可以学习的地方；而一个伟大的社会，除了需要了不起的学校、图书馆、交响乐和剧院，也需要了不起的博物馆。

有两位经验丰富的教师，协助了卡尔弗特学校对《少儿艺术史》系列所进行的修订工作。约翰·帕特森起初本是卡尔弗特学校的一名老师，并由此开始其职业生涯。他认为，卡尔弗特学校为他提供了从事教育工作的架构和基础。由于终生热爱艺术，所以他曾一次又一次地带着学生们到处旅行，实地去参观各种各样的艺术作品。伊兰娜·威肯是本地一所私立学校里的高中艺术史教师。她在国外留过学，并且曾为完成学术项目而到国外考察过；这些经历，帮助她开拓了在艺术、语言和文化领域里的知识面。

在编辑、更新希利尔和休伊两人最初所撰内容的过程中，约翰·帕特森和伊兰娜·威肯一起，都充分利用了各自的经历。我们感谢这两人的专业知识，感谢沃尔特斯艺术博物馆及其员工，尤其是要感谢博物馆馆长加里·威肯。

目录 Contents

SCULPTURE
雕塑篇

Painting
绘画篇

Architecture
建筑篇

SCULPTURE

雕塑篇

Chapter 1 The First Sculpture

When I was in kindergarten, I used to make a bird's nest with round eggs and a bird sitting on top out of clay. Perhaps you have made something similar. That was sculpture, but I didn't know it.

When I was older, in the winter I used to make a snowman with a scarf around his neck, two pieces of coal for eyes, and a carrot for a nose. That was sculpture too, although I didn't know it.

When I was still older, I used to take the soft part of a piece of doughy bread and shape it into a dog with a head, a tail, and feet. That was sculpture, although I didn't know it. My mother didn't know it either, so she sent me to my room for playing with my food.

So I was a sculptor until I was twelve years old — and I have never been a sculptor since.

But other boys and girls did not stop being sculptors when they became young men and women. Once upon a time a boy in a kitchen carved a lion out of a piece of butter and sent it to the table. He became a great sculptor when he grew up. His name was Canova1. I'll tell you about him later.

People have made sculpture ever since the world was young. But at first the sculpture

第1章　第一尊雕像

上幼儿园的时候，我曾经用陶土做过一个鸟窝，其中摆着几枚圆乎乎的鸟蛋，还有一只小鸟趴在上面呢。没准，你们以前也做过类似的什么东西。其实，那就是雕塑；可在当时，我却不知道。

长大了一点儿之后，我在冬天经常会堆上一个雪人，给雪人的脖子挂上围巾，用两块煤炭做眼睛，再用一根胡萝卜做鼻子。其实，那也是一种雕塑；可在当时，我却不知道。

再大一点之后，我又经常用半熟的面包上那软软的一部分做成一只小狗；做出的小狗，既有脑袋、尾巴，也有脚。其实，那也是一种雕塑；可在当时，我并不知道这一点。我的母亲也不知道，所以她会因为我拿着吃的东西玩而罚我回自己的房间去。

因此，在十二岁之前，我都是一名雕塑家；可从那以后，我却再也没有当过雕塑家了。

不过，还有一些男孩子和女孩子，他们直到长大成小伙子、小姑娘之后，都没有停止过当雕塑家呢。曾经有一个男孩，他在厨房里用黄油雕出了一头狮子，然后将它送到了餐桌上。长大以后，他就变成了一名伟大的雕塑家。这个小男孩，名叫卡诺瓦[1]。我在后面会再跟你们介绍他的情况的。

从地球还很年轻的时候起，人们就已经开始制作雕塑了。不过，人们起初制

---

[1] 卡诺瓦（Antonio Canova，1757—1822），意大利古典主义雕塑家，他的作品标志着雕塑艺术从戏剧性的巴洛克时代进入了更加精细的古典主义时代。

that people made was not very different from drawing. The artist first drew his picture on something flat. Then he carved the lines deeper so that, if it were outside, the rain would not wash the drawing away and the weather would not wear it down. This kind of drawing or sculpture is called *sunken relief.*

These sunken-relief drawings have been found in different places around the world, like Peru where pilots flew over them and were quite surprised when they looked down at the ground and saw a whole collection.

Then after that, sculptors rounded the edges of the figures they had carved and cut away some of the background so that the figures stood out a little. This is called *low relief,* or *bas-relief.*

You may have a bas-relief in your pocket right now and not even know it. A penny, nickel, dime, or another coin, medal, or medallion that has figures on it is a bas-relief.

Then sculptors began to round the figure still more and cut away still more of the background so that the figure stood out more. This is called *high relief,* for the figures are halfway out of the background.

Later sculptors cut away the background entirely so that the figure stood out all by itself. This is called *in-the-round* because you can go around it. You will see such pieces of sculpture of men or animals in parks, public squares, and museums.

尼罗河谷地中菲莱神庙的神殿大门
（摄影：加里·威肯）

作的雕塑，与绘画并没有太大的不同。艺术家先是把画在某种非常平坦的东西上绘制下来。然后，他会再将画中的线条刻得深一点儿；这样，哪怕位于室外，雨水也不会把这幅画洗去，而日晒风吹也不会将其湮灭了。这种绘画或者雕塑，称为“凹浮雕”。

这种陷浮雕式的绘画，在世界各地都有发现，比如秘鲁；当飞行员们驾驶飞机飞过这些绘画的上空，往下俯瞰，看到地面上有很多的图画时，都曾惊讶不已呢。

接下来，雕塑家会将自己雕刻出来的图案的边缘打磨圆整，并且切掉一部分背景，从而使得图案稍稍向外凸出来。这种雕塑，就叫“浅浮雕”，或者叫“基线浮雕”。

注意，你们的口袋里可能就有一件基线浮雕，可你们却浑然不知呢。一分钱的、五分钱的、一角钱的硬币或者其他面值的硬币，以及上面刻有图案的纪念章或者大奖牌，都是一种基线浮雕。

接下来，雕塑家开始继续打磨图案，再把更多的背景部分切掉，从而使得图案更加向外凸出。这种雕塑，因为图案的一半都已经凸出于背景之外了，所以就叫“高浮雕”。

再后来，雕塑家们又将背景部分彻底切除，从而使得图案完全独立地凸出来了。这种雕塑，也叫“圆雕”，因为你们可以绕着雕塑的四周去欣赏。你们在公园里、广场上和博物馆里，都会看到这种人物或者动物的圆雕。

Long before the time of Christ, ancient Egyptian artists carved pictures in sunken relief on the walls of their great buildings, such as the Great Temple Gates of the Temple of Philae.

In these sunken reliefs, some figures are sitting and some are standing. All of them may look peculiar to you. Do you know why? They have two things quite unusual about them — two things quite impossible and several things very peculiar.

Here is the first thing: The feet are stepping directly sideways and the faces are all turned sideways too, but the shoulders appear as they are viewed from the front. Now of course, no one really walks that way, with head and feet sideways and shoulders in front view. So the first unusual thing is that the figure is twisted.

The second thing is the eye. What you see is the side of a face — not the front. Yet the eye appears as you would see it from the front, not from the side. All the Egyptian reliefs had the same peculiarly shaped eye and the same twisted bodies. Shoulders and eye are front view while everything else — hips, legs, and feet — are side view.

Can you guess why the Egyptians put the front and side view of a person together? Some say it was a way to show all the important parts of the body doing what they do best — legs walking, eyes looking, and shoulders and chest facing forward.

But there are other strange things to notice about these figures. The man and woman have very little clothing on and, although they are king and queen, they are barefooted. That's because Egypt is a very warm country. In some warm countries even today neither rich nor poor wear shoes and socks. I once went to a dinner party in one of these warm

早在基督降生很久以前，古埃及的艺术家们就在他们那些伟大建筑的墙壁上，用凹浮雕的方式雕刻出了许多图案；比如，菲莱神庙中的神殿大门就是如此。

在这些凹浮雕中，有些人物是坐着的，有些人物则是站立着的。看上去，你们会觉得这些人物图案都古怪得很。知道这是为什么吗？因为在这些图案上，有两个方面都极其异常，也就是说，有两种极其不可能出现的情况；此外，还有几个地方也很古怪。

第一个方面就是，虽说图中人物的双脚都是径直朝着侧面，脸部也全都是朝向侧面，可人物的肩膀却似乎是我们从正面看去的样子。注意，如今是没有人会真的用那种方式走路的，不会是脑袋和双脚侧着，而肩膀却对着正前方地走路。因此，这些浮雕上第一个异常的方面，就是人物图案被扭曲了。

第二个方面就是眼睛。你们在图案上看到的，是一张侧脸，而不是正脸。可图案上的眼睛却让你们觉得，它们似乎是从正面而不是从侧面看上去的样子。所有的古埃及浮雕上，人物都有着这种形状古怪的眼睛和同样扭曲的身体呢。这些浮雕人物的肩膀和眼睛都是朝着前面，而其他的一切，包括臀部、双腿和双脚，却都是朝着侧面。

你们能够猜出，古埃及人为什么要把一个人物的正面像和侧面像糅合到一起吗？有些人认为，这是为了表现出身体各个最重要的部分最擅长的功能，即腿是用来走路的，眼睛是用来看的，而肩膀和胸膛则是朝着正前方的。

不过，这些人物图案上，还有其他一些古怪之处，值得我们去注意。浮雕中的人物不论男女，身上都不怎么穿衣服，并且尽管他们都是国王、王后，却都是光着脚的。那是因为，埃及是一个非常炎热的国家。在一些气候炎热的国家里，即便是

countries and all of the ladies and gentlemen were barefooted. It seemed very peculiar to see the ladies and gentlemen, all gorgeously dressed and wearing many rich jewels, go to the table barefooted!

But to make up for having little ornamentation on their bodies, these Egyptian figures have a lot on their heads — not hats but crowns. These crowns mean something. The woman's crown — she is a queen — looks like a bird cap. The bird is the vulture that feeds only on dead bodies. Above the vulture cap is a moon between two horns. The man's double crown — he is a king — is called a *pschent*. These figures are all sunken relief.

The next kind of relief is called low relief, or bas-relief. The sculpture on the following page of the goddess Isis — the famous goddess of ancient Egypt — is a good example of this type. It shows the goddess Isis sitting. She is wearing a headdress and you can see the shape of the eye and the details of the headdress very clearly. In her left hand she carries a rod, or scepter, to show she is a queen. In her right hand is a strange object called an ankh, an Egyptian symbol of enduring life. The peculiar designs at the top of this illustration are a type of picture writing called hieroglyphics.

The third type of relief is high relief, of which the Temple at Abu Simbel is a good example. It has four huge figures on the front. They are almost cut away from the background but not quite. These figures are colossal — that means gigantic, huge, or mammoth. A real person standing beside one wouldn't reach halfway to the knee.

The Egyptians liked to make giant figures. Notice also that these giant figures are seated in a very stiff position, sitting upright with both feet flat on the ground and both hands

到了今天，富人和穷人也都是不穿鞋子和袜子的呢。我曾经在一个炎热的国家里参加过一场晚宴，席上所有的贵妇、绅士，全都光着脚。看到这些贵妇绅士个个都穿着华丽、戴着许多贵重的珠宝首饰，却光着脚去参加宴会，感觉似乎古怪得很哩！

不过，为了弥补身上几乎没有什么装饰的缺陷，这些古埃及的人物图案里，人物头上却都装饰着很多的东西：不是帽子，而是王冠。那些王冠，都具有某种含义。女性的王冠看上去像是一顶鸟形的帽子，表明她是王后。这种鸟，就是专吃腐尸的秃鹫。而这顶秃鹫帽子的上方，还有一轮处于两个兽角之间的月亮。男性的双层王冠，叫作双重王冠，表明他是一位国王。这些人物形象，全都属于凹浮雕。

第二种浮雕，叫作浅浮雕，或者叫基线浮雕。下面这尊伊西斯女神的雕像，就是这种浮雕的典型例子。伊西斯是古埃及的一位著名的女神。她戴着头巾，你们可以很清楚地看到她眼睛的样子和头巾的细部。她的左手持着一根权杖，或者说“节杖”，表明她是一位王后。她的右手握着一种奇怪之物，被称为“十字生命章”，是古埃及象征着不朽生命的标记。而这幅图案上方那些古怪的图形，则是一种叫作“象形文字”的图画文字。

第三种浮雕便是高浮雕，而阿布辛贝神庙则是这种浮雕一个恰当的范例。神庙的前部有四尊巨型的人物雕像。它们差不多与背景完全分离开来了，当然并未彻底与背景分离。这几尊人物雕像都是庞然大物，即极其巨大、硕大、庞大。一个人站在这种雕像边上，连雕像小腿的一半都摸不到呢。

古埃及人很喜欢制作巨型雕像。注意，这些巨型人物雕像的姿态都非常呆板，

古埃及的伊西斯女神像

flat on the knees. They are all figures of the same king, Rameses II. He is also called Rameses the Great, for he was the greatest of all the Egyptian kings though one of the most cruel.

Rameses II was the pharaoh who lived at the time of Exodus, the book from the Bible that tells the story about Moses growing up in Egypt. Rameses honored himself by building temples and statues of himself. He had the Temple at Abu Simbel cut out of a rocky cliff and huge statues of himself made on the front. The statue to the left is the best preserved. That funny thing on his chin is a beard, which the pharaoh would attach to his face with strings for ceremonies.

Thousands of years later, the Temple at Abu Simbel was cut out of the cliffs and moved in order to make way for construction of the Aswan Dam on the Nile River. The skill of placing the temple just right to catch the Sun, which I'll talk about more in the next chapter, has been lost forever. But at least this great temple has been preserved so you can see it if you should ever travel to Egypt.

阿斯旺附近的阿布辛贝神庙
（摄影：加里·威肯）

都是双脚平平地踩在地上，双手平放于膝上，正襟危坐着。它们都是同一位国王，即拉美西斯二世的雕像。拉美西斯二世也被称为拉美西斯大帝，因为他是古埃及所有国王中最伟大的一位，但也是其中最残忍的一位呢。

拉美西斯二世是古埃及的法老[1]，生活在《出埃及记》所描述的那个时代。《出埃及记》是《圣经》的一部分，讲述了摩西[2]在埃及长大成人的经历。拉美西斯给自己建造了许多的神庙和雕像，以此来纪念自己。他命人在悬崖上雕制出了阿布辛贝神庙，并在神庙前部为自己建造了那四尊巨型雕像。最左边的那一尊，如今保存得最为完整。雕像下巴上那种可笑的东西，其实是胡须；举行庆典的时候，法老就会用绳子将这种胡须挂到下巴上。

几千年后，人们将阿布辛贝神庙从悬崖上切割下来挪走了，目的是给尼罗河上修建的阿斯旺大坝让出位置。让整座神庙全都沐浴着阳光的那种技术，已经永远失传了；而在下一章里，我还会再来说一说这种技术的。不过，起码这座神庙被保存下来了；这样，假如你们有一天到埃及去旅游的话，就可以去看一看这座神庙了。

[1] 法老（pharaoh），古埃及君主的称号，在《圣经》中经常用作专有名称。

[2] 摩西（Moses），《圣经》故事中古犹太人的领袖。在《出埃及记》中，摩西曾带领犹太人逃出埃及，摆脱了埃及法老的奴役。

Chapter 2 Giants and Pygmies

Egyptian sculpture in-the-round was usually either gigantic — as tall as a house — or tiny — only an inch or so high. Statues of kings and important people were usually colossal. Egyptians thought a statue the size of an ordinary man or woman was not big enough for a king or a queen.

The biggest statue in the world is the Great Sphinx1, which is near the three Great Pyramids. It is a huge lion with a king's head. The Egyptians liked to combine men and animals in this way, but more often they put an animal's head on a man's body.

A cat's head or a bird's head on a man's body seems most unusual, like a monster, and may even make us shudder. But a man's head on an animal's body seems only a myth and doesn't shock us as much.

The Great Sphinx was supposed to be the god of the morning and so he faces east toward the rising Sun and gazes at it unblinkingly, as he has done each morning for thousands of years. His nose is as tall as a person. The triangular pieces at the sides of his head are not hair; they form a fancy headpiece for ceremonies much like the beard on the pharaoh at the Temple at Abu Simbel. There are many more sphinxes in Egypt, all of which are much smaller than the Great Sphinx. The smaller sphinxes usually were arranged to form an avenue leading up to a temple, with many of them in a double row.

第2章 巨人和侏儒

古埃及的圆雕，往往要么是庞大无比，与房子一般高，要么便是小得很，只有一英寸[1]左右高。历代国王和要人的雕像，通常都是庞然大物。古埃及人认为，一尊普通人大小的雕像，并不足以体现出国王和王后的重要性来。

世界上最大的雕像，就是位于三大金字塔附近的大斯芬克斯这座狮身人面像。那是一尊巨型狮子像，可狮子的脑袋，却是一位国王的模样。古埃及人很喜欢将人和动物用这种方式联结起来；而他们更常见的做法，还是将动物的脑袋安到人的身体之上。

人的身体上安着一只猫或一只鸟儿的脑袋，样子会非常奇特，就像怪物一样，甚至可能会让我们觉得毛骨悚然呢。可将动物的身体安上人的脑袋，看上去却只会具有神秘感，而不会让我们觉得那么震惊了。

大斯芬克斯被古埃及人认为是黎明之神，因此它朝着东方，并且数千年来，每天清晨都毫不眨眼地凝视着日出的方向。它的鼻子，就有一个人那么高哩。它的脑袋两侧那个三角形的东西，并不是头发；它们其实是一种在庆典时所戴的奇特头巾，就跟阿布辛贝神庙那位法老雕塑上的胡须一样。埃及境内还有许多其他的斯芬克斯雕像，但它们都要比大斯芬克斯小得多。这些较小的斯芬克斯雕像，通常都被安放在通往一座神庙的道路两旁，排成两行，并且其中有许多还是排成双行呢。

[1] 英寸（inch），英制长度单位。1 英寸约等于 2.54 厘米。

Farther up the Nile, there are two colossal figures sitting on thrones side-by-side, gazing out over the plain. Because of their colossal size, they are called the Colossi, and each one is made out of a single stone. They are weather-beaten and broken but you do not need much imagination to see in your mind's eye what they once were.

They, of course, are Egyptian kings — or rather two statues of the same king. These two also face the Sun as it rises in the east. One of them is called Mennon, though Mennon was not the king's name. The king's name was Amenhotep.

吉萨的狮身人面像和哈夫拉金字塔
（摄影：加里·威肯）

We do not know the names of many of the sculptors who made ancient statues, but we do know the name of the sculptor who made these statues of Amenhotep, for he had the same name as the king. Perhaps he was a slave, as a slave was often given the name of his master.

It is believed that around 27 B.C., an earthquake upset the

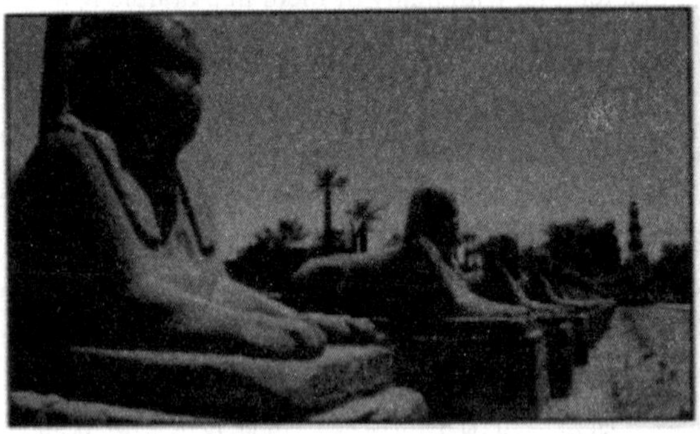

神庙前的狮身人面像大道
（摄影：加里·威肯）

尼罗河上游更远之处，还有两座巨型雕像。它们并排坐在宝座上，眺望着面前的平原。由于尺寸庞大，因此它们被称为“巨像”，而且每一尊巨像都是用一整块石头雕刻而成的。如今，虽说它们因为历经了数千年的日晒雨淋而破碎不堪，但你们不需要太多的想象力，便可以在脑海中想象出它们曾经的样子来。

这两尊雕像，自然也是古埃及国王的雕像，或者说，是同一位国王的两尊雕像。这两尊雕像，同样是面向太阳升起的东方。其中一尊被称为“门农”，但那位国王的名字并不叫“门农”。那位国王，名叫“阿蒙霍特普”。

虽说关于雕制这些古代雕塑的许多雕塑家，我们都不知道他们姓甚名谁，但我们的确知道制作阿蒙霍特普国王这两尊雕像的那位雕刻家的名字，因为这位雕刻家与国王同名，也叫阿蒙霍特普。没准他是一名奴隶呢，因为那时的奴隶经常被赐予其主人的名字。

人们认为，在公元前27年左右，一场地震掀翻了这两尊巨像。结果，太阳升起的时候，其中的“门农”发出了一种声音，可能像是一架巨型风琴的声音，或者是

Colossi. As a result, the Mennon made sounds when the Sun rose, perhaps like the tones of a great organ or a hymn to a new day. The Mennon did not sing every morning or even every year, but when it did sing, it was thought to be a sign of something, or an omen. But an omen of what no one knows.

When a Roman emperor tried to have the Mennon repaired, it ceased its morning song. It has not sung for nearly two thousand years and some people doubt that it ever did, though people at the time used to travel long distances just to hear it sing and were disappointed if it didn't.

Many who did hear it, however, carved their names and the date on the base. So there seems to be little doubt that it did sing once upon a time. Some scientists think the Sun's rays striking the cold stone in the morning wrought some change that made the sound. It is one of the many mysteries of ancient Egypt.

It is also a bit of a mystery that one of the oldest pieces of sculpture in the world is made of wood because wood, of course, does not usually last as long as stone. It's a mystery, too, that this wood sculpture is not a statue of a king, queen, or god, for that is what the Egyptians usually made. What do you suppose it is? A schoolteacher!

The sculpture is the figure of a rather small, fat bald-

塞加拉[1]的布拉克校长

赞美新的一天到来的颂歌。"门农"并不是每天早晨都鸣响，甚至也不是每年都鸣响；可一旦它鸣响起来，人们就认为这是一种要发生某种大事的迹象，或者说是一种预兆。不过，这种预兆意味着什么，却没有人说得清。

而当古罗马帝国的一位皇帝试图修复"门农"之后，这尊雕像却再也不在清晨发出鸣响了。至今它已经有近两千年没有鸣响，因此有些人开始质疑，它以前是不是真的鸣响过；可那时的人却只是为了听一听"门农"的鸣响，就不远千里地跑过去，而若是没有听到，就都失望得很哩。

然而，许多的确听到过它鸣响的人，却将自己的名字和日期刻在了这尊雕像的基座上。因此，它以前的确鸣响过，这一点似乎不容置疑。有些科学家认为，是因为清晨的阳光照到冰冷的石头上后，使石像产生了某种变化，从而使之发出了声音。这可是古埃及诸多谜团中的一个呢。

一座世界上历史最悠久的雕塑作品，竟然是用木头制作而成的，这也有点儿不可思议，因为木头自然难以像石头那样长久保存下来。而令人觉得更加不可思议的是，这尊木制雕塑并非是某位国王、王后或者神灵的雕像，并非是古埃及人通常制作的那种雕像。你们觉得，那会是一尊什么样的雕像呢？它雕刻的，竟然是一位老师！

这尊雕像，刻画的是一个身材相当矮小而肥胖、手持一根长手杖的秃顶男子。

[1] 塞加拉（Saqqara），埃及首都开罗以南的一个村庄，那里有埃及历史上最早的石室坟墓遗址。

headed man carrying a tall walking stick. The statue is smaller than a real man perhaps to show that he was not a king or any important person.

Some people call him The Schoolmaster of Boulac. So you can see what a teacher may have looked like thousands of years ago. But others say there were no regular schools or teachers then, and they believe he was the chief of a tribe. Still others believe he was the boss of a group of workers that worked on the Great Pyramid. So you can take your pick, for no one knows his name or what he was or who made him.

The statue is in a museum in Cairo, the capital of Egypt. Though it was made long ago, it looks much more natural and lifelike than later Egyptian sculpture. It is said that even the old Egyptians thought it so natural that they chained its feet to keep it from walking off!

Another sculpture made about the same time is of a man seated and holding a writing tablet on his lap. It is made of stone and it was painted — guess what color? Red! He was a professional writer — that is, he was one of the few men who knew how to write and made a business of writing for those who could not write, and most people at that time could not. Think of

雕像的尺寸比真人要小，或许是为了表明他既不是国王，也不是什么重要人物吧。

有些人将这尊雕像称为“布拉克校长”。这样，你们就可以看出，几千年前的老师是个什么样子了。不过，还有一些人则说，那个时候世界上并没有正规的学校或者老师，因此他们觉得，这个人应当是某个部落的酋长。还有一些人则认为，这人是一个工头，领着一群工人在大金字塔干活。所以，你们完全可以自己来判定，因为他究竟叫什么、是干什么的、是谁制作了这尊雕像，世界上根本无人知晓。

这尊塑像，如今保存在埃及首都开罗的一座博物馆里。虽说是很久以前制作的，可它却比后来的埃及雕塑显得要自然、逼真得多。据说，连古埃及人也觉得这尊雕像太过栩栩如生，因此还用链子将雕像的双脚拴住，以防它跑掉呢！

坐姿书吏雕像，现存于巴黎的卢浮宫
（摄影：加里·威肯）

差不多同一时期制作出来的另一尊雕像，则是一个坐着的男子，膝头放着一块写字所用的板子。它是一尊石制雕像，并且还上了油漆。你们猜一猜，漆的是什么颜色呢？红色！这个男子，是一位职业文书；也就是说，他是当时为数不多的会写字的人之一，工作就是替那些不会写字的人写东西，因为当时绝大多数人都不会写字。想一想，竟然要雇一个陌生人来替你们写信！这样的人，叫作“书吏”。书吏其实就是一种负责记录口授内容的秘书。当时，

hiring a stranger to write your letters! Such a person was called a *scribe*. He was a kind of secretary who took dictation. Even kings and queens could not write and had to have scribes write for them. This figure is now in the Louvre Museum in Paris.

展翅圣甲虫，
现存于马里兰州巴尔的摩的沃尔特斯艺术博物馆

连国王和王后也不会写字，只得让书吏替他们代写呢。这尊雕像，如今保存在巴黎的卢浮宫博物馆里。

Often Egyptian sculptors went to the other extreme and made tiny statuettes — some only a few inches high — of their kings and queens, gods and goddesses, and sacred animals. Most of these miniature statues were cut out of the hardest kinds of stone — stone that would resist even our modem tools. We suspect that they must have been cut with flint tools instead of steel tools just as a diamond, the very hardest of all stones, has to be cut with another diamond or be shaped by rubbing it with diamond dust.

古埃及的雕塑家们常常还会走向另一个极端，那就是为古埃及的国王和王后、众神和圣兽制作出一些微型的小雕像，有些甚至只有几英寸高呢。这些微型雕像，绝大部分都是用质地最为坚硬的石头制作而成的；这种石头，甚至用我们现代的工具，可能也难以进行雕刻。我们猜想，它们一定是用极为坚硬的燧石工具，而不是用铁制工具雕刻出来的；正如石头中质地最为坚硬的钻石，只能用另一种钻石（金刚石）来切割，或者用钻石的粉末才能打磨成形样。

The beetle was sacred in Egypt and was called a *scarab*. Numerous scarabs made of clay and stone were worn suspended from the neck as a charm. So popular are these charms that they are manufactured today in great quantities and sold to travelers as real antiques.

甲虫在古埃及是一种圣物，被称为“圣甲虫”。无数的人都在脖子上佩戴着用陶土或者石头制成的圣甲虫，把它们当成一种护身符。由于这种护身符大受欢迎，因此如今的人还大批量地生产出这种东西，并把它们当成真正的古董卖给游客哩。

Are there any charms or special treasures you have that you keep or maybe carry with you for good luck? If so, I'll bet it is not an insect such as a beetle!

你们有没有保存着什么护身符和特别珍惜的物品，或者保存着可能给你们带来好运的东西呢？要是有的话，我敢打赌，绝对不会是像甲虫这样的昆虫吧！

Chapter 3 Cherubs and Kings

Can you speak Assyrian? What's that you say? Of course not? But you know one word of Assyrian, I'm sure, even though you may have forgotten the country. Assyria is as old a civilization as Egypt is, and it's a thousand miles to the east of Egypt. The Assyrian word I think you know is *cherub*.

Today an angel head with wings is known as a cherub. Sometimes a sweet baby is also called a cherub. But an Assyrian cherub is neither. It's a fairy-tale animal-either a lion or a bull with a man's head and an eagle's wings. Sometimes the word genie — like the kind that might suddenly appear and ask you for three wishes when you rub a magic lamp — is used to mean the Assyrian type of cherub.

In Assyria cherubs or genies were made out of alabaster, which is a kind of stone that is usually white and softer than most of the stone the Egyptians had.

The Egyptian sphinx was a man-headed lion lying down. The Assyrian cherub was a man-headed lion standing up. The illustration shows an Assyrian cherub. Notice how carefully and tightly the hair and beard are curled.

Here is an easy puzzle. What's wrong with this cherub? He has five legs! The sculptors knew, of course, that a bull had only four legs, but they made him with five legs so that a

第3章 基路伯与国王

你们会讲亚述语吗？说什么？当然不会？但我敢肯定，即便是已经忘记了亚述这个国家，你们也至少知道一个亚述语单词呢。亚述是一个与埃及一样历史悠久的文明古国，位于埃及以东一千英里[1]的地方。我认为你们应该知道的这个亚述语单词，就是“基路伯”。

如今，我们把那种长着翅膀的天使叫作基路伯。有的时候，一个长得非常漂亮的婴儿，也会被人们称为基路伯呢。可亚述语中的基路伯，却既非小天使，也非小宝宝。它是神话传说中的一种野兽，要么是一头狮子，要么是一头公牛，并且都有着人类的脑袋和老鹰的翅膀。有的时候，我们也用“精灵”这个词来指亚述语中的这种基路伯；它们就像是你们摸过一盏神灯后，可能会突然现身并要你们说出三个愿望的那种精灵一样。

在古亚述，基路伯或者精灵都是用汉白玉制作而成的。汉白玉是一种石头，通常都是白色的，并且质地不像古埃及人所用的绝大部分石头那样坚硬。

古埃及人制作的斯芬克斯，是一种卧着的人首狮身雕像。而古亚述人制作的基路伯，则是一尊站立着的人首狮身雕像。下图所示即为古亚述人制作出来的一尊基路伯。请注意，这尊雕像的头发和胡须，卷曲得多么仔细和严实啊。

给你们出一个很容易回答的问题。这尊基路伯雕像的哪个部分有问题呢？答案

[1] 英里（mile），英制长度单位。1 英里约合 1.609 千米。

person looking at him from the front would see two legs together as if he were standing still, and when looking at him from the side a person would see the animal walking.

The next two pieces of Assyrian sculpture are in low relief. Notice the muscles that these men have. They are different from the Egyptian men, who were shown to be slender and with no muscles. The Assyrians thought that beauty was strength and that to be beautiful, a person must be strong, so they showed their kings with big, bulging muscles.

The Assyrians believed also that hair was another sign of strength and that no real man who could grow a beard would choose to have a smooth, less-manly face. Do you know the Bible story of Samson? His great strength was supposed to be due to his long hair. When it was cut off, he became weak.

Here the men have long hair and long beards tightly curled like ropes. Notice that the eyes are like the Egyptians' — front view on the side view of their heads. The men have more clothing on, too, with tasseled shawls or skirts that come to their ankles and half sandals. They are not altogether barefooted.

The two chief things the Assyrian kings liked to do best — their two chief sports —

古亚述人制作的基路伯，
现存于伦敦的大英博物馆

就是：它竟然有五条腿！制作这尊雕像的人当然知道，一头公牛只有四条腿，可他们还是给它雕了五条。原因就在于，这样一来，倘若站在雕像前面，我们就会看到它一共有两条腿，仿佛静静地站在那儿不动似的；而倘若从侧面去看，我们就会看到这头神兽正在走路呢。

下面这两座由古亚述人制作的雕塑，都属于浅浮雕。注意浮雕中那些男子的肌肉。他们不同于古埃及人，后者通常都显得身材修长，并且看不出肌肉来。而古亚述人认为力量就是美，一个人只有身材强壮才算得上美；因此，他们雕刻出来的国王形象都孔武有力，个个都有着大块隆起的肌肉。

古亚述人还认为，头发是力量的另一种标志，并且没有哪一个能够长出一丛胡须的人愿意剃去胡须，愿意让自己的脸庞变得光滑顺溜和没有阳刚之气。你们听说过《圣经》中关于大力士参孙的故事吗？人们认为，参孙之所以力大无穷，就在于他有一头长发。头发剪短之后，他就变得虚弱无力了。

这里的男子都留着长发和长须，并且把它们像绳子一样紧紧地缠了起来。注意，浮雕上人物的眼睛跟古埃及人制作的那些浮雕相似，也是头部是侧像，眼睛却是正面像。浮雕中人物身上穿着的衣物，也比古埃及人制作的雕像人物身上的衣物多，既有垂着穗带且直达脚踝处的披肩或裙摆，脚上还穿着露趾的拖鞋。他们可不是全然光着脚呢。

古亚述的国王们最喜欢干的两件大事，就是猎杀野兽和在战斗中杀戮敌人；这

were hunting animals and killing their enemies in battle, so most of their reliefs show them doing these things. But the best things the Assyrian artists made were figures of animals. They made them much more lifelike than those of the Egyptians. In many reliefs the horses are fine spirited steeds, and their manes and tails are tightly curled.

The Assyrians also made tiny reliefs on the curved surfaces of cylindrical-shaped pieces of stone or clay. A small axle was put through a hole in the center of the cylinder. The cylinder then became a tiny rolling pin that could be rolled over any soft surface such as mud or wax to leave a flat imprint of the picture on the cylinder.

In this way they could make as many small reliefs as they pleased. We think, however, they used these cylinders as seals to sign their writing. They did not write on paper since they had none. They wrote on mud bricks before the bricks were dried, and they stamped their seal at the end instead of signing their names.

Today in Japan and China, artists sign their names with a stamp made of carved stone called a chop. If you have seen a round or square symbol made with red-orange ink on the

阿苏尔纳西尔帕二世的浮雕，
现存于伦敦的大英博物馆
（由波士顿的大学印刷协会提供）

阿苏尔纳西尔帕二世猎狮图，
现存于伦敦的大英博物馆
（由缅因州桑福德的大学印刷协会提供）

也是他们两种主要的娱乐活动，因此他们命人制作出来的浮雕上，绝大部分都是表现他们做这些事情时的场景。不过，古亚述的艺术家们最擅长制作的，还是动物雕像。他们制作出来的动物雕像，比古埃及人制作出来的要逼真得多。在许多浮雕作品中，马匹都是生龙活虎的骏马，而马匹的鬃毛和尾巴也都是严严实实地卷曲着的。

古亚述人也曾在柱状石料或柱状陶土的曲面上制作微型浮雕。他们会用一根细细的轴，穿过一个纵贯柱体中心的洞。这样一来，柱体就变成了一根细细的擀面杖，可以在任何柔软的表面滚动，比如湿泥或者蜂蜡，从而将柱体上的图案浅浅地压印出来了。

用这种办法，他们就可以随心所欲地制作出许多的微型浮雕了。然而，我们却认为，他们是用这些柱状浮雕来做印章，代替他们的签名的。由于当时还没有纸张，因此他们并不是在纸上写字。他们是在还没有干的泥块上写字，而在结尾处也并不是签下自己的大名，而是盖上自己的这种印章。

如今，在日本和中国，艺术家们也都是用一种叫作“图章”的石刻印章来签名的哩。假如在一幅水彩画或者版画的一角看到有一个由橘红色油墨形成的圆形或方

corner of a watercolor or block print, you know just what I mean.

These sculptures of the Assyrians have been dug up from the ruins of their old cities, carried away, and placed in museums. So if you want to see them, you must go not to Assyria but to the British Museum in London, the Louvre Museum in Paris, the Metropolitan Museum of Art in New York, the Walters Art Museum in Baltimore, Maryland, or to other great museums.

From what I have told you of Assyrian sculpture, how would you describe it in a few words?

Huge beasts called cherubs — with five legs
Strong and powerful men and animals
Hair and beards in rope-like curls
Low reliefs showing hunting and fighting scenes
Very natural-looking animals
Small, engraved cylindrical-shaped seals

美索不达米亚的柱状印章，
现存于马里兰州巴尔的摩的沃尔特斯艺术博物馆

古巴比伦的经济文件，
现存于马里兰州巴尔的
摩的沃尔特斯艺术博物馆

形标志，那么你们就会明白我的意思了。

古亚述人制作出来的这些雕塑，被人们从一些古城的废墟之下挖掘出来，带走并放进了博物馆。因此，假如想要看一看这些雕塑，你们大可不必前往亚述古国，只需到伦敦的大英博物馆、巴黎的卢浮宫、纽约的大都会艺术博物馆、马里兰州巴尔的摩的沃尔特斯艺术博物馆，或者其他一些大型博物馆去看看就行了。

根据上面我对古亚述雕塑艺术的介绍，你们又怎样用几句话来加以总结呢？可以参考下面这种方式：

基路伯这种巨兽有五条腿；
男人和动物全都强壮有力；
人物发须卷曲，就像绳子；
浅浮雕呈现狩猎作战场景；
动物形态都非常自然逼真；
还有雕刻的微型柱状章印。

And that's about all we know of Assyrian sculpture. There are not many remains left to tell the tale of the proud, powerful, and cruel tyrants who ruled over millions of people. These monarchs and their subjects have been dead for thousands of years.

Perhaps you think some things you are familiar with will last forever too. Can you name some of them? Imagine that a boy or girl in Assyria must have thought the very same thing about what they saw around them, but those things have practically all disappeared.

对于古亚述的雕塑艺术，我们了解到的情况就是这些了。世界上并没有留下多少遗迹，可以来讲述那些曾经统治着数百万民众、神气十足、强大有力而残酷无比的暴君们的故事。这些暴君，连同他们的子民，都已经死去好几千年了。

你们或许会认为，你们所熟悉的一些东西会永远存在下去。你们能说出一些这样的东西来么？想象一下，亚述古国的一位小朋友对周围所见的一切必定也怀有同样的想法呢；只不过，他所看到的那些东西，事实上都已经消失得无影无踪了。

Chapter 4 Marbles

When I was a boy I once overheard my father talking with a friend about marbles.

"You know," said my father, "the Greeks made the finest marbles in the world."

And his friend answered, "Yes, there is no doubt that the Greek marbles are the finest in the world." I wondered why these grown-up men were talking about marbles, and I wondered who were these Greeks that made such fine marbles and where I could get some, for I played with some very fine marbles myself. I didn't learn until later that they were not talking about marbles to play with, but about statues that the ancient Greeks made out of marble. People call them simply marbles instead of marble bas-reliefs and statues.

Greece was, and still is, a small country in the Mediterranean Sea. But the ancient Greeks and the present-day Greeks are not the same. The ancient Greeks believed in gods and goddesses and heroes, and they told stories about them. This is called *mythology*. The Greeks also made beautiful statues of their gods as they imagined the gods looked and acted, and no one since has been able to make sculpture as beautiful. Sculpture is one of the things that we can't do much better than they did.

The Egyptians usually made their statues of granite that was too hard to carve with great detail. The Assyrians made theirs of alabaster that was too soft and did not last as

第4章 大理石雕塑

小的时候，我曾经无意中听到父亲与他的一位朋友在谈论弹珠[1]的问题。

“您知道，”我的父亲说，“希腊人制作出来的弹珠，可是全世界最精致的呢。”

他的朋友则回答道：“是的，希腊人制作出来的弹珠无疑是世界上最精致的。”我很奇怪，这两个成年人为什么会谈论起弹珠来。我也很想知道，那些能够做出如此精美弹珠的希腊人是谁，要到哪里才能买到这种弹珠，因为当时我自己就有一些非常精美的、好玩的弹珠。直到后来我才明白，他们谈论的并不是用于玩耍的弹珠，而是古希腊人用石头制作出来的雕塑。人们只是将这些雕塑统称为大理石雕塑，而不是称之为大理石浅浮雕和大理石雕像。

希腊曾经是地中海地区的一个小国，如今也仍然是这样。不过，古希腊人和如今的希腊人并不是一回事儿。古希腊人信仰众多的男神、女神和英雄人物，也有许多关于这些神灵和英雄人物的故事流传下来。这些故事传说，被称为“神话”。古希腊人还按照自己想象中的众神的样子和举止，制作出了许多漂亮的神灵雕像；而自那时以后，世界上就再也没有人能够制作出如此漂亮的雕塑作品了。制作雕塑，就是如今的我们没法比古人干得更好的众多事情之一。

古埃及人通常是用花岗岩来制作雕像的；花岗岩质地太硬，人们无法极为精细地进行雕刻。古亚述人曾用汉白玉来制作雕塑，可汉白玉的质地又太软，无法像艺

[1] 弹珠（marbles），亦可指“大理石雕塑”。在孩子听来，大人们谈论的是用于玩耍的弹珠；而实际上，大人谈论的却是大理石雕塑。

long as the artist would have liked. The Greeks made theirs of marble and that was just right. One reason they made such beautiful statues was because they had such beautiful marble to make them from.

In Greece there were several places called quarries where the finest marble in the world was found. One was on a mountain called Pentelicus and another was on an island called Paros. There is still plenty of marble from Pentelicus and Paros, but there is no Greek or other person now living who can make it into such sculpture as did these Greeks who lived two thousand years ago. It takes more than good marble to make a good statue.

迈锡尼古城的石狮城门
（由波士顿的大学印刷协会提供）

But the Greeks did not start off making beautiful statues. The first and oldest piece of Greek sculpture we have is of two lions over a stone gateway at a place called Mycenae. These lions have lost their heads. But even with the heads they once had, they could not have been any finer than some of the Assyrian lions cut in alabaster.

One of the next oldest pieces of Greek sculpture looks almost like something a child might have done, but that is to be expected, for it was made

术家所希望的那样持久保存下去。而古希腊人的大理石雕塑，质地则不软不硬，刚刚好。他们之所以制作出了如此美观的雕塑作品，原因之一便在于他们有非常漂亮的大理石来进行雕刻。

在希腊，有几个地方发现了世界上品质最佳的大理石；这些地方，叫作采石场。其中一个位于一座叫作彭德利康的山上，另一个则位于一座叫作帕罗斯的岛屿上。如今，虽说彭德利康山和帕罗斯岛上仍然储有丰富的大理石，但没有哪个在世的希腊人或者其他人能够像两千年前的古希腊人那样，用这些大理石雕刻出如此美丽的雕塑作品了。制作出一尊优秀的雕像，需要的可不只是品质优良的大理石啊。

可古希腊人并不是一开始就制作出了漂亮的雕塑作品。我们如今能见到的古希腊第一尊，也是历史最悠久的雕像，是位于一个叫作迈锡尼的古城石门上的两头狮子。这两头狮子的脑袋都不在了。不过，就算是安上最初的狮头，它们也不可能比古亚述人用汉白玉雕刻出来的那些狮子更精美。

下一件最古老的古希腊雕塑，看上去差不多就像是一个小孩子做的东西；不过，这一点是必然的，因为这件雕塑就是古希腊初期制作出来的。它表现的是古希腊人关于珀耳修斯[1]和美杜莎[2]的传说。

---

[1] 珀耳修斯（Perseus），古希腊神话中的英雄人物，是宙斯与古希腊公主达那厄所生的儿子，曾杀死蛇发女妖美杜莎，后来又从海怪的手中救出了埃塞俄比亚公主安德罗墨达。

[2] 美杜莎（Medusa），古希腊神话中的三位蛇发女妖之一，据说能够把看到她的人全都变成石头。

when Greece was a child. It tells the Greek story of Perseus and Medusa.

Medusa was a beautiful girl who dared to compete in beauty with Athena, the goddess of wisdom. To punish her, Athena turned Medusa into a horrible-looking creature with hissing snakes that writhed and twisted about her head. So terrible was Medusa's face that anyone who looked at her was turned into stone.

A young hero named Perseus was dared by an enemy of his to cut off Medusa's horrible head. The goddess Athena, who was a friend of Perseus, led him to Medusa. To get there quickly, Perseus borrowed a pair of winged sandals from the god Hermes. When he came to the place where Medusa lay asleep, he borrowed Athena's shield so he could use the shiny inside as a mirror to see how to cut off her head without looking directly at her — and out sprang a winged horse called Pegasus.

In the sculpture, Perseus is shown cutting off Medusa's head as he looks away. Medusa clasps Pegasus in her arms. Athena, on the other side, looks more like a man than a girl, and although she is facing front, her foot is twisted sideways so it would fall inside the block of stone.

雅典娜、珀耳修斯和美杜莎，
现存于巴勒莫的考古博物馆
（摄影：加里·威肯）

美杜莎本来是一个漂亮的女孩，可她竟然敢去与智慧女神雅典娜比美。为了惩罚她，雅典娜便将美杜莎变成了一种样子很恐怖的生物，让她的头上全都是嘶嘶地吐着信子、交错盘旋在一起的蛇。美杜莎的脸极其可怕，会让任何看到她的人都变成石头呢。

当时，有位叫作珀耳修斯的年轻英雄，他的一个敌人用激将法，激他敢不敢去砍掉美杜莎那颗可怕的脑袋。雅典娜女神是珀耳修斯的朋友，便带着他去找美杜莎。为了快点儿到达，珀耳修斯便向赫耳墨斯借了一双长有翅膀的鞋子。他来到美杜莎的老巢后，看到美杜莎躺在那儿睡着了；他借来了雅典娜的盾牌，因为那样的话，就可以把盾牌那光亮的里侧当成一面镜子，从而不用直视美杜莎，便可以将她的脑袋砍下来了。就在砍掉美杜莎的脑袋之后，却突然出现了一匹叫作珀加索斯[1]的飞马！

在这件雕塑作品中，珀耳修斯正在割下美杜莎的脑袋，眼睛却看着别的地方。美杜莎双臂中抱着珀加索斯。而在珀耳修斯另一侧的雅典娜，看上去却更像是一名

[1] 珀加索斯（Pegasus），古希腊神话中美杜莎与海神波塞冬所生的一匹长有翅膀、通常为白色的神马。据说它足蹄踏过的地方有泉水涌出，诗人饮用泉水即可获得灵感。

Medusa's right leg is longer than the left, for the left leg is very short from the knee up. Are you wondering why her legs are such different lengths? To show her walking, one leg had to be made longer so both could remain on the platform and the statue could stand up. Pegasus is depicted as a tiny toy horse and his hind legs are like those of a kangaroo — much longer than his front legs.

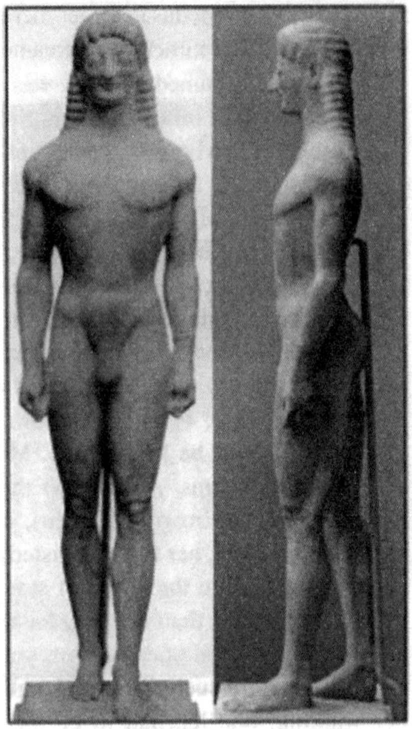

泰内亚的阿波罗，
现存于慕尼黑的州立文物博物馆
（由缅因州桑福德的大学印刷协会提供）

The Lion Gateway and *Perseus and Medusa* are both in high relief, but later the statue *Apollo of Tenea* was made in-the-round. Apollo was the Greek Sun god and, along with Adonis, was supposed to be one of the most handsome of all the gods, but this statue of him may not make you think that he is beautiful. Sometimes ideas about beauty change.

The ancient Greeks thought the human body was the most beautiful thing in the world. They tried to make their own bodies beautiful through sports, exercise, and healthful living, and they made statues of their most famous athletes as examples.

Today we often liken athletic-looking people to Apollo. This statue is probably not of

男子，而不是一位姑娘；并且，尽管她是正脸朝前，可她的双脚却是扭向两侧的，目的是使她的双脚不会凸出到整块石头外面去。美杜莎的右腿要比左腿长，因为左腿的膝盖部分以上非常短。你们是不是觉得奇怪，为什么她的双腿长短会如此不同呢？原因在于，要想雕刻出一尊表现出她走路姿态的雕像，一条腿就必须比另一条腿长才行，因为只有这样，两条腿才能处于同一水平，雕像才能站立起来。珀加索斯被雕成了一匹小小的玩具马，而它的两条后腿，也像袋鼠腿一样，比前腿要长得多呢。

石狮城门、珀耳修斯和美杜莎雕像都是高浮雕，但后来的《泰内亚的阿波罗》却是一尊圆雕。阿波罗是古希腊的太阳神，并且他和阿多尼斯两人被认为是众神当中最英俊的美男子；不过他的这尊雕塑，却可能不会让你们觉得他有多么英俊呢。有的时候，人们对于美的观念是会改变的。

古希腊人认为，人体是世界上最美丽的东西。他们竭尽全力，想要通过运动、锻炼和健康生活，让自己的身材变得漂亮起来；并且，他们还给那些最著名的运动健将制作雕像，把这些人当成自己学习的榜样。

如今，我们常常会将那些体型看上去很像是运动健将的人比作阿波罗。这尊雕

Apollo at all, but just the figure of an athlete such as a runner or a jumper. In this sculpture Apollo is not beefy like the Assyrians or skinny like the Egyptians, but his face has a particular expression, the hair is perfectly placed, and the eyes seem to bulge.

Apollo of Tenea is one of the first statues we have that seems to be smiling. Perhaps the man has just won a race. More likely, the smile is there to show liveliness so that the face, like the figure, looks more natural or real. This early, or *archaic*, sculpture is interesting, but from this point forward the Greek statues are not only interesting but also beautiful in the way we think of beauty nowadays.

像，雕的很可能根本就不是阿波罗，可能只是一个运动员的形象，比如说长跑运动员或者跳高运动员罢了。这尊雕塑中的阿波罗，既不像古亚述人的雕像那样结实、健壮，也不像古埃及人的雕像那样干瘦、苗条；可他的脸上，却有一种特别的神情，头发雕刻得非常完美，而双眼则向外凸出。

《泰内亚的阿波罗》是我们目前拥有的，其中的人物似乎是在微笑的第一批雕像之一。或许，这个人物是刚刚赢得了一场比赛呢。而更有可能的则是，这种微笑是为了让雕像显得很生动，从而让面部跟身体一样，看上去更加自然、逼真。这尊早期的或者“古代的”雕像，雕刻得很有意思；可自此以后，古希腊的雕塑就变得非但有意思，还非常美丽，符合我们如今的审美了。

Chapter 5 Standing Naturally

When I used to recite poetry at school assemblies, I stood like an Egyptian statue of Rameses — hands straight down at my sides and feet close together, flat on the floor.

"Stiff as a poker," my teacher used to say. "Can't you stand more naturally? Put one foot behind the other!"

So I stood like the wooden statue of the Schoolmaster of Boulac, but still with my feet flat on the floor. That was the best that I could do to be natural and that seemed to be the best that sculptors could do with their standing statues — until a Greek named Polyclitus came along.

Polyclitus made a statue of an athlete called *The Spear Bearer*. It was the first statue to have an easy, natural standing position with the weight resting on one leg and one foot behind the other. Polyclitus did this by placing a small wedge beneath the athlete's heel to help hold the leg up in the correct position and to give his leg and the whole statue the support it needed. The Greeks called *The Spear Bearer* the ideal figure because he was perfectly proportioned, and other sculptors used the statue as a pattern and copied its proportions in the statues they made. Indeed, live athletes tried, with exercise, to make their own chests and legs and arms the same size as those of *The Spear Bearer*.

第5章 自然站立

小时候，在学校举行的大会上背诵诗歌时，我都会像古希腊人雕刻的拉美西斯大帝一样地站在台上，双手直直地垂在身体两侧，双脚紧紧并拢，稳稳当当地踩在地板上。

“僵硬刻板得很，”我的老师曾经如此评价道，“你不能站得更加自然一点儿吗？两只脚一前一后！”

于是，我便站得像那尊“布拉克校长”的木雕一样了，可我的双脚，却仍然平平地踩在地板上。这可是我能够保持的最自然的站姿了，而这似乎也是雕塑家们能够让自己制作出来的雕像保持站姿的最佳办法，直到出现了一位名叫波利克里托斯的古希腊雕塑家，这种情况才有所改变。

波利克里托斯制作了一尊运动员的雕像，名叫《执矛者》。这是历史上第一座拥有一种放松而自然之站姿的雕像。其中人物的重心放在一条腿上，并且双脚是一前一后。波利克里托斯是在运动员的一只脚跟下楔入了一小块垫子，让这条腿抬起来，摆出正确的姿势，并且给运动员以及整座雕像以必需的支撑力，从而做到这一点的。古希腊人称《执矛者》是一种理想的形体，因为其中人物的比例非常完美；而其他的雕塑家也纷纷将这座雕像当成典范，模仿它的比例来制作雕像。事实上，一些真正的运动员还想方设法地要通过锻炼，好让自己胸膛、四肢的大小变得像《执矛者》中的那位运动员一样哩。

Polyclitus also made a statue of a woman athlete called an Amazon. The Amazons were a mythological race of warrior women who wanted nothing to do with men — except to fight them in battles and duels.

Other sculptors admired these two statues by Polyclitus and made copies of them in marble. It is fortunate for us they did so, for all we have now are the copies. The ones that Polyclitus himself made have disappeared and no trace of them is left.

Polyclitus made his statues out of a metal called *bronze*. The first metal ever discovered was not gold or silver or iron but copper. Then tin was found, and tin and copper were combined to make bronze. So bronze is not a pure metal. It is a combination of copper and tin. Bronze lasts if kept dry; however, when it is exposed to the weather or dampness, it is gradually eaten away. Bronze could be worked so well that the Greeks loved to make statues and other things out of it. It does not rust like iron, it is not expensive like gold or silver, and over the course of time, it gets a greenish coating called a *patina*.

I have an ancient lamp made of bronze with a beautiful patina that took perhaps two thousand years to form. Some people try to imitate the real patina by treating bronze with acid, but only nature and time can make the real patina.

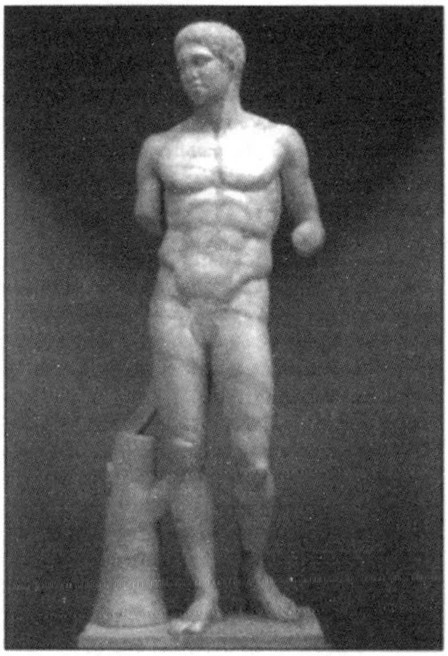
执矛者，波利克里托斯作品的仿制品
（摄影：加里·威肯）

波利克里托斯还制作了一尊叫作《阿玛宗人》的女性运动员雕像。阿玛宗人是神话传说中一个由好战的女性所组成的民族；除了在战斗和决斗中与男子作战，她们可不希望与男子发生任何瓜葛呢。

其他的雕塑家都很崇拜波利克里托斯创作的这两座雕像，因而用大理石制作出了许多的仿制品。对于我们来说，幸亏他们这样做了，因为如今我们只有这两座雕像的仿制品了。波利克里托斯亲手雕刻出来的原作已经不见了，连一丁点儿痕迹也没有留下。

波利克里托斯制作雕像时，用的是一种叫作“青铜”的金属。人类发现的第一种金属，既非黄金、白银，也不是钢铁，而是铜。接着，人们发现了锡。于是，他们便将锡和铜熔化混合，制成了青铜。因此，青铜并不是一种纯金属，而是铜、锡的合金。假如放在干燥的环境里，青铜就能够长久保存；然而，一旦遭到日晒雨淋或者受潮，青铜就会慢慢腐蚀。由于青铜很容易加工，因此古希腊人很喜欢用青铜来制作雕塑或者其他物品。青铜不会像铁那样生锈，也不像金、银那样昂贵；而随着时间的流逝，青铜器上还会长出一层叫作“铜绿”的绿色覆盖物呢。

我收藏着的一盏古代油灯，上面就长了一层漂亮的铜绿；这层铜绿，没准要两千年的时间才能形成哩。如今有些人试图通过用酸性溶液对青铜器加以处理，来仿制出真正的铜绿；可真正的铜绿，只有自然和时间才能造就。

Another Greek sculptor, a friend of Polyclitus, was named Myron. Myron went further than Polyclitus in giving his figures naturalness and action. One of his statues is called *The Discus Thrower*. Discus-throwing is a sport in which the object is to see how far a heavy disk can be thrown underhanded.

The Discus Thrower is shown at the moment just before he hurls the discus. Notice the toes of the front foot gripping the ground and those on the rear foot being drawn along the ground to balance the body. Back then, the discus weighed about two and a half pounds and the record throw was less than one hundred feet. That may not seem very far until you try it. Today the discus has been thrown up to one hundred and fifty-five feet.

掷铁饼者，米隆作品的复制品，
现存于伦敦的大英博物馆
（由缅因州桑福德的大学印刷协会提供）

The Discus Thrower was first made in bronze, but the bronze statue has disappeared and the statue shown here was made in marble from a copy. It is one of several marble copies in museums around the world. The difference between the bronze and marble copy, besides the color, is that marble is so heavy that it breaks if it is not supported. That is why the

还有一位古希腊雕塑家，他是波利克里托斯的朋友，名叫米隆。在赋予雕像以自然感和运动感方面，米隆比波利克里托斯更进了一步。他制作出来的雕塑当中，有一座叫作《掷铁饼者》。掷铁饼是一项体育运动，目的是看一个运动员究竟能手不过肩地将一块沉重的铁饼扔多远。

《掷铁饼者》表现的，是运动员正要将铁饼猛力掷出去的那一瞬间。请注意，雕像前脚五趾紧抓地面，而后脚五趾则抵在地上，目的是保持身体的平衡。当时，每块铁饼重约二点五磅[1]，而投掷距离的最远纪录，也不过一百英尺[2]。除非你们自己去试一试，否则这一距离似乎也不算太远呢。如今，铁饼已经被运动员们掷到了一百五十五英尺远啦。

《掷铁饼者》起初是用青铜制作而成的，可那座青铜原作已经不复存在，所以此处所示的这座雕像，是根据一份复制品用大理石制作出来的。它可是世界上所有博物馆中为数不多的大理石复制品中的一座呢。青铜原作与大理石复制品之间的差异，除了颜色，就是大理石雕像很重，假如没有支撑的话，就会破裂。《掷铁饼者》的大理石复制品上，其中人物一条腿的后面之所以会有一个样子古怪、像树干

[1] 磅（pound），英制重量单位。1 磅约合 0.454 千克。

[2] 英尺（foot），英制长度单位。1 英尺约合 30.48 厘米。

marble copy of *The Discus Thrower* has an odd-looking, tree-trunk shape behind one leg — to hold up the weight and keep the statue from toppling over and breaking.

Myron also made a bronze cow that was so natural it is said to have fooled everybody into thinking it was a real cow. But this cow has disappeared and there are not any copies.

Bronze statues were entirely eaten away or melted down over the course of time. Marble statues often were broken but otherwise lasted, and many have been far luckier than Humpty Dumpty because they have been put back together again.

似的东西，原因就在这里：这个东西，就是为了支撑人物的重量，使整座雕像不至于翻倒、打破才加上去的。

米隆还制作过一座青铜母牛雕像。这座雕像非常自然、逼真，据说还骗过了所有人的眼睛，让大家都以为那是一头真的母牛呢。不过，这座母牛雕塑如今也不复存在了，并且没有留下任何复制品。

随着时间的推移，青铜雕塑要么是被完全腐蚀掉，要么就是毁掉了。可大理石雕塑除非被打碎，否则就能长久保存下去；而许多的大理石雕塑也要比“蛋壳先生”[1]幸运得多，因为后来它们都被人们再次拼合、复原了。

[1] 蛋壳先生（Humpty Dumpty），同名英文童谣中的人物，译名不统一，有“矮胖子”、“鸡蛋男孩”、“蛋头先生”及音译“汉普蒂•邓普蒂”等。这首童谣的原文是：Humpty Dumpty sat on a wall, Humpty Dumpty had a great fall; All the king's horses and all the king's men, Couldn't put Humpty together again（矮胖子，坐墙头，栽了一个大跟斗；国王呀，齐兵马，破蛋难圆没办法）。如今这个词多用于指身材矮胖的人，或者指一经损坏便无法再修复的东西。

Chapter 6 The Greatest Greek Sculptor

Ordinary men are called "Mr." — Mr. Smith or Mr. Jones. Great men are called by their full names without the "Mr." — George Washington, for example. But the greatest men of all are called by just their last names. People have made lists of the one hundred greatest men of all time — the greatest ruler, the greatest writer, the greatest painter, but you probably have never heard of the greatest sculptor. He was a Greek named Phidias — no first name, no middle name — just Phidias.

Polyclitus and Myron made statues of men and women. Phidias made statues of gods and goddesses and godlike men and women. In Athens there is a huge hill called the Acropolis, which means upper city. On this hill the ancient Greeks built a beautiful temple called the Parthenon. It was built just to hold a magnificent statue of Athena, who the Athenians believed gave them many useful things and watched over them and their city as a mother watches over her children.

Phidias was chosen to make this statue of the goddess. Cold marble was not good enough material so Phidias made the statue out of gold and ivory, and he made it seven times taller than a human being. His Athena stood erect in a sleeveless robe that reached to the ground.

On her chest was a breastplate with a border of serpents because serpents were

第6章 古希腊最伟大的雕塑家

普通的人一般被称为“先生”，比如史密斯先生呀，琼斯先生呀。而我们在称呼伟大人物的时候，通常却不加“先生”一词，而是用伟人的全称，比如乔治·华盛顿。可对于全世界最伟大的人物呢，我们通常又只称呼他们的姓。虽说人们早已列出了世界历史上最伟大的一百位人物的名录，比如最伟大的君主、最伟大的作家、最伟大的画家等，但你们很可能从来都没有听说过世界历史上最伟大的雕塑家的情况呢。他是一位古希腊人，叫作菲狄亚斯；这可不是他的名字，而是他的姓，就是菲狄亚斯。

波利克里托斯和米隆制作的，都是凡人的雕像。而菲狄亚斯雕刻的，却是神灵以及圣人的雕像。雅典有一座巨大的山丘，叫作“阿克罗波利斯”，就是“高地城邦”的意思。古希腊人在这个山丘上修建了一座非常漂亮的神庙，叫作“巴台农神庙”。之所以修建这座神庙，只是为了在这里供奉一尊宏伟辉煌的雅典娜神像。古希腊人认为，雅典娜女神赐予了他们很多的有用之物，并且像一位母亲守护着儿女那样，守护着古希腊人和他们的城邦。

菲狄亚斯被推选来制作这尊女神雕像。由于冰冷的大理石并不是十分理想的雕塑材料，因此菲狄亚斯是用黄金和象牙制作出这尊雕像的，并且雕像的高度达到了真人的八倍。他雕刻出来的雅典娜笔直地站立着，身披一件垂到了地上的无袖长袍。

雕像的胸前，有一块边沿雕有毒蛇的胸甲。因为当时的人认为，毒蛇是世界上最聪明的生物。而胸甲的中心，则是美杜莎的头像。你们可能都还记得，前面我跟你们说

supposed to be the wisest of creatures. In the center of the breastplate was the head of Medusa. You may remember I told you that Athena helped Perseus to cut Medusa's head off. Well, around the head of Medusa, between the serpents and the head, a battle between the Amazons and the Greeks was shown. Athena wore a helmet. On top of this helmet was a sphinx and on each side of the sphinx were winged horses.

Athena's left arm rested on a shield and carried a lance, around which coiled another serpent. In her right hand Athena held a statue of Victory, who faced her and offered her a wreath of gold. The statue of Victory was about six feet tall, so you can see how big the statue of Athena herself must have been.

This statue of Athena has entirely disappeared, probably stolen piece by piece for its gold and ivory. We know what it looked like only by a small, probably very poor copy that was made of it. And judging by the copy we have, we cannot quite agree that the statue was as beautiful as the ancient Greeks thought it. A full-size statue was made from that copy. Today it stands in a full-size copy of the Parthenon in Tennessee, not Greece.

Phidias's statue of Athena, as I told you, was inside the Parthenon. All around the four outside walls of the temple, high up near the roof, was a band or strip of sculptured figures in low relief called a *frieze*. This frieze was almost a tenth of a mile long and showed in marble a parade of grand procession that took place in Athens once every four years.

The object of the procession was to bear a gift of a golden dress made by the girls of

过，雅典娜曾经帮助珀耳修斯砍掉了美杜莎的脑袋。而在美杜莎的头像周围，即毒蛇边饰和头像之间，则刻画了阿玛宗人与古希腊人之间的一场战斗。雅典娜戴着一顶头盔。头盔顶上，雕有一尊斯芬克斯。而斯芬克斯的两侧，则各有一匹长有翅膀的飞马。

雅典娜的左臂搁在一面盾牌之上，并且手持一支长矛。长矛之上，缠绕着另一条毒蛇。雅典娜的右手握着一尊胜利女神维克托里亚[1]的雕像。维克托里亚面对着雅典娜，正将一个黄金花环献给她。光是维克托里亚的雕像，就有约六英尺高，由此你们就可以看出，这尊雅典娜雕像本身有多巨大了。

这尊雅典娜雕像已经完全不复存在，很可能是被人一点一点地偷走了，因为这座雕像是用黄金和象牙制作的。我们如今之所以知道它的样子，只是由于我们有一座小型的，很可能做工也非常粗劣的复制品。而从如今拥有的这尊复制品来看，我们可没法完全像古希腊人那样，认为它有多么多么的美丽呢。人们根据这座复制品，制作出了一尊与原件大小一样的雕像。如今，这尊雕像也坐落在按照一比一复制出来的巴台农神庙里；可这座巴台农神庙，并不在希腊，而是在美国的田纳西州。

前面我跟你们说过，菲狄亚斯雕刻的这座雅典娜雕像，被供奉在巴台农神庙里。神庙四面外墙上靠近屋顶的地方，雕有一圈浅浮雕图案，称为“横饰”。这圈横饰，差不多有十分之一英里长，用大理石描绘了雅典每四年举行一次的盛大游行。

举行这种游行的目的，是为了将雅典的姑娘们为雅典娜女神制作的一件黄金礼服，当作礼物献祭给雅典娜；因此，人们会盛况空前地把这件黄金礼服送到神庙里

[1] 维克托里亚（Victory），古希腊神话中的胜利女神，本名尼姬（Nike），“维克托里亚”是她在古罗马神话里的名字。

Athens for their goddess, and it was carried with great pomp and ceremony to the temple. All Athenians — men, women, and children — took their part in the procession. There were horsemen with their horses. There were animals to be sacrificed. There were girls and boys bearing gifts. There were musicians and singers.

The frieze of the procession starts at one end of the Parthenon and proceeds along both sides of the temple to the other end where the entrance is. It is the most perfect relief work that we know anything about. And although there are hundreds of figures of men, women, and animals, Phidias planned it all and, with his students, made it all. There is a tenth of a mile of it and yet, at the time it was completed, there was not one rough or unfinished part in the entire frieze — even the parts that could not be seen were finished. Nothing except perfection was good enough for the temple of this goddess of the Athenians.

When the relief was in place on the Parthenon wall, it could just barely be seen because it was so high up and closed in by the portico of columns that surrounded it. The background and the figures were painted in bright colors so they could be seen better.

Above and between the columns in the Parthenon are spaces or panels called *metopes*. These metopes contain high reliefs illustrating battles, most of which are between gods and animals called centaurs. A centaur is a mythological monster that has the body of a horse and the head and trunk of a man.

There are ninety-two groups of these metopes, and all are now broken! In many cases, an arm or a leg is gone, a nose is broken, or an ear or an eye is missing. So you have to use your imagination to understand what the figure looked like when it was perfect. If you

去。所有的雅典人，不论男女老少，都会参加此次游行。有骑着高头大马的骑士，有准备献祭的牲畜，有捧着礼物的童男童女，还有许多乐师和歌手。

这圈描绘游行盛况的横饰，从巴台农神庙的一端开始，沿着神庙外墙的两侧，直达神庙大门所在的另一端。这是我们知道的，所有作品中最完美的一件浮雕。并且，尽管其中雕有数百个人物和动物的图案，菲狄亚斯却通盘设计，然后带领自己的学生，完美地将它们呈现了出来。虽说整圈横饰长达十分之一英里，可到完工的时候，整圈横饰中却没有一处粗制滥造或者未完成的部分，连那些看不到的地方，也都非常完美。只有完美，才配得上雅典人供奉雅典娜女神的这座神庙呢。

这圈浮雕在巴台农神庙里雕刻到位之后，人们却很难看得到，因为它的位置太高，还被四周的柱廊围挡起来了。因此，浮雕的背景和图案都被涂上了亮丽的颜色，以便让人们看得更清楚一点儿。

巴台农神庙里那些柱子上方和柱子之间的空隙或者嵌板，称为“柱间壁”。这些柱间壁上，都雕有描绘战斗场景的高浮雕，其中绝大部分是众神与一种叫作“半人马”的野兽之间的搏斗。“半人马”是神话故事中的一种怪物，身子是马，但头和上身却是人。

神庙里有九十二组这样的柱间壁饰，可如今它们都已经破损不堪了！在许多情况下，其中的人物要么是一只胳膊、一条腿掉了，或是一只鼻子破了，要么就是少了一只耳朵或一只眼睛。因此，你们得运用自己的想象力，去想象图案完整无缺时是个什么样子才行。假如没有什么想象力，那你们很可能就会惊呼道：“什么！您

have no imagination, you probably will exclaim, "What! You call that beautiful?"

At each end of the Parthenon there is a large triangular space made by the sloping roof called a pediment. In these two triangular spaces were groups of superb, *heroic-size* figures of gods and goddesses. The word heroic-size means bigger than real life. The figures are fully in-the-round — that is, they stand free from the background. Unfortunately, little is left of these sculptures.

The group in one triangular end represented the birth of Athena. Athena was not born as a tiny baby but full-grown and fully armed. And she came from the brain of the king of the gods — that is why she was so wise. Zeus, the chief of the gods, was in the center of this group. Hephaestus, the blacksmith god, had just struck Zeus on the head with his hammer and, according to the story, Athena sprang out of Zeus's head in full armor.

On each side of this central group, the other gods and goddesses are looking on. Some are standing, some are sitting, and some are lying down. The groups were planned to fit the triangular spaces. *Dionysus Reclining* is one of the remaining statues.

Lord Elgin, an English nobleman, saw these sculptures many years ago and thought them so beautiful that he wanted his country

柱间壁饰，源自巴台农神庙细部，
现存于伦敦的大英博物馆
（摄影：加里·威肯）

说那也叫美丽？"

巴台农神庙的两端，各有一个由倾斜屋顶所构成的三角墙，称为"人字墙"。这两座三角墙上，雕有数组宏伟的、尺寸大过真人的众神雕像。所谓的"尺寸大过真人"，就是指尺寸比现实当中的人更大。这些雕像全都是彻彻底底的圆雕；也就是说，它们全都是脱离了背景的雕像。可惜的是，如今这些雕像也几乎所剩无几了。

其中一面人字墙一端的一组雕像，描绘了雅典娜女神降生时的情形。雅典娜出生时，可不是一个小宝宝，而是长大成人了，并且全副武装呢。她是从众神之王的脑袋里生出来的，所以她才这么聪明。众神之首宙斯位于这组雕像的中心。身为铁匠的火神赫菲斯托斯，刚刚用自己的铁锤击打了宙斯的脑袋；而根据神话的说法，此时，全副武装的雅典娜一下子便从宙斯的脑袋里跳了出来。

这组处于中心地带的雕像，周围都是旁观的其他众神。有些神灵站着，有些神灵坐着，还有些神灵则是躺着。这些众神的雕像，都被设计得与整面三角形的人字墙丝丝入扣。下面这尊《斜倚着的狄俄尼索斯[1]》，便是其中保存下来的一座雕像。

英国的一位贵族埃尔金勋爵，在很多年前看到了这些雕塑，觉得它们非常漂亮，因而希望自己的祖国也有这样的雕塑作品。这些雕塑作品在正常的情况下是看

[1] 狄俄尼索斯（Dionysus），古希腊神话中宙斯的儿子之一，也是酒神。

to have them. The sculptures could not be seen properly and they were gradually being destroyed, for there seemed to be no one interested enough to take care of them. So Lord Elgin bought most of them for about two hundred and fifty thousand dollars and took them to England, where they were put in the British Museum. They are now known as the Elgin Marbles.

But the greatest of all the sculpture that Phidias made was not in Athens. It was in a temple at Olympia. For this temple he made a statue of Zeus. It, too, was made of gold and ivory, and it, too, has disappeared. This statue of Zeus was so famous that it was called one of the Seven Wonders of the World and every Greek hoped to see it before he died. When Phidias had completed it, he prayed to Zeus and asked him to show in some way if he liked the statue of himself — whereupon a thunderbolt shot down from the blue sky overhead and struck near the sculptor's feet!

But after all he had done, the great Phidias was put in prison. You'd never guess why! It was because he had carved a picture of himself on the shield of Athena in the Parthenon. To the Athenians, it was a terrible crime for a mortal to put a picture of himself on the shield of their goddess! And so Phidias died in prison. What an end for such a great sculptor.

斜倚着的狄俄尼索斯，源自巴台农神庙细部，现存于伦敦的大英博物馆
（摄影：加里・威肯）

不到的，它们逐渐被损毁了，因为当时似乎没人对保护这些雕塑感兴趣。于是，埃尔金勋爵便花了大约二十五万美元，将其中的大部分都购买下来，并带回了英国，存放到了大英博物馆里。如今，这些雕塑便都被称为“埃尔金大理石雕”了。

不过，菲狄亚斯制作的最伟大的一件作品，却并不在雅典。它位于奥林匹亚的一座神庙里。他曾经为这座神庙制作了一尊宙斯雕像。这尊雕像也是用黄金和象牙雕刻而成的，并且如今也已不复存在了。由于这尊宙斯雕像极其有名，因此它还号称“世界七大奇迹”之一；每个希腊人都希望，自己能够在有生之年去看上一眼呢。菲狄亚斯完工之后，曾经向宙斯祈祷，要求宙斯用某种方式显一显灵，看他是不是喜欢自己的这尊雕像。就在此时，晴天里竟然出现了一道霹雳，从菲狄亚斯的头顶直劈下来，击在这位雕塑家的脚边！

不过，在做完这一切之后，伟大的菲狄亚斯却被关进了监狱。你们可能永远都猜不到原因！这是因为，他竟然把自己的形象，刻在巴台农神庙里雅典娜雕像的盾牌之上了。在雅典人看来，一名凡夫俗子竟然将自己的样子刻在雅典娜女神的盾牌之上，这可是一种严重的罪行！于是，菲狄亚斯后来便死在了监狱里。对于这样伟大的一位雕塑家来说，最终竟是这样一种下场，真是令人惋惜啊。

Chapter 7 After Phidias

Do you have a Greek nose? Do you know what a Greek nose is? It's a nose that, when seen from the side, forms a straight line from the forehead. Look at the people around you and see if any have Greek noses. Very few people have them nowadays and not all of the ancient Greeks had them either. But the Greek sculptors thought this kind of nose was the most beautiful and so they made Greek noses on their statues. A statue of Hermes, the messenger of the gods, shows a perfect Greek nose.

The statue is of a strong and athletic youth. In his arms, Hermes is holding a little boy who Zeus had given him to take care of. Hermes looks thoughtful as he tenderly holds the baby, and you can almost imagine that the baby is reaching up to pull Hermes' curly hair. What the baby is really reaching for is a bunch of grapes that Hermes once held in his hand. This statue has lost parts of its arms and legs, but the head and body are still perfect and probably no broken piece of sculpture in the world is more charming or more beautiful than this. It was made by a Greek sculptor named Praxiteles. If he had made nothing else in his life, this one statue was great enough to make him famous through the ages.

Praxiteles is thought to have made several other statues. One was of a faun — a half-man, half-goat Roman creature, which inspired the title of a book by Nathaniel Hawthorne, *The Marble Faun*. But we are not sure that there are any other sculptures in existence that he himself made.

第7章 菲狄亚斯之后

你们是不是长着一个希腊鼻呢？你们又知不知道，什么叫希腊鼻呢？这种鼻子，倘若从侧面来看，鼻梁很直，从前额往下，呈一条直线。观察一下你们周围的人，看有没有人长着希腊鼻。如今长这种鼻子的人不多，而古希腊人自然也不是全都长着这种鼻子。不过，古希腊的雕塑家却认为，这种鼻子的形状最漂亮，因此他们便将自己雕塑作品中的人物全都雕成了希腊鼻。有一尊雕像，雕刻的是身为众神信使的赫耳墨斯，它就呈现出了一个完美的希腊鼻。

雕像里的赫耳墨斯，是一个身体强壮、体格健硕的年轻人。赫耳墨斯的胳膊中抱着一个小男孩，那是宙斯交给他，让他去照料的。赫耳墨斯显得很细心，因为他是轻轻地抱着那个小男孩；而你们则差不多会以为，那个小宝宝伸出小手，是准备去抓赫耳墨斯头上的卷发。可实际上，那个小宝宝准备去抓的，是赫耳墨斯手中曾经拎着的一串葡萄呢。虽说这尊雕像四肢的一部分已经不见了，可它的头部和身体却依然非常完美；很可能，世界上再也没有哪件破损的雕塑作品，会比它更迷人、更漂亮呢。这件作品，是一个名叫普拉克希特列斯的古希腊雕塑家制作出来的。就算他终生没有雕刻出其他任何作品，这一尊雕塑也足够伟大，足以让他流芳百世了。

人们认为，普拉克希特列斯还制作出了其他数尊雕像。其中之一，便是一尊农牧之神的雕像。农牧之神，是古罗马神话中一种半人半羊的生物。后来，纳撒尼

赫耳墨斯像，普拉克希特列斯作品，
现存于奥林匹亚的考古博物馆
（摄影：加里·威肯）

Perhaps the best known of all statues in the world is that of Venus, the goddess of love and beauty. The sculpture was found on the Greek island of Melos, and so it is called the *Venus of Melos*, or *Venus de Milo*. She, too, has a perfect Greek nose. We do not know who the sculptor was, but some people now think that one of the students of Praxiteles must have made it.

In the statue, Venus has no arms, but a great many people have tried to imagine what the arms were doing when she did have them. Some say that she was holding a bronze shield on her knee and looking into its brightly polished surface to see her reflection. People had no glass mirrors at that time. Instead their mirrors were made of shiny metal. Others say she held a lance or something else or nothing at all, but no one is sure.

Venus de Milo was discovered by accident. A man happened to pass by a limekiln on the island of Melos one day and the statue was lying on the

尔·霍桑[1]写《玉石雕像》时的灵感，就来自这尊雕像呢。但是，我们并不确定，世上还有没有他亲自制作的其他雕像。

或许，全世界所有的雕塑作品中，最广为人知的要算爱情和美貌女神维纳斯的那尊雕像了。这座雕像是在希腊的米洛斯岛上发现的，因此被称为《米洛斯的维纳斯》，或者《米罗的维纳斯》[2]。这座维纳斯的雕像，也有一个完美的希腊鼻。虽说我们搞不清楚是谁创作了这座雕像，但如今有些人认为，这一定是普拉克希特列斯的某位学生雕刻出来的。

这座雕像里的维纳斯没有胳膊。许多人都曾经试图去想象，有胳膊的时候，她的胳膊究竟在干什么。有些人说，她是手持一面青铜盾牌，并将盾牌搁在自己膝上，看着打磨得非常光亮的盾面，在照镜子。当时，世界上还没有玻璃镜面呢。人们都是用闪亮的金属器具来当镜子的。还有一些人则说，她是手持长矛，或者手持其他东西，或者手里根本就没拿任何东西。不过，这些都只是猜测，谁也没法肯定。

《米罗的维纳斯》是在无意当中被人们发现的。有一天，一个人偶然经过了米

[1] 纳撒尼尔·霍桑（Nathaniel Hawthorne，1804—1864），美国十九世纪前半叶最伟大的作家之一。他既是美国心理分析小说的开创者，也是一位浪漫主义和象征主义的小说家，代表作有《红字》《带七个尖顶的阁楼》《福谷传奇》等。《玉石雕像》是他在侨居意大利期间所写的一部探讨人性善恶问题的长篇小说。

[2] 米洛斯（Melos），希腊南部基克拉迪群岛中的主要岛屿之一，亦拼成 Milos 或 Milo，相当于汉语中的异体字。因此，这里虽说叫法不同，但所指的都是同一尊雕像。

ground near the limekiln. A limekiln is a kind of furnace where stone is burned to turn it into lime. The Greek owner of the limekiln, like a good many people today, saw no beauty in the old broken statue and was about to break it up and put it in the furnace to turn it into lime. The man who happened by in the nick of time *did* know how valuable the statue was and he bought it. After some time, France got it and placed it in the Louvre Museum in Paris. It is one of that museum's chief treasures and cannot be bought for any sum of money.

Many believe this statue to be the most beautiful of all women because she is a combination of women who are different ages all at once. She is a young girl, young mother, and mature woman all at the same time. Can you see who's who?

Praxiteles had a friend named Scopas, who also was a sculptor but he liked to make statues that showed people in an emotional state. There are several statues showing the mythological figure Niobe and her children that Scopas may have done, for the statues are the kind he did — they show the emotion of suffering. But some believe Praxiteles did them. Others think the students of one of these two sculptors did them.

The Greek story of Niobe is this: Niobe was the mother of fourteen children — seven boys and seven

米罗的维纳斯，
现存于巴黎的卢浮宫
（摄影：约翰·帕特森）

洛斯岛上的一座石灰窑，发现这尊雕像就躺在石灰窑附近的地上。石灰窑是一种能够把石头烧化成石灰的大火炉。当时，拥有这座石灰窑的那个希腊人就像如今的许多人一样，看不出这尊又旧又破的雕像有什么美感来，所以正准备打碎雕像，将它扔进窑里去烧成石灰哩。在这千钧一发之际碰巧经过的那个人，却知道这尊雕像有多珍贵，所以将雕像买了下来。过了一段时间，这尊雕像被法国购得，成了巴黎卢浮宫的藏品。如今，这座雕像可是卢浮宫的镇馆之宝，出多少钱也买不到了哩。

许多人都认为，这尊雕像是所有女性雕塑作品中最美丽的一座，因为它将同一女性不同年龄段的美丽集于一身。她既是一个少女，一位年轻的母亲，同时也是一个成熟的女人。你们能看出哪个地方说明她是少女，哪个地方又说明她是年轻的母亲和成熟的女人吗?

普拉克希特列斯有一个朋友，叫作斯科帕斯，后者也是一位雕塑家，但他喜欢制作表现人们情感状态的雕塑。有好几尊描述神话人物尼俄柏及其孩子们的雕塑，可能都是斯科帕斯的杰作，因为这些雕塑完全符合他的风格：它们都表现了人物承受苦难时的强烈情感。不过，有些人却认为，这几座雕像都是普拉克希特列斯雕刻出来的。还有一些人则认为，它们是这两位雕塑家的一位学生雕刻出来的。

在古希腊神话中，关于尼俄柏的故事是这样的：尼俄柏是一位母亲，她生了

girls — of whom she was very proud. But she made the mistake of boasting about them to a goddess who had only two children and that made the goddess jealous. As a punishment, all of Niobe's children were killed before her eyes. Niobe, with her arms wrapped around her youngest child, is shown trying to shield her from the arrows of the gods. As her last child was killed, the gods, as a great favor, turned Niobe into stone so she wouldn't suffer any more.

One of the students of Scopas is supposed to have made another very famous statue that we call *Winged Victory*, or *Victory of Samothrace* because it was found on the Greek island of Samothrace. The statue was made to celebrate a victory of the Greeks at sea. The statue shows the goddess of victory standing on the prow of a boat with the wind blowing back her robe. Although she has neither head nor arms, you can see in your mind's eye how she must have looked as she stood triumphantly erect, blowing a trumpet and facing the sea breeze.

Have you ever noticed what someone looks like when he is running fast or perhaps riding a bicycle as fast as possible down a long hill? When you look at *Winged Victory*, you can see her just like that. Her flowing clothes and wings give you a feeling of the wind rushing by. And there is something very unusual too. You can see different parts of her body clearly. Imagine how difficult it is to show that in marble and you will see just why *Winged Victory* is so famous.

You may wonder why someone has not repaired this Greek statue — that is, brought it back to its original condition by putting a new head and arms on it. As a matter of fact, many sculptors have tried to do so. Of course they were not allowed

十四个孩子，七男七女，并且很为自己的这些孩子感到自豪。不过，她犯了一个错误，竟然向一位只生了两个孩子的女神吹嘘自己的孩子们有多了不起，从而让那位女神妒火中烧。作为惩罚，她命人当面杀死了尼俄柏的十四个孩子。雕像中的尼俄柏紧紧地抱着最小的孩子，样子就像是在竭力替孩子挡住众神射过来的箭矢。最后一个孩子也被杀死之后，众神又"大发慈悲"，将尼俄柏变成了石头，以便让她不再受苦。

人们认为，斯科帕斯的一位学生制作出了另一尊极其著名的雕像，我们称这座雕像为《双翼胜利女神》，或者《萨莫色雷斯的胜利女神》，因为这尊雕像是在希腊一个叫作萨莫色雷斯的岛屿上发现的。制作这尊雕像，是为了庆祝古希腊人的一次海战大捷。雕像描述的是胜利女神站在船首，海风将她身上的长袍向后吹拂着的情形。尽管雕像既没有头，也没有胳膊，但你们完全可以想象得出，她欢欣鼓舞地矗立船头，吹着得胜的号角，面对猎猎海风时的模样呢。

你们有没有注意过，一个人正在飞速奔跑，或者骑着自行车飞速冲下一条长长的山坡时的样子呢？观察观察《双翼胜利女神》这尊雕像，你们就会看到，雕像的样子正是如此。她那飘扬的衣裾和双翼，给人一种海风迅速拂过身旁的感觉。这尊雕像还有某种极其罕见之处。你们完全可以清晰地看出女神的各个身体部位来。想一想，用大理石来清晰地表现出各个部位该有多么困难；这样，你们就会明白，《双翼胜利女神》这尊雕像为何会如此有名了。

你们可能会觉得奇怪，为什么没有人修复这尊古希腊的雕塑作品；也就是说，为什么没有人给它安上一个

to experiment on the original statue, but they made copies and added the missing parts as they supposed those parts must have been. It may seem strange, but every such *restoration*, as it is called, has been so unsatisfactory that everyone prefers the broken statue instead of a restored one.

I know a little girl who always puts her hand over the illustrations in a book that she loves to read. "Because," she says, "the picture I see in my mind is so much better than the picture in the book that I don't want the picture I have in my mind spoiled!" Can you picture in your mind how the *Winged Victory* or the *Venus de Milo* once looked?

双翼胜利女神，
现存于巴黎的卢浮宫
（摄影：加里·威肯）

新的脑袋和新的胳膊，从而将它恢复到原貌。事实上，很多的雕塑家都曾经试过这一点呢。当然，他们是不准在这尊雕像的原作上进行试验的；不过，他们制作了许多的复制品，并将他们以为原先一定存在、如今不见了的身体部位补上去。虽说似乎奇怪得很，但每次所谓的“复原”都让人们觉得非常不满意，因此大家都宁愿去看这尊破损了的原作，也不愿再将它复原。

我认识一个小姑娘，她总是会用手遮住自己喜欢看的、书里面的插图。“因为，”她解释说，“我脑海里想象出来的图画，要比书里的好多了，所以不想让书里的插图毁掉我想象中的画面！”你们能在脑海里想象一下，《双翼胜利女神》或者《米罗的维纳斯》这两尊雕像曾经的样子吗？

Chapter 8 Plaster Casts

When I was a boy I used go to a museum that had copies of all the great Greek sculptures made out of plaster — *plaster casts*, they are called. The statues I liked best of all, I learned afterward, were not considered as good as those I've told you about in the last chapter. That seems to be the way with children. They like certain things when they are young and different things when they grow up. My favorite was a statue with a label that read The Dying Gladiator.

"What is a gladiator?" I asked.

A gladiator, I was told, was a swordsman, and gladiators were prisoners or slaves who were made to fight each other or a wild animal until one or the other died. This was done just for the amusement of a crowd of people who gathered in a field surrounded with seats, like a stadium, to watch the sport.

I didn't learn until later that the label on the statue was wrong. It should have read The Dying Gaul and not The Dying Gladiator. The Gauls were a barbaric and uncivilized people who lived in the country that is now France. The Gauls fought the Greeks and this Gaul was killed in battle. He wore a twisted collar or chain called a torque around his neck. That's how we know he was a Gaul, for Gauls wore this particular kind of collar.

第8章 石膏雕塑

小的时候，我经常去一家博物馆，那里有用石膏制作出来的、古希腊所有伟大雕塑作品的复制品；这些复制品，被称为石膏雕塑。后来我得知，人们觉得，其中我最喜欢的那些雕塑，并不像我在上一章已经跟你们提及的那些雕塑作品一样好。孩子们似乎就是这样的。他们小的时候会喜欢某些东西，而长大成人之后，喜欢的却是不同的东西了。我最喜欢的是一尊雕塑，上面贴着一张标签，写着“垂死的角斗士”。

“角斗士是什么人？”我问道。

有人告诉我说，角斗士就是一名武士；很多角斗士都是囚犯或者奴隶，被迫去彼此格斗，或者搏击野兽，直到其中的一个被对方杀死。之所以如此，仅仅是为了娱乐观众；当时，一大群观众会聚集到一个四周都有座位的、像是如今的体育馆的圆形场地里，去观看这项搏击运动呢。

直到后来我才知道，那座雕塑上的标签标错了。它应当是“垂死的高卢人”，而不是“垂死的角斗士”。高卢人是古时一个野蛮的、未开化的民族，生活在如今的法国。当时，高卢人正与希腊人打仗，而这个高卢人则在战斗中阵亡了。他的脖子上戴着一个扭曲了的项饰，或者说项链，称作“项圈”。这正是我们知道他是一个高卢人的原因：因为只有高卢人，才会佩戴这种特别的项圈。

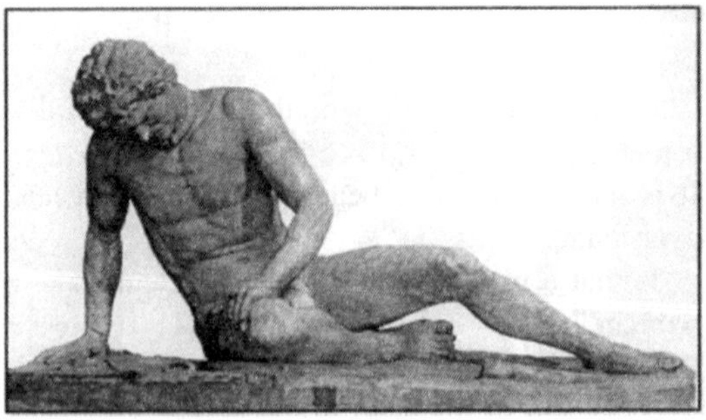

垂死的高卢人，古罗马雕塑复制品，
现存于罗马的卡匹托利欧博物馆
（由缅因州桑福德的大学印刷协会提供）

The statue showed a wound made by a sword in the Gaul's side and the stony blood flowing from it. A sign on the statue read Don't Touch but I could hardly keep from touching the sword wound from which the blood flowed. It seemed so very natural.

"Come away," said my mother. "It's dreadful — a man dying. Let's go see the *Apollo Belvedere*. It is one of the most beautiful statues of a man ever made."

"Is that a man?" I exclaimed. "He looks like a woman."

"That's just because he has long hair and it is piled on top of his head in the way many Greek men wore their hair."

Apollo, as I've told you, was the Sun god and the handsomest of all the Greek gods. We don't know what he is supposed to be doing in this statue. Some say he was holding a bow in his left hand and that he had just pulled the bowstring with his right hand and shot a dreadful dragon-like serpent called a Python, which had killed everyone who had come near it. Others say Apollo was holding the head of Medusa in his left hand to turn his enemy into stone. Apollo, Minerva, and Perseus all had copies of Medusa's head to kill their enemies with.

Belvedere means beautiful to see, but the *Apollo*

贝尔维德勒的阿波罗，
古罗马雕塑复制品，
现存于罗马梵蒂冈的庇护-克莱门蒂诺博物馆
（摄影：加里·威肯）

雕像中的高卢人身体一侧有一处剑伤，还有石制的鲜血从伤口中流淌出来。雕像上挂着一块标牌，写着“请勿触摸”的字样；可我实在没有忍住，还是摸了摸那处流淌着鲜血的剑伤。那处伤口，看上去非常的自然、逼真。

“走吧，”我母亲说。“太可怕了，一个垂死的人。我们还是去看看《贝尔维德勒的阿波罗》吧。那可是人类雕刻出来的最美丽的雕塑作品之一呢。”

“那是个男的吗？”我大声问道，“他看上去很像个女的啊。”

“那只是因为他的头发很长，并且像许多古希腊人一样，将头发盘在头顶上罢了。”

我在前面已经跟你们说过，阿波罗是太阳神，也是希腊诸神中最英俊的一位。我们不清楚这尊雕像里的阿波罗正在干什么。有的人说，他的左手持着一把弓，而右手则拉着弓弦，射出一条可怕的龙形巨蟒；那条巨蟒叫作“皮同”，任何靠近它的人都会被它杀死。还有些人则称，阿波罗的左手提着美杜莎的脑袋，正准备把他的敌人变成石头。阿波罗、密涅瓦[1]和珀耳修斯这三位神灵，都曾经用复制的美杜莎脑袋杀过敌呢。

“贝尔维德勒”的意思，是指看上去很美丽；不过，这尊阿波罗雕像被称为

[1] 密涅瓦（Minerva），古罗马神话中的智慧女神，也就是古希腊神话中的雅典娜（Athena）。

Laocöönis called Belvedere not because he was beautiful to see but because the room in which the statue now stands in the Vatican Museum in Rome is called the Belvedere Room.

But I was more interested in the statues that told a story, especially if the story seemed to be something terrible. There was a big statue of three men caught in the coils of two huge serpents called *Laocöön and His Two Sons*. Laocöön was a Trojan priest who told his people that the Greeks were pulling a trick on them. Just then two huge snakes attacked Laocöön's sons. He went to help them, and all three were killed by the serpents. The people believed this was a sign that Laocöön was not telling the truth about their enemy, although later it turned out — too late — that he was right. Not one but three sculptors are said to have made this statue.

Why is it that some people like to see pictures and statues of suffering and dying? I used to but now I wouldn't have a picture or a statue of such a thing in my house. It is too unpleasant to have around. But in ancient times people were bloodthirsty and loved to see killings as well as statues of killing and suffering. They went to fights and took their lunches along to eat while they watched and gloated over the fighting — especially those that ended in death. There are still people who like to see bullfights in which the bull is killed.

拉奥孔和他的两个儿子，现存于罗马梵蒂冈的庇护-克莱门蒂诺博物馆
（摄影：加里・威肯）

“贝尔维德勒”，却并不是因为阿波罗看上去很漂亮，而是因为如今这尊雕塑存放在罗马梵蒂冈博物馆里一间被称为“贝尔维德勒宫”的屋子里。

不过，我对那些讲述了某个故事的雕塑更感兴趣；而倘若雕塑作品讲述的是个恐怖故事，那就尤其如此了。有一座巨大的雕像，描绘了三个人被两条巨蟒紧紧缠住的情形，叫作《拉奥孔和他的两个儿子》。拉奥孔是特洛伊的一位祭司，他曾经提醒过特洛伊人，说希腊人正在对他们耍花招。就在那时，两条巨蟒袭击了拉奥孔的两个儿子。他跑过去帮助儿子，可最终三人都被巨蟒杀死了。特洛伊人认为这是一种预兆，说明拉奥孔对敌人情况的分析是错误的；虽说结果表明他说得对，可为时已晚了。据说，这尊雕像不是由一位雕塑家完成的，而是三位雕塑家共同创作出来的。

为什么有些人喜欢看描绘人们受苦或者临死时情形的绘画和雕塑作品呢？虽说以前我也喜欢这样，可如今我却不会再在家里保存这样的绘画或者雕塑作品了。看着这样的东西，太让人不舒服了。但在古时，人们却残忍嗜杀，喜欢看到杀戮的场景，喜欢看那些描绘杀戮和苦难的雕塑作品。他们经常打仗，并且会带上午餐，边吃边心满意足地观看战斗场景，尤其是观看那些以死亡告终的场景。如今，仍然有一些人很喜欢观看斗牛比赛呢；在这种比赛中，公牛最终也会被人杀死。

But there was one little statue I've always liked. It is not a statue of a god or a mythical person — not even of a grown-up. It is of a boy pulling a thorn out of his bare foot, and it shows us that boys who go barefooted today are very much like boys who went barefooted two thousand years ago.

Have you ever noticed how people balance when sitting on a stool? They curve this way and that. And if they were sitting there trying to get a splinter out of the bottom of their foot, they would almost fall over. Remember how much trouble sculptors had making statues that were walking forward instead of standing straight up? Well, it's just as hard to make a boy pulling a thorn out of his foot while sitting on a stool without falling off!

Another statue called the Colossus of Rhodes was made around 290 B.C. It was so huge that there was no plaster cast of it. It was a giant bronze statue of the Sun god, about one hundred feet high. According to legend, it was placed so that the god's legs straddled the entrance to the harbor on the island of Rhodes and ships passed between its legs. But in reality, it stood on a pedestal near the harbor. It was one of the Seven Wonders of the World. For some reason, perhaps in an earthquake, the Colossus fell and the broken pieces were sold for junk.

拔刺的男孩，
现存于罗马的康塞巴托里宫美术馆

不过，我一向都很喜欢一座小雕像。它既不是哪位神灵的雕像，不是什么神话人物的雕像，甚至也不是一位成年人的雕像。那是一个小男孩，正在把一根小刺从自己的光脚丫上拔出来。这座雕像向我们表明，如今光着脚走路的小男孩，与两千多年前那些光着脚丫的小男孩是很相像的。

你们有没有注意过，人们坐在凳子上的时候，是怎样保持平衡的呢？他们总是会这样或那样地弓着腰。倘若坐在凳子上时，想要弯下腰将脚掌上的碎片拔出来的话，那么他们几乎就会摔上一跤。还记得雕塑家们是如何费尽心思，才制作出向前走的雕像，而不是直直地站立着的雕像吗？好吧，制作出描绘一个小男孩坐在凳子上将脚掌上的刺拔出来，而不让他摔倒的雕像，也同样麻烦得很呢！

还有一尊名叫《罗得岛巨像》的雕塑，是公元前290年左右制作出来的。这座雕像极其巨大，因此没有任何石膏模型。它是一尊用青铜制成的太阳神巨像，约有一百英尺高哩。根据神话传说，这座雕像的位置很特别：神像的双腿正好跨过罗得岛港的入口，而进出的船只则在其双腿之下驶过。可实际上，它却坐落在港口附近的一个基座上。它也属于世界“七大奇迹”之一。由于某种原因，没准是因为一次地震，这尊巨像倒塌下来，摔成了碎片，然后就被人们当成废品卖掉了。

Chapter 9 Tiny Treasures

For where your treasure is, there will your heart be also.
— Matthew 6:21

I once read a description of a group of sculptured figures that had been made for a public building. The chief thing the newspaper said about the sculpture was that it weighed ten tons. It did not say whether the statues were beautiful or not — just that they weighed ten tons. It might have been ten tons of coal. But mere size doesn't make a thing beautiful. The Greeks made some huge statues and they were beautiful. They also made tiny sculptured figures so small that you have to look at them under a magnifying glass to see how beautiful they are.

Once in a museum I saw a piece of such sculpture. It couldn't have weighed more than an ounce and was no larger than a domino. It was a piece of colored stone through which the light shone and beautiful figures of Greek gods and goddesses were carved into it in low relief. The figures had been cut into the stone with very fine but sharp tools. It had been made by some Greek sculptor whose name no one knows. It was called a gem, the name we give to anything that is very precious although it may be tiny.

The British Museum in London has a whole room of such gems made by sculptors as

第9章 小小珍品

因为你的财宝在那里，你的心也在那里。
——《圣经·新约·马太福音》6：21

我曾经看到过一篇报道，其中介绍了为一座公共建筑而制作出来的一组雕塑。报纸上对这组雕塑的介绍，主要是说它重达十吨。报道并没有评价说这组雕塑究竟是丑是美，只是说它们重达十吨。没准儿是十吨煤炭呢。但是，仅凭尺寸可不会让一个东西美丽起来。古希腊人曾经制作出了一些巨型雕塑，并且都漂亮得很。他们还制作出了一些微型的雕塑作品；这些微雕的尺寸太小，人们只能用放大镜去看，才能看得出它们是多么精美呢。

有一次，我在博物馆里就看到了一件这样的雕塑作品。它的重量绝对不会超过一盎司[1]，尺寸还没有一粒骰子大。那是一颗透光的五彩石子，上面雕刻了古希腊诸神的美丽形象，并且都是浅浮雕。诸神的形象都是用非常精细，但又非常锋利的工具，雕刻在石头上面。它是由某位古希腊雕塑家制作出来的，可如今却无人知道这位雕塑家姓甚名谁了。这件雕塑被称为“宝石”。如今，对于任何小而贵重的东西，我们都称之为宝石哩。

[1] 盎司（ounce），英制重量单位。1 盎司约合 28.35 克。

great as those who made life-size and colossal-size figures. These gems were made for kings and wealthy people, for no others could afford them. Rich people long ago used to collect such gems as you might collect stamps. Today museums — and those who can afford it — still do so.

Often these tiny bits of low-relief sculpture were cut in a stone that had two or three layers of different colors so that the figures were one color and the background another. If one layer was black and the other white, the stone was called *onyx*. If the top layer was reddish and those below it white and black, it was called *sardonyx*. Such sculptured low reliefs were known as *cameos*, and some were very beautiful. Today cameos are made of shells with two color layers and are called *shell cameos*. Some are cut from two or more layers of different-colored stone cemented together or from artificial sardonyx.

There was another kind of gem made in great quantities, in which the figures were hollowed out or sunken instead of being raised. A gem of this sort was called a *seal or intaglio*, which means sunken. The seals were used to stamp a design in wax. The stamped impression made from the sunken relief was raised in wax, and one could

古罗马的石雕“奥古斯都之宝”，
现存于维也纳的艺术史博物馆
（由波士顿的大学印刷协会提供）

伦敦的大英博物馆里有一整间藏室，里面全都是雕塑家们制作出来的这种宝石；而那些雕塑家，也与制作真人大小或者巨型塑像的雕塑家一样伟大。这些宝石都是替国王和有钱人制作的，因为其他人不可能买得起这样的东西。很久以前的有钱人经常收藏这样的宝石，就像你们如今集邮一样。而今天的博物馆，以及那些有经济实力的人，也还在这样做呢。

通常来说，这些微型的浅浮雕作品都是雕刻在一颗有两三层不同颜色的石头上，从而让雕刻出来的人物是一种颜色，背景又是另一种颜色。假如一层是黑色，另一层是白色，这样的石头就被称为“黑玛瑙”。假如最顶上的那一层是红色，而下面的一层是黑白相间的话，就叫作“缠丝玛瑙”。这样雕刻出来的浅浮雕，人们称之为“石雕”，其中有一些作品雕刻得非常精美。如今，石雕都是用有两层颜色的贝壳雕制而成的，因而被称为“贝雕”。有些石雕则是切下两层或者多层不同颜色的石子粘贴起来后再雕刻而成，或者是用人造缠丝玛瑙雕刻而成的。

还有一种大量雕刻的宝石，其中的图案都是镂空或者凹陷下去，而不是向上凸起的。这种宝石被称为“印章”或者“凹雕”；所谓的“凹雕”，就是凹陷下去的雕塑。这种印章，是用于在蜂蜡上压印出图案来。凹雕在蜂蜡上按压后形成的压

make as many stamped impressions with the seal as he or she liked. Each person who could afford it had such a seal with a special design all his own to stamp everything he wished to mark with his own hand. Everyone would then know he alone had made the impression. These seals are similar to the cylinder stamps that the Assyrians, who lived long before the Romans, used to sign their names.

Back in the days when few people knew how to write — or even how to sign their names — these seals were used to make marks that served the same purpose as signatures. Sometimes the seal was fitted into a finger ring that was worn by the owner so that no one else could use it. Such rings were called *signet rings*, or signing rings. Sometimes the seal was not mounted in a ring but was kept in a safe place so that no one but the owner could use it.

Have you ever collected coins? Many people do. Perhaps you would never think of such coins as a kind of sculpture, but that is what old coins are — pieces of low-relief sculpture. The Greeks used to make the most beautiful coins with heads or figures of famous people or gods on them in low relief. First they made a die that was a sunken relief, and then coins were stamped out of metal — gold, silver or bronze — with the die.

One difference between a coin and a gem is that a coin is made from a die and any number of the same coin can be made from one die. But a gem is one of a kind and cannot be duplicated. The coins of some countries today are really beautiful but not quite as beautiful as those the ancient Greeks made. One reason for this is that today our coins have to be made quite flat, or in very low relief, so that they will stack in a pile, for this

痕，是向上凸起的，而人们也可以用印章压出许多的图案来，想印多少就印多少。当时凡是买得起印章的人，都有一枚这样的印章，上面刻有属于自己的专用图案，可以亲手在想要打上标记的任何东西上盖下自己的印章。这样一来，大家便都明白，这个印记是他盖上的了。这些印章，与古亚述人的柱形印章类似；古亚述人所处的时期要比古罗马人早得多，当时他们常常是用柱形印章来签名的。

在还没有几个人会写字，或者说甚至没有几个人会签自己大名的古代，人们用这些印章盖印的作用，与如今的签名是一样的。有的时候，人们会把印章做成戒指戴在手上；这样一来，除了自己，别人就没法使用印章了。这种戒指，就叫“印戒”，也就是签名戒指。有的时候，人们不会将印章镶嵌在戒指上，而是会将其藏在安全的地方，因而除了印章的主人，任何人都别想使用这一印章了。

你们有没有收集过硬币呢？许多人都有这一爱好。或许，你们根本就没有想过，这些硬币也是一种雕塑呢；可古币事实上也是一种雕塑，是一种浅浮雕哩。古希腊人曾经制作出了最漂亮的钱币，上面用浅浮雕的方式雕刻有名人、神灵的头像或者全身像。他们首先会制作出一种凹浮雕模具，然后再用这种模具冲压出金属硬币来；而所用的金属，则是黄金、白银，或者青铜。

硬币与宝石之间的一大区别，便在于硬币是用模具冲压出来的，并且一个模具能够压制出大量的同一种硬币来。可宝石雕品却是独一无二、不可复制的。虽说如今一些国家里发行的硬币确实非常漂亮，可它们还是没有古希腊人制作的那样精美。之所以如此，原因之一便在于，如今我们的硬币必须制作得非常平整，或者说

is necessary in our banks. But it was not necessary to stack the old Greek coins in piles, so they could be made in higher relief.

雕有亚历山大大帝头像的古罗马勋章，
现存于马里兰州巴尔的摩的沃尔特斯艺术博物馆

Coins were, of course, used to buy things, but there were old coin-like sculptures called medals that generally were larger and were not used as money. The figures on medals were often in higher relief and were made by pouring the metal into a mold instead of by stamping the metal with a die. Usually such medals were made for prizes in athletic games, honors in war, or to celebrate some great event, anniversary, or celebration. Medals of this kind are still made today. Perhaps you know someone who has won such a medal and you can see for yourself.

只能用非常浅的浅浮雕工艺，从而让它们可以叠放起来，因为银行需要这样。可古希腊人却不需将钱币堆叠起来，因而硬币上的图案可以制成较深的高浮雕。

钱币自然是用来买东西的，可还有一些样子很像古币的、叫作勋章的雕塑作品，它们虽说尺寸通常都比钱币要大，却不是用来当钱币使用的。勋章上的图案通常都是高浮雕，并且是将金属熔液倒入模具浇铸出来，而不是用模具冲压金属制成的。这种勋章，一般都是为了奖励运动会上的获胜者，表彰战争中的立功者，或者纪念某一重大事件、周年纪念或者庆典而制作出来的。人们如今仍然会制作这样的勋章呢。没准，你们认识的某个人曾经就获得过这样的勋章；那样的话，你们就可以亲自去看一看这种勋章了。

Chapter 10 Baked-Earth Sculpture

Terra cotta means earth baked. A flowerpot and a brick are terra cotta — that is, earth or clay baked until it is brownish red. You may have made things out of mud — cups and saucers — and the old Greeks made figures of people in the same way and out of the same thing, mud or clay. They made little statues of women, smaller than dolls, out of clay and then baked them so that they would not crumble to pieces. The baking process turned them into terra cotta.

It was the custom to place these little figures or little statues — called *figurines and statuettes* — in tombs and graves, and thousands of them have been dug up and are now in museums. Because they were first dug up in a town in Greece named Tanagra, all such statuettes are Tanagra figurines. They are usually figures of ladies carrying a fan or a parasol, all very finely dressed. Yes, the Greek ladies had fans and parasols like the ones you might still see on occasion today in a movie or a play. What is unusual in Greek sculpture is that these female figures are fully clothed.

Most of the statuettes are original but some of them are copies of large statues. As many of the large statues have disappeared, these figurine copies show us what the originals looked like. But they show us more than that. If you want to find out what the Greeks really were like, go to a museum and look at these little figures. The big, famous marble statues are of gods and goddesses, athletes and warriors. They were more nearly perfect

第10章 陶土雕塑

“赤陶”是一种经过烧制的泥土。花盆、砖块，都属于陶土制品；也就是说，它们都是一种经过烧制、变成了褐红色的泥土或者黏土。你们可能都用泥巴做过东西，比如杯子呀，盘子呀；而古希腊人也曾用同样的方法，用同样的材料，即泥巴或黏土，制作过人物雕像呢。他们曾经用黏土制作出比玩具娃娃更小的微型女性雕像，然后再放入火中烧制，从而使得这些雕像不会破碎。烧制的过程，便将这些雕像变成了赤陶。

当时有一种风俗，那就是将这些称为“陶俑”或者“小雕像”的小型人物雕塑品放进坟墓里；人们已经发掘出成千上万件这样的小雕像，并将它们保存进了博物馆。由于它们最初是从希腊一个叫作塔纳格拉的小镇发掘出来的，因此所有这些小塑像都被称为“塔纳格拉陶俑”。它们通常都是手摇扇子或者打着遮阳伞的女性陶俑，并且全部都衣着精美呢。是的，古希腊的贵妇们都有扇子和遮阳伞，与你们如今偶尔还能在电影或者戏剧里看到那种扇子和遮阳伞很相似。但古希腊雕塑与众不同的一点是，这些女性人物身上的穿戴，全都齐整得很呢。

绝大多数小陶俑都是原创作品，但其中也有一些是大型雕塑的仿制品。由于许多的大型雕塑作品都不复存在了，因此这些小型的陶俑仿制品便向我们展示出了原作的模样。不过，它们呈现出来的东西可不仅于此。如果你们想要弄明白古希腊人

than real people. But these terra-cotta statuettes are copied from everyday Greeks. They show ordinary people in everyday activities.

Many of the figurines were painted in bright colors. Some had tiny necklaces of real gold or held bronze ornaments in their hands. But on many of them, the only color left is the brownish red of the clay from which they were formed. To make each figurine the same but a little bit different, they were made of parts like a doll. The heads, arms, and legs were made in separate molds. Then the sculptor would put these parts onto the bodies in different combinations in order to make each figurine the way he thought best.

Figurines were made for the dead; lamps were made for the living. Lamps, which every house had to have, were decorated with figures in low relief. Lamps today, of course, are electric and quite different from those in ancient Greece. These old lamps were very small, seldom larger than your hand, and were made either of terra cotta or bronze. They had a hole in which a twisted piece of string-like cloth was stuffed to make a wick. They held olive

塔纳格拉陶俑

究竟是个什么样子，那就到博物馆里去看一看这些小陶俑吧。那些大型的、著名的大理石雕像，雕刻的都是众神、运动员和勇士。它们差不多全都过于完美，不是真实的古希腊人。而这些小陶俑所描摹的，却都是古希腊人在日常生活中的样子。它们所刻画的，都是普通百姓日常生活的场景。

许多小陶俑上，都漆有亮丽的颜色。有些小陶俑的脖子上，还挂着真金制成的微型项链，或者是手中拿着青铜首饰呢。不过，其中的许多陶俑，如今都只剩下制作这些陶俑所用的黏土本来的那种褐红色了。为了让每尊陶俑都一模一样，只有细微的差别，它们都是像如今制作玩具娃娃的工序一样，用不同的部位组装起来的。头部、胳膊和腿都是用不同的模具进行制作。然后，雕塑家会按照不同的组合方式，将这些部位安装到陶俑身体上去，以便让每尊小陶俑都变成雕塑家心中所想的最佳样子。

这些小陶俑是为死者制作的，而灯具却是为活着的人而制作出来的。每家每户所必需的油灯，上面都雕有浅浮雕的装饰图案。如今我们所用的灯具当然是电灯，与古希腊人所用的油灯已经完全不同了。那些古老的油灯尺寸都很小，几乎大不过你们的手掌，并且要么是用陶土制成，要么便是用青铜制成的。油灯上面有一个孔，人们把一条用布拧成的细绳穿过这个孔，塞入油灯里当灯芯。灯中盛着的是橄

oil or grease that soaked the wick and made it burn when lighted. These lamps gave no more light than a burning match and that was all the light people had at night. Perhaps they did not need more light because they went to bed earlier than we do. The lamps often had Greek gods, goddesses, or other mythological characters on the tops or sides.

Lamps were made in molds, and hundreds or even thousands of lamps were made from one mold. Some of the old molds have been dug up out of the ground and are used to make modern reproductions that are sold today as souvenirs to travelers. Old lamps made of bronze have a patina — a greenish finish showing a softening of the surface that comes with age. New reproductions of lamps made of bronze are sometimes dipped in acid to make them look old, but they have sharper edges than the old lamps and the finish made by the acid bath does not look the same as that eaten away by time. If the reproductions are made of clay, the lamps look cleaner cut and fresher than the old ones. So if you are thinking of buying an ancient lamp, be sure to notice the patina or the freshness of the clay.

Now far away from Greece is another ancient land — China. There was a time when the subjects of the Chinese emperor had their lives saved by terra cotta. Can you imagine how?

Well, in 250 B.C. the first Chinese Emperor Qin Shih Huang Ti made everyone very happy when he decided not to do what his father had done, which was to bury his servants and soldiers alive with him when he died. Instead he had sculptors make life-size terra-cotta replicas of each and every servant and soldier. You see, the emperor had not had an

榄油或者动物油脂，灯芯浸透油脂之后，点着就会燃烧。这些油灯，比一根划着的火柴亮不了多少，可那时的人，晚上全靠这个照明呢。没准他们并不需要太亮，因为当时的人都比我们睡得早。油灯的顶上或者侧面，通常都雕有古希腊众神或其他的神话人物形象。

油灯是用模具制成的，而一个模具可以制造出数百盏甚至数千盏油灯来。我们已经出土了一些古老的模具，并且用它们制造出了现代的仿制品，然后再将这些仿制油灯当成纪念品卖给游客。历史悠久的青铜油灯上，会形成一层铜绿，即一种绿色的表层，表明随着时间的推移，油灯的表面已经软化了。人们有时会把新仿制出来的青铜油灯放入酸液中浸泡，使它们看上去显得古旧；但它们的边缘会比真正的古灯清晰，而经过浸酸做旧形成的表层，看上去也会与长时间腐蚀形成的表层不一样。假如仿制品是用陶土做成的，那么油灯的外形轮廓就会比真正的古灯更清晰，颜色也会更鲜艳。因此，假如打算购买一盏古灯的话，那你们一定得注意油灯表面的铜绿，或者陶土颜色的鲜艳程度才行。

注意，在离古希腊很远的地方，还有另一个古国，那就是中国。曾经有过那么一个时期，陶土还救了中国皇帝及其手下臣民的性命呢。你们想象得出那是怎么一回事吗？

好吧，在公元前250年，中国的第一任皇帝秦始皇决心不走自己父亲的老路，决定自己死后，不再将手下的仆从和士兵活埋来殉葬，这让国人十分高兴。他命雕塑匠人给自己手下的每一个仆从和士兵都制作了真人大小的陶俑。你们都知道，

easy time during his life and he knew he needed protection in the afterlife.

Brightly painted uniformed bowmen, infantrymen, and charioteers had distinct hands and faces, each with different features and expressions. Their hands and heads were detachable, carefully fashioned to match each man in the army just as they were in real life.

Can you imagine how they were found after all this time? Well, one day more than two thousand years later, a farmer was digging for a well. Instead of finding water, he found six thousand terra-cotta warriors — all buried underground in a vast field. Was he surprised! So when you go digging in your backyard next time, remember the farmer in the fields in China just in case you, too, find the surprise of your life.

这位皇帝生前并没有过上什么安逸的日子，因此他明白自己在来生需要这些人的保护。

这些陶俑都涂上了亮丽的颜色，并且着装统一，里面有弓箭手、步兵和驾驶战车的人；它们都有着独特的双手和脸庞，并且每个人都有着不同的容貌和表情。它们的双手和头部是可以拆卸的，并且都经过精心制作，以符合军中每一个人的实际情况。

你们想不想得出，经历这么久的时间之后，人们是怎样发现它们的呢？好吧，两千多年后的一天，一名农夫正在打井。他并没有打出水来，却发现了六千尊兵马俑；它们全都深埋于地下一片广袤的区域内。他惊讶得目瞪口呆！因此，下次你们再在自家后院挖掘的时候，可要记得那个在地里打井的中国农夫哦；说不定，你们也会因此而发现生活中的惊喜呢。

Chapter 11 Busts and Reliefs

Has your mother, father, or teacher ever told you not to say the word *bust*? "If he eats any more, he'll bust!" is very poor English. I agree with your mother or your father or your teacher. What you should say is "burst."

But now I'm going to tell you how you can use the word *bust* so your mother and your father and your teacher will like to hear you use it. In bad English, *bust* means *burst*. In good English, a *bust* is a piece of sculpture showing the upper part of a person — often the head, neck, shoulders, and chest or sometimes just the head and neck. A bust that is made to look like one particular person is called a *portrait bust*. When you see it you can say, "Why that looks just like so-and-so!"

The ancient Egyptians made some very good portrait busts, but the people who made them best were the ancient Romans. The old Roman busts are so lifelike that they look like real people you might see walking down the street today. As you probably remember, the Greeks put Greek noses on most of their statues even though many Greeks didn't have Greek noses. But the Romans liked to make their busts look just like the real person. If a man had a crooked nose or a double chin, the sculptor made that man's bust with a crooked nose or double chin. If the man had a worried look, the sculptor made the bust with a worried look.

第11章 半身像和浮雕

爸爸妈妈或者老师有没有告诉过你们，让你们不要说bust这个词呢？“要是他再吃东西的话，他的肚子就会bust（撑破）了！”这样说，不是正确的英语。我很赞同你们爸爸妈妈或者老师的说法。你们应当说“burst（撑破）”才对。

不过，现在我打算告诉你们正确使用bust这个词的方法；这样的话，你们的爸爸妈妈或者老师，就会乐意听到你们说这个词语了。在不标准的英语里，bust与burst可以混用，指“爆炸，撑破”。但在标准英语里，bust却是指一件只刻画出了一个人上半身的雕塑作品，通常包括头部、脖子、肩膀和胸部，有时也只有头部和脖子，即“半身像”的意思。一尊制作得与某个特定人物看上去很像的半身像，称为人物半身雕像。你们看到这种人物半身雕像时，可能会说：“看上去那真像是某某人呀！”

虽说古埃及人制作出了一些非常优秀的人物半身雕像，但此种雕像制作得最为精美的，还要算是古罗马人。古罗马人制作出来的半身像都非常逼真，看上去就像是你们如今可能看到的正在大街上走路的真人那样。你们很可能都还记得，尽管许多古希腊人并没有长着一个希腊鼻，可古希腊雕塑家还是给绝大多数雕像都安上了希腊鼻。古罗马人则不然，他们喜欢将半身像雕得像真人一样。假如一个人长着歪鼻子或者双下巴，那么雕塑家就会给他雕出一个长着歪鼻子或者双下巴的半身像来。要是那个人满脸愁容，雕塑家也会照葫芦画瓢，把那个人的半身像雕刻得愁容满面。

Each Roman family that could afford it had busts made of all the members of the family. These busts were handed down in the family so that an old family had a great many busts of its ancestors around the house. Whenever there was a death in the family, all the family portrait busts were carried down the street in the funeral procession. If you had watched one of these processions, you could have seen how much a grandson looked like the bust of his grandfather that he was carrying.

Each Roman emperor, including Augustus, had hundreds of busts made of himself to be sent to all the important cities in the Roman Empire.

Except for the busts, the Romans didn't think they were as good as the Greeks at making statues in-the-round. So when they conquered Greece, they brought back to Rome all the famous Greek statues they could find. They brought back Greek sculptors, too, and made them carve statues in Rome. Many of the statues made in Rome were not original but copies of famous Greek statues. It's lucky for us the copies were made because so many of the

奥古斯都大帝的半身像，
现存于马里兰州巴尔的摩的沃尔特斯艺术博物馆

在古罗马，凡是承担得起这笔费用的家庭，都会给所有的家人制作这样一尊半身雕像。这些半身像被家人一代一代地传承下来，因此一个历史悠久的家族，家里会到处都是祖先的半身雕像呢。只要有家人去世，家族的所有半身雕像就会被搬出来，加入大街上送葬的队伍当中。假如亲眼见过一支这样的送葬队伍，那你们一定可以看出，孙子的模样与他手中捧着的爷爷那尊半身雕像有多么的相像。

每一位古罗马皇帝，其中也包括奥古斯都[1]，都曾命人为自己制作过数百座半身雕像，并且将这些雕像分送到罗马帝国的各个重要城市里去。

除了半身雕像，古罗马人都认为他们不像古希腊人那样擅长于制作圆雕。因此，古罗马人征服希腊之后，便把自己凡是能够找到的，古希腊的所有著名雕像都带回了罗马。他们也带回了一些古希腊的雕塑家，让这些人在罗马制作雕像。因此，在古罗马制作的许多雕塑都不是原创作品，而是古希腊那些著名雕塑作品的仿制品。我们倒是觉得，幸亏古罗马人制作出了这些仿制品，因为古希腊许多伟

[1] 奥古斯都，即屋大维（Octavius，前 63—14），古罗马帝国的第一代皇帝，公元前 27 年至公元 14 年在位。

great Greek statues were lost. If we hadn't been able to dig up Roman copies of them, we wouldn't know at all what they were like.

You remember Myron's The *Discus Thrower*. The bronze statue that Myron himself made disappeared and has never been found. But the Romans admired it, described it carefully in writing, and copied it several times in stone, and so we know what it was like. The Romans used stone instead of bronze, maybe because they wanted to save metal for their armies or maybe because it was easier to carve than cast metal. But as you probably remember, stone cannot support itself as bronze can so the figures needed an extra piece of support, like a carved tree stump, to keep it from falling over and breaking.

Although the Romans weren't as good as the Greeks at making statues in-the-round, they did make some excellent bas-reliefs. Many young people like the reliefs showing the campaigns of the Emperor Trajan. They show the Roman soldiers

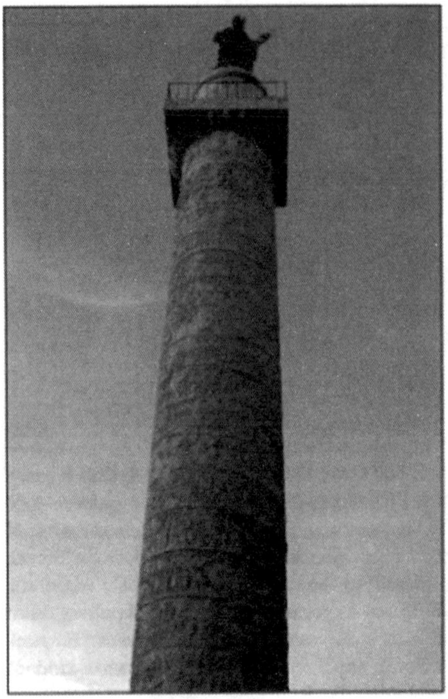

图拉真圆柱，现存于罗马的图拉真广场
（摄影：加里·威肯）

大的雕塑作品都已经遗失了。倘若我们没能发掘出古罗马的这些仿制品的话，那么我们根本就不知道原作是个什么样子了。

你们都还记得米隆创作的那尊《掷铁饼者》吧。米隆亲手制作的那座青铜雕像已经不复存在了，并且此后一直都没有找到。可古罗马人却对这尊雕塑作品崇拜得很，非但在文献资料中详尽地进行了描述，还多次将其复制成石雕，因此我们如今才知道原作是个什么样子呢。古罗马人习惯于用石头而不是用青铜来制作雕塑，或许是因为他们想省下金属来用于军队，又或许是因为石头雕刻起来要比铸造金属更容易一些吧。不过，你们很可能都还记得，石头不如青铜那样能够支撑住自身的重量，因此石雕需要另加支撑物，比如一个雕刻而成的树桩，才能不让雕像倒下来摔碎。

尽管古罗马人不如古希腊人那样擅长于雕刻立体圆雕，但他们也制作出了一些极其精美的浅浮雕。许多年轻人，都喜欢那些描绘图拉真大帝[1]征战四方的浮雕作品。这些浮雕，描绘了古罗马士兵们行军、宿营、作战、攻取城市、抓获俘虏和带

[1] 图拉真大帝（Emperor Trajan，53—117），古罗马帝国皇帝，98年至117年在位。他在位期间，对内巩固了经济和社会制度，对外发动战争，将古罗马帝国的疆域扩张到了历史上的最大范围。由于功绩卓著，因而他获得了罗马元老院赠予的“最佳元首”称号，也是所谓的古罗马历史上的“五贤帝”之一。

marching, camping, fighting, taking a city, capturing prisoners, and carrying off the spoils of war. Trajan's campaign was carved on a marble column and the sculptured band winds around the column from the bottom to the top like a corkscrew. The column is still standing in Rome and is called Trajan's Column. There are so many tiny figures that the story depicted is very difficult for us to interpret as we look up the column. But in the time of the Romans, the scenes were probably seen in the same way that a television account of war might be today.

Another famous relief is carved on the Altar of Peace of Augustus, which the Roman Senate ordered to be erected in 13 B.C. when the Emperor Augustus came back from putting down revolts in the western part of the Roman Empire.

So if anyone should ask you what kind of sculpture the Romans did best, just tell them, "Reliefs and busts."

和平祭坛的浮雕，现存于罗马
（摄影：加里·威肯）

着战利品凯旋的场景。图拉真大帝的征战场景，都雕刻在一根大理石柱上；柱子上那条带状的浮雕图案，就像螺旋一样，从柱子底部蜿蜒而上，直达柱顶。这根石柱，如今依然屹立在罗马，被称为"图拉真圆柱"。柱子上雕有众多的人物形象，因此我们在仰望石柱时，很难说清上面描绘的都是些什么样的情节。可在古罗马时代，人们在观看这些场景的时候，很可能就像如今我们在电视上看战争纪录片一样呢。

还有一件有名的浮雕作品，雕刻在"奥古斯都和平祭坛"上；这座祭坛，是古罗马元老院下令于公元前13年建造而成的，当时正值奥古斯都大帝平定了古罗马帝国西部的叛乱之后，班师返回罗马的时候。

因此，倘若有人问你们，古罗马人最擅长于哪种雕塑艺术的话，你们就可以告诉他们说："是浮雕和半身雕像。"

Chapter 12 Stories in Stone

What would you call men who went around with hammers and broke all the statues they could find? You would probably say they were crazy and should be locked up.

You would be right, and they would be locked up today. But long ago around A.D. 800, such men were not deemed crazy and no one tried to lock them up. They broke statues because they thought statues were too much like idols and that idol worship broke God's commandment "Thou shalt not make graven images," or pictures of God. They thought a church especially should not have such idols or images in it.

In the Greek language, an image is called an *icon* and these men were called *iconoclasts*, a word that means image smashers. They smashed a great many statues, paintings, and mosaics, and the poor artists had to move away from the cities where the iconoclasts were if they still wanted to make statues. Sometimes the artists were hunted down and killed.

The Greek church discussed the smashing, burning, and painting over of icons for more than one hundred years. You may think this is amazing, but after a period of one hundred years, icons were fully accepted and even encouraged by the church.

Here's how it happened. Religious leaders said that if Christ were God taking the form of a man on Earth, to deny having a picture of him as a man would be the same as to deny

第12章 石雕中的故事

对于那些到哪里都带着锤子，把凡是找得到的雕塑统统都砸碎的人，你们会叫他们什么呢？你们很可能会说他们都是疯子，应当把他们都关起来吧。

你们说得对，如今这样的人是会被关起来的。但在很久以前，公元800年左右的时候，人们却并不觉得这样的人是疯子，也没有人想要去把他们关起来呢。他们之所以砸碎雕像，是因为他们觉得，雕塑作品太像偶像了，而崇拜偶像则是没有遵守上帝关于“你们不可制作雕刻的偶像”，或者雕刻上帝形象的诫条。他们认为，教堂里尤其不应当放置这样的偶像或者画像呢。

在希腊语里，“偶像”一词是icon，因此这些人被称为“偶像破坏者”（iconoclast），就是指打碎偶像的人。他们打碎了大量雕塑，毁掉了许多的画作和马赛克作品，而那些可怜的艺术家要想继续创作雕塑作品的话，就只能搬离有偶像破坏者的城市了。有的时候，艺术家们还会被偶像破坏者们抓住并杀掉呢。

对于砸碎、焚毁和掩埋偶像的问题，希腊教会争论了一百多年的时间。你们可能会觉得这样做令人惊讶，但一百年的时间过去之后，教会的确完全接受了偶像，甚至还鼓励人们进行偶像创作呢。

下面我就来说一说教会这样做的理由。一些宗教领袖们说，倘若基督就是上帝在尘世间的化身的话，那么不准世间有他的人形画像，就与否认他是一个人没什么

that he was a man. So images of Christ — flat ones and in low relief — were made once again. It took hundreds of years more before any sculpture in-the-round of Christ would be seen.

Once the church made its decision, many beautiful bas-reliefs of Christ were made in ivory, silver, and gold. The carvings in ivory were used as the covers of books, writing tablets, and little boxes. The place to see them now is in museums where they are kept carefully in glass cases. When you look at them, remember the iconoclasts and why there were no good statues in-the-round or any Christian images at all, in low relief or painted, for a long time after the Romans.

As you learned earlier, some artists left Byzantium — the old name for Constantinople, which in turn was the old name for Istanbul in Turkey — because of the iconoclasts. The next tradition of sculpture took place several hundred years later in France under the great king Charlemagne who was crowned as the Holy Roman Emperor. So it is to France and the Middle Ages that we turn for our next great statues. And, strangely enough, these statues were all carved for churches — just what the iconoclasts didn't want! In fact, the churches were completely covered with statues, which were made of the same kind of stone as the buildings and not of marble like the Greek and Roman statues. These statues were really part of the churches. The cathedral at Chartres in France has no less than ten thousand figures of men and animals on it. They are everywhere — over the doorways, on the columns, on the roof, under the windows, on the walls. Even the waterspouts are carved in the forms of imaginary animals.

两样。因此，人们便开始再次制作基督的形象了，有些是平面形象，有些则是浅浮雕作品。后来又过了几百年，世间才出现为基督所雕刻的立体圆雕。

教会一旦做出决定，人们便用象牙、白银和黄金，雕刻出了许多精美的浅浮雕基督塑像。那些象牙雕塑，多用于做书籍封面、写字板和小盒子。如今，我们只能在博物馆里才能看到这些作品了，它们都被小心翼翼地保存在玻璃箱里。在观赏它们的时候，你们的心中必须记得曾经的那些偶像破坏者，记得古罗马帝国灭亡之后很长一段时间里，为什么世上既无优秀的立体圆雕，也完全没有任何基督教的雕像，无论是浅浮雕还是画像才是。

你们在前面已经得知，由于偶像破坏者的压迫，有些艺术家离开了拜占庭。拜占庭是土耳其君士坦丁堡的旧称，而君士坦丁堡又是伊斯坦布尔的旧称。雕塑艺术的下一种传统，则源自数百年后查理曼大帝统治下的法国；查理曼大帝，曾经还被加冕成为神圣罗马帝国的皇帝呢。因此，接下来那些伟大的雕塑作品，我们便应当转而到法国和中世纪去寻找了。并且，非常奇怪的是，这些雕塑作品都是为各个教堂雕刻出来的，而偶像破坏者却正是不希望看到这种情况呢！事实上，当时各大教堂的外墙上全都布满了雕塑作品，而所用的材料，则是与修建教堂时所用的同一种石头，并不是像古希腊和古罗马雕塑所用的大理石。这些雕塑作品，事实上已经成了教堂的一个组成部分。法国的沙特尔大教堂，竟然雕有一万多个人物和动物形象哩。它们无处不在：教堂入口上方、圆柱上、屋顶上、窗户下、墙上，全都是雕像。连教堂的排水口，也被雕成了人们想象出来的动物形象呢。

Most people in the Middle Ages could neither read nor write, so these sculptures on the churches took the place of books. They told people the stories of the Bible and the saints, and they were useful as well as ornamental.

They are called Gothic figures because churches and cathedrals of the Middle Ages were built in the Gothic style. The Gothic figures on a cathedral are of almost every living thing you can think of. There are scenes from the Bible, statues of saints, carvings of animals and flowers, pictures of the seasons, and images of different kinds of work like farming, writing, wood chopping, and fighting. There are figures of men and women as well as real and make-believe creatures. And each of these figures was made for the particular part of the cathedral where it was placed. The statues were not stuck on after the cathedral was built. They were a part of it, built into it, and made of the same stone.

Have you ever had a sore throat and had to gargle? On the Gothic churches there are statues that gargle. They don't have sore throats, of course, but they gargle every time it rains. They are rainspouts with holes in them so water can run out through their mouths. Like the statues that told the stories of the Bible, they are useful as well as

沙特尔大教堂的哥特式雕塑，
现存于法国的沙特尔市
（摄影：加里·威肯）

在中世纪，绝大多数人都既不认字，也不会写字；因此，各大教堂里的这些雕塑作品，便发挥了书本的作用。它们向人们描述了《圣经》和圣徒们的故事；并且，除了装饰，它们也还具有许多的实际用途呢。

这些雕塑品都被称为哥特式雕塑，因为中世纪的礼拜堂和大教堂，都是用哥特式风格修建起来的。一座大教堂上的哥特式雕塑，几乎涵盖了你们能够想到的所有生物。其中既有《圣经》中的场景、圣徒塑像、动物和花草雕像、关于四季的绘画，也有人物在从事各种劳作的塑像，比如耕田、写字、砍柴以及打仗等。其中既有男人、女人，也有真实的和虚幻的生物。而且，其中的每一种雕塑，都是根据它在整个大教堂所处的特定部位而量身制作出来的。这些雕塑，可不是在大教堂建成之后再粘贴上去的。它们属于教堂的一部分，与教堂融为了一体，并且是用同样的石头雕刻而成的。

你们有没有过喉咙痛，因而必须漱口的经历呢？在哥特式的教堂上，也有漱口的雕塑呢。当然，它们并不是喉咙痛；可每次下雨，它们都会漱口。这些雕塑就是排水口，其中有孔，因而雨水可以通过它们的口中排出去。与那些讲述《圣经》故

ornamental. They are called *gargoyles*, and you could say that they do indeed gargle.

The gargoyles were carved in the shapes of the oddest animals you can think of. Some have heads like monkeys, some have three heads, and some have their tongues sticking out as if they were making faces. Some have claws like eagles while others have hands like men.

The imaginary animals that weren't made to gargle are called *grotesques*. Most of them are up near the roof like the gargoyles and seem to be looking down and laughing at the people on the ground. The sculptors of medieval cathedrals must have enjoyed carving their grotesques and gargoyles. Now what do you think the iconoclasts would say to that?

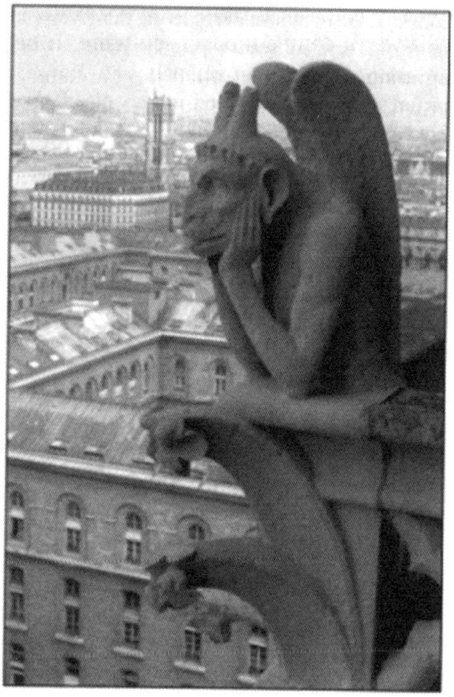

怪兽，现存于巴黎圣母院
（摄影：约翰·帕特森）

事的雕塑一样，它们既有装饰作用，又有实际用途。它们被称为“雨漏”；你们也可以说，下雨的时候，它们的确是在漱口呢。

这些雨漏，都雕成了人们能够想到的最古怪的野兽模样。有些雨漏的头部像猴子，有些雨漏有三个头，还有些雕塑则将舌头伸出来，好像是在做鬼脸似的。有些雨漏上雕着鹰隼般的爪子，还有一些则雕着像人类一样的双手。

而那些不是用于做雨漏、纯属想象出来的动物雕塑，则被称为“怪兽”。其中的绝大多数，都像雨漏一样雕在靠近屋顶的高处，好像是在居高临下地看着并嘲讽地面上的人似的。中世纪建造大教堂的那些雕塑家们，一定都很喜欢雕刻这种怪兽和雨漏吧。如今，你们觉得那些偶像破坏者，对此又会做何评价呢？

Chapter 13 The Gates of Paradise

This story begins with a competition. Not a competition to see who could run fastest or whistle loudest, but a much harder one. It was such a hard competition that each man in it was given a year in which to try to win.

It was a competition in sculpture. It began this way. In Florence, Italy, there is a little eight-sided building called the baptistery. A baptistery is a place where babies, or even grown-ups, are baptized as Christians. This building has four doorways, one of which had a very beautiful pair of bronze doors with reliefs on them at the time of the competition. The civic leaders of Florence decided there should be another pair of bronze doors for one of the other doorways.

There were several good sculptors living then, and the men of Florence could not decide who was the best one to make the new doors, so they held a competition. These were the rules:

Each sculptor had to make a relief in bronze to go on a door.

The relief had to be about Abraham and Isaac from the Bible.

Each sculptor could have a year for the work, and then a group of thirty- four judges would decide the winner.

The winner would make the doors.

第13章 天堂之门

这个故事，是以一场比赛开始的。但这场比赛，并不是看谁跑得最快，或者看谁的哨子吹得最响，而是一场困难得多的竞赛。由于难度太大，因此每个参与比赛的人都有一年的时间，来想方设法赢得比赛。

这是一场雕塑大赛。比赛是如此开始的。在意大利的佛罗伦萨，有一栋规模很小的八边形建筑，叫作“洗礼堂”。所谓的洗礼堂，就是婴儿乃至成年人接受洗礼、皈依成为基督徒的地方。举办比赛的时候，那座洗礼堂有四个入口，其中的一个入口装有两扇漂亮的青铜大门，上面还有浮雕。佛罗伦萨的官员们认为，应当给其余三个入口中的一个也配上两扇青铜大门才是。

当时，佛罗伦萨有好几位在世的优秀雕塑家，而佛罗伦萨人也无法断定，哪一位才是制作新大门的最佳人选，因此他们便举办了一场比赛。比赛规则如下：

每位雕塑家都必须雕刻出一幅与大门搭配的浮雕作品。

这幅浮雕作品描述的内容，必须与《圣经》中的亚伯拉罕和以撒这两个人物有关。

每位雕塑家都有一年的创作时间，然后再由三十四名裁判共同决定谁是获胜者。

最终将由获胜者来制作这两扇大门。

All the sculptors set to work. And all except one kept their work secret from everyone else until the year was up. The one exception was Lorenzo Ghiberti. He worked and worked, and then he asked his friends to come in and tell him how he could make his relief better. Then he worked some more until he had a very beautiful relief indeed.

When the year was up, each sculptor brought his relief to the judges. And what do you think happened? The judges couldn't decide which was the very best! There was a tie for first place. One of the winners was Ghiberti's relief. The other was cast by a famous architect — a person who designs buildings — named Brunelleschi. But Brunelleschi himself thought Ghiberti's relief was better than his own, so he very generously said he would withdraw and let Ghiberti be the winner. Then the judges said Ghiberti could make the doors.

Ghiberti set to work. He worked and worked. One year, two years, five years, ten years passed and still he worked on the doors. You won't believe how long it took to make them. I'll tell you the date when he began and when he finished. He started to work on the reliefs in 1403. He finished the doors in 1424.

"What?" you say. "It took him twenty-one years to make one pair of doors? That is a long time!"

Finally the doors were finished and put in the south doorway of the baptistery. They opened down the middle and had twenty-eight panels fit together into frames to make two enormous doors. Those panels were made up of scenes chiefly from the life of Christ in

所有的雕塑家便开始创作了。他们全都是秘密创作，在一年期满之前都不想让他人知道自己的创作情况，只有一个人例外。这位例外的雕塑家，就是洛伦佐·吉贝尔蒂。他先是不停地工作，然后又将自己的朋友们请过来，就如何将浮雕作品雕刻得更加完美来向他提出意见。接下来，他又继续工作，最终制作出了一幅确实非常精美的浮雕作品。

一年期满之后，所有雕塑家便都带着自己的浮雕作品，来到裁判们的面前。你们觉得，比赛结果如何呢？裁判们竟然无法决定哪一幅是最佳作品！因此，他们选出了并列第一的两幅作品。获胜作品中，有一件便是吉贝尔蒂的那幅浮雕。而另一幅获胜作品，则是由一位名叫布鲁内莱斯基的著名建筑师雕刻的；所谓的建筑师，就是设计和建造建筑的人。不过，布鲁内莱斯基本人却认为吉贝尔蒂的浮雕比自己的作品更好，因此他很大度地说自己退出比赛，让吉贝尔蒂胜出。于是，裁判们便宣布，由吉贝尔蒂去制作那两扇大门。

吉贝尔蒂便开始动手工作了。他不停地工作着。一年过去了，两年过去了，五年过去了，十年过去了，他还在制作那两扇大门。这两扇门做了多久，说出来你们都不会相信呢。我来告诉你们他开工和完工的日期吧。他是在1403年开始制作浮雕的。而他完成这两扇大门的时间，则到了1424年。

"什么？"你们可能会说，"他做两扇大门竟然花了二十一年的时间？那也太久了吧！"

大门终于完工，并被安装到了洗礼堂的南入口上。大门是从中间打开的，上面

relief. Each scene was made separately and then fit together with the rest. Try to imagine doors that are over sixteen feet tall, and each door weighing one and one-third tons.

Ghiberti's doors were a big hit. Everyone liked them so much that the men of Florence asked the sculptor to make another pair of bronze doors for the east doorway to the baptistery. There was no need for a competition this time. They knew Ghiberti was the man for the job.

Ghiberti started on the second pair of doors. He worked and worked and worked. One year, two years, five years, ten years, twenty years, and still he worked on the doors. He began these doors in 1425. He finished them in 1452. What? Twenty-seven years to make one set of doors? That is a long time, of course, so he wanted in some small way to leave his signature behind after so many years. Can you imagine what he decided to do?

Ghiberti included a bust of himself, his son Vittorio, and Vittorio's wife and child — his whole family who had watched as he labored for so very long. So there they are,

天堂之门
洗礼堂东门，吉贝尔蒂作品，
现存于佛罗伦萨洗礼堂
（由波士顿的大学印刷协会提供）

有二十八块嵌板，它们拼合在门框内，形成两扇大门。那些嵌板上的浮雕作品，主要由描述基督生平的场景组成。每幅场景都是独立雕制而成，然后再与其他的浮雕嵌板拼合起来。想象一下吧，这两扇大门有十六英尺多高，并且每一扇都达一又三分之一吨重呢。

吉贝尔蒂制作的这两扇大门，受到了热烈的好评。大家都非常喜欢这两扇门，因此佛罗伦萨市民又请这位雕塑家再为洗礼堂的东入口制作两扇青铜大门。这一次，不用再举行选拔比赛了。他们明白，吉贝尔蒂就是这一工作的不二人选。

于是，吉贝尔蒂开始动手制作第二对大门了。他不停地工作。一年过去了，两年过去了，五年过去了，十年过去了，二十年过去了，他却仍然还在制作那两扇门。他是在1425年开始动手制作这两扇门的。而他完工的时间，则到了1452年。什么？花了二十七年的时间，才制作出了两扇大门？这当然也是很长的一段时间，因此他希望在这么多年后，能够用一种不起眼的方式，在门上留下自己的签名。你们猜得出他决定干什么吗？

在这两扇大门上，吉贝尔蒂为自己，为他的儿子维托里奥、儿媳和孙子们都留下了一尊半身像；这一家人都见证了他在这么久的时间里所付出的辛劳。于是，只

亚伯拉罕的故事，
源自吉贝尔蒂作品“天堂之门”细部，
现存于佛罗伦萨洗礼堂
（由波士顿的大学印刷协会提供）

surrounded by the famous characters from the Old Testament along with frogs, crickets, lizards, and bouquets of flowers just for fun.

But this time, when Ghiberti had finished, the doors were so splendid that many people said they were perfect. Their name, *The Gates of Paradise*, is based on the story that the young Michelangelo, greatly impressed by the doors, described them as worthy to be the gates of Paradise.

The Gates of Paradise has ten scenes from the Old Testament. This illustration is a detail of the scene showing the story of Abraham.

是为了好玩，他们便都置身于大门上那些《圣经·旧约》里的著名人物，以及青蛙、蟋蟀、蜥蜴和花丛之间了。

这一次，待吉贝尔蒂完工之后，由于那两扇大门无比辉煌，因此许多人都说它们非常完美。而这两扇大门之所以被称为“天堂之门”，则源自一则故事：据说，年轻的米开朗琪罗对这两扇大门的印象极其深刻，曾经说过它们可以称得上是“天堂之门”；因此，后来的人便用这个名称，来称呼这两扇大门了。

这座“天堂之门”上，雕有十幅源自《圣经·旧约》中的场景。上图便是描绘亚伯拉罕故事的一幅场景中的细部。

Chapter 14 A Treasure Hunter and a Secret

Have you ever had spring fever? Both kinds of spring fever? Yes, there are two kinds.

Do you remember how lazy and sleepy and tired you have sometimes felt on a warm spring day, when you didn't want to study or work or play or even eat? That's one kind of spring fever.

Then again, do you remember how energetic and healthy and restless you have sometimes felt in the spring? When you wanted to run and shout and turn cartwheels? When sitting still was terrible? When you felt as if you could do anything hard and beat anybody at anything? That's the second kind of spring fever.

Well, after the Middle Ages, the whole world got spring fever. It was the second kind — the full-of-energy spring fever — and it lasted not just a few days in spring but many years.

Italy caught the fever first around 1400. Just as life is born again in the spring after the dark winter and blossoms forth in green leaves and bright flowers, new life was born again in art, literature, architecture, exploration, and trade after the dark of the Middle Ages. This born-again time is called the Renaissance, which means rebirth.

Now one of the germs that had made the world catch this Renaissance fever was the interest people began to take in the skill and learning of ancient times. Statues and

第14章 寻宝者和秘密

你们有没有得过春困症？有没有两种春困症都得过呢？没错，春困症的确有两种。

你们还记不记得，在暖和的春日里，有时你们会觉得非常慵懒、昏昏欲睡、累得很，不想学习、不想工作、不想玩儿，甚至也不想吃东西呢？那就是春困症的一种。

还有，你们记不记得，自己在春天有时会觉得精力充沛、身强力壮并且烦躁不安呢？还记不记得，在这种时候，你们只想跑啊、叫啊、翻上几个跟斗呢？还记不记得，在这个时候，你们会觉得安静地坐上片刻都受不了呢？还记不记得，在这个时候，你们会觉得自己做得到任何难事，能够在任何方面打败任何人呢？这就是第二种春困症。

好吧，中世纪过后，整个世界都得上了春困症。不过，它得的可是第二种，即精力过旺的春困症；并且，这种症状并非只是在春季持续了一天两天，而是持续了多年哩。

公元1400年左右，意大利率先得上了这种春困症。就像阴暗的冬天过后，春天万物再次复苏，到处都是生机勃勃的绿叶和鲜花一样，黑暗的中世纪过后，艺术、文学、建筑、探索和贸易等领域也都再次迸发出了新的生机。这个再次迸发生机的时期，被称为“文艺复兴”时期；而所谓的“复兴”，就是重生的意思。

注意，使得世界陷入“文艺复兴”热潮的根源之一，便在于人们开始对古代的

buildings that had been buried in the ground since Roman times were dug up. Old Roman and Greek writings were brought to light and read again. By learning what the ancients had done in art, the Renaissance people were able to do great things in art too.

One of the first sculptors to make a thorough study of the Roman statues was named Donatello. He lived in Florence, but as a young man, he went to Rome with his friend Brunelleschi, an artist we have already met. In Rome the two friends spent their time hunting through the old ruins for any beautiful Roman artwork they could find. Brunelleschi was more interested in architecture and he measured the old Roman buildings while Donatello looked for sculpture. Soon people called them the Treasure Hunters because they always seemed to be looking for buried treasure.

When the two Treasure Hunters came back to Florence, Donatello made a beautiful marble *cantoria*, or singing gallery, for a choir on the wall at one end of a cathedral. He decorated the outside of the gallery with sculpture of little children who look like cupids dancing and singing. It is a wonderful piece of work, full of life and action.

Donatello's next famous statue was placed outside a church in Florence. It is of Saint George. Saint George was a Christian in the Roman army at a time when it was very unsafe to be a Christian. To show he was not afraid of being a Christian, he carried a shield that had a bright red cross on a white background on it. This symbol has ever since been called the cross of Saint George and is part of the flag of England because the English adopted Saint George as their favorite saint. Saint George was a brave man, and when the

技艺和知识产生了兴趣。那些自古罗马时期以来一直深埋于地下的雕塑作品和建筑，被人们发掘出来了。古罗马人和古希腊人的一些著作被公开发表出来，再次被人们阅读。通过了解古人在艺术方面的成就，“文艺复兴”时期的人也能够在艺术方面取得伟大的成就了。

率先对古罗马雕塑进行全面研究的一位雕塑家，名叫多纳泰罗。他住在佛罗伦萨，但年轻的时候就与朋友布鲁内莱斯基去过罗马；后者是一位艺术家，我们在前面已经提及过了。在罗马，这两位朋友将那些古老的废墟翻了个遍，搜寻能够找到的，所有精美的古罗马艺术品。布鲁内莱斯基对建筑艺术更感兴趣，因此他对古罗马的建筑一一进行了测量，而多纳泰罗则寻找着雕塑作品。不久之后，人们便称他们是“寻宝者”了，因为他们似乎始终都在寻找埋藏在地下的宝物。

这两位“寻宝者”回到佛罗伦萨之后，多纳泰罗便为一个唱诗班制作了一面非常精美的大理石廊台，名叫《唱诗班》，安放在一座大教堂一端的墙上。在这座廊台的外部，他还雕刻了许多载歌载舞的小朋友作为装饰，他们看上去就像是一群丘比特似的。这是一件精美绝伦的作品，既栩栩如生，又充满动感。

多纳泰罗下一件著名的雕塑作品，被安放在佛罗伦萨一座教堂之外。那是一尊圣乔治的塑像。圣乔治是古罗马军中的一名基督徒；而在当时，皈依基督教还是一件很不安全、很可能带来生命危险的事情呢。为了表明自己不惧怕皈依成基督徒，他手持一面盾牌，盾牌上面标有一个鲜艳的白底红色十字架。此后，这个标志便被称为“圣乔治十字架”，并且成了英国国旗的一部分，因为圣乔治是英国人最喜欢的一位圣徒。圣乔治是一个勇敢无畏的人，在古罗马皇帝开始迫害基督徒之后，他

Roman emperor began to persecute the Christians, he went to him and asked him to stop. For this, and because Saint George was a Christian, the emperor had him killed.

Of course Donatello didn't know what the real Saint George looked like because the man who became the saint had lived so long before, so this statue is not a portrait statue. Instead it is what Donatello thought a brave young Christian officer in the Roman army ought to look like. And because so many other people thought this was what Saint George ought to look like, too, the statue became very famous. It is very lifelike.

"There is only one problem with it," someone told Donatello.

"What is that?" asked the sculptor, who was afraid the man had found some fault in the statue.

"The trouble is, it can't speak," said the man.

圣乔治像，多纳泰罗作品，
现存于佛罗伦萨的巴杰罗博物馆
（由波士顿的大学印刷协会提供）

Donatello's most famous work was of a man on horseback. I'll tell you about that in the next chapter, for in this chapter I still have to tell you about a secret. Can you keep a secret?

A sculptor who was a friend of Donatello's had a secret. It was a very good secret and he didn't tell anyone except his adopted son. The adopted son had five sons of his own, and when they grew up they were let in on the

曾跑到皇帝面前，要求皇帝停止迫害呢。正是由于这个，由于圣乔治是一名基督徒，罗马皇帝便命人将他杀害了。

当然，多纳泰罗并不知道圣乔治真正的长相，因为那位圣徒生活在很久很久以前，所以，这尊雕像并不是一座肖像雕塑。相反，雕像的样子是多纳泰罗想象出来的，因为他觉得，古罗马军队中一位勇敢的基督教军官应该就是那个样子。由于许多人也都认为圣乔治应当是那个样子，因此这尊雕像便变得闻名遐迩了。这座塑像，雕刻得也非常逼真。

"只有一个问题。"有人曾经对多纳泰罗说。

"什么问题呢？"这位雕塑家问道。他担心的是，那个人是不是在这座雕塑上找出了什么瑕疵。

"问题就是，他不会说话。"那人回答道。

多纳泰罗最著名的一件作品，是一尊骑马者的雕像。我会到下一章再跟你们来介绍这件作品，因为在这一章，我还得告诉你们一个秘密。你们能够保守秘密吗？

多纳泰罗的一位朋友也是雕塑家，他有一个秘密。那是一个绝妙的秘密，除了

secret too. It was a family secret.

The sculptor with the secret was Luca della Robbia. Like Donatello, he lived in Florence. He was a little younger than Donatello, and so we call him the second great sculptor of the Renaissance. Luca della Robbia made statues in marble and bronze. One of his marble works was a singing gallery for an end wall in the same cathedral as Donatello's marble gallery.

Luca della Robbia carved singing boys on this gallery as Donatello had on his. The two galleries are called the Singing Galleries. Luca della Robbia's looks better than Donatello's when you are close to it because it is smoother and more finished. But when you are looking at the galleries from the floor of the cathedral, Donatello's figures stand out better because they are rougher, so it's about even between them. They are both so valuable that they are now in a museum instead of in the cathedral.

But we've almost forgotten about the secret.

唱诗班廊台，卢卡·德拉·罗比亚作品，
现存于佛罗伦萨的大教堂博物馆
（由波士顿的大学印刷协会提供）

唱诗班廊台细部，卢卡·德拉·罗比亚作品，
现存于佛罗伦萨的大教堂博物馆
（由波士顿的大学印刷协会提供）

自己的养子，他可没跟任何人说过哩。他的养子生了五个儿子，而待这五个儿子长大成人后，他们也获准得知了这个秘密。所以，这算是一个家族秘密呢。

拥有这个秘密的那位雕塑家，名叫卢卡·德拉·罗比亚。跟多纳泰罗一样，他也住在佛罗伦萨。他的年纪比多纳泰罗小一点儿，因此我们称他是“文艺复兴”时期第二位伟大的雕塑家。卢卡·德拉·罗比亚制作了许多大理石雕塑和青铜雕塑。他有一件大理石雕塑作品，也是一座唱诗班的廊台，并且安放在多纳泰罗那座大理石廊台所在的同一座大教堂的另一端。

与多纳泰罗一样，卢卡·德拉·罗比亚也在这座廊台上雕刻了许多唱着赞美诗的小男孩。这两座廊台，合称为《唱诗班廊台》。假如靠近去细看的话，卢卡·德拉·罗比亚的作品似乎还要优于多纳泰罗的作品，因为他雕刻的廊台，要比多纳泰罗的那座廊台更加光滑，打磨得也更加精巧。不过，倘若站在大教堂的地上来看这两座廊台的话，那么多纳泰罗雕刻的人物则更加明显，因为它们都比较粗糙。所以，这两座廊台其实是势均力敌，各有千秋。它们都极其珍贵，因此如今被藏进了博物馆，不再放在大教堂里了。

可我们差点儿都记不起还有秘密这回事了。卢卡·德拉·罗比亚发现，用大理石来雕刻很费工夫，并且大理石购买起来也很昂贵。每次完成作品并获得报酬之

Luca della Robbia found it took a great deal of time to carve in marble, and marble was very expensive to buy. When he finished and was paid for his work, he often found that he hadn't made much money. Bronze had the same drawbacks. He decided to try to find another material that was inexpensive and could be used quickly. He found it. What do you think it was? Not wood or stone, and of course not marble or bronze. It was clay.

"Well," you say, "even the Greeks used clay. I remember the terra-cotta figurines of Tanagra."

True, but wait. Luca della Robbia used terra cotta, but here comes his secret. After he finished a clay statue, he put over it a coating of porcelain, which, when hardened, is something like glass. Then he baked the figure in an oven for just the right length of time. His secret was in mixing the porcelain, or glaze as it was called. When it was finished, the porcelain glaze would resist the rain and bad weather almost as well as marble, whereas the terra cotta without the glaze would soon crumble away. Other sculptors tried it but none did as fine of work in glazed terra cotta as Luca della Robbia. His secret glazing process was very successful.

Most of the sculpture Luca della Robbia did in glazed terra cotta was in relief. The relief part was generally white like marble but the background was a beautiful shade of blue.

Luca della Robbia taught his nephew, whom he had adopted as a son, the secret of the glazed terra cotta. The nephew's name was Andrea della Robbia and he became almost as famous as Luca. Andrea did most of his work in glazed terra cotta and he added many

后，他常常发现自己赚不到什么钱。青铜也存在着同样的问题。于是，他决心找到另一种价格不贵，又能迅速利用的雕刻材料。后来，他的确找到了这样一种材料。你们猜猜，是什么材料呢？它既不是木材，也不是石料，当然更不是大理石和青铜了。这种材料，便是陶土。

“哦，”你们会说，“连古希腊人也用过陶土。我还记得塔纳格拉的小陶俑呢。”

的确如此；不过，你们还是先等一等，听我解释吧。卢卡·德拉·罗比亚用的，的确是陶土；可他的秘密，也正是在这里。雕完一尊陶土雕塑后，他会在雕塑上面涂一层瓷釉；这层瓷釉硬化之后，有点儿像是玻璃。然后，他会将雕像放进一座炉子里，烧制适当的一段时间。他的秘密，便在于调制瓷釉的过程，也就是人们所称的“上釉”。完工之后，这层瓷釉便既能防雨，又不怕日晒风吹，几乎可与大理石媲美了；而没有上釉的陶土制品，却会很快破损。虽说其他一些雕塑家也曾尝试过这种方法，但没有一个人像卢卡·德拉·罗比亚那样制作出了精美的上釉陶土雕塑品。他的这种上釉过程的秘诀，的确获得了巨大的成就哩。

卢卡·德拉·罗比亚制作的绝大部分上釉陶土雕塑品，都是浮雕。通常来说，浮雕部分都是白色的，就像大理石一样；而作品的背景，却是一层美丽的蓝色。

卢卡·德拉·罗比亚把给陶土雕塑上釉的秘诀教给了自己的侄子，也就是他的养子。这位侄子名叫安德里亚·德拉·罗比亚，后来还变得几乎与卢卡一样有名了。安德里亚的绝大部分作品，都是上釉的陶土雕塑；并且，他还给自己制作的

more colors to his reliefs, although he generally left the flesh part of his statues white. His best examples were reliefs of the Madonna and Child.

Andrea did a series of terra-cotta high reliefs of babies in swaddling clothes for the outside of a children's hospital and orphanage in Florence. Swaddling clothes are strips of cloth wrapped around and around the body of a newborn baby to keep it still and quiet. Each baby is on a separate round background. You may have seen plaster casts of these babies, but the plaster casts are white and do not show the colors that Andrea della Robbia put on the originals. Each figure is called a *bambino*, which means baby in Italian.

Luca Della Robbia is also famous for extending the relief by adding to it a frame that looks like a wreath of greens decorated with fruit. Today many wreaths of greens decorated with fruit are called Della Robbia for his famous relief frames.

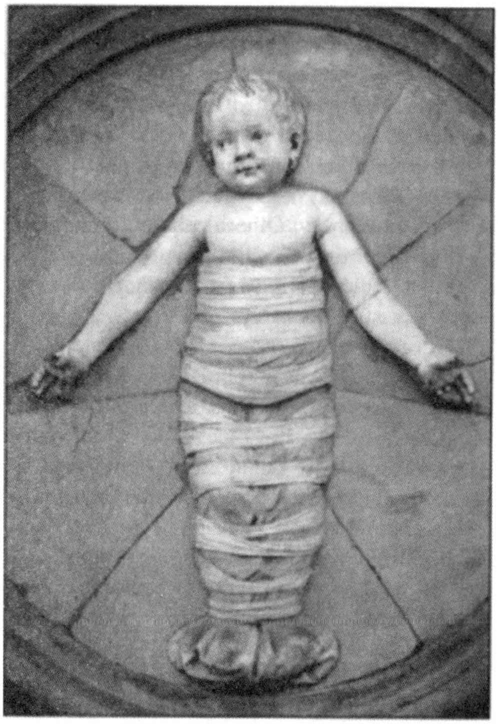

班比诺（彩陶雕塑），
安德里亚·德拉·罗比亚作品，
现存于佛罗伦萨的因诺琴蒂孤儿院
（由波士顿的大学印刷协会提供）

浮雕作品增添了多种颜色，但雕塑的主体部分通常仍是白色的。他的代表作，就是《圣母与圣子》系列浮雕。

安德里亚还为佛罗伦萨一家儿童医院兼孤儿院的外墙创作了一系列陶土高浮雕，其中的形象都是襁褓中的婴儿。所谓的“襁褓”，就是婴儿出生后，为了让婴儿安安静静、不哭不闹而一层层地缠在婴儿身上的那种布条。每座婴儿浮雕，都雕刻在一个单独的圆形基底之上。你们可能已经见过这些婴儿浮雕的石膏复制品了；不过，石膏复制品是白色的，显示不出安德里亚·德拉·罗比亚在原件上创作的各种颜色来。每一座婴儿雕像，都被称为“班比诺”（bambino）；在意大利语中，班比诺就是婴儿的意思。

卢卡·德拉·罗比亚还因为给浮雕作品加上了一个看上去就像是一圈点缀着水果的绿叶外框而变得非常有名。如今，许多点缀着水果的绿叶花环，都因为他那种著名的浮雕边框而被称为“德拉·罗比亚环”呢。

Chapter 15 Among the Best

Have you ever seen a statue of a famous man sitting in a car? No? I haven't, either. And yet in the days when men used horses to carry them from place to place, many statues of great men were made showing them on horseback.

The reason there are no statues of men in automobiles is that a large man-made object like a car is not a suitable subject for sculpture. Very few man-made objects are. A sculptor tries to copy nature. His subjects are things that grow — men, animals, plants, and flowers. A good mechanic with a hammer and chisel could carve an automobile in marble, but it takes an artist to model a horse.

Do you remember the horses and their riders made by Phidias on the Parthenon frieze? They are reliefs. It is much easier to make a horse in relief than in-the-round because in the relief the horse is part of the background and does not have to support all its weight on its legs. A statue of a man on horseback is called an *equestrian statue*. The Romans made better equestrian statues than the Greeks because they knew more about supporting weights. But after the time of the ancient Romans, no good equestrian statue was made for a thousand years.

The man who made the first good equestrian statue after all those years was Donatello. It was bigger than life-size and was made of bronze. It took Donatello ten years to make it and set it up in Padua, Italy. It is such a fine statue that many people call it the second best

第15章 名列前茅

你们有没有见过一尊雕像，描绘的是一位名人坐在汽车里的样子呢？没有？我也没有见过。可是，在人们都是骑着马儿从一个地方跑到另一个地方去的那个时候，许多伟人的雕塑描绘的，却都是他们骑在马背上的情形呢。

之所以如今没有人们开着汽车的雕像，原因就在于，像汽车这样大型的人造物品，并不适合于制成雕塑。事实上，很少有人造的物品适合于制成雕塑。雕塑家试图模仿的，都是自然之物。他们选择的对象，都是自然形成的东西，比如人啦，动物啦，植物啦，花草啦。一名手持锤子、凿子的优秀技工，便可以用大理石雕凿出一辆汽车来；可要想雕刻出一匹马儿，却只有艺术家才做得到。

菲狄亚斯在巴台农神庙的饰带上雕刻出来的那些马匹以及骑马的人，你们都还记得吗？它们都属于浮雕作品。用浮雕手法雕刻出一匹马儿，要比用立体的圆雕手法雕刻出一匹马儿容易得多；因为在浮雕作品里，马儿属于基座的一部分，并不需要依靠四条腿来支撑自身的重量。一尊骑马者的雕塑，称为“骑像”。古罗马人雕制出来的骑像，比古希腊人雕刻出来的更加精美，因为古罗马人更加了解如何支撑塑像的重量。不过，古罗马灭亡之后的一千年里，再也没有出现什么优秀的骑像了。

那么多年过去之后，雕刻出了第一尊优秀骑像的雕塑家，就是多纳泰罗。这座雕像的尺寸比真人要大，并且是用青铜制成的。多纳泰罗花了十年的时间，才将

equestrian statue in the world. You can call it that, too, if you'd like, but what you should really call it is a hard name to pronounce and even harder to spell. The man on the horse was named Gattamelata, and so Donatello's statue is called *Gattamelata*.

Look at the following illustration and notice how heavy and strong the horse is. Gattamelata was a soldier and soldiers' horses in the time of the Renaissance were true warhorses. They were strong so they could carry the weight of a man in armor and heavy so they could charge with great force like the heavy fullbacks on a football team. I have never seen a real horse with his foot on a ball and Donatello hadn't either, but he had to put a ball there to steady the heavy statue. See what a well-balanced, easy seat the rider has in the saddle.

If *Gattamelata* is the second best equestrian statue in the world, what is the best one? Think of all the sculptors who might have made the finest man on horseback. Think of all the hundreds or even thousands of years since sculpture began and you will be astonished to learn that the best and the second best equestrian statues were both made during the Renaissance. They were both made by goldsmiths who lived in

加塔梅拉塔骑像，多纳泰罗作品，
现存于帕多瓦的圣贤广场
（由波士顿的大学印刷协会提供）

它雕制出来，并安放在意大利的帕多瓦。这座雕塑极其精美，因此许多人都称它是世界上第二座最优秀的骑像作品呢。要是愿意的话，你们也可以这样来称呼这座雕像；不过，你们真正应当称呼的，却是一个说起来很拗口，甚至拼写起来也很复杂的名称。骑着马的那个人叫加塔梅拉塔，因此多纳泰罗的这尊雕塑作品，就叫“加塔梅拉塔骑像”。

看一看下面这幅插图，注意那匹马儿的体型有多庞大，身体有多结实。加塔梅拉塔是一名士兵，而“文艺复兴”时期士兵所骑的马匹可都是真正的战马哩。它们都体格健壮，因而驮得起身穿盔甲的士兵；它们都体型庞大，因而能够全力冲锋陷阵，就像橄榄球比赛中的大块头进攻后卫一样。我从来没有见过哪匹真正的马儿踩着一个球，而多纳泰罗应当也没有见过；可他必须在马蹄下放一个球，才能让这座沉重的雕塑保持平衡。看到了吧，骑马者在马鞍上的坐姿是多么的稳当和轻松呀。

要说“加塔梅拉塔骑像”是世界上第二件最优秀的骑像作品的话，那么最优秀的那件骑像作品又是什么呢？你们不妨想一想所有的雕塑家，看谁有可能制作出最精美的骑士雕像来。你们可以回顾一下自雕塑艺术出现以来的那几百年甚至几千年的时间，就会惊讶地发现，这座最优秀的骑像和位居第二的那尊骑像，都是在“文艺复兴”时期雕刻出来的。它们都是由生活在佛罗伦萨的金匠制作而成的。这两

Florence. They were both statues of soldiers on warhorses. And they were both set up in cities in Italy not very far from Florence.

The best statue was made by a sculptor known as Verrocchio. Verrocchio was not his real name. It was the name of the man who taught him to be a goldsmith. Strangely enough, Verrocchio in Italian means true eye. Certainly he lived up to his name. The statue is of a soldier who was commander-in-chief of the armies of Venice. His name was Colleoni. Donatello's *Gattamelata* and Verrocchio's *Colleoni*.

Colleoni was a fine general. He commanded his soldiers and fought well. He was very strong. With his armor on, he could race against the fastest runners in the whole army. He liked to study, he encouraged artists and students at his camp, and he was very courteous. He never ate too much or slept too much, and he was noted for his strict honesty.

When Colleoni died, he left all his fortune to the Republic of Venice on the condition that Venice set up a statue of him in the Square of St. Mark. To put a statue there was against the law of Venice, so the Venetians thought

巴尔托洛梅奥·科莱奥尼的纪念骑像，
韦罗基奥作品，
现存于威尼斯的圣乔万尼和保罗广场
（由波士顿的大学印刷协会提供）

尊雕塑，描绘的都是骑着战马的士兵。并且，它们都被安放在意大利距佛罗伦萨不远的城市里。

世间最优秀的一座雕塑，是由一个叫作韦罗基奥的雕塑家创作出来的。韦罗基奥并不是他的本名。这是教他成为金匠的那位师傅的名字。奇怪的是，“韦罗基奥”在意大利语中是“真正的眼力”的意思。当然，他完全配得上这个名字。他制作的那尊雕像，是一位指挥过威尼斯军队的勇士。这位统帅，名叫科莱奥尼。因此，世界上最杰出的两座雕像，就是多纳泰罗的《加塔梅拉塔》和韦罗基奥的《科莱奥尼》。

科莱奥尼是一位杰出的将领。他指挥着手下的士兵，并且英勇善战。他的体格非常健壮。即便是身披盔甲，他也可以与整支军队里速度最快的那些士兵赛跑。他不但喜欢学习，鼓励军中的艺术人才和学员，还非常礼贤下士。他在饮食上很有节制，从不大吃大喝，而且作息十分规律，不睡懒觉，还以绝对诚实而著称。

科莱奥尼去世后，将所有的财产全都捐赠给了威尼斯共和国，条件是威尼斯应当在圣马可广场上为他修建一座雕像。在那里立一座雕塑是违反威尼斯律法的，因此威尼斯人当时以为，他们是没法得到科莱奥尼的财产的了。可后来，他们却想出

they wouldn't get his fortune after all. Then they had a bright idea. They remembered a building called the School of St. Mark, which had a little square in front of it.

"Why can't that be called the Square of St. Mark too?" they said. So they had Verrocchio make the statue and put it there, and in this way they got the money left by Colleoni.

Verrocchio balanced the statue so well that no ball had to be put under the uplifted forefoot of his horse. Because the statue was on a high pedestal, the sculptor exaggerated Colleoni's features so they would look right when seen from the ground.

Verrocchio's *Colleoni* is one of the most glorious pieces of sculpture in the world — and the best equestrian statue.

了一个绝妙的主意。他们记起，威尼斯有一栋叫作“圣马可学院”的大楼，而这座楼前也有一小块广场。

“为什么不能把那里也叫作圣马可广场呢？”他们说。于是，他们便请韦罗基奥制作了这尊雕像，并将雕像立在这个小广场上；通过这种办法，他们便获得了科莱奥尼的遗产。

韦罗基奥雕刻的这座雕像非常平稳，所以无须在战马抬起的一只蹄子下再放一个球了。因为这尊雕像矗立在一座很高的基座上，因此雕塑家便将科莱奥尼的五官雕刻得非常夸张；这样，当人们站在广场上瞻仰时，科莱奥尼的五官才显得正常。

韦罗基奥的《科莱奥尼》，既是世界上最可称颂的雕塑作品之一，也是世界上最杰出的一尊骑像。

Chapter 16 Four in One

Today there is no famous sculptor who is also a famous painter and architect. But in 1475, a man who would become a world-famous sculptor, painter, and architect was born. He was also a poet and wrote verses that are still published. Not only that, but he is considered the greatest artist of the Italian Renaissance. Many people call him the greatest sculptor since Phidias of ancient Greece.

The name of this wonderful genius was Buonarroti. Have you ever heard of Buonarroti? Very few people know him by that name. We know him as Michelangelo. Michelangelo was trained as a sculptor in marble, and he always spoke of himself as a sculptor in spite of the fact that his most famous works are the frescoes in the Sistine Chapel in Rome.

As a boy he carved a statue in snow that amazed a member of the famous Medici family, the Duke of Florence. The boy was permitted to study the ancient Greek and Roman statues collected by the duke, who later gave him work to do. Some of the statues were those that were dug up from the ground after having been hidden for centuries. Can you imagine the excitement of standing near archeologists as they discover a long-lost famous statue? Michelangelo did just that. He saw the Greek statue of Laocöön pulled out of the ground — a man and his sons strangled by snakes. It's no wonder that Michelangelo

第16章 四项才能，集于一身

如今，世界上没有哪个人既是雕塑名家，同时又是绘画和建筑大师。可在1475年，却诞生了一位后来成了世界著名的雕塑家、画家和建筑设计师的人。他同时也是一位诗人，创作出了许多如今仍在出版印行的诗篇。非但如此，他还被人们公认为意大利“文艺复兴”时期最伟大的艺术家呢。许多人都称，他是自古希腊的菲狄亚斯以来最伟大的雕塑家。

这位了不起的天才人物，名叫博纳罗蒂。你们听说过博纳罗蒂吗？熟悉他这个名字的人可不多呢。我们都只知道他叫米开朗琪罗。米开朗琪罗是学习雕塑出身，因此他总称自己是一名雕塑家，尽管他最有名的作品，其实都是罗马西斯廷教堂里的那些壁画。

小的时候，他就用雪堆雕出了一座塑像，让有名的美第奇家族中的一个人，即当时的佛罗伦萨公爵[1]大感惊讶呢。于是，公爵便允许这个孩子去研究他所收藏的古希腊和古罗马雕塑作品，后来又给米开朗琪罗提供了工作。有一些雕塑作品，是在地下埋藏了数个世纪之后，才再次被人们发掘出来的。你们想象得到，发现一尊早已遗失的、著名的雕塑作品后，站在周围的那些考古学家有多兴奋吗？米开朗琪

[1] 佛罗伦萨公爵（Duke of Florence），即洛伦佐•德•美第奇（Lorenzo de Medici，1449—1492），意大利历史上著名的政治家、外交家和艺术赞助人，同时也是“文艺复兴”时期佛罗伦萨的实际统治者。米开朗琪罗曾在洛伦佐开设的雕塑学校学习。

felt that carving a figure out of marble was like freeing a man from a prison made of stone.

When Michelangelo was only twenty-five years old, he carved a wonderful statue in marble called the *Pietà*. The statue shows Mary holding her dead Son across her lap after his Crucifixion. Some people like it better than Michelangelo's later works because it is quieter and more tranquil than the statues he did afterward. Mary looks like a beautiful young woman instead of a grief-stricken mother of a grown man. Jesus is draped across her lap and his body is completely limp showing that there is no life left in him. People loved, and still love, Michelangelo's idealized, beautiful view of Christ and his Mother.

It is said that during the time Michelangelo was working on the *Pietà*, he overheard two men discussing his work. They said that such a young man could not have carved such a near-perfect sculpture. As a result, Michelangelo took a chisel and hammer and signed his name on the back of the platform of the statue so no one would doubt that he was the artist. He rarely signed his work, for he believed it spoke for itself and all would know who the artist was — but this was an exception.

Some time after finishing the *Pietà*, Michelangelo was able to create a piece of work that made him famous throughout Italy. In Florence there was a huge block of marble that an earlier sculptor had begun to work on but had been unable to finish because the marble was so long and narrow. Michelangelo offered to make a statue out of this block of

罗就有过这样的经历。他曾经亲眼见证了古希腊时期拉奥孔的那尊雕塑出土；这件雕塑，描绘的就是拉奥孔和两个儿子被巨蟒缠死时的情形。难怪米开朗琪罗后来认为，用大理石雕刻出一个人物，就像是把一个人从石头制成的监牢里解放出来一样呢。

米开朗琪罗还在只有二十五岁的时候，便用大理石雕制出了一尊令人惊叹的雕塑作品，名叫《圣母怜子》。这尊雕塑，描绘了耶稣基督在十字架上受难后，圣母马利亚抱着死去的儿子，让他横躺在自己膝上的场景。相比于米开朗琪罗后来的作品，有些人更喜欢这座雕像，因为它比米开朗琪罗后来制作的那些雕像更加朴实，也更加宁静。雕像中的马利亚，看上去像是一位年轻的美丽女子，而不是一个成年人极度悲伤的母亲。耶稣横躺在她的膝上，全身毫无力气，表明他已经没有留下任何生命迹象了。对于米开朗琪罗这尊理想化的，将基督和圣母外表雕刻得非常美丽的作品，以前的人都非常喜欢，而如今人们也依然喜欢得很。

据说，就在米开朗琪罗创作这尊《圣母怜子》雕像期间，不经意中听到两个人在讨论他的作品。那两人说，这样年轻的一个小伙子是不可能雕出如此近乎完美的一座雕像来的。于是，米开朗琪罗便拿了一把锤子和一把凿子，把自己的名字刻在雕像底座的背面；这样，就没有人会再不相信他就是创作这件作品的艺术家了。他很少在自己的作品上签名，因为他相信作品本身就能说明问题，让所有的人都知道，究竟是哪位艺术家创作出了这些作品；可这一次却例外。

《圣母怜子》像完工后，过了一段时间，米开朗琪罗又完成了一件作品，使得他在意大利变得声名大噪了。当时，佛罗伦萨有一块巨大的大理石，以前曾经有一位雕塑家试着雕琢过，可最终并未完成，因为那块大理石的形状实在是太过狭

marble. He was given permission to carve it and went to work. The block was set on end and enclosed by a fence so Michelangelo could work in peace. He finished in three years, and crowds of people came to see what he had done.

The statue was colossal. It was eighteen feet high and showed the Old Testament figure of David with his sling ready to fight the giant Goliath. Strange to say, everyone in Florence called the statue The Giant, although it was of a man who killed a giant. It *is* gigantic in size, weighing nine tons. People loved this statue of an ideal young man — the shepherd boy who defeated a giant and who would become king and compose the Psalms that so many know.

大卫像，米开朗琪罗作品，
现存于佛罗伦萨艺术学院美术馆
（摄影：约翰·帕特森）

Michelangelo was a very careful student of anatomy — the study of the muscles and other parts of the body. He studied the bodies of people and even cut up dead bodies so he could learn about the muscles under the skin, which were key to making a statue look lifelike. He knew so much about muscles that he carved some of his statues in strained and unusual positions, showing the proper play of muscles under the skin.

You can see how Michelangelo's understanding of anatomy helped him make *David* look so lifelike. The original statue of David is in the Galleria

长了。米开朗琪罗提出，由自己来将这块大理石雕刻成一尊雕像。他获得了允许，便开始雕刻了。人们将这块大理石立起来，并用篱笆围住，好让米开朗琪罗可以安静地工作。三年之后，米开朗琪罗完工了，人们便蜂拥而至，都想看看他雕的究竟是什么。

这座雕像的尺寸异常庞大。它高达十八英尺，描绘的是《圣经·旧约》中大卫这个人物手持弹弓，准备与巨人哥利亚战斗时的场景。说来也怪，尽管这尊雕像实际上描绘的是一位杀死了巨人的英雄，可佛罗伦萨人却全都将这尊雕像称为“巨人”呢。它的尺寸的确异常巨大，竟然重达九吨。人们都很喜欢这座描绘了理想中的年轻小伙子的雕像；其中的大卫本是一个牧童，却打败了巨人哥利亚，后来还当上了国王，并且创作出了众所周知的《诗篇》。

米开朗琪罗还认真地研究了解剖学，这是研究人体肌肉和其他身体部位的一门学科。他研究了人们的身体结构，甚至还解剖过死尸，以了解皮肤之下肌肉的情况；而这一点，正是让一座人体雕像显得栩栩如生的关键之处。由于他对人体肌肉了如指掌，因此还雕刻出了一些姿势不太自然、比较罕见的雕塑作品，表现出了皮肤之下肌肉的特有变化。

你们可以看出，米开朗琪罗娴熟的解剖学知识，极大地帮助了他，才使他将《大卫》这尊雕像雕刻得栩栩如生。这座雕像的原件，如今保存在艺术学院美术

dell'Accademia, a school of art in Italy, where it stands under a dome and is bathed in natural light from a window above. I remember the first time I went to see the statue. After waiting in the long line that gathers every day, I entered the gallery, turned the comer, and saw this famous statue in the distance at the end of a long hall. It was so lifelike that I thought I saw *David's* chest move as if he were breathing. Perhaps that may be one reason many consider Michelangelo's *David* to be the most famous statue of all.

For the tomb of one of the popes in Rome, Michelangelo carved a statue of Moses, the Old Testament figure who led the Jews out of Egypt and received the tablets of the Ten Commandments from God. Of course, Michelangelo did not know what Moses really looked like. He had no pictures of Moses to go by, so he carved what he thought a hero like Moses ought to look like. He even carved horns on his Moses! You can see them in the picture. You remember, perhaps, how the Bible says the face of Moses shone with light when he came down from Mount Sinai. In early Italian versions of the Bible, the rays of light coming from the head of Moses were called horns due to a mistranslation of the Hebrew word *light*. And for this reason, people of Michelangelo's time thought Moses had horns. The statue is forceful,

摩西像，米开朗琪罗作品，
现存于罗马的圣伯多禄锁链堂
（摄影：约翰·帕特森）

馆里，那是意大利的一所美术学校。这座雕像，矗立在一个圆形屋顶之下，沐浴在由天窗透下来的自然光线中。我还记得，自己第一次看到这尊雕像时的情形。在每天都有的长长队伍里等候多时之后，我进入了美术馆，拐过了一个角落，便远远地看到，这尊著名的雕塑作品屹立在长长的大厅的那一头。雕像极其逼真，我觉得自己好像看到大卫的胸膛在起伏，仿佛他正在呼吸一样。或许，这就是许多人认为米开朗琪罗的《大卫》是有史以来最著名的雕塑作品的一个原因吧。

米开朗琪罗还给罗马一位教皇的坟墓创作了一尊摩西的雕像。摩西是《圣经·旧约》中的一个人物，曾经率领犹太人逃离埃及，并得到了上帝赐予的、刻有《十诫》的那块石板。当然，米开朗琪罗并不知道摩西真正的长相是个什么样子。他没有摩西的画像可以参考，因此便按照自己心中所想的，像摩西这样的英雄人物应有的样子来雕刻。他雕刻出来的摩西，头上竟然还长着两只犄角呢！在下图中，你们就可以看到这两只犄角。没准你们都还记得，《圣经》中说，摩西从西奈山上下来时，脸上闪烁着光芒。在早期的意大利文版《圣经》中，由于误译了希伯来语中的“光芒”一词，所以摩西头上发出的光芒，就被误称为“犄角”了。因此，米开朗琪罗那个时代的人，都以为摩西头上是长着犄角的。这尊雕像非常有力，既宏伟

majestic, and powerful. All who see it, remember it.

Michelangelo made statues for the tombs of two members of the Medici family that are as famous as Moses. The Medici family was one of the most powerful in all of Florence. They were patrons — wealthy or influential supporters who provided everything artists such as Michelangelo needed to live and work. These tombs are in the Medicis' private chapel in Florence. Michelangelo placed two figures, a man and a woman, on each tomb. The two figures on one of the tombs are known as *Morning* and *Evening* and those on the other are known as *Day* and *Night*. Above these figures, Michelangelo placed portrait statues of the men whose tombs they were. One of the portrait statues is known as *The Thinker* and the other as *The Warrior*.

Michelangelo lived to be eighty-nine years old and died in 1564. He is remembered not only for his sculpture but also for his paintings, such as those on the ceiling of the Sistine Chapel, and for his architecture, such as the dome of St. Peter's Basilica in the Vatican.

洛伦佐·德·美第奇墓前雕塑，
米开朗琪罗作品，
现存于佛罗伦萨圣洛伦佐的新圣器安置所
（由波士顿的大学印刷协会提供）

庄严，又威风凛凛。所有的人看过这尊雕像后，都会终生难忘呢。

米开朗琪罗也给美第奇家族中两位成员的坟墓制作过雕像，它们都与《摩西像》一样，声名赫赫。美第奇家族是佛罗伦萨历史上最有势力的家族之一。他们都是所谓的“恩主”，即给像米开朗琪罗这样的艺术家提供生活和创作所需一切的有钱人，或者有权有势的资助者。这两座坟墓，都位于佛罗伦萨美第奇家族的私人小教堂里。米开朗琪罗为每座坟墓都雕刻了一男一女两尊人物雕像。其中一座墓地的两尊雕像，分别叫作《晨》与《昏》，而另一座墓地的两尊雕像，则称为《昼》与《夜》。在这几座雕像的上方，米开朗琪罗还为墓主人制作了肖像雕塑。其中的一尊肖像雕塑被称为《思想家》，而另一尊则称为《勇士》。

米开朗琪罗活到了八十九岁高龄，逝世于1564年。如今，由于他那些高超的雕塑艺术作品，还有像西斯廷教堂天花板上的绘画，以及像梵蒂冈圣彼得大教堂这样的建筑，米开朗琪罗被世人永远铭记着。

Chapter 17　Cellini Makes His Perseus

A man named Benvenuto Cellini became known as the best goldsmith in Italy. His work in gold, silver, and precious stones was so wonderful that the few examples we have now are all in museums and are considered priceless.

Cellini was a goldsmith but he believed he could create good sculpture too. Although he was very boastful about it he made good on every boast because his bronze statues turned out to be just as good as he said they would be.

Cellini lived in Florence, and the Duke of Florence asked him to make a bronze statue of *Perseus beheading Medusa*, the hideous monster. Cellini worked hard and long on the clay model for Perseus Beheading Medusa until he thought it was just right. Then came the work of casting the statue in bronze.

Today when a sculptor wants to make a bronze statue, he makes a clay model first and then sends it to a bronze foundry that makes the statue in bronze. This is easier for the sculptor because he can spend all his time on modeling statues and not have to do the work of bronze casting. But during the Renaissance a sculptor like Cellini generally had to make the bronze cast himself as well as the clay model. This was often a very hard thing for a sculptor to do.

Cellini's *Perseus Beheading Medusa* was to be larger than life-size and many people in Florence said that it would be impossible for Cellini, a goldsmith, to make a good bronze

第17章　切利尼创作“珀耳修斯”

意大利有一个家喻户晓的、技术最高超的金匠，名叫本韦努托·切利尼。由于他用黄金、白银和宝石雕琢而成的作品都极其精美，因此如今我们保存下来的为数不多的那几件样品，全都保存在博物馆里，被人们认为是无价之宝呢。

虽说切利尼是一位金匠，可他却觉得，自己也可以创作出优秀的雕塑作品来。尽管他很喜欢吹嘘这一点，可他总能兑现每一句大话，因为后来表明，他的青铜雕塑确实像他自夸的那样优秀哩。

切利尼住在佛罗伦萨。当时的佛罗伦萨公爵要他制作一尊青铜雕塑，描绘珀耳修斯砍掉美杜莎这个丑陋怪物脑袋时的情形。切利尼努力工作了很久的时间，才制作出了一个他认为刚好合适的《珀耳修斯砍下美杜莎头颅》的陶土模型来。接着，他便开始用青铜来浇铸这尊塑像。

如今，一位雕塑家倘若想要制作一尊青铜雕塑的话，首先会制作出一个陶土模型，然后再将陶土模型送到青铜铸造厂，由铸造厂去浇铸塑像。这对雕塑家来说较为轻松，因为他可以将所有时间都放到制作雕塑模型上，而不必亲自去用青铜浇铸出雕像来。可在“文艺复兴”时期，像切利尼这样的雕塑家，通常既需制作陶土模型，还得亲自去用青铜浇铸出雕像。雕塑家去干这种事情，通常都是很不容易的。

切利尼的这尊《珀耳修斯砍下美杜莎头颅》，尺寸原定比真人大；可当时佛罗

casting of such a big statue. Even the Duke of Florence told Cellini he thought it would be unwise for a goldsmith who is used to working with tiny jewels to cast a large bronze statue.

All this discussion, however, made Cellini all the more anxious to do the bronze statue. He began by building a furnace to melt the bronze. Then he dug a pit to put the mold in and connected it with tubes so that the melted bronze could run down into the mold and harden. The mold was just the shape of the statue. To make it easier, Cellini cast the Medusa part of the statue first. Medusa turned out very well indeed.

Then Cellini began casting Perseus. This was much harder to do because of its greater size and peculiar shape. The fire in the furnace melting the bronze got so hot that the roof of Cellini's house caught fire. Cellini himself had to work like a fiend to keep the fire burning in the furnace. He became so exhausted that he suddenly became ill and had to go to bed, telling his helpers what to do. He felt so sick he thought he was going to die.

Before long, one of the helpers came to Cellini's room and told him the statue was ruined, as the bronze was not melting right. Cellini, in spite of his sickness, jumped out of bed and ran to the furnace. He was a very hot-tempered man and now he was so angry with his helpers that he frightened them and they jumped every time he spoke.

During his rage, a storm had moved in and it began to rain. Cellini sent two men out for more wood for the furnace fire and then the fire got so hot that the roof caught fire again. Cellini ordered some of the helpers to put up boards or carpets to help keep off the rain.

伦萨的许多人都说，切利尼这位金匠是不可能浇铸出这样一尊大型的青铜雕塑来的。连佛罗伦萨公爵本人也曾对切利尼说，他觉得，让一位习惯于制作小型珠宝的金匠来浇铸一尊大型的青铜雕像，可能有点儿失策呢。

然而，这些指指点点，反而使得切利尼更加心切地要制作出这尊青铜雕像了。他首先建造了一座用于熔化青铜的炉子。接着，他又挖了一个大坑来放置模具，并用管道将模具与炉子连接起来，好让熔化的青铜顺着管道下流到模具里，然后冷却、硬化。模具的外形，就是成品雕塑的样子。为了省时省力，切利尼首先浇铸的是雕塑上的美杜莎这一部分。结果表明，美杜莎这一部分的确浇铸得很不错。

接下来，切利尼开始浇铸珀耳修斯这一部分。这一部分要难浇铸得多，因为它的尺寸比美杜莎大很多，形状也很特别。由于熔化青铜的炉火烧得过旺，因此切利尼家的屋顶都被点着了。切利尼自己必须像传说中的恶魔一样，尽力让炉火不致熄灭。因为太过劳累，他一下子病倒了，只能卧床休息，吩咐帮工去干。他病得极其厉害，一度以为自己快要死了呢。

不久后，一名帮工跑到切利尼的房间里来，对他说那尊雕像毁了，因为青铜熔化得不合适。尽管生着病，切利尼还是从床上一跃而起，向熔炉跑去。他的脾气本来就很暴躁，此时更是对着帮工们大发雷霆，把他们都吓坏了，因此他每说一句话，帮工们都会吓得跳起来。

就在他大发脾气的过程中，一场暴风雨降临，开始下起雨来。切利尼派两人出去，搬来了更多的木柴，把炉火烧旺；可之后弄得火势过猛，又一次把房顶点着了。切利尼命令几名帮工将板子或毡毯搭起来挡雨。然后，他们又用很长的铁棍搅

Then they stirred the bronze with long iron rods until it began to be the right thickness again.

Suddenly there was a great flash of light and the crash of an explosion. They were all too scared to move. Then Cellini saw that the cap of the furnace had blown off and the bronze was bubbling over the top. So he quickly opened the tubes that would let the metal flow into the mold below.

Still the bronze didn't flow freely. Cellini thought the great heat had eaten up the metal that was mixed with the copper to make it flow. What was he to do? You'll never guess what he did.

He got all the pewter platters, bowls, and dishes in the house and threw them into the melting bronze. Pewter is a soft metal that was often used for dishes. The pewter melted and mixed with the bronze. The bronze flowed and soon the mold was filled. The scheme had worked. Cellini was so pleased he forgot all about his sickness. The next morning the servants had to go out and buy new dishes before they could serve breakfast.

珀耳修斯砍下美杜莎头颅，切利尼作品，
现存于佛罗伦萨的兰齐敞廊
（由波士顿的大学印刷协会提供）

拌炉中的青铜熔液，直到熔液开始再次达到合适的稠度。

突然之间，天空中划过一道巨大的闪电，然后又是咔嚓一声炸雷。他们都吓得不敢动弹。后来，切利尼看到炉顶被大风刮掉了，青铜熔液升到了炉顶，不断翻滚着。于是，他马上打开管道的阀门，让青铜熔液顺着管道流向下面的铸模。

可是，青铜熔液流动得仍然不够顺畅。切利尼认为，是炉中的高温熔掉了混入铜液之中、用于让熔液流动起来的那种金属。他该怎么办呢？你们永远都猜不到他采取的办法呢。

他马上将家里所有的白镴[1]盘子、碗碟找出来，全都丢进了青铜熔液当中。白镴是一种质地较软的金属，通常都用于制作盘子。白镴熔化之后，便与青铜熔液混合起来了。青铜熔液流淌起来，很快便注满了模具。这种办法奏效了。切利尼大感欣慰，完全忘掉了自己的病。第二天早上，他的仆人只得出去买来一些新的碗碟，然后大家才有碗碟吃早饭呢。

[1] 白镴（pewter），指锡与铜的合金，尤指锡、铅合金。它既可以焊接金属，也可制造器物。亦称锡镴。

In the finished statue of *Perseus Beheading Medusa* — cast in bronze with so much bragging and trouble and excitement by Cellini — Perseus holds up the head of Medusa that he has just cut off. He is not looking at it because that would turn him to stone. The statue was set up in Florence and there it still stands, admired all the more by those who know how hard the artist Cellini worked to cast it.

这尊完工后名叫《珀耳修斯砍下美杜莎头颅》的雕像，是切利尼在夸下海口之后，既经历了巨大的困难，又经历了一个个激动人心的时刻，用青铜浇铸而成的；作品描绘的是珀耳修斯刚刚砍下美杜莎的脑袋，将其提在手中的情形。作品中的珀耳修斯并没有看着美杜莎的脑袋，因为只要看上一眼，他就会变成石头。这尊雕塑坐落在佛罗伦萨，并且如今依然屹立在那里；而人们在得知切利尼这位艺术家经历了那么多艰辛才浇铸出这尊塑像之后，对这件作品就更加景仰了。

Chapter 18 A. M. — After Michelangelo

What goes up must come down. Sculpture had been going up. It had been getting better and better since the beginning of the Renaissance. Renaissance sculpture was at its peak with the work of Michelangelo.

Then

it

came

down!

For two hundred years after Michelangelo, there were hundreds of sculptors but only a few good ones. One of the good ones was Cellini, the goldsmith who made the bronze *Perseus Beheading Medusa*. Another was John of Bologna from Belgium.

第18章 米开朗琪罗之后[1]

凡事都是有起有落，绝不会一帆风顺的。雕塑艺术一直都在向上发展。自“文艺复兴”发端之后，雕塑艺术始终都在朝着日益完美的方向发展。而“文艺复兴”时期的雕塑艺术，以米开朗琪罗的作品为标志，达到了巅峰状态。

接下来，

它

就

开

始

走

下

坡

路

了！

米开朗琪罗之后的两百年里，尽管出现了数百位雕塑家，可其中优秀的雕塑家，却是屈指可数的。其中一位就是切利尼，即浇铸了青铜塑像《珀耳修斯砍下美杜莎头颅》的那位金匠。另一位则是博洛尼亚的约翰，他是比利时人。

[1] 本章题目中的 A.M. 仅是 After Michelangelo（米开朗琪罗之后）首字母的缩写，与英语中常用的表示“上午，午前”的 A. M. 不同。

飞行的墨丘利，博隆亚作品，现存于佛罗伦萨的巴杰罗博物馆（由波士顿的大学印刷协会提供）

John of Bologna was born in Belgium but he didn't stay there. He moved to Italy and lived in Italy the rest of his life. All of his important work was done in Italy. When a famous fountain he made was placed in the city of Bologna in Italy, people began to think he was a man of Bologna and called him Giovanni da Bologna, which means John of Bologna.

When people get joyful news, you may have heard them say, "I'm walking on air!" That is really pretty hard to do. Don't try it. But Bologna made a statue that is walking on air. How? A statue can't walk on air any more than a person can! But this statue is walking on air. It is Bologna's masterpiece and it is called *Flying Mercury*.

Now to make Mercury fly through the air, there shouldn't be anything but air to hold him up. So Bologna held Mercury up by the wind. The wind is a bronze wind and is shown coming out of the mouth of a bronze wind god. The wind is blowing on the bottom of Mercury's foot. Look closely and you can see the head of the wind god facing up toward the sky.

博洛尼亚的约翰出生于比利时，可他并没有一直待在国内。后来，他来到了意大利，并在意大利度过了自己的余生。他所有的重要作品，都是在意大利完成的。他曾经为意大利的博洛尼亚修建了一座有名的喷泉；此后，人们便开始将他视为博洛尼亚人，纷纷称他为“乔瓦尼·德·博隆亚”[1]，意思就是“博洛尼亚的约翰”。

你们可能听到过，人们在得知喜讯的时候，会说：“我高兴得飘上天了！”可实际上，要飘到天上去，要漫步云端，却是件很不容易的事情呢。你们可别去试啊。但是，博隆亚却的确制作出了一件飘在空中的雕塑作品。这是怎么回事呢？连人都不能飘在空中，更何况是一尊雕塑呢。可是，那尊雕像，却真的是飘在空中！这件雕塑，就是博隆亚的名作，叫作《飞行的墨丘利》[2]。

注意，要让墨丘利在空中飞行，那么他的脚下就不该有其他东西，只应当有空气。于是，博隆亚便用风来支撑雕像中的墨丘利。当然，这阵风是用青铜雕制而成的，从同样是用青铜铸就的一位风神嘴中吹出来。这阵风，就在墨丘利的脚底下吹

[1] 博隆亚（Bologna），就是意大利地名“博洛尼亚”，都是音译。译者在此处稍加变化，是为了将人名与地名区分开来。

[2] 墨丘利（Mercury），古罗马神话中众神的信使，也是商业之神，对应于古希腊神话中的赫耳墨斯（Hermes），其形象一般是头戴插有双翅的帽子，脚穿飞行鞋，手持魔杖，并且行走如飞。如今，属于太阳行星之一的水星，就是以墨丘利之名命名的，以示其运行速度很快。

Mercury really looks as if he were running in the air as well as flying with his winged cap and sandals and his caduceus — a winged staff or wand with two snakes curling around it. Mercury was the messenger of the gods in Roman mythology. He was also the god of commerce, thievery, travel, and science. If you ever want to think of someone considered to be very important, think of Mercury.

His caduceus is a Roman symbol of truce and neutrality. When animals or people quarreled, the caduceus was supposed to make them friends again. Mercury once saw two snakes fighting. He threw his staff down between them and the two snakes curled peacefully around it. So Mercury kept them there to show the power of his staff. Today the caduceus is used as the symbol of doctors in the United States Army.

Now when people think of Mercury, they generally think of *Flying Mercury* by Bologna. That statue fits my idea of how flying Mercury should look. Does it fit yours?

拂着。仔细观察，你们就能看出，风神的头部朝上，正对着天空。

的确，这尊雕塑中的墨丘利看上去就像是在空中飞奔着，头上戴着那顶长有双翅的帽子，脚穿飞鞋，手持节杖飞行着；他的节杖，就是一根长有翅膀，上面还盘着两条蛇的棍子或者魔杖。在古罗马神话里，墨丘利是众神的信使。他还是掌管商业、盗窃、旅行和科学的神灵。假如你们希望自己了解哪位公认的重要人物，那么，想一想墨丘利就行了。

墨丘利手持的那根节杖，是古罗马时期停战和中立的标志。如果动物之间或者人们之间发生了争执，据说这根节杖就可以让他们重新言归于好呢。墨丘利曾经看到两条蛇在打架。他将自己的节杖扔到两条蛇中间，那两条蛇便一起缠到了节杖之上，和平共处了。于是，墨丘利便让那两条蛇一直盘绕在节杖上，以此来表明他的节杖具有魔力。如今，美国陆军仍然用这根节杖来作为军医的标志呢。

现在，人们一想到墨丘利，便会想起博隆亚创作的这尊《飞行的墨丘利》。这尊雕塑，完全符合我想象中的、飞行着的墨丘利应有的样子。它与你们想象中的样子，是不是也相符合呢？

Chapter 19 An Italian and a Dane

The best Italian sculptor since the time of Michelangelo was named Antonio Canova. He lived from 1757 to 1822. Canova was brought up by his grandparents and, as his grandfather was a stonecutter, the boy had the chance to be a sculptor. When he was only eight years old, he carved two small shrines in marble. When he was about ten, he is said to have carved a lion out of butter for the banquet of a rich nobleman. The nobleman liked it so much he became Canova's patron.

Canova studied hard to become a sculptor. By the time he was a man, he was doing a great many good statues that brought him fame and fortune. He spent the money by giving it away to poor people, establishing art schools, helping sculptors, and giving prizes for good sculpture.

Canova's statues are very smooth and pretty rather than strong in appearance. He carved a great many of the ancient gods and goddesses and seemed to imitate the old Greek and Roman art. He also carved portrait busts of famous men, including George Washington.

Canova's *Perseus With the Head of Medusa* may remind you of another Perseus. Canova's *Perseus* isn't as good as Cellini's, in my opinion, but many believe it is just as famous. Which one do you prefer?

When Canova was at the height of his fame, a young man from Denmark came to Italy.

第19章 一个意大利人和一个丹麦人

自米开朗琪罗那个时代结束以来，意大利最优秀的雕塑家，就要算安东尼奥·卡诺瓦了。他生于1757年，逝于1822年。卡诺瓦是由爷爷奶奶带大的；由于他的爷爷是一名石匠，因此这个小男孩便有了成为一名雕塑家的机会。还在只有八岁的时候，他便用大理石雕刻出了两座小小的神龛。到了十岁左右的时候，据说他还在一位富有贵族举办的宴会上，用黄油雕刻出了一头狮子呢。那位贵族由于非常喜欢他雕刻出的这头狮子，因此后来还成了资助卡诺瓦上学和创作的恩主。

卡诺瓦刻苦学习，立志要成为一名雕塑家。成年后，他创作出了许多优秀的雕塑作品，从而名利双收。后来，他又用自己赚到的钱，既给穷人捐款，同时还开设艺术学校，资助其他雕塑家，奖励优秀的雕塑作品。

卡诺瓦的雕塑作品，线条都非常平滑，外形优美，但力度感并不是很强。他雕刻了许多古代的神灵雕像，看上去似乎是在模仿古希腊和古罗马时期的艺术风格。他也为许多名人制作过半身像，其中还包括乔治·华盛顿呢。

卡诺瓦创作的《手持美杜莎头颅的珀耳修斯》，可能会让你们想起另一座关于珀耳修斯的雕塑作品来。在我看来，卡诺瓦的这件珀耳修斯，不如切利尼的《珀耳修斯砍下美杜莎头颅》那样好；可许多人却觉得，两件作品堪称齐名。你们更喜欢哪一件呢？

就在卡诺瓦的名气达到顶峰之时，一位年轻人从丹麦来到了意大利。抵达意

Soon after arriving, he became famous as a sculptor. He liked Italy so much he stayed there for twenty- three years. Who was this Dane? His name was Thorvaldsen. He knew Canova and, like Canova, imitated the style of the statues of ancient Greece and Rome. He was the most successful of the imitators. Some of his works, like *The Lion of Lucerne*, were not in ancient style.

手持美杜莎头颅的珀耳修斯，卡诺瓦作品，现存于罗马的梵蒂冈博物馆（摄影：加里·威肯）

When Thorvaldsen returned to Denmark after spending twenty-three years abroad, he had become so famous that he was asked to make a colossal statue of Christ and twelve colossal statues of the apostles for a church in Copenhagen. Colossal, you remember, means tremendously large. Thorvaldsen completed these huge statues in Italy twenty years later and sent them to Copenhagen. Many copies of his Christ statue were made and they can be found throughout the world, including at the Johns Hopkins Hospital in Baltimore, Maryland. When a famous work of art is

大利之后不久，他便成了一位赫赫有名的雕塑家。他非常喜欢意大利这个国度，因此在该国整整待了二十三年之久。这个丹麦人是谁呢？他叫托瓦尔森。他认识卡诺瓦，并且曾经与卡诺瓦一样，模仿过古希腊和古罗马时期的雕塑艺术风格。他是所有模仿者中成就最大的一位。但他有些作品，比如《卢塞恩狮子纪念碑》[1]，也并不是古代雕塑的风格。

卢塞恩狮子纪念碑，托瓦尔森作品，现存于卢塞恩（由波士顿的大学印刷协会提供）

在国外侨居了二十三年之后，托瓦尔森返回了丹麦；此时，由于他的名气已经蜚声国内外，因此哥本哈根的一座教堂延请他去制作一尊巨型基督雕像和十二尊巨型使徒像。你们都还记得吧，巨像就是指尺寸极其巨大的雕像。二十年后，托瓦尔森在意大利完成了这组巨像，并将它们运回了哥本哈根。后来，他的这尊基督巨像出现了许多的仿制品，世界各地都有，连马里兰州巴尔的摩的霍普金斯医院里也有呢。倘若一件名作被仿制出来进行展示并

[1] 《卢塞恩狮子纪念碑》（The Lion of Lucerne），1819年托瓦尔森为瑞士创作的一件作品，表现的是一头垂死的狮子躺在破裂的法国王室徽章上，目的是为了纪念法国大革命期间为保卫杜伊勒里宫而牺牲的六百多位瑞士卫兵。由于它保存在瑞士的卢塞恩，故称《卢塞恩狮子纪念碑》。

copied and displayed for all to see, it tells us that the original work and its artist helped art develop in important ways.

When Thorvaldsen died, he left much of his fortune for the building of an art museum in Copenhagen. There most of his works are kept, and in the courtyard the sculptor himself is buried.

供众人观赏，那就向我们说明，原作以及创作这件作品的艺术家，都在一些极其重要的方面促进了艺术的发展。

托瓦尔森去世时，将自己的大部分遗产都捐赠出来，用于在哥本哈根修建一座艺术博物馆。他的绝大部分作品都保存在这座博物馆里，而这位雕塑家本人，也被安葬在这座博物馆的院子里。

Chapter 20 On a Stamp

When I was a boy, I collected stamps. Now I'm grown up but I still have the stamps I collected, and I still like to get new ones to put in my album.

If you collect stamps, you may have one with a side view, or profile, of George Washington's head. This profile of Washington was first used on postage stamps in 1851. It has been used on several issues of ordinary United States postage stamps since then.

All these profile pictures on stamps were made from a bust of Washington. The bust itself was made by the French sculptor Jean-Antoine Houdon. Houdon went to Mount Vernon, Washington's home in Virginia, and stayed with Washington until he had made the bust that the portrait on the stamp is copied from.

An expert at making realistic-looking busts, Houdon was one of the best sculptors France had had for two hundred years. When he was a boy, he studied art in Paris, and when he was twenty, he won a prize for sculpture. The prize gave him enough money to study art in Italy for four years, so he went to Italy. He liked Italy and stayed there ten years instead of four. Then he came back to France. Isn't it interesting how many artists went to Italy to study art and how many stayed on longer than they had planned?

Houdon said he believed that a sculptor should try to make true likenesses of men who had brought glory and honor to their country so that people would always know what these men looked like. Houdon became just as successful at making portrait statues as the

第20章 邮票上的雕塑

小的时候，我曾经集过邮。如今，虽说已经长大成人，可我却仍然保存着当时收集的邮票，并且仍然喜欢搜集新的邮票，来充实我的集邮册呢。

假如你们也集邮的话，那你们可能会藏有一张印有乔治·华盛顿侧面头像的邮票。华盛顿的这幅侧面头像，是1851年首次用于邮票上的。从那时以来，美国已经在数批普通邮票上用过这幅侧面像了。

所有这些印在邮票上的侧面像，都是根据华盛顿的一尊半身像制作而成的。那座半身雕像，是法国雕塑家让-安东尼·乌敦制作的。乌敦曾经来到华盛顿位于弗吉尼亚州弗农山庄的家中，一直跟随在华盛顿左右，直到最终制作出那尊半身像；而后来邮票上的侧面头像，正是根据这尊半身像复制而成的。

乌敦极其擅长于制作惟妙惟肖的半身雕像，是法国两百年间最杰出的雕塑家之一。小的时候，他曾在巴黎学习美术，并且在二十岁的时候，就荣获了一项雕塑艺术奖。奖金很丰厚，足以让他到意大利去学习四年的美术，于是他便去了意大利。他非常喜欢意大利这个国度，因此在那里待了整整十年，而不是最初所定的四年。然后，他回到了法国。许许多多的艺术家都曾到意大利来研习艺术，并且很多艺术家在意大利逗留的时间也都比原先计划的要久，这难道不是一种很有意思的现象吗？

乌敦曾经说过，他认为一位雕塑家应当尽量给那些为本国带来了辉煌和荣耀的

乔治·华盛顿半身像，乌敦作品，
现存于巴黎的卢浮宫
（由波士顿的大学印刷协会提供）

Romans had been. Some people think he was even better than the Romans. The most famous statue Houdon made was of a French writer named Voltaire, who is shown seated in a chair.

Have you ever wondered why so many statues have eyes without pupils? One reason the eyes are blank is because the sculptor tried to make the exact shape of the eyes. As you know, there isn't a hole in a real eyeball and so the sculptor felt it would not be right to make a hole in the statue's eyeball. If a sculptor wanted to show the iris — the colored part — and the pupil — the dark center — he painted them on the eyes or put glass or crystal eyeballs in the statue. Carving the eyes without pupils was good sculpture, but it did make the eyes look blank. Michelangelo very lightly carved a circle and dot on his *David's* eyes, but most of his other statues have blank eyes.

But Houdon thought, just as you probably do, that a portrait statue ought to have eyes with

人物制作出逼真的雕像，从而让民众始终牢记这些英雄人物的长相。在制作半身塑像方面，乌敦取得的成就，就像古罗马人曾经取得的成就一样伟大。有些人甚至认为，他比古罗马人更加优秀哩。乌敦最有名的一件作品，就是法国作家伏尔泰[1]的雕像，它描绘了伏尔泰坐在椅子上的情形。

你们有没有奇怪过，许多雕塑作品上，人物的眼睛里为什么会没有瞳孔呢？人物眼睛里空洞无物的一个原因，在于雕塑家都试图准确地将眼睛的原样雕刻出来。大家都知道，真正的眼球上是没有洞的，因此当时的雕塑家们都认为，在雕像的眼球上刻一个洞是不合适的。假如要表现出眼睛里的虹膜（即有颜色的那一部分）和瞳孔（即黑色的中心部位）来，雕塑家就会给塑像的眼睛涂上颜色，或者给塑像装上玻璃或水晶做的眼球。虽说雕刻没有瞳仁的眼睛是一种高超的雕塑艺术，可这样做，却会让人物的眼睛看起来空洞无神。米开朗琪罗在创作《大卫》这尊雕塑时，曾经轻轻地在人物的眼睛上刻了一个圆圈和一个点；不过，他其他绝大多数雕塑作品中的人物，眼睛却都是空空的，什么也没有。

但是，乌敦却认为，对于一尊半身像来说，人物的眼睛里应当有虹膜和瞳仁才对；你们很可能也会这样认为呢。于是，乌敦便发明了一种雕刻方法。他将瞳孔雕

[1] 伏尔泰（Voltaire，1694—1777），原名弗朗索瓦 - 马利 • 阿鲁埃（François-Marie Arouet），法国著名的思想家、文学家、史学家和哲学家，是法国十八世纪资产阶级启蒙运动的旗手，曾经被誉为“法兰西思想之王”、“欧洲的良心”等。

irises and pupils. So Houdon invented a way of his own for doing this. He made a deep hole for the pupil and made the iris in relief. He also left some of the marble for the white part of the eye a little raised so it would catch the light. Houdon's idea worked very well. His portrait busts look alive. Some of the busts even seem to have a twinkle in their eyes. Do you see what I was saying about how artists can make a difference in important ways? Houdon did this by showing other artists how to make the eyes of a statue look more lifelike.

When Benjamin Franklin was in France, he had a portrait bust made by Houdon. Franklin liked the bust of himself so much that he asked Houdon to travel to the newly formed United States to make a statue of George Washington. It took Houdon and Franklin almost two months to sail from France to America, and that was on a fast trip in 1785. Some of the side views of Franklin on U.S. stamps have also been taken from Houdon's bust of Franklin. That is especially fitting, as Franklin was the first U.S. postmaster.

Houdon's bust of Washington has never left Mount Vernon, and you can still see it

伏尔泰坐像，乌敦作品，
现存于巴黎的法兰西大剧院
（由波士顿的大学印刷协会提供）

成一个很深的洞，再用浮雕手法雕刻出虹膜。他还留下了一部分大理石，使得眼球中的眼白部分稍稍上凸，从而能够被光线照到。乌敦的这种方法，效果非常好。他雕刻出来的半身像，个个都很逼真，都显得栩栩如生。其中有些半身像，眼睛里甚至似乎还在闪闪发光呢。我在前面说过，艺术家如何能够在一些极其重要的方面对艺术产生重要的影响，如今你们明白这句话的意思了吗？乌敦发挥了重要的作用，就在于他向其他艺术家表明了将一尊雕塑的眼睛雕刻得更加逼真的方法。

本杰明·富兰克林在法国的时候，也曾请乌敦制作过一尊半身像。富兰克林非常喜爱自己的这座半身像，便邀请乌敦到刚刚成立的美国一行，去给乔治·华盛顿制作一尊雕像。乌敦和富兰克林在海上航行了差不多两月之久，才从法国抵达美国；而在1785年那个时候，这趟旅程还算是很快的呢。美国邮票上所印的富兰克林的侧面像，有一些也是取自乌敦为富兰克林所制的那尊半身像。这种做法尤其实至名归，因为富兰克林正是美国的第一任邮政总长。

乌敦为华盛顿制作的那座半身像，一直都保存在弗农山庄，因此你们如今倘若去参观华盛顿故居的话，就能看到那尊雕像呢。乌敦还为华盛顿制作了一尊大理石

乔治·华盛顿像，乌敦作品，
现存于美国里士满的州议会大厦
（由波士顿的大学印刷协会提供）

when you visit the home of Washington. Houdon also made a full-length marble statue of Washington that is now in the Virginia State Capitol in Richmond.

And now, even if you are not a stamp collector, you know more about the portrait on one stamp than many stamp collectors know.

全身像；如今，这尊全身像保存在弗吉尼亚州里士满的州议会大厦里。

现在，即便不是集邮爱好者，你们对一枚邮票上所印肖像的了解程度，也已经超过许多集邮爱好者了。

Chapter 21 A Lion, a Saint, and an Emperor

Do you like to go to the zoo? Almost everybody likes to look at animals, play with animals, or draw animals. A man named Barye liked to make statues of animals.

Barye lived in Paris. He worked in a jewelry shop and was a goldsmith, as were so many of the Renaissance sculptors of Florence. But Barye lived much later than the Renaissance. He lived in the 1800s.

Barye loved to go to the zoo in Paris. He used to take paper and crayons to the zoo and draw pictures of the animals. Then he would go home and make little statues of the animals he had drawn. When he was at work in the jewelry shop, he often made tiny gold animals for watch chains and necklaces and bronze animals to go on clocks. In this way Barye practiced until he became the best animal sculptor of his time in the world. Americans especially liked his lions and tigers. On the street corners of American towns, men used to sell plaster casts of Barye's *Walking Lion*.

Many of Barye's bronzes show action and cruelty. He seemed to like making statues depicting the survival of the fittest in the animal kingdom, such as a tiger eating an alligator or a jaguar eating a rabbit.

Many of Barye's bronze animals are much too small for monuments, but people still call his work monumental sculpture. This means that Barye modeled his statues in the same way large monuments that you see in parks were modeled. They are not filled with

第21章 狮子、圣徒和皇帝

你们喜欢去动物园参观吗？可以说，几乎每一个人都喜欢观看动物，喜欢与动物嬉戏或者画出动物的样子呢。而一个名叫巴耶的人，却是喜欢制作动物雕塑。

巴耶是巴黎人。他在一家珠宝店里工作，就跟“文艺复兴”时期佛罗伦萨的许多雕塑家一样，也是一名金匠。不过，巴耶在世的时间，却要比“文艺复兴”时期晚得多。他生活在十九世纪。

巴耶很喜欢去巴黎的动物园。他去动物园时，经常会带上纸张和蜡笔，给动物画像。然后，回到家里后，他又会根据自己所画的动物，制作出一座座小型的雕像。他在珠宝店上班时，经常制作一些小小的动物金像，挂在怀表链条或者项链上，并且还制作过一些用于钟表上的青铜动物雕塑品。巴耶一直这样练习着，后来成了当时世界上最杰出的动物雕塑家。美国人尤其喜欢他制作出来的雄狮和猛虎作品。在美国一些城镇的街道拐角处，经常可以看到人们在售卖巴耶那尊《行走的狮子》的石膏复制品呢。

巴耶的许多青铜雕塑作品，表现的都是动物的行为和残忍。他似乎很喜欢制作描绘动物世界里适者生存法则的雕塑，比如一头猛虎正在吞噬一条鳄鱼，或者一头猎豹正在吞吃一只野兔。

巴耶创作的许多青铜动物雕塑都太小，没法做高大的纪念碑，但人们却仍然

行走的狮子，巴耶作品，
现存于马里兰州巴尔的摩的沃尔特斯艺术博物馆

tiny details. I wonder if you would know what I meant if I told you they are heavy in shape. Being heavy in shape doesn't mean they are not graceful, but it does mean that a Barye bronze looks beautiful at a distance as well as close up.

Another Frenchman named Frémiet made statues of people as well as of animals. His statues of people on horseback — equestrian statues — proved to be his best ones. His most famous equestrian statue is *Joan of Arc*. Joan is clad in armor and holds aloft the flag of the King of France as she leads the king's soldiers to battle.

忒修斯[1]杀死半人马，巴耶作品，
现存于明尼阿波利斯的明尼阿波利斯艺术学院

称他的作品是“具有纪念碑意义的雕塑”。这就是说，巴耶创作雕塑作品的方式，与你们在公园里看到的那些大型纪念碑的制作方式是一样的。这些雕塑作品上面，并没有充斥着过多的细节。要是我告诉你们说，这些雕塑作品的形状都很厚重的话，不知道你们明不明白我的意思。所谓的形状厚重，虽说并不是指它们不优美，但的确是说巴耶的青铜雕塑作品远看、近观时都很漂亮。

还有一位法国人，名叫费密尔，他既创作过动物雕像，也制作过人物雕像。他制作出来的那些表现人们骑在马背上的雕塑——即骑像——后来被人们认为是他最杰出的作品。而他最有名的一尊骑像作品，就是《圣女贞德像》。在这尊塑像中，贞德全副武装，身披盔甲，手执法国国王的旗帜，正在率领着国王的士兵，准备战斗。

[1] 忒修斯（Theseus），古希腊传说中雅典的国王和英雄人物。

Frenchmen are proud of Joan of Arc. They consider her to be a saint. Frenchmen are proud, too, of another leader of French armies, although he certainly wasn't a saint. His name was Napoleon.

You might already know the story of Napoleon, the boy from Corsica who went to a military school, became a lieutenant in the French army, and then rose to be a famous and successful general. He made himself Emperor of France and became the most powerful man of his time in all the world. In the end, he was defeated and went to live on Elba, an island in the Mediterranean. From Elba he suddenly returned to France. His old soldiers rallied around him. He raised an army to fight the English and the Prussians. He was beaten at the Battle of Waterloo and sent to a different island this time — St. Helena, which was far away in the South Atlantic.

圣女贞德像，费密尔作品，
现存于巴黎的金字塔广场
（摄影：约翰·帕特森）

圣女贞德是全法国人的骄傲。他们认为，贞德是一名圣徒。而法国军队的另一位领袖，也是全法国人的骄傲；当然，这位领袖并不是圣徒。他的名字，就是拿破仑。

你们可能都已经听说过拿破仑的故事了：他是一个出生于科西嘉岛上的小男孩，后来上了一所军校，变成了法国陆军中的一名中尉；然后，他一步步崛起，成了一位名满天下、成就斐然的将领。他自封为法兰西帝国皇帝，变成了他那个时代整个世界上权力最大的人。最后，他被敌人打败了，流放到了地中海的厄尔巴那个小岛上。再后来，他又突如其来地从厄尔巴岛回到了法国。他原来的那些老部下，都齐心协力地来辅佐他。他招募了一支军队，与英国人和普鲁士人作战。可在滑铁卢之战中，他又被打败了。这一次，他被流放到了一

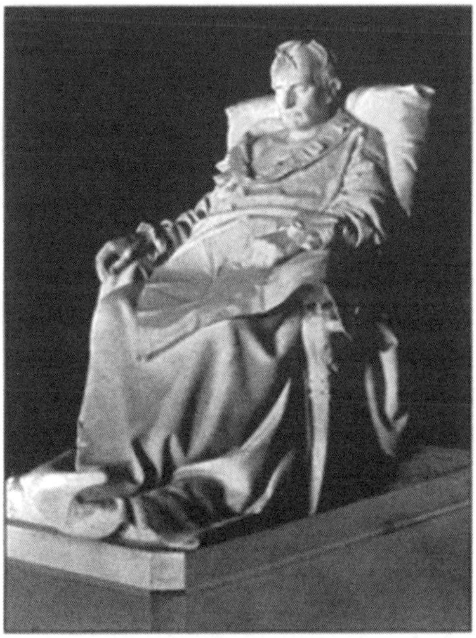

拿破仑的最后时光，贝拉作品，
现存于里格诺内托的贝拉博物馆

There Napoleon spent the last six years of his life longing to return to lead his armies once more to victory. And there he died.

The Last Days of Napoleon shows the former emperor at St. Helena with a map of Europe spread on his knees. One hand is clenched in rage at his loss of power and the other is loosely open, showing how hopeless he feels his chance of returning is.

The statue was done by a sculptor named Vincenzo Vela, who was born in Switzerland. Do you like it? It is called a *dramatic statue* because it shows something happening. It is not just Napoleon, but Napoleon wishing to return and win back his past glory.

个不同的地方，即遥远的南大西洋上的圣赫勒拿岛上。拿破仑在这个岛上度过了一生中最后的六年，一直都渴望着回到法国，率领手下的军队再次走向胜利。最终，他死在圣赫勒拿岛上。

雕塑作品《拿破仑的最后时光》，表现的就是这位前法国皇帝困在圣赫勒拿岛上，膝上搁着一幅欧洲地图时的情形。他的一个拳头紧握着，表明他因自己的失势而愤怒不已；另一只手掌则无力地摊开在那里，表现出了他觉得回国的希望极其渺茫的心态。

这件雕塑作品，是一个出生于瑞士、名叫文森佐·贝拉的雕塑家所作的。你们喜欢这尊雕塑吗？由于表现的是正在发生的某件事情，因此这种雕塑作品被称为情景雕塑。这件雕塑作品，表现的不仅仅是拿破仑这个人物，还表现了拿破仑希望回到法国、重新赢得过去之辉煌的心情。

Chapter 22 A Handsome Present

Have you ever been inside a statue? Most big bronze statues are hollow, and often there is room inside for a person — if there were only a way of getting in. But there is one statue in the world that hundreds of thousands of people have been inside. Thousands of people couldn't all get in at one time, but forty people could get into the head at one time. You've probably already guessed what I'm talking about. It is the *Statue of Liberty*.

The Statue of Liberty stands on a pedestal, or stone base. The pedestal stands on a little island at the entrance of New York Harbor. Every ship that goes in or out of New York passes near the statue. Even in the dark, the passengers on a ship can see it, for at night it is lit up with strong searchlights. American travelers coming back from abroad know they are home when they see the Statue of Liberty.

What would you think if you saw a woman as tall as a ten-story building? A woman whose hand is sixteen feet long, whose eyes are each two and one-half feet wide, whose uplifted right arm is forty-two feet long, and whose finger is as long as an elephant is high! If you wanted that woman to wear a ring, the ring would have to be as big as a hoop. If you wanted the woman to wear gloves, the material for the gloves would spread over more space than a tennis court!

Such a woman is Liberty. She is officially called *Liberty Enlightening the World*. This is because Liberty holds a lighted torch in her raised right hand. The torch is so big that a

第22章 气派的礼物

你们有没有到雕像里面去过呢？绝大多数大型的青铜雕像都是中空的，并且里面通常都有容得下一个人的空间，要是只有一个地方可以进去的话。不过，世界上却有过一尊雕像，成千上万的人都进去过哩。当然，不可能是成千上万人同时进去；不过，雕像的头部一次可以容纳四十个人。你们很可能已经猜出，我说的是哪尊雕像了。没错，它就是美国的自由女神像。

这尊自由女神像，建在一个基座或者说石制底座上。这个基座屹立在纽约港入口处的一个小岛上。进出纽约港的每一艘船只，都会从雕像附近经过。即便是在黑暗中，船上的乘客也看得见它，因为这座雕像在夜间会点亮许多功率强大的探照灯。从国外回来的美国游子一看到自由女神像之后，就明白自己回到家里了。

假如看到一位女士的个子有十层楼那么高，你们会做何感想呢？自由女神像上的这位女士，手掌有十六英尺长，两只眼睛中的每一只都有二点五英尺宽，而那只高高举起的右臂长四十二英尺，并且一根手指就有一头站立着的大象那样高呢！如果你们希望这位女士戴上一枚戒指的话，那么这枚戒指必须像你们所玩的铁圈那样大才行哩。假如你们希望这位女士再戴上一双手套，那么用于制造这双手套的布料，展开之后的面积，会比一个网球场还大！

这样的一位女士，就是这尊自由女神像。她的正式称呼，应当是《自由照亮整个世

自由女神像，巴托尔蒂作品，
现存于纽约州的纽约港
（摄影：加里·威肯）

person could climb a ladder inside the right arm and walk around the torch as if it were a porch. You might make a rhyme of it:

Liberty's torch,
Can be used as a porch.

Held in Liberty's left arm is a tablet. On the tablet, which is much bigger than a dining room table, are these letters:

界》。之所以起这个名称，是因为自由女神高高举起的右手中，擎着一支燃烧着的火炬。这支火炬极其巨大，以至于一个人可以沿着女神像右臂里面的一架梯子爬上去，绕着火炬走上一圈，仿佛那是一条游廊似的。你们完全可以就此写上一首韵诗呢：

自由女神手里举着的那支火炬，
可以当成游廊，任我们爬上去。

自由女神像的左臂里，挽着一块牌匾。这块面积比一张餐桌还要大得多的牌匾上，刻着这样两行字：

JULY IV
MDCCLXXVI

Do you know what they mean? If you don't know, I'm not going to tell you so you can have a puzzle to work out.

The Statue of Liberty can be seen from a long way off, but you can't get very close to it unless you take a ferry. When you get off the ferry, you walk up some steps to the pedestal. Inside is an elevator to the top of the pedestal. Then there are stairs inside the statue that reach all the way up to Liberty's crown where you can look out of the windows. The stairs wind around and around inside the statue like a snail's shell. And the framework, made of rods of steel, is built around the stairs. The outside of the statue is made up of separate pieces of copper that have been welded together.

The man who made the huge statue was a Frenchman named Bartholdi. It was a gift from the people of France to the people of the United States. Bartholdi chose the setting for Liberty and then went back to France and made a model. The model was used to make the huge copper pieces of the statue itself. These pieces were brought by ship to the United States and put together on the island. It was like fitting together a gigantic three-dimensional puzzle, for each piece of copper was a different shape.

I think it was a very effective and friendly present for France to give to the United States, don't you?

JULY IV
MDCCLXXVI（1776年7月4日）

你们知道这两行字是什么意思吗？要是不知道的话，我可不会告诉你们答案；这样，你们不妨把它当成一个字谜，好好猜一猜去吧。

人们从很远的地方以外就可以看到自由女神像，可要想靠得很近地去观赏的话，我们必须坐船才行。下船后，你就会踏上几级台阶，一直通往雕像的底座。进去之后，有一架电梯通往底座的顶部。接下来，雕像内部又有一条长长的楼梯，一路往上，直达自由女神像所戴的王冠；在那里，你们可以透过窗户向外眺望。楼梯在雕像内部呈螺旋形蜿蜒而上，就像蜗牛壳似的。而雕像的整个框架都由钢条制成，围绕着楼梯而建。雕像的外部，则是用独立的铜片焊接起来制成的。

制作出这尊巨型雕像的，是一个名叫巴托尔蒂的法国人。这尊雕像，是法国人民赠送给美国人民的一件礼物。巴托尔蒂选定了自由女神像的安放地点之后，便返回了法国，制作出了一个模型。这件模型，是用于制造雕像主体上的那些巨大铜片的。这些铜片经由船只运到美国，然后在岛上将它们焊接起来。这一过程，就像是拼接一幅巨大的三维拼图似的，因为每块铜片的形状都不一样。

我觉得，这是法国赠送给美国的一件非常感人而友好的礼物，你们是不是也这样认为呢？

Chapter 23 Thoughts for Thinkers

Suppose you were a sculptor and wanted to make a statue expressing thought. Thought is an idea. In grammar we would call it an abstract noun. How, then, could a sculptor make as solid a material as bronze or marble represent an abstract idea like thought?

Of course a sculptor could make a statue of a person sitting as one sits when thinking. He could label this statue Thought, but without the label it might just as well be Sleep or Rest or Fatigue.

The Greeks solved the problem in their own way by imagining a goddess of thought or wisdom and then making a statue of the goddess. The statue would look wise, but it would still be just a likeness of a goddess, not of thought. Any thoughtful or wise-looking woman might serve as the model.

Let's try another way. A person who does a lot of thinking is generally able to think easily. Often, if he is a very wise and thoughtful person, you may not see him thinking at all. He would probably not look as if he were thinking because he could think so easily. He thinks with his brain and not with his muscles.

But watch a child who is not very good at math trying to do a math problem. He does not think easily. He sticks out his tongue. He twists his legs about his chair. He bends his head to one side. He holds his pencil so tightly his fingers hurt. You can see him thinking

第23章 思想家的思想

假设你是一位雕塑家，想要制作一尊表达思想的雕塑作品。所谓的思想，就是人的想法。在语法里，我们称之为“抽象名词”。那么，雕塑家如何才能用青铜或大理石这样具体的材料，来制作出一尊表达思想这种抽象观念的雕塑呢?

当然，雕塑家可以根据一个人坐着思考时的样子，制作出一尊人物坐像来。但是，虽说雕塑家可以给这尊雕塑贴上“思想”的标签，可要是没有这个标签的话，它也可以叫作“睡眠”、“休息”或者“疲乏”呢。

古希腊人用自己的办法解决了这个问题。他们先是想象出一位思想女神或者智慧女神，然后再给这位女神制作出雕像。虽说这种雕像的外表看上去会很聪明，可它仍然只是女神的样子，而不是思想的样子。任何一个陷入沉思，或者外表聪明的女性，都是可以当成这种雕塑的模特的。

我们来想想其他的办法吧。一个经常思考的人，往往也能轻松地想出办法来。通常来说，倘若一个人非常睿智、很有思想，那你们可能根本看不出他正在思考。他很可能完全不像是在思考，因为他思考起问题来非常轻松。他是用大脑在思考，而不是用肌肉在思考。

但是，观察观察一个数学成绩不好的孩子努力做算术题时的样子吧。他思考起来，可一点也不轻松呀。他会把舌头伸出来。他的双腿会在椅子周围不停地扭来扭去。他的头会偏向一边。他会紧握铅笔，弄得手指都疼起来。你们看得出他正在思

because it is hard for him to do it.

Now instead of the child, imagine a cave man. His muscles are big and powerful. You may think he is more like an animal than a man. Because he is a man, however, he has a soul and sooner or later he will wonder about his life and what is going to come of it. Why is he here in this world? What happens when he dies? Does he just go out like a dying fire or does part of him live on in some other world that he knows nothing about? He begins thinking, wondering, pondering with his brute-like mind. You can see him thinking even more than the child. And the first thing you would say if you saw him would be, "He is thinking so hard!"

A statue of such a caveman would show thinking much better than a goddess of thought or a brilliant thinker. The sculptor who expressed thought by creating a statue of someone trying hard to think was a Frenchman named Auguste Rodin. His most famous statue is called *The Thinker*. The statue isn't thinking — the man is thinking. He's a thinker. It is probably as near as anyone can get to show thinking or thought.

The Thinker isn't smooth and pretty like Canova's *Flying Mercury*. It is roughly modeled.

思想者，罗丹作品，
现存于巴黎市的罗丹美术馆

考，因为思考对于他来说很艰难。

现在，我们不再想这个孩子，再来想想一位穴居人吧。他的肌肉非常强壮发达、结实有力。你们可能会觉得，他更像是动物，而不像是人类哩。然而，正因为他是人类，所以他有自己的思想，并且迟早会对自己的生活感到奇怪，想知道未来是个什么样子。他为什么会来到这个世界上？他死后又会变成什么？他死的时候，是会像火焰熄灭那样变得无影无踪呢，还是会有一部分身体在其他某个一无所知的世界里继续生存下去呢？于是，他用自己那个尚处于野兽阶段的大脑，开始思考、怀疑和回想。你们可以看出，他思考时的样子，甚至比前面所说的那个孩子更明显呢。倘若看到这样一个人，你们所说的第一句话，可能就是："他思考得多么认真啊！"

给这样一个穴居人所制作出来的雕像，可能会比思想女神，会比才华横溢的思想家的雕像作品更好地表达出"思考"这个抽象概念呢。有位雕塑家是法国人，名叫奥古斯特·罗丹，他创作出了一尊描绘一个人苦苦思索的雕像，来表达"思考"这一概念。他最著名的那件雕像作品，名叫《思想者》。当然，不是雕像在思考，而是雕像中所描绘的那个人在思考。他是一位思想者。很可能，几乎没有其他艺术家能够如此贴切地表达"思考"或者"思想"这种概念了。

《思想者》并不像卡诺瓦的《飞行的墨丘利》[1]那样平滑和漂亮。它雕刻得很

[1] 此处应为作者笔误。《飞行的墨丘利》为博隆亚的作品，而不是卡诺瓦的作品。

This rough modeling helps make the man look coarser and not used to thinking. He sits, head in hand, pondering so intensely that even his toes are tightly clutching the ground.

Rodin loved contrasts. Often he carved delicate and beautiful forms as though they were just coming out of the uncarved marble block, like those of Michelangelo whom he admired. The beauty is increased by the contrast of the finished part with the unfinished part.

粗糙。这种粗糙的雕刻手法，使得雕像中的人物显得粗野，显得这是一个不常思考的人。他坐在那儿，一只手托着脑袋，紧张地沉思着，连脚趾也紧紧地抓在地上。

罗丹很喜欢用对比的手法。他通常雕刻的都是一些精细而美丽的形象，好像它们都是刚刚从未经雕琢的大理石中走出来似的，就像他所崇拜的米开朗琪罗雕刻的那些作品一样。大理石上雕刻出的部分与未经雕琢的部分形成对比，从而增添了整座雕像的美感。

Chapter 24 American Sculpture

I've told you about sculpture from Egypt and Assyria, Greece and Rome, Italy and France, but not a thing about sculpture made in the United States. I did tell you that Houdon made his bust of George Washington at Mount Vernon, but Houdon himself was not an American.

The reason I haven't told you about American sculpture yet is because it was late in starting. Probably the last thing the early settlers would have thought of bringing across the ocean to America would have been a statue. Statues aren't easy to carry around and the ships were small and crowded. Then, when the settlers got here, they were too busy even to try to make statues. They had to chop down trees, build homes, plant crops, fight the Native Americans, and explore the country. Two hundred years after the first colonial settlement, America could boast of no real sculptors or sculpture of their own.

At that time, ships were built along the seacoast to bring back goods from other countries and to hunt whales. These were splendid, square-rigged sailing vessels. The owners were proud of their ships and decorated the ships' bows — the front part — with wooden figures called *figureheads*. These figureheads were generally the figures of mermaids or sea nymphs and seemed to sprout out of the bows of the ships. Some figureheads were full-length figures, some were carved from the waist up, and some were simply busts. Figureheads were almost always brightly painted.

第24章 美国的雕塑

我已经给你们介绍过了从古埃及和古亚述、古希腊和古罗马到意大利和法国的雕塑艺术，但其中却没有一件雕塑作品是美国人制作出来的。我也的确说过，乌敦曾经在弗农山庄制作出了乔治·华盛顿的半身像，可乌敦本身却不是美国人。

至今我还没有向你们介绍美国的雕塑艺术的原因，在于美国的雕塑艺术起步很晚。很有可能，早期殖民者最不愿意带着漂洋过海、来到美洲的东西，就是雕塑了。雕塑很不容易携带，当时的船只也又小又拥挤。而后来，殖民者来到美洲之后，他们又忙碌得很，根本就不会想起要制作什么雕塑。他们必须砍树、建房、种庄稼、与美洲的土著作战，并且探索美洲这片土地。首次殖民二百年后，美国仍然没有出现真正的雕塑家，没有出现美国人亲手制作出来的雕塑作品呢。

那个时候，船只都是在沿海地区制造，以便从其他国家运回货物，或者出海捕鲸。这些都是很威风、装有横帆的帆船。船东们都以自己的船只为傲，将船首（即船只的前部）装饰上木质图案，称为“船头雕饰”。这些船头雕饰，通常都是美人鱼或者海仙女的形象，好像都是从船头上长出来的似的。有些船头雕饰有真人大小，有些则是从腰部往上的形象，还有一些则只是半身像。这些船头雕饰，几乎都刷上了亮丽鲜艳的颜色。

The best of the figurehead carvers was named William Rush. He was America's first real sculptor. When he was a young man, he was a soldier in the American Revolution, and afterward, an important citizen of Philadelphia. Rush made many figureheads, but he also carved a life-size statue of George Washington in wood. His best carving in wood is the *Spirit of the Schuylkill River*. Later the *Schuylkill* statue was cast in bronze and today it stands in Fairmount Park in Philadelphia.

斯古吉尔河的水仙女和鹭鸟，
拉什作品，现存于宾夕法尼亚州费城的费尔蒙特公园
（由波士顿的大学印刷协会提供）

The next important American sculptor was Horatio Greenough. He, too, did a statue of George Washington and it was his most famous. Greenough worked on it for seven years in Italy. It is now in Washington, DC, and if you ever see it, you'll never forget it. In the statue, Washington isn't dressed in his own clothes. He is dressed only in a kind of sheet, just as if he were a Greek god. Zeus was the head of the Greek gods and Washington was the head of the United States. So Greenough carved this statue with the body of Zeus and the head of Washington. It looks very unusual to us now. It was made in marble and is larger than life-size.

雕刻这些船头雕饰的人当中，最优秀的一位名叫威廉·拉什。他堪称美国第一位真正的雕塑家。年轻的时候，他曾经当过兵，参加过美国革命战争；后来，他又成了费城一位重要的市民。拉什制作出了许多的船头雕饰，但他还雕刻出了一尊真人大小的乔治·华盛顿木雕。他最优秀的木雕作品，便是《斯古吉尔河[1]的水仙女和鹭鸟》。后来，《斯古吉尔河的水仙女和鹭鸟》这尊木雕被浇铸成了青铜雕像，如今屹立在费城的费尔蒙特公园里呢。

美国第二位重要的雕塑家，就是霍雷肖·格里诺。他也制作了一尊乔治·华盛顿的雕像，并且这也是他最有名的一件作品。格里诺在意大利花了七年的时间，才把这件作品雕制出来呢。这件作品如今保存在华盛顿特区，倘若见了它，你们是永远都不会忘记的。在这尊雕像里，华盛顿并未穿着自己的衣服。他身上只披着一条单子，就像古希腊的一位神灵那样。宙斯是古希腊诸神的领袖，而华盛顿则是美国各州的领袖。因此，格里诺便用宙斯的身体、华盛顿的头制作出了这尊雕像。如今在我们看来，这一点是很不寻常的。这尊雕像用大理石制作，尺寸也比真人要大。

[1] 斯古吉尔河（Schuylkill），美国宾夕法尼亚州东南部的一条河流，流程约 209 千米，大致向东南方向流入费城的特拉华河。

Then came a sculptor named Thomas Crawford. He was given the job of making figures for the pediment at one end of the new Capitol that was being built in Washington, DC. Crawford called the figures that he made for this pediment *The Progress of Civilization*. Sometime I am sure you will make a trip to Washington, DC. When you do, be sure to look at Crawford's statues. They are on the Senate end of the Capitol.

While you are in Washington, take a look at the statue on the very top of the dome of the Capitol. It looks like a Native American from the ground and many people think it is supposed to be a Native American. But it really is a statue of Freedom. It also was done by Thomas Crawford.

Do you remember that I told you about *monumental sculpture*? With so many sculptures, Washington, DC, can be called a monumental city.

乔治·华盛顿像，格里诺作品，
现存于华盛顿特区的史密森学会
（由波士顿的大学印刷协会提供）

自由雕像，克劳福德作品，
现存于华盛顿特区的美国国会大厦

接下来，出现了一个名叫托马斯·克劳福德的雕塑家。当时，华盛顿特区正在修建新的国会大厦，克劳福德被任命去为国会大厦一端的山墙制作雕塑。克劳福德将自己为这座山墙所雕刻的作品命名为《文明的进步》。我相信，你们有朝一日都会到华盛顿特区去游玩的。要是真去了，一定要记得去看一看克劳福德的那些雕塑作品哦。它们位于国会大厦靠近参议院的那一端。

倘若到了华盛顿特区，你们不妨还看一看国会大厦圆顶上的那座雕像。从地面往上看去，这座雕像很像是一位美洲土著印第安人，而许多人也都认为那应当是一位美洲的土著印第安人。不过，它其实是一尊自由雕像。它也是由托马斯·克劳福德创作的。

你们还记不记得我曾经跟你们介绍过的纪念性雕塑呢？由于有这么多的雕塑作品，因此华盛顿特区完全可以称为一座具有纪念性的城市呢。

Chapter 25 Among America's Best

Now I'm going to tell you about Saint-Gaudens. Saint-Gaudens wasn't a Christian martyr or an apostle; he wasn't a saint at all. His last name was Saint-Gaudens just as it might have been Adams or Von Hindenburg. His first name was Augustus.

When I told you Saint-Gaudens wasn't a saint, I didn't mean for you to think he was bad. Saint-Gaudens was a fine man and a very fine sculptor.

There is one way we know he was a truly great sculptor — his work is liked by so many different kinds of people. Young people and grown-ups alike praise the statues that Augustus Saint-Gaudens made.

Saint-Gaudens' first great statue was of Admiral Farragut. Admiral Farragut was an officer in the United States Navy during the Civil War. The statue, which stands in Madison Square Park in New York City, shows the admiral as he must have looked standing on the deck of his ship. His feet are apart to brace him against the roll of the ship on the sea. His coat is blown back by the wind. His cap is pulled tight on his head on account of the stiff sea breeze. His face is strong and he looks determined, as if he had made up his mind to win no matter what.

Now look at the pedestal on which the statue stands. Most pedestals are just big blocks

第25章 美国最杰出的雕塑家

现在，我打算给你们说一说圣-戈登斯。圣-戈登斯既非基督教的殉道者，也非基督教使徒；他根本就不是一位圣徒。只是因为他姓“圣-戈登斯”，就像有的人可能姓亚当斯或者姓冯·兴登堡一样。他的名字，叫作奥古斯塔斯。

虽然我跟你们说圣-戈登斯不是一位圣徒，但我并不是要让你们觉得他这个人很坏。相反，圣-戈登斯是一个很好的人，也是一位非常杰出的雕塑家。

从一个方面来看，我们便知道，他是一位真正伟大的雕塑家，因为有如此之多不同的人都喜欢他的作品。对于奥古斯塔斯·圣-戈登斯创作的雕塑作品，年轻人和成年人可都是同样地赞不绝口呢。

圣-戈登斯第一件伟大的雕塑作品，便是海军上将法拉格特[1]的雕像。法拉格特上将是南北战争时期美国海军的一名将领。这尊雕像坐落在纽约市的麦迪逊广场公园里，表现的是这位海军上将站在军舰甲板上时必定拥有的那种威风凛凛的模样。他的双腿微微分开，牢牢地对抗着海船的起伏。海风将他的外套吹向后方。由于海风猛烈，他的帽子紧紧地扣在头上。他的面容坚强，看上去毅然得很，似乎已经下定了决心，不管前面是什么，都要获得胜利。

---

[1] 法拉格特（David Glasgow Farragut，1801—1870），美国南北战争中著名的海军将领，曾在1862年率军攻占了新奥尔良，并于1864年参加了莫比尔湾海战，功勋卓著，为美国的统一做出了重要的贡献。他也是美国历史上的第一位海军上将。

of stone to hold the statue high. But Admiral Farragut's pedestal is really part of the statue. An architect helped Saint-Gaudens design the pedestal. The ripples and the dolphins in the pedestal make you think of the ocean. And the naval sword in the front carries your eye up to the admiral. Notice that Admiral Farragut is in his uniform, which includes long pants called trousers.

This is the first statue we've looked at that shows a figure in trousers. In George Washington's time, sculptors put their bronze or marble men in knee breeches. When men began to wear long pants, the sculptors had a hard time because the pants are apt to look like stovepipes or logs instead of like cloth leg coverings. But Saint-Gaudens didn't let tree- trunk trousers spoil his statues. His statues are good even in trousers.

And there's another statue of his in trousers to prove it. Saint-Gaudens' *Abraham Lincoln* is one of the best-loved statues in America. It stands in Lincoln Park in Chicago. A copy of the statue was given to Great Britain by the United States and was put up near Westminster Abbey in London. Lincoln stands before a chair of state, or a president's chair. He looks as if he has just stood up to say something to the people before him. Lincoln's face is serious. It is a face that has in it both strength and gentleness, as though Lincoln knew that

法拉格特上将像，圣-戈登斯作品，
现存于纽约的麦迪逊广场
（由波士顿的大学印刷协会提供）

现在，请大家看一看这尊雕像的基座。绝大多数雕像的基座，都只是一块块巨大的石头，好让雕像高高屹立罢了。但是，《法拉格特上将像》这尊雕塑的基座，实际上却是整座雕像的一部分。是一位建筑师，协助圣-戈登斯设计出这个基座的。基座上的波浪和海豚，令人想起茫无天际的海洋。而前部的海军之剑，则带领着我们的目光往上，去瞻仰这位海军上将。请注意，法拉格特上将身着制服，包括长裤。

这是我们见过的、其中人物身着长裤的第一尊雕塑作品。在乔治·华盛顿的那个时代，雕塑家们制作出来的青铜或大理石人物雕像，都是穿着短裤的。人们开始穿长裤之后，雕塑家们可犯了难，因为长裤雕刻出来后，看上去很容易像是大烟囱或者圆木，而不像是人们腿上所穿的裤子。但圣-戈登斯并没有让这种树干似的长裤，毁掉自己的这件雕塑作品。即便是其中的人物穿着裤子，他创作出来的雕塑也是很优秀的。

他还有一尊穿着长裤的雕塑作品，可以证明这一点。圣-戈登斯创作的《亚伯拉罕·林肯》，是美国民众最喜爱的雕塑作品之一。这件雕塑，坐落在芝加哥的林肯公园里。美国曾经把这尊雕塑的一件复制品赠送给英国，立在伦敦威斯敏斯特大

millions of anxious people were depending on him to lead them and comfort them. Do you know what the words *dignity* and *simplicity* mean? Saint-Gaudens' *Abraham Lincoln* has dignity. And it has simplicity.

The Farragut and Lincoln statues are of Civil War leaders. Saint-Gaudens was much too young at the time to be in the Civil War himself. But after the war, people wanted statues of the war heroes and Saint-Gaudens was chosen to make some of them.

The next statue is also of a Civil War leader. Saint-Gaudens made a statue in memory of Colonel Shaw, who commanded the first African American regiment from Massachusetts. The statue stands in Boston on the spot from which Colonel Shaw and his soldiers started out for the war.

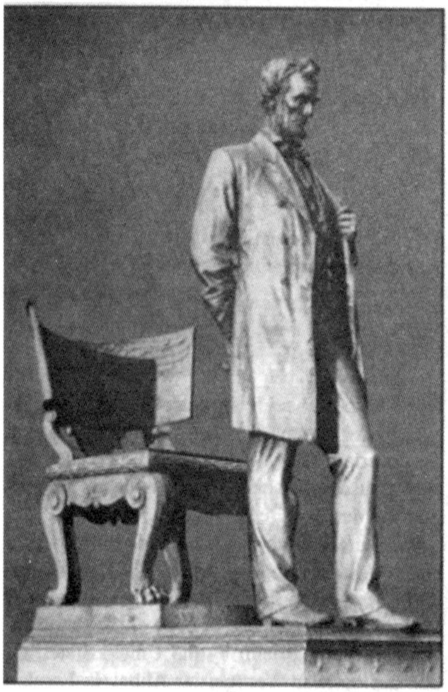

亚伯拉罕·林肯像，圣-戈登斯作品，
现存于芝加哥的林肯公园
（由波士顿的大学印刷协会提供）

The Shaw Memorial is in relief. It shows the young colonel mounted on a horse and riding beside the marching African American men in his regiment. Above in the sky flies the angel of death. Saint-Gaudens put the angel of death there because Colonel Shaw was killed in battle with many of his soldiers.

The sculptor worked on this relief for fourteen years. Again and again he made

教堂附近呢。作品中，林肯站在国家元首宝座前，或者说总统宝座之前。他似乎是刚刚站起身来，要向面前的民众说点儿什么。林肯的面容非常严肃。这张面庞，既饱含力量，又充满了亲切和善之情，仿佛林肯明白，千百万忧心如焚的民众正在倚赖着他，需要他的率领，需要他的鼓舞。你们知不知道，“庄严”和“朴素”这两个词的意思呢？圣-戈登斯的《亚伯拉罕·林肯像》，就显得既庄严，又朴素。

法拉格特上将像和林肯像，描绘的都是美国内战中的领导人。当时，圣-戈登斯还太小，没法参加这场内战。可战争过后，美国民众希望为战争中的这些英雄人物雕刻塑像，便选定圣-戈登斯来为其中的一些领袖制作雕塑了。

下一尊雕像，刻画的也是美国内战中的一位领导人。圣-戈登斯制作了一尊雕像，来纪念那位曾经指挥过马萨诸塞州第一支美籍非裔军团的肖上校。这件雕塑，坐落在波士顿，就在肖上校曾经率军开始出征的那个地方。

《肖上校纪念碑》是一件浮雕作品。它描绘了这位年轻的上校骑在马上，在手下那个美籍非裔军团进军时驰骋一旁的情形。天空中，飞翔着死亡天使。圣-戈登斯之所以雕上死亡天使，是因为后来肖上校与手下许多的士兵全都英勇阵亡了。

圣-戈登斯花了十四年的时间，才完成了这尊浮雕。他一遍又一遍地修改，直

changes until he felt that every part of the statue was right. In fact, he was so careful to make it a good memorial that he spent more money making it than he was paid for doing it. The marching soldiers, the slanting rifles, the spirited horse, the forward look of the rider, and the drawn sword give such swing and movement to the whole statue that you can almost hear the tramp of the feet and the beat of the drums.

Do you still remember the equestrian statue that is called the best in all the world? And the equestrian statue called the second best? Now we come to the equestrian statue that has been called the third best equestrian statue. The sculptor was Saint-Gaudens. The statue is of General Sherman. General Sherman was a Union leader in the Civil War. The statue shows General Sherman riding forward behind the angel of victory.

The Sherman statue is made of bronze but it is painted with gold paint, or *gilt*, so it isn't the same color as other bronze statues. It stands near the entrance to Central Park in New York City for all to see. It was made by one of the best American sculptors of all.

肖上校纪念碑，圣-戈登斯作品，
现存于波士顿的波士顿公园
（由波士顿的大学印刷协会提供）

到自己觉得雕塑的每个部分都没有问题才罢手。事实上，他太过谨慎，想要让这件作品成为一座优秀的纪念碑，因此花出去的钱比创作这件雕塑赚到的工钱还要多哩。行进中的士兵、他们斜斜扛着的步枪、那匹精神饱满的战马、骑马者急切的面容，以及他拔出来的那把利剑，给整座雕像赋予了强烈的节奏感和运动感，以至于你们几乎都可以听得到进军步伐的声音，听得见战鼓的轰鸣。

你们还记不记得那件被称为世界上最杰出的骑马雕塑作品呢？还记不记得那尊号称世界第二杰出的骑马雕塑呢？如今，我们碰到的，则是被称为世界第三的骑马雕塑作品了。雕刻出这件作品的，就是圣-戈登斯。而这件雕塑作品，就是谢尔曼将军[1]像。谢尔曼将军是美国内战中的一位领导人。这尊雕塑，描绘的就是谢尔曼将军骑着战马，跟在胜利天使之后前进的情形。

谢尔曼将军纪念像由青铜浇铸而成，但上面涂成了金色；也就是说，它是一尊镀金青铜像，因此它的颜色与其他青铜雕塑作品并不一样。它屹立在纽约市中央公园的入口，供万人瞻仰。它也是由美国历史上这位最杰出的雕刻家雕制出来的。

[1] 谢尔曼将军（William Tecumseh Sherman，1820—1891），美国南北战争中北军的著名将领，被历史学家普遍认为是“全面战争”的早期倡导者。美国内战后，他曾担任美国陆军总司令。

Chapter 26 Daniel Chester French

The Great Sphinx is the biggest statue in the world. However, the biggest marble statue in the world is in the Lincoln Memorial in Washington, DC. The Lincoln Memorial is a beautiful marble building built by the United States in memory of President Lincoln. The statue inside is a huge figure of Abraham Lincoln. It is made up of twenty large pieces of marble so carefully carved and fitted together that the statue seems to be all one piece.

Now just because a statue is big doesn't mean that it is beautiful. A little piece of sculpture as big as your hand may be much more beautiful than a statue that is as big as a house. But this huge marble statue is considered by many to be beautiful. It is great in other ways than just size.

The Lincoln statue is the only statue in the building. Do you remember another great shrine with a single statue inside? The inner walls of the Memorial are decorated with huge paintings, but the whole building seems to be made just to hold this one statue. Lincoln is seated in a chair that looks like a throne. He sits facing the door so that you stand before him when you enter.

The whole memorial is so impressive yet so simple that you feel as if the spirit of Lincoln himself were in the building. The sculptor of this wonderful statue of Abraham Lincoln was Daniel Chester French.

第26章 丹尼尔·切斯特·法兰奇

大狮身人面像是世界上最大的一尊雕塑作品。然而，世界上最大的一座大理石雕塑，却位于华盛顿特区的林肯纪念堂里。林肯纪念堂是美国修建的一栋美丽的大理石建筑，目的就是为了纪念林肯总统。这座纪念堂里，有一尊巨大的人物雕像，即亚伯拉罕·林肯像。它由二十块巨大的大理石组成；这些巨石，都经过精心雕刻和细致镶嵌，从而使得整座雕像看上去浑然一体。

注意，一尊雕塑尺寸巨大，并不意味着这尊雕像一定会很漂亮。巴掌大的一件小雕塑作品，可能会比一件大如房屋的雕塑作品要漂亮得多呢。不过，许多人却认为，这尊硕大的大理石雕像非常美观。除了尺寸，这尊雕塑有其他的一些方面，也很了不起呢。

这尊林肯雕像，是林肯纪念堂里唯一的一座雕塑。你们记不记得，还有一个了不起的圣地，里面也只有一尊雕像呢？虽说纪念堂的内墙上，装饰有一幅幅巨大的油画，可整栋纪念堂建起来似乎只是为了容下这一尊雕塑似的。林肯坐在一张像是王座的椅子上。他面朝大门坐着，因此游客一进门，就正好站在雕像面前。

整座纪念堂既令人印象深刻，又朴素无华，令人觉得林肯的精神似乎已经与整栋建筑融为了一体。而制作出这尊精妙绝伦的雕塑作品的，是雕塑家丹尼尔·切斯特·法兰奇。

林肯像，法兰奇作品，
现存于华盛顿特区的林肯纪念堂里
（由波士顿的大学印刷协会提供）

民兵，法兰奇作品，
现存于康科德的康科德桥
（由波士顿的大学印刷协会提供）

Daniel Chester French also carved the *Minuteman*, which stands on the American Revolutionary War battlefield in Concord, Massachusetts. Where the statue stands, the road crosses a little wooden bridge over a stream. It was at this crossing that the New England farmers fired "the shot heard round the world" on the British soldiers. The *Minuteman* was placed there in memory of those men. They were called minutemen because they were ready to fight the enemy at a minute's notice. The statue shows a minuteman who is plowing when the call to arms comes. He leaves the plow in the field as he snatches his musket. It was French's first statue, made when he was twenty-three

丹尼尔·切斯特·法兰奇还雕刻出了一尊叫作《民兵》的雕塑作品，如今屹立在马萨诸塞州康科德的美国革命战争战场遗址上。雕像所在之处，有一条公路与一座横跨小河的木桥交叉而过。正是在这个交叉口，新英格兰地区的农民向英军士兵开出了“传遍整个世界的一枪”。在这里安放《民兵》这尊雕像，就是为了纪念那些农民。他们之所以被称为“民兵”，是因为他们随时准备着与敌作战，只要提前分分钟通知就行了[1]。这座雕塑，表现的是一位正在耕地的民兵听到作战命令时的情形。他将犁铧留在地里，一把抓起自己的步枪。这是法兰奇的第一件雕像作品，

[1] 民兵（minuteman），由 minute（分钟）和 man（人）构成，本义指“高度警觉的人，随时准备行动的人”，后专用于指美国独立战争时期那些招之即来的民兵。

years old.

Do you remember what the word *icon* means? It means image. But when I say that the *Minuteman* is an icon, I don't mean a holy image or a symbol on a computer. Instead, Daniel Chester French's *Minuteman* takes on another meaning that is important to a great many people. This statue looks the way many of us feel about an ordinary man who was ready to fight for freedom and liberty. In that way, it is an icon about freedom.

是在他二十三岁那一年雕刻而成的。

你们还记得“偶像”这个词是什么意思吗？它指的就是肖像、图标。但是，我之所以说《民兵》这件雕塑作品是偶像，却并非指它是一尊圣像，也不是说它是电脑上的一个图标。相反，丹尼尔·切斯特·法兰奇的《民兵》，对许多人来说，却具有另一种极其重要的意义。这尊雕塑，表达了我们当中许多人对于一个普通人随时准备着为自由和解放而战斗的感受。从这个意义上来说，它就是自由的一种象征。

Chapter 27 Women's Work

Men have made so many good statues that there isn't room in one book to tell you about them all. Perhaps you notice that I said men have made so many good statues. What about women? It is true that all the statues I have told you about so far have been made by men. Not many women were known as good sculptors. Generally they have not been good sculptors because they have not been sculptors at all — until recently.

The first person to make portrait statues in America was a woman whose name is now forgotten by most people. Her portrait statues were very lifelike. They were made of wax and were colored to look like real people. In fact they were the same size as real people. She even dressed them in real clothes, just like the wax figures in a clothing store. And then later a woman named Madame Tussaud made the same kind of wax figures of famous people in history. Madame Tussaud's Waxworks are in London, New York, Amsterdam, and other cities. You can go there and see such men as Napoleon and President John F. Kennedy all looking so lifelike that they seem ready to speak. Most people go there with a camera so that they can have their photo taken next to their heroes!

But waxworks aren't considered real sculpture any more than a photograph is considered real painting, even though photography is considered an art form.

第27章 女性的作品

男人们已经创作出了如此之多优秀的雕塑作品，而一本书是没有那么多的篇幅去为你们一一介绍的。或许你们注意到了，我说的是“男人们”已经制作出了如此之多优秀的雕塑作品。女性的情况又如何呢？的确，迄今我给你们介绍的所有雕塑作品，都是男性雕塑家制作出来的。女性当中，以杰出雕塑家出名的不多。通常来说，女性都不是优秀的雕塑家，因为她们根本就没有当过雕塑家，直到近来这种情况才有所改观。

美国第一位制作人物肖像雕塑的人，就是一位女性；可她的名字，如今却已被绝大多数人忘记了。她制作出来的肖像雕塑，个个都惟妙惟肖得很。它们都是用蜂蜡制成，并且涂上了颜色，看上去就跟真人一样。事实上，这些雕像的尺寸与真人一般大小。她甚至还给雕像穿上真正的衣服，就像服装店里的蜡像模特一样。后来，一位名叫杜莎夫人的女性，又给历史上的名人制作了同样的蜡像。如今，伦敦、纽约、阿姆斯特丹以及其他的城市里，都有杜莎夫人蜡像馆。你们可以去那里，观看诸如拿破仑、约翰·肯尼迪总统这些人的蜡像；它们一个个看上去都栩栩如生，似乎想要开口说话呢。绝大多数人前去参观时都会带上照相机，这样就可以站在自己崇拜的英雄人物身边拍照了！

不过，人们认为蜡像并不是真正的雕塑作品，就像虽说人们认为照相是一种艺术形式，但他们还是觉得照片并非真正的绘画那样。

After the early waxworks, more and more women studied to be sculptors, especially in the United States. One of these two was Anna Hyatt Huntington. She had two favorite subjects for her statues and is famous for her animal statues and for her Joan of Arc statues. The statue in the following illustration combines both subjects. It is of Joan of Arc on a horse. Art critics — people who write about art — say that this statue is the best Joan of Arc statue that anyone has ever made.

Most statues of Joan of Arc show her as too old or too big or too grown-up looking. Joan of Arc was only seventeen years old when she led the French armies against their enemies. In Huntington's statue, Joan looks just that — seventeen. Then again, people who know about the kind of armor worn in the time of Joan of Arc say that Huntington was the first sculptor to put exactly the right armor and equipment on Joan and on Joan's horse.

Perhaps you think the horse is too big for Joan. But it's probably closer to the kind of horse that Joan really rode than others that have been depicted. I told you warhorses had to be big and strong to carry men in armor and to charge through the enemy. It's very likely that when Joan took command of the army she was

圣女贞德像，亨廷顿作品，
现存于罗彻斯特的罗彻斯特大学纪念艺术画廊

经历了早期的蜡像作品制作之后，越来越多的女性，尤其是美国的女性，便开始通过学习，变成了雕塑家。这两个方面中最著名的一位，就是安娜·海耶特·亨廷顿。她的雕塑作品，最喜欢表现两大主题，而她也因为擅长创作动物雕塑和圣女贞德塑像而著称。下图中的雕塑作品，就表现了这两个主题。这是一尊描绘圣女贞德骑在马背上的雕像。艺术评论家们，即那些写作艺术评论文章的人都说，这件作品是人类最杰出的一尊圣女贞德雕像哩。

绝大多数关于圣女贞德的雕塑作品，不是将她表现得太老，就是将她的体型雕刻得过大，或者样子过于成熟。圣女贞德在领导法军对抗敌人的时候，才十七岁。在亨廷顿的雕塑作品里，贞德的模样恰如其时，即十七岁。再者，那些了解圣女贞德时期士兵身上所穿盔甲的人说，亨廷顿也是第一个将圣女贞德及其战马身上的盔甲、装备雕刻得正确无误的雕塑家。

或许，你们会觉得那匹战马相对于贞德来说，体型实在太大了。不过，与其他人的作品相比，这件雕塑中的战马，很可能更加接近于贞德当时真正所骑的战马呢。我曾经对你们说过，当时的战马必须体型庞大、强壮有力，才能驮得动身穿盔甲的士兵，才能在敌人中冲锋陷阵。很有可能，在贞德指挥军队的时候，她骑的战

given a man's warhorse to ride. Before fire trucks, large and beautiful horses pulled water wagons from the firehouse to the fire. The horse used as a model for this statue was a fire engine horse in Gloucester, Massachusetts.

The other woman sculptor I want you to know about is Gertrude Vanderbilt Whitney. She won the competition for a monument in memory of the people who drowned when the *Titanic* sank. You probably know that the *Titanic* was a great new ocean liner in 1912. On her first trip across the Atlantic, she ran into an iceberg, which ripped a hole in her hull. She sank before other ships could reach her and more than fifteen hundred people died. The memorial Whitney designed shows a human figure standing erect with arms outstretched.

And now for Buffalo Bill. Yes, the famous Buffalo Bill, the daring Western scout, has an equestrian statue in his honor. Buffalo Bill's real name was William Cody and his statue stands in the little town of Cody, Wyoming, which he founded. The statue, made by Whitney, shows Buffalo Bill looking down into a valley signaling with his rifle to the

"泰坦尼克"号沉船事故纪念碑，
惠特尼作品，
现存于华盛顿特区的麦克奈尔堡

马本来是男子所骑的。在救火车出现之前，运水车也是用又高大又漂亮的马匹拉着，从消防队驶往火灾现场呢。这尊雕像所用的马匹模型，正是马萨诸塞州格洛斯特的一匹消防用马。

我希望你们了解的另一位女性雕塑家，就是格特鲁德·范德比尔特·惠特尼。在一场为纪念"泰坦尼克"号沉船事故中溺水者而进行的纪念性雕塑比赛中，她拔得了头筹。你们很可能都知道，"泰坦尼克"号是1912年一艘了不起的远洋轮船。在横渡大西洋的处女航行中，这艘轮船撞上了冰山，船体被撕开了一个大洞。没等其他船只赶来救援，"泰坦尼克"号便沉没了，有一千五百多人丧了命呢。惠特尼设计的那座纪念碑，描绘的是一个人直直地站立着，双臂伸开。

现在，我们来说一说"野牛比尔"[1]吧。没错，就是大名鼎鼎的"野牛比尔"，就是那个勇敢无畏的西部侦察兵，人们也为他雕刻了一座纪念性的骑像。"野牛比尔"本名威廉·科迪，而他的这尊雕像，就坐落在怀俄明州的一个小镇上，即他建立的科迪镇上。这尊雕塑由惠特尼创作，描绘的场景则是"野牛比尔"

[1] 野牛比尔（Buffalo Bill），原名威廉•科迪（William Cody，1846—1917），美国陆军侦察兵。据说他善于猎杀野牛，曾在八个月的时间里杀死了五千头野牛，因此获得了这一外号。他是美国"蛮荒西部"（Wild West）的代表性人物，人们曾拍摄过一部同名电影来讲述他的传奇故事。亦译作"水牛比尔"。

"野牛比尔"像，惠特尼作品，
现存于怀俄明州的科迪镇

wagon train that he is guiding through the lands of Native Americans. Where the statue stands in Cody, however, there is no valley right below and so perhaps Buffalo Bill is looking at the hoof prints of horses on the trail beside him. It is a very good statue. The horse was modeled from one of Buffalo Bill's own horses.

Although I've mentioned only two women sculptors so far, remember that there are many more women who are making excellent statues.

正在俯瞰着一条峡谷，用自己的步枪向他护送通过美洲土著印第安人领地的那支马车队发信号。然而，科迪镇那尊雕像所立之处，下面却没有什么峡谷；因此，"野牛比尔"或许是在察看身后小径上的马蹄印儿呢。这真是一件非常优秀的雕塑作品。其中的马儿，就是用"野牛比尔"手下的一匹马儿做的模型哩。

尽管到现在为止，我只提及了两位女性雕塑家，但你们可要记住，还有许多女性，正在创作出许多的优秀雕塑作品。

Chapter 28 Twentieth-Century Sculpture

Modern sculpture can be nonrealistic just as modem painting can be. *Nonrealistic sculpture* gives the idea, the thought, or the impression of something. The sculptor doesn't try to make an exact copy of something he sees.

The sculpture called *Bird in Space* is an example of nonrealistic sculpture. It doesn't look like a bird, but it does give you the idea of flight. The flight of a bird depends upon wings, and this sculpture seems to be all wings. At least most people think it looks wing-like. Highly polished, it is a smooth, streamlined wing shape. Constantin Brancusi, its sculptor, did not carve a body, a head, a tail, or even feathers into it. Some people think that a piece of sculpture called a bird should look like a bird. In this sculpture, however, the sleek flight of a bird, not the bird itself, is the important idea.

Nonrealistic, conceptual sculpture is a type of twentieth-century sculpture. Brancusi was one of the first to develop this style. He was born in Romania and studied art there as a young man. Then he went to Paris and worked in the studio of the great French sculptor Rodin. At first his sculptures were realistic like Rodin's. But he became interested in

空中之鸟，
布朗库西作品，
现存于纽约的
现代艺术博物馆
（由缅因州桑福德的
大学印刷协会提供）

第28章 二十世纪的雕塑艺术

现代的雕塑艺术，可以与现代的油画艺术一样，变成非现实主义。非现实主义雕塑艺术这个词汇，说明了人们的某种观念、思想或者印象。非现实主义的雕塑家，不会试图去制作出与自己所见之物完全一样的复制品。

一件名叫《空中之鸟》的雕塑作品，就是非现实主义雕塑艺术的一个例子。虽说这件雕塑的外形并不是一只鸟儿，但它的确给了我们飞翔的感觉。鸟儿飞翔，凭借的是双翼；而这尊雕塑作品，似乎满眼都是鸟翼呢。起码来说，绝大多数人都觉得它看上去像是鸟翼。这件雕塑经过高度抛光，因而是一种平滑而呈流线型的鸟翼状。创作出这件作品的，是雕塑家康斯坦丁·布朗库西。他并没有雕刻出鸟儿的身体、头部、尾巴，甚至羽毛。有些人认为，一件名叫“鸟儿”的雕塑作品，看上去应当像一只鸟儿才是。然而，这件雕塑中的重要理念，却是鸟儿那种线条明快、流畅的飞翔，而不是鸟儿本身。

非现实主义的、概念性的雕塑，是二十世纪雕塑艺术的一种形式。而布朗库西则是率先发展了这种艺术形式的雕塑家之一。他出生于罗马尼亚，年轻时曾在国内学习艺术。然后他去了巴黎，在伟大的法国雕塑家罗丹的工作室里工作。起初，他的雕塑作品与罗丹的一样，也属于现实主义。但后来，他开始对非现实主义雕塑艺术产生了兴趣，因此很快就不再创作现实主

nonrealistic sculpture and soon stopped making realistic statues.

Brancusi not only made new forms of sculpture but he tried using many different materials. He made sculpture in wood, bronze, marble, stone, glass, and steel. *Bird in Space* is his best-known work.

It's fun to find a piece of sculpture that is not too dignified and serious. In the past most sculpture has been very dignified and very serious. There are the busts of powerful men like the Roman emperors and the statues of Greek gods, heroes on horseback, and Christian saints. There are imaginary figures called Victory, Liberty, or Justice. These are all very solemn and impressive statues because the artists were following the rule about making art with a worthy subject or moral lesson. People, however, like familiar and amusing things. Look back at the Greek sculpture of the *Boy With Thorn* in Chapter 8. Even two thousand years ago some sculptors had found it fun to make a familiar, everyday amusing sculpture.

Statues of people or things we see every day are often appealing. One modem sculptor who plays with familiar objects is Claes Oldenburg. He surprises us by taking an ordinary small object and sculpting it in large

晒衣夹，欧登伯格作品，
现存于费城的中央广场
（由波士顿的大学印刷协会提供）

义雕塑作品了。

布朗库西不但开拓了雕塑艺术的新形式，而且尝试使用许多不同的材料来制作雕塑。他曾用木头、青铜、大理石、宝石、玻璃和钢铁创作过雕塑。而《空中之鸟》，则是他最负盛名的一件作品。

看到一件不太庄重、严肃的雕塑作品，是一件很有趣的事情。过去，绝大多数雕塑作品都是非常非常庄严、肃穆的。其中，既有像古罗马皇帝那样有权有势之人的半身像，有古希腊诸神的雕像，有骑在马背上的英雄人物雕像，也有基督教圣徒的雕像。还有像胜利女神、自由女神、正义之神这种想象中的人物雕像。之所以有这些非常庄严肃穆、令人印象极其深刻的雕塑作品，是因为当时的艺术家遵循的创作准则，就是要让雕塑作品拥有一个有价值的主题，或者说具有道德意义。然而，人们其实也喜欢常见和有趣的事物。请回过头去，看一看第八章中的那座名叫《拔刺的男孩》的雕塑作品吧。即便是在两千多年前，一些雕塑家就已经发现，创作出一尊大家非常熟悉、日常所见且颇具趣味的雕塑，也是一件乐事呢。

我们日常所见的那种人物雕像或者物品雕塑，通常都是很有吸引力的。用常见之物来制作雕塑作品的一位现代雕塑家，就是克拉斯·欧登伯格。他喜欢将普通的

scale like a monument, and even making it out of an unexpected material. For example, he made a giant sculpture of a clothespin out of stainless steel.

Another kind of modem sculpture that makes you smile is called a *mobile*. Mobiles are moving sculpture. They often look like the models of the solar system that you sometimes see when you study the planets or the little mobiles that are hung in a crib to amuse a baby.

Alexander Calder is one of the most famous mobile artists of the twentieth century. In his earlier mobiles, Calder installed motors to move the hanging pieces. Then he became more interested in natural movement and constructed his later mobiles to move with air currents. But they all change, moving slowly or quickly in time. You could try to make your own simple mobile using a hanger and string.

You don't have to go to a museum to see all different kinds of sculpture. Every city has sculptures in parks and on monuments and on the outside of buildings. Because these sculptures are outdoors, they are easy to photograph and make good subjects for your camera.

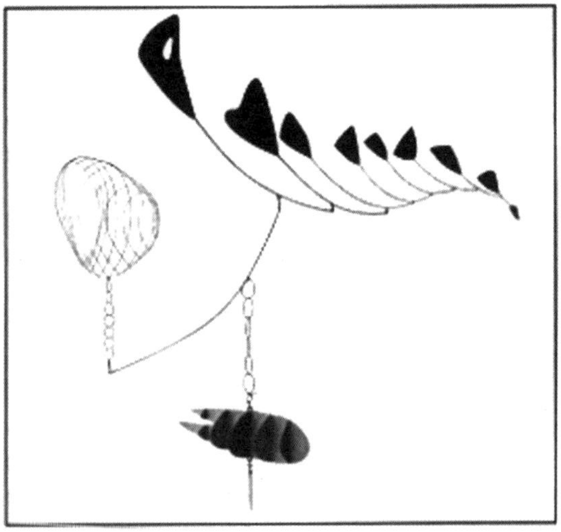

龙虾笼子和鱼尾，考尔德作品，
现存于纽约的现代艺术博物馆
（由缅因州桑福德的大学印刷协会提供）

小物体雕制成大型的纪念碑，甚至用某种意想不到的材料来制作雕塑，从而给我们带来惊喜。比如说，他曾经用不锈钢，制作了一个尺寸巨大的晒衣夹雕塑呢。

另一类会让你们微笑的现代雕塑，称为“活动雕塑”。所谓的活动雕塑，便是移动的雕塑。它们经常就像是你们在研究行星，或者观察挂在婴儿床边哄宝宝的那些小挂件时，有时可以看到的太阳系模型那样。

亚历山大·考尔德就是二十世纪最伟大的活动雕塑艺术家之一。在他早期的活动雕塑作品中，考尔德曾经装上发动机，来让悬挂着的雕塑部件运动起来。后来，他对自然运动越来越感兴趣，因此后期的活动雕塑便都是随着气流而运动了。不过，它们都会变化，会适时地运动得快或慢下来。用一把衣架和一根绳子，你们也可以试着亲手制作出一件简单的活动雕塑来呢。

你们不必非得到博物馆去，才能看到所有不同的雕塑作品。每座城市的公园里、纪念碑上、建筑外墙上，都有雕塑作品。由于这些雕塑作品都在户外，因此你们完全不难将它们当成不错的拍照对象而用相机拍下来呢。

PAINTING

绘画篇

Chapter 1 The Oldest Pictures in the World

I was listening to the teacher but I had my pencil in my hand. There were two little dots about an inch apart on my desktop. Absentmindedly, I twisted my pencil point into one dot and then into the other. The two dots became two little eyes. I drew a circle around each eye, and then I joined the two circles with a half-circle to make a pair of glasses.

The next day I made a nose and a mouth to go with the eyes and glasses.

The next day I finished the face and added ears and some hair.

The next day I added a hat.

The next day I added a body with arms, legs, and feet.

The next day I went over the drawing again, bearing down on my pencil. I traced the lines over and over again until they became deep grooves in my desktop.

The next day my teacher caught me and I caught *it*!

The next day my father got a bill for a new desk and I got — well, never mind what I got.

"Perhaps he's going to be an artist," said my mother.

"Heaven forbid!" said my father. "That would cost me much more than a new desk." And heaven did forbid.

I know of a school that has a large board in the hall for its students to draw on. The

第1章 世界上最古老的绘画

我一边听着老师讲课，手里一直玩着铅笔。我的课桌上，有两个相距约一英寸远的小圆点。我心不在焉地用笔尖绕着一个小圆点画了画，然后又绕着另一个小圆点画了画。于是，那两个小圆点便变成了两只小眼睛。我在每只眼睛周围画了一个圈，然后又用一个半圆将这两个圆圈连起来；这样，它们就变成了一副眼镜。

第二天，我又加上了一个鼻子和一张嘴巴，以配上那双眼睛和那副眼镜。

第三天，我画完了整张脸，还加上了耳朵和部分头发。

第四天，我加上了一顶帽子。

第五天，我加上了身体，画上了胳膊、双腿和双脚。

第六天，我重新审视了一下整幅图画，全部精力都放在自己的铅笔上。我一遍又一遍地描着那些线条，最后它们在我的课桌上变成了一条条深深的沟槽。

第七天，老师发现了我，而我也明白了！

第八天，我的父亲接到了要买一张新课桌的账单，而我则得到了——哦，别去管我得到什么了。

“没准，儿子打算将来当一位画家呢。”我的母亲说。

“但愿不会这样！”我父亲说，“那样的话，我要花的就不止一张新课桌的钱了。”而后来，我的确也没有成为画家。

我曾听说，有一所学校的礼堂里设有一块巨大的牌子，供学生在上面涂鸦呢。

following sentence hangs above the board: If you just must draw, don't draw on your desk, draw on this board.

If you put a pencil in anyone's hand, he just has to draw something. Whether he is listening to a teacher or talking on the phone, he will draw circles and faces or triangles and squares on the pad — if there is a pad. Otherwise he draws on the desktop or his hand, because he just has to draw something. It's human nature. The urge to draw shows you are a human being.

Now animals can learn to do many things that human beings can do, but one thing an animal can't learn is to draw. Dogs can learn to walk on two legs and fetch the newspaper. Bears can learn to dance. Horses can learn to count. Monkeys can learn to drink out of a cup. Parrots can learn to speak. But human beings are the only animals that can learn to draw.

Every boy and girl who has ever lived has drawn something at some time. Haven't you? Perhaps you have drawn a horse or a house, a ship or an automobile, or a dog or a cat. The dog may have looked just like a cat or a caterpillar, but even this is more than any animal can do.

Even people who lived long ago when there were no houses, only caves, to live in — people who were almost like wild animals with long hair all over their bodies — could draw. There were no paper or pencils then. The pictures were not framed and didn't hang on the walls. They were drawn right on the walls of the cave and on the ceiling too.

Sometimes the pictures were just scratched or cut into the wall, and sometimes they were painted in afterward. The paints those people used were made of a colored clay

牌子上面挂着这样一条标语：假如你们非得要画，那就不要在课桌上画，到这块牌子上来画吧。

若是将一支铅笔塞到任何一个人的手里，他都会画点儿什么的。不管是在听老师讲课还是在打电话，他都会在便笺本上（要是有便笺本的话）画点什么的：圆圈呀，人脸呀，长方形呀，正方形呀。不然的话，他就会在课桌或者自己的手掌上画，因为他就是想画点儿什么。这是人的天性。有画画的欲望，就说明你是一个人。

如今，虽说动物也可以学会做人类能做的许多事情，可任何动物都学不会画画。小狗可以学会用两条腿走路和取报纸。熊可以学会跳舞。马儿能够学会数数。猴子可以学会用杯子喝水。鹦鹉能够学会说话。但是，人类却是唯一能够学会画画的一种动物。

有史以来，任何一个小朋友都曾经在某个时间画过某种东西。你们画过没有呢？你们或许画过一匹马儿、一座房子、一艘小船、一辆汽车、一只小狗或者一只小猫。你们画出的小狗，可能看上去就像是一只小猫或者一条毛毛虫；但即便是这样，其他动物也都做不到呢。

甚至很久很久以前的人，也会画画；哪怕当时他们还没有房子，只有洞穴可以居住，身上覆盖着长长的毛发，看上去几乎跟野兽没什么区别，也是这样。当时也没有纸张和铅笔。他们的图画没有裱上画框，也没有挂在墙上。人们都是将它们画在自己所住洞穴的洞壁上，或者是画在洞穴顶上。

有的时候，这些图画只是胡乱地刻在洞壁上；而有的时候，人们过后还会给图画涂上颜色。那些人所用的涂料，是用一种彩色黏土与油脂混合起来制成的，通常

mixed with grease, usually simply red or yellow. Or perhaps the paint was just blood, which was red at first and then turned almost black. Some of the pictures look as if they had been made with the end of a burned stick as you might make a black mark with the end of a burned match. Other pictures were cut into the horns of deer or ivory tusks.

Now what do you suppose these cave dwellers drew pictures of? Suppose I ask you to draw a picture of anything — just anything. Try it. What you have drawn is probably one of five things. A cat is my first guess, a sailboat or an automobile is my second, a house is my third guess, a tree or a flower is my fourth, and a person is my fifth. Are there any other kinds?

Well, the cave dwellers drew pictures of only one type of thing. Not men or women or trees or flowers or scenery. They drew chiefly pictures of animals. And what kind of animals do you suppose? Dogs? No, not dogs. Horses? No, not horses. Lions? No, not lions. They were usually big, strange animals. But they were drawn well enough that we know what the animals looked like. The following picture was drawn by a cave dweller thousands of years ago.

You can see it's a picture of some animal, and it's not a cat or a caterpillar. It is a type of animal that lived in those days. It looks like a huge elephant with long hair. But its ears were not big like those on elephants today. And elephants now have skin or hides but hardly any hair. The animal pictured is called a mammoth. It had long hair because the average temperature was colder in those days and the hair kept the animal warm. And the mammoth was much, much bigger than elephants are today.

都只有红或者黄这样的单色。有的时候，涂料没准还是鲜血哩；鲜血起初是红色的，然后就会慢慢变成几乎全黑色。有的图画看上去，似乎是用烧焦的木头一端画成的，就像你们可以用点过后的火柴棍一端在纸上画一个黑点那样。其他一些图画，则是刻在鹿角上或者象牙上。

现在，你们觉得，这些穴居人画出的图画中，会有些什么东西呢？假设我要求你们画一幅画，内容随意。你们试一试吧。你们画出来的，很可能是五样东西。我猜位于第一位的是小猫，第二位则是帆船或汽车，第三位则是一栋房子，第四位是一棵树或者一朵花，而第五位则是一个人物。还有其他的东西吗？

注意，穴居人画出来的，却只是一种东西。这种东西，既不是男人、女人，也不是树木、花草或者风景。他们画的，主要是动物。你们觉得，他们画出的都是些什么样的动物呢？小狗？不，不是小狗。马儿？不，不是马儿。狮子？不，不是狮子。它们通常都是体型很大的、奇怪的动物。不过，它们都画得很好，足以让我们了解那些动物的样子。下面这幅画，就是几千年前的一位穴居人画下来的。

你们都看得出，画中所画的是某种动物；但它既不是小猫，也不是毛毛虫。这是一种生活在当时的动物。它的样子像是体型庞大的大象，全身都长着长毛。不过，它的耳朵并不像如今大象的耳朵那样大。并且，如今的大象有皮肤，即兽皮，身上几乎也没有什么毛发。图中所画的这种动物，叫作猛犸象。它之所以全身长满长毛，是因为当时的平均气温比如今要寒冷得多，毛发则可以让这种动物保暖。而且，猛犸像的体型也要比今天的大象大得多哩。

There are no mammoths alive now, but people have found their bones and have put them together to form huge skeletons. Today any very big thing is called mammoth. You've probably heard of Mammoth Cave in Kentucky. It is called mammoth not because mammoths lived in it — which they didn't — but because it is such a huge cave.

The cave dwellers drew other animals besides the mammoth. One was the bison, a type of buffalo. You can see a picture of a buffalo on an old-fashioned nickel. It looks something like a bull. One day a little girl went to a cave in Spain with her father to search for arrowheads. While her father was looking on the ground, she was looking at the ceiling of the cave. She saw what she thought was a herd of bulls painted there. She called out, "See the bulls!"

Her father, thinking she had seen real bulls, cried, "Where? Where?"

Cave dwellers also drew other animals that are like those that are alive today — reindeer, deer with big antlers, bears, and wolves.

It was quite dark in the caves where the cave dwellers drew these pictures because there were no windows. The only light

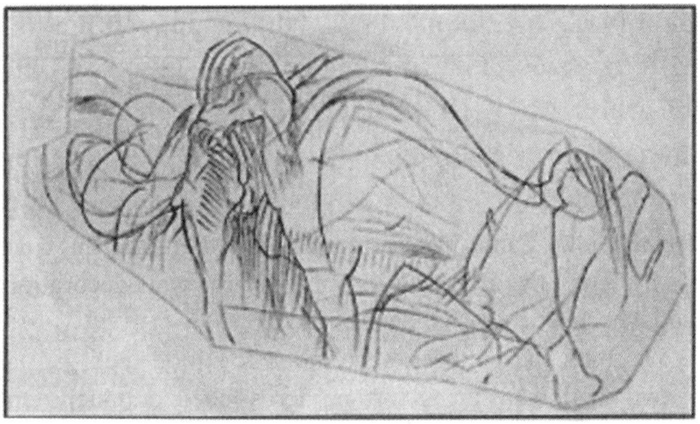

进攻的猛犸象，
法国玛德莱娜教堂一支长牙上所刻的图案，
现存于巴黎植物园的考古博物馆
（由波士顿的大学印刷协会提供）

如今，世界上已经没有活着的猛犸象了；可是，人们发现了猛犸象的骨骼，并将它们重新拼合，拼成了巨大的猛犸象骨架。如今，任何体型非常硕大的东西，都被称为猛犸象似的庞然大物呢。你们很可能都听说过肯塔基州的“猛犸洞穴”吧。之所以称为“猛犸洞穴”，并不是因为曾经有猛犸象在那里生活过（事实上，其中也没有住过猛犸象），而是因为那个洞穴极其巨大。

除了猛犸象，穴居人还画过其他的动物。其中有一种，便是野牛，它属于水牛的一种。在一种旧式的五美分硬币上，你们可以看到一幅野牛的图画。野牛的样子，与公牛有点儿像。有一天，一个小姑娘跟着自己的爸爸来到西班牙的一个洞穴里，去寻找箭簇。当她的父亲正盯着地上四处搜寻时，小姑娘却抬着头，看着洞穴顶部。她看到了一幅图画，觉得画着的是一群公牛。于是，她就叫了一声：“看那群公牛！”

她的父亲以为她看到的是真正的公牛，便大喊道：“哪儿？哪儿？”

穴居人还画过其他一些动物。那些动物，跟如今有些动物一样，比如驯鹿，即长有两只大角的鹿；再比如熊，比如狼。

穴居人画有这些图画的那些洞穴里都很黑暗，因为洞穴里没有窗户。唯一的光

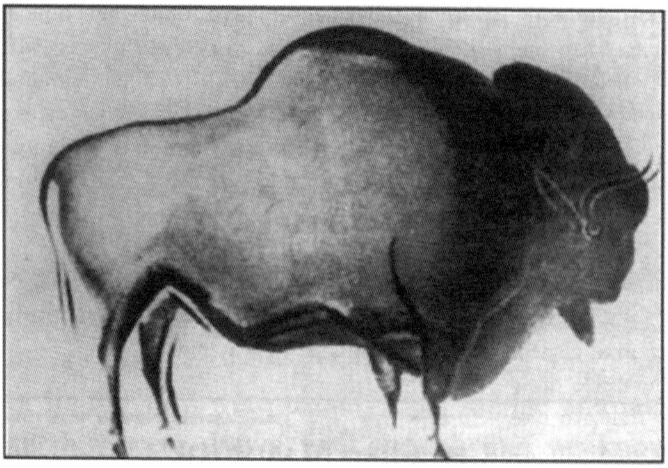

站立的野牛，现存于法国的枫德戈姆洞窟
（由波士顿的大学印刷协会提供）

was a smoky flame from a torch. Why, then, did the cave dwellers draw pictures at all? Such pictures couldn't have been just for wall decorations, like those you have on your walls, because it was so dark in the cave.

We think the pictures were made for good luck, just as some people put a horseshoe over their door to bring fortune across their doorstep. Or perhaps they were put there to tell a story or make a record of some animal the cave dweller had killed. But perhaps the cave dweller just had to draw something, just as boys and girls draw pictures on the walls of a garage or even sometimes on the walls of their own houses or, worse yet, on their desktops.

The pictures made by these cave dwellers are the oldest pictures in the world, and the artists who made them have been dead for thousands of years. Can you think of anything you might ever make that would last as long?

亮，便是一支火把上冒着浓烟的火苗。那么，穴居人究竟为什么要画这些图画呢？这些图画，不可能只是为了装饰洞壁，不可能像你们家中墙壁上的图画那样，因为洞穴里的光线非常黑暗，装饰了也没什么用处。

我们认为，穴居人画这些图画，是为了祈求好运；就像如今有些人将马掌挂在家门口，以便将财富引进家门似的。或者，穴居人画这些图画，没准是为了讲述一个故事，或者是为了记录下他们猎杀过的某种动物。不过，没准也是因为穴居人只是想要画点儿什么，就像小朋友们在车库墙壁上涂鸦，或者甚至有时还会在自家墙上涂鸦，或者像更糟糕的情形，在自己的课桌上涂鸦那样。

穴居人画下的这些图画，就是世界上最古老的图画；而创作这些图画的艺术家呢，却都已经死了好几千年了。你们想象得出，自己做的什么东西能够保存如此长久的时间吗？

Chapter 2 What's Wrong With This Picture?

The cave dwellers made pictures on the walls and ceilings of their caves. But the ancient Egyptians didn't live in caves. They lived in houses where they didn't draw pictures on the walls or ceilings. Their houses were usually mud huts. These huts were not much better than the caves that the cave dwellers lived in, but the Egyptians were not interested in the houses they lived in. They were interested only in the tombs they were buried in or in the temples they built for their many different gods.

Most dead people are buried in the ground nowadays, but the Egyptians thought the ground was not the best place for the dead. Besides much of Egypt was under water for almost half of each year because the Nile River flooded the country regularly every summer. That would have been bad for graves.

The Egyptians believed their bodies would come to life again, and so kings and those who could afford it built tombs above the ground. And they built them to last — never out of wood or anything like that but out of solid stone or brick. They wanted to put their bodies in a safe place, something like a safe-deposit vault. When they died, their bodies were preserved using a process called embalming so that they would not decay.

These embalmed bodies were called mummies, and the mummies were put in coffins that were shaped like very big versions of the bodies. On the coffins, or mummy cases, and on the plaster walls of their tombs and temples, the Egyptians drew and painted thousands

第2章 这幅画有什么问题呢?

穴居人在自己所住洞穴的洞壁和洞顶上画画。不过，古埃及人却没有住在洞穴里。他们都是住在房屋里，而他们也没有在自己所住房屋的墙壁和天花板上画画。他们所住的房屋，通常都是小土屋。虽说这些小土屋比穴居人所住的洞穴好不了多少，可古埃及人的兴趣，却并没有放在自己所住的房屋上。他们只对自己死后所葬的坟墓，或者他们为众多不同神灵所建的神庙感兴趣。

如今，绝大多数死者都埋葬在地下；可古埃及人却认为，地下并不是最适合于死者待的地方哩。除此之外，埃及的许多土地一年中几乎有一半的时间都是淹没在水下，因为尼罗河每年夏季都会很有规律地发洪水，淹没这些土地。对于墓地来说，发洪水可真是糟糕得很呢。

古埃及人相信，他们的肉体会重生；因此国王和那些有钱有势的人，便在地面之上为自己建造了陵墓。并且，他们建造的坟墓都能持久保存下去，因为这些坟墓根本不是用木头或其他类似的东西建造的，而是用坚固的石头或砖块建成的。他们都想把自己的尸体，保存在一个安全得就像是保险金库似的地方。而他们死后，尸体会用一种称为“尸体防腐”的方法进行处理并保存下来，从而确保尸体不会腐坏。

这些经过防腐处理的尸体，叫作“木乃伊”，它们都盛放在外形很像是极大号人体的棺材里。古埃及人会在棺材或者木乃伊盛放匣上面，在坟墓或者神庙的灰泥

of pictures to cover every bit of space. And these pictures were made while the people that were to be buried there were still alive.

These pictures that the Egyptians made on the mummy cases and on the walls of tombs and temples were not like the pictures of wild animals that the cave dwellers drew. Some were of animals but most of the pictures were of people — men and women, kings and queens, gods and goddesses.

There is a way to find out how old boys and girls are without asking their age. The children are shown drawings of three faces from each of which something has been left out. The first face has no eyes, the second has no mouth, and the third face has no nose. Then the children are asked if they can tell what is left out. Now you might think anyone could tell what was wrong with these pictures, but until children are old enough, they can't see that anything at all is left out.

The following illustration is an Egyptian picture that has something wrong with it. It's a picture of a seated man making a lance. He is a lance maker. I wonder if you are old enough to see what's wrong with this picture before I tell you.

造长矛的人

Here's the answer: The eye is drawn as it is seen from the front, but the face is drawn as it is seen from the side. So it is a front view of an eye on a side view of a face. Another peculiar thing about this picture is that the body is twisted. The

抹墙上，画上或者涂上成千上万幅图画，遮住每一条细小的缝隙。而这些图画，都是在死者仍然在世的时候就画上了的呢。

古埃及人在木乃伊盛放匣上、坟墓与神庙墙壁上所绘的图画，与穴居人所绘的野兽图画并不相同。虽说其中也有一些动物，但绝大部分图画描绘的都是人物，包括男人、女人、国王和王后，以及男神和女神。

我们有一种办法，不用经过询问就可以得知小朋友们的年龄。给孩子们出示三幅人脸图，每幅图上都漏掉了某些东西。第一张人脸图上没有眼睛，第二张上没有嘴巴，第三张的脸上则没有鼻子。然后，问孩子们能不能说出每幅图画上漏掉的都是什么部位。注意，你们可能会觉得，大家都说得出这些图画上有什么不对的地方；可实际上，除非孩子长到一定的年龄，否则他们是看不出图画上漏掉了什么部位的。

下图就是古埃及人描绘的，其中存在不对之处的一幅图画。这幅图画，描绘的是一个坐在那里制造长矛的人。他是一个打制长矛的人。我可不知道，你们的年龄是不是够大，能不能在我告诉你们答案之前，看出图画有什么问题来。

答案如下：图中所画人物的眼睛，似乎是正面看去的样子，可整张脸却是侧面像。因此，这幅画就是在一张侧面人脸像上画着一只正面的眼睛。这幅图里，还有一个奇特之处，那就是整个人体也是扭曲的。图中的肩膀画成了正面看去的样子，

shoulders are drawn as they are seen from the front, but the hips, legs, and foot are drawn as they are seen from the side. See if you can sit that way yourself. I'll bet you can't!

In ancient Egyptian times, artists were taught to draw people this way. Can you guess why the Egyptians would combine the front view of a person with the side view? Some say it was a way to show all the important parts of the body doing what they do best — the eye looking right at you, the legs positioned to be walking, and the strong chest and shoulders facing you straight on.

Have you ever noticed the pictures on magazine covers? Some are just pictures of fashion or buildings or gardens. But some of the pictures tell a story, or part of a story. Some of these storytelling pictures have words underneath to tell what the picture means, but some don't need any words underneath. The picture tells the story without any words. This type of picture is called an *illustration*.

Egyptian pictures are chiefly illustrations. They tell a story either with or without words — a story of the life of some dead king or queen, his battles, his hunting parties, his parades. And above, below, or at the side of the picture there are often words in Egyptian writing that describe the pictures. These words look very much like pictures themselves, for the Egyptian writing is a type of picture writing. These picture words are called *hieroglyphics*.

狩猎场景，现存于贝尼哈桑的柯南姆霍特普二世墓
（由波士顿的大学印刷协会提供）

而人物的臀部、双腿和脚，却画成了侧面看去的样子。你们能不能用那种姿势坐着呢？我敢打赌，你们肯定做不到！

在古埃及时期，画家们描画人物时，都是这样的。你们猜不猜得出，古埃及人为什么会把人物的正面像和侧面像画在一起呢？有些人说，这是体现人体所有重要部位最擅长之功能的一种方式；比如眼睛径直看着你，双腿能够走路，而强壮的胸膛和肩膀则正对着你。

你们有没有注意过杂志封面上的图片呢？其中有些只是时装图片，或者是建筑、公园等的图片。但其中有些图画，却会讲述一个故事，或者故事的一部分。这些讲述故事的图片下方都有文字，说明图片表达的意思；还有些图片，则不需要任何文字说明。也就是说，图片无须任何文字，就讲述了整个故事。这种图片，称为“插图”。

古埃及人的图画，主要都属于插图。它们都讲述了一个故事，或有文字说明，或无文字说明；比如某位已故国王或王后的生平，他所经历的战斗、狩猎活动和游行盛况。而图画的上方、下方或者侧面，通常都有古埃及文字，说明了图画的内容。这些文字的样子，与图画本身都很相似；这是因为，古埃及文字本身就是一种图画文字。这种图画文字，称为“象形文字”。

向图坦卡门[1]致敬，现存于底比斯的胡伊墓
（由波士顿的大学印刷协会提供）

When Egyptian artists drew a king with common people around him, they made the king very large and the other people very small. The king was made to be a giant — two or three times as large as the common people — to show he was a really important man.

When the Egyptian artists drew pictures of crowds, they didn't show figures farther back in the picture by drawing them smaller and raising them just a little bit. Instead, they drew all the figures the same size but put those who were supposed to be farther back right above the figures in the front.

We have hundreds of colors and shades, but the Egyptians preferred four bright colors: red, yellow, green, and blue. They also had black, white, and brown. And their colors

古埃及画家在描绘一个国王身边围着普通百姓的时候，都会把国王画得很大，而把其他人画得很小。国王通常被画成巨人，有普通百姓的两三倍大，以表明那是一位真正重要的人物。

古埃及画家在描绘人物群像时，不会将人物画得很小，或者将人物位置绘得稍高一点点，来表明这些人物处于画中的远处。相反，他们是把所有的人物都画成一般大，而把那些本应位于远处的人物画在位于前方的人物上方。

我们如今有成百上千种颜色和明暗层次，可古埃及人却喜欢四种亮丽的颜色：红色、黄色、绿色和蓝色。当然，他们也有黑色、白色和棕色。而且，他们所用的颜料能够保存很久，不易褪色。我们都知道，找到一种不褪色的颜料有多困难。如

[1] 图坦卡门（Tutankhamen），古埃及第十八王朝的法老，约公元前 1361—公元前 1352 年在位，因其陵墓于 1922 年被完整发现而闻名于世。

lasted, We all know how hard it is to find any color that doesn't fade. Window curtains, sofa covers, and even the colors of dresses fade unless they are colorfast, or fixed not to fade. But the pictures the Egyptians made are almost as fresh and bright as when first painted thousands of years ago because they were hidden away in the dark tombs where the Sun could not fade them. The pictures were drawn and painted on the plaster walls, and the colors were very bright — not like nature. It didn't matter whether something really had any color or what the particular color should be. The ancient Egyptians painted it the way they thought it looked best. They might paint a man's face bright red or even green!

When you think of all these old pictures that were not meant to be seen by anybody, you may wonder why the Egyptians made them. And yet today when we build a great building such as a church, school, or government building, we might put the daily newspaper, photographs of people, and other artifacts into a cornerstone — a hollow stone in a building's foundation. Why? The building is expected to last for ages, and the cornerstone will not be opened until the building comes down. Why? Our idea may be something like the ancient Egyptians' idea after all.

今，窗帘、沙发面，甚至是衣物，除非不掉色，或者经过固色处理，否则还是会褪色的呢。可是，古埃及人所绘图画的颜色，如今却几乎仍然像几千年前最初画下时那样新鲜、亮丽呢；因为它们都被藏在漆黑的墓穴里，太阳晒不到，故不会褪色。这些图画都是绘制或者漆刷在灰泥墙壁上，色彩非常亮丽，当然不像自然形成的色彩。东西的真实颜色是什么，应当用哪种特定的颜色，都不要紧。古埃及人觉得看上去怎样最合适，就怎样画。他们可能会把一个人的脸绘成亮红色，甚至还会漆成绿色呢！

倘若考虑到这些古画本来就不是给人看的，那么你们很可能会觉得奇怪，古埃及人又为什么要绘这些图画呢？不过，如今修建一座大型建筑，比如说一座教堂、一所学校或一栋政府办公楼时，我们可能还会把一些日报、人物照片和其他的人造物品一起放入一块奠基石，即埋在建筑物地基下一块中空的石头里。为什么要这样做呢？这是因为，人们希望所建的这栋建筑能够持续保存几个世代，而除非这栋建筑垮塌下来，否则奠基石就不会打开。为什么要这样做呢？因为我们的想法，终究与古埃及人的想法可能有点儿相似呢。

Chapter 3 Palace Picture Puzzles

An inch away from Egypt on a map but a thousand miles away on the ground was another ancient civilization called — well, there were several civilizations there with hard-to-pronounce names. Egypt was a civilization with one river. These other civilizations, a thousand miles off to the east, had two rivers so let's bunch them together and call them, for short, the Two-River Civilization. In case you're interested, the real names of these countries were Mesopotamia, Chaldea, Babylonia, and Assyria. This is the part of the world where the Garden of Eden is thought to have been.

The One-River Civilization and the Two-River Civilization are the two oldest civilizations in the world. The largest and most important cities of the ancient world — very big cities like New York or London or Tokyo today — were once in the Two- River Civilization. These cities were ruled by mighty but cruel kings. Yet there isn't one single building from these old cities left.

Because there was very little stone in the Two-River Civilization, buildings weren't built of stone. Instead, they were built of bricks made of mud. But the bricks were only dried in the sun, not baked by fire the way the Egyptian bricks were to make them last and last.

You know how mud pies dried in the Sun soon crumble to pieces. Well, these buildings

第3章 王宫里的拼图

在地图上距埃及仅一英寸远，可实地却达一千英里的地方，有着另一种古代文明；这个地方，先后出现过好几个文明古国，而名称也都难念得很。古埃及是一个只有一条河流的文明古国。而这些位于古埃及以东一千英里远的其他文明古国，却拥有两条河流；因此，我们不妨将它们合并起来，简称为“两河文明”。假如你们感兴趣的话，那我不妨告诉你们：这些古国的真正名称，分别是美索不达米亚、迦勒底、巴比伦尼亚和亚述。这一地区，就是人们认为“伊甸园”[1]曾经所在的地方。

“一河文明”与“两河文明”，就是世界上两种最古老的文明。古代世界规模最大和最重要的城市，都位于“两河文明”地区；那些大城市的规模，都堪比如今的纽约、伦敦和东京哩。那些城市，全都由一些强大有力却残暴无比的君主统治着。不过，那些古城里，却没有一座建筑保存至今。

由于“两河文明”地区很少有石头，因此那里的房子都不是用石头筑成的。相反，它们是用湿泥制作的砖头砌成的。不过，这些砖块都只是在太阳底下晒干了，而不是用火烧制出来的，不像古埃及人所烧制的砖块，因而后者可以长长久久地保存下去。

[1] 伊甸园（Garden of Eden），基督教《圣经》故事中人类始祖亚当和夏娃所居的花园。现多喻为“乐土，乐园”。

made of sun-dried bricks have all crumbled away, and where magnificent cities once stood, there are now only mounds of brick dust that today look like natural hills.

You may wonder why the people of these civilizations didn't bake their bricks in fire, for fire- baked bricks last longer than almost anything else. The reason is that they didn't have much wood or much other fuel to make fire with. On some bricks, however, they painted pictures and decorations. They covered these bricks with a glass-like substance called a glaze and then baked the bricks in fire so that they became colored tiles. These tiles have lasted and have been found by men digging down in the mounds that were once cities of brick buildings.

In Egypt, as I told you, the artists painted pictures chiefly for the dead. In the Two-River Civilization, the artists didn't care about the dead people. They painted pictures for live people to see.

The Two-River kings didn't build tombs. They weren't interested in what was to become of them after they were dead. Instead, they built great palaces for themselves and great temples for their gods. These palaces and temples were built of brick, but a mud palace or temple was not very beautiful so the artists covered the walls with tiles that had pictures on them.

These tiles were made of a beautiful stone called *alabaster*. Alabaster — which can be either pale yellow, creamy white, white with pink, or white with gray — is so soft that it can be cut into easily. So the artists carved pictures into the alabaster tiles and painted

你们都很清楚，太阳晒干的泥团很快就会碎裂成许多小块。所以，这些用晒干的砖块砌成的房屋全都荡然无存了；而那些辉煌无比的城市曾经所在的地方，也只剩下一堆堆由砖土形成的土墩，以至于如今看上去，它们就像是一座座自然形成的小丘呢。

你们可能会觉得奇怪，这些文明古国里的人，为什么不将砖块用火烧制；因为经火烧制出来的砖块，几乎比其他任何建材都保存得更久。原因在于，他们那时没有什么木柴，也没有什么其他燃料来生火。然而，在有些砖块上，他们却绘制了图画和装饰。他们将这些砖块涂上一种类似于玻璃的，叫作“釉料”的物质，然后将砖块放入火中烧制，从而使得它们变成了瓷砖。这些瓷砖能够保存很久，而人们在发掘过去那些城市里砖砌房屋所在之处的土墩时，也的确找到了一些这样的瓷砖。

我已经跟你们说过，古埃及的画家主要是为死者绘画。而在“两河文明”地区，画家却并不在意那些已经逝去的人。他们绘画，是给活着的人看的。

“两河文明”地区的君主没有修建陵墓。对于自己死后会如何，他们并不感兴趣。相反，他们为自己修建了许多了不起的宫殿，为他们信奉的神灵修建了许多了不起的神庙。这些宫殿和神庙都是用砖头砌成的；不过，用泥砖砌成的宫殿和神庙却不是很漂亮，因此画家们便将瓷砖贴在土墙上，并在砖上绘画。

这些瓷砖都是用一种很美丽的，叫作汉白玉的石头制成的。汉白玉或是淡黄色，或是乳白色，或是灰白色；它们的质地都非常柔软，能够轻松进行雕刻。因此，当时的画家便把图画刻在汉白玉制成的瓷砖上，然后再涂上颜色。他们会在每块瓷砖上画出整幅图画的一部分，然后再将许许多多的瓷砖拼接在一起，形成一幅

them. Part of a picture was drawn on each tile, and then a great many tiles were put together to form a larger picture, just as picture puzzles are put together from separate pieces.

There is a type of picture made of many tiny pieces of different colored stones called a *mosaic*. The people who lived in the Two-River Civilization were the first to work in mosaics.

The Egyptian pictures on the inside walls of the tombs or temples are still there, but those on the mummy cases have been put in museums. The alabaster and tile pictures of the Two-River people were dug up from under the mounds that once were buildings, and they, too, have been put in museums.

These alabaster and tile pictures made in the Two-River Civilization tell stories about what the king and his courtiers, the advisors who served him, liked to do — hunt wild animals and fight battles. So there were many pictures of battles and hunting parties.

The pictures found in the Two-River Civilization are like the Egyptian pictures in some ways. As in Egypt, the front view of an eye is on a side view of a face, but in the Two-River Civilization the shoulders are drawn as seen from the side. When an artist wished to show men behind those in front, he drew the figures above them as the Egyptian artists did. But in some of their pictures, the Two-River artists did try to show figures in the background by raising them in the picture, making them smaller, and partially covering those behind with those in front. This technique of showing distance in a picture is called *perspective*.

更大的图画，就像我们用许多碎片拼成一幅幅拼图那样。

如今有一种图画，是由许多颜色不同的小石子拼合起来的，叫作“马赛克”。而世界上率先制作马赛克的，就是生活在“两河文明”地区的人。

古埃及人在陵墓或者神庙内壁上所绘的图画，如今依然留在这些地方；而那些绘制在木乃伊盛放匣上的图画，则已经保存进了博物馆。“两河文明”古国的人用汉白玉和瓷砖制成的图画，被人们从本是建筑的那些土墩之下挖掘出来后，也保存进了博物馆。

“两河文明”地区制作出来的这些汉白玉和瓷砖画，都讲述了一国君主以及服侍他的朝臣、顾问们喜欢做的一些事情，比如猎杀野兽、打仗。因此，这些图画中，有许多描述的都是战斗和狩猎场景。

“两河文明”地区发掘出来的这些图画，在某些方面与古埃及人的图画很相似。与古埃及人的绘画一样，这些图画中人物的眼睛也是正面像，而脸部则是侧面像；不过，“两河文明”地区的图画中，人物的肩膀却画成了侧面像。倘若画家想要表现某些人位于前面的人身后，他也会像古埃及画家一样，将后面的人物画在前面人物的上方。不过，在其中一些画作中，“两河文明”地区的画家也的确尝试过，在画面上将人物提升，使他们变得较小，并且让前面的人物部分遮挡住后面的人物，来表明某些人物处于后面。在画作上显示距离的这种技术，就称为“透视”。

“两河文明”地区画家所描绘的人物类型，并不同于古埃及人所绘的人物形

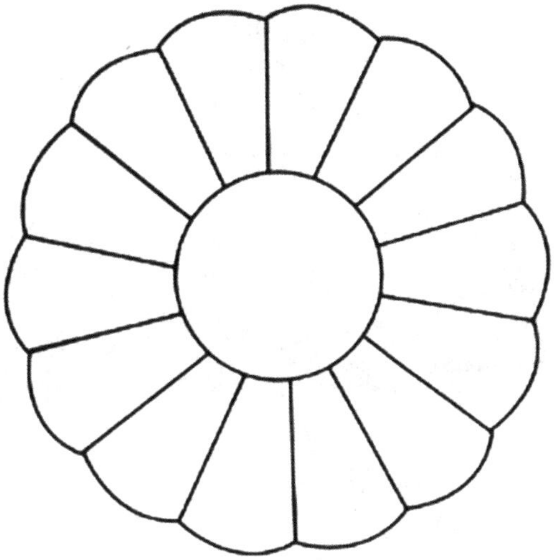

圆形花饰

The type of men that the Two-River artists drew was different from those the Egyptians drew. The Two-River artists admired strength and strong men, and they thought all strong men had long hair and beards. So they pictured the kings with bulging muscles and long hair and beards — every lock of which was carefully curled. The curls were regular corkscrew curls, as if freshly done with a curling iron!

The pictures of animals the Two-River people made are much more natural than those the Egyptians drew. They liked to paint the lion and the bull best because these animals are so strong.

The Two-River people were especially good at making designs and decorations for borders on buildings. One such decoration is called a *rosette*. It is a circular ornament of leaves or flowers, and it is still used today.

象。“两河文明”地区的画家崇尚力量和身体强壮的人，并且他们还认为，所有强壮的男子都长着长长的须发。因此，他们描绘的国王，全都有着隆起的肌肉和长长的头发、胡须，并且每一绺须发都精心地缠扎起来了。而那卷曲着的绺绺须发，全都呈规则的螺旋状，仿佛是刚刚用卷发钳烫出来似的呢!

“两河文明”地区的人所绘的动物图画，比古埃及人所画的动物要显得自然、逼真得多。他们最喜欢画狮子和公牛，因为这两种动物都非常强壮。

“两河文明”地区的人尤其擅长于给建筑物的四周绘制图案和装饰画。其中一种装饰画叫作“圆形花饰”。这是一种用树叶或者花朵构成的圆形装饰图案，如今的人还在使用这种图案呢。

生命树纹饰

The Two-River people also created a design called the *guilloche'*. Versions of this design are used today in tiles for floors and for the halls of public buildings. Even placemats in some restaurants have this type of repeating pattern as a border.

Another design the Two-River people made that has been copied by artists of many other countries is called *tree of life*. This tree is not like those that grow in the ground. It has many different kinds of leaves and other ornamentation. It is often used in designs on rugs and in embroidery. We don't know what it means or why it is called tree of life, so you'll just have to guess why.

“两河文明”地区的人，还创造出了一种叫作“扭索纹饰”的图案。如今人们也仍然用这种纹饰的不同图案，来装饰地板瓷砖和公共建筑的大厅呢。连一些旅店的餐具垫子上，也会用这种重复的图案来做边饰。

“两河文明”地区的人还创造出了另一种图案，一直被其他各国的画家竞相模仿，称为“生命树”。这种树，可不像地里生长出来的那些树呢。树上长着各种各样的叶子，以及其他的装饰物。它通常用于做地毯上的图案和刺绣图案。我们不知道这种图案的意思是什么，不知道人们为什么称之为“生命树”，因此你们也只能自己去猜测其中的原因了。

Chapter 4　April Fool Pictures

I once had a cat I used to tease by holding her up to a mirror. When she saw what she thought was another cat, she would arch her back and spit. I thought it was very funny. But here is a strange thing: If you showed her a picture of a cat, she didn't appear to see it at all. Dogs are the same. They will growl when they see themselves in a mirror, but if you show them a picture of another dog or even a cat, they will pay no attention to it at all. Animals, though they have eyes to see things, do not see things in pictures.

Some people are like that. They look at pictures but do not see them for what they are. So there is a difference between looking and seeing, just as there is a difference between hearing and listening. That's what the Bible means when it says there are those who "have eyes and see not."

When I was a boy, there was a candy shop on the comer. On the counter was a painted silver dollar. It was painted so naturally that everyone tried to pick it up. I thought it wonderful and that the artist who had done it must be a wonderful artist too.

I also remember being taken to an art gallery where there was one picture that I liked best. To me it was a marvel. It was the picture of a door half open with a lady peeking out from behind it. When I first looked at it, I was startled. The picture was so lifelike I could hardly believe it was not a real person looking out from behind a real door. I thought that must be the greatest kind of art — to paint something so natural and lifelike that a person

第4章　错视画作

我曾经养过一只猫，并且经常把它举到一面镜子前逗弄它。它看到自己在镜中的样子后，还以为那是另一只猫，便会弓起背来，呜呜直叫。我觉得这太有意思了。不过，有一件很奇怪的事，那就是：倘若把一张猫的图片放到它面前，那么它就会表现得熟视无睹似的。小狗也一样。它们看到镜中的自己后，会吠个不停；可要是你把另一条狗或者甚至是一只猫的照片放到它们面前，那么它们根本就不会注意到照片。尽管动物有眼睛，能够看到东西，可它们却看不见图画上的东西。

有些人，也跟猫和狗一样。他们会看着图画，却看不出图画中有些什么。所以，“观看”和“看到”之间还是有区别的，就像“听到”和“倾听”之间有所差异那样。《圣经》中说过，有些人“有眼睛，却什么也看不到”，指的就是这个意思。

我小的时候，街角有一家糖果店。糖果店的柜台上，画着一个银质的一美元图案。由于画得非常逼真，因此每位顾客都想要把它捡起来。当时我觉得这非常了不起，觉得那个绘制了这枚银元的画家，也必定是一位很了不起的画家。

我还记得，大人曾经带我去一家画廊参观，那里有一幅画作我最为喜欢。在我看来，那幅画作就是一大奇迹。第一次观看的时候，我还吓了一大跳呢。那幅画非常逼真，我几乎难以相信那不是一个真人正在从一扇真正的门后向外望去。我觉得，那一定是最了不起的一种艺术，才能把某种东西画得如此逼真和栩栩如生，才

would be fooled into thinking it was real.

Well, the old Greek painters seemed to feel the same way about pictures. Greece, as you know, is across the Mediterranean Sea from Egypt. You may not know, however, that the Greeks are thought by many to be the greatest sculptors who have ever lived and were also great architects. Many of their pictures were this kind of April Fool painting that I've described. They tried to paint pictures that would fool people into believing they were real. These April Fool pictures are called *trompe l'oeil* or paintings that fool the eye.

In Egypt and Assyria we know the most famous wall paintings but not the names of the painters who did them. In Greece we know the names of the painters but not the paintings they did. Here is the name of the first painter whose name we do know. He was a Greek. It is a hard name because, for some of us, Greek names are not familiar. But as he is called the father of Greek painting, you might want to remember his name. It is Polygnotus.

The writers of the time of Polygnotus tell us that he was a wonderful painter, but not one of his pictures remains so we have to take their word for it. As a matter of fact, we have very few Greek paintings. One reason for this is that most of the pictures were painted on something that could be moved from place to place, like the pictures we hang on our own walls. These movable pictures have all been lost or destroyed.

One of the most famous April Fool painters was a Greek artist named Zeuxis, who lived around 400 B.C. It is said that he painted a boy carrying a bunch of grapes that looked so real the birds came and pecked at them, trying to eat them.

能使得它可以骗过人的眼睛，令人以为那种东西是真的呢。

好吧，古希腊人似乎对图画也有着与此相同的感受。大家都知道，希腊与埃及隔着地中海相望。然而，你们可能不知道，许多人都认为，古希腊人既是有史以来最伟大的雕塑家，也是那些兼为伟大建筑设计师的人当中最为伟大的呢。他们的许多画作，就是我刚才描述过的那种能够愚弄人的绘画。他们都曾努力绘制出能够骗得人们信以为真的画作。这些愚弄人的画作，称为“错视画”，也就是能够骗过人眼的画作。

对于古埃及和古亚述，我们了解那些最有名的壁画，却不知道绘制那些壁画的画家姓甚名谁。而对于古希腊，我们却是知道画家的名字，却不了解他们所绘的那些画作。下面就是我们的确知道其名字的第一位画家。他是古希腊人。他的名字很难念，因为我们中的一些人并不熟悉希腊人名。不过，由于他被称为希腊的“绘画之父”，因此你们可能也希望记住他的名字吧。他叫波吕格诺图斯。

与波吕格诺图斯同时期的作家告诉我们说，波吕格诺图斯是一位了不起的画家；可他所绘的画作，却一件也没有留存下来，因此我们只好相信这些作家的话了。事实上，我们没有保存下几件古希腊时期的绘画作品。原因之一，便在于当时的绝大多数画作，都是绘在可以从一个地方搬到另一个地方去的东西之上，与我们如今挂在墙上的那些装饰画没什么两样。这些可以移动的绘画作品，如今都已经佚失殆尽，或者是毁掉了。

最著名的错视画家，是一位名叫宙克西斯的古希腊人，他生活在公元前400年左右。据说，他曾经绘制了一幅画作，画中是一个手中拿着一串葡萄的小男孩；由

Zeuxis entered his picture in a contest with a rival painter named Parrhasius to see who was the greater artist. Everyone was sure that Zeuxis would get the prize because the birds were fooled into thinking the grapes he had painted were real. Parrhasius's picture had a curtain drawn across the front of it.

"Now," said Zeuxis to Parrhasius, "draw back the curtain and show us your picture."

To which Parrhasius replied, "The curtain is my picture. Even you, a human being, were fooled into thinking it was real. So I win. You fooled the birds, but I fooled you. And besides, the boy you painted holding the grapes wasn't so lifelike or he would have scared the birds away."

The best and worst Greek painting was on the floor of a famous hall. It was a painting of fruit peels and other pieces of food as if they had fallen from the table and hadn't been swept up. It was called *Unswept Floor*, and the Greeks thought it was the best because it tricked them into thinking that the food was real. But it was also the worst! How could the Greeks have thought this subject — the mess from a meal — beautiful no matter how naturally and realistically it was painted?

The greatest of all the Greek painters was named Apelles. He was a great friend of the precocious young ruler and general Alexander the Great, and he painted Alexander's portrait. And yet we know him more by two of his famous sayings than by his pictures.

A shoemaker once criticized the way Apelles had painted a sandal in one of his pictures. Apelles was glad to have expert advice from one who knew sandals and he made the

于绘制得非常逼真，以至于鸟儿都飞过来啄食，想要吃画中的葡萄哩。

宙克西斯曾经用他的这幅画作，与另一位名叫巴尔拉修的画家进行过一场比赛，看谁更了不起。大家都断定宙克西斯会获胜，因为连鸟儿都受了蒙骗，以为他画的葡萄是真的。而巴尔拉修的画作前面，却有一道帘幕挡着。

“现在，”宙克西斯对巴尔拉修说，“把帘幕拉开，让我们瞧瞧您的画作吧。”

巴尔拉修回答道：“这道帘幕，就是我的画儿呀。连您这个人都被骗过了，以为那是一道真的帘幕。所以是我获胜了。您骗过了小鸟，而我骗过了您。此外，您画的那个手持葡萄的小男孩也不够逼真；否则的话，他就会把小鸟吓走的。”

古希腊时期最好的，也是最糟糕的一幅画作，就绘制在一座著名城堡的地板上。画中到处都是果皮和其他的食物残渣，好像是从餐桌上掉下来，一直没有清扫似的。这幅画，叫作《未清扫的地板》。古希腊人之所以觉得它最好，是因为这幅画作骗过了他们的眼睛，让他们以为画中是真正的食物残渣。可这也是最糟糕的一幅画呢！不管画得多么自然、逼真，古希腊人怎么能够把这样一种主题，即就餐后的狼藉场面，认为是一种美呢？

而古希腊画家中最伟大的一位，名叫阿佩利斯。他是亚历山大大帝这位少年老成的年轻君主兼将领的密友，曾经给亚历山大大帝画过肖像。不过，我们更为熟知的，却是他的两句名言，而不是他的画作。

有一次，一名鞋匠批评阿佩利斯，说他在一幅画作中拖鞋的画法不对。听到这样一个了解拖鞋的人提出的专业建议，阿佩利斯很高兴，便对画作进行了修改。第

correction. The next day the shoemaker criticized another part of the same picture. But this time Apelles did not like the criticism, for he felt the shoemaker didn't know what he was talking about. So he exclaimed, "Let the shoemaker stick to his last." This meant, let him stick to his own business — to things he knows about. A last is the form on which shoes are made. Let him, therefore, criticize only the things he knows about.

Apelles was a very hard worker and made it a rule never to let a day go by without doing some worthwhile work. So he used to say, "No day without a line." Even though more than two thousand years have passed since he lived, we still quote his sayings. They have become proverbs, or wise sayings. They have lasted but none of his paintings have, though everyone who lived at his time honored him and called him the greatest painter of Greece.

Here's another story to show how skilled Apelles was in handling a brush. It is said that one day he visited a friend of his who was also an artist. The friend was not at home, so Apelles picked up a brush, dipped it in paint, and drew an extremely fine, thin line across the artist's easel to see if his friend would know who'd been there.

His friend returned, and when he saw the painted stroke on his easel, he exclaimed, "Apelles has been here. No one else in the world could make such a fine and beautiful brushstroke as this — except myself."

Then he painted an even finer line on top of the first line that Apelles had made, splitting it in two. Later Apelles returned. When he saw the finer stroke down the middle of his own line, he picked up the brush once more and with another stroke did what

二天，那名鞋匠却又批评他说，同一幅画中有另一个部位画得不对。可这一次，阿佩利斯却不喜欢鞋匠的批评意见了，因为他觉得，鞋匠根本就不知道自己在说些什么。于是他大声说道："鞋匠还是只说自己的鞋楦子为好。"意思就是说，鞋匠应该只评价自己的本行，即只说自己了解的东西。"鞋楦子"，就是制鞋时所用的模子。因此，阿佩利斯的意思，就是人们应该只对自己熟知的东西发表批评意见。

阿佩利斯工作起来非常勤奋，总是一天都不虚度，每天都要做点有意义的事情。因此，他常常说："每日一行。"即便是距他生活的时期已经过去了两千多年，如今的我们却仍然在引用他的这些名言呢。它们已经变成了格言，或者说至理名言。这些格言恒久流传，可他的画作却一件也没有留传下来；尽管如此，与之同时期的每一个人都非常敬重他，称他为希腊最伟大的画家。

还有一个故事，很能说明阿佩利斯运用画笔的娴熟程度。据说有一天，他去拜访自己的一位朋友；这位朋友，也是一位画家。由于朋友不在家，因此阿佩利斯便拿起一支画笔，蘸上颜料，在那位画家所用的画板上绘出了一条极精致、极细小的线条，看他的朋友回来后知不知道谁来过他家。

他的朋友回来后，看到自己画板上的那条细线，便大声说道："阿佩利斯来过了吧。世界上没人能够画出这样精细、漂亮的线条，除了我自己。"

于是，他便在阿佩利斯所画的第一条细线上面，画了一条更加精细的线条，将阿佩利斯的那一笔平分成两半。后来，阿佩利斯又过来了。等他看到画布上那条将自己所画线条分成两半、更加精细的线条后，便再次拿起画笔，画出了看似不可能

seemed impossible. Again he divided the fine line lengthwise. Splitting hairs, we might say.

I can show you no pictures with this chapter because there are no pictures to show. What a pity none of these pictures are left, so that we might judge for ourselves and see if they really were so wonderful!

的一笔。他竟然将那位朋友所画的线条从头到尾又分成了两半！我们完全可以说，这真是像在分割发丝一样呢。

这一章，我没有办法让你们观看绘画作品，因为根本就没有绘画作品可以展示。这些画作没有留传下来，是一种多么巨大的遗憾啊；要是有的话，我们就可以自己来做出判断，看它们是不是真的那样神奇了！

Chapter 5 Jars and Jugs

One type of Greek painting has lasted through the years, examples of which are in many museums. These surviving paintings were made on vases.

Today vases are made out of glass, china, or copper and are usually for one purpose — to hold flowers. We don't often paint or even decorate the outside. But Greek vases were made out of clay, and they were not used for flowers at all. They were used to hold anything liquid — water, wine, oil, ointments, perfumes — as we would use jars and jugs, bottles and bowls, cups and kettles, pitchers or tin cans.

Greek vases were made in many beautiful vase shapes. Some were tall and thin; some were short and fat. Some had one handle like a cup; some had two handles. Our pitchers and kettles and bowls today, whether they are made of glass or silver or china, are copies of many of the Greek vase forms.

The Greeks had names for most of the shapes, and though some of the names may be hard to pronounce, you might like to learn them so that you may surprise your friends by calling the vases, bowls, pitchers, or dishes in your own house by their Greek names.

The *kylix* was a flat vase with a stem and two handles. It was used for drinking. Even today you might find some children in France drinking hot chocolate out of a shallow cup that is similar to a kylix, a vessel used over two thousand years ago.

第5章　坛坛罐罐

有一种古希腊时期的绘画作品，一直延续了下来，因而如今许多博物馆里都有这种绘画作品的例子。这些留存下来的绘画作品，都是画在花瓶上的。

如今的花瓶，都是用玻璃、瓷器或者黄铜制成的，并且通常都只有一种用途，即盛放鲜花。我们一般都不会在花瓶外表面上绘画，不会对花瓶外表面进行装饰。但古希腊时期的花瓶，却是用陶土制成，并且根本就不是用来盛放鲜花的。它们通常都是用于盛放液体的，比如水、酒、油、软膏、香水之类，就像我们如今会用坛坛罐罐、瓶子和碗、杯子水壶、水缸或锡罐来盛放这些东西一样。

古希腊时期的花瓶，有着许许多多种漂亮的形状。有些花瓶又高又细，有些则又矮又粗。有些只有一个把手，就像一只杯子；而有些花瓶上则有两个把手。如今我们所用的水缸、水壶、碗，不论是用玻璃、白银还是瓷器制成的，都是仿照古希腊时期的许多花瓶样式做出来的。古希腊人给许多的形状都取了名称；尽管有些名称很难念，你们可能还是想要知道那些名称，以便在自己家里冷不丁地把花瓶、碗碟、水缸、盘子的希腊名称叫出来，让你们的朋友都大吃一惊呢。

基里克斯杯是一种有一个杯脚和两个把手的扁形杯。它是用来喝酒的。即便是如今，你们也能看到，法国的一些小朋友会用一种很浅的杯子喝热巧克力；而那种杯子，与两千多年前人们所用的基里克斯杯这种器皿是很相似的。

The *askos* was a low vase with a spout and a handle across the top. It was used to fill lamps with oil. It was, in other words, an oil can — only it was not made of metal.

The *amphora* was a rather fat vase with two handles on the hips.

The *oinochoë* was a pitcher-shaped vase.

The *lekythos* was a tall, thin bottle-shaped vase with one handle.

All the better vases were painted with pictures all around the outside. The pictures were not of kings and queens. In Egypt the kings and queens would have been pictured. In Assyria there would have been pictures of kings. But at that time, the Greeks had no royalty and no use for kings and queens. So they painted Greek gods and heroes in scenes from their mythology. Many of these pictures on the vases are like illustrations in a book and are very graceful and lovely, but they do not fool you and make you think they are real. To fool you, a picture has to be the same size as the person or object.

The pictures were usually in two styles. In the first style, figures were black or dark brown on a reddish or clay-colored background. In the second style, the background was black and the pictures were reddish or clay-colored, as if the whole vase had been painted black

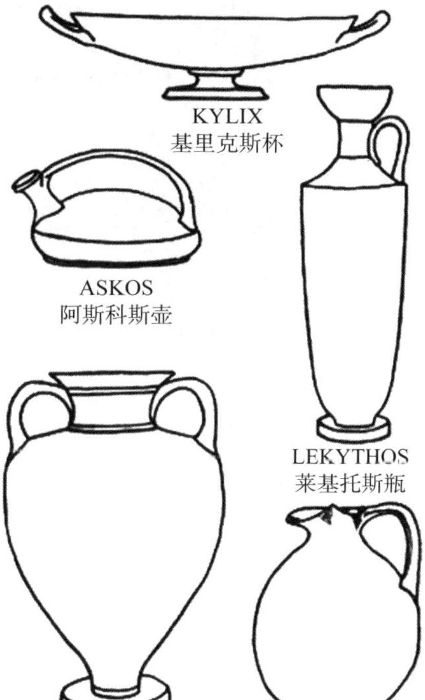

阿斯科斯壶是一种有一个壶嘴、顶上有一个把手的矮壶。这种壶，是用来给油灯添油的。换句话来说，它是一把油壶，只不过这种油壶不是铁制的罢了。

安芙拉罐是一种瓶肚上有两个把手的、瓶体相当粗的罐子。

陶土酒坛是一种样子像是水缸的坛子。

莱基托斯瓶是一种又高又细、有一个把手、外形就像酒瓶一样的瓶子。

在所有较好的瓶瓶罐罐上，整个外表面全都绘有图画。这些图画上，绘的可不是国王和王后。在古亚述，可能会有描绘国王的画作。但在当时，古希腊人却没有王室，因而也不需要什么国王和王后。所以，他们便根据神话传说中的场景，绘制希腊诸神以及古希腊的英雄人物形象。这些绘在瓶子上的图画中，许多都像如今的书籍插图，并且非常优雅、漂亮；但是，它们都不会欺骗你们的眼睛，不会让你们以为它们是真的。要想骗过你们的眼睛，一幅画作的尺寸，必须有所绘的真人或物体那样大才行呢。

这些绘画作品，通常有两种风格。在第一种风格里，人物都是黑色或者深褐色，而背景则是红色或者陶土色。在第二种风格里，背景是黑色的，而图画则是红

基里克斯杯内壁的雅典娜为赫拉克勒斯斟酒图，
现存于慕尼黑的州立文物博物馆
（由波士顿的大学印刷协会提供）

and then the picture had been scraped out so that the clay color was left to form the picture.

Every city-state, or community, in ancient Greece produced pottery, but only a few main centers produced such finely decorated pieces like the one pictured here. The art of painting vases was often passed on from father to son. These pottery artists were not looked up to in the same way the April Fool's painters were. Some of these artists might have even been slaves. But now we admire them for making such beautiful pictures that tell us about life in ancient Greece.

色或者陶土色的，仿佛是整个瓶子都被漆成了黑色，然后再在上面刮磨出图画，从而留下陶土的颜色，形成整幅图画似的。

古希腊的每一个城邦，或者说社区，都出产陶器；不过，只有少数主要的中心城邦，才能生产出装饰得如此精美的陶器，就像上面所示的这件基里克斯杯。在瓶瓶罐罐上绘画的这门艺术，通常都是父子相传的。可是，人们并不像尊重错视画家那样地尊重这些陶器画家。这些画家当中，有一些人很可能还是奴隶呢。不过，如今我们却很钦佩他们；是他们绘制出了如此漂亮的画作，我们才能得知古希腊人的生活是个什么样子。

Chapter 6 Pictures of Christ and Christians

The name we know best in all history is that of Christ. Yet no one knows what Jesus looked like. More paintings have been made of him than of anyone who has ever lived but they are all from the imaginations of the painters. If we did have an actual picture of Christ, it would probably be the most valuable picture in the world. The earliest picture of him was made long after the time when he lived. It was painted by artists who never saw him so they had to guess how he looked.

The greatest city in the world at the time of Christ was Rome, Italy, and soon there were more Christians in Rome than in the country where Christ was born and had lived. The early Christians were a secret society. Their society had to be secret because the rulers of the people thought them dangerous and tortured them and even put them to death on the slightest excuse.

So the Christian society in Rome made hiding places by cutting tunnels and cellar-like rooms — thousands of them — underneath the ground. There they held meetings. They were buried there, too, in places cut into the walls. These dark, damp caves, lighted only with small, dim oil lamps made of clay, are called the Catacombs.

On the ceilings and sides of the Catacombs, the Christians painted pictures. Some of these pictures were from the Jewish tradition showing stories from the Old Testament, like

第6章 关于基督和基督徒的绘画

在整个历史长河中，我们最熟悉的一个名字，就是基督。不过，却没有哪个人知道耶稣基督长得是个什么模样。虽说人们描绘基督的画作，比描绘有史以来其他任何人的画作都要多，可这些画作中的基督形象，都源自画家的想象。要是我们的确有一张基督的真正画像的话，那么它很可能就是世界最为珍贵的一幅画作了。最早的基督画像，也是在他生活的那个时代过去很久之后，才绘制出来的。这幅画作，也是由那些从未见过基督的画家绘制的，因此他们也只能去猜测基督究竟是个什么样子。

基督在世时，世界上最大的城市是意大利的罗马；而不久之后，罗马城中的基督徒数量，便超过基督出生并生活的那个国家了。早期的基督徒，形成了一个隐秘的社团。他们的这个社团必须隐秘，因为当时统治民众的各国君主都认为基督徒很危险，因而对他们严刑拷打，甚至还会以最微不足道的借口，将他们处死哩。

因此，罗马的基督社团便通过在地下挖掘地道，挖出一个个地窖般的房间（有好几千个呢），修建了许多的藏身之所。他们在这些地方集会。他们死后，也被葬在这些地方，葬在这些房间墙壁上挖空了的地方。这些洞穴阴暗、潮湿，只有小型而昏暗的陶制油灯照明，被称为“地下墓穴”。

在“地下墓穴”的穴顶和四周墙壁上，基督徒绘制出了许多的图画。这些图画的内容，有一些源自犹太人的传说，描绘的是《圣经·旧约》中的故事，比如“但

好牧人，马赛克半月画，
现存于拉文纳的加拉・普拉西狄亚陵墓
（由缅因州桑福德的大学印刷协会提供）

Daniel in the Lion's Den or Jonah and the Whale. Some were pictures showing Greek and Roman gods, like the story of Orpheus charming the wild animals with his magic music. But most were from the New Testament, the part of the Bible that tells the story of Christ and his followers.

One was a mosaic of Christ as the Good Shepherd to show how we are sheep that he guards. And when artists did paint the face of Christ, where do you suppose they got the face they used for Christ? It was the picture of what they thought a Greek god looked like!

以理狮穴脱险”[1]，或者“约拿与鲸鱼”[2]的故事。有些图画描述了古希腊和古罗马诸神的故事，比如俄耳甫斯[3]用自己魅力十足的音乐迷住野兽的故事。不过，大部分画作的内容却都源自《圣经・新约》中讲述基督及其信徒们故事的那一部分。

其中有一幅画，就是关于“好牧人”[4]基督的马赛克画，目的是说明我们为何都是基督所放牧的绵羊。而当画家们绘制基督的脸部时，你们觉得，他们会用什么人的脸庞来做基督脸部的原型呢？告诉你们吧，竟然是从他们觉得描绘了古希腊一位神灵模样的图画中选取出来的！

[1] 但以理狮穴脱险（Daniel in the Lion's Den），《旧约・圣经》中的故事。但以理是基督教中的先知。《但以理书》中称，古巴比伦新王任命了一百二十位省长和三位监督，但以理是监督中的主席，因而被人嫉恨。那些人设计让国王将但以理投入了狮坑。不过，但以理得神护佑，毫发无损。

[2] 约拿与鲸鱼（Jonah and the Whale），《旧约・圣经》中的故事。约拿也是基督教中的一个先知。《约拿书》中称，约拿曾逃避神的指示，后来被人丢下大海，在鲸鱼腹中待了三天三夜。

[3] 俄耳甫斯（Orpheus），古希腊神话中的著名诗人兼歌手。他是太阳与音乐之神阿波罗和史诗女神卡莉俄帕（Calliope）之子。据说阿波罗曾送给他一把宝琴，弹奏起来能使人神共醉，连洪水猛兽听了也会变得温柔和顺、俯首帖耳起来。

[4] 好牧人（the Good Shepherd），《圣经・新约・约翰福音》中对耶稣基督的称呼。

But most of the paintings in the Catacombs were not what you would call real paintings of people. They were more like signs or symbols that had some meaning to a Christian. They made pictures of a dove because it represented the Holy Spirit, which they believed came down from heaven in the form of a dove. They painted the cock that crowed when Peter denied that he knew Christ. They painted an anchor, which meant their religion was like an anchor that keeps a boat in a storm from being dashed on the rocks. They painted a vine because Christ said, "I am the vine." And so on.

Perhaps the most important symbol used by early Christians was the fish. They painted a fish because in the Greek language the initial letters of the word *fish* form an acrostic that refers to Christ: *Iesous Christos Theou Yios Soter*, or Jesus Christ, Son of God, Saviour. When early Christians had to worship in secrecy, these symbols let other Christians know whether a place was safe for them.

About three hundred years after Christ died, a Roman emperor named Constantine became a Christian himself. Then, for the first time, the Christian society no longer needed to be secret. The Christians had no further fear of harm so they came out of the Catacombs to worship openly. They built churches above ground and covered the inside walls with pictures and mosaics. Then, for over a thousand years, they painted pictures of people and scenes from the Bible.

Most people at this time in history could not read. So the scenes in the churches helped

但是，"地下墓穴"中的绝大部分画作，都不是我们所称的真人油画作品。它们更像是对于基督徒具有某种意义的符号或者标志。他们之所以绘制鸽子，是因为鸽子象征着圣灵；基督徒认为，圣灵就是化身为一只鸽子，从天堂下到凡间的。他们绘制了彼得否认自己认识基督时那只啼叫的公鸡[1]。他们绘制了一只船锚，意味着自己信仰的宗教就像是一只船锚，能够在暴风雨中让船只不至于撞上岩石。他们还绘制了一株葡萄树，因为基督曾经说过："我是真葡萄树。"[2]诸如此类。

或许，早期基督徒所用的最重要的一种标志，就是鱼。他们之所以画鱼，是因为在希腊语里，"鱼"这个词的首字母构成了一首涉及基督的藏头诗："*Iesous Christos Theou Yios Soter*"，即"耶稣基督，上帝之子，尘世救星"。在早期基督徒还只能秘密地礼拜上帝的那个时代，这些标志可以让其他的基督徒明白，某个地方是不是安全。

距基督受难升天大约三百年后，一位名叫康斯坦丁的罗马皇帝自己也皈依了基督教。于是，基督教团体第一次不用再隐秘行事了。基督徒再也不用担心受到迫害了，因此他们纷纷走出"地下墓穴"，开始公开礼拜上帝。他们在地上修建起了教堂，并且给教堂的内墙绘上了图画和马赛克。接下来，在一千多年的时间里，他们绘制的就是人物画和描述《圣经》中场景的画作了。

这一历史时期的绝大多数人都不识字。因此，教堂墙壁上绘制的场景，便有助于

[1] 基督教《圣经》的四卷《福音书》中都提到，基督被犹大出卖后，使徒彼得曾经三次否认自己认识主（即基督）。后来，一只公鸡啼叫，才让彼得警醒过来。

[2] 我是真葡萄树（I am the vine），引自《圣经·新约·约翰福音》15：1。

people learn about Jesus' miracles, the saints, and stories from the Bible.

The Greeks painted pictures chiefly of people without any clothes on because they thought the human figure was the most beautiful thing in the world and they did not want to cover it up. The Christian painters thought such figures were not modest, and in the pictures they made, they covered up the entire body with clothing so that only the face, hands, and feet showed.

《林迪斯芳福音书》[1]中一页：
圣徒马太[2]，现存于伦敦的大英博物馆
（由波士顿的大学印刷协会提供）

The Christian painters spent all their efforts trying to make the face not just beautiful but also spiritual and holy. Often the background was painted in gold. Sometimes the pictures, instead of being painted, were made of mosaics. Paintings on plaster walls would peel, crumble, and rub off but mosaics would last. Mosaic pictures were often made on the floors of churches because such a picture made of small pieces of stones fitted together was the only kind that would stand the tread of countless feet. It would not wear out and it would not wear off.

人们了解耶稣的种种神迹，有助于他们了解圣徒们的经历，以及《圣经》中的其他故事。

古希腊人绘制的画作，之所以主要都是不穿衣服的人物画像，是因为他们认为，人体是世界上最美的东西，他们不想把这种美丽的东西遮挡起来。而基督徒画家则觉得，这种画作不太端庄，因此在他们绘制的画作中，他们会把整个人体都用衣物遮盖起来，只有脸、手和脚露在外面。

基督教画家都竭尽全力，想要让画出的人脸不只是漂亮，还要显得崇高和神圣。画作的背景通常都是金色的。有的时候，一些画作不是用画笔绘出来的，而是用马赛克拼出来的。灰泥墙壁上的绘画会剥落、碎裂、擦掉，但马赛克画却能持久保存下去。马赛克画一般都是绘制在教堂的地板上，因为只有这种用许多细小石子拼凑形成的画作，才能经得起无数双脚的踩踏。它们既不会被人踩坏，也不会磨损。

[1] 《林迪斯芳福音书》（Lindisfarne Gospes），7世纪晚期为英国诺森伯里亚岛的林迪斯芳修道院制作的一种四卷本手抄插画福音书，由林迪斯芳主教埃德弗里斯设计并制作，其中的插画为爱尔兰-撒克逊风格，体现了爱尔兰、古典主义和拜占庭风格这三种元素的完美融合。

[2] 圣徒马太（Saint Matthew），耶稣的十二使徒之一，属于早期基督教的传教史家，于公元42年左右著写了《马太福音》，是《圣经·新约》中的四大福音书之一。公元91年，马太遇刺殉教。又译“圣玛窦”。

But perhaps the best paintings the Christian artists made were tiny illustrations or decorations for their Bibles and holy books. Some of these pictures were no larger than a postage stamp. Most of them were made by monks — religious men who gave their lives to the service of the church. Because the printing press had not yet been invented, all books were written manually, or by hand. Hence, these books are called *manuscripts*.

These manuscripts were illustrated with bright and decorative pictures using gold and bright colors. The pictures were called *illuminations* because they seemed to light up or illuminate the page. The pages were made of vellum, a very thin material made from animal skin that has lasted until today. Perhaps you have seen an illuminated manuscript in a museum you have visited.

不过，基督教画家绘制得最好的画作，可能还是他们为各种版本的《圣经》和经典著作所绘的插图或者装饰画。其中，有些插图还不到一张邮票大呢。它们中的绝大部分，都是由修道士绘制出来的；所谓的修道士，就是那些终生都为教会服务的神职人员。由于当时还没有发明印刷机，因此所有书籍都是人工抄写而成的，或者说是手工抄写出来的。所以，这些书籍就被称为“手抄本”。

这些手抄本上，都有用金色或者其他亮丽颜色绘制出来的、鲜艳且具有装饰作用的插图。这些插图被称为“照明画”，因为它们看上去似乎照亮了书籍中的页面。当时的书页都是用皮纸做成的；那是一种用动物皮制成的、非常薄的材料，一直保存到了今天。或许，你们在博物馆里早已见过这种含有照明画的手抄本了呢。

Chapter 7 The Shepherd-Boy Painter

Perhaps you have never seen a great painting. Some people have if they were lucky enough to visit a large art museum. But the ones who have not had that chance have only seen pictures of such paintings. That is about the same as seeing a picture postcard of Niagara Falls instead of seeing the Falls themselves. We know what the Falls look like, and we know what some of the great pictures look like, but that's not the same as seeing the real thing. So you have to use your imagination to understand what a great picture is like when all you can see is a small copy of it.

The father of Greek painting, you may remember, was a man named Polygnotus. About two thousand years later, there lived a man who is called the father of Italian painting. His name is Cimabue. Cimabue lived in Florence, which means the City of Flowers. It is in the central part of Italy. There are very few of his paintings in existence, and we are not sure certain pictures that still exist are really his. And you may not even see from the paintings we have why he was supposed to be such a great painter.

If Cimabue were painting now, he probably would not be considered great, but in his time he was thought very great because he was so much better than any other painter had been for a thousand years before him. When he had finished painting a large picture of the Virgin Mary, the mother of Jesus Christ, it is said that the people of Florence thought it so beautiful they formed a procession and, with trumpets sounding and banners flying,

第7章 牧童画家

你们也许从来没有见过一幅伟大的画作。假如运气好，在参观大型美术馆时，有些人没准碰到过。不过，那些没有机会去大型美术馆的人，就只见过这些画作的照片了。这跟看印有尼亚加拉大瀑布的明信片，而不能亲眼看到这道瀑布本身一样。我们都知道尼亚加拉大瀑布是个什么样子，我们也都知道一些伟大的画作是个什么样子，可这跟亲眼看到实物还是不可同日而语。因此，倘若只能看到这些作品的小型复制品，那我们就只能充分发挥自己的想象力，才能理解一幅伟大的画作究竟是个什么样子了。

你们可能都还记得，古希腊的“绘画之父”是一个叫作波吕格诺图斯的人。大约两千年之后，又出了一个被称为意大利“绘画之父”的人。他名叫契马布埃。契马布埃住在佛罗伦萨；在意大利语里，“佛罗伦萨”就是“花城”的意思。该城位于意大利的中部地区。如今他的画作少有存世，而我们也不清楚如今存世的某些画作究竟是不是真的是他所作。从如今存世的画作里，你们甚至可能也看不出，他为何会成为如此伟大的一位画家呢。

倘若契马布埃如今仍在绘画的话，那人们很可能不会认为他很伟大了；可在他那个时代，人们却认为他非常伟大，因为他比一千年以来其他所有的画家都要优秀。据说，他画完一幅描绘耶稣基督之母，即圣母马利亚的巨幅画像之后，由于佛

carried the picture through the streets from his house to the church where it was placed.

Another picture that Cimabue painted is of a monk named Saint Francis. Monks were holy men who spent their whole life trying to be good and do good. Saint Francis started a society of monks named after him. They were called Franciscans. Those who joined the society promised to try to live as Christ had lived. They could own nothing. They could have no money. They could not marry. They spent all their time doing good.

The Franciscans worked to earn their daily bread and lodging. They shaved the top of their heads, leaving a circular place called a tonsure bare like a bald spot. They kept it shaved so that everyone would know they were monks. They wore a rough brown robe with a hood, and they held the robe closed with a coarse rope tied round the waist.

One of the most surprising parts of paintings of Saint Francis is the circle around his head called a halo. A halo was painted round the heads of saints to show that they were holy persons. The spots on this saint's hands are not an accident. It is said that Saint Francis wanted so to be like Christ that an angel came to him and made nail holes on his hands and

圣母与天使及圣方济各，契马布埃作品，
现存于阿西西圣方济各教堂的下教堂
（由波士顿的大学印刷协会提供）

罗伦萨人都认为这幅画像非常漂亮，因此还吹着鼓乐、挥舞着旗帜，抬着那幅画像，沿着从他家到安放画像的教堂那条街道，举行了一次盛大的游行呢。

契马布埃绘制的另一幅画作，是为一位名叫圣方济各的修道士所绘的画像。修道士都是一些终生致力于为善、行善的神职人员。圣方济各创立了一个以自己的名字命名的修道士团体。团体中的修道士，因此便叫方济各会修士。凡是加入方济各会的修道士，都誓言尽力像基督那样去生活。他们不能拥有任何东西。他们不能拥有钱财。他们不能结婚成家。他们的所有时间，全都用于行善。

方济各会修士都是通过劳作，来挣得每日的衣食住行所需。他们会剃掉头顶的头发，形成一个叫作“削发光顶”的、就像一块秃斑的圆圈。他们始终让头顶的这一圈光着，以便让大家都知道他们是修道士。他们身穿粗糙的、带有兜帽的长袍，并且在腰间用一根粗糙的绳子，将长袍系住。

在圣方济各的那些画像中，最令人惊讶的地方，就是他的头部周围都有一个叫作“光环”的圆圈。之所以在圣人的头部周围画上光环，是为了表明他们都是圣洁之人。而这位圣徒双手上的斑点，则不是偶然为之的。据说，圣方济各变得完全像基督一样，因此一位天使来到他的面前，在他的手上和脚上留下许多钉眼，就

feet like those that Christ had received on the cross. These famous nail marks are called stigmata.

But Cimabue is not famous for what he did himself. Rather he is known chiefly as the teacher of someone who became a much greater artist. One day Cimabue was walking in the country not far from Florence when he came upon a shepherd boy tending his flocks. The boy, while watching his sheep, was drawing pictures of them on a piece of slate with a sharp stone. Cimabue, looking over the boy's shoulder, was amazed at the picture he saw and asked the boy his name.

"Giotto," the boy replied.

Cimabue asked Giotto if he would like to go to Florence and study drawing and painting. The boy was delighted to have such a chance. So after getting permission from his father, he went to live and study with Cimabue. When Giotto grew up, he painted many famous pictures of Christ, the Virgin Mary, and especially of Saint Francis, whom Cimabue had also painted.

Saint Francis lived in a town on the top of a high hill near Florence called Assisi. In Assisi there is a church built in his honor. In

圣方济各像，《圣母与天使及圣方济各》细部，契马布埃作品，
现存于阿西西圣方济各教堂的下教堂
（由波士顿的大学印刷协会提供）

像基督在十字架上受难时留下的那些钉眼一样。这些大名鼎鼎的钉眼，被称为“圣疤”。

不过，契马布埃之所以闻名，倒不是在于他自己的绘画作品。不如说，他之所以出名，主要在于他是一位后来变得比他更加伟大的画家的老师。有一天，契马布埃正在距佛罗伦萨不远的一处乡间散步，偶然碰到了一位正在放羊的牧童。那位牧童一边照看羊群，一边用一块尖尖的石子在一块石板上画着羊群的样子。契马布埃从牧童的肩膀上看过去，对自己看到的那幅画大感讶异，便问那位牧童叫什么。

“我叫乔托。”牧童回答道。

契马布埃便问那牧童，愿不愿意到佛罗伦萨去学习绘画。有这样的机会，那个牧童当然是高兴坏了。于是，在得到父亲允许之后，他便随契马布埃而去，跟他一起生活，并向他学习绘画。乔托长大成人后，创作了许多著名的基督画像、圣母马利亚画像，尤其是像契马布埃一样，创作了许多关于圣方济各的绘画作品。

圣方济各住在距佛罗伦萨不远的一个叫作阿西西的小镇的一座高山上。阿西西有

fact, there are two churches, one on top of the other. In the upper church, Giotto painted a series of pictures along the walls that told stories from the life of Saint Francis. Among the many wonderful things Saint Francis did was to preach sermons to the birds that gathered around him to listen. Giotto's painting *Saint Francis Preaching to the Birds* shows him doing this.

In those days, the paint was not what we have now. Today paint is usually made by mixing colored powder with oil. We call it oil paint and artists use it to paint pictures on canvas. But in those days, oil was not used in making paint and painting was not done on canvas. Instead artists mixed their powdered colors with water and painted on freshly plastered walls. Or they mixed their colors with something sticky like eggs or glue and painted on dry plaster, wood, or copper. The first kind of painting on fresh plaster is called *fresco*, which means fresh. The second kind of painting is called *tempera*, which means mixed.

A story is told that the pope wished to have a picture painted so he sent a messenger to Giotto to ask for a sample of the artist's work. Giotto dipped his brush in some paint and, with a single swinging stroke, painted a perfect circle on a piece of wood, and then he sent it to the pope to show how skilled he

圣方济各向鸟儿布道，乔托作品，
现存于阿西西圣方济各教堂的上教堂
（由波士顿的大学印刷协会提供）

一座教堂，就是为了纪念他而修建的。事实上，那里有两座教堂，并且其中一座建在另一座的上方。在上面的教堂里，乔托沿着四周墙壁，绘制了一系列的画作，讲述了圣方济各的生平。在圣方济各的诸多异事里，有一件就是他曾经布道给聚集在他身边的小鸟听。乔托的《圣方济各向鸟儿布道》这幅画作，描述的正是这件事情。

那个时候，绘画所用的颜料并不是目前我们所用的颜料。如今，颜料通常都是用彩色粉末混合油脂制成的。我们称之为油画颜料，而画家则用颜料在画布上作画。可在那个时代，制作颜料时却不用油脂，而画家也不是在画布上作画。相反，画家是将彩色的粉末用水调制而成，并在刚刚粉刷过灰泥的墙壁上作画的。不然的话，他们就是用某种黏稠的，像是蛋清或者胶水的液体来调制颜料，并在已经干了的灰泥墙壁、木器或者铜器上作画。第一种绘画作品，即画家在刚刚刷过的灰泥墙壁上所绘的画作，叫作湿壁画，就是指趁墙还湿着的时候所绘的壁画。第二种油画则叫丹配拉画，意思就是混合颜料画。

有个故事说，教皇曾经想请人给自己画张像，便派了一个使者到乔托那里去，要这位画家给他一幅作品样本。乔托用画笔蘸了一点儿颜料，任意地大笔一挥，在

was. Do you think you could draw a perfect circle with one stroke of a pencil without a compass? Try it. Then try doing it with a brush.

But even if you can do this, it does not mean you are a great artist. For many, it is easy to trace a drawing. It is not much harder to copy a drawing without tracing. Thousands of people can paint a basket of fruit, a vase of flowers, or a view of the sea or the land. That is just a copy. Thousands can copy the painting of a great artist so well that you can hardly tell the copy from the original. But very few people are able to invent a picture out of their own heads and put the parts together to make a beautiful painting. That is what takes genius!

一块木头上画了一个完美的圆圈，然后送给了教皇，以此来表明他的技艺娴熟。你们觉得，自己可不可以不用圆规，只用一支铅笔，一笔就画出一个完美的圆圈来呢？试一试吧。然后，你们不妨再用画笔来试一试。

不过，就算你们做得到这一点，也并不意味着你们就是伟大的画家了。在许多人看来，描摹一幅画作是件轻而易举的事情。而不用描摹，仿制一幅画作也难不了多少。成千上万的人都能画出一篮子水果、一瓶鲜花，或者大海和陆地的景色来。那不过是一种复制品罢了。成千上万的人也可以将一个伟大画家的作品仿制得极其逼真，以至于让人们分不清哪是原作，哪是仿制品来。可是，很少有人在自己的脑海里想象出一幅图画，并将各个部分组合起来，形成一幅漂亮的画作呢。而这一点，需要的就是天赋！

Chapter 8 The Angel-Like Brother

The houses where monks live together are called monasteries. Monks are known as brothers because they are supposed to treat one another and everyone else as such. In some churches the members call one another brother and sister.

In Florence, the City of Flowers, was a monastery called St. Mark's. In this monastery lived a monk who, because he was so very good and holy, was called the angel-like brother — which is Fra Angelico in Italian. It may seem strange that a monk should become a great artist, but Fra Angelico had a talent for drawing and painting. He painted Bible pictures on the walls of the rooms in his monastery.

The rooms where the monks slept were called cells because they were so plain and bare that they were almost like cells in prison. There were forty of these cells, and Fra Angelico spent most of his life painting them so that the monks would have scenes from the Bible to look at and think about. These pictures were painted in fresco. Fra Angelico also painted movable pictures on wooden panels in tempera, which, as I have told you, is color mixed with something sticky like egg or glue.

Fra Angelico lived about a hundred years later than Giotto but his style was much like Giotto's style. It is said that before starting to paint a picture, he always prayed long and earnestly. Then when he did set to work on a painting, he never changed a brushstroke. He left everything he did just as he first put it down. He believed that the Lord had guided

第8章 天使般的兄弟

修道士们集体居住的地方，叫作修道院。众所周知，修道士们都被称为兄弟，因为他们应当像兄弟一样彼此相待。在有些教会里，所有修道士都互称兄弟和姐妹呢。

在佛罗伦萨这座花城里，有一座叫作“圣马可”的修道院。在这座修道院里，有一个修道士，由于他非常善良、非常圣洁，因此被人称为“天使一般的兄弟”；而在意大利语里，这个称呼就是“弗拉·安杰利科”。虽说一名修道士最终变成了一位伟大的画家，这事儿看起来可能有点儿奇怪，可弗拉·安杰利科却很有绘画天赋。他在自己所在的那座修道院的墙壁上，绘制了很多与《圣经》有关的画作呢。

修道士们睡觉的房间，称为“小间”；因为这些房间都非常简陋，几乎没有什么家具，因此与监狱里的单人牢房差不多。圣马可修道院里有四十个这样的小间，而弗拉·安杰利科几乎终生都在给这些房间绘画，以便修道士们都可以看到《圣经》中的故事场景，并且引发他们去思考。这些画作都是用湿壁画法绘制的。弗拉·安杰利科也用丹配拉画法在木板上绘制过一些活动画作；前面我已经跟你们说过，所谓的丹配拉画法，就是用某种黏稠得像蛋清或胶水的液体调制而成的颜料来绘制画作。

弗拉·安杰利科生活在乔托之后大约一百年，可他的绘画风格，却与乔托非常相似。据说，在开始绘制一幅画作之前，他总是会极其虔诚地祈祷很长的时间。然后，待真正开始绘制作品之后，他就决不会再改动一笔了。他相信主会引导着他的

圣母领报，弗拉·安杰利科作品，
现存于佛罗伦萨圣马可教堂的上层走廊
（由波士顿的大学印刷协会提供）

his hand and, therefore, no correction should be made. Of course, being such a religious man, he painted nothing but religious pictures — pictures of saints and angels — and he received no pay whatsoever for his work.

One religious subject that painters of the time loved to paint was the Annunciation — the announcement to Mary that she was to be the mother of Christ.

Fra Angelico painted an Annunciation picture, which I think you'll agree is very lovely. In it, the Virgin Mary is seated on a stool on the porch of her home with her arms folded across her breast. An angel messenger, who has just descended from heaven, kneels halfway to tell Mary that she is to have a Divine Son.

手，因此，绘完后根本无须对画作进行修改。当然，由于他是一个极其虔诚的人，所以他只绘制宗教画作，即圣徒和天使的画像，除此之外，别无其他；并且，无论他绘制什么作品，都是无偿的。

当时的画家很喜欢绘制的一个宗教主题，就是“圣母领报”[1]，即马利亚接到通知说，她即将成为基督的母亲。

弗拉·安杰利科也绘制过一幅《圣母领报》图；我觉得，说这幅画作非常漂亮，你们都会没有意见的。在这幅画作中，圣母马利亚坐在自家门廊里的一条凳子上，双手交叉抱在胸前。一位刚刚从天堂降临下界的天使信使屈膝半跪，对马利亚说，她即将诞下一位圣子。

[1] 圣母领报（Annunciation），《圣经》中的故事。《路加福音》中称，天使加百列曾向马利亚通报，耶稣基督即将通过马利亚成胎而降生。亦译“天使传报”、“天使报喜”等。如今每年的 3 月 25 日就是西方的“圣母领报”节。

殉道者彼得告诫保持安静，
弗拉·安杰利科作品，
现存于佛罗伦萨的圣马可博物馆

Now what would happen if Mary stood up? Would her head hit the ceiling? Fra Angelico was less interested in the exact space in which Mary is placed than in the quiet, spiritual, mystical feeling of that moment.

The monks of St. Mark's were not allowed to talk to one another except at certain times as a special treat. Think about keeping silent for one single day or even for one hour! The rule was made so that the monks would keep their thoughts always on God and religion and not waste their time in gossip or other worthless talk. Over a doorway in St. Mark's monastery, Fra Angelico painted a picture of Saint Peter with his finger on his lips to remind the monks that they must be silent.

St. Mark's monastery is now a museum for the paintings of Fra Angelico. It contains most of his movable paintings as well as the fresco paintings on the cell walls. One of the

注意，倘若画中的马利亚站起身来，又会出现什么样的情况呢？她的头会不会碰到上面的天花板呢？弗拉·安杰利科注重的，可不是马利亚所处的准确位置，而是当时那种静谧的、精神上的、神秘的氛围。

圣马可修道院里的修道士，只有在某些时候才能彼此交谈，这可是一种特殊待遇呢。想象一下，安静无语地待上一天，哪怕是待上一个小时，会多么令人难受啊！修道院里的规定就是这样，目的是让修道士们始终都想着上帝和宗教，而不会把时间浪费在闲谈或者其他毫无意义的交谈上。在圣马可修道院一扇门的上方，弗拉·安杰利科还绘制了一幅圣徒彼得的画像；画中，圣彼得把一根手指放在嘴唇上，提醒修道士们必须保持安静。

如今，圣马可修道院变成了一座收藏弗拉·安杰利科画作的博物馆。其中藏有他的绝大多数活动画作，以及他在修道院小间墙壁上所绘制的湿壁画。这些活动画

吹奏乐器的天使，
《利奈奥尼圣母祭坛三联画》细部
弗拉·安杰利科作品，
现存于佛罗伦萨的圣马可博物馆

movable paintings is a picture of the Virgin Mary with the Christ Child. The Virgin Mary is called Madonna, which is Italian for my lady. So such a picture is called a *Madonna*.

For hundreds of years, thousands of pictures of the Madonna were painted. In fact, every artist painted at least one Madonna and often many more. Each church had to have one or more Madonnas. And every family that could afford to have any painting at all had a Madonna hanging on the wall, just as many families these days have a Bible in the house.

The Madonna that Fra Angelico painted is framed by a broad gold border on which the artist painted angels playing different musical instruments. Thousands of colorful postcards and other copies of these angels have been made.

作中，有一幅画的是圣母马利亚抱着儿时基督的情形。圣母马利亚又被称为“玛丹娜”，在意大利语里，就是“圣母”的意思。因此，这样的画作便都被称为“圣母像”。

在几百年的时间里，人们绘制了成千上万幅圣母像。事实上，每位画家起码都绘制过一幅圣母像，并且通常来说，他们绘制的可远不止一幅。每座教堂都必须绘制一幅或者多幅圣母像。而凡是买得起画作的家庭，也都会买上一幅挂到自家的墙上，就像如今许多家庭都会买上一本《圣经》摆在家里一样。

弗拉·安杰利科所绘的圣母像上，有一道很宽的金边；画家在这道金边上绘制了许多弹奏着不同乐器的天使。人们已经根据这些天使，制作出了成千上万的彩色明信片，以及其他的复制品呢。

Chapter 9 Born-Again Painters

The ancient Egyptians believed they would come to life again after they had died, but they never did. The ancient Greeks didn't think much about coming to life again, but about two thousand years after the ancient Greek artists had died, some people born in Italy were in many ways like those old Greeks — so much so that it seemed as if the Greeks had been born again and were living once more. This period is called the born-again time, or the *Renaissance*, because art, literature, and learning were reborn.

One of the first artists of the Renaissance was a boy who had a very insulting nickname. Now nicknames stick to some people when they grow up. But it seems strange that this boy, who became a great painter, was always called by his insulting nickname. To this very day we know him by the name Masaccio. That may not sound very insulting unless you speak Italian. It means Big Tom, but not in a complimentary way.

Masaccio was very absentminded and did not care about the way he looked. Perhaps he was so absorbed with his artwork that he did not pay attention to himself and other people. He certainly did not pay attention to money, for he was always in debt. But after he died at a very young age, people thought differently about him. Great artists thought his paintings were so good that they went to the place where they could be seen to study and copy them.

第9章 复活的画家

古埃及人以为，他们死后还会重新活过来，可实际上他们却从来没有复活过。古希腊人虽说对重生这一点考虑得不是很多，可在古希腊的那些画家们死了大约两千年后，出生于意大利的一些人却在某些方面与这些古希腊人极其相似，简直就像是古希腊人获得了重生，重新活过来了似的。这个时期，就称为重生时期，或者称“文艺复兴”，因为这是一次艺术、文学和知识的复兴。

“文艺复兴”时期的第一批画家中，有一位是一个绰号曾经极其不雅的小男孩。注意，有些人的绰号，只会陪伴到他们长大成人。但奇怪的是，这个小男孩变成一个伟大的画家之后，人们却始终还是用这个不雅的绰号称呼他。直到如今，我们都知道他叫马萨乔。这个名字听上去似乎并不是很具侮辱性，可倘若你们懂意大利语的话，就不会这么想了。它指“大个子”[1]，但并不是一种恭维。

马萨乔很健忘，并且不太注意自己的外表。没准儿，这是因为他太过专注于自己的绘画创作，因而根本注意不到自己和他人所致。他自然也不关心钱的问题，因为他总是负债累累。不过，在他英年早逝之后，人们对他的看法却发生了改变。许多伟大的画家都认为，他的画作非常优秀，因而纷纷前往看得到这些画作的地方，去进行研究和临摹呢。

[1] 大个子（Big Tom），英语国家中对块头大的人的称呼，含有“头脑简单，四肢发达”的贬义，相当于我们所说的“傻大个”。“汤姆”（Tom）是英语国家中常见的人名。

The reason other artists studied and copied his pictures is that Masaccio had found out how to do something that no artist before him had been able to do. Masaccio's pictures did not look flat. He painted pictures so that you could see right *into* them, as if looking through a window into the distance. Perspective, you may remember, is what we call that special artist's technique.

For thousands of years, artists had never shown the depth of space and real-looking figures that come with perspective. Do you remember why? It's because the size of the person or where he was positioned in the frame indicated to the viewer who was more important and who was less important. But in the Renaissance, artists changed and wanted to know just how Masaccio figured out the rules of perspective.

逐出伊甸园，马萨乔作品，
现存于佛罗伦萨卡尔米内的布兰卡契教堂
（由波士顿的大学印刷协会提供）

One of Masaccio's famous frescoes was a picture of the angel driving Adam and Eve out of the Garden of Eden.

One of the painters who studied Masaccio's frescoes was a monk named Fra Filippo — that is, Brother Filippo. Fra Filippo was not, however, a good and holy monk like the religious painter Fra Angelico. Fra Filippo was a good painter but a bad brother. It

其他画家研究并临摹马萨乔画作的原因，在于马萨乔找到了一种前辈画家从未做到的绘画方法。马萨乔的画作，看上去很有层次感。马萨乔绘制的画作，我们可以看进去，就像透过一扇窗户，向远处望去似的。透视画法，你们可能都还记得吧；这就是我们对这位特别的画家所创造的画法的称呼。

几千年来，所有画家都从未在画作中用符合透视的手法，表现出空间的深度和人物的真实模样。你们还记得原因吗？这是因为，画框中人物的大小或者人物所处的位置，向观看画作的人表明了画中人物哪个更加重要、哪个不那么重要。可到了“文艺复兴”时期，许多画家都改变了想法，都希望了解马萨乔是如何想出透视画法的了。

马萨乔绘制的著名湿壁画中，有一幅描述的是天使将亚当和夏娃两人逐出伊甸园时的情景。

而研究过马萨乔湿壁画作品的画家当中，有一位还是修道士，名叫弗拉·菲力波，即“菲力波兄弟”。不过，弗拉·菲力波与虔诚的画家弗拉·安杰利科可不一样，他并不是一位善良、圣洁的修道士。虽说弗拉·菲力波是位优秀的画家，可他也是一位不好的兄弟。据说，他因为厌烦了为善，厌烦了当修道士，所以还逃出

is said that he was bored with being good and with being a monk so he ran away from his monastery. After many wild adventures, he was captured by pirates and made a slave. Then one day he drew a picture of his master with a piece of charcoal. The likeness was so good that his master set him free.

Once free, do you know what he did next? Fra Filippo made his way right back to Italy and was hired to paint a picture of the Madonna for a convent. A convent is a building where women called nuns live. Nuns live together in the same way monks do in a monastery.

One of the nuns in this convent, a beautiful young girl, posed as the model for Fra Filippo's painting of the Virgin. Now neither a monk nor a nun is supposed to fall in love with anyone. But in spite of what he was not supposed to do, Fra Filippo fell in love with the nun and they ran away together. They had a son whom they named Filippino, which means Little Filippo. Filippino became a great painter too — even greater than his father.

Another artist of this time was Benozzo Gozzoli.

In the city of Pisa, there is a peculiar tower that does not stand straight but leans to one side. In the same city is another peculiar thing — a cemetery. The peculiar thing about this cemetery is that the ground for it was brought all the way from Jerusalem so that people could be buried in the same holy earth that Christ had trod. It took fifty- three shiploads of this holy earth to make the cemetery. It is called the Campo Santo, which means Holy Field.

Around the Campo Santo is a wall, and on the inside of this wall, Benozzo Gozzoli

了修道院呢。在经历了数次疯狂的冒险之后，他被海盗抓住，变成了奴隶。接下来有一天，他用一块木炭给主人画了一幅画像。由于他画得非常逼真，因此主人便放了他。

获得自由之后，你们猜得出他接下来做了什么吗？弗拉·菲力波想法径直回到了意大利，并受人雇用，为一座女修道院绘制了一幅圣母像。女修道院，就是那些叫作“修女”的女性修道士所住的地方。与男修道士在修道院里一样，修女在女修道院里过的也是集体生活。

这座女修道院里有一位修女，是个年轻漂亮的姑娘，由她来做弗拉·菲力波这幅圣母像的模特。注意，男修道士也好，修女也罢，都是不应该爱上任何人的。可尽管不应该这样做，弗拉·菲力波还是爱上了那位修女，于是他们便一起私奔了。后来他们还生了一个儿子，取名为菲力皮诺，即“小菲力波”。菲力波诺后来也成了一位了不起的画家，甚至比他的父亲更了不起哩。

这一时期还有一位艺术家，叫作贝诺佐·戈佐利。

在比萨市，有一座奇怪的高塔，它并不是直立着，而是向一侧倾斜着的。这座城市里，还有另外一个奇怪的地方，那就是一处墓地。这块墓地的奇怪之处，在于墓地的土全都是从耶路撒冷一路运过来的，目的是让人们死后能够葬在基督曾经走过的同一种神圣土地之下。人们总共运了五十三船的这种圣土，才建成这座墓地呢。这个墓地被称为“圣土公墓”，也就是“圣地”的意思。

“圣土公墓”四周有一道围墙，而贝诺佐·戈佐利则在这道围墙的内壁上，绘

painted twenty-four subjects from the books of the Old Testament — the story of Noah, the Tower of Babel, David, Solomon, and so on. In the background of each picture are crowds of people and often buildings.

In most of the pictures that Benozzo Gozzoli painted, as well as in those of other painters of this time, the clothing was not the kind that the people of Bible times wore. And the buildings in the background were not those of Bible times or Bible places at all. The artists had not visited Bible lands and didn't know what kind of clothes the Bible people wore or what kind of buildings they built, so they made the clothes and buildings like the Italian clothes and buildings of their own time.

So here are three painters to begin the Early Renaissance, the hundred years from 1400 to 1500. These three painters may not seem to you much like ancient Greeks born again, but be sure to remember them — Big Tom, the bad brother, and the cemetery painter. All of them lived and worked just before Columbus discovered America.

制出了源自《圣经·旧约》中的二十四个主题，比如诺亚的故事、通天塔、大卫王、所罗门王，诸如此类。每幅画作的背景上，都是一群群的人物，并且通常还有建筑物。

在贝诺佐·戈佐利所绘的大部分画作，以及这一时期其他画家的大部分画作中，人物身上所穿的衣物，都不属于《圣经》时期的服装。并且，背景中的建筑物也根本不是《圣经》时期的建筑，或者《圣经》时代的地点。这些画家并没有实地到过《圣经》中提到的那些地方，不知道《圣经》中的人物当时穿的是何种服装、修建的是何种建筑，因而只能将画中人物的衣着和建筑，画成当时意大利的服装和建筑样式。

因此，开启“文艺复兴”初期的是三位画家；这一时期，从公元1400年至公元1500年，长达一百年。虽说在你们看来，这三位画家可能不太像是古希腊画家的复活，可你们还是应当记住他们：“大个子”、坏兄弟和墓地画家。他们三人生活和创作的时间，刚好都是在哥伦布发现美洲之前。

Chapter 10 Sins and Sermons

One of the first dates that every boy and girl learns is 1492, the year that Columbus discovered America. Columbus was an Italian, but most of the people in Italy at that time were not interested in Columbus or what he was doing. They were interested in just two things. First, they were interested in having a good time. Second, they were interested in art. They were interested in Greece and its art, literature, and learning — not in discovering new countries. This time is known as the High Renaissance, which began around 1492.

When you look at a globe of the world, you can hardly find Italy. It is no larger than your little finger sticking down into the Mediterranean Sea. And yet in this little finger of land lived the greatest artists there have ever been. We call these artists Old Masters. It may seem strange that the greatest artists had been born and had lived in Italy all within a few miles of one another. One explanation is that Italy was the center of the Christian religion and, up to this time, Italian artists painted no pictures but religious ones.

An artist named Botticelli was one of the first Italian artists to paint pictures of things that were not told about in the Bible. Botticelli painted religious pictures too, but he especially liked to paint pictures of Greek gods and goddesses and other nonreligious subjects, for, as I've told you, the Renaissance was a time when everyone was interested in Greek art, literature, and learning.

第10章 罪孽与布道

在每一位美国小朋友最先了解到的日期当中，有一个就是1492年，即哥伦布发现美洲的那一年。哥伦布是意大利人，可当时的绝大多数意大利人，对哥伦布和他所做的事情却并不感兴趣。他们只关心两件事情。第一，他们关心的是让自己过得快活。第二，他们对艺术很感兴趣。他们关注的是古希腊以及古希腊的艺术、文学和知识，而不是去发现新的国度。这一时期从1492年左右开始，被称为“文艺复兴的全盛期”。

你们在看地球仪的时候，是很难找到意大利的。在地球仪上，意大利还没有你们的小手指头大，向下伸入了地中海。然而，在这个小手指大的国度里，却生活着许多有史以来最伟大的画家呢。我们称这些画家为“早期的绘画大师”。最伟大的一些画家都出生并生活在意大利，彼此之间相距不过数英里，这一点看上去可能很奇怪。有一种解释就是，意大利属于基督教的中心，并且直到这一时期，意大利的画家绘制的都是宗教画，而没有其他方面的画作。

有位名叫波提切利的画家，就是一位率先创作不是讲述《圣经》故事的绘画作品的画家。虽说波提切利也曾创作过宗教绘画，但他尤其喜欢绘制关于古希腊诸神以及其他非宗教主题的画作，因为我在前面已经跟你们说过，“文艺复兴”是一个大家都关注古希腊艺术、文学和知识的时代。

Botticelli had a peculiar style of painting. The women in his paintings usually had long legs and seemed to be dancing or floating along the ground instead of standing or walking. They were clad in very filmy, gauzy gowns as thin as a veil that showed their figures almost as if they had nothing on. *Allegory of Spring* is a good example.

春天的寓言，波提切利作品，
现存于佛罗伦萨的乌菲齐美术馆
（由波士顿的大学印刷协会提供）

Now at the time of Columbus, a monk named Savonarola was living and preaching in Florence. Some people thought he was mad. At any rate, he was such a powerful preacher that those who heard his sermons would do almost anything he told them to. He seemed to hypnotize them. Most of the people in Florence were very wicked by his standards. They thought of nothing but pleasure and having a good time, no matter how bad they were when they had a good time.

Savonarola preached against the sins of this world and prophesied death for those who did not repent and mend their ways.

《春天的寓言》细部，波提切利作品，
现存于佛罗伦萨的乌菲齐美术馆
（由波士顿的大学印刷协会提供）

波提切利有一种非常独特的画风。在他的画作中，女性的腿都很修长，仿佛是在跳舞，或者是在地面上飘浮着，而不是简单地站立着或者走路。她们都穿着朦胧、轻薄透明如绸纱的长袍，她们的胴体若隐若现，仿佛身上什么也没穿似的。《春天的寓言》这幅画作，就是一个典型的例子。

注意，在哥伦布那个时代，佛罗伦萨有位名叫萨伏纳罗拉的修道士，在城里四处布道。有些人觉得他是一个疯子。不管怎么说，他都是一位非常有影响力的传教士；凡是听他布道的人，都会对他言听计从呢。好像是他给人们施了催眠术似的。按照他的标准来说，佛罗伦萨的绝大多数人都非常邪恶。他们除了享乐和过得快活，什么也不考虑，也不管他们在享乐的时候有多么堕落。

萨伏纳罗拉抨击这个世界上的所有罪孽，并且预言说，那些不进行忏悔、不改变自己行为方式的人，必将灭亡。他抨击那些玩牌赌博、脸上化妆、佩戴珠宝

He preached against people who played card and dice games, used makeup on their faces, wore jewelry, danced, sang songs that were not hymns, or wrote books or painted pictures that were not religious. The people of Florence began to repent, and then one day they brought all their jewelry, trinkets, fancy clothes, and bad books to the public square and made a huge bonfire of them.

Botticelli had heard Savonarola preach, and he felt that he, too, had committed a sin by painting pictures of gods and goddesses and other subjects that were not religious. So he brought his paintings that were not religious and threw them on the bonfire. Fortunately for us, only a few of Botticelli's pictures were burned and his best ones are still preserved in museums.

One of Botticelli's religious paintings is called *Madonna of the Magnificat*. Two angels are placing a crown on Mary to show that she is the Queen of Heaven. She is writing a song in a book while the infant Jesus seems to be guiding her hand. The song she is writing — titled "Magnificat" — is a thanksgiving to God for he has chosen Mary from among all the women in the world to be the mother of Jesus.

The boy holding the inkwell and the one holding the book were real boys. They did not live in the time of Christ but in the time of Botticelli. It may seem strange that they were put in the

圣母颂，波提切利作品，
现存于佛罗伦萨的乌菲齐美术馆
（由波士顿的大学印刷协会提供）

首饰、跳舞、唱非赞美诗的歌曲、写非宗教书籍或绘制非宗教画作的人。佛罗伦萨的人便纷纷开始忏悔，直到有一天，他们把自己所有的珠宝、首饰、花哨的服装和不良的书籍全都带到了该市的公共广场上，然后将它们付之一炬。

波提切利听说过萨伏纳罗拉的布道，因此他也觉得，自己创作古希腊诸神以及其他非宗教题材的绘画作品，就是一种罪孽。于是，他便将自己那些非宗教画作都投入了大火之中。令我们觉得幸运的是，波提切利只有少量画作被烧掉了，而他最优秀的一些画作，如今仍然保存在博物馆里呢。

波提切利绘制的宗教画作中，有一幅叫作《圣母颂》。在这幅画作中，两位天使正给马利亚戴上皇冠，表明她是天国之母。马利亚正在书上写下一首诗歌，而襁褓中的耶稣似乎正在引导着她的手。她正在写下的那首诗歌，即标题中的"颂歌"，是对上帝的感恩，感谢上帝从世间所有女性中选择了她来做耶稣的母亲。

图中那个捧着墨水瓶的男孩，以及那个拿着书的男孩，都是真实存在的。但他们并没有生活在基督那个时代，而是生活在波提切利的那个时代。他们会被画进油

picture, but the Old Masters often did that sort of thing. When these two boys grew up, they became popes.

Notice that the picture is circular in shape, not square as most are. A circular picture is called a *tondo*, which means round.

Eventually the people who Savonarola said were so wicked could stand him no longer, and even some of his own followers turned against him. He was hanged and his body was burned. Not satisfied with that, the people then threw his ashes into the river.

There was a young painter in Florence who, as Botticelli had done, had also burned all of his pictures that were not religious. He was so shocked by the way in which Savonarola had been treated that he gave up painting and became a monk himself. He took the name of Fra Bartolommeo and went to live at St. Mark's monastery where Fra Angelico and Savonarola had lived before him.

For six years, Fra Bartolommeo never painted a stroke or touched a brush. He did nothing but pray. Then he was persuaded to start painting

吉罗拉莫·萨伏纳罗拉像，
弗拉·巴托洛米奥作品，
现存于佛罗伦萨的圣马可博物馆

画里，这一点看起来很奇怪，可古时的绘画大师却经常干这种事呢。这两个小男孩长大之后，都成了教皇。

大家都注意到了吧，这幅画是圆形，而不是像绝大多数画作那样是方形的。圆形画作被称为“通多”（tondo），这个词的意思就是指圆形画。

最后，萨伏纳罗拉所称的那些极其邪恶堕落的人再也受不了他，连他自己的一些信徒也开始反对他。他被人们处以绞刑，而他的尸体也被烧掉了。即便是这样，人们也还不满意，于是将他的骨灰都扔进了河里。

当时，佛罗伦萨有一位年轻的画家，他曾经像波提切利一样，将自己创作的非宗教画作全都付之一炬。他对人们这样对待萨伏纳罗拉大感震惊，因此放弃了绘画，自己成了一名修道士。他给自己起名弗拉·巴托洛米奥，住进了圣马可修道院；在他之前，弗拉·安杰利科和萨伏纳罗拉都曾在这座修道院里修行。

在长达六年的时间里，弗拉·巴托洛米奥再也没有画过一幅画，再也没有动过一下画笔。他什么也不干，一心祈祷。后来，有人劝说他，他才再次开始绘画，并

once more, and he made many beautiful pictures — all of them, of course, religious.

Fra Bartolommeo painted a picture of his hero, Savonarola. Now Savonarola was not handsome at all. In fact, he had a very big nose and was quite ugly — so ugly that his enemies used to joke about it. But the painting of him by Fra Bartolommeo shows that a picture can be great without being pretty. Fra Bartolommeo didn't change Savonarola's features at all. He painted the man just as he was, but the picture is beautiful because it shows someone who was able to face the most terrible suffering and agony for what he believed was right.

When drawing or painting pictures, most artists have real men or women pose for them as models. Instead of live models, Fra Bartolommeo used a wooden jointed doll that he dressed and arranged in the position he wanted the figure to be. This type of wooden doll is called a *lay figure*.

Fra Bartolommeo was the first painter to put baby angels at the foot of his pictures of the Madonna, and other painters copied this idea. Many of the most famous painters are those who were the first to think of a new way of doing things just like Fra Bartolommeo did.

圣母与圣婴，弗拉・巴托洛米奥作品，
现存于卢卡的圣马蒂诺大教堂

且创作出了许多美丽的画作；当然，这些画作全都是宗教画。

弗拉・巴托洛米奥还为他自己崇敬的英雄人物萨伏纳罗拉绘制了一幅画像。注意，萨伏纳罗拉根本就谈不上英俊。事实上，他长着一个硕大的酒糟鼻子，相貌也极其丑陋，连与之为敌的人也经常用他的丑貌来取笑他呢。不过，弗拉・巴托洛米奥为他绘制的这幅画像却说明，一幅画作，即便所画人物不漂亮，也可以是一件杰作。弗拉・巴托洛米奥一点儿也没有改动萨伏纳罗拉的面貌特征。虽说他是真实地描绘了这个人物的样子，可整幅画作却很漂亮，因为它描绘了一个为了坚持自己认为正确的教义而能直面最可怕的苦难和痛苦的人。

在绘制画作的时候，绝大多数画家都会让别人摆出姿势来当模特。可弗拉・巴托洛米奥却没有用活人当模特，而是用一个木质的活动玩偶来当模特；他给玩偶穿上衣服，并且摆出他所想要的姿势。这种木偶，称为人体模型。

弗拉・巴托洛米奥是第一位在其创作的圣母画底部绘制天使宝宝的画家，后来其他画家便纷纷效仿他的这一做法。许多最伟大的画家，正是率先构想出某种新画法的人，就像弗拉・巴托洛米奥这样。

Chapter 11 A Great Teacher and a Great Student

Many cities are named for people — Washington, St. Louis, Jacksonville, and others. But it is not often that people are named for cities; however, one famous painter was. The city was Perugia in Italy, and the man was called Perugino. He wasn't named Perugino when he was born, but most people have forgotten what his real name was. Perugino wasn't even born in Perugia, but he went to live in that town and started a school for painters there.

Sometimes you can tell who sent you a letter before you even open it just by the handwriting on the envelope. In the same way, you can tell a picture was painted by Perugino even if his name isn't on it. He painted Madonnas and saints, and after you have seen several of them, you can recognize others he did. Usually the figures have their heads bent to one side, a sweet expression, and one bent knee.

Perugino painted many beautiful pictures but he is also famous because of one of his students. This student was a boy some people feel became the greatest painter of all time. His name is Raphael and he studied with Perugino for three years.

By the time Raphael was nineteen years old, he had learned everything that his master could teach him so he struck out on his own. He died when he was only thirty-seven years old, but he was such a hard worker that he had painted or drawn over a thousand pictures

第11章 了不起的老师和了不起的学生

很多城市都是用人物的名字来命名的，比如华盛顿、圣路易斯、杰克逊维尔，还有其他一些城市。可人物用城市来命名的现象却不常见；然而，有位著名画家的情况却正是如此。这座城市，就是意大利的佩鲁贾，而这位画家，则叫佩鲁吉诺。他出生时，父母给他起的名字可不是佩鲁吉诺，但后来人们都忘记了他本来的名字。佩鲁吉诺甚至也不是在佩鲁贾出生的，只是他后来住在那座城市里，并在那里开设了一所绘画学校。

有的时候，在拆开信封之前，你们就可以根据信封上的笔迹，猜出这封信是谁写来的。同样，就算没有名字在上面，你们也能看出某幅画作是佩鲁吉诺创作的。他绘制了许多的圣母像和圣徒像，而你们欣赏过其中的数幅作品之后，就可以辨认出他的其他作品了。他的作品中，人物的头部通常都会偏向一侧，带着甜美的表情，并且常常都屈着一膝。

虽说佩鲁吉诺绘制过许多漂亮的画作，但他之所以闻名遐迩，也是因为他有一位很了不起的学生。这名学生，当时还是个小男孩；有些人认为，后来他却变成了世界有史以来最伟大的画家。他叫拉斐尔，在佩鲁吉诺的手下学习了三年。

到了拉斐尔十九岁的时候，他已经把老师的所有本领全都学到了手；于是，他便开始出去自谋生计了。后来，虽说他刚刚三十七岁便英年早逝了，但由于他非常勤奋，因此到去世的时候，他已经绘制了一千多幅画作呢。实际上，有些人还说，

by that time. Indeed, some say that he died from overwork.

Raphael must have painted about one picture a week, and some of his paintings are very large and have many figures in them. The only way he could have made so many was to have his students help him, and we know he did it this way. Raphael always painted the faces himself but his students painted the clothes and hands and other less important parts of the pictures.

It would take several books with a picture on each page to show all of Raphael's paintings. One of the most famous is *Madonna del Granduca*. It is called so because it was bought by a grand duke who prized it more highly than all his riches. In fact, he was not willing to leave it hanging on the wall of his palace or put it in a vault for safekeeping. He wanted it with him all the time and is said to have carried it with him in his carriage wherever he went so that it would never be out of his sight.

The grand duke is now dead, of course, and *Madonna del Granduca* is in an art gallery in Florence where everyone can see it as often as he or she likes.

庄严圣母，拉斐尔作品，
现存于佛罗伦萨的碧提宫
（由波士顿的大学印刷协会提供）

他就是因为积劳过度，才英年早逝的。

拉斐尔当时一定是每个星期就差不多绘制出一幅画作，而他的有些画作，尺寸还非常巨大，里面描绘的人物也非常众多呢。他能够绘制出如此之多画作的唯一途径，便是请自己的学生来帮忙；而我们也很清楚，他的确这样干过。拉斐尔经常亲自绘制画作中人物的脸部，而让学生去绘制人物的衣着、双手以及其他一些不那么重要的部位。

就算每一页上都印一幅画，也要好几本书，才能囊括拉斐尔的所有画作哩。其中最著名的画作之一，便是《庄严圣母》。之所以叫这个名称，是因为这幅画作后来曾被一位大公[1]收购，并且大公认为这幅画作价值连城，超过了他的所有财产。事实上，他既不愿意把这幅画作挂在公爵府的墙上，也不愿把它放在保险库里妥善保管起来。他希望这幅画整天都陪伴在自己左右，据说无论去哪里，他都会把这幅画放在自己的马车里带着，好让它一刻都不离开自己的视线呢。

这位大公如今当然是死了，而《庄严圣母》这幅画作则被保存进了佛罗伦萨的一家美术馆，任何人只要想看，就可以去看个够。

[1] 大公（grand duke），王朝爵位之一，地位仅次于国王。后用于指沙皇俄国时代的太子。《庄严圣母》（Madonna del Granduca）本为意大利语，指“大公的圣母像”，其中的 Granduca 就是“大公”的意思。

Raphael painted another Madonna called *The Madonna of the Chair*. It is a tondo. Do you remember what this is? It is a round picture.

The story is that Raphael was walking one day in the country when he saw a young mother sitting in a doorway with her little baby.

"What a beautiful Madonna!" Raphael said to himself. "I must paint her now, on the spot where she is before she changes."

He looked around for something to paint on and saw the round top of a barrel in the trash nearby. So he sketched the young woman and her baby then and there on that round piece of wood with nothing more than a pencil. And as soon as he reached his home, he made the round painting of them.

But perhaps the most famous picture by Raphael is another Madonna called *Sistine Madonna*. It is named after the convent where it was first placed. It is not there now, however, but in a gallery in Dresden, Germany, where it is in a room all by itself for no other picture is thought worthy to be hung in the same room.

Many of the Madonnas that I have shown you are beautiful, but the Holy Child in the pictures may not be beautiful at all. He often looks like a little old man or just a very fat baby and not what we feel the Son of God should look like. However, the Christ Child in Raphael's *Sistine Madonna* is very beautiful.

Leaning on the edge of the frame beneath the feet of the Madonna are two little angels or cherubs. Raphael got the idea to put two angels in the picture from Fra Bartolommeo,

拉斐尔还创作了另一幅圣母像，叫作《椅中圣母》。这是一幅“通多”。你们还记得“通多”是什么吗？就是圆形画啊。

据说，有一天拉斐尔正在乡间散步的时候，看到了一位年轻的母亲；她抱着自己的小宝宝，坐在门口。

“多么美丽的一位圣母啊！”拉斐尔自言自语地说，“我必须马上画下来，在她改变姿势之前就地画下来。”

他环顾四周，想找到什么能画画的东西，后来发现附近的垃圾堆里有一个圆圆的桶盖。于是，他便只用一支铅笔，当场将那位少妇和她的小宝宝素描在那块圆形木板上。待他一回到家，便根据素描，创作出了《椅中圣母》这幅圆画。

不过，拉斐尔最著名的画作，可能是另一幅圣母像，叫作《西斯廷圣母》。这个画名，是根据最初放置画作的那座女修道院的名字起的。然而，如今这幅画可不在那座修道院里了，而是保存进了德国德累斯顿市的一座美术馆。在美术馆里，这幅画作还被单独保存在一个房间里；因为人们觉得，没有其他哪幅画作，配得上与这幅画挂在同一个房间里呢。

虽说我给你们看过的许多圣母像都很漂亮，可那些画中的圣子可能根本就说不上漂亮。他的样子经常像个小老头儿，或者只是一个胖乎乎的婴儿，而不是我们想象中圣子应有的模样。然而，在拉斐尔的《西斯廷圣母》这幅画作里，襁褓里的基督却非常漂亮。

而在圣母脚下的画框边上，倚靠着两个小小的天使，即小天使。拉斐尔之所以在画中绘上两个小天使，是受了他的密友弗拉·巴托洛米奥的启发。这两个小天使

西斯廷圣母，拉斐尔作品，
现存于德累斯顿的德累斯顿美术馆
（由波士顿的大学印刷协会提供）

who was a great friend of his. These cherubs are very famous. They are often seen on popular greeting cards, posters, and even clothing.

The two other people in the picture are Pope Sixtus and Saint Barbara. They, of course, did not live during the time of Christ. If you were to draw a picture of your family or friends, who would you like to introduce them to in your picture just for fun?

可是大大有名哩。它们经常出现在流行贺卡、招贴画甚至是人们的衣服上。

画中的其他两个人物，一是西斯笃教皇，一是圣徒巴巴拉。他们二人，自然也不属于基督那个时代的人。倘若你们要给自己的家人或者朋友画一幅画，而纯属好玩的话，你们又会将他们当中的哪一个人画进画中呢？

Chapter 12 The Sculptor Who Painted Pictures

During the Renaissance young girls used to wear golden garlands or wreaths around their heads, just as girls today wear bracelets around their wrists or rings on their fingers. One goldsmith was so famous for the garlands he made that he was called Ghirlandajo, which means maker of garlands. Ghirlandajo gave up making garlands and began to paint pictures instead. He made many very fine pictures, but the chief thing he made was the artist Michelangelo. Michelangelo studied with Ghirlandajo for three years, and the teacher paid the student instead of charging for his teaching!

Ghirlandajo was probably a good teacher of painting, but young Michelangelo liked making statues better than painting pictures. So he left Ghirlandajo's workshop and began to study sculpture.

Now Michelangelo was not a very easy person to get along with. He didn't mind saying what he thought, even if it hurt other people's feelings. One day he said he thought another young sculptor's statue wasn't much good. This might have been true but the other young sculptor got very angry and hit Michelangelo on the nose. He punched him so hard that he broke Michelangelo's nose. Michelangelo had a crooked nose for the rest of his life.

Michelangelo soon became famous as a *sculptor* — one who makes statues or sculpture. He moved from Florence to Rome and there he worked for the pope, who liked Michelangelo's work so much that he didn't want him to make statues for anyone else.

第12章 会绘画的雕塑家

在“文艺复兴”时期，年轻姑娘的头上，往往都戴着金质的花环或者花冠，就像如今的姑娘都喜欢戴手镯、戒指一样。有位金匠，因为他所打制的花环极其出色而变得非常著名，因此人们都称他为“吉兰达约”，即“花环制造者”的意思。可后来，吉兰达约却不再打制花环，而是转行开始画画了。他绘制出了许多极其精美的画作，可他最主要的一件杰作，却是画家米开朗琪罗。米开朗琪罗曾经跟着吉兰达约学习了三年；可奇怪的是，竟然是老师付钱给学生，而不是向学生收取学费！

吉兰达约很可能是一位优秀的绘画老师，可年轻的米开朗琪罗却喜欢制作雕塑，而不那么喜欢绘画。于是，后来他便离开了吉兰达约的工作室，开始学习雕塑去了。

注意，米开朗琪罗可不是一个很好相处的人。他心直口快，不在意自己说出来的话会不会伤到他人的情绪。有一天他说，他觉得另外一位年轻雕塑家的雕塑作品不是很好。这可能是实情，但那位年轻的雕塑家却很生气，就一拳打在了米开朗琪罗的鼻子上。他出手太重，把米开朗琪罗的鼻子都打折了。于是，米开朗琪罗在余生中便一直顶着一个歪鼻子了。

很快，米开朗琪罗便成了一位著名的雕塑家，即制作雕像或者塑像的人。他从佛罗伦萨搬到了罗马，然后在罗马开始专门替教皇效力；当时的教皇非常喜欢米开朗琪罗的作品，不想让他再替其他任何人去制作雕塑。

This pope wanted to have pictures painted on the ceiling of the Sistine Chapel in Rome. The Sistine is a chapel in the Vatican, the palace of the popes. It has a very high curved ceiling called a barrel-vaulted ceiling. The pope asked Michelangelo to paint the pictures on the ceiling, but the artist said that he was a sculptor and didn't want to paint at all. Then some enemies of his spread around the story that he didn't want to do it because he wasn't good enough at painting and was afraid to try. This made Michelangelo angry. He made up his mind that he would show he could do the work as well as any painter in the world.

First of all, he had to have scaffolding built in the chapel. The scaffolding was a wooden framework with boards across the top near the ceiling so that Michelangelo could climb up on the boards and paint.

If you stop to think a moment, you will see how hard it must have been to paint pictures on a ceiling. The painter had to lie on his back or lean backwards all the time. He had to be so close to the ceiling that he could only see the part right above him. The only way for the painter to see the whole picture would be to climb down the ladder to the floor and look up.

The ceiling of the Sistine Chapel is very large. The pictures on it had

米开朗琪罗像，无名画家作品

这位教皇，想请人给罗马西斯廷教堂的屋顶绘上画作。西斯廷是梵蒂冈的一座小教堂，也是历代教皇的宅邸。这座教堂，有一个高耸的弧形屋顶，叫作桶形穹顶。教皇请米开朗琪罗为教堂的屋顶绘画，可米开朗琪罗却说自己是搞雕塑的，根本就不想去画。接下来，他的一些对手便开始散布流言，说他之所以不想画，是因为他画得不好，根本就不敢去尝试。这让米开朗琪罗很生气。于是，他便下定决心，要让人们看一看，他可以画得并不逊色于世界上其他的任何一位画家。

首先，他必须在教堂里搭一座脚手架。这座脚手架，是用木头扎好框架，再在顶上靠近天花板的地方搭上木板；这样，米开朗琪罗便可以爬上木板，坐在上面绘画了。

要是停下来想一想的话，你们就会明白，给屋顶绘画必定是极其困难的。画家必须始终仰面躺着，或者斜靠着，才能绘画。他必须离屋顶很近才行，但这样一来，就只看得见自己头顶上的那一小块地方了。画家观察整幅画作的唯一办法，就是爬下梯子，站到地面往上看。

西斯廷教堂的屋顶很大。因此，所绘的画作也必须很大才行，这样人们站在下

to be large so people could see them plainly from the floor down below. How would you like to draw the head of a man when you could not see where his feet were to be? Even if you were a very good painter that would be hard to do. And if Michelangelo put too much paint on his brush, the paint would drip down all over him. No wonder he didn't want to do the job!

But once he had started, nothing could stop him. At first he had other artists help him, but he found that the helpers couldn't do the work just as he wanted it so he sent them away and kept on all by himself.

The pope kept telling him to hurry, and Michelangelo even moved his bed into the chapel so he would be able to spend more time painting. It took him four and a half years to finish the ceiling, and that was really a very short time when you think of the work that had to be done!

The pope also kept telling him how the pictures should be done. Michelangelo didn't like this because he felt he knew more about such things than the pope did. So one day when the pope was standing on the floor calling up advice to the painter, Michelangelo let a hammer drop from the scaffolding. He was careful to let it fall without hurting the pope but near enough to scare him. After that, as the story goes, the pope stayed out of the chapel while Michelangelo was painting!

Finally, the ceiling was almost finished. Michelangelo wanted to add some touches of gold paint, but the pope was so anxious to have the chapel opened that the scaffolding was

面的地板上，才能看得清楚。倘若连人物的脚在哪里都看不到，你又怎样去画出这个人物的头部呢？就算你是一位极其优秀的画家，要做到这一点也是很困难的。而倘若米开朗琪罗的画笔上颜料蘸得太多的话，颜料又会滴得他满身都是呢。难怪他不想干这事！

不过，一旦开始工作，就没有什么能够阻止他了。起初，他还请了其他一些画家来帮忙；可后来他发现，这些帮忙的画家根本就没法按照他的想法去做，于是他便把他们都打发走，自己一个人来干了。

教皇不停地催促他，要他快点干，因此米开朗琪罗把床都搬进了教堂，以便能够将更多的时间花在绘画上。他花了四年半的时间，才画完整座屋顶；假如你们想一想这件工作的难度，那么四年半真的要算是很短的一段时间呢。

教皇还不停地对他指手画脚，说要怎样怎样画。米开朗琪罗很不喜欢这样，因为他觉得在这个方面，自己比教皇懂得更多。因此，有一天教皇正站在地上向画家大声提出建议的时候，米开朗琪罗故意让一把锤子从脚手架上掉了下去。他很小心，使得锤子掉下去时，不会砸到教皇，但落在距教皇不远的地方，吓了教皇一大跳。据说，自那以后，只要米开朗琪罗正在绘画，教皇就再也没有进过那座教堂了！

最后，待整个屋顶差不多全部完工时，米开朗琪罗本想再添上几笔金色，可教皇却已急不可耐，想要开放教堂，因此不待画家添上这几笔金色，便命人将脚手架拆了。

接下来，整个罗马的人便纷纷来到这座教堂，想看一看这位著名的雕塑家究竟画

taken down before the gold was put on.

Then people came from all over Rome to see what the famous sculptor had done as a painter. What they saw was a painting of Bible pictures. Around the edges of the ceiling were huge figures of the prophets who had foretold the coming of Christ. Down the middle of the ceiling were pictures of the Old Testament stories — the Creation, Noah's Ark and the Flood, and others. The pictures were drawn so well that people were astonished.

But it was difficult to see the pictures from far below because there are only a few windows in the chapel and those that are there are small and near the ceiling itself. So to see the pictures better, people took torches into the chapel to bring in more light, but with the burning torches came black smoke that over time built up and covered the brilliant colors Michelangelo used when he painted all of those famous scenes.

Centuries passed and the paintings became darker and darker. One pope after the next wondered what to do. Finally a plan was developed to restore the entire chapel by carefully cleaning the smoke off the paint, but it took many years and many artists. The artists would clean tiny parts one by one, each the size of your fingernail. At last the whole ceiling looked as it once did when the people of Rome came in to see it for the first time.

If you were to look at before-and-after pictures of the ceiling painting, you may notice that even the smoke damaged paintings are very beautiful. In fact, some people prefer them that way.

The men and women that Michelangelo painted on the ceiling look strong and solid.

了些什么。他们看到的，是一幅根据《圣经》中的图画绘制出来的画作。房顶四周的边沿，是先知们的巨像；他们曾经预言了基督的降生。再往上一点，屋顶中部则是一些描述《圣经·旧约》故事的图画，比如创世纪的故事、挪亚方舟和大洪水的故事，以及其他的故事。这些图画都绘制得非常精美，因此前来参观的人全都惊讶不已。

但是，站在相距甚远的地上，人们却很难仰头看清屋顶上的这些画作，因为教堂里窗户不多；而已有的那些窗户非但很小，距屋顶本身又很近。因此，为了更好地观赏这些画作，人们便带着火把来到教堂里，想让教堂里更亮堂一点；可是，燃烧的火把却冒出黑烟，并且随着时间的推移而越积越多，盖住了米开朗琪罗最初绘制这些闻名遐迩的画作时所用的亮丽色彩。

数个世纪过去了，这些画作也变得越来越黑。一任又一任教皇全都束手无策，不知道该怎么办才好。最后，人们制定了一个计划，打算通过细心清除画作上的烟尘，从而恢复整座教堂的原貌；可这种修复工作，却需要耗费多年的时间，需要许多画家合力才能完成。这些画家只能一小部分、一小部分地逐一清理，每次都只能清理指甲盖大小的范围。最终，这座教堂的整个屋顶终于恢复了原貌，宛如罗马人第一次前来观看时那样焕然一新了。

如果你们对比一下西斯廷教堂屋顶油画以前的样子和如今的样子，那你们可能会注意到，即便是那些被烟雾毁掉了的画作，如今也变得非常漂亮了。可事实上，有些人却宁愿这些画作保持着被烟毁坏时的样子呢。

米开朗琪罗在西斯廷教堂屋顶上所绘的人物，不论男女，看上去都很强壮、结实。这些人物，线条清晰，轮廓分明，因此看上去很像雕塑，而不只是没有层次感

The figures have such definition and shape that they look like statues, not just flat pictures. So Michelangelo's paintings are called *sculpturesque*, or like sculpture.

The following picture shows a famous part of the ceiling painting called *Creation of Man*. Notice what great shoulders and muscles Adam has.

Almost thirty years after the ceiling was painted, Michelangelo was asked to paint a picture on the wall over the altar at one end of the Sistine Chapel. The wall was already covered with a painting by Perugino, but Michelangelo's painting replaced it. This painting, called *The Last Judgment*, is one of the most famous ever painted, though it is not so great as the ceiling pictures. The painting is crowded with the figures of men and women rising from the dead on Judgment Day as it was described in the Bible.

Michelangelo painted very few other pictures. The only small finished painting that we are

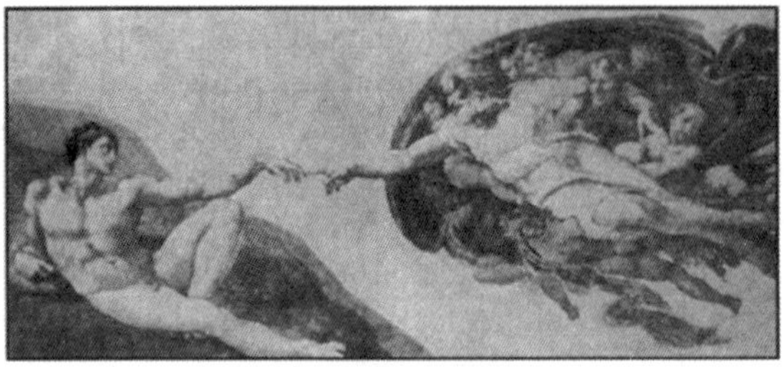

创造亚当，米开朗琪罗作品，
现存于罗马梵蒂冈西斯廷教堂的屋顶上
（由波士顿的大学印刷协会提供）

最后的审判，米开朗琪罗作品，
现存于罗马梵蒂冈西斯廷教堂的东墙上
（由波士顿的大学印刷协会提供）

的平面画像。由此，人们便称米开朗琪罗的画作具有雕刻风格，或者说，就像雕塑一样。

下图所示的，就是西斯廷教堂屋顶油画中很有名的一个部分，叫作《创造亚当》。请注意，画中亚当的肩膀宽阔，肌肉非常结实。

西斯廷教堂屋顶油画绘制完工差不多三十年后，米开朗琪罗又被请去给西斯廷教堂一端祭坛上方的墙壁绘制一幅壁画。那堵墙壁上面，本来已经有了一幅由佩鲁吉诺绘制的油画，可后来却用米开朗琪罗的画作替换了它。这幅壁画，叫作《最后的审判》，是人类有史以来最著名的画作之一，尽管它并不像西斯廷教堂的屋顶壁画那样有名。这幅画作上，全都是根据《圣经》所述的故事，描绘了许多人物在审判日从死者复活时的情形。

米开朗琪罗绘制的其他画作并不多。唯一一幅小型的、完整的，我们确定系他

神圣家庭，米开朗琪罗作品，
现存于佛罗伦萨的乌菲齐美术馆
（由波士顿的大学印刷协会提供）

sure was done by him is a tondo of the Holy Family. It shows the Madonna on her knees holding her little son over her shoulder so that Joseph can see him. The picture shows that Michelangelo liked to paint people in unusual yet interesting positions.

Michelangelo lived to be a very old man. As he grew older, he seemed to grow more cross and harder to get along with than ever. Although he was a cranky old man, everyone respected him and admired him as one of the greatest artists in the history of the world.

所绘的油画，是关于“神圣家庭”的一幅圆形画。画作描绘的是圣母跪在地上，将自己的小儿子举到肩上，好让约瑟能够看到这个小儿子的情形。这幅画作说明，米开朗琪罗很喜欢绘制人们姿势不寻常，却很有意思时的样子。

米开朗琪罗活到了很大的年纪。随着年纪越来越老，他似乎也变得比以前越发乖戾，越发难以相处了。尽管他是一位脾气暴躁的古怪老头儿，可大家都很尊重他、钦佩他，认为他是世界历史上最伟大的艺术家之一。

Chapter 13 Leonardo da Vinci

Hold this page up in front of a mirror so that you can read the following line more easily.

?SIHT DAER UOY NAC

This is what people found they had to do with notes written by a very great man named Leonardo da Vinci. It was not because he wrote from right to left that we call him a very great man though. It is because he knew how to do more things well than most anyone in the whole world. Many imagine that he wrote from right to left because he was left-handed. Others think that maybe he wanted to keep his notes secret so he wrote backwards and from right to left. Try doing it yourself and then check it with a mirror. I'll bet it's hard!

Leonardo da Vinci lived in Italy during the Renaissance. He was born some years before the painter Raphael and died a year before Raphael did. Painting was among the many and varied things that Leonardo da Vinci did well. Some people still think he was the best painter that has ever lived. And yet, because he was interested in doing so many other things besides painting, he only painted a few pictures during his lifetime.

One of Leonardo's paintings is in the Louvre, a famous art museum in Paris. The picture is called the *Mona Lisa*. About a hundred years ago this priceless painting was

第13章 列奥纳多·达·芬奇

将这一页举到一面镜子前，这样你们就可以比较容易地看出下面这行字说的是什么了。

?SIHT DAER UOY NAC

（你们能读出这一句话吗？）

这就是人们在看一个名叫列奥纳多·达·芬奇的伟大人物所写的笔记时，发现他们不得不去干的事情。当然，并不是因为他能够从右向左写字，我们才称他是一个非常伟大的人物。许多人都曾猜想，他之所以从右向左写字，是因为他是一个左撇子。还有一些人则认为，可能是因为他想让自己的笔记保密，因而才用相反的方向，从右向左写。你们不妨试上一试，然后用镜子来看一看自己所写的字。我敢打赌，你们是很难做到这一点的！

列奥纳多·达·芬奇是"文艺复兴"时期的意大利人。他比画家拉斐尔稍早出生几年，去世也比拉斐尔早了一年。绘画，只是列奥纳多·达·芬奇擅长的诸多不同领域中的一种。如今还有一些人，认为他是人类有史以来最杰出的画家呢。不过，由于除了绘画，他还对其他诸多领域感兴趣，因此他一生中只创作了为数不多的一些画作。

列奥纳多有一幅画作，如今保存在巴黎的卢浮宫这座著名的美术馆里。这幅画

stolen right from the wall of the Louvre. Newspapers all over the world printed the story with headlines as big as those announcing that a great king had died or a big ship had sunk at sea. Luckily the painting was finally found and put back in the Louvre.

The *Mona Lisa* is the picture of an Italian woman. On her face is a faint smile. If the artist had changed the painting the least bit, there might have been no smile there at all. It is a puzzling smile. Mona Lisa seems to be smiling at something that no one else knows anything about.

There are other things to notice besides the smile. The woman looks solid — not flat like a cardboard cutout. Leonardo could make her look real because he understood how to use dark and light and how to make the bright part fade into the shadows. This technique is called *chiaroscuro*. Leonardo was the first painter to understand how to do this.

Also worth mentioning is the background of the picture. It is a landscape with a stream and hills and mountains. When you look at a real landscape, you know you can't see things far away quite as clearly as things close to you. That is because of all the air between you and the things that are far away.

蒙娜·丽莎，达·芬奇作品，
现存于巴黎的卢浮宫
（由缅因州桑福德的大学印刷协会提供）

作，名叫《蒙娜·丽莎》。大约一百年前，这幅无法估价的油画竟然被人从卢浮宫的墙壁上偷走了。全世界的报纸都用大幅标题报道了这一消息，规格堪比那些宣布某位伟大国王去世或者一艘大型船只在海上沉没的消息。幸好，人们最终还是找到了这幅画，让它重新回到了卢浮宫。

《蒙娜·丽莎》是一位意大利女性的画像。她的脸上，流露着一丝淡淡的微笑。哪怕画家只在画法上稍稍改变一点儿，她的脸上根本就不会出现笑容了。那是一种谜一般的微笑。画中的蒙娜·丽莎，似乎正在因某件无人知晓的事情而微笑着。

除了微笑，画中还有其他一些方面，也值得我们注意。画中的女性看上去很有立体感，而不是像用纸板剪成的人物那样没有层次感。列奥纳多之所以能够让她显得非常逼真，在于他明白如何运用明暗对比，如何让画中明亮的部分逐渐隐入暗部。这种技法，被称为明暗对比法。列奥纳多就是第一位明白如何运用这种方法的画家。

还值得一提的，是这幅画作的背景。背景是一幅风景画，其中有一条小溪，还有土丘和山脉。在观看一种真实的风景之时，你们都明白，相距太远的东西看起来

最后的晚餐，达・芬奇作品，
现存于米兰感恩圣母堂的饭堂里
（由缅因州桑福德的大学印刷协会提供）

Although you can't see this air, you can understand that the more air you look through, the dimmer things seem. Leonardo da Vinci was a great enough painter to make the landscape look as if it really were far away. He was also the first painter who understood how to do this.

Another painting by Leonardo is not in an art museum, where it would be carefully taken care of, but is in a low, damp room in a monastery in Italy where it has been badly damaged by moisture. It is one of the world's greatest paintings, but it will never be put in an art museum because Leonardo painted it directly on the wall.

The picture is known as *The Last Supper*. It shows Christ and the twelve apostles seated at a long table. Leonardo chose to picture the moment when Christ said, "One of you will betray me."

是不会像近处的东西那样清晰的。那是因为你和远物之间，隔着一层空气所致。尽管看不见这层空气，但你们也能理解，需要穿透的空气越多，远处之物看起来就会越模糊。列奥纳多・达・芬奇真是一位极其了不起的画家，能够将一道风景画得看上去像是它真的处于很远之地一样。因此，他也是第一个真正明白如何做到这一点的画家。

列奥纳多所绘的另一幅画，如今却并未保存在哪座博物馆里，并未保存在能够细心保管好这幅画作的地方，而是在意大利一座修道院一间低矮而潮湿的房间里，已经被潮气损毁得非常严重。这幅画，虽属于世界上最伟大的画作之一，可它永远都无法保存进哪座美术博物馆里，因为列奥纳多是把画作直接绘制在房间的墙壁之上。

这幅画作众所周知，名叫《最后的晚餐》。它描绘的是基督和十二使徒坐在一张长桌旁时的情景。列奥纳多选取描绘的，就是基督说出“你们当中有个人将会出卖我”这句话的那一瞬间。

Can you imagine the apostles' reaction to the thought of one of them betraying their beloved master? Through their gestures and facial expressions, Leonardo shows how each apostle feels when he hears the words.

To show what men feel in a painting is not easy. A painter cannot, of course, make the people in his pictures say what they feel. If he wants to show their feelings, he must do it by showing how people look when they are thinking a certain thing.

Leonardo visited deaf people who could not speak well because they could not hear words in order to imitate them. He did this to learn how they showed their feelings when they were excited, happy, frightened, or angry. This helped him make the people in his pictures show the feelings he wanted them to, even if they could not speak.

Not many years after *The Last Supper* was painted, the paint began to come off the plaster of the wall. One reason for this was that Leonardo painted on dry plaster. Michelangelo and other wall painters always had painted on plaster when it was still fresh and damp. When they did this, the paint sank into the fresh plaster and wouldn't peel off unless the plaster came off with it.

You remember I told you this kind of painting is called fresco. Leonardo was interested in trying new ways of painting, and so unfortunately, he didn't paint *The Last Supper* in fresco.

When the paint had flaked off in many places, other artists painted over the picture where they thought it needed touching up. After a time, a large portion of Leonardo's

你们想象得出，十二使徒想到他们当中有一个人会出卖他们挚爱的主时的反应吗？通过他们的手势和面部表情，列奥纳多生动地描绘出了每位使徒在听到这句话后心中的感受。

要想在画作中表现出人物的感受，可不是一件容易的事情。画家自然没法让笔下的人物在画中说出他们的感受来。假如想要表现他们的感受，画家就必须描绘出人物在思考某件事情时的神态。

列奥纳多曾经拜访过一些耳聋的人；因为听不到别人说的话，无法进行模仿，因此这些聋人说话都不太利索。他之所以这样做，是想了解这些人如何表达自己兴奋、高兴、害怕或生气等情绪。这有助于他在自己的画作中让人物表达出他所希望的情绪，即便这些人物无法开口说话。

《最后的晚餐》绘制出来没有多少年之后，便开始从灰泥墙上剥落了。之所以如此，原因之一便在于列奥纳多是在干了的灰泥墙上绘制出这幅画作的。米开朗琪罗以及其他一些壁画画家，一向都是趁着墙上的灰泥刚刚涂上，还很潮湿的时候去绘画的。他们绘制壁画作品的时候，颜料会渗入刚刚涂抹上去的灰泥里，因此除非整层灰泥都剥落下来，否则这些壁画就不会脱落。

你们都还记得吧，我曾经告诉过你们，这种油画叫作湿壁画。列奥纳多对尝试新的绘画方法很感兴趣，因此很可惜，他并没有将《最后的晚餐》画成湿壁画。

待这幅画作的许多地方都剥落了之后，其他一些画家便对他们认为需要修改的地方重新着色，进行了修复。过了一段时间后，列奥纳多那幅画作的一大部分，便都成了这些画家所绘的，技艺没那么娴熟的修复画了。而最糟糕的是，修道院里的

painting was covered by the less-skilled paintings of these artists. Worst of all, the monks decided to cut a door in the wall. The top of the doorway was made right in the middle of the lower part of the painting, and the hammering to make a hole through the stone wall jarred off more of the paint. And worse still, when Napoleon led his armies into Italy, some of his soldiers used the room where *The Last Supper* is as a stable for their horses!

So year by year this wonderful painting became more and more a ruin until there was a danger that it would be lost altogether. Finally a wise Italian found a way of making the remaining paint cling to the wall so it would not come off. Then he managed to take off all the paint put on by the other painters so that the picture was in better condition than it had been for hundreds of years. But unfortunately that, too, did not last.

The room where it can be found is called the refectory, which is another word for dining room. For many years, the monks who lived there thought the best way to keep the painting from fading was to cover it with a velvet curtain.

Have you seen velvet? If you have, then you know it has one very soft side and another side that is quite rough. Well, the monks liked the soft side better so they put the rough side near the painting. This curtain kept even more moisture in and the rough side scraped paint off every time it was moved. Just like the Sistine Chapel, this painting was restored little by little in tiny squares until, at long last, it was as beautiful as when it was first painted.

Only about three or four other paintings by the great Leonardo da Vinci have survived

修道士竟然决定在这面墙上开出一扇门来！这扇门的门楣，正好开在壁画下半部分的中间；为了在这堵石墙上用锤子敲出一个门洞，就震掉了更多的油漆。而雪上加霜的是，拿破仑率军攻入意大利后，他手下的一些士兵竟然还将《最后的晚餐》所在的那间房子，当成了关战马的马厩！

于是，一年又一年过去，这幅神奇的画作便逐渐变成了一片废墟，直至有一天，出现了彻底消失的危险。最后，有位聪明的意大利人找到了一种让幸存下来的那一部分画作留在墙上、不致剥落的办法。接下来，他又设法将其他画家所绘的颜料剥离下来，从而让这幅画作处于一种比数百年来更好的状况。可不幸的是，即便那样，这幅画作也保存不了多久。

这幅画作所在的那个房间，被称为“饭堂”，换言之就是餐厅。在许多年间，住在那座修道院里的修道士都以为，不让这幅画褪色的最好办法，就是用一道天鹅绒窗帘将它遮住。

你们见过天鹅绒吗？假如见过，那你们就很清楚，天鹅绒窗帘的一面非常柔软，而另一面则十分粗糙。好吧，因为修道士们更喜欢柔软的一面，因此他们便让窗帘粗糙的一面贴着那幅画作。这道窗帘吸收了更多的潮气，而它每掀动一次，粗糙的那一面就会把画上的颜料蹭掉一些。与西斯廷教堂里的屋顶油画一样，这幅画作也被人们一点一点、一小块一小块地进行了修复，最后总算又像起初绘制出来时那样漂亮了。

伟大的列奥纳多·达·芬奇所绘的画作中，只有三四幅其他的作品幸存下来，

until today. One that many people admire is called *The Virgin of the Rocks*. It shows the baby Jesus and his mother seated on the ground with an angel and John the Baptist as a child. They seem to be in a place of caves and dark rocks. Through openings in the rocks we can see the bright blue of a waterfall and the green of plants.

Leonardo knew more about plants and flowers than anyone else of his time. He understood that nature has simple ideas that are found again and again. For example, the radiating petals of a flower are like the crystals of a snowflake. Leonardo also drew anatomical illustrations, such as *The Vitruvian Man*. In this famous notebook drawing, Leonardo used geometric principles to illustrate the proportions of the human body.

Do you think he stopped there? No! As an inventor, he sketched out ideas for machines that were not invented until many years later. He even drew a type of a helicopter!

How often have you heard someone be called a genius? When you think about every famous person you have studied in school, how many can you name that you would call a genius? Perhaps Leonardo is one because he was a scientist, inventor, and artist all in one.

保存到了如今。其中，许多人交口称颂的一幅，叫作《岩间圣母》。它描绘的是襁褓中的耶稣和母亲一起坐在地上，身边还有一位天使，以及儿时的“施洗者约翰”[1]。透过岩石间的空隙，我们可以看到一道瀑布的亮蓝色，以及植物的绿色。

列奥纳多比同时代的其他人更了解植物和花草。他明白，大自然的一些理念非常简单，到处都可以一再发现。例如，一朵花呈辐射状的花瓣，就像雪花的冰晶一样。列奥纳多还画过解剖图，如《维特鲁威人》。在这幅著名的笔记式画作上，列奥纳多利用几何规则，说明了人体各部分的比例。

你们觉得，他的成就到此为止了吗？没有！他还是一个发明家，构想出了一些机械设备；而这些机械设备，过了多年后才被人发明出来呢。他甚至曾经画过一种直升机！

你们有没有经常听到人们称某人为天才呢？倘若想一想在学校了解到的所有著名人物，你们又会称哪些人是天才呢？列奥纳多或许就是其中的一位，因为他既是科学家、发明家，同时也是一位画家。

[1] 施洗者约翰（John the Baptist），基督教中的先知。他是耶稣基督的表兄，耶稣开始传播福音之前，他就在旷野中对犹太人进行劝勉，后来又为耶稣基督施洗。他同时也是伊斯兰教的先知。亦译“圣若望洗者”、“施洗的约翰”等。

Chapter 14 Six Venetians

Venice is a city in which canals are streets and one often must take a boat instead of a car to go from place to place. Today Venice belongs to Italy, but during the Renaissance Venice was an independent state, a republic that governed itself. Venice had its own army and navy, its own ruler called the Doge, and its own way of doing things. It had its own great painters too — painters still famous above all others for the wonderful colors they gave to their pictures.

In the Early Renaissance, there was a painter in Venice named Bellini, and he had two sons who also became painters. The sons were even better painters than their father. One of the Bellini brothers taught painting to two young men who became better painters than any of the Bellinis. These two men were called Giorgione, which means Big George, and Titian. Three Bellinis, one Giorgione, and one Titian — five men and only three names to remember.

I wish I had room to tell you more about the Bellinis. I think you would like their pictures of the Doges, the rulers of Venice. But there isn't room in this chapter for all of them, so we'll begin with Giorgione.

Giorgione is called one of the greatest of painters. Like Leonardo da Vinci, he left very few pictures that we are sure he himself painted. A famous painting called *The Concert* is

第14章 六个威尼斯人

威尼斯是一座城市，其中以水路为街道，人们从一地到另一地常常得坐船，而不是坐公共汽车。如今，威尼斯隶属于意大利；可在“文艺复兴”时期，威尼斯却还是一个独立的国家，是一个自治的共和国呢。当时的威尼斯拥有本国的陆军和海军，有本国的统治者，称为总督，并且拥有本国的政策。当然，威尼斯也出了一些伟大的画家；那些画家，如今由于他们在画作上所用的绝妙色彩，而比其他所有画家都更加有名呢。

在“文艺复兴”初期，威尼斯有一位画家，名叫贝利尼；他有两个儿子，后来也都成了画家。他的这两个儿子，画艺甚至比父亲更优秀呢。而贝利尼家这两兄弟中的一位，还教导过两位年轻人绘画，后来那两位年轻人又成了比贝利尼兄弟更优秀的画家。这两位年轻人，一个叫作乔尔乔涅，意思就是“大个子乔治”，另一位叫作提香。三个贝利尼，一个乔尔乔涅，一个提香；总共五个人，但你们只要记住三个名字就可以了。

我本来希望有足够多的篇幅，能给你们多介绍一点儿三位贝利尼的情况。我觉得你们可能会喜欢他们所绘的总督画像，即威尼斯统治者的画像。不过，这一章没有篇幅来全部介绍他们，所以我们还是从乔尔乔涅开始吧。

乔尔乔涅被人们称为最伟大的画家之一。像列奥纳多·达·芬奇一样，他也没有留下几幅我们可以确定是他本人所绘的画作。大多数人都认为，一幅名叫《音乐

thought by most people to have been painted by Giorgione, but others think it was painted by Giorgione's friend Titian.

The Concert shows the head and shoulders of three men. One of these men is seated at a clavichord. Do you know what a clavichord is? It is a musical instrument like a piano that was used before pianos were invented. The second man has a violin in his hand, and the third wears a big hat with feathers on it that makes him look like a woman.

Unfortunately Giorgione didn't live long enough to paint many pictures. A terrible disease called the plague spread through Venice. Giorgione caught the plague and died when he was only about thirty-two years old.

His friend Titian lived to be a very old man, and so he had time to paint many more pictures than Giorgione. Titian was especially good at painting *portraits* — pictures of people that usually just show their heads. He painted many noblemen of his time. One of these portraits is called *The Man With the Glove*. No one knows who the man with the glove was, but almost everyone likes the picture. How do you like it?

Titian could paint other kinds of pictures besides portraits. He painted a picture called *The Assumption* for an altar in a Venetian church. The painting shows the Madonna entering heaven. The Venetians liked it tremendously. They

戴手套的人，提香作品，
现存于巴黎的卢浮宫
（由波士顿的大学印刷协会提供）

会》的名画是乔尔乔涅创作的，可也有一些人认为，这幅画是乔尔乔涅的朋友提香创作的。

《音乐会》描绘的是三个人的头部和肩部。其中一人坐在一架翼琴边上。你们知道翼琴是什么东西吗？它是一种像钢琴的乐器，在钢琴还没有发明出来的时候，人们弹的就是翼琴。第二个人手里拿着一把小提琴，而第三个人则戴着一顶饰有羽毛的大帽子，使得他看上去像是一位妇人。

可惜的是，乔尔乔涅寿命不长，没能绘制出很多的画作。当时，一种叫作“鼠疫”的可怕疾病席卷了威尼斯。乔尔乔涅染上了鼠疫，只有三十二岁左右便去世了。

他的朋友提香则很长寿，因此他创作的绘画作品比乔尔乔涅多得多。提香尤其擅长于绘制肖像画，即通常只是描绘人物头部的绘画作品。他给当时的许多贵族都画过肖像。其中有一幅肖像画，叫作《戴手套的人》。虽然没人知道这个戴手套的人是谁，但差不多每个人都很喜欢这幅画。你们喜不喜欢呢？

除了肖像画，提香也能绘制其他类型的画作。他曾给威尼斯一座教堂里的祭坛创作了一幅叫作《圣母升天》的画作。这幅画描绘的是圣母马利亚升入天国时的情形。威尼斯人都极其喜欢这幅画。他们尤其喜欢这幅画作上那种浓丽、鲜亮的色

especially liked its rich glowing color because Venice itself was full of color with its deep blue sea on every side and its marble palaces gleaming in the brilliant sunlight.

Venetians even liked pictures painted on the outside of their buildings to add to the bright colors of the town. Both Giorgione and Titian made many paintings on the outside walls of buildings, but all these have now disappeared, washed away by the weather.

At last, after a long life of painting, Titian died — some say from the plague, the same disease that had killed Giorgione.

There were still great artists left in Venice, however. One of these was called Tintoretto1, which means little dyer, because his father was a dyer — one who dyes things different colors. Tintoretto was much younger than Titian. When he was a boy, he was sent to Titian's studio to learn painting. For some reason, Titian only let him stay at his studio for ten days. After that Tintoretto had to teach himself to paint.

Tintoretto also painted many pictures on the outside walls of buildings, but these have washed away like Giorgione's and Titian's. Titian had always been careful to make good deals when he sold his paintings, but Tintoretto didn't seem to care for money. He was satisfied to take much less for his pictures than they were worth. Often he even gave them away.

One of Tintoretto's greatest undertakings was to paint pictures for the walls of a building called the Scuola di San Rocco in Venice. Michelangelo had made his wall paintings on wet plaster. Leonardo had made his on dry plaster. But Tintoretto made his on canvas, and then the painted canvas was fastened to the wall. The San Rocco pictures were fastened to the

彩，因为威尼斯本身就是一座颜色丰富的城市，四周都是深蓝色的大海，而市里那些大理石宫殿也在灿烂的阳光下闪闪发光呢。

威尼斯人甚至还喜欢给自己的房屋外墙绘上图画，以增添整座城市的鲜艳色彩。乔尔乔涅和提香两人都曾在建筑物的外墙上绘制了许多画作，可这些画作由于风吹雨打，如今全都不复存在了。

最后，度过了长久的绘画生涯之后，提香去世了；有人说他是死于鼠疫，即让乔尔乔涅去世的同一种疾病。

然而，威尼斯还有其他一些伟大的画家。其中一位叫作丁托列托，意思就是“小染工”，因为他的父亲是一位染工，即给东西染上不同颜色的人。丁托列托比提香年纪小得多。小的时候，他就被送到提香的工作室去学习绘画。可由于某种原因，提香只让他在工作室里待了十天。此后，丁托列托便只能自学绘画了。

丁托列托也在一些房屋的外墙上绘制了许多的画作，可这些画作也像乔尔乔涅和提香的作品一样，因为日晒雨淋而不复存在了。提香在出售自己的画作时，一向都很谨慎，以达成划算的交易，可丁托列托却似乎并不在意金钱。哪怕得到的比自己的画作价值少得多，他也心满意足。而且，他甚至常常还免费给别人绘画。

丁托列托最了不起的一项任务，便是给威尼斯一座叫作圣罗科教堂的建筑外墙绘制画作。米开朗琪罗曾在未干的灰泥墙上绘制过画作。列奥纳多则在干了的灰泥墙上绘制过画作。可丁托列托却是在画布上绘画，然后再将画布粘到墙壁上。圣罗科教堂的画作，正是粘贴在墙上的。

wall.

Tintoretto used to make little clay figures to use as models when he painted. He worked very quickly so he was able to paint a great many pictures in his lifetime. Most of them are full of energy and action. Some of his figures seem to be rushing through the air. So much action and movement made his pictures very different from the quiet ones of early Italian painters. Tintoretto's pictures were more like Michelangelo's energetic paintings, but Tintoretto also had the glowing colors of Titian.

Over his studio door Tintoretto put these words: The drawing of Michelangelo and the color of Titian. Sometimes he went beyond Titian, whose colors were golden browns and rich reds and greens. Tintoretto's later pictures contained soft shades of gray and had a silvery finish rather than a golden glow.

One of Tintoretto's famous paintings is called *The Miracle of Saint Mark Freeing the Slave*. The story goes that Saint Mark had a faithful servant who was sentenced to be tortured to death for being a Christian. Saint Mark was away when this happened. The servant was stretched on the ground in front of the judge's chair and the torture was about to begin. Suddenly the tools broke in the executioner's hands as Saint Mark appeared in the air above. He had come to save his servant.

Tintoretto's picture shows Saint Mark flying through the air above the executioner but nobody in the picture except a little baby has noticed him. Everyone else is looking at the broken tools of the executioner.

When Tintoretto was an old man, he was given the order to paint a huge picture of

丁托列托绘画的时候，经常制作小型的黏土人物来当模特。他绘画的速度很快，因此一生中绘制出了大量的画作。其中绝大部分画作都充满了表现感和动感。他绘制的一些人物，看上去似乎是在空中急速前行呢。这种丰富的动感，使得他的画作与早期意大利画家那些非常宁静恬淡的画作在风格上大相径庭。丁托列托的画作，更像是米开朗琪罗那些活力四射、充满动感的作品，不过丁托列托的画作还有着提香画作的那种鲜亮色彩。

在自己那座工作室的门楣上，丁托列托写了这样一句话：“米开朗琪罗的画法，提香的色彩。”有的时候，他甚至比提香走得更远。提香在绘画中所用的，主要是各种各样的金褐色、浓烈的红色和绿色。而丁托列托晚期的一些画作中，还包括了一系列柔和的灰色，并且用银色而不是亮金色来做表面处理。

丁托列托最著名的一幅画作，叫作《圣马可解救奴隶的神迹》。传说，圣马可有一个忠心耿耿的仆人，这位仆人因为信奉基督教而被当局判处了死刑。此事发生的时候，圣马可并不在家。那个仆人的四肢被绑上绳子向四周拉伸，躺在法官面前的地上，当局准备开始折磨他了。突然之间，圣马可在刑场之上的空中现身，行刑者手中的刑具便坏了。原来，圣马可来解救自己的仆人了。

丁托列托的这幅画作，描绘的是圣马可正在行刑者上方的空中飞过，可画中除了一个小男孩，并没有人注意到他的情景。画中的其他人，都正在看着行刑者手中的刑具呢。

丁托列托年老后，还受命绘制过一幅巨大的天堂画作。这幅画作的尺寸非常巨

Paradise. The picture was to be large enough to cover a wall space thirty feet high and seventy-four feet long.

Tintoretto set to work and finished the largest painting on canvas in the world. His *Paradise* shows Christ and the Madonna seated on clouds in heaven. Below them are crowds of saints and angels — more than five hundred figures altogether. This painting was Tintoretto's last great work. He died soon after finishing it.

Some of Tintoretto's paintings were, of course, much better than others. The Venetians used to say he had three pencils — one of gold, one of silver, and one of iron. By this they meant that some of his pictures were wonderfully done, some were only fairly well done, and some were poorly done. Perhaps this is why people have had so many different opinions about Tintoretto.

Venice had great painters after Tintoretto. But certainly the Bellinis, Giorgione, Titian, and Tintoretto are enough great men to squeeze into one little chapter!

圣马可解救奴隶的神迹，丁托列托作品，现存于威尼斯美术学院画廊
（由波士顿的大学印刷协会提供）

大，必须盖满一堵三十英尺高、七十四英尺长的墙面。

丁托列托受命后便开始动手，最终创作出了世界上面积最大的，绘制在画布上的作品。他的这幅《天堂》，描绘了基督和圣母坐在天堂里的云端之上时的情景。他们的下方，是众多的圣徒和天使，总计五百多个人物形象呢。这幅画，是丁托列托最后创作的一幅杰作。完成这幅画作后不久，他便去世了。

当然，在丁托列托的画作当中，有一些比其他作品要优秀得多。威尼斯人曾称，丁托列托有三支铅笔：一支金笔，一支银笔，一支铁笔。他们这样说，是指他的画作有些属于无上妙品，有些只算尚可，还有一些则质量低劣。或许，这就是人们如今对丁托列托一直褒贬不一的原因所在吧。

丁托列托去世之后，威尼斯又出现了许多伟大的画家。不过，三位贝利尼、乔尔乔涅、提香和丁托列托都伟大得很，自然值得我们用短短的一章来介绍他们！

Chapter 15 A Tailor's Son and a Master of Light

If your name were Andrea, and if your father were a tailor, and if you were called Andrea of the Tailor, people would always ask, "Can you paint pictures?" For Andrea the son of the Tailor was a famous painter, one of the Renaissance painters of Florence. Italians, of course, didn't use English words for their painter's name. What they called him was Andrea del Sarto, which is the Italian way of saying Andrea of the Tailor.

When this son of the tailor grew up, he married, strange to say, the widow of a hatter — one who makes hats. We can imagine he loved her very much, but there was one thing he could not love — she spent Andrea's money as fast as he could make it.

Two of Andrea's paintings were sent to France, and when the King of France saw them, he wanted the painter to come to France and paint for him. So Andrea went to France. The king was pleased with his work and paid him well, but soon Andrea got a letter from his wife telling him to come back to Italy. The king made him promise he would return to France very soon and gave him money to buy some pictures in Italy to bring back to France.

And now we see that Andrea's pictures were better than he was, for Andrea was a troubled man caught between a king and his wife! When he got home to Italy, his wife made him build her a fine house. And when Andrea found his own money wasn't enough

第15章 裁缝的儿子和光影大师

如果你的名字是“安德利亚”，而你父亲曾经是裁缝，并且人们都叫你“裁缝安德利亚”的话，那么人们常常就会问你：“你会画画吗？”这是因为，裁缝的儿子安德利亚曾经是一位非常著名的画家，是“文艺复兴”时期佛罗伦萨的画家之一。当然，意大利人是不会给他们的画家起个英文名字的。他们称这位画家为“安德利亚·德尔·萨托”；在意大利语里，就是“裁缝安德利亚”的意思。

当这位裁缝的儿子长大成人之后，说来也怪，他却娶了一位制帽匠的遗孀；所谓的制帽匠，就是制作帽子的人。我们想象得到，虽说他一定很爱这个寡妇，但有一件事情，却肯定是他爱不起来的，那就是：安德利亚挣多少钱，她就能花多少钱。

安德利亚的两幅画作，曾经被送到法国。法国国王看到了之后，便想请画家到法国去为他绘画。于是，安德利亚便到法国去了。法国国王很满意安德利亚的画作，给了他丰厚的报酬；可不久之后，安德利亚便接到了妻子的来信，让他回意大利去。法国国王让安德利亚承诺他很快就会回法国去，还给了他很多钱，让他在意大利代购一些画作，并带回法国去。

如今，我们就可以看出，安德利亚的画作比他本身的为人要好，因为安德利亚成了一个陷在法国国王和他妻子之间的倒霉蛋了。回到意大利的家中之后，他的妻子让他给她建了一座漂亮的房子。而当安德利亚发现自己的钱不够建起那座房子之

for the house, he used the king's money! Of course, after such dishonesty, he was afraid to ever go to France again.

In Italy Andrea painted frescoes on the walls of monasteries. You may remember what a fresco is — a picture painted on plaster while it was still wet so the colors would soak into the wall. If a painter made a mistake in painting a fresco, he couldn't rub it out because the picture was part of the plaster. So most artists touched up their frescoes after the plaster was dry. Andrea, however, never did this. He could paint so well that he didn't have to correct mistakes after the picture was finished. There weren't any mistakes to correct.

Andrea painted in oil as well as in fresco. Do you remember that the Early Renaissance painters used to mix their paints with egg or glue? Then someone discovered that it was better to mix paints with oil instead of egg or glue, and soon all the painters were using oil paints except when they painted in the fresco technique.

In the egg or glue way of painting, artists had to paint on a board covered with a kind of smooth plaster called gesso. With oil paints they could paint their pictures on canvas or boards without using gesso. This was much easier, and it also made the pictures look shinier.

Andrea's most famous oil painting is a Madonna. The baby Christ is in her arms. On one side stands Saint Francis and on the other Saint John with two little angels between them. The picture has a peculiar name. It is called *Madonna of the Harpies*. Do you know what harpies are? Harpies are make-believe animals — birds with women's heads. The

后，他竟然动用了法国国王给他买画的钱！当然，做出此种不诚实的事情之后，他也没胆子再回到法国去了。

在意大利，安德利亚给许多修道院的墙壁绘制过湿壁画。你们可能都还记得湿壁画是什么吧；它就是一种趁着墙上的灰泥还没有干透的时候绘制的壁画，这样，颜料就可以渗进墙壁里面。不过，倘若画家在绘制湿壁画的过程中出了差错，他是没法把错的地方擦掉的，因为壁画已经成了灰泥的一部分。所以，绝大多数画家都是等灰泥干透之后，才去对湿壁画进行修改。然而，安德利亚却从来没有这样干过。他画得非常完美，因此无须在画作完成之后再去改正其中的错误之处。他绘制的壁画里，根本就没有错误。

除了湿壁画，安德利亚也绘制油画。你们还记不记得，“文艺复兴”初期的画家常常用蛋清或胶水来调制颜料呢？后来有人发现，用油脂来调制颜料，要比用蛋清或者胶水来调制颜料更好；于是，所有画家很快便开始使用油画颜料，只在湿壁画上才不用了。

用蛋清或胶水调制的颜料绘画时，画家必须在一块盖有一层光滑的，叫作“石膏底子”的灰泥板子上作画。而有了油画颜料后，他们就可以在画布或者木板上作画，不需要用到石膏底子了。这样一来，非但绘制画作变得容易了，而绘制出来的画作也会显得更加亮丽。

安德利亚最著名的一幅油画作品，是一幅圣母像。画作中，圣母胳膊中抱着儿时的基督。她的一侧站着圣方济各，而另一边则站着圣约翰，他们之间还有两个小天使。这幅画作有一个很古怪的名称。它叫《鸟身女妖圣母》。你们知道“鸟身女

Madonna in Andrea's picture is standing on a block or pedestal that is decorated with two little harpies.

The Madonna in this picture is supposed to look like Andrea's wife. He painted her likeness in almost all his pictures, but when poor Andrea finally caught the plague and became very ill, his wife was so afraid of catching the disease that she left him alone and uncared for until he died.

Andrea del Sarto was named for his father's trade. Now we come to a painter who was named for his hometown. Do you remember Perugino, who was named for the city where he lived? Well, not a great distance from Perugia is the city of Correggio, where there lived a painter known everywhere by the name of his city.

We don't know much about Correggio's life, but we can admire his pictures. Like Andrea del Sarto, Correggio painted both in fresco and in oils. All his frescoes are in the city of Parma, Italy, where he worked on the cathedral and the churches.

The cathedral in Parma has a round tower on top called a cupola, and Correggio painted

《鸟身女妖圣母》细部，安德利亚作品，
现存于佛罗伦萨的乌菲齐美术馆
（由波士顿的大学印刷协会提供）

妖”是什么吗？这是人们虚构出来的一种动物，就是长着女人脑袋的鸟儿。而安德利亚所绘的这位圣母，就是站在饰有两位小“鸟身女妖”的一个底座上。

这幅画中的圣母，据说看上去很像是安德利亚的妻子。他创作的几乎所有画作中的圣母，模样都跟他的妻子差不多；但后来可怜的安德利亚染上了鼠疫，病得很厉害时，他的妻子却因为害怕自己也染上鼠疫而离开了他，让他没人照料，自生自灭，直到去世。

安德利亚·德尔·萨托以他父亲所从事的行业为名。现在，我们再来看一看一位以自己故乡为名的画家。你们还记不记得佩鲁吉诺呢？他是一位以自己生活的城市为名的画家。好吧，距佩鲁贾不远的地方，有一座叫作科雷乔的城市；那里出了一位画家，世界各地的人都用他生活的这座城市的名字来称呼他。

尽管我们对科雷乔的生平了解得不是太多，但我们还是可以称颂他的画作。与安德利亚·德尔·萨托一样，科雷乔既绘制过湿壁画，也创作过油画。他创作的湿壁画，全都位于意大利的帕尔马市；他给那里的各个大教堂和小礼拜堂都绘制了许多的湿壁画呢。

帕尔马市的大教堂顶上有一座圆形的塔楼，叫作“穹顶”；科雷乔曾经为这座穹顶的内壁绘制了一幅画作。这幅画作是圆形的，以便适合那座穹顶的内壁。由于

a picture for the inside of the cupola. The picture was circular so it would fit into the ceiling of the cupola. Because it could only be looked at from the floor below, Correggio decided to make the angels and other figures in the picture look like real figures flying through the air. If you were to look straight up and see an angel flying above your head, the soles of the angel's feet would be closer to you than his head would be. You would see just the opposite view if you looked down on the top of someone's head.

To paint a figure seen from below was something that very few artists knew how to do. Correggio first had a sculptor make some models in clay so he would know how people would look from this position. This technique of painting is called *foreshortening*.

Correggio did other foreshortened cupola pictures. People who saw them didn't quite know what to make of them. Actually it was a lot like the April Fool pictures that the Greeks had painted centuries earlier. It was such a new way of painting that at first it wasn't liked very much. But the painter Titian came to Parma, and when he saw Correggio's cupola picture in the cathedral, he said, "Turn the cupola upside down and fill it with gold and even that will not equal what the picture is worth."

Correggio's oil paintings are noted for their wonderful light and shade. He was what we call a master of light and shade. The people in his paintings are graceful, smiling, pretty, and happy- looking, and so almost everybody likes them. The main fault people find with them is that they do not seem to mean very much. Correggio was not a great thinker like Michelangelo and Leonardo da Vinci.

Another one of Correggio's paintings is called *The Marriage of Saint Catherine*. Saint

人们只能站在地下往上观看画作，因此科雷乔决定将画中的天使以及其他人物，画得像是真人在空中飞过那样。要是你们抬头往上看去，见到一位天使在你们头顶飞翔的话，那么天使的脚底应该会比天使的头离你们更近。而倘若你们站在某人的头顶往下看去，那么情况就会正好相反。

当时，还很少有画家知道怎样去绘制一个从下面往上看去的人物。科雷乔先是请一位雕塑家用陶土制作了一些模型，从而了解到以这种角度看上去，人物会是个什么样子。这种画法，被称为前缩透视法。

科雷乔还用前缩透视法绘制了其他一些穹顶画。当时的人看了以后，都很不明白怎么才能画成这样。事实上，这种画作很像是古希腊人在数个世纪以前所绘的那种错视画呢。这是一种全新的画法，因此起初人们都不太喜欢这种画作。不过，后来画家提香来到了帕尔马，他看到科雷乔给那座大教堂所绘的穹顶画后，说了这样一句话："哪怕将整座穹顶翻过来，装满黄金，也抵不上这幅画作的价值啊。"

科雷乔的油画作品，以其中有着精美绝伦的明暗对比而著称。他就是我们所称的光影大师。他绘制的画作中，人物都很优雅，或是微笑着，或是很漂亮，或是样子很幸福，因此几乎人见人爱。人们在其画作中发现的主要缺陷，就是这些画作都没有什么意义。科雷乔与米开朗琪罗和列奥纳多·达·芬奇不一样，他并不是一个伟大的思想家。

科雷乔的另一幅画作，名叫《圣加大勒纳的婚姻》。圣加大勒纳曾经梦见自己正在嫁给儿时的基督，而这幅画作描绘的，则是小基督正在玩耍圣加大勒纳在梦中

圣加大勒纳的婚姻，科雷乔作品，现存于巴黎的卢浮宫
（由波士顿的大学印刷协会提供）

Catherine dreamed she was being married to the baby Christ, and the picture shows the baby playing with the wedding ring that Saint Catherine had seen in her dream.

A strange story is told of Correggio's death, but we do not know if it is true. According to this story, Correggio was paid for one of his paintings in bronze coins. You know that if you pay in pennies for something expensive, it takes a lot of pennies. And this payment to Correggio took so many bronze coins that it made a very heavy load.

Correggio started out to carry this load of coins home. It was a hot day, and the heavy load made Correggio so overheated and tired that he became ill. He had to go to bed and soon after died. And that was the end of this master of light and shade, but his paintings have lived on after him to give pleasure to all who see them.

所见的那个婚戒。

关于科雷乔的死，有一种很离奇的说法，可我们不知道这种说法究竟是不是真的。根据这种说法，有人用铜钱去买科雷乔的一幅画作。你们都知道，要是用分币去买贵重物品的话，就得用大大的一堆分币才行呢。而这个人付给科雷乔那么多的铜钱，以至于装了满满一大车呢。

于是，科雷乔便开始将这一大车铜钱拉回家去。那天天气非常炎热，因此那一大车铜钱让科雷乔拉得又热又累，后来就病倒了。他只得卧床养病，不久后就去世了。这位光影大师的结局就是这样；可他的作品却留传下来，给每一个看到它们的人带来了快乐。

Chapter 16 Flemings

Do you know what a Fleming is? It isn't some strange animal you see in the zoo. In fact, a Fleming isn't any stranger than you are yourself, for a Fleming is a Flemish person — a person of Flanders. The only strange thing about a Fleming is that he is also bound to be either a Frenchman, a Belgian, or a Dutchman as well as just a Fleming, for Flanders is now partly in France, Belgium, and the Netherlands.

An interesting thing about the Flemings is that they had great artists who were painting at the same time as the Early Renaissance artists in Italy. There weren't quite as many great artists in Flanders at that time as there were in Italy, but there were many more than in any other country. If you want to find this country of Flanders on the map, look for Belgium along the North Sea.

The first of the famous Flemish artists were two brothers with the last name Van Eyck. Hubert was the older brother and Jan, the younger. They worked in the city of Bruges, which was one of the largest and richest cities in Europe at the time.

These two brothers painted a magnificent altarpiece for a church in Ghent, a city not far from Bruges. An altarpiece was not like an ordinary picture. An altarpiece had a central panel with wings or shutters on each side like a folding screen. These shutters could be closed like the shutters of a window, and so the Van Eycks painted pictures on the back

第16章 佛兰芒人

你们知道佛兰芒是什么吗？这可不是你们在动物园里看到的什么怪兽。事实上，佛兰芒并不比你们本身更奇怪，因为佛兰芒指的就是佛兰芒人，也就是佛兰德斯[1]人。佛兰芒人唯一奇怪的地方，就在于他们除了只是佛兰芒人之外，要么还是法国人，要么还是比利时人，要么就是荷兰人，因为佛兰德斯包括如今法国、比利时和荷兰的部分地区。

关于佛兰芒人，一个有趣的现象就是，他们当中有一些伟大的画家，与意大利“文艺复兴”之初的那些画家属于同一时期。虽说当时佛兰德斯的杰出画家并不像意大利那样多，可这一地区涌现出来的画家，却比其他国家都要多得多呢。倘若想要在地图上找到佛兰德斯这个国家，那你们不妨找一找比利时的北海沿岸地区。

佛兰芒人画家中，最先出名的是一对姓“凡·艾克”的兄弟。其中的哥哥叫休伯特，而弟弟则叫扬。他们都在布鲁日市工作；当时，布鲁日市还是欧洲最大和最富庶的城市之一。

两兄弟为距布鲁日不远的根特市里的一座教堂绘制了一幅精美绝伦的祭坛画。祭坛画与普通的画作不同。一幅祭坛画，有一面处于中央的主嵌板上，两侧各有一

[1] 佛兰德斯（Flanders），中世纪西欧的一个国家，属于一位伯爵的领地，包括如今法国西北部的部分地区，比利时的东佛兰德斯省、西佛兰德斯省，以及荷兰西南部的部分地区。

of them as well as on the front. Hubert was the one who planned the paintings on this altarpiece, but before he had finished them all, he died. Then Jan completed the work.

The altarpiece was so admired that several cities wanted it for their museums. So it was taken apart and for a long time the central part was in one city and each of the shutters in another. After World War I, the pieces were brought back to Ghent to make a complete altarpiece again. The altarpiece is almost all we have to show us how good an artist Hubert Van Eyck was. But Jan's paintings have been better preserved, and there are several very famous ones in museums.

Both the Van Eycks painted with oil. In fact, they used oil so well to bring out the colors and to keep the paintings fresh looking that many people believed the brothers invented oil painting. This isn't exactly true, but they did improve oil painting so much that today they are often regarded as the fathers of oil painting. It is from them that the Italians learned to paint with oil.

The Van Eyck brothers were followed by other good painters in Flanders, but I'm going to have to skip them and tell you about another great Flemish artist who lived two hundred years later than the Van Eycks. His name is Peter Paul Rubens, and he lived from 1577 to 1640.

Rubens must have been a very bright boy, for he learned to speak Latin, French, Italian, Spanish, English, German, and Dutch! Do you know anybody who can speak seven languages?

翼，或者说遮板，就像折叠屏风那样。这些遮板可以像百叶窗那样合起来，因此凡·艾克兄弟既要在遮板正面绘画，还得在遮板背面绘画。这幅祭坛画是休伯特设计的，可还没等这幅画作整体完工，他便去世了。于是，扬便完成了这幅画作。

人们对这幅祭坛画都交口称颂，好几个城市都想把这幅画收藏到本市的博物馆里。于是，人们便把这幅画拆开，中央嵌板保存在一个城市里，而两扇侧板则各自存放在其他城市里，这种情况保持了很长的一段时间呢。第一次世界大战结束后，人们将这些分散的部分归还了根特市，重新形成了一幅完整的祭坛画。我们差不多只要看一看这幅祭坛画，便可以明白，休伯特·凡·艾克是位多么优秀的画家了。不过，扬的一些画作保存得更好，有些博物馆还保存着他的好几幅名作呢。

凡·艾克兄弟创作的都是油画。实际上，他们的油画绘制技法极其高明，既发挥出了色彩的魅力，又让画作的外观始终保持着鲜艳亮丽，以至于许多人都以为，是这对兄弟发明了油画艺术呢。虽说这种看法并不确切，但他们的确极大地改良了油画技法，因此如今他们经常被称为“油画之父”。正是从他们那里，意大利画家才学会了用油画颜料绘制画作呢。

凡·艾克兄弟之后，佛兰德斯又涌现出了其他一些优秀的画家，但我不得不略过他们，而给你们介绍另一位伟大的佛兰芒画家；他所在的时期，是凡·艾克兄弟的两百年后。他叫彼得·保罗·鲁本斯，生于1577年，1640年去世。

小的时候，鲁本斯一定是个非常聪明的孩子，因为他竟然学会了多种语言，会说拉丁语、法语、意大利语、西班牙语、英语、德语和荷兰语！你们认识的人当中，有没有人能说七种语言呢？

As a young man, Rubens worked for a duke in Italy for several years. The duke liked his work so much that he would not give Rubens permission to leave. One day, however, Rubens had a message from Flanders telling him that his mother was very ill. He started for home at once without the duke's permission.

The rulers of Flanders were glad Rubens had come back. They not only gave him orders for pictures but made good use of him in other ways. He was entrusted with important diplomatic missions to carry out in Spain, France, and England. He won friends everywhere he went. The King of Spain made him a knight. The King of England also made him a knight. Honors were heaped upon him.

Rubens continued to paint hundreds of pictures. In his house was a huge studio where he had many young artists helping him and learning from him. He liked to paint big pictures best, and the stairway of his studio was made very large so that his largest paintings could be taken from the studio after they were painted.

Rubens is noted for the rich, bright colors of his paintings. He could paint all kinds of pictures — portraits and landscapes, animals and battles, religious scenes, and mythological and historical figures. Some are so full of action they make you excited just to look at them. *The Lion Hunt* is a good example. It shows men on horseback with spears attacking lions. The picture lets you know that hunting lions is a sport for only those who are remarkably brave and strong. Rubens learned to draw lions by using a real live lion for a model.

Like most painters of his time, Rubens didn't mind painting people of the past in the

年轻的时候，鲁本斯曾经替意大利的一位公爵工作了好几年的时间。那位公爵非常喜欢他的画作，因此不肯让鲁本斯走。然而，有一天，鲁本斯接到了佛兰德斯的来信，说他的母亲病得非常严重。于是，他没有获得公爵的允准，便马上动身回家去了。

佛兰德斯的君主们都很高兴，因为鲁本斯终于回来了。他们不但命令他去作画，在其他方面也充分地利用了他。他被委以重任，去西班牙、法国和英国完成外交任务。所到之处，他都结交了许多的好朋友。西班牙国王曾经授予他爵士爵位。英国国王也授予了他爵位。他的身上，堆满了各种各样的荣誉。

但鲁本斯继续创作了数百幅画作。他的家，就是一间巨大的画室，有许多年轻的画家来协助他并向他学习绘画技艺。他最喜欢绘制尺寸巨大的画作，因此他那间工作室的楼梯也非常宽大，以便一些尺寸最大的画作完成之后，可以搬出画室。

鲁本斯以其画作色彩丰富、鲜艳亮丽而著称。他能够绘制各种各样的画作，肖像、风景、动物、战斗、宗教场景、神话和历史人物，全都不在话下。其中有些作品极富动感，因此只要看到这些画作，就会让你们热血沸腾呢。《猎狮》这幅画就是个很好的例子。这幅画描绘的是人们骑在马上、手持长矛，向狮群发动攻击时的情景。这幅画作让你们明白，猎狮是一种只属于那些异常勇敢者、强壮者的活动。鲁本斯还是用一只真正的活狮子当模特，学会绘制狮子的呢。

与同时期的绝大多数画家一样，鲁本斯也将古时人物的衣着，画成当时人们所穿的衣物。当时似乎没有人觉得奇怪，一幅画作中的古希腊人竟然穿着十七世纪时

same kinds of clothes that people wore in his day. No one seemed to think it was peculiar to see a painting of an ancient Greek in the costume of the Flemings of the seventeenth century, but painters nowadays always try to have their figures wear clothes that would have been worn at the time the figures were supposed to have lived.

Another well-liked painting is one that Rubens did of his two sons. The older boy was eleven years old and the younger boy was seven years old when Rubens painted their portraits.

They look very lifelike, don't they? Indeed they look very much like boys of today except that their clothes are not the kind boys wear now, even when they are dressed up to go to a party or have their pictures taken.

Rubens was just the opposite of lazy. He worked hard and fast, but even then he had orders for more pictures than he could finish. Sometimes he let his students paint parts of his pictures to save time and also to give them practice. He was always ready to help other artists and sometimes bought their pictures only because they needed money. He even bought some of the paintings of a certain artist who had been very unfriendly to him, just because he felt sorry for him.

Rubens taught so many young men in his

画家的儿子阿尔伯特和尼古拉，
鲁本斯作品

佛兰芒人所穿的衣服；可如今的画家，却始终尽量将画作中人物的衣着，画成与人物所处时代相符的衣物呢。

鲁本斯还有一幅广受人们喜爱的画作，画的是他的两个儿子。鲁本斯给他们绘制肖像的时候，大儿子十一岁，小儿子才七岁。

两兄弟看上去逼真得很，不是吗？实际上，除了身上穿着的衣服与如今的孩子不同，以及如今的孩子化了妆去参加晚会或者拍照时不像之外，这两兄弟的模样，与如今的孩子很是相像呢。

鲁本斯一点儿都不懒惰。他工作起来极其勤奋，而且速度很快；可即便这样，别人订购的画作，也多得让他应付不过来。有的时候，为了节省时间，同时也让学生们练练手，他会让学生绘制画作中的某些部位。他时刻都乐意对其他画家施以援手，有时仅仅因为一些画家缺钱，就将他们的画作购买下来。他甚至还买下了一位曾经对他非常不友好的画家的画作，只是因为他同情那位画家呢。

鲁本斯的画室里，年轻弟子众多，因此其中有些弟子后来自然也成了非常著名

查理一世的孩子们，范·戴克作品，
现存于伦敦温莎城堡的王室藏阁中
（由波士顿的大学印刷协会提供）

studio that some could hardly help becoming famous painters too. The best painter of all who studied under Rubens was Anthony Van Dyck. Van Dyck went to England to live and there he painted for the king, who knighted him for his work. Sir Anthony Van Dyck is most noted for his portraits of kings, noblemen, and their families, such as the painting *Children of Charles I.*

Sir Anthony Van Dyck became so famous for painting portraits of noblemen who wore small pointed beards that even now people call such beards Van Dyck beards.

Most of the hands in Van Dyck's portraits are long and slender, and it is said he copied his own long and slender hands for his pictures. In addition to portraits, Van Dyck also painted many religious pictures.

的画家。在鲁本斯手下学习过绘画的弟子当中，最杰出的一位便是安东尼·范·戴克。范·戴克后来去了英国生活，为英国国王绘画，后来英国国王也因他的画作而授予了他爵位。安东尼·范·戴克勋爵最为著称的，便是他给国王、贵族及其家人所绘制的画像，比如《查理一世的孩子们》。

安东尼·范·戴克勋爵因为他所绘的贵族肖像画而变得闻名遐迩了；由于那些贵族都长着一小撮尖尖的胡子，因此即便是到了如今，人们还是称这种胡子为“范·戴克胡子”呢。

范·戴克所绘制的肖像画里，人物的手臂都又细长又苗条；据说，他是仿照自己那双又细又苗条的手来绘制画作的。除了肖像画，范·戴克还绘制了众多的宗教画作。

I wish I had room to tell you of other Flemish painters. With only this one chapter about them you may think Flemings are not as important in the story of painting as they really are. But I must tell you the last names of three Flemish painters who came between the time of the Van Eycks and Rubens. They were a father and two sons all with the last name Brueghel.

Almost everyone likes the Brueghels' paintings because there is so much going on in them. You can study them closely and still see new things every time. Some of their more famous paintings are *The Harvesters, Haymaking*, and *Landscape with the Fall of Icarus*.

And now I've really told you of more Flemings than I expected to — seven in all. Here they are.

2 Van Eycks
3 Brueghels
1 Rubens
+ 1 Van Dyck
7 Flemings

我真希望，有足够多的篇幅来向你们介绍其他一些佛兰芒画家。只有这区区一章来介绍他们的话，你们可能会以为，佛兰芒画家在绘画历史上并没有他们实际上那么重要呢。不过，我还得跟你们提一下三位佛兰芒画家的姓，他们都生活在凡·艾克和鲁本斯之间的那一时期。这三个人当中，一位是父亲，其余两位则是儿子，都姓勃鲁盖尔。

几乎所有的人都很喜欢勃鲁盖尔父子的画作，因为他们的画作内容都非常丰富。你们可以仔细研究研究他们的画作，而每次研究都会有新发现的。他们较为著名的画作有《收割者》《晒牧草》和《有伊卡鲁斯坠落的风景》。

至此，我向你们介绍过的佛兰芒画家，已经多过我的预期了，总共是七位。他们就是：

2位 凡·艾克
3位 勃鲁盖尔
1位 鲁本斯
+1位 范·戴克
7位 佛兰芒画家

Chapter 17 Two Dutchmen

Next door to Flanders on the shore of the North Sea is the country called the Netherlands — the land of wooden shoes and windmills, tulips and hyacinths, canals and dikes. Often people speak of the Netherlands as Holland, but that is not quite correct because Holland is just a part of the country. The people of the Netherlands are called the Dutch.

The Dutch also had a Renaissance but it was later than the Italian and the Flemish Renaissance. When it did come, it produced some of the very best artists in the world.

The Dutch artists painted pictures that were different from those of the Italians and the Flemish. The Dutch religion had become Protestant instead of Roman Catholic, and the Dutch did not believe in decorating their churches as much as the Catholics did. So the Dutch artists painted very few religious pictures. Instead they painted portraits, landscapes, and pictures of everyday people and objects.

Their pictures differed in other ways too. In older paintings from Italy and Flanders, for instance, most of the people had natural expressions on their faces. You can think of one of these artists saying to someone who was having his portrait painted, "Now just sit still and don't move, and I'll paint your portrait."

But some of the Dutch artists had different ideas about portrait painting. A Dutchman named Frans Hals painted portraits of people who you know were not told to sit still and

第17章 两个荷兰人

与佛兰德斯相邻的北海之滨，是一个叫作尼德兰的国家；那是一个有着木屐和风车，有着郁金香和风信花，有着运河与堤坝的国度。人们通常将尼德兰叫作荷兰，但这种叫法其实不太正确，因为荷兰只是尼德兰的一部分。尼德兰的人，因此也叫作荷兰人。

虽说荷兰人也经历了一个“文艺复兴”的时期，但这一时期比意大利和佛兰德斯的“文艺复兴”都要晚。不过，这一时期到来之后，荷兰便涌现出了许多非常杰出的画家。

荷兰画家的画作，与意大利画家和佛兰芒画家的画作都不同。荷兰人信奉的是新教，而不是罗马天主教；并且，荷兰人也并不像天主教徒那样热衷于装饰他们的教堂。因此，荷兰画家绘制的宗教画作很少。相反，他们主要绘制肖像和风景画，以及关于日常人物的画作。

他们所绘的画作，在其他一些方面也与众不同。比如，在意大利和佛兰德斯一些历史较为悠久的画作中，绝大多数人物脸上的表情都很呆板。你们完全可以想见，这些画家中的一位，在对一个想要请画家绘制自己肖像的人说：“现在，请安安静静地坐着，不要动，我来给您画像。”

可是，一些荷兰画家对于肖像画，却有着不同的理念。你们都知道，有位名叫

look natural. What his portraits captured is called a fleeting expression. He caught a smile, or a grin, or a scowl — expressions that last only a second or two. Hals made his pictures look as though in another second the expression would change.

Some pictures by Hals were different in still another way. They showed the strokes of the paintbrush not smoothed out but left in the picture as if the artist wanted you to see that he had painted the portrait quickly and caught the fleeting expression on the face with a few quick strokes of his brush. Not all his pictures are like this. Some are just as smoothly and carefully finished as can be.

A portrait called *The Laughing Cavalier* is one of his most famous pictures. It shows the lace on the man's cuffs in detail — and lace is not an easy material to make let alone paint in a picture. *The Laughing Cavalier* really isn't laughing. He seems to have a self-satisfied smile instead of a laugh on his lips.

Another picture by Hals shows the quick brushstroke work that he could do so well. It is called *Malle Bahhe* and features a woman and her owl. The old

马勒·巴伯，哈尔斯作品，
现存于柏林的国家博物馆
（由波士顿的大学印刷协会提供）

弗兰斯·哈尔斯的荷兰画家；他绘制的人物肖像画，可不是那种要求人物安安静静地坐着，看上去表情很呆板的画作。他的画作中捕捉到的，都是所谓的短暂的表情。他会捕捉一丝微笑、一种露齿大笑或者某种皱着眉头的愁容，即那些只会持续一两秒钟的表情。哈尔斯绘制的画作中，人物的表情看上去，都好像再过一秒钟就会改变似的。

哈尔斯的画作，还有一个方面也与众不同。这些画作的笔触，并非很平滑地隐出画外，而是留在画中，似乎是画家有意让你们看出，他是以很快的速度画出这幅肖像，用寥寥数笔就迅速捕捉住了人物脸上的短暂表情似的。当然，并不是他的所有画作都是这种风格。有些作品画得非常平滑，并且尽可能地进行了仔细的表面处理。

他最著名的画作之一，是一幅名叫《笑容骑兵》的肖像画。这幅画，细致地描绘出了骑兵袖口上的饰带；这种饰带，制作起来都并非易事，更不用说将它在画作中绘出来了。《笑容骑兵》中的那名骑兵，其实并不是正在大笑。他脸上浮现出来的，似乎是一种沾沾自喜的微笑，而不是一种咧嘴大笑。

哈尔斯的另一幅画作，则说明了他非常擅长的那种快笔画作品。这幅画叫《马勒·巴伯》，刻画了一位带着猫头鹰的女士。那位老太太脸上的表情一点儿也不高

woman isn't a bit pleasant-looking. Sometimes the picture is even called *The Witch of Haarlem*. Haarlem is a Dutch city just outside of Amsterdam where Hals lived.

At the time Hals lived and painted, the Netherlands had recently become a free and independent country. To make sure that they would be strong enough to keep their freedom, the Dutch citizens were trained to act as companies of soldiers in case of need. Gunpowder and guns were so new that some of these companies still called themselves archers or crossbowmen. The officers of each company generally had their portraits painted all in one picture, and Hals painted several group portraits of the archers and other companies. Hals is generally spoken of as the greatest of all Dutch portrait painters — except Rembrandt.

Rembrandt did most of his work in Amsterdam; however, he did not just do portraits. He painted almost every kind of subject an artist could paint. Rembrandt created a light in his pictures that was unlike real daylight or lamplight but which makes his pictures marvels of light and shadow.

Rembrandt worked hard, lived happily, and — unlike so many artists who became famous long after they died — earned money and fame during his lifetime. But he spent so much money in collecting beautiful things that he finally owed more than he could pay. After many years, tastes changed and his pictures became unpopular, so he found it hard to make money in his old age.

You wouldn't think, would you, that a picture that is now considered one of the great pictures of the world would be laughed at and disliked and would make the painter unpopular when it was painted? But that is what happened when Rembrandt painted The

兴。有的时候，这幅画甚至还被人叫作《哈勒姆的女巫》呢。哈勒姆是荷兰的一座城市，就在哈尔斯所居住的阿姆斯特丹外围。

哈尔斯在世并绘制画作的那个时候，尼德兰刚刚成为一个自由和独立的国家。为了确保实力强大到足以维护自身的独立和自由，荷兰人都接受过训练，一旦需要，就可以组成连队行动起来。当时，火药和枪炮都是新鲜事物，因此有些连队仍然自称弓箭连或者长弩连。每个连队的长官，通常都会请人为连队绘制一张集体画像，因此哈尔斯曾经替这些弓箭连和其他连队画过集体像。人们通常都说，哈尔斯是除伦勃朗之外，荷兰最伟大的画家呢。

伦勃朗的绝大部分画作，都是在阿姆斯特丹创作的；然而，他并非只是绘制人物肖像画。凡是画家可以绘制的题材，每一种他差不多都涉猎过。在他的画作中，伦勃朗创造出了一种光线；虽说它不像真正的日光或者灯光，却让他的画作变成了光与影的奇迹。

伦勃朗工作勤奋，生活幸福，并且不像那些死后很久才出名的画家，而是在生前就名利双收了。不过，由于他在收藏方面花的钱太多，因此最终欠下了巨额债务。过了许多年后，人们的品位改变了，他的画作不再受到人们欢迎，所以他便发觉，自己在晚年很难赚到什么钱了。

你们可能不会想到，如今被人们认为属于世界名作的一幅油画，在刚刚绘制出来的时候却被人们笑话和讨厌，使得绘制这幅作品的画家不受欢迎，对不对？可

Night Watch.

The painting was ordered by one of the companies of men who acted as guards for the city in times of danger. It was to hang in their meeting hall, and each member of the guard was to pay his share for having the picture painted.

Rembrandt wanted to show the stir and excitement as the guards marched out, and he painted the picture with the captain and his lieutenant in the front and the members of the guard hurrying out behind them with guns and spears. Children are there to watch the show and even a dog appears in the picture. The light is very bright on some of the figures and the rest are in the darkness of night. Yet the light is so different from ordinary light that some think the picture is a daytime scene and should not be called *The Night Watch*.

When the members of the guard saw the picture, they did not like it. "We paid to have our portraits painted," they said, "and here the artist has stuck us in the background where it is so dark we can hardly even be recognized."

Other Dutchmen laughed at the picture. "We can't tell whether it represents night or day," they said. And from that

夜巡，伦勃朗作品，
现存于阿姆斯特丹的国家博物馆
（由波士顿的大学印刷协会提供）

是，伦勃朗在绘制《夜巡》这幅画的时候，情况却正是这样呢。

这幅画，是一个在危险时期担任阿姆斯特丹市警戒任务的连队订购的。这幅画本打算挂在这个连队队部的会议厅里，并且每个队员都要付一部分钱给绘制这幅画作的伦勃朗。

伦勃朗希望描绘这个警卫连队出营行军时的激动和兴奋情景，因此他将连长及其手下的中尉画在前面，后面则是匆匆涌出、手执枪支长矛的士兵。画中还绘制有观看这一阵仗的孩子们，甚至还有一条狗，也出现在画作里。其中一些人物身上的光线非常明亮，而其他人则隐藏在夜幕的黑暗之中。不过，由于画中的光线与普通光线大不一样，因此有些人觉得这幅画描绘的是白天的场景，不应当叫作《夜巡》呢。

可是，当整个连队的人看到这幅画作后，他们却很不喜欢。“我们付了钱，要画自己的肖像，”他们都说，“可画家却把我们画在后面，那儿黑得很，几乎没人认得出我们呢。”

还有一些荷兰人，则对这幅画作进行了嘲讽。“我们可看不出，这幅作品画的是晚上呢，还是白天。”他们说。从那时起，购买伦勃朗画作的人就越来越少了。

time on, Rembrandt sold fewer and fewer pictures.

Wouldn't you like for me to show you a list starting with the very best artist in the whole world followed by the second best, then the third, and so on down to the twentieth or fiftieth or hundredth best artist? Well, I'm not going to show you any such list. Not because I don't want to but because no one in the world can make such a list. If I did, it would be only my opinion of course. It wouldn't be the best artist and the next best and so on, but the artist I think is best and the one I think is next best. And just because I think he is the best doesn't make it true. No one artist is so much greater than all the other artists that everyone can say, "He is undoubtedly the best."

But if all the people who know most about such things made their own private lists of the best, I'm pretty sure all the lists would have Rembrandt somewhere near the top.

So remember how great an artist people think Rembrandt was, and if you ever in your whole life get a chance to see one of his real pictures — not just a copy in a book — be sure to look at it long and thoughtfully. Then see where he would come on your list of great artists.

你们是不是希望我出示一份名单，从整个世界上最杰出的画家列起，接下来是位居第二的杰出画家，然后又是位居第三的画家，并且依此类推，直到第二十位、第五十位至第一百位的杰出画家来呢？好吧，我可没打算给你们看这样的名单。并不是因为我不想，而是因为世界上没人能够列出一份这样的名单来。就算我列出来了，那自然也只能说是我一个人的看法。列在这张名单上的，不会是什么最杰出的画家、位居第二的杰出画家以及依此类推地列举出来的画家，而是我认为属于最杰出或者位居第二的画家。仅凭我认为这位画家最杰出，并不说明这位画家就真的最杰出。没有哪位画家比其他所有画家都更伟大，从而让大家异口同声地说："他无疑是世界上最杰出的画家。"

不过，倘若让那些最了解这一艺术领域的人各自列出一份最佳画家的名单，那我倒是完全可以肯定，所有人都会把伦勃朗列入最前面的几位呢。

因此，你们就该记住，人们认为伦勃朗是一位非常了不起的画家；倘若一生中有机会去亲眼欣赏欣赏他的一幅真迹，而不只是看看书籍里印着的照片的话，那你们一定要长时间、细细地看上一番才是。然后，你们就可以再来看一看，倘若要你们列出一份伟大画家的名单，他又会排在名单中的第几位呢？

Chapter 18 Ü and Jr.

"Don't forget to dot your *i*'s. Be sure to cross your *t*'s."

Has your teacher ever said that to you? I used to have a hard time remembering to dot all the *i*'s when I wrote compositions at school. But suppose I had gone to school in Germany. There the students have to be careful about dotting *u*'s as well as *i*'s! For in Germany there are two kinds of *u* — a plain *u* like the one in English and a *u* with two dots on it like this: *ü*. A *ü* with two dots, which are called an umlaut, is pronounced something like the English *u* in *pure*.

I wanted to tell you about the dotted ü at the beginning of this chapter because, if I didn't, I know you would ask what the two dots are for when you see them on the name of the German artist Albrecht Dürer. He lived and painted at the same time as Titian, Tintoretto, Michelangelo, and Leonardo da Vinci. In fact, he knew some of the great Italian artists personally, for he took a trip to Venice and stayed there for some time. Germany was having a Renaissance just as Italy, Flanders, and later the Netherlands had had, and Albrecht Dürer was the great artist of the German Renaissance.

Dürer didn't paint quite like the Italians. He painted many kinds of pictures but his portraits are most famous. And in addition to paintings, Dürer made engravings and woodcuts.

第18章 "ü"和"小"

"可别忘了i上要打个点。一定要记得t上有一横。"

你们的老师有没有这样叮嘱过你们呢？我以前在学校写作文的时候，可有过一段时间，根本就记不住要给i加上一点呢。不过，倘若我是在德国上学的话，那里的学生除了对i这个字母，对u也必须小心才是哩！这是因为，在德语里有两种u：一种与英语里的一样，就是一个简单的u；而另一种，上面还带有两个点，也就是这样：ü。带有两个点的ü，叫作变元音，而它的读音则有点像是英语里pure（纯粹的）这个单词里u的发音。

我之所以在本章的一开头就要给你们介绍这个带有两点的ü，是因为倘若不这样做的话，我知道你们在看到德国画家阿尔布雷希特·丢勒（Albrecht Dürer）的名字时，是肯定会问我，其中字母u上面的两点有什么用的。他在世和绘画的时间，与提香、丁托列托、米开朗琪罗以及列奥纳多·达·芬奇都属于同一时期。事实上，这些伟大的意大利画家中，有些人他还认识呢，因为他曾经到过威尼斯，并在那里待了一段时间。当时，德国与意大利、佛兰德斯以及后来的尼德兰一样，正处于"文艺复兴"时期，而阿尔布雷希特·丢勒，则正是德国"文艺复兴"运动中涌现出来的一位杰出画家。

丢勒的画作，与意大利画家的风格不太一样。虽说创作过各种各样的画作，但他最著名的，却还是肖像画。而除了绘画，丢勒还创作过版画和木刻呢。

To make an engraving the artist cuts the lines of a picture in wood or copper. Then he puts ink in the lines and presses the wood or copper on a piece of paper. A picture that is printed this way is called an *engraving*.

Dürer made many engravings, and he is one painter who is as celebrated for his engravings as he is for his paintings. Some of his engravings, such as *Melancholy*, are as well known all over the world as his best paintings.

Dürer's woodcuts are also famous. A *woodcut* is just the opposite from an engraving. In a woodcut, lines are drawn on wood and then the wood is cut away from the lines so that the lines are left raised. Then the raised lines are inked and pressed on paper. Both techniques allow the artist to easily make several copies of the same picture.

Dürer was using these techniques at about the same time that Gutenberg developed the printing press. As a result of this invention, books like the Bible could be copied more quickly by machine instead of slowly by hand, as had been done for so long. Now lots of people,

丢勒父亲的肖像，丢勒作品，
现存于佛罗伦萨的乌菲齐美术馆
（由波士顿的大学印刷协会提供）

制作版画时，画家先是在木板或铜板上刻出一幅画作的线条。然后，再用油墨涂满这些线条，并将整块木板或铜板压到纸上。这样制作出来的一幅画，就称为版画。

丢勒创作了许多的版画作品，所以他也是一位因油画和版画而著称的双料画家。他的一些版画，比如《愁思》，与他那些最优秀的油画作品一样，享誉了全世界呢。

丢勒创作出来的木刻，也非常有名。木刻与版画的创作方法正好相反。制作木刻画时，画家先是在木板上绘出画作的线条，然后将线条之外的木头剔去，使得留下的画作线条凸起。接下来，画家将这些凸起的线条涂上油墨，并按印到纸张上。这两种技术，都可让画家轻而易举地用同一幅画作制作出多幅复制品来。

就在古登堡[1]开发印刷机的同一时期，丢勒正在用这两种方法绘制画作。而印刷机发明出来之后，像《圣经》这样的书籍，便可以用机器迅速复印，而无须再像过去以来一直所做的那样，用人工去慢慢抄写了。这样一来，许多人就都买得起

[1] 古登堡（Johannes Gensfleisch zur Laden zum Gutenberg，1397—1468），德国发明家，西方活字印刷术的发明者。他的发明引发了一次媒介革命，迅速推动了西方科学和社会的发展。亦译“古腾堡”、“谷登堡”、“古滕贝格”等。

instead of a wealthy few, could afford to have a Bible.

When Dürer made the trip to Venice that I mentioned, he was welcomed and honored by the Venetians as a famous man. The Venetian artist Bellini, who was then an old man, asked Dürer one day if he would give him one of the special brushes he used to paint the hair in his portraits. Dürer said, "Certainly." And he gave Bellini the brush he was using.

"Why," said Bellini, "this is just an ordinary brush. Do you really paint those wonderful hairs with a brush like this?"

Dürer took the brush and with it painted some hairs as only he could paint them.

Dürer admired the works of the Italian painters, but when he returned to Germany, he continued to paint in his own way without trying to make his pictures have an Italian look.

Dürer painted several *self-portraits*, or pictures of himself. He was able to do this, of course, by looking in a mirror and painting what he saw in the glass. From these self-portraits we know he was a very handsome man. Several of the other portraits he painted are equally famous, such as the painting of his father.

Dürer was apt to put a great deal of detail into his pictures. He filled the paintings with all kinds of odds and ends, and every tiny button is painted as carefully as if it were as important as the person's face. Most of the German artists did this, and in many of their pictures so much detail is a drawback. Your eye is drawn from the important things to the unimportant ones. But although Dürer often had just as much detail as other German painters, he was a great enough artist to keep the little things in the picture from becoming

《圣经》，而不是只有少数富人买得起了。

我在前面已经提到过，丢勒曾经去过威尼斯；而当他到了那里之后，威尼斯人都把他当成名人，热烈地欢迎和尊敬他。有一天，当时已是老年的威尼斯画家贝利尼问丢勒说，能不能将他自己所用的一支特殊画笔送给贝利尼，好让贝利尼去绘制肖像画中人物的头发。丢勒回答道："当然可以呀。"于是，他便把自己所用的画笔送给了贝利尼。

"哎呀，"贝利尼说，"这只是一支普通的画笔呀。难道您真的是用这样一支画笔，画出了那么精妙绝伦的头发？"

丢勒便拿起那支画笔，画出了数缕头发，表明他就是用这样的画笔画出来的。

虽说丢勒很钦佩意大利画家的画作，可他返回德国后，却是继续用自己的风格绘制画作，并没有试图让自己的画作带上意大利风格。

丢勒还创作了好几幅自画像，也就是他本人的肖像画。当然，他是做得到这一点的：站在镜子面前，将自己在镜中的样子画下来就可以了。从这些自画像，我们可以看出，丢勒长得很英俊呢。他创作的其他几幅肖像画也同样著名，比如他父亲的肖像画。

丢勒常常会在自己的画作中描绘大量的细节。他的画作中，充斥着各种各样的零碎之物，连每一颗细小的纽扣也是精心绘制，仿佛它们与人物的脸部一样重要似的。绝大多数德国画家都这样，而在他们的许多画作中，此种细致实际上已经变成了一种缺点。观众的注意力，将会从重要的部位分散到不重要的地方。不过，尽管

too important.

The second great Renaissance artist of Germany also did portraits and woodcuts. His name was Hans Holbein. We have to speak of him as Hans Holbein the Younger because his father was also an artist named Hans Holbein.

The Holbeins moved to Switzerland and Hans Holbein the Younger became the friend of a very famous man who lived there — Erasmus. Erasmus was a great thinker and writer. Holbein painted five portraits of Erasmus. The following portrait is the one most people prefer.

The painting shows a side view, or *profile*, of Erasmus writing at his desk. There do not seem to be very many details in this portrait. But in another famous portrait by Holbein, called *Portrait of Georg Gisze*, there are about twenty- five things to look at besides Gisze himself. And yet, like Dürer, Holbein was able to keep them in their place so that Gisze is the chief thing your eye looks at. Indeed, he left the unimportant details out of the faces of his portraits, putting in only the lines that would tell the most.

Holbein found his painting business was not doing so well in Switzerland so he decided to take a bold step. He got a letter of introduction from Erasmus and went to England. The English liked his work, and he painted portraits of most of the important Englishmen of the time, including King Henry VIII.

Boys and girls usually like the portraits by Holbein more than those by any other painter, except perhaps Frans Hals. And that is true for a great many grownups too. So I'm pretty sure you will like them yourself and that you would enjoy a picture book of portraits

丢勒经常也像其他德国画家一样面面俱到，但他毕竟是一位了不起的画家，能够不让画作中无关紧要的部位变得太过喧宾夺主。

德国“文艺复兴”时期第二位伟大的画家，同样是既创作过肖像画，又创作过木刻。这位画家，名叫汉斯·荷尔拜因。我们得称他为“小汉斯·荷尔拜因”才行，因为他的父亲老汉斯·荷尔拜因也是一位画家。

荷尔拜因一家搬到了瑞士，而小汉斯·荷尔拜因则与当地一个大名鼎鼎的人物伊拉斯谟交上了朋友。伊拉斯谟是一个伟大的思想家和作家。小荷尔拜因曾经给伊拉斯谟绘制过五幅肖像画呢。下面这幅肖像，就是绝大多数人最喜欢的一幅。

这幅画作描绘的，是从侧面看去，伊拉斯谟坐在书桌前写作时的样子；或者说，它是一幅侧面像。在这幅肖像画中，我们看不到过多的细节。可在小荷尔拜因另一幅叫作《格奥尔格·吉斯泽肖像》的著名画作中，除了吉斯泽本人之外，我们还可以看到大约二十五件其他的东西呢。不过，与丢勒一样，小荷尔拜因也很有本事，能够让这些细节各安其所，从而让观众把注意力放在吉斯泽这个主体上。事实上，他将那些不重要的细节都放在肖像画中的人物脸部以外，脸部则只有表现力最强的线条。

后来，小荷尔拜因发现自己在瑞士的绘画业务不是很多，便决定踏出大胆的一步。他请伊拉斯谟写了一封推荐信，然后去了英国。英国人都很喜欢他的作品，于是他便替英国当时的绝大多数权贵绘制了肖像画，其中还包括英王亨利八世。

小朋友们通常都更喜欢小荷尔拜因绘制的肖像画，而不太喜欢其他画家的作品；或许，只有弗兰斯·哈尔斯属于例外。许多的成年人也是这样。因此，我完全

伊拉斯谟像，小荷尔拜因作品，
现存于巴黎的卢浮宫
（由波士顿的大学印刷协会提供）

by this master portrait painter.

But don't forget Dürer. You'll like his pictures too.

Albrecht Dürer and Hans Holbein the Younger — I wonder which one you are going to like better.

可以肯定，你们也会喜欢他的画作的；要是有一本这位肖像画大师的肖像作品集，你们也会很高兴的。

不过，可别忘了丢勒。你们也会喜欢上他的作品。

我倒是很想知道，在阿尔布雷希特·丢勒和小汉斯·荷尔拜因这两人当中，你们更喜欢哪一位呢。

Chapter 19 Forgotten and Discovered

All anyone knows about the life of one of the very great painters of the world can be written in a few sentences. Most great painters have had whole books written about their lives, but there isn't enough known about the life of the Dutchman Jan Vermeerl to fill even a few pages. But I will tell you what is known about him.

Vermeer was born in 1632 in Delft, which is in Holland in the Netherlands, and died there in 1675, leaving a widow and eight children. There it is in one sentence — the life of Vermeer of Delft. Nobody even knows how many pictures he painted because some pictures he is thought to have painted may have been painted by someone else.

But the pictures that we are sure were painted by him are considered to be extraordinary. Most are of indoor scenes. Only one, as far as we know, is a landscape.

Many of Vermeer's indoor paintings show a woman doing a common, everyday thing like reading a letter, sewing, playing the clavichord, or even just looking out of a window. Perhaps his wife or one of his daughters posed for Vermeer's pictures. In some pictures there are two women, and in a few there are men. In most cases the person in the picture is shown near a window.

The wonderful way Vermeer could paint light coming into a room through a window is one of the first things people notice about these paintings. Some people say it is the finest daylight that any painter has ever put into an indoor scene.

第19章　遗忘与发现

对于世界上任何一位极其伟大的画家，我们所了解的生平，都可以用寥寥数行文字概括出来。尽管对于绝大多数伟大的画家来说，都曾有人给他们写过整本整本的生平传记，但人们对荷兰画家扬·维米尔的生平却所知不多，连几页内容都填不满呢。不过，我还是会将我们所了解的情况，给你们介绍介绍。

维米尔1632年出生于尼德兰霍兰德的代尔夫特，1675年去世，留下了一位遗孀和八个孩子。代尔夫特的维米尔的生平就是这样，一句话就概括完了。甚至没人知道，他一生中创作了多少幅画作，因为有些原本以为是他绘制的画作，其实可能是由别人绘制的。

不过，我们确定是他创作出来的那些画作，却都被世人公认为非凡之作。其中绝大部分画作的内容，都是室内场景。据我们所知，其中只有一幅风景画。

维米尔的许多室内场景画，描绘的都是一位女性正在从事普通日常之事时的情景，比如看信、做针线活、弹翼琴，或者甚至只是望着窗外。没准，他是让妻子或者一个女儿摆出姿势做模特来绘制画作的。有些画作中有两名女性，还有少数几幅画里甚至还有男子。而绝大多数情况下，画中的人物都位于窗户边上。

维米尔用一种精妙的手法，描绘了从一扇窗户透进房间里来的光线；这是人们在这些画作中率先注意到的一个方面。有些人还说，这是有史以来所有画家在

Next, one notices how well Vermeer could show what material an object is made of — that is, its *texture*. The lace cuff, silk dress, wooden chair, silver pitcher, ripe fruit, shiny drinking glass, pearl necklace, and blue china plate are all done so well that no one could doubt what each is made of. One could almost tell how each object feels to the touch. And the daylight from the window streams over all, binding the parts of the picture together. Certainly Vermeer was able to paint as few artists could.

Young Woman With a Water Pitcher is one of Vermeer's pictures. It is simply a woman pausing by a window but it is painted so well that it has become famous. It looks so real that you may be wondering if this is another April Fool picture, but it's not. Can you remember why? April Fool pictures are very real, and they are the same size as the objects in the painting.

Vermeer did not make his paintings life-size, but he did make them look so real that when people stand in front of them they cannot stop noticing all the details. In many ways, his paintings seem even more real than the real things do themselves!

拿着水罐的少妇，维米尔作品，
现存于纽约的大都会艺术博物馆
（由缅因州桑福德的大学印刷协会提供）

室内场景画中描绘得最为精妙的日光呢。

接下来，人们又注意到，维米尔能够完美地表现出物体的材质，也就是说，表现出物体的质地。饰有花边的袖口、丝质的衣服、木质的椅子、银质的水罐、成熟的水果、擦得锃亮的酒杯、珍珠项链、蓝色的瓷器盘子，全都描绘得惟妙惟肖，以至于没有人会怀疑每样东西的材质。我们甚至几乎说得出，每样东西摸上去的感觉呢。而从窗户透进来的阳光，则如流水般均匀地洒在所有物品上，将画作中的各个部分连成一个整体。当然，维米尔的这种绘画本领，是没有几位画家能够做到的。

《拿着水罐的少妇》就是维米尔创作的一幅画作。虽说画中只有一位少妇伫立在窗前，但由于绘制得非常精美，因此这幅画作后来变得非常有名了。画作看上去极其逼真，以至于你们可能会很想知道，这会不会是另一种错视画呢；但它并不是错视画。你们还记得这是为什么吗？错视画非常逼真，而画中的人和物，也应与所绘的人、物尺寸一般大。

维米尔并没有绘制过与真人大小相当的画作，可他确实画得非常逼真，因此人们站在画作前观看的时候，都会情不自禁地注意到所有的细节。在许多方面，他的画作看上去似乎比真的事物本身更加逼真呢！

Vermeer didn't use his imagination; he painted only what he saw. He never, for instance, made his women prettier than they really were. I don't believe he could have painted a dragon or Saint George without looking at a real dragon (as if there were such a thing!) or at Saint George himself.

Why is so little known about so fine a painter? It seems mysterious, doesn't it? Vermeer's pictures were well liked at the time they were painted, but then for some reason they were almost forgotten about for two hundred years. No one took the trouble to write down anything about the artist. Then his pictures were "discovered" again and became so valuable that it took a great deal of money to buy one. Most of Vermeer's paintings are now carefully kept in museums.

This chapter is far too short for so important a painter. But there aren't any stories to tell about him unless I just make them up. Vermeer didn't use his imagination in painting his pictures, and I'm not going to use mine in telling you made-up stories. We'll just have to let Vermeer's pictures speak for him.

戴珍珠耳环的少女，维米尔作品，
现存于海牙的莫瑞泰斯皇家美术馆
（由波士顿的大学印刷协会提供）

维米尔在绘画时，并没有运用自己的想象力；他只是将自己的所见画下来。比如，他从来都不会将画中女性的容貌画得比现实中的本人漂亮。我觉得，假如没有亲眼见过一条龙（就算世界上真的存在这样一种东西的话），没有亲眼见过圣乔治本人，他是不可能画出一条龙，不可能画出圣乔治来的。

对于一位如此杰出的画家，我们了解的为何会这么少呢？这一点，似乎很不可思议，对不对？当时的人都很喜欢维米尔的画作，可接下来却由于某种原因，人们几乎将这些画作遗忘了近两百年呢。没有人费点儿心，将这位画家的情况记录下来。然后，他的画作又被人们再一次“发现”，并且变得非常珍贵，要花上一大笔钱才能买到一幅了。如今，维米尔的绝大部分画作，都被精心保存进了博物馆。

对于一位如此重要的画家来说，这一章的介绍实在是太简短了。但我并没有其他的故事来告诉你们，除非我捏造事实。维米尔在绘制画作的时候，没有运用过想象力，因此我也不打算运用自己的想象力，跟你们说一些捏造出来的东西。我们只能让维米尔的作品，来替他说话啊。

Chapter 20 Speaking of Spaniards

This chapter is about Spain. But I'm going to begin by telling you about Crete, which hasn't anything at all to do with Spain.

Crete is an island south of Greece. It belongs to Greece and the people of Crete speak the Greek language. Around the mid-1500s a baby was born who was to become a celebrated painter. You have never heard of his name and might not even find it easy to pronounce even if you had. I'll tell it to you just to show you but don't try to remember it, for this painter is never spoken of except by his nickname. His real name is Domenikos Theotocopoulos.

He was a mysterious man and no one knows very much about his life. He seems to have left Crete and gone to Venice to study art under the great Titian. The next we hear of him he was in Rome, and then he popped up in Spain and settled in the city of Toledo just south of Madrid.

In Spain he remained and in Spain he died in 1614. But he always thought of himself as a Greek rather than a Spaniard and he signed his most important paintings in Greek letters. The Spaniards could hardly be expected to call him Domenikos Theotocopoulos any more than you are expected to. They just called him the Greek, which in Spanish is El Greco.

第20章 西班牙值得一提的画家

这一章，介绍的是西班牙的画家。不过，在开始的时候，我打算先跟你们说一说克里特岛的情况；这个地方，跟西班牙可是八竿子都打不着呢。

克里特岛是希腊南部的一个岛屿。这里属于希腊，而岛上之人说的也是希腊语。在十六世纪中期左右，这里诞生了一个婴儿，后来这个婴儿又变成了一位大名鼎鼎的画家。你们都还没有听说过这位画家的名字呢；而就算是听说过，你们可能也会发现，他的名字不太容易念出来。我之所以会将他的名字告诉你们，只是让你们知道，而不是要你们去记住；因为人们很少提起这位画家的本名，只会说他的绰号。他的真名，叫作多明尼科斯·底欧多科普洛斯。

这是一位很神秘的人物，没有人十分了解他的生平。后来他好像离开了克里特岛，前往威尼斯，到伟大的提香手下去学习过绘画。关于他，我们了解的第二件事情，便是他到了罗马，后来又突然出现在西班牙，并在马德里以南的托莱多这座城市里定居了下来。

后来，他便一直住在西班牙，直到1614年去世。不过，他一向都认为自己是希腊人，而不是西班牙人，并且他在绝大多数重要画作上的签名，用的都是希腊文。当时的西班牙人就像你们一样，也不希望叫他的本名多明尼科斯·底欧多科普洛斯呢。他们只是简单地称他为“希腊人”；而在西班牙语里，“希腊人”就是“埃尔·格列柯”。

El Greco painted pictures that are so different from other artists' paintings that you may think they are not beautiful when you first see them. All his people are too long and thin to be like real people. Some say that the figures in El Greco's paintings look elongated because the artist had something different about his eyes that caused him to see people that way so that's how he painted them.

But shape is not the only difference. The colors he used are distinctive from the colors used by other artists. El Greco's colors often have a yellow tint to them. Just as many people suspect his unusual figure shapes are due to the way he saw things, they also imagine he may have seen colors differently than others. Once you have seen a few of his paintings, the shapes and colors are so distinctive that you will always be able to say "That's an El Greco" and know that you are right.

When you see a picture by El Greco, you must remember that he is not trying to make you see a picture of things as they would look in a photograph. His paintings of men and scenes represent the spirit, or idea, of them, which is not what you would see with your eyes if you looked at real people and real scenes.

This is hard for many people to understand. They think a painting should always show you exactly what real things look like — as if a camera took the picture. But many artists like El Greco paint not what they see but what they think will look best as a picture.

When El Greco died, the man who was to become the greatest Spanish painter of all — Diego Velásquez — was still only a boy of fourteen.

埃尔·格列柯绘制的画作，风格与其他画家的画作都大为迥异，因此乍一看去，你们可能会觉得他的画作并不漂亮。他绘制的所有人物，身材都太高、太瘦，看上去并不像现实生活中的人。有些人说，埃尔·格列柯画作中的人物之所以看上去都被拉长了，是因为这位画家的眼睛与常人不同，使得他看到的人物就是画出来的那种样子。

不过，人物体型并不是埃尔·格列柯画作唯一的与众不同之处。他所用的色彩，也明显有别于其他画家所用的色彩。埃尔·格列柯所用的色彩中，通常都有一抹淡淡的黄色底子。就像许多人怀疑他所绘的那种与众不同的人物体型是因为他看事物的方式所致一样，人们也猜想，这位画家看色彩的方式可能也与他人不同。一旦你们欣赏过他的一些画作，由于这些画作中人物的体型和色彩都与众不同，因此你们以后就总是能够分辨出"这是埃尔·格列柯的画"，并且知道自己说得正确了。

看到埃尔·格列柯的画作时，你们必须记住，他并不是想要让你们像看照片一样，看到事物的本来面目。他的人物画作和场景画作，代表的是人物和场景的精神，或者说人物和场景的意义；而这种精神或者意义，并不是你们亲眼看到真实的人物和真实的场景时能够看出来的。

这一点，对于许多人来说，都是难以理解的。他们认为，一幅画作始终都应当准确地描绘出真实事物的本来面目，就像用照相机拍照那样。不过，许多画家，比如埃尔·格列柯，描绘的其实不是他们看到的东西，而是他们心中所想的一幅画作的最佳样子。

埃尔·格列柯去世的时候，接下来即将成为西班牙最伟大画家的那个人，即迪

Velásquez was born in the city of Seville in 1599, the very same year that Van Dyck was born in Holland. After Velásquez grew up and after he had painted for some time, he decided to visit Madrid, the capital of Spain. The King of Spain, Philip IV, saw some of his work and liked it, and so the next year Velásquez was sent for. The painter moved to Madrid for good and became the king's painter.

We know very well what this King of Spain looked like because Velásquez painted many pictures of him. That was one of the duties of the king's painter. The camera had not been invented yet and so portraits were a record of important people like kings.

When you see a portrait of King Philip IV, the first thing you notice is his large mustache that curls up toward his eyes. It must have been a nuisance because King Philip had to put leather cases on it at night to keep it shaped right. I wonder what the king looked like when he got his fancy mustache caught in the rain!

Almost all the portraits of the king and his nobles show a wide stiff white collar that sticks out from around each man's neck. King Philip was very proud of this kind of collar, and for a very special reason — he invented it himself!

Velásquez also painted portraits of the king's family, including his daughter Princess Margarita in *The Maids of Honor*.

Velásquez was very different from El Greco in his painting. El Greco painted things as he wanted them to look in order to give his idea of them. El Greco used his imagination instead of putting down on canvas just what he saw with his eyes. But Velásquez painted

亚哥·委拉斯贵兹，却还只是一个年仅十四岁的小男孩。

委拉斯贵兹1599年出生于塞维利亚市，与荷兰的范·戴克是同一年出生的。委拉斯贵兹长大成人，并且从事了一段时间的绘画之后，决定前往西班牙的首都马德里游历。西班牙国王腓力四世看到了他的一些画作，非常喜欢，便在第二年派人去延请委拉斯贵兹。于是，这位画家便搬到马德里，永久定居下来，成了国王的御用画师。

我们很清楚这位西班牙国王的模样，因为委拉斯贵兹为他绘制了许多画像。这可是国王御用画师的职责之一呢。当时，照相机还没有发明出来，因此画像就是把像国王这样的重要人物的模样留存下来的手段。

观看国王腓力四世的画像时，你们首先注意到的，就是他那朝着眼睛向上卷起来的大胡子。这胡子一定很让人心烦，因为腓力国王晚上睡觉时，必须给胡子套上皮套，才能让胡子保持合适的形状。我倒是很想知道，要是那奇特的胡子淋了雨，这位国王会是个什么样子呢！

这位国王和他手下那些王公贵族的画像里，几乎所有人物的脖子上都戴着一个宽大、硬挺并且向前凸出的领结。腓力国王对这种领结感到非常自豪，而原因也很特殊：这种领结，就是他本人发明的！

委拉斯贵兹还给这位国王的家人绘制了许多画像，其中包括玛格丽塔公主的画像《小公主》。

委拉斯贵兹的绘画风格，与埃尔·格列柯大不相同。埃尔·格列柯是按照自己想要呈现的样子去描画事物，从而传达出自己对于所画之物的想法的。埃尔·格列柯绘画时，会运用自己的想象力，而并非只是将自己眼睛所见的东西，如实地绘在画

objects to look like real objects. A painter who does this is called a realist because he paints only what he really sees.

When Rubens came to Madrid, the king asked Velásquez to show the Italian painter the art treasures of Spain. Rubens and Velásquez got along together very well. Rubens admired Velásquez's paintings and Velásquez admired Rubens' paintings.

Velásquez wanted to see the famous paintings of the great Italian artists and, fortunately for him, the king sent him on trips to Italy where he made copies of some paintings by Tintoretto, Michelangelo, and Titian. While he was there, he also bought many paintings for the king's royal collection, which later became part of the Prado Museum in Madrid.

You may wonder what all those paintings cost. Well, while it is difficult to say what the cost would be today, we do know that on his shopping spree in 1650, he spent two million dollars in gold! The money he spent could have been used for art that was not the best of all, but Velásquez had what we call a wonderful "eye" for art and selected only the finest from his time. It is no wonder that the Prado is one of the most famous museums in the world.

Velásquez also painted a portrait of Aesop, who wrote such famous fables as "The Fox

《小公主》细部，委拉斯贵兹作品，
现存于巴黎的卢浮宫
（由波士顿的大学印刷协会提供）

布上。但是，委拉斯贵兹却将事物描绘得完全就像是真实的绘画对象。这样做的画家，被称为现实主义画家，因为这类画家只会描绘出眼睛所见的、事物的真实模样。

鲁本斯来到马德里后，国王曾经让委拉斯贵兹把西班牙的美术珍藏品出示给那位意大利画家看。鲁本斯和委拉斯贵兹两人相处得非常融洽。鲁本斯很钦佩委拉斯贵兹的画作，而委拉斯贵兹也对鲁本斯的画作赞不绝口。

委拉斯贵兹很想看一看鲁本斯这位伟大画家的名作，而幸运的是，腓力国王后来还派他出使了意大利；在意大利，他仿制了丁托列托、米开朗琪罗和提香等人的一些作品。他在意大利的时候，他还替腓力国王购买了许多画作，充实皇家收藏；而后来，这些藏品都成了马德里普拉多博物馆的一部分。

你们可能很想知道，所有这些画作花了多少钱。好吧，虽然很难说清那笔钱如今究竟值多少，但我们的确知道，他在1650年的这次疯狂收购，竟然花掉了价值二百万美元的黄金！虽说他的这笔钱，可能并不是全都花在最好的美术作品上，但委拉斯贵兹对美术作品，却的确拥有我们所称的那种绝妙“眼光”，挑选的全都是当时最精美的一些作品。难怪，普拉多博物馆是如今世界上最著名的博物馆之一呢。

委拉斯贵兹还创作了一幅伊索的肖像画；伊索就是那个写出了《狐狸和葡萄》《马槽里的狗》及《龟兔赛跑》等著名寓言故事的人。当然，画中的人物并不是真

and the Grapes," "The Dog in the Manger," and "The Hare and the Tortoise." Of course, the picture is not of the real Aesop. Velásquez just painted the picture as he thought Aesop might have looked, for Aesop himself lived two thousand years before Velásquez.

Velásquez has been called the painters' painter because so many painters have admired and praised his work. He was the greatest of the Spanish painters, greater than El Greco and greater than the next Spanish painter I'm going to tell you about, whose name was Murillo.

Murillo, like Velásquez, was born in Seville. He went to Madrid where Velásquez encouraged him in his painting and got him permission to study the paintings in the king's picture gallery. After two years there, Murillo went back to live in Seville. He was still poor and unknown.

Now about that time, the Franciscan monks in Seville were looking for an artist who would decorate one of their buildings with paintings. They wanted a famous artist but they had too little money to pay a famous artist's prices. So they decided to let Murillo do the work. Murillo painted eleven pictures for the monks, and everyone liked them so much that he was asked to do more pictures. Then Murillo painted eleven pictures for another building. These were even better than the first eleven and they made

伊索像，委拉斯贵兹作品，
现存于马德里的普拉多博物馆
（由波士顿的大学印刷协会提供）

正的伊索。委拉斯贵兹只是将自己想象中伊索的样子画下来罢了，因为伊索生活在委拉斯贵兹所处时代的两千年前呢。

委拉斯贵兹被人们称为“画家中的画家”，因为许多画家都非常崇拜他，并且赞扬他的作品。他是最伟大的西班牙画家，比埃尔·格列柯，比我接下来要给你们介绍的、名叫牟利罗的这位画家，都要伟大哩。

牟利罗跟委拉斯贵兹一样，也是出生于塞维利亚。后来，他去了马德里；而在马德里，委拉斯贵兹不但鼓励他绘画，还帮他得到了去西班牙国王画馆里学习的许可证。在马德里过了两年之后，牟利罗又回到了塞维利亚。此时，他仍然穷困潦倒，默默无闻。

注意，差不多就在此时，塞维利亚的方济各会修道士正在寻找一位画家，想要这位画家替修道院绘制装饰画。他们本来想找一位名气很大的画家，可他们的钱不多，没法雇用哪位有名的画家来绘画。于是，他们决定请牟利罗来干。牟利罗为这些修道士们绘制了十一幅画，大家都非常喜欢，便请他绘制更多的画作。接下来，牟利罗又给另一座修道院绘制了十一幅画作。后面的这些画作，比原先的那十一幅画更精美，因而使得牟利罗声名鹊起了。

him famous.

Like Velásquez, Murillo's pictures were also very realistic. In fact, one picture of a priest with a spaniel at his feet was so lifelike that when a live dog saw the painted spaniel, he thought it was real and growled at it. This reminds us of the story of the birds who pecked the grapes in Zeuxis's picture.

Murillo was very good at painting children and Madonnas. His Madonnas generally have dark hair and eyes. *The Children of the Shell* is one that all children seem to like. It shows the baby Christ and little Saint John getting a drink of water out of a seashell. The little lamb in the comer of the picture looks as if he is thirsty and wants a drink too.

Murillo was so successful at selling his pictures that he made a large fortune, but he was a very generous man and gave much money to the poor. He had been poor once himself and he knew how much help they needed.

One day when he was old, he was getting up on scaffolding to paint the higher parts of a large picture when he stumbled and fell. He was so badly hurt that he never got well and the picture was left unfinished.

The people of Seville never forgot their famous painter, and even today in Seville they call any beautiful picture a Murillo.

玩贝壳的孩子们，牟利罗作品，
现存于马德里的普拉多博物馆
（由波士顿的大学印刷协会提供）

与委拉斯贵兹一样，牟利罗的画作风格也是非常写实的。事实上，其中有一幅，画的是一位牧师的脚边有一只西班牙猎犬；由于画得极其逼真，因此当一只真正的小狗看到画中的猎犬后，还以为那是一只真的小狗，便朝着画作狂吠起来呢。这不由得让我们想起小鸟去啄食宙克西斯画作中葡萄的故事呢。

牟利罗极其擅长绘制关于儿童和圣母马利亚的画作。他创作出来的圣母，通常都有着黑色的头发和眼睛。《玩贝壳的孩子们》就是所有小朋友似乎都很喜欢的一幅画作。画中描绘的是儿时的基督和儿时的圣约翰正在从一只海贝中喝水时的情景。画作一角的那只绵羊，看上去似乎也很口渴，也想喝水似的呢。

牟利罗的画作销路很好，因此赚了很多的钱；可他是个非常慷慨的人，捐了很多的钱给穷人。以前他自己一度也很穷困，因此明白穷人很需要别人的帮助。

年老后，有一天，他正在脚手架上绘制一幅画作中较高的部位，却突然跸了一跤，从上面摔了下来。他受了很重的伤，后来一直没有复原，而那幅画作也一直没有完成了。

塞维利亚人民永远都不会忘记他们这些伟大的画家；因此，就算是到了如今，塞维利亚人还称漂亮的画作为“牟利罗”呢。

Chapter 21 Landscapes and Shop Signs

Fire escapes are part of the scenery in a city. Land*scapes* are the scenery in the country. Fire escapes have nothing to do with painting. Landscapes have a great deal to do with painting. But once upon a time, landscapes had as little connection with painting as fire escapes have now.

It seems strange that from the time the cave dwellers made their animal pictures thousands of years ago all the way up to the middle of the seventeenth century almost no one in Europe painted a real landscape. Italy had great painters during the Renaissance. Italy had beautiful landscapes. But the great painters never thought of painting the beautiful landscapes. If there was any country scenery at all in the Italian pictures, it was always as a background for the figures in the foreground.

The Van Eycks in Flanders had come close to real landscapes in their famous Ghent altarpiece. But the things happening in their picture were more important than the scenery. Some landscapes had also been painted in Germany around 1500 but they didn't attract much notice.

It seems strange that the first two painters of Italian landscapes were not Italians but Frenchmen. One was named Nicolas Poussin. He was interested in the stories of the ancient Greeks and in Roman ruins. His pictures generally have Greeks in the foreground but the backgrounds are closer to true landscapes.

第21章 山水画与商店招牌

“火灾逃生出口”是城市风景的一部分，山水则属于乡村里的风景。火灾逃生出口与绘画艺术没有什么关系，山水却与绘画艺术有着莫大的关系。可在很久以前，山水却与如今的火灾逃生出口一样，与绘画没有什么联系呢。

自从几千年前穴居人绘制动物画以来，一直到十七世纪中期，欧洲几乎没有谁绘制过一幅真正的山水画，这一点似乎奇怪得很。“文艺复兴”期间，意大利涌现出了很多伟大的画家。意大利也有优美的山山水水。不过，那些伟大的画家，却从来没有想过要把这些美丽的山水绘制下来。就算意大利画家的画作当中有一点儿乡间的山水，那也不过是作为前景中人物的背景罢了。

佛兰德斯的凡·艾克兄弟那幅著名的根特祭坛画，已经近似于真正的山水画了。不过，画作中描绘的故事，却比其中的风景重要得多。在公元1500年左右，德国也已有人绘制出了一些山水画；可这些画作，却没有引起人们太多的注意。

最先创作意大利山水风景画的两位画家，都不是意大利人，而是法国人，这一点似乎很奇怪。其中一位名叫尼古拉斯·普桑。他对古希腊人的传说，对古罗马的废墟都非常感兴趣。他创作的油画里，通常都是以古希腊人为前景，而背景则很接近真正的山水画。

普珊的画作《阿卡迪亚的牧人》，说明了他对古希腊人的看法。

Poussin's picture *Shepherds of Arcadia* shows his view of the Greeks.

Do you know where Arcadia is? Arcadia used to be a country of ancient Greece known for its kind, happy, simple country people and shepherds. These shepherds that Poussin painted seem to be talking about the marble tomb in the picture. One is pointing to some words on the tomb. The words are hard to read here, but in the real picture they mean "I, too, have been in Arcadia."

The other French artist who painted landscapes in Italy is known as Claude Lorrain. His real name was Claude Gellée, but as he came from Lorraine, France, he is always called Claude Lorrain.

The story goes that he was once a pastry cook and later worked for a painter in Italy. One of his duties was to clean the paintbrushes. This interested him in painting. The painter gave him lessons and soon Claude Lorrain was a painter himself.

Claude Lorrain had people in his pictures but generally they were small and unimportant. The landscape was the important thing, even more important than it had been with Poussin. So Claude Lorrain is sometimes called the father of landscape painting. He liked to paint pictures of the sea even more than landscapes, so we might call him a seascape painter too.

阿卡迪亚的牧人，普桑作品，现存于巴黎的卢浮宫
（由波士顿的大学印刷协会提供）

你们知道阿卡迪亚在哪儿吗？阿卡迪亚曾经是古希腊的一个城邦，以那里的乡民与牧人和善、快乐、朴素而著称。普桑绘制的这些牧人，似乎正在谈论画中的那块大理石墓碑。其中一人正指着墓碑上的字。我们在这里很难看清上面的字，但在原作中，墓碑上文字的意思是："我，也曾到过阿卡迪亚。"

另一位在意大利创作山水风景画的法国画家，人称克劳德·洛林。他的真名本是克劳德·热莱，可由于他出生于法国的洛林，因此人们总是叫他克劳德·洛林。

据说，他曾经是一名面点师，后来又到意大利替一位画家工作。他的工作任务之一，便是清洗画笔。这让他对绘画产生了兴趣。那位画家便给他讲课，教他绘画；于是，克劳德·洛林不久后也成了一位画家。

克劳德·洛林的画作中虽然绘有人物，但这些人物通常都很小，很不重要。画中的山水风景才是重点，其重要性甚至超过了普桑画作中的风景。因此，克劳德·洛林有时还被人们称为"风景绘画艺术之父"。相比于山水的秀丽，他更喜欢绘制大海的壮阔，因此我们也可以称他为海景画家呢。

The next important French painter lived about one hundred years later than Poussin and Lorrain. His name was Jean-Antoine Watteau. One of his more famous paintings, *Gersaint's Shop Sign*, was a sign for an art dealer.

Poor Watteau led a miserable life. In the beginning he was very poor. When he arrived in Paris to paint, he worked hard but he was paid so little that he almost starved. At last, when he had become well known as a painter and was making enough money to live comfortably, he was so ill that he could not enjoy himself much and sadly he died.

Now I'm telling you about the sad things of Watteau's life for this reason: The pictures he painted are just the opposite of sad. Instead of painting poor people, he painted young men and women clothed in silks and satins. Instead of painting hard-working people like himself, he only painted people having a good time — dancing, picnicking, playing at garden parties, and falling in love. Instead of painting sickly people like himself, he painted people who are almost too graceful and pretty and polite. No one could be quite so free from worries and cares as Watteau's people seem to be. When an artist paints a person to look better than he really could look, we call that an *idealized* view of the person.

Chardin was a French painter who was born a little later than Watteau. He, too, painted a shop sign. Perhaps he got the idea from Watteau, but Chardin's sign was for a surgeon's office instead of an art dealer. It showed a crowd of people in a street looking on while a surgeon binds up the wound of a man hurt in a sword fight.

Chardin liked to paint *still lifes*. Still lifes are pictures of objects that have no life to them, such as fruit, dead fish, cut flowers, pots, pans, and so on. He was also a portrait

接下来这位重要的法国画家，所处的时间比普桑和洛林大约晚了一百年。他名叫让-安东尼·华托。他较为著名的一幅画作，叫作《乔森特商店招牌》，是一家美术商店的店牌。

贫困的华托过着一种不幸的生活。起初他非常潦倒。而他到达巴黎开始绘画之后，虽说努力工作，但赚钱很少，因而总是挨饿。最后，当他成了一位声名赫赫的画家，并且赚了很多钱，生活过得很舒心之后，他却生了重病，根本无法享受生活，痛苦地去世了。

注意，我之所以给你们说华托生活中的可悲之事，原因在于：他所绘制的画作，风格却一点儿也不悲哀。他画的不是贫苦人民，而是穿着绫罗绸缎的年轻小伙子、小姑娘。他绘制的不是像他自己这种辛勤劳作的人，而是只描绘一些非常快乐的人；比如他们在跳舞啦，野餐啦，在花园里举行舞会啦，或者坠入了爱河。他绘制的不是像自己这样的病人，而是那些体态优美、漂亮、彬彬有礼的人。没有哪个人，能够像华托笔下的人物看起来那样豁达，那样无忧无虑。倘若一位画家描绘的某个人物看上去比实际的模样更好，那我们就称这是对那个人物一种理想化的呈现。

夏尔丹也是一位法国画家，他出生的时间，要比华托稍晚一点儿。他也绘制过一幅商店招牌画。或许，是华托给了他灵感吧；不过，夏尔丹绘制的，是一座诊所的招牌，而不是美术商店的招牌。这块招牌上描绘的，是大街上一群人正在看着一位医生给一名在决斗中受伤的男子包扎伤口时的情景。

夏尔丹很喜欢绘制静物画。所谓的静物画，是指其中所绘的是无生命之物的

玩陀螺的男孩，夏尔丹作品，
现存于巴黎的卢浮宫
（由波士顿的大学印刷协会提供）

painter.

But the third kind of painting that Chardin liked to do is the kind he is best known for — scenes of people inside their houses doing everyday things. Usually there are children in these pictures. One painting shows a mother teaching her little girls to say grace before meals. Another shows a mother telling her son to be careful with his new hat when he goes out. Yet another shows a little boy spinning a top on a table.

Though the people in Chardin's time dressed differently from us, we can say when we see his paintings, "They look like real, everyday people." We feel he didn't try to show us something astonishing or exciting but just ordinary scenes in ordinary French families.

画作，比如水果、死鱼、剪下的花朵、罐子、盘子，诸如此类。他还是一位肖像画家。

不过，夏尔丹喜欢绘制的第三种画作，也正是他最为人们称道的一种，就是人物在自己家里做日常之事的室内场景画。这些画作中，通常都有儿童的形象。有一幅画，描绘的是一位母亲教自己的小女儿在餐前做祷告时的情景。还有一幅画，描绘的是一位母亲告诉儿子出去时要小心自己的那顶新帽子时的情形。还有一幅，描绘的则是一个小男孩正在桌子上玩陀螺时的样子。

尽管在夏尔丹那个时代，人们的衣着与我们如今不同，但我们可以说，在看到他的画作后，“他们看起来都像是真正的、日常生活中的人物”。我们认为，夏尔丹并没有想要向我们呈现什么惊人的或者令人兴奋的东西，而只是向我们展示了普通的法国家庭日常生活中的普通场景。

Chapter 22 Stirring Times

It was the year 1793. Just a few years before in 1789, the French Revolution had overthrown the government of the King of France. The common people had stood hardships and injustice until they could stand them no more. Then they had forced the government to change. France was made a republic. The heads of hundreds of people — enemies of the republic — were being cut off. The king and his family had been put in prison. It was voted that they, too, should lose their heads.

One of the men who voted yes to the question "Shall the king be executed?" was Jacques Louis David. David was a painter. He believed the revolution was necessary even though he had been one of the court painters chosen by the king.

Some of the revolutionaries had read about the ancient Roman Republic that you have read about in your history books. They liked to think of themselves as being as strong and brave as the ancient Romans. And they liked to think of their new republic as being similar to the ancient Roman Republic. So it became the fashion in the revolution to imitate ancient Roman heroes.

David had actors in theaters wear Roman costumes instead of French clothes. Soon other people were dressing like the Romans. They even made their furniture in imitation of Roman furniture. David found that the people wanted Roman pictures so he painted many pictures of scenes from Roman history.

第22章 动荡的时代

此时正是1793年。就在几年之前，就在1789年，法国大革命推翻了王室政府对法国的统治。法国的普通民众已经承受了无数的艰难困苦和不公待遇，最终再也忍受不下去了。于是，他们便迫使政府进行了改革。法国被迫变成了一个共和国。成百上千名与共和国为敌的人，都被砍掉了脑袋。国王及其家人都被关进了监狱。后来经过投票决定，他们也应当被砍掉脑袋。

对“国王应当被处决吗？”这个问题投了赞成票的人当中，有一位就是雅克·路易·大卫。这个大卫，是一名画家。虽然他曾经是国王钦定的宫廷画师之一，但他认为革命是必需的。

有些革命者曾经阅读过古罗马共和国的历史，也就是你们如今在历史书中阅读到的古罗马共和国的历史。他们喜欢自认为像古罗马人那样强大和勇敢。并且他们认为，这个新的共和国与古时的罗马共和国很相似。因此，模仿古罗马时期的英雄人物，便成了这次革命中流行的做法。

大卫让剧院里的演员都穿着古罗马的服装，而不是法国服装。不久之后，其他人的穿着便都像古罗马人一样了。他们所用的家具，甚至也是仿制古罗马时期的家具。大卫发现，人们都很想购买古罗马时期的画作；于是，他便根据古罗马的历史，绘制了许多场景画。

Today David's paintings are not considered to be as wonderful as the revolutionaries thought them to be. But they are important because they set a style in painting. The ancient Roman and Greek days are known as the classical times, and so this style that David made so popular is called *neoclassicism*.

David and the other neoclassical artists said that no other kind of painting was worth doing. They made many rules for painting that they expected all good artists to follow. For example, the subject of a painting had to be important and worthy of being painted. A painting that shows a great historical moment was felt to be more worthy than one about everyday life. Another rule was that the surface of the picture had to be smooth and sleek so that you could hardly see the brushstrokes the artist had made.

David had begun painting pictures of the Romans even before the revolution. One of these paintings is called *The Oath of the Horatii*.

If you have read your Roman history carefully, you will remember that the Horatii were three brothers who were champion fighters. Rome was at war with another city. Instead of letting the two armies fight, which would have meant the death of many men, each side agreed to pick three fighters and let them fight it out to see

贺拉斯兄弟的誓言，大卫作品，
现存于巴黎的卢浮宫
（由缅因州桑福德的大学印刷协会提供）

如今，人们觉得大卫的画作并不像当时的革命者所认为的那样奇妙了。不过，他的画作还是很重要，因为它们开创了一种绘画风格。由于古罗马和古希腊时期被称为古典主义时代，因此由大卫推广开来的这种风格，便被称为“新古典主义风格”。

大卫和别的新古典主义画家都称，其他形式的绘画风格都毫无价值。他们制定了许多的绘画规则，并且希望所有优秀的画家都遵循这些规则。例如，绘画对象必须很重要，有绘画的价值才是。他们认为，一幅描绘重大历史场合的画作，要比一幅描绘日常生活场景的画作更有价值。另一条规则，就是画作的表面必须流畅平滑，从而让观众几乎看不出画家所运用的笔触来。

还是在法国大革命爆发之前，大卫就开始创作绘画了。他在这一时期创作的绘画当中，有一幅叫作《贺拉斯兄弟的誓言》。

假如仔细学习过古罗马的历史，那你们就会记得，贺拉斯兄弟有三个，他们都是在战斗中获胜的斗士。当时，罗马正与另一个城邦交战。双方并没有让两个城邦的军队开战，因为那样就会带来大量的伤亡，而是同意双方各派三名战士，让他们相互格斗，看哪个城邦应当赢得此次战争。

罗马这一方派出的就是贺拉斯三兄弟；他们发下庄严的誓言，要为罗马赢得胜

which city should win the war.

The Romans chose the three Horatii brothers, who took a solemn oath to win for Rome or die trying. David's picture shows them taking this oath. When the fight was over, two of the brothers had been killed. But the third had managed to kill the other three fighters and win the war for Rome.

David was also a portrait painter. He painted a portrait of a French lady named Madame Récamier. She is shown lying on a couch. The couch is Roman in style and the Madame Recamier's dress shows the type of Roman fashions that French women wore then.

David painted a portrait of his friend Marat, who was killed during the French Revolution in a most unusual assassination — while sitting in his bathtub with a wet cloth on his head! David shows the dead Marat with only a drop of red for blood, and we feel that we are in the presence of a hero cut down in his prime. Other pictures of this scene show the maids, dogs, piles of books, and all sorts of things. But David decided to portray only the most important parts of the scene in order to heighten the moment.

After the revolution came Napoleon. Napoleon made himself Emperor of France. David admired Napoleon greatly and painted several pictures of him. He painted him on a battlefield, and he painted him on a rearing horse, crossing the Alps.

One of the most interesting paintings of Napoleon is of his coronation, or crowning.

利，否则就尽力战死。大卫的这幅画作，描绘的就是他们发下这一誓言时的情景。格斗结束后，其中的两兄弟战死了。不过，第三位兄弟却成功地杀死了对方的三名战士，从而为罗马打赢了这场战争。

大卫也是一位肖像画家。他曾经为一位名叫雷卡米娅夫人的法国贵妇绘制过一幅肖像。画作中，雷卡米娅夫人正倚在一张躺椅上。这张躺椅是古罗马风格的，而雷卡米娅夫人身上的服装，则正是当时法国女性所穿的、古罗马式的服装。

大卫还给他的朋友马拉[1]绘制了一幅肖像。马拉在法国大革命中被人刺杀了；那是一次极其不同寻常的暗杀行动，因为马拉遇刺时，正坐在浴缸里，头上盖着一块湿布。大卫描绘了死去的马拉，画上只有一滴红红的鲜血；而我们在观看这幅画作时，都会觉得身临其境，仿佛自己就站在这位壮年英雄被刺杀的现场似的。其他描绘这一场景的画作当中，还有女仆、小狗、一堆堆的书籍，以及其他各种各样的东西。但大卫决定只绘制出这一场景中最重要的那些部位，以便增强这一场合本身的重要性。

法国大革命过后，拿破仑上台了。后来，拿破仑还自行加冕，成了法国皇帝。大卫极其崇拜拿破仑，因而创作了好几幅表现拿破仑的画作。他创作过战场上的拿破仑肖像，也创作过描绘拿破仑骑在一匹殿后的战马上，翻越阿尔卑斯山脉时的画作。

在描绘拿破仑的那些画作中，最有意思的一幅，便是描绘他的加冕礼，或者说

---

[1] 马拉（Jean Paul Marat，1743—1793），瑞士裔法国革命家，他于1789年创办了《人民之友报》，支持法国大革命。1792年他被选为国民公会成员，但在第二年被一名吉伦特分子刺杀身亡。

The pope had traveled from Rome to Paris for the ceremony at the Cathedral of Notre Dame. Napoleon was expected to kneel in front of the pope, bow his head, and wait for the pope to crown him to show that France was under the religious leadership of the Roman Catholic Church. But Napoleon surprised everyone. He approached the pope, remained standing, took the crown from the pope's hands, and in front of everyone, crowned his own head!

David's huge painting shows Napoleon crowning his wife. To be sure everyone knew of the power he now had, even more than the church, Napoleon's mother is painted into the picture as if she were there to see such an historic moment. But in truth, she had passed away before that time.

After Napoleon came another king. Although this new king was from the same family as the poor king who had lost his head, David wasn't a court painter to him — not after having voted for the old king's death! In fact, David had to run away from France and lived in Brussels, Belgium, for the rest of his life.

But the strict rules of the neoclassical style of art lived on. David had many students, and some of them became famous painters too. One of these students was the artist Ingres.

Ingres was a wonderful draftsman. That means the lines that he drew were beautifully done. He thought more about the lines in a picture than the color or the light. All neoclassical painters tried to make the lines and shapes in their pictures more important

描绘他的登基典礼的画作。当时，教皇还从罗马赶到了巴黎，来参加在巴黎圣母院举行的这场典礼呢。拿破仑本应在教皇面前跪下，低下头，等待教皇给他加冕，以示法国服从罗马天主教会的宗教领导。可拿破仑却让所有的人都大吃了一惊。他走到教皇身边，依然直立着，从教皇手中接过皇冠，然后当着众人的面，把皇冠戴到了自己的头上！

大卫有一幅巨型画作，描绘了拿破仑给他的妻子加冕时的情形。为了确保所有的人都明白他此时所拥有的巨大权力，明白他的权力甚至大过了教会，大卫还把拿破仑的母亲也绘进了画中，仿佛她是在那里见证这一历史时刻似的。可实际上，她在此时之前早已去世了。

拿破仑之后，法国又有过一位国王。尽管这位新国王是之前那位可怜的、掉了脑袋的国王的家人，但大卫却不再是他的御用画师了；自从他投票赞成处死那位老国王之后，他就不再是御用画师了！事实上，大卫还不得不逃离法国，在比利时的布鲁塞尔度过了自己的余生。

不过，新古典主义艺术风格那些严格的规则，却继续延续下来了。大卫收了很多的学生，其中一些后来也都成了伟大的画家。这些学生当中，有一位便是画家安格尔。

安格尔简直就是一位令人称奇的绘图员。这是说，他绘制的线条非常完美。相比于色彩或者光线来说，他考虑得更多的，就是画中的线条。所有的新古典主义画家，都是尽力让画作中的线条和形状显得比色彩更加重要。因此，他们画作中的色彩，都是很不鲜明、很呆板的。

安格尔最为人称道的，很可能就是他绘制的肖像画了。而他只用铅笔绘制，根

than the colors. So their colors are dull and lifeless.

Ingres is probably best known for his portraits. And the portraits that he drew in pencil and did not paint at all show how great a draftsman he was. He made magnificent drawings even as a teenager!

Now we come to a French painter who did not believe at all in neoclassical painting. The strict rules that the neoclassical painters said all artists should follow made this artist rebel. He was Delacroix. Delacroix led a revolt against the neoclassical style of painting. Painters who thought as Delacroix did were called *romanticists*.

The romanticists didn't see any sense in painting Greeks and Romans. They wanted to paint what was going on in the world at that time. The romanticists revolted against the neoclassical style in another way. They believed in color. They thought color, not line, was the fundamental principle in painting.

Of course the neoclassical painters disagreed with the romanticists and tried to do all they could to stop them. But Delacroix and his followers became more and more popular, and finally they took the place that the neoclassical artists had once held.

Delacroix painted pictures of the Crusaders, Bible stories, northern Africans, the war between the Greeks and the Turks, and many other subjects. His picture *Christ on the Sea of Galilee* shows a scene from the Bible. Delacroix's drawing was not always as good as that of other artists but his coloring was very good indeed. And since his time, many painters have agreed with his idea that painting is all about color.

本就没有再用画笔添色的那些素描肖像画，正好说明了他是多么伟大的一位制图员。甚至还是在十几岁的时候，他就已经创作出了许多绝妙的画作呢！

现在，我们再来说一说一位根本就不信奉新古典主义绘画规则的法国画家。新古典主义画家称所有画家都应当遵循的那些严格规则，使这位画家产生了反感。这位画家，就是德拉克洛瓦。德拉克洛瓦领导了一场反抗新古典主义绘画风格的革命。而那些与德拉克洛瓦想法相同的画家，则被称为“浪漫主义派”。

浪漫主义派认为，绘制古希腊和古罗马风格的画作没有任何意义。他们希望创作的，是关于当时世界上正在发生的事情的画作。在另一个方面，浪漫主义派画家也很反感新古典主义风格。他们崇尚色彩。他们认为，绘画艺术的基本原则是色彩，而非线条。

新古典主义画家自然并不同意浪漫主义派的这些观点，因而竭尽全力地要阻止他们。但是，德拉克洛瓦及其追随者变得越来越受人们欢迎，并且最终取代了新古典主义派一度拥有过的地位。

德拉克洛瓦创作过关于十字军、《圣经》故事、北非人、希腊人与土耳其人的战争以及其他许多主题的画作。他的画作《加利利海[1]上的基督》，描绘的就是《圣经》中的一个场景。虽说德拉克洛瓦的画作并非总是像其他画家的作品那样优秀，但他对于色彩的运用，的确非常娴熟呢。而自他那个时代以来，许多画家实际上都已经认同了他的观点，即绘画只与色彩相关的观点。

[1] 加利利海（the Sea of Galilee），即位于以色列和叙利亚之间的太巴列湖（Lake Tiberias）。加利利是以色列北部的一个地区，曾是基督教徒心中的圣地之一。

加利利海上的基督，德拉克洛瓦作品，
现存于马里兰州巴尔的摩的沃尔特斯艺术博物馆

Another painting by Delacroix is called *Liberty Leading the People*. It depicts a scene that took place in the streets of Paris in 1830 when, once again, there was fighting between the people and the soldiers of the king. It is a stirring picture, full of action and movement. One lady is larger than everyone else in the picture because she is not a real person like the others in the painting. Rather she represents the idea of Freedom and Liberty.

But the painting has a double meaning. The neoclassical style of painting that tried to keep all other styles of painting out of France needed to be overthrown too. And this picture may be thought of as Liberty leading romantic art against the too- strict rules of neoclassical art.

德拉克洛瓦创作的另一幅油画，叫作《自由领导人民》。这幅画作，描绘的是1830年巴黎街头发生的一幕。当时，巴黎人民与国王手下的军队再次爆发了战斗。这是一幅描绘动荡场景的画作，其中充满了动感。在画作中，有位女士的形象比其他人物都大，因为她与画作中的其他人不一样，不是一个真正的人物。她象征着自由和解放的观念。

不过，这幅油画有着双重含义。那种试图将其他绘画风格通通赶出法国的新古典主义绘画风格，也需要推翻才行。而这幅画作，也可以看成是自由女神正在领导着浪漫主义艺术，反抗新古典主义那些严格的规则。

Chapter 23 A Late Start

Do you know what an international painting exhibition is? It is a group of pictures brought together from different countries so that people can see how alike and how different the paintings are.

Imagine it's the year 1700 and all the great countries in western Europe have decided to hold an international painting exhibition. We'll call it a make-believe show because the various countries never thought of such a thing in those days. So let's make our own rules. Each country can send only one picture and the best will get a prize.

Now let's say that all the paintings have arrived.

A Titian from Venice	威尼斯的提香 1幅
A Michelangelo from Rome	罗马的米开朗琪罗 1幅
A Velásquez from Spain	西班牙的委拉斯贵兹 1幅
A Rubens from Flanders	佛兰德斯的鲁本斯 1幅
A Rembrandt from the Netherlands	尼德兰的伦勃朗 1幅
A Dürer from Germany	德国的丢勒 1幅
A Poussin from France	法国的普珊 1幅

But where is England's picture? Every important country except England has sent a famous painting.

Now in 1700 England is one of the greatest countries. But all we got from England is a letter saying that she is very sorry but she can't send us a picture by a famous English artist because they do not have any famous artists. What? One of the greatest countries in

第23章 迟来的发端

你们知道国际美术展览是什么吗？所谓的国际美术展览，就是将不同国家的画作聚集到一起，从而让人们能够看出，各国的画作有哪些相似之处，又有哪些不同之处。

假设现在是公元1700年，西欧各个大国都决定举办一次国际美术展览。我们将其称为一次虚构的展览，因为当时的各国其实从未想过要举办这样的一次展览呢。因此，不妨让我们自己来制定参展规则。每个国家都只能送一幅画作参展，而最佳画作则会获得奖品。

现在，我们不妨假定所有的画作都已经抵达展览现场。

可是，英国的参展画作在哪里呢？除了英国，每一个重要国家都已经送来了一幅名作。

注意，在公元1700年的时候，英国已经是欧洲最大的国家之一了。可我们只收到了英国寄过来的一封信，说抱歉得很，该国无法送来一幅由著名的英国画家绘制的画作，因为英国根本没有什么著名画家。什么？位居欧洲最大国家之列的英国竟

Europe has no painters? It is true: England was a country mostly of words, not of pictures.

Though England had had no famous painters by 1700, she soon made up for lost time. Her first famous artist was three years old in 1700. His name was Hogarth. And after Hogarth came other artists. If we had held our make-believe international picture show in 1800, England would have had plenty of paintings to choose from.

Hogarth began as an engraver of silver. Then he learned to engrave on copper and make prints from his copper plates. These prints were very popular and he sold enough of them to make a good living. But all the time he wanted to be a painter. So he painted pictures, but he was so well known as a printmaker that very few people considered him a great painter. They preferred his prints and engravings. He found that he could make engravings of his paintings and sell the prints much more readily than the paintings themselves. Today we think of him as a great painter — the first great English painter.

Probably all students like to read the comics. A newspaper comic strip is generally quickly and roughly drawn. You could hardly call it fine art. And yet Hogarth used the same idea as the comics in some of his paintings. He made a series of six or eight pictures about the same people that showed what happened to them over time. But in addition to being funny, Hogarth's pictures also revealed how bad certain things were in England at that time. This kind of humor is called *satire*.

Hogarth printed one series of pictures about a man who was trying to be elected to Parliament. One picture shows the man making a speech. Another shows him hiring men

然没有画家？是的，当时的英国，主要是一个文学发达的国家，而不是一个绘画艺术发达的国家。

尽管英国到公元1700年的时候还没有出现什么著名的画家，可该国不久便迎头赶上来了。该国第一位著名的画家，公元1700年还只有三岁大哩。这位画家，名叫贺加斯。而贺加斯之后，又涌现出了许多其他的画家。如果我们把这次假想的国际绘画展放到公元1800年来举行，那么英国可以选择来参展的画作就很多了。

贺加斯起初是一位银器雕刻师。接下来，他又学会了雕制铜器，学会了用铜版来制作版画。这些铜版画很受人们欢迎，因此他出售了很多，生活变得优裕起来。但是，他一直都想要当一名画家。因此，他也绘制过画作；不过，由于他是一位赫赫有名的版画大师，所以很少有人认为他是一个伟大的画家。人们更喜欢他的版画。后来他发现，他可以将自己绘制的画作制成版画；而卖掉这些版画，也要比卖掉他的画作更加容易呢。如今，我们认为他既是一个伟大的画家，也是英国第一位伟大的画家。

十有八九，所有的同学都喜欢看漫画作品。报纸上的连环漫画，通常都是在短时间里草草画出来的。可是，贺加斯在他的一些画作中，却运用了与连环漫画相同的手法。他曾绘制过由六张或八张画作构成一套的作品；这些画作中的人物都相同，用以说明在一段时间内这些人物身上发生的事情。不过，除了有趣，贺加斯的画作也揭露了当时英国一些极其不好的现象。这种幽默，就称为讽刺。

贺加斯曾经绘制过一套讽刺画，描绘了一个人想方设法要当选议员的经过。其中一幅画描绘的是那个人正在演讲。另一幅画描绘的是他雇用了一些手持棍棒

with clubs to force people to vote for him. And another shows him bribing voters — that is, paying them to vote for him.

Each of the pictures is a good painting by itself but the whole series was supposed to be seen together like the different pictures in a comic strip. And these pictures made a great impression on the Englishmen of Hogarth's time. Perhaps they did help make things better as Hogarth hoped they would. Nowadays elections are certainly run as fairly in England as anywhere in the world.

Hogarth painted portraits too. He painted a portrait of himself with his little dog. He also painted *The Shrimp Girl*. Today we buy shrimp in a store or at the market, but in London in Hogarth's time, people bought shrimp from girls who carried them around in a basket on their heads.

Hogarth has caught the shrimp girl's smile as Hals caught the smiles in the portraits he painted — with quick, sure strokes of the brush. If you put this painting side by side with Dürer's portrait of his father, it looks unfinished. And yet it tells you as

卖虾姑娘，贺加斯作品，
现存于伦敦的国家美术馆
（由波士顿的大学印刷协会提供）

的人，正在强迫人们投票选他。还有一幅画，则描绘了他正在贿赂选民，即付钱给选民，让选民选他时的情景。

虽说其中每张图片本身都是一幅优秀的画作，但整套图画应当连起来看，就像一期连环漫画里不同的图片似的。因而，这些画作给贺加斯那个时代的英国人留下了深刻的印象。或许，他们的确像贺加斯所希望的那样，在看了这些画作之后，的确促进了社会形势的进步。如今，英国的选举当然与世界上其他地方一样，已经非常公正了。

贺加斯也绘制过肖像画。他曾经绘制了一张他带着小狗的自画像。他还绘制了一幅《卖虾姑娘》。如今，我们都是去商店或者市场里买虾，可在贺加斯那个时代的伦敦，人们却是从那些把装着小虾的篮子顶在头上、四处走动的姑娘们手里买虾呢。

贺加斯用迅速而坚定的数笔，捕捉到了卖虾姑娘脸上的笑容，就像哈尔斯在他绘制的肖像画中捕捉到了人物的微笑那样。假如你们将这幅画与丢勒给他父亲所画的肖像画并排放到一起的话，那么这幅画就像还没有画完似的。尽管如此，它却让你们了解到了真实生活中那位卖虾姑娘的情况，就像丢勒的那幅肖像画让你们了解

much about the real shrimp girl as Dürer's picture tells you about his father. I like it that way. Do you?

About the middle of the eighteenth century, while Hogarth was still painting, two other Englishmen were rising to fame as great painters. One was Sir Joshua Reynolds and the other, Thomas Gainsborough. Both were best known as portrait painters. Sir Joshua Reynolds was a few years older than Thomas Gainsborough, and so I'll tell you about him first.

I'll begin this story with an African pirate. But please don't get excited. There isn't a pirate fight in the story, much as I know you'd like to hear one. The pirate was holding up ships in the Mediterranean. The British sent a captain with a squadron of ships to talk things over with the pirate.

悲剧女神西登斯夫人，雷诺兹作品，
现存于圣马力诺的亨廷顿藏品馆
（由波士顿的大学印刷协会提供）

Now the captain was a friend of Reynolds' and he invited the artist to come along on his warship. Reynolds accepted the invitation, and when he got to Italy, he stayed there to study the great paintings of Michelangelo, Titian, Correggio, and Raphael. He liked Michelangelo best, and so he spent a lot of time in the Sistine Chapel studying Michelangelo's paintings.

Reynolds went back to London and

到了他的父亲一样。我很喜欢这种风格。你们喜不喜欢呢？

差不多到了十八世纪中叶，当贺加斯仍在绘画的时候，有两个英国人即将成名，变成伟大的画家。其中一位是乔舒亚·雷诺兹勋爵，而另一位则是托马斯·庚斯博罗。两人都以肖像画最为著称。乔舒亚·雷诺兹勋爵比托马斯·庚斯博罗年长几岁，因此我将先给你们介绍他的情况。

我要从一个非洲海盗说起。不过，请大家不要激动。这个故事里并没有海盗打仗的情节，尽管我也清楚得很，你们都喜欢听这种情节。这名海盗，当时正在地中海上拦截和劫掠过往船只。英国便派了一名上校，率领一支舰队，去与那名海盗谈判。

注意，这位上校是雷诺兹的一个朋友；他邀请雷诺兹登上战舰，与他一同前往。雷诺兹接受了邀请；而当他抵达意大利后，便留在那里研究米开朗琪罗、提香、科雷乔和拉斐尔等大师的伟大画作。他最喜欢米开朗琪罗的作品，因此在西斯廷教堂花了大量的时间，对米开朗琪罗的画作进行了研究。

雷诺兹回到伦敦后，成了该市最受人欢迎的肖像画家。由于当时还没有发明照

became the favorite portrait painter of the city. There were still no cameras in those days so no one could have a photograph taken. Instead, people went to an artist and had their portraits painted. Poor people could not afford portraits by such an expensive painter as Reynolds so most of his portraits are of lords and ladies and their children.

The king knighted him and he became known as Sir Joshua Reynolds. Sir Joshua worked hard and tried to make every picture he painted better than the one before. He was especially good at painting women and children.

Unfortunately Reynolds was always trying out new kinds of paints and oils so many of his pictures have become faded or cracked. Some even faded soon after he painted them. But this didn't make him less popular. A friend of his said, "A faded portrait by Reynolds is better than a fresh one by anybody else."

The following picture of angel heads by Sir Joshua Reynolds shows five different views of the same little girl.

The other portrait painter, Thomas Gainsborough, made the people he painted look so graceful and charming in their portraits that he was in great demand. Gainsborough's colors are not so rich and glowing as Reynolds'. Instead they are more silvery and gray.

天使头像，雷诺兹作品，
现存于伦敦的国家美术馆
（由波士顿的大学印刷协会提供）

相机，因此人们都没法照相。于是，人们便请来画家，让画家把他们的肖像绘制下来。由于穷人没钱雇请像雷诺兹这样收费昂贵的画家来画肖像，因此他的绝大多数画作，都是贵族、贵妇及其孩子们的肖像画。

英国国王授予了他爵位，于是他便摇身一变，成了乔舒亚·雷诺兹勋爵。乔舒亚勋爵工作勤奋，尽力让自己绘制的每一幅画作都比前一幅优秀。他尤其擅长于描绘女性和儿童的形象。

可惜的是，由于雷诺兹一直都在尝试新的画风和颜料，因此他的许多画作后来都褪了色，或者开裂了。他的有些画作甚至刚刚绘制好，很快就褪色了。不过，这一点并没有让他失去人们的青睐。他的一位朋友曾经说过：“雷诺兹一幅褪了色的肖像画，也比其他任何人刚刚绘制出来的画作要好。”

下面这幅由乔舒亚·雷诺兹勋爵绘制的天使头像画，呈现了对同一个小姑娘的五种不同的视角。

另一位肖像画家托马斯·庚斯博罗，则将肖像画中的人物都绘制得极其优雅、迷人，因此请他的人络绎不绝。庚斯博罗画中所用的色彩，并不像雷诺兹的画作那样丰富和亮丽。相反，他的画作较多使用银色和灰色。

西登斯夫人，根兹伯罗作品，
现存于伦敦的国家美术馆
（由波士顿的大学印刷协会提供）

Gainsborough painted portraits of many of the same people that Reynolds did. They both, for example, painted Mrs. Siddons. It would be hard to say which of the portraits of these two ladies is better. Which one do you prefer?

庚斯博罗为许多的人绘制过肖像画，而他们也正是雷诺兹为之绘制肖像的那些人。比如，庚斯博罗和雷诺兹都为西登斯夫人[1]绘制过肖像。我们很难说，他们各自绘制的那两幅贵妇肖像中，哪一幅更好。你们喜欢哪一幅呢？

[1] 西登斯夫人（Sarah Siddons，1755—1831），英国著名的女演员，因其扮演莎士比亚剧作中的人物角色，尤其是麦克白夫人这一角色而著称。

Chapter 24 Three Englishmen Who Were Different

Ghosts! Do you like ghost stories? Stories of haunted houses, chains clanking at midnight, misty white shapes that you can see right through? Of course the best time to read a ghost story is at night. Then, though you know the story can't be true, it makes you feel creepy.

But I'll tell you of one ghost that won't make you feel creepy. This ghost won't even make you tremble in your boots. It's the ghost of a flea. It makes one smile just to think of the ghost of a flea coming back to haunt perhaps the dog who scratched him to death. This flea ghost isn't in a ghost story. He's a more unusual ghost than that, for this ghost had his portrait drawn by a celebrated artist.

The artist who drew the picture of *The Ghost of a Flea* was William Blake. He was an Englishman who was living in London at the time the American colonies were fighting their Revolutionary War.

William Blake was very different from any artist I've told you about so far. For one thing, besides being an artist, he was a poet. For another thing, William Blake's pictures are not at all like the pictures of any other artist. For still another thing, William Blake saw visions. A vision is something like a dream — it is a sight a person sees only in his mind. Some people say that Blake was a little crazy. Perhaps he was only different.

Blake had always wanted to be an artist. He studied engraving for many years until he

第24章 风格迥异的三位英国画家

幽灵鬼怪！你们喜欢听鬼故事吗？喜欢听那种关于闹鬼的房子、半夜里有铁链子叮当作响、有一眼就能看个对穿的模糊人影的故事吗？读鬼故事的最佳时间，当然是在晚上。这样的话，就算你们知道故事不可能是真的，但也会让你们觉得毛骨悚然呢。

不过，我会跟你们说说一个并不会让你们觉得毛骨悚然的鬼。这个鬼，甚至不会让你们双腿打战哩。这是一只跳蚤鬼。一只跳蚤鬼回来到处游荡，让原来可能是挠死了它的那条狗不得安宁；只要想一想这个，就会让人觉得很好笑。这只跳蚤鬼可不是鬼故事里的主角。它比平常的鬼更加不同寻常，因为有位著名的画家还为这只鬼绘制了一幅肖像画呢。

创作这幅《跳蚤鬼》的画家，就是威廉·布莱克。他是英国人，住在伦敦；当时，正值美洲诸殖民地进行革命战争的那个时代。

威廉·布莱克与迄今为止我给你们介绍过的所有画家都大不相同。一方面，他除了身为画家，还是一位诗人。另一方面，威廉·布莱克创作出来的画作，与其他所有画家的画作一点儿都不相同。第三，威廉·布莱克看得见幻象。所谓的幻象，有点儿像是梦境，也就是一个人只能在脑海里才看得到的景象。有些人说，布莱克的精神有点儿不正常。或许，他只是与众不同罢了。

布莱克一直都希望成为一名画家。他学习了多年的版画技术，后来成了一名非

became an expert engraver. And then when he set up in business for himself, he engraved his poems and his pictures together on one copper plate. This was a new idea that he himself invented. Before then, the pictures in a book were engraved on a metal plate but the words of the book were printed with a printing press. Blake made both pictures and words on the same plate, so the story was really part of the pictures and the pictures were part of the story.

He made and engraved pictures not only for his own poems but for many other books also. The most famous of all his pictures are the ones he made to illustrate the Book of Job in the Bible. The pictures of Job and his troubles are hard to forget once you have seen them. Every time I think of Job, I think of the pictures that Blake made.

Most of Blake's pictures that you see in books look like drawings. That is because they are made up of lines. An engraving has to be made with lines. But Blake generally made a painting for each picture before he engraved it, and these paintings show he could use colors as well as lines.

Blake had new ideas about painting, and soon there were other English artists who had new ideas. One such painter was John Constable who tried to give his pictures the

主在旋风中回答约伯的祈祷，
布莱克作品，
现存于爱丁堡的苏格兰国家美术馆
（由波士顿的大学印刷协会提供）

常专业的版画师。然后，待亲自开业从事版画制作之后，他便将自己的诗作和画作都刻在一张铜版上。这个新点子，是他亲自发明出来的。在此之前，书籍上的插画是用金属制版，而书籍中的文字则是用印刷机印刷的。布莱克将图画和文字刻在同一块版上，使得书籍所讲述的故事真正成了图画的一部分，而图画也成了故事的一部分。

他不但为自己的诗作制作版画，还给其他许多的书籍制作了版画。他所有的画作中，最著名的便是为《圣经》中的《约伯记》所作的插图。一旦你们看过这些插图，约伯的形象和他所经历的种种困苦，便再也难以忘怀了。每当我想到约伯，都会想起布莱克绘制的那些画作来呢。

你们在书籍中看到的，由布莱克创作的绝大多数画作，看起来都像是素描画。那是因为，这些画作都是用线条构成的。版画只能用线条来绘制。不过，布莱克在制作版画之前，通常都会绘制出每幅版画的油画原作；而这些油画原作，说明除了线条，他也能将色彩运用得非常娴熟。

布莱克在绘画艺术方面有很多的新想法，而不久之后，英国其他的画家也萌发出了新的念头。这些画家当中，有一位便是约翰·康斯太勃尔；他试图在画作中呈现出自己在现实风景中所见到的色彩。这一点，说起来容易，做起来就难了。即便

colors he saw in real landscapes. This sounds easier to do than it really is. Even the whitest white a painter can put in a picture isn't nearly as bright as a dull sky on a rainy day. And if the picture sky can't be as bright as the real sky is, all the other colors have to be made a little darker than the real colors to make the sky look bright enough. For the darker the dark parts of a picture are, the brighter the bright parts will look next to them.

Being darker doesn't keep the picture from being beautiful but it does keep it from looking exactly like the real landscape. And if a way could be found to make the colors in a painting look brighter, then artists could make an outdoor picture look more real. And that is what Constable did. He found a way to make paints look brighter. Instead of putting the paint on smoothly, he put it on in little dabs of thick color, so that if you were allowed to touch one of his paintings with your finger, it would feel rough.

Constable found that when he used little dabs or spots of color the whole picture became brighter. The old way of painting a green field, for instance, was to paint it all green. Constable's way was to paint the field with separate little spots of green and yellow and blue. And strange to say, these make the field look all green, unless you get too close to the picture. When you do get too close, you can see the separate spots, but at a little distance, the whole field becomes one color — a brighter green than if it had been painted a smooth, solid color in the first place.

My gracious! If you have read all that, you are a good reader! So we remember Constable for improving landscape painting. He made pictures brighter by using rough little spots of paint in place of smooth, solid colors.

是画家能够在画作中运用最白的白色，也不会像下雨时的阴暗天空那么鲜亮。而若是画作中的天空无法像真正的天空那样明亮的话，那么其他的所有色彩就必须比实际的色彩稍暗一点儿，才能让画中的天空看上去足够鲜亮。因为画作中的暗部越暗，那么与之相邻的亮部看上去就会显得越亮。

颜色较暗，虽说并不意味着会让画作不漂亮，但会让画作看上去与真正的景色不一样。因此，倘若能够找到一种方法，使画作中的色彩看上去鲜亮的话，那么画家绘制的户外风景画便会显得更加逼真了。康斯太勃尔所致力的，就是这个方面。他找到了一种让画作显得更鲜亮的方法。他并不是用颜料在画布上平滑作画，而是用画笔蘸着浓丽的颜料，一点一点地轻拍在画布上；因此，倘若允许你们用手指去摸一摸他的画作，那你们就会发现，感觉是很粗糙的。

康斯太勃尔发现，要是用小笔颜料或点状颜料绘制的话，整幅画作就会变得更加亮丽。比如，在绘制一片绿地时，原来的办法是将这块地全都绘成绿色。而康斯太勃尔的方法，却是分别用一个个绿色、黄色和蓝色的点状来绘制这片绿地。说来也怪，这样做竟然会让整片土地看上去全都是绿色，除非你们贴到画作边上去细看。虽说靠得很近的时候，人们能够看出这些独立的点状颜料，可要是离得稍远一点儿的话，整片土地便变成了一种颜色，变成了一种比原先用平滑而一致的颜料去绘制后更加鲜亮的绿色。

我的老天啊！如果把上面所有的内容都看完了，那你们可真是一个不错的读者呢！因此，我们要记住康斯太勃尔，因为他改进了风景画的绘画艺术。他用粗糙

Many people believe the best English painter was the landscape painter Turner — Joseph Mallord William Turner. He came nearer than any other painter to catching the brightness of color and natural light. He loved to paint the sea and the Sun.

Now of course the Sun itself is so much brighter than any paint that no one can ever put it in a picture and expect it to look like the real dazzling, brilliant Sun. But a painter can paint something that people will know is meant to be the Sun. Turner often did something that Claude Lorrain had sometimes done. He painted into the Sun. That is, he painted a scene with the Sun ahead of him instead of behind him. Generally he put the Sun behind a cloud or in a mist or at sunset so that its brightness would not look too unlike the brightness of the real Sun.

We know very well that no painter can find bright enough colors for a sunset, but people who saw Turner's sunset pictures said they were too bright to be true. They aren't true but not because they are too bright, as these people said. It is because they aren't bright enough.

Turner could also paint the sea maybe better than anyone before him. He was a painter of seascapes as well as landscapes. Before he

干草车，康斯太勃尔作品，
现存于伦敦的国家美术馆
（由波士顿的大学印刷协会提供）

的小点状颜料，取代了纯粹、一致的色彩，把画作绘制得更加亮丽了。

许多人都认为，英国最优秀的画家是风景画家透纳，即约瑟夫·马洛德·威廉·透纳。他的画作，比其他所有画家都更加真切地捕捉到了色彩和自然光线的亮丽。他很喜欢创作关于大海和太阳的画作呢。

注意，太阳本身自然会比任何画作上的太阳要亮得多，因此没有人能够让画作中的太阳像真正的太阳那样耀眼和灿烂。不过，一位画家却能够绘制出一个太阳，让人们都认为那必定就是太阳。透纳经常干的，就是克劳德·洛林有时偶尔为之的事情。他经常将太阳补入画中。也就是说，在他绘制的风景画中，太阳总是位于人物之前，而不是在人物之后。他通常会将太阳画在云层后面，或者薄雾当中，或者描绘日落时的情景；这样一来，画作中太阳的亮度，看上去就不会与真太阳的亮度相差太大了。

我们都很清楚，任何画家都找不到亮度足够的色彩，来绘制日落时的情景；可是，人们在看过透纳的日落画作之后，都说这些画作太亮，简直令人难以置信。不过，之所以令人难以置信，并不是因为它们像这些人所说的那样太亮。这是因为，画作中的色彩还不够亮。

透纳所画的海洋风景，可能也比前人更加优秀。他既创作过陆地风景画，也绘

战舰“无畏号”，透纳作品，
现存于伦敦的国家美术馆
（由波士顿的大学印刷协会提供）

painted the sea he really studied it — how it looked when it was calm and how it looked in a storm, how it looked in the rain and how it looked in sunshine. Once he even had himself lashed tight to the mast of a ship in a storm so he could study the sea without being washed overboard.

One of Turner's most famous paintings is called *The Fighting Temeraire* because that was the name of the old warship in the picture. The *Temeraire* had become too old for further use and the picture shows her being towed by a puffing tug to the dock for salvaging. It is sunset and the water of the harbor reflects the gorgeous orange and yellow of the sky. It is the end of the day and the end of usefulness for the old ship that has served her country for many years.

Hopefully, one day you will be able to see the painting at the National Gallery in London. Then you will get an idea of the brilliant sunset that Turner painted.

制过海上风景画。事实上，他在描绘海洋的风景之前，还进行过仔细的研究，即研究海上风平浪静时是个什么样子，海上暴风肆虐时又是个什么情景，雨中的大海是个什么样子，艳阳高照时海上又是个什么样子。有一次，他甚至还将自己紧紧捆在暴风雨中一艘船只的桅杆上，从而可以在不被冲上甲板的大浪卷走的情况下，仔细地观察大海呢。

透纳最著名的画作之一，叫作《战舰“无畏号”》，因为画中那艘旧战船的名字，就叫“无畏号”。当时，“无畏号”太过老旧，没法再用了；而这幅画作，描绘的就是这艘战舰被一条喷着烟雾的拖轮拖向船坞，准备回收时的场景。当时正值日落时分，港口里的海面上，倒映出了黄昏天空中那种绚烂瑰丽的橙色和黄色。此时，正是一日的终结，也是那艘为祖国服役了多年的战舰的终结。

但愿，你们有朝一日能够在伦敦的国家美术馆里看到这幅画作。那样的话，你们就会认识到透纳绘制的那种精彩绝伦的日落景象了。

Chapter 25 Some Very Poor Painters

Why should I tell you about very poor painters? If a painter can't paint good pictures, why mention him at all? Well, because these poor painters in this chapter did paint good pictures. They were poor in money, not poor in painting.

One of these poor, good painters was a Frenchman named Corot. He was poor because no one would buy his paintings. Not until he was fifty years old did he sell a single picture. He wasn't quite as poor as that sounds, however, because his father gave him an allowance every year. It was a very small allowance, but Corot managed to get along on it.

After Corot finished school, he wanted to be a painter. But his father was in the linen business, and into the linen business the son had to go. Still he kept hoping he could be a painter, and finally his father let him stop selling linen and begin studying painting. Corot went to Italy for several years and became a landscape painter. Then he went back to France. He painted many fine landscapes but no one seemed to want to buy them.

At this time some other painters who were also poor found they could live more cheaply in the little village of Barbizon, a short distance south of Paris, than they could in the city. And they found, too, that the country around Barbizon was a much better place in which to paint landscapes. There they could see the forests and streams and fields that

第25章 穷困潦倒的画家

我为什么要向你们介绍一些穷困潦倒的画家呢？如果一位画家创作不出优秀的画作来，那我们为何还要提到他们呢？好吧，这是因为本章介绍的这些穷困潦倒的画家，的确绘制出了许多优异的画作。他们只是在钱财方面穷困潦倒，而不是绘画技艺差劲[1]。

这些穷困而又优秀的画家当中，有一位就是法国画家柯罗。他之所以穷困，是因为没人愿意购买他的画作。直到五十岁的时候，他才卖出了自己的第一张画。然而，他并不像听上去那样潦倒，因为父亲每年都会给他一笔生活费。虽说这笔生活费很少，但柯罗还是设法靠这笔钱生活着。

柯罗完成学业后，就想要当一名画家。可他父亲从事的是布匹生意，因此儿子也得子承父业，去从事布匹行业才行。尽管如此，他还是希望日后自己能当一名画家；于是，父亲便不让他卖布，任他转而学习绘画去了。柯罗到意大利留了几年学，成了一名风景画家。接下来，他便回到了法国。他创作了许多精美的山水风景画；可在那时，似乎没有人愿意购买这些画作呢。

当时，其他一些同样穷困潦倒的画家发现，在巴黎南部不远的巴比松镇，生活成本要比巴黎低得多。他们还发现，巴比松镇周围的乡村也更适宜他们创作风

[1] 英语中，“穷困”与“差劲”都是用poor来表示。作者为避免孩子们误解，才在此处进行了解释。

they loved to paint. So these poor-in-money painters moved to little cottages in and around Barbizon. They are called the Barbizon painters.

It was Corot's idea to live in Barbizon. He liked to get up early in the morning and go out to study the trees and fields in the early light of dawn when the dew was on the ground and everything looked misty. He would make *sketches*, or quick drawings, of what he saw and then come home and paint. He liked twilight and moonlight, too, and often painted twilight and moonlight landscapes. His pictures have a magical, dreamy beauty that has made them famous.

When he was an old man, Corot's pictures began to sell. Money and fame came rolling in at last. Corot had always loved to help other people in any way he could, so now that he was wealthy, he had a fine time giving most of his money away to people who needed it.

Although his landscapes often seem dreamy and sad, Corot was always cheery and happy with his friends. Everyone loved him and called him Father Corot, and so it is pleasant to learn that he finally became so famous.

意大利留念：宁芙的舞蹈，柯罗作品，
现存于格拉斯哥市立美术馆
（由波士顿的大学印刷协会提供）

景画。在那里，他们可以看到自己喜欢绘制的森林、小溪和田地。于是，这些穷困潦倒的画家便纷纷搬到了巴比松镇和该镇周围的村舍里。由此，他们便被称为巴比松画派。

住到巴比松镇，正合柯罗的意。他喜欢一大早就起床出门，在晨光中，在地上还留有露水，一切看上去都朦朦胧胧的时候，去研究树木和田野。他会把自己的所见绘制成素描，或者说速写，然后回家再创作成油画。他也很喜欢暮色与月光，并且经常创作含有暮色与月光的风景画。他的画作，有一种迷人的、梦幻般的美感；正是这种美感，让他的画作后来变得闻名遐迩了。

步入老年之后，柯罗的画作开始有了销路。金钱和名誉，终于滚滚而来了。柯罗一向都喜欢竭尽所能地帮助别人，因此一旦富裕起来，他便能够尽情地将自己的绝大部分钱财都捐赠给那些需要帮助的人了。

尽管他的风景画看上去常常带有梦幻、忧郁的色彩，但柯罗本人与朋友们在一起时，却一向都很活泼、乐观。大家都很喜欢他，称他为“柯罗前辈”；因此，得知他终于有了名气，真是可喜可贺啊。

Another Barbizon painter was much poorer in money than Corot. Jean Francois Millet was one of the first to go to Barbizon. He took his wife and children and lived in a little three-room house that had no wooden floors, just packed earth. Yet he was one of the greatest painters of France.

Millet had always been poor. His father was a farmer and when Millet was a boy, he worked on his father's farm. When he saw some pictures in an old Bible, he started to draw. During the rest hour in the fields, the workers would all take naps but young Millet would spend the time drawing pictures. Finally the village where he lived gave him a little money to go to Paris to study art.

When Millet got to Paris, he had a terrible time. He was very shy and not used to city ways so he didn't get along well at all. He barely made enough money for food by selling little pictures he painted. He liked best to paint poor peasants whose lives he knew so well, and at last when he was almost starving, someone bought one of his peasant paintings. This gave him enough money to get out of Paris and go to Barbizon, and there he lived for the rest of his life.

Millet's pictures of peasants at work were painted in an unusual way. The painter would go out on the farms and watch the people at work — digging, hoeing, spreading manure, sawing wood, churning butter, washing clothes, or sowing grain. Then he would come home and paint what he had seen. His memory was so good that he could paint at home without a model and get all the movements of his figures right. When he did need a live model, he would ask his wife to pose for him.

而另一位巴比松派画家，却要比柯罗穷困得多了。让·弗朗索瓦·米勒是第一批搬到巴比松镇的画家之一。他带上了自己的妻儿子女，住在一栋只有三个房间的屋子里，地板不是木质的，而是压实的泥土地面。尽管如此，他仍属于法国最伟大的画家之一。

米勒一直都很穷。他的父亲是位农民；米勒还小的时候，就到父亲的农场里干活了。后来，他在一本旧《圣经》上看到了一些画作，于是开始绘画。在地里干活间隙的休息时间里，其他的工人全都在睡午觉，可小米勒却会利用这段时间来画画。后来，他所在的那个村庄给了他一小笔钱，让他到巴黎去学习绘画艺术。

米勒到达巴黎后，过了一段很艰难的日子。他非常腼腆，又不习惯城市里的生活方式，因此根本就与其他人合不来。他通过出售自己绘制的小幅画作，勉强维持着生计。他最喜欢描绘关于贫苦农民的画作，因为他非常了解这些人的生活；而到了他最后几乎就要挨饿的时候，终于有人购买了他的一幅农民画作。这让他有了足够多的钱搬出巴黎，来到巴比松镇；而后来，他也在那里度过了自己的余生。

米勒那些描绘劳作中农民的画作，都是用一种非同寻常的手法绘制出来的。画家会出门来到田野上，观察人们劳作时的情景，比如翻地啦，锄草啦，施肥啦，伐木啦，搅制黄油啦，洗衣服啦，或者播种啦。然后，他会回到家，将自己所见到的情景画下来。他的记性特别好，因此回到家后，根本不用模特，就能将画中人物的一举一动都绘制得准确无误。倘若确实需要一位现场模特，他便会请自己的妻子为他摆出所需的姿势。

拾穗者，米勒作品，
现存于巴黎的卢浮宫
（由波士顿的大学印刷协会提供）

One of Millet's paintings is called *The Sower*. It shows a man planting seed. Have you ever seen a farmer sowing a field by hand? The sower's hand keeps time with his step. He reaches into his bag for seed and then swings his hand back to scatter the seed, and with each swing of his hand, the sower strides forward.

In Millet's picture, the sower has been working hard but his swinging step and outflung arm still move smoothly in time like a machine. Only the man's head shows how tired he is. Millet made several pictures of *The Sower*, all of which are somewhat alike.

Another picture that is as famous as *The Sower* is called *The Gleaners*. A gleaner is someone who picks up grain left in the field after the wheat has been harvested. When farmers are very poor, as they were near Barbizon, even the little bits that the gleaners can find are helpful. You can see from Millet's picture what backbreaking work gleaning must be.

米勒创作的油画中，有一幅名叫《播种者》。这幅画作，描绘的是一名男子正在播种时的情景。你们见过农民用手在地里播种时的情景吗？播种者的手，会与自己的步伐保持一致。他将手伸进袋子，掏出种子，然后向后扬起手来，把种子播撒出去；而每扬一次手，播种者便会向前走上一步。

在米勒的画作中，虽说播种者一直在辛勤劳作，可他的步伐和后扬的胳膊，却依然像是一台机器那样，一举一动都非常流畅。只有那个人的头部，才说明了他有多累。米勒创作过好几幅名叫《播种者》的画作，它们的风格和内容都差不多。

米勒另一幅与《播种者》齐名的画作，叫作《拾穗者》。所谓的拾穗者，就是麦子收割完后，在地里捡拾掉落的麦穗的人。当时巴比松镇附近地区的农民都很穷，因此拾穗者哪怕捡到一点点儿麦穗，也是件好事。你们可以从米勒的画作上看出，捡拾麦穗一定是一种极其累人的活儿呢。

收土豆，米勒作品，
现存于巴尔的摩的沃尔特斯艺术博物馆

Like Corot, Millet was at last recognized as a great painter before he died. But unlike Corot, he always remained poor. When Millet died, his friend Corot helped his widow.

Some of the other Barbizon painters became famous too. They all used to meet in a big bam where they had tacked drawings on the walls, and there they would talk about the painting they all loved to do.

像柯罗一样，米勒最终也在去世前被人们公认为一位伟大的画家。可与柯罗不一样的是，他始终都穷困潦倒。米勒去世后，他的朋友柯罗还资助过他的遗孀呢。

还有其他的一些巴比松派的画家，后来也出了名。他们常常会在一座大谷仓里集会，将自己的画作钉在谷仓的墙壁上，并且对大家都热爱的绘画艺术展开讨论呢。

Chapter 26 The Most Important Person

And now I'm going to have to blindfold you. I won't ask you to look at some pictures blindfolded. You can enjoy music that way but hardly pictures. But let's suppose you really are blindfolded. I'm going to guide you, blindfolded as you are, out to a field this morning. I'm going to stand you so you are facing a haystack, and then I'm going to take the blindfold off your eyes and let you look at the haystack for five minutes. Then I'll blindfold you again and lead you back. It's a funny kind of a game, isn't it? Something like Blindman's Bluff.

Let's play it once more. The first time when you looked at the haystack, it was ten o'clock in the morning. This time I'll let you look at the same haystack for five minutes at about five o'clock in the afternoon. And this time the haystack will look quite different from the way it looked at ten o'clock.

It's the same shape but the colors and light and shadows have changed. As the Sun and clouds move across the sky during the day, the haystack changes in color and brightness. That's why I let you look at it for only five minutes at a time — so the light would not change and give your eye another picture.

Now I'm sure you can see that if an artist painted a picture of the haystack for every hour of the day, he would have many pictures of the same haystack but each picture would be different from all the others.

第26章 最重要的人物

现在，我打算蒙住你们的眼睛。当然，我是不会要你们蒙起眼睛来观看某幅画作的。你们可以蒙上眼睛去听音乐，可蒙上眼睛是欣赏不了画作的。不过，不妨假定你们真的被蒙上了眼睛。今天上午，我打算领着蒙上了双眼的你们出门，来到一片田野之上。我会让你们站在一个地方，使得你们正好面对着一堆干草，然后摘下你们的眼罩，让你们对着那堆干草看上五分钟。接下来，我会再次蒙上你们的眼睛，并领着你们回去。这是个很有意思的游戏，不是吗？有点儿像是捉迷藏呢。

我们不妨多玩一次。你们第一次看到那个干草垛时，是上午十点钟。而这一次，我会让你们在下午五点钟左右的时候，再对着那个干草垛看上五分钟。这一次，那座干草堆的样子，会与上午十点钟时看到的样子大不相同呢。

此时，干草垛的形状还是一样的，可它的色彩、光线和明暗都已经发生了改变。随着白天太阳、云朵横过天空，干草堆的颜色和亮度也会相应地发生变化。而我之所以每次只让你们看上五分钟的原因，就是免得光线会改变，从而让你们看到另一幅图景。

现在，我敢肯定你们都已经明白，倘若一位画家在一天之中，每隔一个小时便绘制一幅描绘那堆干草的画作，那么，虽说他会绘制出多幅描绘同一堆干草的画作，可每幅画作都会与其他的画作不一样。

That is just what some French artists did. Then they exhibited their work by hanging their paintings on the walls of a room so that people could come and see them. The people who came found these paintings to be very different from any they had ever seen before. The pictures were like your quick view of the haystack. They showed the colors and light that the artists had seen in quick views of the things they were painting. These views are called impressions. And so the painters soon got the name of *impressionists*.

Earlier painters never thought of doing such a thing. They painted a horse one color and a haystack another no matter whether the light always made them look that color or not. But in reality, a black horse or a yellow haystack is not black or yellow. The color depends on the light. The light shining on a black horse may make him look blue in places. But because you know that a horse isn't blue, you don't notice how blue he really may be in a certain light!

Painters always used to paint shadows brown or gray or black. But if you look carefully at a real shadow, it is often not brown or gray or black at all. It's just as apt to be green or blue or purple or some other color.

Of course bright light and color on an object outdoors was always hard to paint because paints are not nearly as bright as light. But if you remember what I told you about the painter Constable, you will see how these impressionist artists made their colors look bright like sunlight. They put the colors on in little dots and dashes.

Putting colors on in dots and dashes really does make them look brighter. They almost

一些法国画家正是这样干的。后来，他们还展出了这些画作，将它们全都挂在一个房间的墙上，以便人们前来观赏。那些前来观画的人都发现，这些画作与他们以前见过的所有画作都大不一样。这些画作，就像是你们将干草堆的照片一幅幅地进行回放那样。它们呈现出了画家快速捕捉到的、所绘之物的色彩和光线。这些捕捉到的视图，被称为“印象”。因此，那些画家很快便得到了“印象派”的名称。

早期的画家从来都没有想过要干这样的事情哩。他们总是将马儿画成一种颜色，将干草堆画成另一种颜色，而不管光线是不是始终会让所画之物保持着那种颜色。可实际上，一匹黑色的马儿或者一堆枯黄的干草，并不是纯黑或者纯黄色的。它们的色彩，取决于光线。照在一匹黑马身上的光线，没准会让马儿的某些部位呈现出蓝色来呢。可是，由于大家都知道马儿不会是蓝色的，因此大家也都不会注意到，在某种光线之下，这匹马儿实际上可能变成一种蓝色！

过去的画家，往往把阴影绘成棕色、灰色或者黑色。可是，倘若仔细观察一下真正的阴影，你们就会发现，它们常常根本就不是棕色、灰色或者黑色的。真正的阴影，很容易呈现出绿色、蓝色、紫色或者其他的颜色。

当然，户外物体上那种明亮的光线和色彩，一向都是很难描绘出来的，因为绘画所用的颜料，本来就不像光线那样明亮。不过，若是你们都还记得前面我给你们介绍过的康斯太勃尔那位画家的话，你们就会看出，这些印象派画家是如何让他们绘制出来的色彩显得像阳光那样亮丽的。他们是把颜料弄成微小的点状或者条状，在画布上绘制出来的。

把颜料弄成点状或者条状绘在画布上，的确使得画作看上去更加亮丽了。它们

seem to shimmer like real sunlight. But it also makes the pictures look quite different from the older kind of painting.

For this reason, the people who saw the French exhibition of the impressionists weren't very pleased. These people had been used to one kind of painting, and the change was so great that they didn't like the new kind nearly as well at first.

But after a while the impressionists came to be understood better. People saw that they were trying out a new way of painting and that what they were doing might be very worthwhile. One of the impressionists named Claude Monet used to go out with a carriage full of canvases and spend all day painting the same scene. He used a different canvas each time the light changed the color and appearance of the thing he was painting. For instance, Monet painted fifteen pictures of the same haystacks and each one had a different color and light effect.

Monet also painted twenty pictures of the front of a French cathedral and each picture was different. The paintings make for an interesting series. Monet was interested in light and color, not especially in form or shape. The whole series shows how the cathedral stayed the

白杨树，莫奈作品
（由波士顿的大学印刷协会提供）

显得差不多和真正的日光一样，闪闪发亮呢。不过，这种画法也让画作与以前的油画显得大相径庭了。

正是由于这个原因，那些观看法国印象派画展的人都不是很满意。这些人都习惯了欣赏一种绘画风格，而这种改变又过于巨大，因此他们并不像一开始那样喜欢这种新的风格了。

但是，过了一段时间之后，人们开始更加理解那些印象派画家了。人们明白，他们正在尝试一种新的绘画方式；而他们所做的尝试，可能也是很有意义的。印象派画家中，有一位叫作克劳德·莫奈；他经常带着一马车的画布外出，整天对着同一种场景绘画。每次光线改变了绘画对象的色彩和样子，他都会换上不同的画布。例如，莫奈曾就同一堆干草，绘制了十五幅画作，而每一幅的色彩和光影效果，都很不一样呢。

莫奈还给法国一座教堂的前门绘制了二十幅画作，并且每幅画作都各不相同。这些画作，形成了一个很有意思的系列。莫奈关注的是光线和色彩，而不是特别注意形式和造型。整个系列所描绘的，是那座大教堂的造型虽说保持不变，但随着

same but looked entirely different depending upon the light and sky and time of day.

Another impressionist had a name much like Monet. His name was Manet. In fact, Manet was the painter who really started the impressionist style, or *impressionism*. Manet didn't break his pictures up into so many little glittering spots as Monet did. Indeed, it was only in the last ten years of his life that Manet even tried that way of painting. Someone once asked Manet who was the chief person in one of his impressionist pictures.

"The most important person in any picture," Manet answered, "is the light." And that was what the impressionists tried to show in their paintings.

One of Manet's more famous pictures is *The Fifer*. People at first thought that the fifer boy looked flat like a cutout paper doll, and he seemed to be floating in space without any background at all. But now we don't even notice this because we are used to seeing flattened-out paintings.

Can you guess where the idea of flattening out figures was developed? It was in Japan where woodblock prints were made. The French loved these woodblock

吹短笛的少年，马奈作品，
现存于巴黎的卢浮宫
（由波士顿的大学印刷协会提供）

白天时间的推移，随着光线和天空的变化，而会呈现出的完全不同的模样。

还有一位印象派画家，他的名字与莫奈很像。他叫马奈。实际上，马奈才是真正开创了印象派风格，或称印象主义绘画艺术的画家。马奈并没有像莫奈那样，把自己的画作分割成许多闪亮的小点。实际上，只是在他生命中的最后十年里，马奈才去尝试了这种绘画方法。有人曾经问马奈，他创作的一幅印象派画作中，哪个人才是主体。

“任何画作中最重要的人物，”马奈回答道，“就是光线。”而这一点，正是印象派画家试图在画作中表现出来的东西。

马奈较为著名的一幅画，就是《吹短笛的少年》。人们起初认为，那个吹短笛的男孩毫无层次感，就像剪纸玩偶似的，并且那个男孩似乎飘浮在空中，根本就没有任何可以凭依的背景。不过，如今我们根本就不会注意到这一点，因为我们已经习惯于看平面画作了。

你们能不能猜出，平面人物的概念是从哪里发展起来的呢？是从制作木版镌刻画的日本发展起来的。法国人很喜欢这种木刻画，而日本于十九世纪六十年代后首

prints, which they finally got to see when Japan first began to trade with the West after the 1860s. The rage for all things Japanese was like the craze for all things Roman during the neoclassical period.

The Japanese prints inspired many French painters in many ways. One way was to flatten out the figure to emphasize shapes, designs, patterns, and broad outlines. Another way was to look at the figure from an odd angle as if through a keyhole. And yet a third way was to let the figure float without a ground line so that the floor and wall or the Earth and sky almost blend. That's where Manet and the impressionists found a new way of looking at things.

次开始与西方各国展开贸易的时候，他们便终于见到这种木刻画了。人们对日本的一切东西都很狂热，就像新古典主义时期人们对古罗马的一切都很狂热一样。

日本的木刻画，在许多方面都给许多法国画家带来了启发。一个方面就是将人物平面化，以突出造型、构思、格局和大致的轮廓。第二个方面，就是从一种古怪的角度，仿佛是从一个锁孔里来观察人物。而第三个方面，就是让人物在没有基线的情况下飘浮着，从而使得地板和墙壁、地面和天空几乎融为了一体。马奈和其他的印象派画家，正是从这里发现了一种看待事物的新方法。

Chapter 27 Postimpressionism

Postimpressionism doesn't have anything to do with fence posts. The *post* part of the title of this chapter means *after*. So the title might be After Impressionism to describe the new styles of painting that came after the impressionist paintings. You remember that Monet's work is impressionist, where light is the most important person.

The father of postimpressionism was Paul Cézanne. He was a Frenchman like Manet and Monet. At first he was an impressionist himself, but then he said he wanted to make impressionism something solid and lasting like the art of the Old Masters.

Cézanne worked hard all his life at painting but he never became popular as a painter until after his death. Luckily for him, he had enough money to live on without having to sell his paintings, for he found he couldn't sell them.

Cézanne wasn't interested in showing light at different times of the day or in different seasons. He preferred to recreate the solid, geometric shapes of nature. He built them up through broad patches of color instead of small dabs. He didn't use lines to show depth so you first see his space as flat and then you see it as deep. He loved Japanese prints. A famous subject in many of those prints is Mount Fuji. Similarly, Cézanne also painted a mountain — the Mont Sainte Victoire in Provence, the region where he lived in southern France.

第27章 后期印象派

后期印象派，与栅栏柱子可没有什么关系[1]。本章标题中的post这一部分，是“后”的意思。因此，本章标题其实就是“印象派之后”，用于说明印象派画作之后，出现的一些新的绘画风格。你们都还记得吧，马奈的作品属于印象派，其中最重要的主体就是光线。

后期印象派的奠基者，是保罗・塞尚。他与马奈和莫奈一样，都是法国人。起初，他本来是一位印象派画家；可后来他说，自己希望让印象派变成某种具体的东西，并且像古时那些大师的艺术一样，永世流传下去。

塞尚终生都在勤奋创作；可作为一名画家，他一直都没有受到大家的追捧，直到去世之后才名声大噪。幸运的是，他积蓄颇丰，不用卖画便能生活下去，因为他发现自己的画作根本就卖不出去。

塞尚对表现一天或者四季中不同时间的光影并不感兴趣。他更喜欢重现大自然中那些具体的几何造型。他用大片的色彩，而不是微小的点状颜料，来构成这些造型。他没有用线条来呈现深浅，因此乍一看去，他绘制的空间是没有层次感的；可接下来你们才会看出，他笔下的空间具有深度。他很喜欢日本的版画。其中许多版画都有一个著名的主题，即富士山。同样，塞尚也有一幅描绘一座大山的画作；这

[1] 在英语中，表示“后”的前缀 post- 与表示“柱子”的 post 词形相同，因此作者才这样说。

Another postimpressionist who was younger than Cézanne had a very different kind of life. This other painter didn't live quietly on a farm in southern France as Cézanne did. His name was Vincent van Gogh. He was a Dutchman.

Van Gogh tried working for an art dealer, but if he thought his customers wanted to buy poor pictures, he talked them out of it and lost the sale. So he tried being a schoolteacher for a few months. I don't believe he could have been a very good teacher because he had a bad temper.

Then he decided to be a minister. This didn't work either because he soon got so tired of the college for ministers where he was studying that he did not finish his studies. And so he set out as a missionary to help the workers in the Belgian mines. He felt so sorry for these poor miners that he gave away all his money and nearly starved. At that time he began to sketch the people he wanted so much to help.

His brother sent him money to live on and encouraged him to go to Paris to study art. Then Van Gogh went to live in a little town in Provence in southern France, and there he painted many pictures. The postimpressionists loved the light and color of southern France.

The paintings that Van Gogh did in southern France are made up of thick, bold lines of paint instead of the dabs of paint that the impressionists had used or the patches of paint in Cézanne's work. Van Gogh's brushstrokes show that he pressed down hard, forcefully, and worked fast using pure, bright colors, sometimes right out of the tube.

座山，就是圣维克多山，位于塞尚所生活的，法国南部的普罗旺斯地区。

还有一位比塞尚年轻的后期印象派画家，却过着一种完全不同的生活。这位画家，并没有像塞尚那样，平静地生活在法国南部的一个农场里。他叫文森特·凡·高，是荷兰人。

凡·高曾经努力工作，想要成为一位画商；不过，一旦觉得顾客希望购买的是质量低劣的画作，他就会尽力劝说，让客户不要购买，从而丢掉那笔生意。于是，他又试着去一所学校当了几个月的老师。我可不相信，那几个月里他会是一名很好的老师，因为凡·高的脾气很坏。

接下来，凡·高又决定做一名牧师。这也没用，因为他很快便厌烦了自己就学的那所神学院，于是他没有完成学业便跑了。接下来，他开始当传教士，去帮助比利时的矿工。他很同情那些贫穷的矿工，因此倾其所有，将身上的钱全都捐给了他们，自己差点儿就要挨饿了。就在那时，他开始用素描将这些他很想帮助的人记录下来。

他的弟弟给他寄了生活费，并且鼓励他到巴黎去学习绘画。于是，凡·高便到了法国南部普罗旺斯地区的一个小镇，在那里住了下来，并且创作了许多油画。后期的印象派画家，都很热爱法国南部绚丽的阳光和多姿的色彩呢。

凡·高在法国南部创作出来的油画，都是用颜料绘制出厚重、粗大的线条所构成；它们既不是印象派画家曾经所用的点状画法，也不像塞尚的作品那样，不是用大片颜料堆砌而成的。凡·高的笔法，表明他下笔有力，并且是用纯粹而亮丽的色彩，有时甚至是用直接从颜料管里挤出的颜料，一挥而就的。

阿尔勒市公园入口，凡·高作品，
现存于华盛顿特区的菲利普收藏馆
（由波士顿的大学印刷协会提供）

A friend of his said, "He paints so fiercely that it is terrible to watch him." His pictures look as if he had painted them with great intensity. He expressed his emotions through vivid color and firm brushstrokes. Like Millet, he loved the farmland. You can tell that by looking at his painting *The Sower*. He, too, loved Japanese prints and wanted to emphasize the surface pattern and the odd angles as they did.

And now comes a sadder part of Van Gogh's life. His mind began to give way. He began to go crazy. One day a friend of his who was a waitress in a cafe asked him for a present. Just in fun she said to him, "Well, if you can't give me anything else, you might give me one of your big ears." And just before Christmas, the woman received a package. She thought it was a Christmas present. But when she opened it, out fell — an ear! The woman was horrified. Poor Van Gogh was found in bed, completely out of his mind. He

他的一位朋友曾经说道："他绘画的时候，样子就像是在拼命，看着他还真是令人生畏呢。"他的画作，看起来就像是用了很大的力气画出来的。他用鲜艳的色彩和坚定的笔触，表达出了自己的情感。他与米勒一样，也很喜欢田野。从他的画作《播种者》，我们就可以看出这一点。他也很喜欢日本的版画，并且希望像日本艺术家一样，突出表层格局和奇特的视角。

接下来，凡·高的生活便开始变得凄惨起来。他的大脑开始失去控制。他开始精神错乱。有一天，一位在咖啡馆里当女服务员的朋友问他要一份礼物。只是为了好玩，她对他说："好吧，如果您给不了我别的东西，也可以把您的一只大耳朵送给我呀。"就在那个圣诞节前夕，这位女士收到了一个包裹。她还以为那是一份圣诞礼物呢。可打开一看，包裹里面竟然掉出了一只耳朵！这位女士吓坏了。后来，人们发现可怜的凡·高躺在床上，已经完全失去了意识。他竟然用剃刀割下了自己

had cut off his right ear with a razor.

Of course he had to be taken to an asylum where he finally got well enough to paint some more pictures. But the periods of instability kept coming back and during one of them Van Gogh shot himself.

A third postimpressionist was Paul Gauguin. Gauguin was a different Frenchman than Cézanne, and he led a life almost as strange as Van Gogh's. When he was a boy, Gauguin ran away from home, got on a ship, and went to sea. He made several voyages as a sailor to different parts of the world. Then he came back to Paris and went into business.

Perhaps Gauguin would never have become a painter if he had not run away to sea. For one day when he was walking down the street, he came to a shop window that had some paintings in it. These paintings had the brightness and color that Gauguin had seen in the faraway Pacific isles. They brought memories of his voyages back to him so he asked who the artists were. Thus he became acquainted with the postimpressionists who had painted these pictures.

Gauguin then began to paint too. He became a friend of Van Gogh and even lived in Provence with him for a while before Van Gogh became sick.

Later Gauguin moved to Brittany — the part of northern France that sticks out into the Atlantic Ocean — and there he, too, painted peasants and the French countryside. And he, too, flattened out his pictures — but with even larger areas of solid saturated color and odder angles.

But Gauguin could not forget the beautiful tropic islands of the Pacific that he had

的右耳。

自然，人们不得不把他送进了一家精神病院；在那里，他的身体最终恢复了一些，从而让他又创作出了一些作品。不过，后来他的病情一直都很不稳定，不时复发；而在一次发作过程中，凡·高用枪结束了自己的生命。

第三位后期印象派画家，就是保罗·高更。高更是一个与塞尚不同的法国画家，而他的生活，则差不多像凡·高的生活那样怪异哩。还在很小的时候，高更便离开了家，上了一艘船出海去了。在当水手的那段时间里，他曾远航了数次，到过世界各地。后来，他回到巴黎，开始做生意。

或许，倘若高更没有出海远航过，他可能永远都不会成为一名画家。有一天，正当他在街上散步的时候，他经过了一家商店；那家商店的橱窗里，陈列着一些画作。画作上的鲜亮色彩，正是高更曾经在遥远的太平洋地区一些岛屿上见到过的。它们让高更记起了自己那些远航的经历，于是他便询问店主，绘制这些画作的画家都是谁。这样，他便结识了绘制这些画作的一些后期印象派画家。

接下来，高更也开始绘画了。他成了凡·高的好朋友，甚至还在凡·高生病之前，到普罗旺斯与凡·高生活了一段时间呢。

后来，高更搬到了布列塔尼，就是法国北部伸进大西洋中的那个地区；在那里，他也创作了一些关于农民和法国乡村风景的画作。而且，他的画作也属于平面画，但画作中用纯粹而饱和的色彩的面积更大，呈现的视角也更为与众不同。

不过，高更始终都无法忘记自己在航海过程中看到的，太平洋上那些美丽的热

上帝之日，高更作品，现存于芝加哥的芝加哥艺术博物馆
（由波士顿的大学印刷协会提供）

seen on his voyages. One day he packed up again and sailed for the island of Tahiti in the South Seas. There the painter found the life he liked best. He lived like one of the native islanders. And there he painted some of his best pictures.

The Tahitian paintings are bright with the color of the tropics and show the people of the islands at work, rest, and play. These South Sea pictures made Gauguin famous.

带岛屿。于是，有一天，他重新整理好行装，坐船前往南太平洋上的塔希提岛。在那里，这位画家找到了自己最喜欢的那种生活。他住了下来，像当地土著一样生活着。而在那里，他也创作出了一些最杰出的画作。

高更在塔希提岛上创作的那些油画，全都具有热带地区的亮丽色彩，描绘了岛屿上的人们劳作、休息、玩乐时的情景。正是这些描绘南太平洋风情的画作，使得高更成了一位著名的画家。

Chapter 28 Early Americans

Now we come to painting in America. I have to tell you right off that there is much more American painting and many more American artists than I have room to tell you about in this book. America has had artists since before the American Revolution, and today we have as many good painters at work as any country in the world.

The first American artist to become really famous was Benjamin West. Benjamin West's family lived in Pennsylvania when Native Americans inhabited its forests. There he was born and there he grew up.

When Benjamin West was a boy, he loved to draw pictures. The Native Americans were pleased when he drew pictures of them. Of course he didn't have any paints or paintbrushes or even any pictures to look at. There weren't such things in the little frontier village where he lived. So the boy was delighted one day when the Native Americans gave him some of the yellow and red paint that they used to paint their faces.

Benjamin ran home and showed the paints to his mother. Then his mother gave him the bluing color that she used for laundry. Now he had yellow, red, and blue paint, but no paintbrushes. How do you think he got a brush? He used the cat!

Yes, he cut some hairs off the cat's tail and made them into a paintbrush. When the first brush wore out, he got some more hairs from the cat. After a while the poor cat had hardly

第28章 早期的美国画家

现在，我们再来说一说美国的绘画艺术。在这里，我得先告诉你们，美国绘画艺术的内容很多，美国的画家也很多，但本书可没有那么多的篇幅来一一进行介绍。还在独立战争之前，美国就已经有了很多的画家；而如今，我国正在创作的优秀画家，数量也不逊于世界上的其他各国呢。

美国第一位真正变得家喻户晓的画家，就是本杰明·韦斯特。本杰明·韦斯特一家居住在宾夕法尼亚州，而当时的印第安人还住在该州的森林里。本杰明·韦斯特在那里出生，又在那里长大成人。

本杰明·韦斯特小的时候，便很喜欢绘画。他给印第安人画像的时候，那些印第安人都很高兴。当然，那时的他既没有颜料，没有画笔，甚至也没有可以参考的画作。他所生活的那个小小的偏远山村里，是没有这些东西的。因此，有一天那些印第安人给了他一些黄色的、红色的颜料之后，这个小男孩非常高兴；那些颜料，是印第安人用来涂在自己脸上的。

本杰明马上跑回家，把这些颜料给妈妈看。然后，妈妈又给了他一些用来染制衣物的蓝色颜料。这样，他有了黄色、红色和蓝色三种颜料，只是没有画笔。你们猜猜看，他后来用什么做成了一支画笔呢？竟然是用一只猫！

是的，他从猫尾巴上剪下一些毛来，然后用这些猫毛做成了一支画笔。第一支画笔用坏了之后，他就再剪下一些猫毛，又做了一支。过了一段时间之后，那只可

any hair left on her tail and was beginning to look very ragged in other places.

When Benjamin West grew up, he went to live in Philadelphia, and there he worked hard to become a good painter. Then he decided to go to Europe where he could see and study famous paintings. When he reached Rome, he was taken to see a statue of a Greek god called the *Apollo Belvedere*.

"It looks like a Mohawk warrior," he said, thinking of the strong and graceful braves of Pennsylvania.

West then went to England and settled in London where he became a very popular painter. King George III liked West and his work so much that he made him court painter. And so Benjamin West never returned to America. But he always welcomed American artists who came to London and was very generous and helpful to them. In fact, his studio was a kind of school for young men learning to paint and many well-known American painters studied there. He was like a father to them all.

West's pictures often were very large and generally were filled with many figures, though he also painted smaller portraits. They were admired by everyone, and some people even said they promised to be as great as the paintings of Michelangelo.

Today we think West's paintings are not really as great as Michelangelo's, but isn't it pleasant to hear of an artist's pictures being so well thought of while he was alive and could enjoy their success? Many painters have had to struggle all their days as nobodies

怜的小猫的尾巴上，就几乎就没剩下多少毛，而其他部位也开始变得参差不齐了。

本杰明·韦斯特长大后，去了费城，并在那里住了下来，笔耕不辍，想要成为一名优秀的画家。然后，他决定去欧洲游历一番；因为那样的话，就可以看到并研究许多的名作了。抵达罗马之后，他便由人领着，去观赏一尊描绘一位古希腊神灵的雕塑，即《望楼的阿波罗》。

"它看上去像是莫霍克族[1]的一名武士呢。"他说，因为他想到了宾夕法尼亚州那些身体强壮的勇士。

接下来，韦斯特去了英国，在伦敦定居下来，并在那里变成了一个广受人们欢迎的画家。英王乔治三世很喜欢韦斯特及其画作，因此延请他为御用画师。这样，本杰明·韦斯特便再也没有回美国了。不过，他对那些来到伦敦的美国画家都很热情，并且非常慷慨，经常帮助他们。事实上，他的工作室就是一所学校，非但有许多年轻人在那里学习绘画，许多知名的美国画家也曾在那里研习过。对于这些人来说，本杰明·韦斯特就像是一位父亲。

韦斯特绘制的画作，通常尺寸都很大，其中充斥着各种各样的人物；但是，他也绘制过一些尺寸较小的肖像画。大家都非常推崇这些画作；有些人甚至还说，它们必定会像米开朗琪罗的作品那样伟大呢。

如今我们觉得，韦斯特的画作并不是真的像米开朗琪罗的作品那样伟大；不过，听到一位画家的画作在他活着并且能够享受成功的时候就得到了人们如此之高的评价，不也是一件乐事吗？许多画家生前都默默无闻，一生坎坷，只是到了

[1] 莫霍克族（Mohawk），印第安人的一支，主要分布在北美洲，因居住在莫霍克河边而得名。

only to have their pictures admired after they died, so I'm glad the opposite happened to this painter.

One of West's best-known paintings is *The Death of General Wolfe*. General Wolfe was the leader of the British soldiers during the war with France over Canada. The British won but General Wolfe was shot. Both the French and English were helped by Native American warriors. Notice the Native American in the picture. West had grown up with Native Americans, you remember, so he could paint them even in England with the nearest Native American three thousand miles away.

The picture caused a great stir in London because the soldiers are dressed in their regular uniforms. In England it was thought that all pictures of history should show people dressed as Greeks or Romans. Even the king told West he shouldn't put his figures in such modem dress. But when the picture was finished, everyone, including the king, decided that West did the right thing. After that, artists painted their figures in the clothes that their subjects actually wore.

沃尔夫将军之死，韦斯特作品，
现存于渥太华的加拿大国家美术馆
（由波士顿的大学印刷协会提供）

死后，他们的作品才得到人们的推崇；因此，对于这位情况正好与此相反的画家，我感到非常欣慰。

韦斯特最负盛名的一幅画作，就是《沃尔夫将军[1]之死》。沃尔夫将军是英国与法国因加拿大而爆发的那场战争中的英军将领。此战中，英军虽然获胜，但沃尔夫将军却中弹阵亡了。当时，法军和英军都得到了印第安武士的协助。请注意画作中的那个印第安人。韦斯特从小跟印第安人一起长大，你们都还记得吧。因此，即便是在英国，他也能够把远处三千英里以外的印第安人描绘得毫厘不差呢。

这幅画作在伦敦引起了巨大的轰动，因为画作中的士兵都穿着常规的军装。在英国，人们觉得所有历史题材的画作中，人物的衣着都应当按照古希腊或古罗马时期的服装来描绘。连当时的英国国王也对韦斯特说过，不应当让画作中的人物穿着如此现代的服装。不过，待这幅画作最终完成后，所有的人，包括英国国王，便都认为韦斯特做得对了。自那以后，所有画家便都在画作中按照绘画对象实际所穿的服装来描绘人物了。

[1] 沃尔夫将军（General Wolfe，1727—1759），英国十八世纪时的一位名将。1756 年，英法之间争夺殖民地和海上霸权的斗争日益激烈，终于导致了七年战争的爆发，并波及了两国在美洲的殖民地。在北美战场，到 1758 年底，英国已经打开了通往加拿大的门户。1759 年，英国开始远征加拿大。此战最终以沃尔夫将军率领的英军在魁北克城下击败法军而告终，但沃尔夫却在战斗中中弹身亡。韦斯特的这幅画作，再现的就是将军战死时的场景。

乔治·华盛顿像，斯图尔特作品，
现存于波士顿的波士顿美术馆
（由波士顿的大学印刷协会提供）

One of the young Americans who studied under West in London was Gilbert Stuart. He was born and raised in New England before the American Revolution. He, too, thought he could do better in England so he traveled to London. There he became a painter of fine portraits. People then thought Benjamin West a much better painter than we now think he was, but Gilbert Stuart's paintings are just as well thought of today as they were when he painted them.

After living many years in England, Gilbert Stuart came back to America. It was now the United States of America, for the Revolution had been fought and won. He said he had come back to paint the portrait of George Washington, whom he greatly admired.

在伦敦师从过韦斯特的那些年轻的美国人当中，有一位便是吉尔伯特·斯图尔特。他出生于美国独立战争之前的新英格兰地区，并在那里长大。他也认为自己到英国去更有发展前途，因此来到了伦敦。在伦敦的时候，他成了一名以精美的肖像画著称的画家。虽说当时的人比如今的我们更看重本杰明·韦斯特，认为他是一位非常了不起的画家，可在吉尔伯特·斯图尔特进行创作的当时与如今，人们也都一致认为他的画作非常优秀呢。

在英国生活了多年之后，吉尔伯特·斯图尔特回到了美国。此时，美国已成了美利坚合众国，因为独立战争已经打完，并且美国获得了胜利。他说，自己之所以回去，是为了给自己极其崇拜的乔治·华盛顿绘制肖像。

Washington posed for three portraits by Gilbert Stuart. The last of these three is the most famous and best-loved picture of Washington. It was put on the three-cent stamp in 1932. Although it is not on a stamp anymore, this portrait is still featured on the United States one-dollar bill.

You may wonder why the portrait of Washington is unfinished. The reason is that Gilbert Stuart liked it so well that he wanted to keep it. He had promised the portrait to Washington when it was finished but it never was. Instead of the original, Washington agreed to take a copy that Stuart made of it for him. As a matter of fact, the artist painted about fifty copies of the portrait from time to time and sold a copy whenever he needed money.

Gilbert Stuart went to live in Boston and never returned to England. He painted five other presidents besides Washington so he is sometimes called the painter of presidents.

Now there were, of course, other American painters in the early days of the United States. Most of them were portrait painters because so many people wanted portraits. There were still no cameras to take photographs. It is from the portraits of these early painters that we know what Americans of those days looked like.

These early portraits have become very valuable and many of them are now in museums. Some, however, still belong to the families whose ancestors had their portraits painted.

乔治·华盛顿摆出姿势，让吉尔伯特·斯图尔特绘制了三幅肖像画。在这三幅肖像中，最后一幅最有名，也是人们最喜欢的一幅华盛顿肖像画。1932年，这幅肖像画被印到了三美分的邮票上。尽管如今已经不再用于邮票上，可这幅画作依然是美国一美元纸币上的主角呢。

你们可能很想知道，为什么华盛顿的这幅肖像没有画完。原因在于，吉尔伯特·斯图尔特极其喜欢这幅画作，因此想要自己保留下来。本来，他已经答应华盛顿，说完工后就把这幅画送过去，可这幅画却一直都没有画完。后来，华盛顿同意，不要斯图尔特为他绘制的原作，只要一幅仿制品就行了。事实上，这位画家后来却制作了五十幅仿制品，每当自己需要用钱，就时不时地卖上一幅呢。

吉尔伯特·斯图尔特后来住在波士顿，再也没有回过英国了。除了华盛顿，他还替五位美国总统绘制过肖像；因此，人们有时还称他为“总统画家”呢。

注意，在美利坚合众国建国的初期，当然也出现过其他的一些画家。他们当中，绝大多数人都是肖像画家，因为那时有很多人都想请画家给自己绘制画像。当时，仍然没有发明照相机，人们仍然没法拍照。正是通过早期这些画家的肖像画，我们才了解到那个时代的美国人是个什么样子哩。

如今，这些早期的肖像画已经变得非常珍贵，因此其中的许多画作都保存进了博物馆。然而，有些画作却依然由祖辈曾经请人绘制了这些肖像画的一些家庭保留着。

Chapter 29 More Americans

I know you've heard of Robert Fulton, the inventor of the steamboat. But have you ever heard of Robert Fulton the painter? Does it seem strange they should have the same name? Then it ought to seem even stranger that they were born the same year. Stranger yet — they died the same year.

It's actually not strange at all because the painter and the inventor were the same Robert Fulton. Robert Fulton's first profession was portrait painting. He studied under Benjamin West in London.

I know you've also heard of Samuel Morse. He invented the telegraph. But have you ever heard of Samuel Morse the painter? The painter and the inventor were also one and the same. Morse's first profession was portrait painting. He, too, studied under Benjamin West in London.

Both Fulton and Morse were inventors. Both were painters. Both were taught by West. And they weren't bad painters either. Of course they weren't nearly as good portrait painters as Holbein or Hals or Dürer.

I wish I could tell you more about these and the many other early American portrait painters. I would tell you about Rembrandt Peale, for instance, who was the first to light an American city with gas streetlights and who also studied under Benjamin West. Or about his father, Charles Willson Peale, who had a famous museum of all kinds of unusual

第29章 更多的美国画家

我知道，你们都听说过罗伯特·富尔顿这个曾经发明了汽轮的发明家。可是，你们有没有听说过画家罗伯特·富尔顿呢？两人完全同名同姓，是不是有点儿奇怪呢？更加奇怪的是，两人还是同一年出生的。还有更加奇怪的呢，他们竟然是同一年去世的！

其实，这一点儿也不奇怪，因为画家罗伯特·富尔顿与发明家罗伯特·富尔顿实际上就是同一个人。罗伯特·富尔顿起初的职业，就是绘制肖像画。他曾经也到伦敦师从过本杰明·韦斯特呢。

我知道，你们也都听说过萨缪尔·摩尔斯这个人。他发明了电报。可你们听说过画家萨缪尔·摩尔斯没有呢？这位画家与发明家，也是同一个人。摩尔斯最初的职业，也是绘制肖像画。他也到伦敦师从过本杰明·韦斯特。

富尔顿与摩尔斯两人都是发明家。两人都是画家。两人也都曾师从过韦斯特。并且，两人的画艺都并不坏。当然，相对于荷尔拜因、哈尔斯或丢勒这样的杰出肖像画家来说，他们肯定是没法与之相提并论的。

我希望能够多给你们介绍介绍这些画家，以及美国其他许多早期画家的情况。比如，我愿意给你们介绍介绍伦勃朗·皮尔，他是率先让美国的一座城市用煤气来点亮路灯的人，并且也在本杰明·韦斯特的手下学习过。或者，介绍介绍他的父亲

things. Or about — but I'll have to stop, for it's time to tell you instead about the next group of American painters. They were landscape painters.

Most of the early American landscape painters are not quite as well known as the portrait painters. These landscape painters tried to put all the little details that they saw in nature into their pictures. Every stick and stone and bush were painted in very carefully, and their pictures as a whole weren't as good as if the painters had left out the little things so you could look at the picture all at once. Instead your eye sees the picture piece by piece.

They generally painted scenes that were very impressive, like views of mountains and big rivers and valleys seen from hilltops. Finally, however, one landscape painter changed this. He painted everyday peaceful scenes like meadows or trees. He left out the unimportant details so you could see a beautiful picture instead of just a copy of a piece of real country.

I don't mean for you to think that the real country isn't beautiful. A real outdoors scene is beautiful — more beautiful, generally, than any picture of it could be. But, you see, a painter can never make his picture look exactly like the real, beautiful scenery itself, so it's often better for him to make his painting a beautiful thing and not try to make it exactly like a real scene. A painter has to do this mostly by trying to make you feel what he felt when he saw the scene rather than trying to show you every little thing he saw.

So this painter of everyday peaceful scenes, whose name was George Inness, tried to make people feel how beautiful he thought the scene was. George Inness used very

查尔斯·威尔逊·皮尔也行，因为他拥有一座赫赫有名的博物馆，其中收藏了各种各样的稀奇之物。或者，介绍介绍……不过，我得打住了，因为现在我必须转而给你们介绍下一批美国画家了。这些画家，都是风景画家。

美国早期的风景画家，绝大多数人都不像肖像画家那样有名。这些风景画家，都努力将他们在大自然中所见的每一个小细节都描绘到自己的画作中去。每一根枯枝、每一块石头、每一丛灌木，他们都会细细进行描绘；而倘若他们略去这些细节，从而让观众一眼就看得完整幅画作的话，那么整幅画作就没那么优秀了。相反，你们得一点一点儿地去细看他们的画作才行。

他们绘制的，通常都是那些令人印象深刻的场景，比如从山顶俯瞰到的崇山峻岭、大江大河和深沟巨壑。然而，最终有位风景画家却改变了这种做法。他绘制的，都是日常生活中的宁静景色，比如草地或者树林。他忽略掉了其中一些不太重要的细节，从而让观众可以欣赏到一幅美丽的画作，让观众看到的不只是现实乡村风景的翻版。

我可不是要你们认为现实中的乡村不美。现实中的户外景色是很美的，并且通常都比任何画作中描绘出来的景色更美。不过，你们也明白，一名画家是永远不可能将画作绘制得与现实的美景本身一模一样的；因此，将自己的画作绘制成一件美的作品，而不是努力绘制得跟现实风景一模一样，这种做法对画家来说往往更可取。一位画家，必须是主要通过尽量让观众体会到画家看到某种景色时的感受，而不是尽力去向观众呈现出画家看到的任何细微之处，来做到这一点才行。

因此，这位创作日常的宁和之景、名叫乔治·英尼斯的画家，正是努力想让观

平静和富饶，英尼斯作品，
现存于纽约的大都会艺术博物馆
（由波士顿的大学印刷协会提供）

beautiful colors that harmonized, or went well together. If there were some bits of color in the real scene that would not harmonize with the other colors in the picture, he left them out. If the picture looks better without every detail clearly put in, why not paint it without the detail? This is what George Inness thought. And so his landscapes gradually became better and better pictures as he learned to leave out the things that would prevent the pictures from being beautiful.

Do you still know what I'm talking about? I know it is pretty hard to understand. I hope you will go to a museum someday and see one of Inness's paintings. Then you will be able to enjoy the colors as well as the shapes of what he painted.

For instance, in a famous picture of his called *Peace and Plenty*, you can see the shapes but I can only tell you of the warm, glowing, golden light that streams across the original painting.

众感受到，他觉得画中的景色有多么美丽。乔治·英尼斯运用的，都是很和谐，或者说搭配得很完美的色彩。如果现实景色中有某些色彩与画作中的其他色彩并不协调，那么他就会剔除掉这些色彩。如果不把所有细节全都清清楚楚地绘进去，而画作反而显得更漂亮的话，那我们为什么不去剔除掉这些细节呢？乔治·英尼斯正是这样想的。于是，随着学会忽略掉那些会让画作变得不美的东西，他绘制的风景画，也逐渐变成了越来越优秀的画作。

你们能明白我说的是什么意思吗？我知道，这个方面是很难理解的。我希望，有朝一日你们能去博物馆，看一看英尼斯的一幅画作。那样的话，你们就能够欣赏到他画作中的色彩和造型了。

例如，在他那幅叫作《平静和富饶》的名作中，虽说你们都看得见其中的造型，但我能告诉你们的，却只是流淌在原作之上的那种温暖、鲜艳的金色阳光。

I can only tell you, too, that George Inness was one of the best American landscape painters. You will have to see some of his paintings in person before you can really appreciate their true beauty.

Winslow Homer was a very different painter than George Inness. Homer is famous for painting the sea. But he didn't care to paint quiet seas. He preferred stormy ones. His pictures of waves dashing high against the rocky New England coast have been called the best sea paintings that any artist has done. Homer loved the sea. He built his house on the rocky coast of Maine where he could always watch the ocean.

Homer loved to hunt and fish too, and he often went into the Adirondack Mountains in New York State — they were really wild in those days. There he painted hunting scenes, canoes shooting the rapids, and guides at work.

When Homer took a trip on the ocean south toward Bermuda and the West Indies, he painted sea scenes of stormy weather there too. He was also fond of painting the fishermen who went to fish on the Grand Banks out at sea in their schooners. His picture *The Fog Warning* shows you one of these fishermen.

The fisherman is in a boat called a dory that has been sent out from a schooner. You can see the fish the man has caught. But fog is creeping in and the fisherman has to row hard and fast to get back to his schooner so as not to be caught in the fog. If the fog catches him, he can only hope to get safely back by listening for the foghorn on the ship and rowing blindly toward the sound. It is dangerous business alone in an open boat on the

我也只能对你们说，乔治·英尼斯是美国最著名的风景画家之一。你们必须亲自去看一看他的画作，才能真正欣赏到它们真正的美。

温斯洛·霍默则是一个与乔治·英尼斯风格迥异的画家。霍默以绘制海景而著称。不过，他并不喜欢绘制平静的大海。他更喜欢狂暴的大海。他那些描绘了滔天巨浪高高地拍打着新英格兰地区岩石耸立的海岸的画作，被人们誉为有史以来最优秀的海洋画作。霍默热爱海洋。他甚至把自家的房屋建造在缅因州岩石嶙峋的海岸边，从而让他能够常常观察大海。

霍默还很喜欢打猎和捕鱼，因此经常到纽约州的阿迪朗代克山脉中去；在那个时代，阿迪朗代克山脉可还是荒无人烟呢。在那里，他创作出了一些描绘狩猎场景、坐着独木舟漂流以及描绘向导工作场景的画作。

而当霍默坐船在大海上南行，前往百慕大群岛和西印度群岛时，他又创作出了一些描绘暴风雨肆虐时的海景画。他也很喜欢描绘去大浅滩[1]捕鱼的渔民驾着帆船出海时的情景。他创作的《大雾警报》，便向观众呈现了一位渔民的形象。

画中的渔民，坐在一艘从帆船上放下来的小船上；这种小船，叫作“平底船”。你们可以看到这位渔民打到的鱼儿。可是，大雾正在他的身后悄悄逼近，因此那位渔民不得不使劲划桨，迅速向他的帆船划去，以免被大雾困住。如果大雾赶上来，他就只能寄望于听着帆船上的雾角之声，并在看不清方向的情况下朝着发出声音的地方划船，才能安全回到帆船上去了。独自划着敞口船，留在即将起雾的大

[1] 大浅滩（Grand Banks），北美洲纽芬兰岛东南岸外大西洋上的浅滩，是世界著名的大渔场。

大雾警报，霍默作品，现存于波士顿的波士顿美术馆
（由波士顿的大学印刷协会提供）

Atlantic with the fog rolling in. Let's hope he reached the schooner.

Now instead of simply telling you that these two painters, George Inness and Winslow Homer, were fine painters, I'll say it this way: The more you see of their paintings, the more, I'm sure, you will like them.

And I'll add this: You don't have to wait until you're grown up to understand and like their pictures. Inness and Homer painted pictures that young people surely must like. That's what I think.

西洋上，是一件很危险的事情哩。让我们祈祷他安然回到帆船之上吧。

现在，我不会简简单单地跟你们说，乔治·英尼斯和温斯洛·霍默二人都是优秀的画家，而要这样说：你们见到他们的画作越多，我敢肯定你们就会越喜欢这两位画家。

并且，我还要补充一句：你们并不是非得等到自己长大成人之后，才能理解和喜欢他们的作品。英尼斯和霍默二人都创作了一些画作，年轻人肯定都非常喜欢。至少，我是这么认为的。

Chapter 30 Two European Americans

Paintings sometimes go visiting. In 1932 a famous painting was carefully taken from its home in the Louvre in Paris, put on an ocean liner, and allowed to go on a visit to New York. The last time this painting had been in the United States was fifty years before. Then no one thought enough of it to pay the one thousand dollars that its painter was asking for it.

On its second visit to New York, it was treated as an honored guest. Crowds of people went to see the painting, and if anyone had offered many, many thousands of dollars for it, he could not have bought it, for it is now considered a great art treasure and is not for sale.

The man who painted this visiting picture named it *Arrangement in Gray and Black, No. 1*. But it became too well loved to be called by such an uninteresting name. So now everyone simply calls it Whistler's Mother.

James McNeill Whistler was an American but he spent most of his life in Europe. He quarreled with his friends and seemed to like to cause a little trouble wherever he went. This probably helped him to become famous because it kept people talking about him. He was always news. Perhaps that is why he wore a monocle, which is an eyeglass for just one eye, and why he carried an extra long cane and signed his pictures with a butterfly. He liked to be talked about. He liked to be news.

第30章 两位欧裔美国画家

有的时候，人们会将画作进行巡回展出。1932年，一幅名画被人们小心翼翼地从巴黎卢浮宫的原保存地取出来，放到一艘远洋轮船上，获准前往纽约进行访问展出。这幅名画上一次来到美国，还是五十年前的事情了。当时，可没有人想过要答应画家的出价，用一千美元就将这幅名画买下来呢。

第二次造访纽约的时候，这幅画作就被美国人当成贵宾了。人们蜂拥而至，都想一睹这幅画作的丰采；就算有人出价成千上万美元，也不可能再买到这幅画，因为它此时已经被人们视为一件伟大的艺术瑰宝，属于非卖品了。

创作出这幅访展名作的那位画家，将这幅画命名为《灰与黑的组合，第1号》。不过，由于人们太过喜欢这幅画，因此再用这样一个毫无意思的名称就不太好了。于是，如今大家都只称之为《惠斯勒的母亲》。

詹姆斯·麦克奈尔·惠斯勒本是美国人，但他一生中的绝大部分时光，却是在欧洲度过的。他常常和朋友们争吵，并且似乎到哪里都喜欢惹出点麻烦来。这一点，很可能在他出名的过程中发挥了作用，因为这让人们总是在谈论他。他一向都是新闻焦点。或许，他之所以总是戴着一副独眼眼镜（即只能戴在一只眼睛上的那种眼镜），并且总是随身携带着一根超长的手杖，在画作上的签名就像是一只蝴蝶，原因就在这里。他喜欢被人们谈论。他喜欢成为新闻人物。

But of course, no matter how much people talked about him, Whistler would not have been a great artist if he had not painted great pictures. And everyone agrees that *Whistler's Mother* is a great picture. It is a different kind of portrait than those that other artists had painted before. That is why it wasn't admired as much at first as it is now. Whistler's mother is shown sitting beside a wall. On the wall hangs a picture in a black frame. You can see that everything in the painting is drawn with straight lines except the old lady herself.

How big would you guess the portrait of Whistler's mother is? Would you be surprised to hear that the mother in the picture is life-size? Now that you know she is life-size, you can understand that the painting is a rather large one.

灰与黑的组合，第1号：画家母亲的肖像，惠斯勒作品，
现存于巴黎的奥赛博物馆
（由波士顿的大学印刷协会提供）

If you could see some of Whistler's paintings in person, I think you would be surprised at the way he used colors. Some of his pictures are almost all blue in color — dark blues and light blues and medium blues, all blended to make a picture that is unlike any by artists who used many different colors. Some of

不过，无论人们怎么谈论他，倘若没有创作出了不起的作品，惠斯勒自然也是成不了一名伟大的画家的。而人们都一致认为，《惠斯勒的母亲》是一幅伟大的画作。它是一幅风格与以前其他画家的作品完全不同的肖像画。而它起初之所以并不像如今一样受到人们的推崇，原因也在于此。画作中，惠斯勒的母亲坐在墙边。墙上挂着一幅有着黑色外框的画作。你们都看得出，除了老太太本人，画作中的一切都是用直直的线条绘制出来的。

你们猜猜看，惠斯勒母亲的这幅肖像画，尺寸究竟有多大呢？倘若听说画中的那位母亲有真人大小，你们会不会觉得惊讶呢？既然你们都知道画中的母亲有真人大小，那你们就能想到，这幅画作的尺寸是非常巨大的。

如果你们能够亲自去看一看惠斯勒的一些作品，那么，我觉得你们很可能会对他运用色彩的方式感到惊讶。他的一些画作所用的色彩，几乎全都是蓝色：深蓝、浅蓝、间蓝，全都融合在一起，组成一幅画作。这与运用各种颜色的其他画家的作品全都不同。惠斯勒还有一些画作则全是白色的。比如，《白色交响乐1号》描绘的，就是一个身穿白色连衣裙的女孩站在白色的背景之中。你们自然猜得出，这可

Whistler's pictures are almost all white. *Symphony in White, No. 1*, for instance, shows a girl in a white dress against a white background. You can guess that it was not the easiest kind of picture to paint and that Whistler must have been skillful to do it successfully.

Another famous American painter who lived most of the time in Europe was John Singer Sargent. Isn't it interesting that all the American painters used to go to Europe to study art? In fact, so many travelers and artists visited the masterworks and famous sites in Europe that it was called the Grand Tour. Wouldn't it be fun to go on a Grand Tour?

Sargent was born in Florence, Italy, to American parents and spent his childhood growing up traveling from city to city throughout Europe. His mother loved traveling so much, in fact, that his father had to give up being a doctor just to keep up with her.

At age seventeen, Sargent settled down in Paris and began to paint works everyone found remarkable. He would present his latest painting or collection in a setting called a *salon*, a place to exhibit artwork. Everyone would praise his works as if he could do no wrong — until one painting was presented that shocked everyone.

Sargent had completed a portrait of a woman who was well known for her very unusual style of clothing, makeup, and hair. She was someone many people found too extreme to accept, so the portrait of her became too extreme to accept too. Sargent left Paris immediately and refused to paint a person or scene that would cause rejection ever again.

Most of Sargent's portraits are admired very much, but I like his murals at the Boston Public Library best of all. When the library was built, Sargent was asked to decorate the

不是最容易绘制的一种画作；因此，惠斯勒必定技艺精湛，才能成功地创作出这幅画呢。

还有一位著名的美国画家，他的一生中绝大多数时间也是在欧洲度过的；这位画家，就是约翰·辛格·萨金特。所有的美国画家都曾去欧洲学习过绘画艺术，这一点难道不是很有意思吗？实际上，由于许多游客和画家都瞻仰过欧洲的杰作，都参观过欧洲那些著名的遗址，因此这种游历还被称为“大旅行”呢。进行这样一次“大旅行”，难道不是很有趣吗？

萨金特出生于意大利的佛罗伦萨，但父母都是美国人；他的童年，就是在整个欧洲从一座城市搬到另一座城市的过程，而他也在这一过程中慢慢长大了。事实上，他的母亲非常热衷于旅行，因此父亲不得不放弃医生的职业，跟着她到处跑呢。

长到十七岁的时候，萨金特在巴黎安顿下来，开始绘画；而他的作品，大家都觉得非常出色。他会将自己最新的画作或者画集放到一个叫作“沙龙”的地方；所谓的沙龙，就是展出艺术作品的地方。大家都交口称赞他的作品，好像他画得毫无缺陷似的；直到后来，他展出的一幅画作震惊了所有的人。

当时，萨金特完成了一幅肖像画；画中是一位女士，她因在穿着、化妆和头发风格上都与众不同而著称。许多人都觉得她过于极端，令人难以接受；因此，她的这幅肖像画也被人们认为过于极端而令人难以接受了。于是，萨金特马上离开了巴黎，并且自此以后，再也不愿去创作那种会引发反对意见的人物画或者风景画了。

虽说萨金特的绝大部分肖像画都备受人们推崇，可我却最喜欢他为波士顿公共

walls on the third floor. He decided to paint a history of religion and called it *Triumph of Religion*. One wall shows the children of Israel worshiping the old false gods. Underneath is a long row of Hebrew prophets from the Old Testament. These prophets seem to be lamenting the evils of their people's ways.

On another wall Sargent painted saints and angels with the crucified Christ in the center. He painted these figures with bands of real gold around their heads and with the figure of Christ carved like a statue as well as painted. People who saw the paintings marveled that a portrait artist could paint these large murals so splendidly. Now visitors to Boston go to the library just to admire the murals. I encourage you to see them, too, if you ever go to Boston.

穿着起绒粗呢的先知们，
《宗教的胜利》壁画细部，萨金特作品
现存于波士顿的波士顿公共图书馆

During his lifetime Sargent became the most famous living painter of portraits. He painted portraits of many rich and important people in Britain and America. Indeed, it was considered an honor to have Sargent paint your portrait. At one time, he had a waiting list that would have taken him forty years to complete!

图书馆所创作的壁画。这座图书馆建成后，萨金特被请去给三楼的墙壁绘制装饰画。他决定绘制一幅宗教历史画，并将其命名为《宗教的胜利》。其中一面墙上，画着以色列的孩子们正在崇拜旧伪神时的情景。其下则是《圣经·旧约》中提到的一长队希伯来先知。这些先知，似乎正在痛惜这个民族所犯下的罪孽呢。

在另一面墙上，萨金特画上了圣徒和天使，而钉在十字架上受难的基督，则位于画作的正中央。他在绘制圣徒和天使这些人物时，竟然用了一圈圈的真金围在人物头上；而基督这个人物呢，则既像是画作，又像是雕刻出来的一尊雕像呢。凡是看到过这些画作的人都很惊奇，一位肖像画家竟然能够将这些大幅的壁画绘制得如此辉煌壮观。如今，游客前往波士顿图书馆，都只是为了瞻仰这些壁画。我劝你们，要是有机会去波士顿的话，不妨也去看一看。

萨金特在生前就已经成了最为声名赫赫的一位肖像画家。他替英国和美国的许多富人、要人绘制过肖像。实际上，人们认为，能请到萨金特为自己绘制一幅肖像画，就是一种莫大的荣耀了。曾经有过一段时间，一大波人都等着他去绘制肖像；而他要绘完这些肖像的话，足足要花上四十年呢！

Chapter 31 Real-People Artists

What American pictures do you like best? Do you like pictures of the Wild West? Pictures of Native Americans with their horses and dogs and rolled-up tepees taking the trail to new hunting grounds? Pictures of cowboys with their six- shooters and lariats, riding the herd or roping broncos? Pictures of hunters with their fur caps and trusty rifles, making their way through a heavy snowstorm? Pictures of soldiers of the United States Cavalry patrolling the country to keep order and protect property?

Are these the kinds of pictures you like?

If they aren't, I'll be disappointed, for I like them very much. Even if they were painted by a poor painter, I'm afraid I'd like such pictures just because I can't help liking Native Americans and cowboys and soldiers.

Luckily there was an American artist who painted such pictures very well. His name was Frederick Remington. Frederick Remington didn't sit home in a studio and ask Native Americans to come and pose for him. He went out to the Wild West and painted them as he saw them living their daily lives. Even if Frederick Remington had never written books about his life in the cowboy country, we should know by his paintings that he had lived there among real cowboys and Native Americans.

At first Remington didn't paint. He drew. He was an *illustrator*. An illustrator's job is to draw pictures in black and white or color for magazines and books. Remington was

第31章 平民画家

你们最喜欢美国的哪种绘画作品呢？你们喜欢描绘“狂野西部”的画作吗？喜欢描绘印第安人带着马匹、猎狗，卷起他们的圆锥形帐篷，沿着小径前往新狩猎场地的画作吗？喜欢描绘牛仔们带着他们的六发式左轮手枪和套马索，赶着牛群或者套捉野马的画作吗？喜欢描绘猎人戴上皮帽，带着可靠的步枪，在肆虐的暴风雪里艰难前进的画作吗？喜欢描绘美国骑兵部队的战士们在乡间巡逻，以维持社会秩序和保护民众财产的画作吗？

你们喜欢的，是不是这些类型不同的画作呢？

如果不是，那我会觉得很遗憾，因为我非常喜欢这样的画作。即便是由一位技艺低劣的画家所作，恐怕我也会喜欢的，只是因为我是不由自主地喜欢印第安人，喜欢牛仔，并且喜欢士兵。

幸亏，有一位美国画家，很擅长于绘制这样的画作。他名叫弗里德里克·雷明顿。但是，弗里德里克·雷明顿并不是在自己的工作室里舒适地待着，让印第安人前来摆出姿势做他的模特，而是亲自来到“狂野西部”，将自己看到的印第安人日常生活时的情景描绘下来。就算弗里德里克从来没有写过描述他在牛仔乡村生活的著作，我们通过他的画作，也能明白他在那里跟真正的牛仔和印第安人一起生活过。

起初，雷明顿并没有创作油画。他只是勾勒。他是一位插图画家。插图画家的

something like a human camera, trained to put down on paper with pen and ink life in the West just as it was so that people in the East could know what it was like.

Often illustrators do not become great painters, and at first Remington wasn't a great painter. When he began to paint with colors instead of simply drawing with pen or pencil, he depicted the cowboys and Native Americans accurately but the colors he used were too bright and glaring.

Of course on the plains and badlands of the West, the colors that he saw were really bright and glaring in the brilliant sunlight and clear atmosphere. Gradually, however, his pictures became better paintings as he learned to use the bright colors better. His later pictures are really fine paintings, I think, and not just brightly colored illustrations.

Frederick Remington didn't only paint exciting events. He also liked to paint Native Americans as plain, everyday people — not always dressed in feathers and war paint. In other words, his pictures show us real Native Americans and not just the picture-book kind you often see in the movies.

His soldiers are not always dressed up for a parade or marching to a stirring band like picture- book soldiers. They are simply real men, cooking their suppers over the campfire, guarding wagon trains, and cleaning their horses. His cowboys are real cowboys working for a living, not just the sort of cowboys we see in old movies. "Men with the bark on" is what Remington called these rough and ready men of the West.

And as for horses, Frederick Remington, let me tell you, could paint real horses. People

工作，就是替杂志和书籍绘制黑白或者彩色插图。雷明顿有点儿像是一台“活人相机”，学的就是将西部的生活用笔和墨忠实地记录在纸上，以便东部的人能够了解到西部生活是个什么样子。

插图画家一般都成不了伟大的画家，因此起初雷明顿也不是一位了不起的画家。他开始用油彩来绘画，而不是只用钢笔或铅笔素描的时候，虽说准确地描绘出了牛仔和印第安人的模样，但他所用的色彩，都太过亮丽和醒目了。

当然，在西部的平地和荒原上，在灿烂的阳光和清澈的空气中，他所见到的色彩本来的确是亮丽而耀眼的。然而，随着他学会更加自如地运用那种亮丽的色彩，他的插图便慢慢地变成质量更佳的画作了。我觉得，他后期创作的一些作品，确实都是一些非常精美的油画，而不仅仅是一些颜色鲜艳的插图。

弗里德里克·雷明顿并不是只描绘那些激动人心的场景。他也喜欢将印第安人描绘成简简单单、普普通通的人，而并非始终都是那种头插羽毛、身涂颜料的印第安人。换句话来说就是，他的画作为我们呈现出了真实的印第安人，而不是你们在电影中经常能够看到的那种连环画式的印第安人。

他笔下的士兵，也并非始终都是像连环画中的士兵一样，排列得整整齐齐地准备操练，或者准备向骚乱地区进军。他们完全都是真实的人，在营火上做晚饭，护卫军需车队，给自己的战马梳洗。他笔下的牛仔，也都是真真实实、为了谋生而辛勤劳作的牛仔，并不是我们在老电影中所看到的那种牛仔。雷明顿把这些粗犷而机敏的西部人，都称为“质朴的人”。

至于马儿，我不妨告诉你们，弗里德里克·雷明顿也能塑造出非常逼真的马儿

aren't all alike. Neither are horses. Frederick Remington's horses aren't just picture-book horses any more than his Native Americans are picture-book figures. Each horse is a special horse, different from any other horse. They are slow or bright, high-spirited or gentle, lazy or full of energy, just as real horses are.

Besides being a wonderful illustrator, a writer, and a good painter, Remington was a sculptor. He made statues of men on horseback that seem full of life and action.

So if you want to see what the real Wild West was like, find a book illustrated by Frederick Remington. You'll really enjoy the pictures.

Remington was an American painter who painted American people. So was a later painter named George Bellows, He also painted the kind of pictures I think you'll like, only his pictures are of the eastern part of the country, especially in and around New York City.

Bellows was such a good baseball player on his college team that he almost became a professional ballplayer, but he decided to be a painter instead. Just the same, he always liked sports. Some of his pictures show men and boys swimming along the New York waterfront, some are of polo games, and some very well-known ones are of boxing matches.

西部原野上发起冲锋的骑兵，雷明顿作品，
现存于纽约的大都会艺术博物馆
（由波士顿的大学印刷协会提供）

形象。人与人的长相都不一样。马儿也是如此。与他笔下的印第安人都不是图画书中的那种印第安人一样，他笔下的马儿，也不是图画书中的那种马儿。他笔下的每一匹马，都有自己的独特之处，都不同于其他的马匹。它们有的蠢笨、有的机灵，有的脾气暴烈、有的温和驯服，有的懒惰无比、有的精力充沛，就像真正的马儿一样。

除了是一位令人叹服的插图画家、作家和优秀的画家，雷明顿还是一位雕塑家呢。他创作出了许多骑在马上的人物雕像，而这些雕像看上去也全都充满了活力和动感。

因此，如果你们想要看一看真正的“狂野西部”是个什么样子的话，不妨找一本由弗里德里克·雷明顿绘制插图的书籍来看看。你们会真正喜欢上这些画作的。

雷明顿是一位描绘普通民众的美国画家。而后来一位名叫乔治·班洛斯的画家，也是如此。他还创作了一些画作，我觉得你们都会喜欢的；只是这些画作描绘的都是美国东部地区，尤其是纽约市内和周围地区的风情人物。

班洛斯上大学时，是校队里一位优秀的棒球运动员，还差点儿成了一名职业棒球手；可后来，他却决定要当一名画家。尽管如此，他还是一直都很喜欢体育运动。他的一些画作，描绘了男人和男孩子们沿着纽约海滨游泳时的情景，有些画作描绘了人们进行水球比赛的场景，还有一些非常著名的画作描绘的则是拳击比赛。

He was an illustrator, too, as Remington was, but Bellows' illustrations were made in a very different way. They were made first on smooth stone and then printed from the stone with ink onto paper. This kind of picture is known as a *lithograph*. Bellows was an unusually fine lithographer.

One of Bellows' most well-known paintings is of the real boxing match between Jack Dempsey and Luis Firpo for the heavyweight championship of the world. Firpo was a strong South American boxer. He was called the Wild Bull of the Pampas because of his tremendous strength.

班洛斯母亲肖像，班洛斯作品，
现存于哥伦布市的哥伦布美术馆
（由波士顿的大学印刷协会提供）

Once during the match, Firpo knocked Dempsey right through the ropes and down into the laps of the people looking on. But this didn't seem to damage Dempsey much, for he finally won the match. Bellows' picture shows Dempsey sailing out of the ring after Firpo's powerful punch. The picture is very dark in some places and very bright in others because all the light was turned on the ring like a big spotlight on a stage. The picture shows how well Bellows could paint furious action.

George Bellows and Frederick Remington are just two of the many American artists who should

虽说跟雷明顿一样，也是一位插图画家，但班洛斯所绘的插图，却是用一种大不相同的方式创作出来的。这些插图，是先刻在光滑的石板上，然后再用墨水从石板上拓印到纸上的。这种画作，被称为石版画。班洛斯就是一位异常优秀的石版画家。

班洛斯最负盛名的一幅画作，描绘的是杰克・邓普希与刘易斯・费尔波两人之间争夺世界重量级拳击冠军的那场拳击比赛。费尔波是南美一位极其厉害的拳击手。由于力大无穷，他还被人们称为“潘帕斯草原[1]上的野牛”呢。

在这场比赛中，费尔波有一次将邓普希直接击出了场外，后者掉到了观众的膝盖上。不过，这一拳似乎并没有让邓普希受太大的伤，因为他最终还是赢得了这场比赛。班洛斯的那幅画作，呈现的正是受到费尔波的有力一击之后，邓普希摔出场外时的情景。画作中，有些部位非常阴暗，而其他一些地方又非常明亮，因为所有灯光就像舞台上一盏巨大的聚光灯那样，全都转到了赛场上。这幅画作，说明班洛斯非常擅长于描绘激烈的场景。

乔治・班洛斯和弗里德里克・雷明顿，仅仅是应当列入艺术史书籍的众多美国

[1] 潘帕斯草原（the Pampas），概指南美大草原，尤指位于阿根廷境内的大草原。

be in an art history book. I wish I could tell you about the other American painters, but to tell about them alf would make this book too thick, and no one likes too fat a book.

I have hardly mentioned the murals that decorate rooms in many American buildings. Almost every large city in the United States has good mural paintings in some of its buildings. If you live in a city, try to find out where these mural paintings are and then go see them. They are very interesting. When you learn the name of the artist who painted them, see how much you can learn about him and his other paintings.

You can have fun on a rainy day making a scrapbook of American paintings and statues. Look for pictures of them in magazines and advertisements. Often there are pictures of paintings there.

American art isn't mostly in the past. It's being created right now. Real artists are even painting pictures for advertisements.

Many people like to collect things, and a collection you could be proud of would be a scrapbook of American art. I know scrapbooks are fun to make because I've made them myself. I'm making one now. Try one yourself and get some fun out of all this art that is being created in your country.

And if you like American artists, don't forget Remington and Bellows.

邓普希与费尔波，班洛斯作品，
现存于纽约的现代艺术博物馆

画家当中的两位罢了。我要是能够将其他的美国画家全都介绍给你们就好了；可要是全都介绍的话，这本书就会太厚了：没有人会喜欢一本书的内容太多呢。

我几乎还没有提及过那些装点了美国许多建筑物的壁画呢。美国几乎每一座大城市里，一些建筑物的内部都有优秀的壁画作品。如果你们住在城市里，那么不妨试着找出这些壁画所在的地方，然后去观赏观赏吧。它们都非常有意思。待你们得知绘制这些壁画的画家姓甚名谁之后，再来看看你们能够了解到多少关于这位画家，以及他们的其他绘画作品的内容吧。

在一个雨天，制作出一本关于美国绘画和雕塑作品的剪贴本，你们可能会很开心的。到一些杂志和广告中去搜集这些作品吧。那些东西上面，通常都印有油画作品的照片呢。

美国的绘画艺术，并非主要存在于过去。就在此时此刻，人们也在进行创作呢。一些真正的画家，甚至还在创作广告画呢。

很多人都喜欢收藏东西，而你们可以为之感到自豪的一种收藏，便是一本关于美国艺术的剪贴簿。我知道制作剪贴簿很好玩，因为我自己以前也制作过。现在，我还在制作一本剪贴簿呢。你们不妨也亲自试着制作一本，从你们的祖国正在创造的这种艺术当中，得到某种乐趣吧。

而且，如果你们喜欢美国的画家，那就不要忘了雷明顿和班洛斯这两个人。

Chapter 32 Nons and Surs

"Why, a six-year-old child could paint a better picture than that!" said the man.

"At least it has plenty of bright colors," said the woman. "Look at all that yellow and orange. I like it. Perhaps it's supposed to be a sunset."

"It looks more like a fried egg to me," the man said.

The man and woman were in an art museum. They were standing before a painting that really didn't look much like either a sunset or a fried egg. It was made of all yellow and orange paints except for a small dark blue square near one comer. As they moved on to the next painting, the man shook his head. "Modem art is too much for me," he said. "I just don't understand it."

Many people are puzzled by paintings that are not realistic pictures of objects. Such paintings are called *nonobjective*, or *abstract*, paintings. Nonobjective paintings are not supposed to look like sunsets or fried eggs or people or houses or any other objects.

Have you ever tried to find pictures of objects in the clouds? Did you ever see a cloud that looked like a lion? Many times one can see clouds that look like a landscape with hills and valleys and harbors and islands. But seeing objects in the clouds doesn't make the clouds more beautiful. The clouds are beautiful whether or not we can use our imagination to see pictures in them.

Nonobjective paintings can be beautiful also. They don't have to look like some object

第32章 非写实主义和超现实主义

“哎呀，一个六岁的孩子都能绘制出一幅比那个更好的画作来！”男人说。

“起码来说，这幅画用了大量鲜艳的色彩呢，”女人说，“瞧瞧那种黄色和橙色。我很喜欢。没准，它应该是日落时分的情景呢。”

“在我看来，它可更像是一个煎鸡蛋。”男人说。

这对男女正在一座美术馆里。他们站在一幅油画前面，而那幅油画，看上去也的确不太像是日落或者煎鸡蛋。整幅画作都是用各种黄色和橙色颜料绘制而成的，只在一个角落附近有一小块方形的深蓝色。他们走向下一幅画作的时候，男人摇了摇自己的头。“我可理解不了现代美术，”他说，“我就是搞不明白。”

许多人对那些不属于现实主义的画作都感到困惑。这样的画作，被称为非写实画，或者抽象画。属于非写实主义风格的画作，看起来本来就不该像日落、煎蛋、人物、房屋或者其他的任何物体。

你们有没有曾经试图在云朵中找出什么东西的形状来呢？你们有没有看到过一朵像是雄狮的云朵呢？人们经常可以看到一些云朵的样子，就像是一幅幅有山有谷、有港湾有小岛的风景画呢。不过，看着云朵像是某种东西，并不会让云朵变得更加美丽。无论我们有没有运用自己的想象力，在其中看没看出什么画作来，云朵都是美丽的。

非写实主义的画作，也是可以非常漂亮的。它们根本就没有必要像是我们认得

that we can recognize. You can enjoy them more if you don't worry about what objects they are supposed to look like. Just remember they are not supposed to look like anything — except a nonobjective painting. They are about color, shape, design, rhythm, texture, and materials.

Artists who paint nonobjective paintings sometimes say, "A camera can make a picture of an object. A photograph will look like the real object. It will have realism. Why should a painter always try to make a picture look realistic? Why should a painter try to do something that a photographer can do with a click of the camera's shutter?"

Jackson Pollock painted a work called *Autumn Rhythm* by spattering, dripping, splashing, and dragging the paint on the canvas. You could say he applied the paint to the canvas just like the wind blows autumn leaves on the landscape.

How can a person tell whether a nonobjective painting is a good painting or a poor one? Why is one building beautiful and another ugly?

People who try making nonobjective pictures themselves usually find they are fun to make. If you try one, you may find it easier to use crayons instead of paints. Put the colors on strong and thick. Don't use a pencil, just the crayons. Don't just scribble; make different shapes.

When you show your nonobjective picture to other people, they'll probably say, "What is it supposed to be?"

And you can answer, "Why it's not supposed to be anything. It's a nonobjective, abstract picture."

出来的某种东西。倘若不费神去想这些画作应该像什么东西的话，你们倒是可以更好地去欣赏它们呢。只要记住，它们除了是一幅非写实主义画作，并不是非得像什么东西这一点就行了。它们呈现出来的，就是色彩、造型、构思、节奏、纹理和材质。

一些创作非写实主义画作的画家，有时会说："相机能够给物体拍照。照片中的物体，跟现实当中的物体是一样的。照片就是现实主义。那么，画家为什么总是要试图创作出看上去很真实的画作呢？拍照的人只要咔嗒一声按下相机快门就能做到的事情，画家又为什么要去做呢？"

杰克逊·波洛克曾经通过将颜料泼、滴、溅、拖在画布上，创作出了一幅叫作《秋韵》的画作。我们完全可以说，他在画布上运用颜料时，就像秋风扫落叶一样洒脱呢。

那么，人们又如何来判定一幅非写实主义画作究竟是好还是不好呢？为什么某栋建筑看起来很漂亮，而另一栋建筑看上去却很丑陋呢？

那些试图创作出非写实主义画作的人，自己通常都觉得这样做很好玩。如果你们也试一试的话，就会发现用蜡笔要比用油画颜料来绘制画作更加容易呢。将画上的色彩涂得又浓又厚。不要用铅笔，只用蜡笔就行。不要只是乱涂乱画，而要绘出不同的形状来。

待你们将自己绘制的非现实主义画作给别人看了之后，他们很可能都会这样问："您画的是什么呢？"

而你就可以这样回答他们："哦，什么都不是。这是一幅非写实的抽象画。"

Of course, many artists still paint pictures of objects. All modem paintings aren't nonobjective.

There are many modem paintings of objects, however, that are just as puzzling to some people as nonobjective paintings. That's because some people think a painting should show objects just the way they look to your eye or to a camera. They think the objects in these paintings should look real — that they should be realistic.

But a painter may not want to paint objects realistically. He may want to get into the picture some of the feeling he himself has about the object. He may want to use his imagination about the object.

Perhaps the artist may want to show all four sides of the object in the same picture, like the Egyptians did when they showed the most important views of the human figure. Usually when you look at an object, you don't see more than two sides. When you look at a table, for instance, you know it has four legs but often you can see only two legs at once.

One of the best-known modem painters first painted pictures that showed people and objects as they really looked. They were realistic paintings. Then he got tired of painting realistic pictures. He tried other ways of showing objects. Some of his paintings, for example, show the front view and side view of a person's face in the same picture like the Egyptians had done.

This modern painter's name is Pablo Picasso. Picasso was born in Spain but most of his work was done in France. Look at the two pictures by Picasso in this chapter. The first one is a realistic painting. See how differently the second one is painted. It is not

当然，许多画家同时仍在创作写实画。并非所有的现代油画，都属于非写实主义画作。

然而，也有许多写实的现代油画，就像非写实主义画作一样，让人们感到迷惑。那是因为，有些人认为，一幅画作所描绘的物体，应当是我们眼睛所见或者相机所见的本来面目。他们觉得，这些画作当中的事物，应当看起来很逼真，也就是说，它们应当“写实”才是。

但是，画家可能却不想完全按照现实去描绘对象。他可能希望在画作中置入自己对绘画对象的某种情感。他可能希望发挥出自己对于绘画对象的想象力。

或许，画家可能还希望在同一幅画作中呈现出物体的四面，就像古埃及人在画作中呈现出人物最重要的部位那样。通常来说，在看着一个物体时，你们顶多只能看到物体的两面。比如说，倘若正面看着一张桌子，虽说你们都知道它有四条腿，可一眼看去，常常却只能看到两条桌腿。

有一位著名的现代画家，率先创作出了一些正是按照本来面目来呈现人物和物体的画作。这些画作，全都属于现实主义风格。后来，他开始厌倦绘制现实主义画作了。于是，他开始尝试用别的手法来呈现对象。例如，他的一些画作就是像古埃及人做的那样，在同一幅画作中呈现出了一个人物脸部的正面像和侧面像。

这位现代画家，名叫巴勃罗・毕加索。毕加索出生于西班牙；但他的绝大部分油画，却都是在法国创作出来的。看一看本章中毕加索的这两幅画作吧。第一幅是现实主义风格的画作。然后再看看第二幅画的风格，看它与第一幅有多大的

realistic at all. You could never mistake this picture for a photograph of three musicians. The three musicians are there in the picture all right, but you can see they are not painted realistically.

Which picture do you like better? Do you think the nonrealistic picture is more interesting than the realistic one?

Would you say *Three Musicians* is a nonobjective picture? It isn't because it shows objects — musicians, instruments, and the like. We can simply call it a *nonrealistic* picture.

Another way of painting is called surrealism. In a dream anything can happen. In a surrealist painting anything can happen too. People can have heads made of cabbages, bodies made of bureau drawers, or trees growing out of their ears — just as in a dream.

One famous surrealist painting called *The Persistence of Memory* shows several watches. They look exactly like real watches except for one thing: they're limp like pancakes. It's as if they were melting. And there are ants in one

美食，毕加索作品，
现存于华盛顿特区的国家美术馆
（由波士顿的大学印刷协会提供）

差异吧。这幅画，根本就不属于现实主义画作。你们也绝不会搞错，这幅画其实就是三位音乐家的相片。虽说那三位音乐家确确实实存在于画作当中，但你们都能看出，他们并不是用现实主义的手法绘制出来的。

你们喜欢哪一幅画作呢？你们有没有觉得，那幅非现实主义的画作比那幅现实主义画作更有意思呢？

你们会不会认为，《三个音乐家》是一幅非写实主义的画作呢？其实，它并不是一幅非写实主义的画作，因为它呈现了音乐家、乐器等绘画对象。我们只能称之为一幅非现实主义的画作。

三个音乐家，毕加索作品，
现存于纽约的现代艺术博物馆
（由缅因州桑福德的大学印刷协会提供）

而另一种绘画风格，则被称为“超现实主义”。在梦境中，什么事情都有可能发生。而在一幅超现实主义画作中，也是什么事情都有可能出现的。就像做梦一样，画中人物的脑袋可以是一棵卷心菜，身体可是以抽屉，而树木也可以从人物的耳朵里长出来。

有一幅名叫《永恒的记忆》的超现实主义名画，描绘了数块手表。它们与真正

of the watches. Why should ants be in a watch? There doesn't have to be a reason because the painting is surreal.

This painting was made by a man named Salvador Dalí, who was born in Spain but came to live in the United States. Dalí is the best known of the surrealist painters. Most surrealist paintings are clearly and smoothly painted with great skill. They are realistic paintings except that the objects in the pictures are often impossible objects. If there were limp watches, however, that's the way they would look.

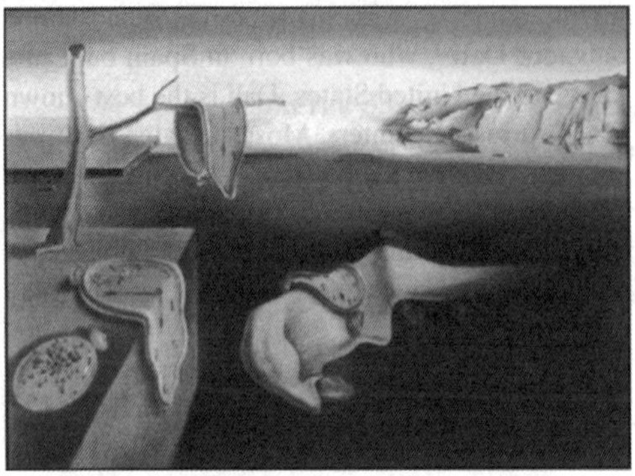

永恒的记忆，达利作品，
现存于纽约的现代艺术博物馆
（由缅因州桑福德的大学印刷协会提供）

Surrealist paintings are puzzling just as a dream is puzzling. They are interesting and fun to look at just as a dream is fun — unless it's a nightmare. Often the artists who paint surrealist pictures make them still more puzzling by giving them strange titles. The title of the limp watches is *The Persistence of Memory*. What does that mean? Your guess is as good as anyone's.

When you next visit an art museum, see how many nons — nonobjective and nonrealistic paintings — and surs — surrealist pictures — you can pick out.

的手表根本没什么两样，只有一个方面除外，那就是它们都像煎饼一样柔软。其中一块表里，还有很多蚂蚁。蚂蚁为什么会跑到表里去呢？这根本就不需要什么理由，因为这是一幅超现实主义的画作。

这幅画作，是由一个名叫萨尔瓦多·达利的人创作的；他出生于西班牙，后来移民到了美国。达利是最负盛名的一位超现实主义画家。绝大多数超现实主义画作，都既清晰又流畅，绘画手法高超。除了其中的物体通常都不可能存在这一点之外，这种画作其实就是现实主义画作。然而，倘若世界上的确存在柔软的手表，那它们看上去就会是那个样子的。

像梦境令人困惑一样，超现实主义画作也是让人感到困惑的。观赏这些画作，就像进入梦境那样（除非那是一个噩梦），既有意思，又好玩得很。那些创作超现实主义画作的画家，常常还会给自己的画作取上一个古怪的名称，从而让这些画作更让人们觉得莫名其妙呢。比如这幅描绘柔软手表的画作，就叫《永恒的记忆》。这是什么意思呢？你们猜去吧。而你们的猜想，与其他人的猜想一样，都是合理的呢。

下次再去参观美术馆时，你们就不妨看一看，能够找到多少幅属于非写实主义、非现实主义的画作，又能够找出多少幅属于超现实主义的画作来吧。

Chapter 33 More Modern Painters

Everybody likes the circus.

Clowns! Elephants! Trained horses! Peanuts!

Everybody likes the circus.

Acrobats! Tightrope walkers! Camels! Band music!

Suppose you had a choice of going to the circus or painting a picture. Which would you choose? You'd choose the circus. Everybody likes the circus.

But if you were an artist you might think it more fun to paint a picture. Artists like the circus, but they also love to paint. That's why they are artists.

An artist named John Steuart Curry loved to paint pictures. Painting was his business. He also loved the circus. The circus was his hobby so for a while he combined the two. He joined the circus and traveled with it so he could paint pictures of it. He painted pictures of the acrobats, trapeze performers, elephants, and equestrians.

John Steuart Curry was born in Kansas. Besides circus pictures, he painted many pictures of his home state, especially of farm life.

John Steuart Curry's pictures are modem paintings, but they are not at all like the modem art that you read about in the last chapter. Modem art includes many kinds of paintings. Painters keep trying new ways of painting, and it's a good thing they do.

第33章 更多的现代画家

大家都很喜欢马戏团。

那里有小丑！有大象！有驯马！还有花生米吃！

大家都很喜欢马戏团。

那里有杂技！有走钢丝的人！有骆驼！还有乐队演奏的音乐！

假设让你们来选择，是去马戏团看马戏呢，还是绘制一幅画作。你们会选哪个呢？你们当然都会选去看马戏。因为大家都很喜欢看马戏。

不过，倘若你们是画家的话，那你们可能就会觉得，绘制画作比看马戏更好玩呢。虽说画家也喜欢看马戏，可他们也热爱绘画啊。这就是他们成为画家的原因。

有位名叫约翰·斯图尔特·柯里的画家，非常热爱绘画。绘画就是他的职业。他也很喜欢马戏团。马戏则是他的业余爱好。因此，有一段时间，他将二者结合了起来。他加入了一个马戏团，随着马戏团周游各地，以便自己能够创作出关于马戏团的画作来。后来，他绘制了许多描绘杂技、秋千表演者、大象和马术表演者的画作呢。

约翰·斯图尔特·柯里出生于堪萨斯州。除了那些描绘马戏团的油画，他还创作出了许多关于自己故乡的画作，尤其是描绘农场生活的一些画作呢。

虽说约翰·斯图尔特·柯里的画作都是现代油画，但它们一点儿也不像你们在上一章看到的那种现代美术。现代美术，包括了风格多样的油画。画家们一直都在尝试新的绘画方法；而他们这样做，也是一桩好事。如果画家们始终都墨守成规，

If artists always painted the way artists painted in the past, their paintings would get tiresome.

Nonobjective and nonrealistic paintings were new ways of painting when they were invented. But they aren't the only kinds of modem art. In this chapter all the paintings are modem, but you can tell easily that they are not like nonobjective, nonrealistic, or surrealist paintings.

马戏团里的大象，柯里作品，
现存于华盛顿特区的国家美术馆

One very famous painting by an artist named Grant Wood is called *American Gothic*. It shows an elderly Iowa farmer and his wife looking straight out from the picture. Behind them is a wooden house with Gothic-style trimmings that some American houses still have. The man and woman look like serious, honest, kind, hardworking people. How do I know they are Iowa people? Because Grant Wood's home was in Iowa and he liked to paint pictures of his own state.

Both Grant Wood and John Steuart Curry were from the Midwest in the United States. Another famous painter from the central United States is Thomas Hart Benton. He

美国哥特式，伍德作品，
现存于芝加哥的芝加哥美术馆
（由缅因州桑福德的大学印刷协会提供）

像过去的画家那样去创作的话，那他们的画作就会变得令人生厌了。

非写实主义和非现实主义的画作在刚刚发端的时候，都属于新画法。可现代美术并非只有这两种画法。本章中介绍的所有画作，全都属于现代美术的范畴；可你们很容易就能看出，它们与非写实主义、非现实主义或超现实主义风格的画作都不一样哩。

有位名叫格兰特·伍德的画家，创作出了一幅叫作《美国哥特式》的画作。这幅画，描绘的是艾奥瓦州一位年老的农民和他的妻子，他们都在画中直勾勾地盯着观众。他们身后，是一栋装饰风格为哥特式的木屋，如今美国一些房屋的装饰风格仍是这样呢。画中的这对夫妇，看起来都是正经、诚实、和善、勤劳的人。我怎么知道这对夫妇是艾奥瓦州人呢？这是因为，格兰特·伍德的家就在艾奥瓦州，而他也很喜欢创作关于自己家乡风情人物的画作。

格兰特·伍德和约翰·斯图尔特·柯里两人，都出生于美国的中西部地区。还有一位著名的画家，则是出生于美国的中部地区；这位画家，就是托马斯·哈

painted pictures of his native state of Missouri. Many of his paintings are murals in public buildings.

Huck Finn and Jim is part of one of these murals. Mark Twain's book *Huckleberry Finn* tells of Huck's trip down the Mississippi on a raft with his friend Jim, who was escaping from slavery. The picture shows them on their raft. It's a good picture to remember when you read the book.

Another modem painter is Edward Hopper. His pictures are mostly of the eastern part of the United States. Hopper's painting *New York Movie*, however, might fit a movie theater in any large city. It shows the inside of a movie theater with a girl usher standing near the stairway of the balcony.

It is an unusual subject for a painting. For one thing, it's generally pretty dark in a movie theater. For another thing, painters are not often inspired by the beauty of a movie theater. But in spite of these handicaps, the painting turned out to be a very good one because of the skill of the artist.

One of the differences between many modem artists and artists of the past is that artists now so often paint common, everyday subjects

刘麦，本顿作品，现存于圣路易斯的圣路易斯美术馆
（由波士顿的大学印刷协会提供）

特·本顿。他创作了许多描绘其故乡密苏里州的画作。他的许多画作，都属于公共建筑物里的壁画。

《哈克费恩和吉姆》就是这些壁画中有一幅的一部分。马克·吐温的《哈克贝利·费恩历险记》一书，描述了哈克与自己的朋友、逃亡的奴隶吉姆坐着筏子，沿着密西西比河而下的历险过程。这幅画作刻画了他们坐在筏子上的情形。倘若你们去看这本书，那就记住这幅优秀的画作吧。

另一位现代画家就是爱德华·霍珀。他的画作，描绘的主要是美国东部地区的情况。然而，霍珀的画作《纽约电影院》描绘的情景，却可能适合于任何一座大城市里的电影院呢。画作描绘了一家电影院内部的情况，还有一名年轻的女引座员站在通往包厢的楼梯边。

油画选用这种题材，是很不常见的。一方面，电影院里通常都很阴暗。另一方面，一座电影院就算很漂亮，也常常不会激发出画家的创作灵感。可尽管有这些不利因素，此画最终还是由于画家高超的技术，而变成了一幅非常优秀的作品。

许多现代画家与过去那些画家之间存在的一种差异就是，如今的画家经常创作出描绘普通、日常题材的画作，即描绘我们大家都很熟悉的人物和地点的画作。在“文艺复兴”时期，以及此后很长的一段时间里，画家们选取的创作主题都是宗教

纽约电影院，霍珀作品，
现存于纽约的现代艺术博物馆

— people and places that are familiar to all of us. During the Renaissance and for a long time afterward, most of the subjects chosen by painters were religious subjects, beautiful scenery, or important people such as kings and queens. Ordinary people and scenes were seldom painted. A few painters like the Brueghels in Flanders, Hogarth in England, and Millet in France did paint the kind of people that most artists found uninteresting. But now most artists paint people and scenes that are part of the everyday life of their countries.

Do you know any artists? Real, live artists? There are thousands of painters in America today. You have more chance of knowing a real artist now than ever before in history. Certainly more people are painting now than ever before. The paintings of Curry, Wood, Benton, and Hopper are merely samples of many that could have been chosen for this chapter.

Many people are painting just for the fun of it. Painting isn't their chief job. They just

题材、美丽的风景，或者像国王、王后那样的重要人物。他们很少创作关于普通民众和场景的画作。只有像佛兰德斯的勃鲁盖尔父子、英国的贺加斯、法国的米勒等少数几位画家，才确实创作过关于普通民众的画作；而绝大多数画家却都认为，这种题材是很没意思的。但是，如今的绝大多数画家，选取的题材却都是属于各国日常生活一部分的普通民众和场景了。

你们有认识的画家吗？就是真正的、还活着的画家？现在，美国有几千位画家呢。如今，你们比过去更有机会去结识一位真正的画家了。当然，如今从事绘画创作的人，也比过去更多了。柯里、伍德、本顿和霍珀的画作，都只是例子罢了，因为还有许多其他画家的画作，也可以选入这一章里。

如今，许多人从事绘画创作，只是为了好玩。绘画创作并不是这些人的主业。

like to paint. For example, Winston Churchill, the great prime minister of Great Britain during World War II, took up painting as a hobby and became very good at it.

One country that hasn't been mentioned in this book is Mexico. Between World War I and World War II, Mexican artists became known all over the world for their paintings. The most famous Mexican artist is Diego Rivera. He painted many of his pictures on the walls of buildings. Most of these murals are in Mexico, but some are on walls in the United States. He liked to paint pictures of working people — especially Mexican laborers.

Notice that in the picture called *Detroit Industry* the whole painting is filled with people and machinery. This painting is on a wall in Detroit.

What you have read about in the last two chapters is this: There are many kinds of modem painting. Some are called nonobjective, nonrealistic, or surrealist. Others are realistic. And today's artists are always experimenting with new ways of painting. There are more artists now than ever before. The United States has many good painters.

What you haven't read in the last two chapters is this: All countries in the world have good painters. So wherever you go, you should be able to find paintings worth looking at.

他们只是喜欢绘画罢了。比如，第二次世界大战期间英国那位伟大的首相温斯顿·丘吉尔，也曾把绘画当成业余爱好，并且后来绘画技艺还变得非常娴熟了呢。

本书中没有提到一个国家，那就是墨西哥。在第一次世界大战到第二次世界大战期间，墨西哥的画家还曾因为他们的画作而变得举世闻名哩。最负盛名的墨西哥画家，就是迭戈·里维拉。他创作出来的许多作品，都属于建筑物上的壁画。这些壁画当中，绝大部分都位于墨西哥境内，但美国也有一些。他喜欢创作描绘劳动人民，尤其是描绘墨西哥劳工的画作。

请大家注意《底特律工业》这幅画作；这幅画上，全都是人物和机器设备。这幅油画，就绘在底特律市的一堵墙壁上。

在本书最后的两章中，你们已经看到的内容，就是：现代的绘画艺术风格是多种多样的。有些风格被称为非写实主义、非现实主义或者超现实主义。其他的则属于现实主义。而且，如今的画家，始终都在尝试新的绘画手法。而如今的画家，人数也比过去更多。美国就有不少优秀的画家。

而在最后两章中，你们没有看到的内容，则是：世界各国，都拥有许多优秀的画家。因此，无论你们走到哪里，都能够找到值得一观的画作。

ARCHITECTURE

建筑篇

Chapter 1 The Oldest House

Some men were talking about houses. "How old is your house?" one of them asked me.

"Five years old," I replied.

"Well, my house is over 100 years old," said the man. "It's in Massachusetts."

"Only 100 years old!" exclaimed another man. "My house is 200 years old. It's in Virginia."

"That doesn't seem old to me," still another man said. "I live in Santa Fe, New Mexico, and in my town, there is a house that is more than 800 years old. It is considered the oldest house in America and was built by Native Americans in the *pueblo* style. Native Americans in that area lived in pueblos before the Spanish arrived. And even older than that house are the villages of the cliff dwellers in Mesa Verde, New Mexico, that were first built in 600 A.D."

"Well, how about this?" said another man. "If you count buildings abroad, I've been in one that's 1,000 years old. It's a church in France."

"Only 1,000 years old?" said an Englishman, who seemed bent on outdoing us. "I've been in a building made 2,000 years ago. It's a temple in Greece. They call it the Parthenon."

"Well," said I, not to be outdone, "I can beat that. I've been in two different types of

第1章 历史最悠久的房子

一群人正在谈论房子的事情。"您家的房子建起多少年了？"有人问我道。

"五年了。"我回答说。

"哦，我家的房子有一百多年了，"那人说，"是在马萨诸塞州。"

"才一百年！"另一个人大声说道，"我家的房子有二百年了呢。是在弗吉尼亚州。"

"在我看来，你们的房子历史都不算久，"又有另一个人说道，"我家在新墨西哥州的圣达非，在我们镇里，有座房子竟然有八百多年的历史了呢。人们认为，那是美国历史最悠久的一座房子，是印第安人按照普韦布洛风格建造起来的。在西班牙人到来之前，那个地区的印第安人都是住在普韦布洛风格的村庄里。而比那座房屋历史更加悠久的，是新墨西哥州梅萨维德那些悬崖洞人所建的村庄，那些村庄，还是公元前600年的时候修建起来的呢。"

"哦，那么听听这个如何？"又有一人说道，"要是国外的建筑也算上的话，那我还到过一座有一千年历史的房子呢。那是法国的一座教堂。"

"只有一千年的历史？"一位英国人说道，似乎一心要压过我们，"我还到过一座二千年前建起的房子里呢。那是希腊的一座神庙。人们称它为巴台农神庙。"

"好吧，"我说道，并没有要压倒他的意思，"我说的房子，历史可比那个还要久呢。我曾经到过两座类型不同的房子里，它们都位于同一个大洲，而其历史也

houses a continent apart that are between 6,000 and 7,000 years old. One is in Jericho, near the city of Jerusalem, and the other is in a village of 100 houses in Ban Po, near the city of Xi'an in China."

"Well, no one can beat that, but I still have one for you," said the man from Santa Fe. "It's a house built for the dead."

"What!" everyone exclaimed. "For the dead?"

"That's exactly what I said. It's in Egypt. They call it a pyramid."

"Well, I thought the 7,000-year-old houses were the winners of this contest, but houses for the dead? Tell me more!"

Long ago, people expected to live for only about fifty years or so. They did not have jobs as we know them, but had to find the food and clothing they needed by farming and herding in just one place or hunting and gathering by moving from place to place. They did not own land as we do today, for they just lived on the land.

Not only did people not own land, they did not own houses on the land that could last and be passed down to their children. You see, if they built portable houses, then they could take them along. Some Native Americans called these tent-like houses *tepees*, and some called them *wigwams*. The Mongolians called theirs *gurts*.

If people wanted to stay in one place for the whole season, then they built houses of mud and straw. Many Africans did this. Their mud huts with straw roofs worked well in the dry season but could wash away in the rainy season.

都有六千年到七千年之久呢。其中一座在耶路撒冷城附近的杰里科，而另一座则在中国西安附近的半坡村，那是一个有着一百户人家的小村庄。”

“哦，尽管没人能够说出胜过这一点的建筑来，可我还是知道有一座房子的历史胜过你所说的，”那名居住在圣达非的人说道。“那是一座为死者修建的房子。”

“什么！”大家都惊呼道，“为死者建造的？”

“我说的正是这样。那座房子位于埃及。人们称之为金字塔。”

“哦，我还以为那两座建起了七千年的房子是历史最悠久的呢，可竟然还有为死者建造的房子？再给我们多说一说它的情况吧！”

很久以前，人类的寿命平均只有五十岁左右。当时的人并没有像我们现在所知的种种工作，而是只能在一个地方种地、放牧，或者从一个地方转移到另一个地方，一路打猎、采集，才能获得生活所需的粮食和衣物。他们并不像我们现在这样拥有土地，因为他们只是在土地上生活罢了。

当时的人非但不拥有土地，而他们在土地之上，也并未拥有那种能够长久保存并传给子孙后代的房屋。你们都知道，要是他们建造活动房屋的话，那就可以随身带着这些活动房屋迁徙了。有些印第安部落称这些帐篷式的房屋为“锥形帐篷”，有些则称之为“窝棚”。蒙古人则把他们的帐篷称为“蒙古包”。

如果人们想要在某个地方待上整整一个季节，那他们就会用湿泥和稻草，建造起房屋。许多古非洲人正是这样做的。他们用湿泥建造的、屋顶为稻草的小屋，在旱季时很有用处，可一到了雨季，就会被雨水淋坏。

Building things that lasted or things to pass on to their children or be remembered was not something important to many people long ago.

But the Egyptians were different from so many others because they built houses that still last today. Even more surprising is that these houses were built for the dead. Egyptians thought the houses had to last forever because of what they believed. You see, the Egyptians, thousands of years before Christ, believed in resurrection from the dead. They believed their dead bodies would, in fact, come back to life again, so they built the pyramids out of stone to last. Egyptians had their bodies *embalmed* — that is, preserved, making them into what we call *mummies* — to last forever, and to be housed inside the pyramids.

Now, the pyramids are still there in Egypt, but the mummies that were once in them are not in them anymore. They have been stolen or have been taken away and put in museums — in museums for anyone and everyone to gaze upon, in spite of all the care that the tomb builder took to have his body undisturbed.

Today we do not pay as much attention as the ancient Egyptians did as to how and where people are to be buried. There were over a 100 pyramids built near the river Nile by Egypt's rulers (or *pharaohs*), but the largest is one built by King Khufu — the pharaoh who is often called Cheops — about 5,000 years ago. This pyramid is one of the Seven Wonders of the Ancient World and is almost 500 feet high. That is a length of about two football fields! It used to be 480 feet high, to be exact, but the top has been broken off, and it is now only 451 feet. In spite of that, it is by far the largest stone building in the world

对于很久以前的许多人来说，建造能够长久保存，或者能够传给子孙后代，或者具有纪念意义的房屋，这一点根本就不重要。

可古埃及人却与其他许多古代民族都不同，因为他们建造了一些一直保存至今的房屋。而更令人惊讶的是，那些房屋竟然是给死者建造的。由于信仰的问题，古埃及人认为这些房屋必须能够永世长存才行。大家都知道，在基督降生以前的几千年里，古埃及人都相信，死者终有一天是会复活的。事实上，他们相信自己死去的尸体会再次活过来，因而用石头建造出了能够长久保存的金字塔。古埃及人会把他们的尸体进行防腐处理，也就是进行腌制，制成我们所称的木乃伊，从而把尸体永久保存下来，存放在金字塔里。

如今，那些金字塔仍然屹立在埃及境内，可曾经存放在其中的木乃伊，却不再留在里面了。尽管建造这些陵墓的人当时都小心翼翼地不让自己的尸体受到打扰，可那些木乃伊要么被人盗走，要么便是被人们带走，保存进博物馆了。在博物馆里，大家都可以前去观看这些木乃伊呢。

现在，对于如何埋葬死者、把死者埋葬在哪里的问题，我们不再像古埃及人那么关注了。古埃及的历代君主（或者称为法老）在尼罗河附近修建了一百多座金字塔，但其中最大的一座，则是大约五千年前的国王胡夫修建的，他就是人们常称为“基奥普斯”的那位法老。这座金字塔，属于古时的世界“七大奇迹”之一，有差不多五百英尺高哩。这一高度，几乎相当于有两个足球场那么长呢。准确一点来说，它以前有四百八十英尺高，可塔尖已经掉了，因此如今只有四百五十一英尺高了。

— a mountain of stone.

The pyramid of Cheops is built of solid rock on a natural rock foundation, but as there was no rock nearby for building the pyramid itself, it had to be brought from quarries, some of which were 50 miles away and others as much as 500 miles away. The rock had to be dragged those 50 miles or 500 miles from the quarry. Some of the huge stones weighed two and a half tons. That is more than an eighteen-wheel truck, and it took several years to drag the rocks to the site of the pyramid. It seems the only easy part was when the stones were put on barges to carry them down the Nile River, for transportation was much easier on water than on land.

You see, there was no machinery in those days — no pulleys, no tracks or trucks, no engines or mechanical devices to lift and carry huge loads — so every block of stone had to be pushed or pulled by sheer brute force over rows of logs used as rollers. Hundreds of men tugged from in front and hundreds shoved from behind. And then each block had to be lifted and moved into place. Probably a ramp the size of a roadway was built right up the side of the pyramid, but at not too steep an angle because the huge stones had to be dragged upwards, to where the blocks could be slid into position. It is supposed to have taken at least 20 years to build the pyramid for Cheops, and the pharaoh may have employed over 50,000 men to do the job.

When it was finished, the outside of the pyramid was smooth, polished stone — pearly white limestone. But long ago all this covering of polished stone was stolen and carried off to make other buildings, so that the sides of the pyramid are now rough, irregular

尽管如此，它也是世界上最大的石制建筑，并且当之无愧，完全就是一座石山。

胡夫金字塔是在一处天然的岩石地基上，用坚固的岩石修建起来的，可由于附近地区并没有用于修建金字塔本身的岩石，因此只能从采石场运来。有些采石场，与金字塔建造地相距五十英里，其他一些采石场甚至还在五百英里以外呢。这些岩石，都得从这五十英里或者五百英里以外的采石场拖过来。其中有些巨石竟然重达两吨半，比一辆有十八个轮子的卡车还重，因此花了好多年的时间，才将所需的石料拖到建造金字塔的地方。唯一比较容易的部分，似乎就是将这些石头放入驳船上，然后顺着尼罗河而下的时候，因为水上运输比陆地运输要轻松得多。

你们都知道，那个时候是没有机械设备的：没有滑轮，没有轨道或卡车，没有发动机或机械设备来抬升和运送巨大的重物，因此，每一块巨石都只能放在用一排排圆木上做成的滚轴上，用纯粹的蛮力来推动或者拉拽。前面用几百人拉，后面再用几百人推。而接下来，每块巨石又必须抬起来，放置到位。很可能，当时的人在金字塔一侧上还修建了一条大小像如今的快车道那么宽的坡道，但坡道的角度不是很陡，因为人们必须将巨石拖上去，拖到巨石可以滑入其应在位置的高度。据说，人们起码花了二十年的时间，才建好胡夫金字塔，而这位法老，可能也役使了五万多人来进行修建呢。

完工之后，金字塔的外侧全都是光滑、经过打磨的石头，都是像珍珠般白晰的石灰石。不过，很久以前，这层经过打磨的石头便被人盗走并拿去修建其他建筑了，因此如今这座金字塔的四面外层，才成了粗糙而不规则的阶梯，每一级都高达

steps, each one three or more feet high. You could climb to the top on any side simply by climbing from one tall step to another. But it's not quite that easy, for many of the "steps" are over five feet tall.

The limestone that once covered the pyramid made each side look like a single, smooth triangle. The limestone blocks fit into the rough steps, their angled sides forming a kind of giant sliding board from the *pinnacle* on top straight down to the desert floor below.

If it were sliced through the center, the Great Pyramid, as we call it, would show three small rooms, one above the other, and some slanting passageways leading into the three rooms. The rest would be solid rocks, pieced tightly together with no mortar or sticking material between them.

The topmost room was for the king's own mummy, and in order to make sure that the weight of stone above would not crush through the room where his mummy was, five ceilings of stone were built, one above the other, with a space above each ceiling and then a slanting ceiling above them all. The two lines slanting upward from the king's room to the sides are small air passages. The room underneath is known as the queen's chamber, even though the queen had her own, smaller pyramid.

The room underneath

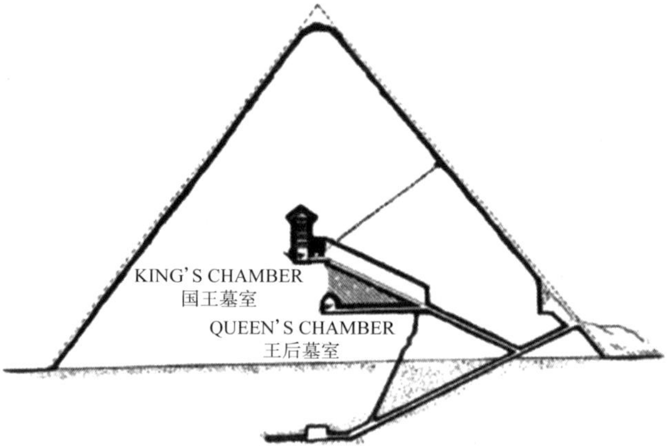

金字塔内的小房间

三英尺，甚至更高。你们只需从一级高高的台阶爬到另一级上，就可以沿着任何一面爬到这座金字塔的塔顶上去。但是，其实并没有那么容易，因为许多“台阶”都有五英尺多高呢。

那些曾经覆盖在表面的石灰石，让这座金字塔的每一面看上去都像是一个平滑的三角形。这些石灰石，都是嵌盖在粗糙的台阶里，而台阶有角的那一面，则形成了一个巨大而光滑的平面，从最上面的“尖顶”，一直延伸到下面的沙漠之中。

倘若从中劈开的话，这座我们所称的“大金字塔”里，就会出现三个上下排列的小房间，还有一些倾斜的、通向这三个房间的通道。其余部分则是实心的岩石，一块接一块地紧紧拼合在一起，中间根本没有灰浆或者黏合材料。

最上面的那个房间，用于存放国王胡夫自己的木乃伊，而为了确保不会因为上面的石块太重而压垮木乃伊所在的这个房间，还修建了五块石制的天花板，上下排列，并且每块天花板上都留有空隙，然后再用一块斜着的天花板盖在它们的上面。两条斜斜向上、从存放国王木乃伊的那个房间通往两侧的通道，就是小型的通风道。而下面的那个房间，则被称为王后墓室，但王后其实也修建有属于自己的、规模较小的金字塔。

the queen's chamber, in the cellar or foundation of the pyramid was, perhaps, for nobody. That was, for a while, the great mystery of the Great Pyramid, but now we think we have guessed the riddle. You see, there was only one passageway starting from the outside. From this one passageway, another secret passageway led off to the pharaoh and queen's chambers. The passage that went straight ahead led down to the room that had nothing in it. Cheops was afraid that after he had been buried in this tomb, some enemy might try to steal his mummy and prevent him from coming to life again. So he had all the passageways filled up with stone after he was buried. Then the entrance was covered, so that no one could find where or how to get in.

But Cheops figured that just in case someone did find the entrance and began to dig out the passageway down to the cellar, this straight passage would lead him off the right track. Then when the intruder did reach the empty room, he would find nothing — sort of an April Fool's joke.

Above all, the pharaoh wanted to ensure that his spirit would always be able to find his body in the afterlife. That is why his body was embalmed, put into a mummy case, which was itself put inside another mummy case, and often yet a third case. And, if somehow, all those mummy boxes were disturbed, there

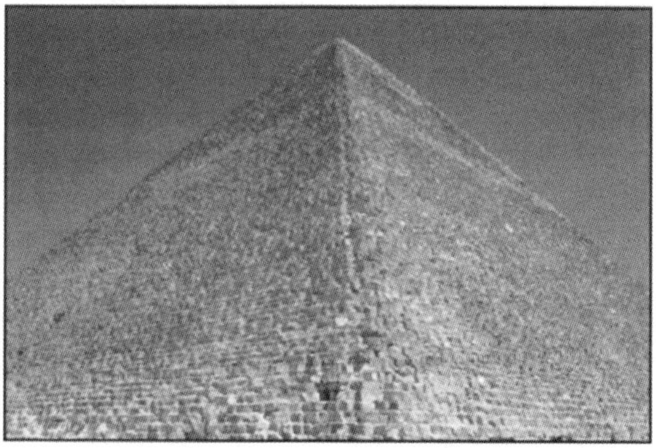

大金字塔，现存于埃及的吉萨
（摄影：加里·威肯）

王后墓室下面的那个房间，位于整座金字塔的地下或者地基里，可能不是为任何人修建的。曾经有过一段时间，这一点还成了“大金字塔”最大的一个谜呢，可如今，我们认为已经猜出谜底了。你们都看得出，从外部进入金字塔，只有一条通道。而由这条通道出发，还有一条秘道，通往法老墓室和王后墓室。而那条直行的通道，则往下通向那个空空如也的房间。基奥普斯担心，自己葬入这个墓穴之后，某个敌人可能会设法盗走他的木乃伊，从而阻止他获得重生。因此，他便命令，在他下葬后，将所有通道全都用石头堵死。这样一来，由于入口被堵，就没人能够找到入口，也没人能够进入墓穴了。

但基奥普斯认为，就算万一有人发现了入口，开始挖开通往墓穴地窖里的那条通道的话，那么，这条直道就会将他们领入歧途。那样，待闯入者来到那间空荡荡的墓室后，就会什么也找不到：这倒有点儿像是愚人节的把戏呢。

最重要的是，法老希望确保自己的灵魂在来生始终都找得到自己的躯体。他的尸体之所以要进行防腐处理，然后装入一个木乃伊盛放匣，再将这个木乃伊盛放匣又放入另一个木乃伊盛放匣里，并且通常还会再装入第三具木乃伊盛放匣里，原因就在于此。并且，就算由于某种原因，这些木乃伊盛放匣全都坏了，墓穴中也还会

would also be many statues of the pharaoh as substitutes for his body and its mummy cases. His name was inscribed on all these cases and statues, itself protected with a circle around it.

But in spite of all these extraordinary precautions that Cheops took to prevent anyone finding his mummy, all these passageways and rooms were later discovered and opened and the mummies were removed — to where and by whom no one knows.

Here is another interesting bit of information. Although, as I told you, there are over 100 pyramids, not all of them have the true pyramid form. That is, not all of them are triangular. In some pyramids the sides slope in very little at the bottom and then, as if the builder had changed his mind, they slope in faster toward the top.

The pharaoh who built his tomb like this may have been in a hurry. Perhaps he was sick and afraid he was going to die before the pyramid was finished. Or maybe his builder made a mistake in the design. In the earliest pyramid the sides zigzag toward the top in several giant-like steps.

拉美西斯二世的椭圆形名字碑，现存于埃及
（摄影：加里·威肯）

有许多的法老塑像，用以取代他的尸体和那些木乃伊盛放匣。这些木乃伊盛放匣和雕像之上，全都刻上了他的名字，并且名字周围还刻有一个圆圈来加以保护。

不过，尽管基奥普斯费尽心思地采取了这些非同寻常的措施，来防止有人找到他的木乃伊，但后来这些通道和墓室全都被人们发现并打开，其中的木乃伊也被挪走了，至于它们被挪到哪里去了，是什么人挪走的，却都无人知晓了。

还有一件很有意思的事情。我已经跟你们说过，尽管埃及有一百多座金字塔，但它们并非全都是真正的金字塔形。也就是说，它们的外形并非都是三角形。有些金字塔的侧面坡度，在靠近底部的地方非常平缓，可接下来仿佛是建造者改变了主意似的，它们的坡度会突然陡升，直到塔顶。

这些法老可能是在匆忙之中，才把自己的陵墓建造成这种样子的。或许是因为法老生病了，害怕金字塔还没建好自己就一命呜呼了，或许是法老手下负责建造金字塔的人在设计时犯了错误。最早的那座金字塔，四面都只有寥寥几级巨人似的台阶，然后呈之字形地直达顶部呢。

左塞的阶梯金字塔，现存于埃及的塞加拉
（摄影：加里・威肯）

Perhaps the pyramid builders were just figuring out how to go from the shape of one burial mound that looked like a large step; to a pile of steps, as if the pharaoh could climb up to the Sun god; and finally, to a smooth-sided pyramid, that took the shape of a real mountain.

Some of the pyramids are built of brick instead of stone. Perhaps the pharaohs who built such pyramids were poor.

But all of these ideas are just guesses. Until archeologists, who are detectives of the past, find more clues, all we have are guesses. I'll bet you have a guess of your own, don't you?

Now it's time to get back to our story. And so, the three greatest pyramids stand close together on the sands of the desert in giant majesty as they have stood for ages past and will for ages to come, to thrill the beholder with their sublime grandeur.

Keep in mind, though, that mere size doesn't make a thing beautiful. A big thing may be

没准，修建金字塔的那些人，只是想出了如何从一种看上去就像是巨大的一级台阶似的坟丘变成多级台阶坟丘的办法，仿佛法老可以顺着台阶爬上去，爬向太阳神似的。最终，这种坟丘才变成了侧面平滑、样子像是真正的大山的金字塔。

有些金字塔是用砖头建成，而不是用石头建成的。或许是因为建造这种金字塔的法老都很穷吧。

但是，这些全都不过是猜想罢了。在考古学家这些探究过去的人发现更多线索之前，我们所想的一切全都属于猜测。我敢打赌，你们也有自己的猜测，对不对？

现在，我们该回到正题上来了。于是，那三座最大的金字塔相距很近，一起屹立在沙漠当中的沙地之上，威风凛凛，它们在过去已经屹立了数个世代，将来还会世世代代屹立下去，让看到它们的人全都因为其宏伟、庄严而激动不已。

不过请你们记住，仅凭大小，可不会让一件东西变得漂亮起来。体型庞大的东

本尼哈珊的克努霍特普石窟陵墓，现存于埃及
（由波士顿的大学印刷协会提供）

very ugly. But the pyramids are monuments to man's attempt to make something lasting, and their builders succeeded in making the most lasting thing ever built by man.

The pyramids are also monuments to the belief in a life after death. And when we think of the millions of people who have come and gone, lived and died, since these mighty monuments were built, and the countless millions who will come and go while the pyramids still stand, it sets us thinking of the shortness of our little lives and the awesome length of eternity — and that is ART.

All the pyramids were tombs, but not all tombs were pyramids. That is, some tombs were not pyramid-shaped at all, as I told you. Some were rather small stone buildings with flat tops. Furthermore, some tombs were simply caves cut into the rock cliffs on the west side of the Nile. These rock tombs were hollowed out on the west side of the river so that the entrance would face east, toward the rising Sun.

西，有可能非常丑陋呢。但是，金字塔是一种丰碑，纪念的是人类制造持久之物的尝试；而它们的建造者，也成功地建造出了人类有史以来最持久的东西呢。

金字塔也是古埃及人对于来生这种信仰的一座座纪念碑。倘若想一想自这些宏伟的金字塔建起以来，已经来过去过、生过死过的千千万万人，以及在这些金字塔仍然屹立的将来，还会有千千万万、数不胜数的即将来去的人，我们就会想到自己生命的渺小和短暂，以及令人叹为观止、悠长久远的永恒，而这种永恒，就是艺术。

所有的金字塔都是陵墓，但并非所有陵墓都是金字塔。也就是说，有些陵墓根本就不是金字塔形，这一点我在前面已经跟你们说过了。有些陵墓，是规模很小的平顶石制建筑。而且，还有一些陵墓，不过是在尼罗河西侧的悬崖上凿出来的一个个洞穴罢了。这些石窟陵墓，都是在尼罗河西岸的悬崖上开凿出来的，目的是让入口朝着东方，朝着太阳升起的地方。

The Egyptians never had their tombs face any other way, for they thought the Sun god could not wake the dead unless the tomb faced him as he rose in the east. If the tomb faced him, he would wake the people who were dead, just as the rising Sun shining into east windows wakes a sleeper in the morning.

In ancient Egypt no one even lived on the west side of the river. People would come across the river each day to farm the fertile soil near the edge of the river, and build the tombs, the great big ones and the little ones. Then they would cross back to the east side of the river, leaving behind the dead, ready to be awakened by the Sun.

Here is such a rock-cut tomb — one of the most famous — a tomb at Beni-Hasan.

It is particularly interesting because it has two columns in front, two columns cut out of the rock. None of the pyramid tombs had columns.

So now you know more about these very old Egyptian houses, built just for the dead.

古埃及人从来不会让他们的坟墓朝向其他的任何方向，因为他们认为，除非坟墓朝着东方，否则太阳在东方升起的时候，太阳神就无法唤醒死去的人。倘若坟墓朝着东方，那么太阳神就可以唤醒死者，就像早上初升的阳光透过东窗，唤醒沉睡的人那样。

在古埃及，甚至没有人居住在尼罗河的西岸呢。人们会每天渡河过去，耕种河滨那些肥沃的土地，修建大大小小的陵墓。然后，他们又会渡河回到尼罗河东岸，而将死者留在西岸，等着被太阳神唤醒。

本尼哈珊就有一座这样的石窟陵墓，它也是古埃及最著名的石窟陵墓之一。

这座陵墓特别有意思，因为它的前面有两根柱子，那是两根从岩石中雕凿出来的石柱。而金字塔式的陵墓前，都没有这样的柱子呢。

这样，对于古埃及那些历史非常悠久的、只是为死者而建的房屋，你们就更加了解了。

Chapter 2 Houses for Gods

At some time or other, all of you have probably built a house. It may have been a house of cards that blew over very easily, or it may have been made of books, or it may have been made of building blocks. Perhaps it was a shed in the backyard.

Every house must have walls and a roof. If you lean two blocks or cards together, you have the walls forming a roof and the roof forming the walls. That is the simplest way — a tent, as in a *tepee* or a wigwam. The word tepee comes from the Native American tribes of the Great Plains. The term wigwam comes from the word the Algonquian tribe of Native Americans used for *dwelling*. So, like a tepee or wigwam, the sides of the pyramids, too, were both walls and roof. A pyramid was shaped something like a tent, but it was built solid except for the small rooms in the center.

You may remember that I told you some of the very old buildings in the world are tombs. But there are other very old buildings called *temples* — houses men built for their gods. Look at the picture of the ruin of what we think was a temple. It is called Stonehenge and it's in England instead of Egypt. It probably never had a roof, but you can see several stone crossbeams still in place.

第2章 神灵的房屋

你们所有的人，很可能都曾经在某个时候修建过一座房子。这座房屋，或许是用纸牌搭成的，风一吹就倒；或许是用书本搭起来的；或许是用积木搭建的；又或许，是你们家后院的一个小棚子呢。

所有房屋都必定有几面墙、一个屋顶。倘若你们把两块积木或两张纸牌斜靠在一起的话，那么这两块积木或者纸牌，便既是屋顶、又是墙壁了。这是最简单的一种建筑办法，建成的就是一顶帐篷，像印第安人的锥形帐篷或者活动窝棚那样。“锥形帐篷”（tepee）这个词，源自北美大平原地区[1]的印第安部落。而“窝棚”（wigwam）一词，则源自印第安人中的阿尔冈昆部落[2]用于指“住所”的那个词。与锥形帐篷和窝棚一样，金字塔的四面也既是墙壁，又是屋顶。虽说金字塔的外形有点儿像帐篷，但除了中心的那几间小室，金字塔其他部位却都是实心的。

你们可能都还记得，我在前面曾经告诉过你们，世界上有些历史非常悠久的房屋，它们都是陵墓。不过，世界上还有其他一些历史也极其悠久的建筑，叫作神庙，是人们为神灵建造的房屋。看一看下面这幅废墟图片吧，人们认为，这堆废墟原本应是一座神庙呢。此处被称为“巨石阵”，它位于英国，而不是在埃及。这座神庙很可能根本就没有屋顶，但你们可以看到，有几根石制横梁仍然留在原来的地方呢。

---

[1] 大平原（Great Plains），指北美中西部的平原和河谷地区。

[2] 阿尔冈昆部落（Algonquian tribe），北美印第安部落之一，因说属于印第安语族的阿尔冈昆语而得名，最初定居于如今美国俄亥俄河谷中部地区。

I am showing it to you here because the stones still standing show very well how it was built — not as the pyramids were built, but by putting one stone across two standing stones. This is the second way of building. Think of it as two posts topped by a flat roofline.

Stonehenge looks very much like something a child might build out of blocks — two blocks standing up with one laid across. But these blocks are of stone, immense stones many times bigger than a man. Stonehenge was built by a group of people called Druids, and probably was built just to enclose a space they set aside as holy ground. Ancient people would have come there to worship their Sun god, even long before the Egyptian pharaohs ruled.

One of the greatest and oldest of temples, however, is in Egypt. It is the temple at Karnak, part of which was built by Rameses the Great. It is one of the most beautiful ruins in the world. You may feel that a ruin could not be beautiful. A broken down and dilapidated house is not usually beautiful. Why do you suppose this ruin of Karnak is called beautiful?

The main columns at Karnak that once supported the roof were almost seventy

巨石阵，现存于英国
（摄影：尤因·加洛维）

我之所以向你们介绍这个地方，是因为这里仍然屹立着的那些石头，非常清楚地说明了这座神庙的建筑方法：它不像修建金字塔时所用的那种方法，而是将一块石头横着架在两块直立的石头之上。这就是第二种建筑方法。我们不妨把它看成是在两根柱子顶端搭上一个平平的屋顶。

“巨石阵”的样子，很像是小朋友们用积木搭建起来的那种东西，也就是把两块积木直立起来，然后再用一块积木横着搭在上面。只不过，“巨石阵”里所用的“积木”都是石头，都是比人体还要大上许多倍的巨石罢了。“巨石阵”是由一群叫作“德鲁伊特教徒”[1]的人建成的，而他们之所以建造这个“巨石阵”，很可能是为了把他们预留出来的、准备用作圣地的那个地方封上，古时的人会去那里敬奉太阳神。而他们这样做的时间，甚至比法老开始统治古埃及还要早得多呢。

然而，世界上规模最大、历史最悠久的一座神庙，却还是位于埃及。它就是卡纳克神庙，其中有一部分还是拉姆西斯大帝建造的。它也是世界上最美丽的一处废墟遗址。你们可能会认为，废墟不可能很美丽。一栋垮塌并且荒废了的房子，通常都不会好看。那么，你们觉得，我为什么会说卡纳克神庙的废墟很漂亮呢？

卡纳克神庙曾经支撑庙顶的那些主立柱，差不多都有七十英尺高（大约是一

[1] 德鲁伊特教徒（Druid），指古代英国、爱尔兰、高卢地区信奉德鲁伊特教的凯尔特人。

feet high (about twelve times as high as a man standing up) and twelve feet wide (twice a man's length when he is lying down). These columns were made to look either like a single lotus flower or a bouquet of lotus flowers. Lotus flowers were water lilies that grew in the Nile. Sometimes the columns were made to look like *papyrus*, another plant that grew in Egypt. So the columns were like tree trunks, with their tops like flowers or plants.

There are other, smaller Egyptian temples, but all were built in somewhat the same way. First there was an avenue of *sphinxes*, or creatures with a human head and a lion's body. The name *sphinx* means strangler — a frightening thought, indeed. The largest, most famous one is called the Great Sphinx, but that is not the only one in Egypt. All along this avenue leading to the temple is a row of sphinxes on either side, ending before two obelisks. An *obelisk* is a tall, upright four-sided stone pointed at the top, as if a little pyramid sits upon it, and it was supposed

卡纳克神庙复原后的立柱大厅，现存于埃及
（由波士顿的大学印刷协会提供）

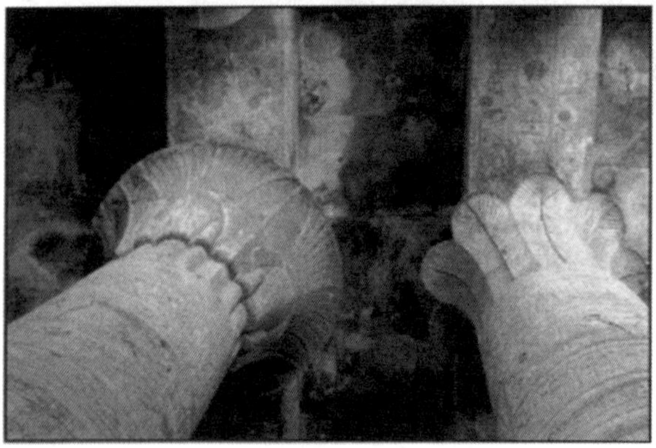

主立柱，现存于埃及的卡纳克神庙
（摄影：加里・威肯）

个人身高的十二倍），直径达十二英尺（相当于一个人身高的两倍）。这些立柱的样子，要么像一朵盛开的莲花，要么就像是一束莲花。莲花就是荷花，是尼罗河里生长的一种水生植物。有的时候，这些立柱还制作得像纸草，而纸草也是埃及的另一种植物。因此，这些立柱就像树干，而顶端则像花朵或者植物。

埃及还有其他一些较小的神庙，可它们的建筑方式，或多或少都是相同的。首先，神庙前面是一条立有斯芬克斯像，即一种人首狮身生物的大道。“斯芬克斯”这个名称，本义是指“扼杀者”，实际上就是一种令人害怕的思想。其中尺寸最大、名气最盛的一座斯芬克斯像，被称为“大斯芬克斯”，不过，它自然也并非埃及境内唯一的一座斯芬克斯像。而在这条通往神庙的大道一侧，有一排斯芬克斯像，一直排到两座方尖碑为止。所谓的“方尖碑”，就是一种高高直立着的、有四面的石制尖顶碑，好像上面顶着一座小金字塔那样，象征着被一缕阳光抚摸着的大地。用来制作方尖碑的巨

to represent the Earth being touched by a ray of Sun. The heavy stone used to build the obelisk was dug out far away from the temple in a quarry like the one on the right. It was then put on a boat to go down the Nile. If the stone cracked in its quarry, it was just left behind.

Behind the obelisks was the gateway to the temple. This was made with two huge towers or gateways called *pylons*, one at each side of the door. The pylon walls slant inward, and if they went higher they would meet like a pyramid. It is thought that the ancient astrologers — men who told fortunes from the stars — used to go up on top of these pylons to "read the stars." The front of these pylons had figures cut into the rock face.

石，都是从距神庙很远的采石场开采出来的，并且左右两侧的方尖碑都是如此。然后，人们再将开采出来的巨石搬到船上，顺着尼罗河而下。倘若巨石在采石场的时候就破裂了，那么人们就会将它们弃而不用。

两座方尖碑之后，就是神庙的大门了。大门由两座巨型塔楼，或者称为"桥塔"的门楼组成，一边一座。桥塔的墙壁都是向内倾斜的，倘若它们更高一点儿的话，四面墙壁就会相互连接起来，构成一座金字塔似的形状。人们认为，古时的占星家，也就是那些根据星相来算命的人，会经常跑到这些桥塔之上，去"观察天象"呢。而这些桥塔正面的岩石上，都刻有人物形象。

莲花和纸草
（摄影：加里・威肯）

斯芬克斯大道，现存于埃及的卢克索
（摄影：加里・威肯）

采石场里的方尖碑，现存于埃及的阿斯旺
（摄影：加里・威肯）

卢克索神庙，现存于埃及的卢克索
（摄影：加里·威肯）

多柱厅，现存于埃及的卢克索
（摄影：加里·威肯）

协和广场上的方尖碑，现存于巴黎
（摄影：约翰·帕特森）

Behind the gateway was a walled courtyard, and behind that was a hall of columns, a room that looked like a forest of stone columns, called a *hypostyle hall*, and behind that was the most sacred place of all — called the Holy of Holies — where the statue of the god was kept.

Some people bring home souvenirs when they travel. Well, nations have done the same thing. Travelers, adventurers, archeologists, collectors of art — and those who just wanted to make a lot of money — carried away many of the obelisks in Egypt and took them to their own countries. Sometimes these souvenirs have been given to a museum, sometimes they have been bought by a collector, and sometimes they have just been stolen. As a matter of fact, there is an Egyptian obelisk in Central Park, New York, and there is another in London on the bank of the river Thames. These two obelisks are called "Cleopatra's Needles," although they were made long before the queen of Egypt named Cleopatra lived, and they look more like giant pencils than needles.

大门之后，是一个四周有墙的院子。而院子后面，则是一个充满立柱的大厅，其间石柱林立，宛若森林，称为“多柱厅”。再往后，便是那个最神圣的地方了，它被称为“至圣所”，就是安放神像的地方。

有些人在旅游的时候，都会带点儿纪念品回去。好吧，各国的人都干过同样的事情。游客、探险家、考古学家、艺术品收藏家，以及那些只想发大财的人，都拿走了古埃及的许多方尖碑，将它们带回了各自的国家。有的时候，这种纪念品会送给博物馆，有的时候会被收藏家购买并收藏起来，有的时候则是被人偷走了。实际上，纽约市的中央公园里就有一座古希腊的方尖碑，而伦敦泰晤士河岸上也有一座呢。这两座方尖碑，尽管它们是在古埃及那位叫作克里奥帕特拉的王后之前很久制作出来的，但还是被称为“克里奥佩特拉之针”，它们的样子，也更像是两支巨大的铅笔，而不太像是两根针呢。

还有一座方尖碑，位于巴黎那三条通往一座

Another obelisk is in Paris in the center of a beautiful circle where three roads come together as they lead to the royal palace that is now the Louvre Museum. There are many more in Rome.

When you look at one of these giant "pencils" in stone, you may wonder how they were originally taken somewhere after construction, then put upright for all to see. Figuring that out was a very complicated puzzle indeed. Can you imagine how builders managed to do such a thing?

The builders amazed everyone and built a gigantic catapult that would not throw something high and fast, but instead lift slowly and precisely. This was such an amazing feat, that there is a picture of how this was done carved right into the base of the Cleopatra's Needle obelisk that is in the heart of Paris. To be sure that everyone knows how important these Egyptian builders were, who were able to put the obelisk exactly in the right place, with the square sides perfectly lined up to face the palace and three roads leading to it, the carved story is lined in gold leaf, or a piece of gold so thin it can be made to take any shape at all.

万神殿前的方尖碑，
现存于罗马
（摄影：约翰·帕特森）

圣彼得大教堂前的方尖碑，现存于罗马
（摄影：约翰·帕特森）

皇宫的道路在交汇之处形成的美丽圆圈正中央，而那座皇宫，就是如今的卢浮宫博物馆。罗马的方尖碑，则还要多得多哩。

看到这种巨型的石制“铅笔”时，你们可能会感到奇怪：开凿制成之后，它们又是如何被运到某个地方，然后直立起来供大家瞻仰的呢？要想出解决办法，的确是一件很复杂的难事。你们想不想得出，当时的建造者们是如何设法做到这一点的呢？

那些建造者，让每个人都吃了一惊：他们建造了一台巨大的投石车，但并不是为了用它来把什么东西投掷得又高又快，而是用它来缓慢而精准地抬升东西。由于这是一件极其令人惊讶的盛事，因此当时的人还将这一过程刻成了图画，雕在如今巴黎市中心那座“克利奥佩特拉之针”方尖碑的底座上呢。为了确保所有的人都明白这些古埃及的建造者有多重要，明白他们有本领将方尖碑准确安放到位，并且让方尖碑的四面完美排列，正对着皇宫以及通往皇宫的那三条道路，这座方尖碑底座上所刻图画的周围，还排列着一行金叶子，也就是那种极薄的、能够打造成任何形状的金片呢。

Chapter 3 Mud Pie Palaces and Temples

In the Bible, *Chaldeans* were the wise men and priests of what you and I call the Two-River Civilization, or Mesopotamia. In Greek, the name *Mesopotamia* means "between two rivers." Do you remember that is the land between the Tigris and the Euphrates Rivers? Chaldea was one of the countries in Mesopotamia along with Assyria and Babylonia. Assyria was a littler farther north than Babylonia and Chaldea, but all three countries were very much alike and sometimes all three were under just one powerful king.

Mesopotamia was able to create a whole network of canals. Since it was between two rivers, the land was very fertile. The finest crops in the entire world grew there, and many large cities were built on the plains. Today these plains are dry and desert-like, for the canals have not been taken care of, and without water, crops fail to grow. On the plains one can now see big mounds or low hills where once the palaces and cities stood.

These are all that is left of the handsome buildings of this ancient land, and they crumbled into dust because they were made of mud, as the chapter title tells you. Imagine a king's palace made of mud — mud baked in the Sun like a mud pie!

But you may remember learning that the Mesopotamian people covered their mud walls with glazed tiles and slabs of stone. The tiles were bright colored, like bathroom tiles, and

第3章 用泥巴建造的宫殿与神庙

在《圣经》中，迦勒底人都很聪明，是我们如今所称的“两河文明”（或者美索不达米亚）地区的祭司。在希腊语中，美索不达米亚这个名称就是指“两条河流之间”。你们还记不记得，这就是底格里斯河与幼发拉底河之间的那片土地呢？迦勒底曾经是美索不达米亚地区的一个国家，此外，这一地区还有亚述古国和巴比伦王国。虽说与巴比伦王国和迦勒底相比，亚述的位置要偏北一点儿，但这三个国家都极其相似，因此，有的时候这三个国家还是由一位实力强大的君主统治着哩。

美索不达米亚地区厉害得很，形成了一个完整的运河网络。由于该地区位于两条河流之间，因此土地非常肥沃。当时全世界最好的粮食作物，全都产自这里，而广袤无垠的平原之上，也建起了一座座大型的城市。可是，如今这些平原都非常干旱，变得像是沙漠一样了，因为人们并没有维护好那些运河。没有了水，庄稼自然也没法生长了。在这些平原上，如今我们还能看到一些巨大的土堆或低矮的土丘，而这些地方，原来却都是宫殿和城市呢。

这片古老的土地上曾经有过的那些漂亮建筑，如今却只剩下一个个土堆了。它们之所以碎成尘土，是因为它们都是由泥土筑成的，正如本章标题所说的那样。想象一下，一位国王的王宫竟然是用泥土筑成的，这种泥土，就像泥团一样，都是在太阳底下晒干的呢！

不过，你们可能都还记得，前面已经说过，美索不达米亚地区的人还会用上过

the slabs of stone were carved in low relief, so that even a mud palace could become a handsome building.

But with only mud bricks the Mesopotamian builders were handicapped. They could not make mud-brick houses more than one story high. The houses would have tumbled down had they been higher. The walls were not strong enough to hold a second story. Since a one-story house would not look very palace-like, the Mesopotamians first made a hill with a flat top or platform of dried mud and placed the palace on that. The palace then seemed much higher.

The sides of the platform were very steep — almost straight up and down. To reach the top of the platform, a slanting, ramp-like roadway was built against its side.

As mud walls were so crumbly, the builders had to make their palace walls very, very thick. Some were as much as twenty feet thick. The Sun is very hot in that part of the world, and these thick walls helped to keep out the heat. To further keep out the heat, the Mesopotamian people made their palaces without windows, so the rooms were lighted only by oil lamps.

We usually think of palace rooms as large and spacious, but the rooms in the Mesopotamian mud palaces were very small. They had to be, because of the lack of stone and of wooden beams long enough to stretch across a wide space. In a palace, however, the builders made up for the smallness of the rooms by having a great number of them.

The temples that the priests built were made of mud bricks, too, but the single platform

釉的瓷瓦和石板覆盖墙面。那些上过釉的瓦片，颜色都很鲜艳，就像如今我们浴室里所用的瓷砖一样，而石板上也雕刻有浅浮雕，因此，一座宫殿即便是用泥土筑成，也可以变成一栋漂亮的建筑。

但是，由于只有土砖，美索不达米亚的建造者还是遇到了困难。他们无法用土砖建造超过一层楼高的房子。倘若建得再高一点儿，房子就会塌掉。这种房子的墙壁不够坚固，无法支撑第二层的重量。由于仅有一层的房屋不太像是宫殿，因此美索不达米亚人会先用干土堆砌出一个平顶的土丘，形成一个平台，然后再在上面修建宫殿。这样一来，宫殿看上去就要高得多了。

这个平台的四面都非常陡峭，几乎是上下垂直的。为了爬到平台顶上，人们又在平台侧面修建了一条倾斜的、像坡道似的道路。

由于土墙极其松脆易碎，因此建造者们只能把宫殿的墙壁筑得非常宽厚。有些宫墙，甚至厚达二十英尺呢。这一地区日照强烈，气候炎热，而这些厚厚的土墙则有助于隔热。为了进一步隔热，美索不达米亚人所建的宫殿还没有建窗户，因此里面的房间只能用油灯来照明。

我们通常都认为，宫殿里面的房间应该都是又大又宽敞才是，不过，美索不达米亚地区那些用泥土筑成的宫殿里的房间，却都狭小得很哩。它们是只能如此啊，因为那里既没有石头，也没有长度能够满足大跨度所需的木质横梁。然而，建造者在宫殿里设计了众多的房间，从而弥补了房间过小的不足。

而祭司们建造的神庙，也是用土砖筑成的，不过，只用一个平台来做地基还不够，因此他们会修建好几座平台，使得平台之上又是平台。这样做，就让它看

for a foundation was not enough, so they built several, one on top of another. This gave the effect of a terraced pyramid, as each platform was set back from the one below it. In New York and some other cities today, architects have built tall buildings in this ancient way — the stories stepped back, as we call it.

Do you remember the Bible story of Noah and the ark he built to survive the Flood? Do you also remember the story of the Babylonians building the Tower of Babel so that people could climb to the top and escape drowning in case of another flood? Well, the Tower of Babel was not built straight up and down. It had stories that were stepped back, too. It was like a set of blocks of different sizes piled one on top of another, each one a little smaller than the one below. Each was reached from the other by a ramp. On the topmost and smallest platform was placed the temple or shrine for an idol to be worshipped.

亚述古国的神庙（复原图）

The Tower of Babel was supposed to have had seven giant steps or terraces. Seven was a magic number. Each step was in honor of one of the heavenly bodies. The topmost terrace, in honor of the Sun, was covered with gold. The next, in honor of the Moon, was covered with silver. Those below, in honor of each of the five known planets, were painted in different colors.

The Chaldeans were the first to make a study

起来像是一座梯田式的金字塔那样。因为每座平台，都在下面那一座的基础上缩进去了一些。在如今的纽约和其他一些城市里，有些建筑师仍然按照这种古老的方式，即我们所称的“逐层缩进”，建造了许多高楼大厦呢。

你们还记得《圣经》里面关于挪亚以及他建造方舟以在大洪水中幸存下来的那个故事吗？你们还记得古巴比伦人修建了“通天塔”，以便万一再来一场大洪水的话，可以让人们爬到塔顶，不至于溺死的那个故事吗？哦，“通天塔”可不是上下垂直的。它也是一层一层地逐层缩进的。这就好像是用大小不同的积木，一块一块地上下堆砌起来，并且每块都比下面的那一块小一点儿似的。每层都可以通过坡道，到达上面的那一层。而安放着用于供奉的偶像的神庙或者神殿，就建在顶层那个面积最小的平台上。

据说，“通天塔”本来是应当有七级巨大的台阶，或者说七个梯级的。“七”可是个有魔力的数字啊。其中的每一级，都是为了向一个天体致敬呢。最顶端的那一级，是向太阳致敬，上面都铺满了黄金。接下来的一级，是向月亮致敬，上面铺满了银子。而往下的那几级，则是为了分别敬奉人类已知的其余五大行星，并且都绘有不同的颜色。

迦勒底人是世界上最先对日月星辰以及它们在天空中的运行情况进行研究的一

of the stars and their movements in the sky, and they gave many of the stars names that we still use. We call such people *astronomers*. The Chaldean astronomers used the temple on top of these terraced pyramids or towers for an observatory — that is, a place from which to observe the heavenly bodies. That is why the Chaldeans came to be known as the wise men of Mesopotamia.

There is an old saying, "Necessity is the mother of invention." That means if you don't have what you need, you will invent something to satisfy that need. It was necessity that made the Assyrians invent one of the most important ways of building that we use today. This way of building is based on the principle of the arch.

The Assyrians had no stones long enough to stretch from one side to the other of a large room to form the ceiling, so they had to invent a way of covering a room or a doorway with small pieces of stone or bricks. You might call an open doorway an arch, but one piece of stone or wood laid across an opening does not make an arch. An arch must be made of several pieces.

Now, you can't cement bricks or small stones together strongly enough to make them into one piece that will stretch from wall to wall and not fall.

But if you arrange the stones in an arch — set in a curve or half circle — they will not fall.

By this simple arrangement, the stones are made to stay in place, not because they are stuck together, for they will stay in place whether cemented or not; but because each stone, pressing downward, trying to fall through, presses against the stones at each side. They

个民族，并且还给其中的许多星辰命了名，而我们如今仍然还在使用这些名称呢。我们将这些人称为“天文学家”。迦勒底的天文学家，把这些阶梯金字塔或高塔顶端的神庙当成观象台，也就是说用于观察天体的地方。这就是迦勒底人后来被称为“美索不达米亚智者”的原因呢。

有一句古老的格言：“需要乃发明之母。”这是指，如果没有得到自己需要的东西，人们就会发明出某种东西，来满足这种需要。正是有了需求，才让古亚述人发明出了最重要的建筑方法之一，而我们如今也仍在使用这种方法呢。这种建筑方法，是在拱形原理的基础上发明出来的。

由于古亚述人没有能够从一个大房间的这一边横跨到那一边、从而形成屋顶的长石，因此他们不得不发明了一种用小块石头或者砖块来覆盖一间房子或者一道门的方法。虽说你们可以把一扇敞开的门称为拱门，但仅用一块石头或者一根木头横放在一扇门上，却不会形成一道拱门。拱门一定是由好多块石头或者木头搭建而成的。

注意，人们无法将砖头或小石块粘得紧紧的，使之成为一个整体，并且让它横跨在两堵墙壁之上而不会垮塌下来。

但是，如果你们将这些石块排成拱形，即排列成一道弧形或者一个半圆的话，它们就不会塌掉了。

通过这种简单的排列方式，我们便可以让那些石块纹丝不动了。这倒不是因为它们都紧密地结成了一个整体，因为事实上，无论其间有没有用混凝土进行黏合，

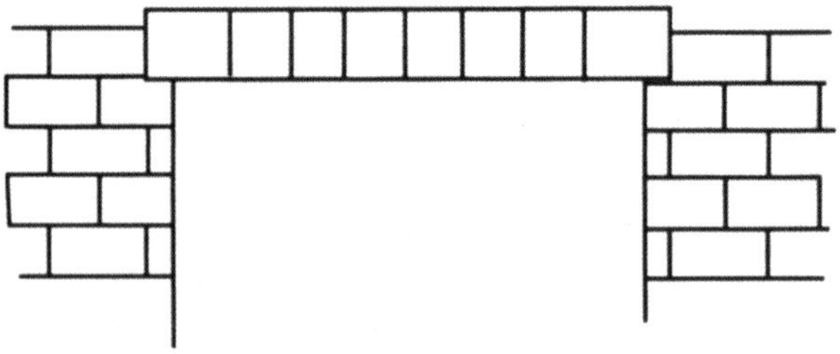

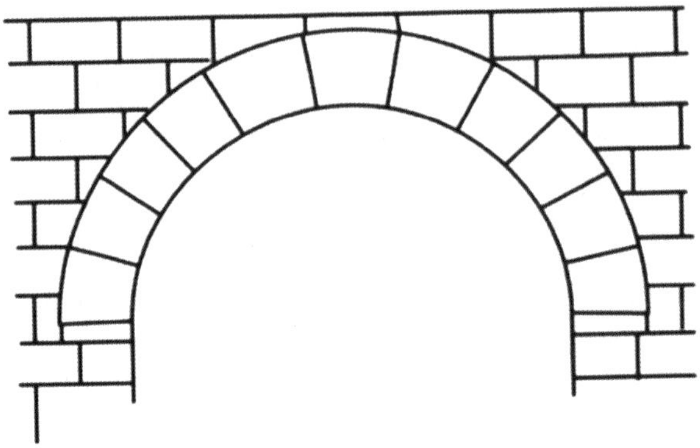

are all so tightly jammed together that none can squeeze through and fall. The heavier the weight on top of the arch, the more firmly are the stones held in place, provided there is no way for them to push against the walls on either side and widen the space.

Try to hold half a dozen upright books in your hands by squeezing them together. If you can squeeze them tight enough, they'll not slip, but release your pressure and they fall. So to prevent the stones of an arch from slipping, the sidewalls of arches were made very heavy and thick.

Not only doorways but whole rooms could be covered in this way. When a room was covered, the arch became what was called a *barrel vault*, as the ceiling of such a vaulted

它们都会纹丝不动的，由于每块石头都向下沉、试图掉下去，从而对两侧的石块形成了挤压。它们都紧紧地相互挤压在一起，从而没有哪块石头能够挤出并掉下去。拱形顶上的东西越沉重，形成拱门的那些石块便会挤压得越牢固，越发纹丝不动。当然，条件是它们不会将两侧的墙体挤开，不会增大两堵墙壁之间的距离。

你们不妨试一试，用双手夹紧竖着的六本书，不让它们掉下去。假如你们能够夹得很紧的话，书本就不会滑动，可一旦松下劲来，它们就会掉下去。因此，为了不让构成拱门的那些石块滑动，人们就得把拱门两侧的墙壁修建得又重又厚。

不仅门厅可以这样来建，而且整间房子也可以用这种办法来盖顶。一个房间用这种方法封顶之后，其拱顶就是人们所称的“桶形穹顶”，因为有这种穹顶的房

room was like half a barrel. You may have seen a barrel vault when you have gone through a tunnel with a curved ceiling.

If a room itself had circular walls, the ceiling became a bowl turned upside down. We call the bowl a dome, but the principle is the same — the principle of the arch. If you take an arch and turn it to make a circle, you end up with a dome shape.

You may wonder how pushing and pulling will hold things better than lifting and holding things up. To understand this even more, there is something you can try. Get a whole group of people together and stand in an open circle so that your hands can touch the next person's shoulder. Next, everyone needs to take one medium-sized step back, then clasp the next person's forearm while they clasp yours. When everyone is ready, slowly lean out and keep the circle a circle. You will see how the whole circle is held together with pressure instead of effort. Domes are doing just what you are doing, but they have been doing it a lot longer!

While an arch or vault or dome was being built, it was necessary to have something to build the stones upon, for until the last stone was in place, the arch would not hold. Usually a temporary framework of wood, shaped like a half circle and called *centering* was placed across from one wall to the other. On top of this, the arch was built, starting at each side and working toward the top. When the last stone at the top — called the *keystone* — was put in place, then, and not until then, could the centering be knocked down and the arch would stand alone. The keystone is one of the most important discoveries in building.

间，房顶的形状就像是半只水桶呢。假如你们曾经钻过顶上呈弧形的那种隧道，那么，你们可能就已经见过这种桶形穹顶了。

倘若房间的墙壁本身是圆形的，那么屋顶就会变得像是一个倒扣的碗了。虽说我们将这个“碗”称为穹顶，但其所依据的基本原理还是一样的，还是拱形原理。倘若拿来一个拱形，并将它变成一个圆周的话，那么，你们最终就会看到一个穹顶的形状。

你们可能会感到奇怪，为什么推、拉会比抬、举能够更牢固地控制住物体。为了更好地理解这一点，你们可以试一试下面这个。召拢一群人，让他们站成一个敞口的圆圈，从而让每个人的双手都能碰到两边的人的肩膀。接下来，每个人都适当地退后一步，然后抓住两边的人的胳膊。大家都准备就绪之后，就慢慢地探出身体，将整个圆圈合拢。这样，你们就会看到，这个圆圈是如何被压力而非作用力结合在一起的了。穹顶的原理，与你们这样做的原理是一样的，只不过穹顶坚持的时间，要比你们久得多罢了！

在建造拱门、拱顶或穹顶时，必须先有个支撑点，才能将石块砌上去，因为除非最后一块石头砌放就位，否则拱门就会垮掉。人们通常会将一个临时的木质支架放在两堵墙之间，这个木架是半圆形，称为拱架。拱门就建在这个拱架上，并且是从两边开始，向着顶端砌拢。当顶端的最后一块石头（称为拱顶石）砌放就位后，就可以拆掉拱架，而拱门也会自行屹立，不致倒塌了，也只有到了这个时候，拱架才能拆掉。因此，拱顶石也是建筑领域里最重大的发现之一。

In Assyria, however, there was so little wood for making centering that few arches or vaults were made, and it was not until 1,000 years or so later that arches were frequently used.

In Egypt, the pyramids are still standing because they were made of stone and built in the most lasting shape there is. They cannot topple over or fall down. In Mesopotamia very few palaces or temples are still standing because the bricks of which they were built often have crumbled into dust, so that all that is now left are the mounds of earth overgrown with weeds.

It seems impossible to believe that our great cities of today may one day become just heaps of dirt, grown over with weeds like the old Assyrian and Babylonian cities, or that the millions of people now living in the houses and thronging the streets could ever disappear. Yet the people who lived in Assyria probably thought the very same thing.

然而，由于古亚述没什么木材来搭建拱架，因此这里修建的拱门或穹顶很少，直到差不多一千年之后，人们才开始频繁地修建拱门。

在埃及，那些金字塔如今仍然屹立着，因为它们都是用石头修建，并且是用世界上最持久、最稳定的形状建成的。它们既不可能倒塌，也不可能垮掉。而在美索不达米亚，那些宫殿或者神庙却没有几座保存下来，因为修建它们所用的土砖，往往已经碎裂成了齑粉，因此如今剩下的，便都是长满杂草的一个个土堆了。

我们如今的这些大城市，有朝一日也有可能变成一个个土堆，就像古亚述和古巴比伦的那些城市一样长满杂草，而如今生活在千家万户里、挤满了大街小巷的千千万万人，有朝一日也将永远逝去，这一点似乎令人难以置信。然而，生活在古亚述时期的人，很可能也想过同样的问题呢。

Chapter 4 The Perfect Building

If you make a mistake in mathematics or composition, you can correct it, or tear it up and do it over. If a picture or a statue is ugly, it can be put out of sight, hidden, or destroyed. But if a building is ugly, there it stands for everyone to see. Its ugliness, its mistakes cannot be covered up until it falls down or is torn down. An architect once committed suicide just as the great temple he had planned was finished. He left a note saying that he had made five mistakes in the building, and as they could not be corrected and could not be covered up, there they were for everyone to see forever. He could not stand the disgrace.

Most buildings that are erected have many mistakes, many things that are ugly about them, though few people, few passers-by may notice anything wrong. Architects, after all, are just like the rest of us who sometimes notice our own mistakes when no one else can.

But there was one building that was erected over 2,000 years ago that has no mistakes. It is one of the few perfect buildings in the world. It was built by men, but built for a woman, in honor of a Greek goddess, the goddess of wisdom whose name was Athena Parthenos. And so the building was called the Parthenon after her last name. It is on a high hill in the city of Athens, in Greece, and although it has been partly destroyed, people come from all over the world to see what a perfect building looks like.

第4章 完美的建筑

假如在做算术题时做错了，或者在写作文时写了错别字，你们可以改正，或者撕下那一页重新来过。要是一幅画作或者一尊雕像不好看的话，我们也可以将它收起来、藏起来，或者干脆毁掉。但是，如果一栋建筑不好看的话，它却会一直矗立在那里，大家都看得到。除非倒塌或者拆除，否则这栋建筑的难看和错误是藏不住的。有位建筑师，曾经在自己设计的那座神庙刚刚完工后，就自杀了呢。他留下了遗言，说他在设计这栋建筑时犯了五个错误，因为这些错误既没法改正，也没法掩盖，因此大家永远都看得到。他实在无法忍受这种丢脸的事情，因此才自杀的。

如今世界上的绝大多数建筑，都有许许多多不完善的地方，都有许多的部位设计得很丑，只是很少有人、很少的路过者会注意到这些不完善之处。毕竟来说，建筑设计师也像我们其他人一样，只能偶尔在其他人都看不出的情况下，注意到自己犯下的错误呢。

不过，有一座两千多年前修建的建筑，却没有任何不完善的地方。它属于世界上为数不多的完美建筑之一。虽说是男人们修建起来的，可它却是为一个女人而建，是为了供奉古希腊的一位女神，即智慧女神雅典娜·巴台农的。因此，这座建筑便以她的姓来命名，称为巴台农神庙。这座神庙，位于希腊雅典城的一座山丘上，尽管其中有些部位已经损毁，但人们还是从世界各地不远万里而来，都想看一看一座完美的建筑是个什么样子呢。

The Egyptian temples had flat roofs because there is little or no rain in Egypt, and so a sloping roof to shed the rain was not necessary. The Greek temples had to have slanting roofs, for Greece has rain. So the Parthenon had a sloping roof.

The Egyptians built their temples with the columns on the inside. The Greeks turned the Egyptian temple inside out and put the columns on the outside. The Greek temple was not to hold people, but to protect the statue of the god or goddess. People didn't go inside to worship as they do in churches, synagogues, or mosques. They stood on the outside. The columns the Greeks used were not like those the Egyptians used. They were simpler, but perhaps even more beautiful.

Greek temples had three kinds of columns, but the kind used in the Parthenon was sometimes called the Man's Style column. It is also called *Doric* after a very old Greek tribe. Not only the column but the style of building that always went with it was strong, simple, plain. That's why it is called the Man's Style. There were many Doric buildings in Greece, but the Parthenon was considered the most beautiful of all.

A Doric building is built on a terraced or stepped platform and is not made of mud bricks plated with *alabaster* (a precious marble) or tile as

巴台农神庙，现存于雅典

古埃及的神庙都属于平顶，这是因为埃及少雨，有些地方甚至一年到头都不下雨，因此没有必要修建挡雨的坡顶。可古希腊的神庙却必须建有坡顶才行，因为希腊雨水很多。所以，巴台农神庙的屋顶也是坡顶。

古埃及人修建的神庙内部都有立柱。而古希腊人却是反埃及神庙之道而行之，将立柱都建在神庙外部呢。古希腊人修建的神庙，并不是为了容纳人们，而是为了保护诸神的雕像。与去教堂、犹太会堂或者清真寺做礼拜不一样，古希腊人无须进入神庙里面去供奉神灵。他们都是站在神庙外面。古希腊人所用的立柱，也与古埃及人所用的立柱不同。前者更简单，不过可能也更加漂亮呢。

古希腊的神庙里，通常有三种立柱，巴台农神庙里所用的，却是有时被人们称为"男子汉式"的那一种立柱。这种立柱，也叫作"多利克式"立柱；多利克是希腊一个古老的部落的名称。非但是这些立柱，而且整个建筑的风格也都很强壮、简单而朴实。此种风格之所以被称为"男子汉"风格，原因也在于此。古希腊有许多属于多利克式的建筑，可巴台农神庙却被人们认为是其中最美丽的一座。

一座多利克式的建筑，通常都修建在一处阶梯状、或者说有台阶的平台上，并且与美索不达米亚人修建的神庙不同，不是用镶有汉白玉（这是一种很珍贵的大理

the Mesopotamian people built their temples, but of solid stone, sometimes marble. In the Greek buildings, there was no covering of cheap materials with a surface of fancier materials. Styles in clothes change often, as you know, but the Doric style of building has lasted over 2,000 years, and we are still using it today. I'll try to describe it so you can remember which one it is it when you see one for yourself.

The Doric column has no base but rests directly on the platform. It tapers slightly as a tree trunk does, so its sides are not perfectly straight. They may look straight, but they bulge slightly. This bulge is called *entasis*; and a column was given entasis because one that had straight sides, one without entasis, looked as if it were thinner in the middle. That is so because your eyes play tricks on you sometimes. So, when you look at a Doric column, you think it goes straight up, but it does not. Tricks like this are called optical illusions.

Some architects of the present time, noticing this ever-so-slight bulge in the Doric column, have thought they would improve on it by making the bulge greater. (When the doctor says to take one pill, some people take two, reasoning that if one pill is good for you, two will be better.) But the Greek entasis was just exactly enough, and more entasis makes a column look fat instead of straight by using an optical illusion.

The sides of the Doric column were then *fluted* — that is, cut with grooves so as to make slender, lengthwise shadows from top to bottom of the column, taking away from the plainness that a perfectly smooth column would have. Most columns today have no fluting. You can imagine how difficult it is to cut such channels in marble without making

石）或瓷瓦的土砖建成的，而是用一些很牢固的石块建成的，有时用的还是大理石呢。古希腊的建筑中，没有哪个部位会表面材料花哨，而其下的材料却很廉价。你们都知道，服装风格经常变化，可这种多利克式的建筑风格，却已经持续两千多年了，而如今我们仍然还在利用这种建筑方式呢。下面我就来介绍介绍这种建筑风格，以便日后你们亲眼看到后，能够想起那是属于哪一种建筑风格。

多利克式立柱没有基座，而是直接立在平台上。它们像树干一样，越往上直径越细，因此其表面并不是完全垂直的。虽说它们看上去可能很直，但实际上它们的表面却是稍微有点儿凸起的。这种凸起，叫作柱微凸线；而之所以在立柱上加上柱微凸线，是因为表面平直、没有柱微凸线的立柱，中部会显得较细。这种现象，是因为人眼有时也会跟我们玩把戏呢。这种把戏，就叫视错觉。

目前，有些建筑设计师在注意到多利克式立柱上这种极其细微的凸起之后，曾经以为他们通过加大这种凸起，便可以改善这种立柱的样子。（这就好比是医嘱服用一粒药，有些人就会服两粒，因为他们觉得，既然服一粒有好处，那么服两粒就会更好。）可是，古希腊人制作的那种柱微凸线，其实已经恰到好处了，倘若制造更多柱微凸线，反而会因为视错觉的原因，令立柱显得更粗而不是更细。

当时，多利克式立柱的侧面都有压槽，也就是说，都刻有一条条的凹槽，使之看上去更加细长，立柱从上到下，都有纵向的条纹，从而避免了上下完全光滑的那种立柱的单调。如今的绝大多数立柱上，都没有压槽了。你们完全可以想象得出，在大理石立柱上雕刻这样的凹槽而不能出现任何差错，该有多么困难。一点儿差错

a single slip. One single slip would ruin the column and it couldn't be repaired.

To make things even more challenging, the Greeks built their columns in pieces and then stacked them up on a post. Can you see why it would be so difficult? Builders had to get the bulge and the flutes to match perfectly all the way up.

If you see a column built like this, you can see the seams between those thick sections, called *drums*, which are all stacked up.

The top of the column is called the *capital* because capital means head. The capital was made of a piece shaped like a saucer, above which was a thin square block. You'll have to look at the picture to understand the rest.

There is probably a Doric building where you live, for as I have said, we are still using this style today. It may be a bank or a library, a courthouse or some other building. When you see a Greek building that's not in Greece, it is called Greek Revival because it is a model of the perfect Parthenon and other similar buildings throughout ancient Greece.

When you do see a building with Doric columns, examine it and see if it has all these things that a perfect Doric building has and only these things. Consider the following.

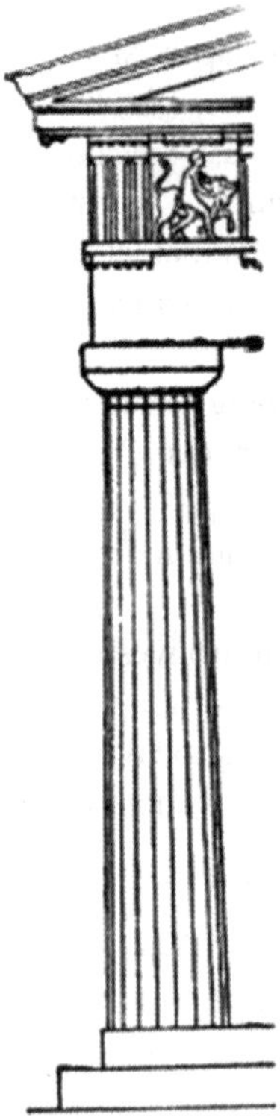

多利克式立柱

就会毁掉整根立柱，并且无法再进行修补呢。

而更难的是，古希腊人还是将立柱一截一截地完成，然后再将它们在一根柱子上堆叠起来的。你们明白为什么会这么难吗？建造立柱的人不但必须雕出柱微凸线来，还得让压槽从下到上衔接得严丝合缝呢。

如果看到一根这样的柱子，你们就能看出两个厚部之间的接缝了。这些厚部，叫作“圆鼓石”，都是一块一块地堆砌起来的。

立柱的顶端称为“柱顶”；因为“顶”这个词，指的就是“头”。柱顶是一块形如茶托的石块，它的上面还有一块薄薄的方石。你们得先看一看图片，然后才能去了解其他的部位。

你们家附近，很可能会有一栋多利克风格的建筑，因为正如前面已经说过的那样，如今我们仍然在运用这种风格呢。你们家附近的，可能是一家银行，或者是一座图书馆、法院大楼或者其他的建筑物。你们在希腊以外的地方看到的希腊式建筑，都被称为“希腊复古式”建筑。因为这种建筑的形式，就是完美的巴台农神庙，以及整个古希腊时期其他类似建筑所用的样式。

倘若你们确实看到了一栋拥有多利克式立柱的建筑，那就不妨仔细地观察观察，看它是不是集中了一栋完美的多利克式建筑的所有特征，是不是只拥有这些特征。同时，想一想下面的问题：

⊙ Are the columns of stone or only of wood?
⊙ Are they fluted or only plain?
⊙ Do the columns have proper capitals and other parts as in the true Doric style?

People have tried ever since the time the Parthenon was built to improve on the Doric temple, but it seems impossible to do so. Every change they make from the original is less beautiful.

One of my earliest recollections is a picture of the Parthenon that hung on the wall of my classroom. I had seen it day after day for months. One day I asked my teacher what the picture was.

"It's a picture of the most beautiful building in the world," she replied.

"What! That old wreck?" I exclaimed. "I don't see anything beautiful about it."

"You wouldn't," she answered.

That expression — "You wouldn't" — made me want to argue why it wasn't beautiful, but she wouldn't even argue.

She said, "Wait until you grow up."

Even though I was a child, I hated to be treated like I couldn't understand what was beautiful and what wasn't, so I set about trying to find out why the Parthenon was not beautiful. But the more arguments I tried to find, the less I found.

And then one day, twenty-five years later, when I first looked upward at that great Doric temple itself, standing against the blue sky, a traveler at my side remarked, "I don't see

⊙ 这些立柱是石制的呢，还是木质的?
⊙ 这些立柱上面有压槽呢，还是平的?
⊙ 这些立柱的柱顶和其他部位，是不是像真正的多利克式立柱那样呢?

自巴台农神庙建成以来，人们一直都在试图对多利克式神庙进行改善，可这一点似乎是不可能做到的。他们在原作上所进行的每一种改动，都没有原作那样漂亮。

我儿时最早的记忆之一，便是挂在我们教室墙上的一幅巴台农神庙的照片。我日复一日地看着那张照片，过了好几个月呢。有一天，我问老师，照片上是什么东西。

"那是世界上最漂亮的一栋建筑的照片。"她回答道。

"什么! 就是那座又旧又破的房子?"我大声说道，"我可看不出它哪里漂亮呢。"

"你当然看不出来。"她回答道。

她脸上的那种表情——"你当然看不出来"——让我很想争一争，说说它为什么不漂亮，可她连争都不跟我争。

她只是说："等你长大后，就能看出来了。"

尽管我那时还是个小朋友，可我很不喜欢别人认为我理解不了什么是美、什么是丑，于是我开始想要弄清楚，为什么巴台农神庙不漂亮。不过，我找出的证据越多，却越觉得自己没理了。

接下来，二十五年后的一天，当我第一次抬起头来，仰视着那座屹立在蓝天之下的多利克式神庙本身时，我身边的一位游客说道："我可瞧不出这堆垮塌得七零

anything beautiful about that broken-down old ruin."

And at that, I turned and just kept myself from saying, "You wouldn't."

Even a young child can tell whether a person is beautiful, but some adults can't tell whether a building is beautiful or not. If they could really tell the difference, we wouldn't have so many buildings that aren't beautiful. Anyone who draws knows whether the proportions are right or not, but it takes a good eye to tell when a building's proportions are right or wrong.

Now, some buildings have parts that are all out of proportion with each other. Have you seen such a building? Perhaps the windows were too small or the door and porch were just too large, or something was not right, but you couldn't put your finger on it. And other times, you may see a building you think is so beautiful you want to go there or see it again and again. Perhaps it makes you feel welcomed or amazed, but you just don't know why.

Even if you don't know why something seems right or wrong, but you know it's beautiful, you have what is called "a good eye." Some people can't tell when a picture is hanging straight on the wall. They may even measure the distance and declare it straight, but a person with a "good eye" can detect what the ruler may not show — that it is tipped the smallest bit, just a hair's breadth perhaps.

It is a gift to have a good eye, but you can learn to have one, too. You can learn to see, and not just look. So, let's continue to find out just what to look for, shall we?

八落的旧废墟有什么漂亮的地方呢。"

听到这话，我转过身去，费了好大的劲才忍住，没有这样说："您当然看不出来。"

连小孩子也能分辨出一个人的美丑，可有些成年人，却愣是分不清一座建筑是丑是美哩。要是他们真的能够辨别出其间的差异的话，我们就不会有那么多不好看的建筑了。任何一个绘画的人，都知道所绘比例正不正确；可要看出一坐建筑的比例正不正确，却需要很好的眼力了。

如今，在一些建筑上，有的部位彼此之间完全不相称。你们看没看到过这样的建筑呢？要么是窗户太小，要么就是门或走廊太大，或者还有其他不合理的地方，可你们没办法确切地指出来。还有的时候，你们也有可能看到一座自己觉得非常漂亮的建筑，因而希望一次又一次地去那儿，一次又一次地看到那座建筑呢。或许，它会让你们觉得很暖心或者感到惊讶，可你们就是不知道为什么。

如果你们虽然不知道某种东西是对是错的原因，却仍然知道它很漂亮，那么你们就是拥有了所谓的"好眼力"。有些人甚至分不清墙上的一幅画是不是挂歪了。他们会量一量距离，然后才说这画挂正了。可那种拥有"好眼力"的人，却能看出尺子说明不了的一些问题，哪怕只是挂歪了一点点，或许只是歪了发丝那么宽，他们也看得出来呢。

虽说眼力好是一种天赋，可你们也可以学会拥有好眼力。你们可以学会观察，而不再停留在走马观花的水平上。因此，我们不妨继续去发现那些我们需要寻找的东西，好不好呢？

如今，每位建筑工都有两件重要的工具，即铅锤线和水平仪。铅锤钱能够表明

There are two important tools that every builder today uses — a *plumb line* and a *level*. A plumb line tells whether a wall or a column or anything else supposed to be straight up and down is really straight up and down or vertical, as it is called. A level, which has a little bubble in a glass on its edge, tells whether a floor or a sill or anything else supposed to be level is really level or horizontal, as it is called. You can't fool a plumb line or a level.

But the Greeks said you couldn't believe the plumb line or the level, for columns that are really vertical seem to lean out and floors that are really horizontal seem to sag in the middle. Do you now know why? That's because our eyes make them seem so. As it is our eyes that have to see buildings, the Greek builders of the Parthenon built it as they wanted the eyes to see it; and so, though all lines may seem to be vertical, horizontal, level, or straight, there is really not a vertical line or a horizontal line or a perfectly straight line in the Parthenon. Changes were made to trick our eye, and make the building more beautiful than it would have been using really straight lines. That's one of the things that makes the Parthenon so extraordinary — it is full of optical illusions!

一堵墙、一根立柱或者其他应当上下笔直的东西是不是真的上下笔直，也就是人们所称的“垂直”。水平仪的边沿则是一根玻璃管，里面有一个小小的气泡，它能够表明一处地板、一个窗台或者其他应当保持与地面平行的东西是不是真的与地面平行，也就是人们所称的“水平”。你们可骗不过铅锤线和水平仪呢。

不过，古希腊人却称，我们不能相信铅锤线或水平仪，因为那些真正垂直的立柱，看上去却似乎是倾斜的，而真正水平的地板，中心部位看上去却像是向下凹陷的。你们知道这是什么原因吗？是我们的眼睛，才使得它们看上去成那样呢。由于观看建筑的是我们的眼睛，因此古希腊建造巴台农神庙的建筑者，便将它建造得似乎是人们的眼睛希望看到的那个样子。于是，尽管所有边线看上去可能都是垂直的、水平的、与地面平行的或者直的，但其实巴台农神庙里却没有一根真正的垂直线、水平线，或者说没有一根彻底的直线。他们做出了改变，以便骗过我们的眼睛，并且使得整座神庙更加漂亮，倘若用真正的直线，神庙就不会这么漂亮了。这一点，也是使得巴台农神庙变得如此非凡的一大原因：整座神庙里，到处都充满了视错觉的效果！

Chapter 5 Woman's Style Building

It may seem rather far-fetched to say a building is like a woman, but the ancient Greeks had farfetched imaginations. In one of the famous stories of Greek mythology, they imagined, for instance, that a vain boy had been turned into the flower we call the narcissus; that a girl who dared to love the beautiful Sun god was turned into a sunflower; and that a nymph had been turned into a laurel tree. So it was not such a great stretch of the imagination, after all, for them to say that a woman had been turned into a certain kind of column, or that a certain kind of marble column was like a woman.

A Roman architect named Vitruvius who lived 2,000 years ago said that the two curls on the head of this column were the locks of the woman's hair; that the grooves or flutings in the body of the column were the folds of her gown; and that the base was her bare feet. They called this kind of column *Ionic* because it was first made in Ionia, a colony of Greece across the sea in Asia Minor, or what today is known as Turkey.

But the best Ionic building was in Athens on the Acropolis, near the Doric temple, the Parthenon. It was called the Erechtheum because it was built in honor of Erechtheus, who was supposed to have been a king of Athens in days long past.

The Parthenon is a Man's Style building built in honor of woman. The Erechtheum is a

第5章 阴柔风格的建筑

说一栋建筑像个女人，这种说法似乎有点太过牵强了，可是，古希腊人的想象力，却更不靠谱哩。比如说，在古希腊一个著名的神话故事里，他们曾经想象过，一个自负的小男孩被人变成了一种我们称之为“水仙花”的花朵；一个敢于爱上英俊潇洒的太阳神的女神，被人变成了一朵向日葵；还有一位宁芙，则被人变成了一株月桂树。因此，他们说一名女性被人变成了某种立柱，或者说某种大理石立柱像是一个女人，这种想象力也就不足为奇了。

两千年前，一位叫作维特鲁威[1]的古罗马建筑师曾经说过：下面这根立柱柱头上的那两个卷状装饰，是女人头上的两缕卷发；柱身上的凹槽或者压槽，是女人长袍上的褶皱；而底下的基座，就是女人光着的双脚。人们把这种形式的立柱，称为“爱奥尼亚式”立柱，因为，这种立柱最初是在爱奥尼亚这个地方制造出来的。爱奥尼亚是古希腊的一个殖民地，位于地中海对面的小亚细亚，也就是如今的土耳其。

不过，最杰出的爱奥尼亚式建筑，却是在雅典的“卫城”，离巴台农这座多利克式的神庙不远。这座建筑，叫作厄瑞克修姆神庙；因为修建这座神庙，是为了供奉厄瑞克修姆这个人的。据说，他曾经是古时雅典的一位国王呢。

巴台农神庙是一座具有阳刚之气的建筑，供奉的却是一位女神。而厄瑞克修姆

[1] 维特鲁威（Marcus Vitruvius Pollio，生卒年不详），古罗马时期的建筑师和作家。他的《论建筑》（*De Architectura*）是古代建筑理论方面唯一保存下来的一部著作。

Woman's Style building built in honor of a man.

Ionic columns are on three sides of the Erechtheum, but on the fourth end of the same building there are six statues of women in place of columns, and they hold the roof on their heads. It is called the Porch of the Maidens. So we get in the same temple, not only the Woman's Style columns, but the actual women's figures. The women's figures are called Caryatids.

The story of the Caryatids is that they represented captives from Carya condemned to stand in this position, holding the roof on their heads forever. One of the Caryatids was taken away to England, and in its place was put a copy made of painted terra cotta. Then the other Caryatids were put into a museum in Athens, and replacement copies were put on the Erechtheum, all to protect the statues from city pollution.

The largest and most famous Ionic temple in the world was not in Greece itself. It was in Ionia, in the city of Ephesus in Asia Minor. The Temple of Artemis was built to Diana, the goddess of the moon, and was so magnificent that it was called one of the Seven Wonders of the Ancient World. It is the second wonder I have told you about. The Bible tells us that Saint Paul nearly started a riot there by preaching against Diana, who was one of many gods and goddesses instead of the one God he taught about.

The angry mob wouldn't listen to Paul, but just to drown out what he

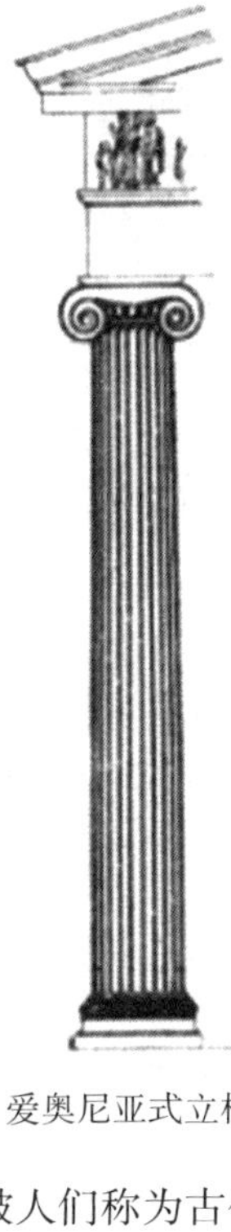
爱奥尼亚式立柱

神庙是一座具有阴柔风格的建筑，供奉的却是一位男性国王。

厄瑞克修姆神庙有三面都建有爱奥尼亚式的立柱，可在第四面的一端，却是六尊女性的雕像，而不是立柱，并且是用雕像的头部支撑着庙顶呢。这个地方，被称为“女像柱廊”。这样，在这同一座神庙里，我们既能看到具有女性阴柔风格的立柱，也能看到真正的女性雕像。这些女性雕像，就称为“女像柱”。

关于这些女像柱，传说她们都是卡律亚[1]女神的俘虏，被迫用这种姿势站在那里，永远用自己的头去支撑着庙顶。其中一座女像柱被带往了英国，因此人们便用彩陶做了一个仿制品取而代之。后来，其余的女像柱都被搬到了雅典的一座博物馆里，因此如今厄瑞克修姆神庙里便全都是后来的仿制品了，好让那些雕像原件不再受到城市的污染。

世界上最大和最有名的爱奥尼亚式神庙，却并不在希腊国内，而是在小亚细亚以弗所这座城市里的爱奥尼亚。阿耳忒弥斯神庙是给月亮女神狄安娜修建的，由于它极其宏伟、壮丽，因而还被人们称为古代世界的“七大奇迹”之一呢。这是我给你们介绍的第二大奇迹。《圣经》中说，圣保罗曾经在那儿反对狄安娜，因为狄安娜属于诸神之一，而不是他所宣传的单一上帝，所以差点儿还引发了一场骚乱呢。

那些愤怒的暴民不肯聆听保罗的传道，而为了消除他对这位女神所说的坏话，

[1] 卡律亚（Carya），古希腊神话中的榛树女神。“女像柱”（Caryatid）一词即由此派生而来。

was trying to say against their goddess, they kept chanting for two hours: "Great is Diana of the Ephesians! Great is Diana of the Ephesians!"

All but the floor of the temple has since disappeared, but the sayings of Saint Paul, which the Ephesians tried to drown out, still last. Buildings may not last, but the written word endures.

The third wonder was another Ionic building at a place called Halicarnassus. It was not a temple, however, but a tomb built for King Mausolus by his widow. While this tomb no longer exists, we still call any very large tomb today a *mausoleum*, named after the tomb of Mausolus.

You don't have to go all the way to Greece to see Ionic columns, however. There are probably many Ionic buildings where you live. You can, however, see if they are the true Ionic, or if they are what we call *hybrid*, which means a mixture, or a hybrid of styles.

Today our architects copy the Ionic style more often than they do the Doric, so if you try to count the number of Ionic and Doric columns you can find in the place where you live or places where you may visit, you will probably count several times as many Ionic as Doric columns. Can you imagine why? They are easier to build. Can you name the reasons why?

女像柱廊，现存于雅典的厄瑞克修姆神庙
（摄影：加里·威肯）

他们还反复颂唱了两个钟头："以弗所人的狄安娜伟大！ 以弗所人的狄安娜伟大！"

这座神庙里，除了地面，其他部位早已不复存在了；可以弗所人曾经尽力排斥的、圣保罗传播的教义，如今却仍然流传着。建筑物可能不会永久存在，但写下的文字却能永世长存。

第三大奇迹也是一栋爱奥尼亚式的建筑，位于一个叫作哈利卡纳苏斯的地方。然而，这座建筑并不是神庙，而是摩索拉斯的遗孀为他修建的一座陵墓。尽管这座陵墓已经不复存在，但如今我们仍然会根据摩索拉斯的名字，将一座大型的墓穴称为"摩索拉斯大陵墓"呢。

然而，你们并不是非得亲自前往希腊，才能看得到爱奥尼亚式立柱。你们的家乡，很可能也有许多爱奥尼亚式风格的建筑。不过，你们可以看一看，它们是真正的爱奥尼亚式风格呢，还是属于我们所称的"混合式"。而所谓的混合式，就是指不同风格的混合。

如今，我们的建筑设计师们常常仿照爱奥尼亚式风格，而不那么经常仿制多利克式风格，因此，倘若在自家附近或者游览的地方去数一数那些能够找到的爱奥尼亚式立柱和多利克式立柱的话，你们很可能就会发现，爱奥尼亚式立柱的数量会有多利克式立柱的好多倍呢。你们知道这是什么原因吗？原因就在于，它们容易建造一些。你们能说出这又是什么原因吗？

Chapter 6 New Styles in Building

People get tired of seeing the same styles of clothing and try to start something new. We might look to Paris or Milan or New York for the newest style. In the same way, architects used to go to Greece for their styles in buildings. Some architects have tried to start new styles in columns just to have something new and different, but the columns they have invented are all less beautiful than the two Greek columns I have described.

The Greeks started a new style of column called the *Corinthian*, but they didn't like it very much themselves and hardly used it at all. The Roman architect Vitruvius, who told us the story of the Ionic column, tells us another to explain the Corinthian capital.

Vitruvius said that a basket of toys with a tile covering the top was placed on the grave of a little girl in Corinth, as was the custom in those days. By chance, the basket had been placed directly over a thistle plant and the leaves of the thistle grew up around the basket. An architect, seeing this basket with the leaves curling round it, thought it would make a good design for a capital of a column, so he copied it in marble and put it on an Ionic column in place of the Ionic capital. In this way the Corinthian column was invented.

So the Corinthian column is just an Ionic column with a different capital. The Greek thistle is called the *acanthus*, so the leaves that curl upward and outward on each side of the Corinthian capital are acanthus leaves. Just underneath the tile are four corner scrolls

第6章 建筑上的新风格

同样风格的服装穿久了之后，人们就会厌倦起来，想要开创出新的款式。我们可能会很注意巴黎、米兰或者纽约那些最新的款式。同样，建筑设计师们以前也经常到希腊去寻找建筑风格的灵感哩。有些建筑师曾经试图用新的风格来建造立柱，只是为了弄点儿新的、与众不同的东西出来。可他们发明设计的那些立柱，却都没有我跟你们说过的那两种古希腊风格的立柱这么漂亮。

虽说古希腊人后来又发明了一种新的立柱风格，叫作科林斯式风格，可他们自己不是很喜欢这种风格，因此很少使用这种风格的立柱。古罗马时期的建筑设计师维特鲁威曾经向我们说明了爱奥尼亚式立柱的历史，也向我们解释了科林斯式柱顶出现的历史。

维特鲁威称，科林斯一个早夭的小姑娘的坟墓上，曾经放着一篮子玩具，上面还盖有一块瓦片，因为当时的风俗就是那样。而那个篮子，恰巧又放在一篷蓟草上面，因而蓟草叶子绕着篮子长了一圈。一位建筑设计师看到这个草叶盘绕的篮子之后，觉得用这种样式来做柱顶很不错，便照着那个样子用大理石制作出来，放在一根爱奥尼亚式立柱之上，取代了原来那个爱奥尼亚式的柱顶。这样，就发明出了科林斯式立柱。

因此，科林斯式立柱实际上就是一种爱奥尼亚式立柱，只是加上了一个不同的柱顶。希腊的那种蓟草叫作“茛苕”，因此沿着科林斯式柱顶每一面向上、向外盘

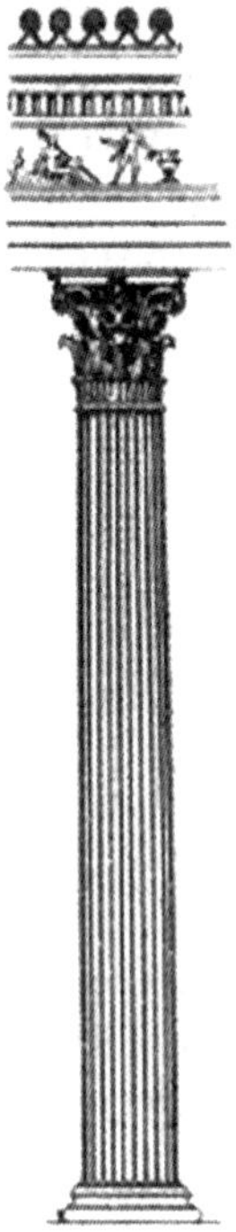
科林斯式立柱

or curls. The Ionic curls face front and back, but the Corinthian curls face cornerwise.

Many people think the Corinthian capital more beautiful than either the Doric or the Ionic, but others find it too fancy and not natural to have stone beams seeming to rest on leaves. At any rate, although the Greeks invented the Corinthian column, they hardly used it.

The Greeks finished all their great buildings about 300 years before Christ was born, and one might say that no more great Greek architects lived after that time.

You know from your geography that Greece is nearly an island, but not quite since it is surrounded on only three — not four — sides by water. It is a peninsula jutting out into the Mediterranean Sea. Next door to Greece is another near-island or peninsula called Italy. The capital of Italy was (and still is) Rome, and after Greece had lost her power, Rome became the capital — that is, the head — of most of the Western world.

The Greeks were great architects, but the Romans were great builders. There is a difference. The Romans liked the Corinthian column better than either the Doric or the Ionic. The Romans also made another column, composed of both Ionic and Corinthian capitals, and so this column is called *composite*. It had the large curls, or *volutes*, of the Ionic and the acanthus leaves of the Corinthian.

绕的那种叶子，就是莨苕叶。而顶上那块瓦片下方的四个角上，则是涡卷形饰，或者说卷状物。爱奥尼亚式立柱的卷状装饰是向前或向后卷起，但科林斯式立柱的卷状装饰物，却是向四个角上卷起。

许多人都认为，科林斯式立柱的柱顶比多利克式或爱奥尼亚式的柱顶都要漂亮；可还有一些人，却认为这种柱顶太过花哨，而叶子上面的长石，也显得不太自然。不管怎么说，虽然古希腊人发明了科林斯式立柱，他们却很少使用这种立柱呢。

古希腊人所有的伟大建筑，都是在距基督降生大约三百年前就出现了；而我们也可以说，自那以后，希腊再也没有出现过更加伟大的建筑设计师了。

从地理课上，你们都知道，希腊差不多就是一个小岛；但它并非全然是一个岛屿，因为那里只是三面环海，而不是四面环海。它是一个伸向地中海里的半岛。紧挨着希腊的，是一个同样近乎岛屿、实际上却是半岛的国家，叫作意大利。意大利的首都曾经是（如今也是）罗马，而待古希腊走下坡路后，罗马就变成整个西方世界的首都，即领袖了。

古希腊人都是些伟大的建筑设计师，而古罗马人也都是一些伟大的建设者。他们之间，有一处不同。相比于多利克式立柱和爱奥尼亚式立柱来说，古罗马人更喜欢科林斯式立柱。古罗马人还结合爱奥尼亚式立柱的柱顶和科林斯式立柱的柱顶，设计出了另一种立柱，因此这种立柱便叫作“组合式立柱”。这种立柱的柱顶，既有爱奥尼亚式那种大型的卷曲形装饰，或者说涡卷形饰，同时又有科林斯式柱顶的那种莨苕叶饰。

Often it is hard to tell whether a column is Corinthian or composite. In the composite column, the Ionic top is larger than in the Corinthian; that is all. The Romans also changed the Doric column; they gave it a base and left out the flutings and the saucer-shaped part of the capital. This kind of Roman column was called *Etruscan Doric* or *Tuscan*.

The Romans made other changes in their styles of building — some would say, changes for the worse. In order to make columns seem higher than they were, they frequently put a box-like base or pedestal beneath each column. They also placed split half-columns against walls. Such half-columns built against the wall are called *engaged columns*. Other columns they flattened out against the wall so that they appeared square. A column so flattened out is called a *pilaster*. You can remember the name by thinking of *plaster* and putting an i between the p and l.

Perhaps the greatest thing the Romans did for building was to use the arch. As you know, the Assyrians invented the arch but used it very little because they had very little stone with which to build arches. But they never rested their arches on columns. The Greeks and other architects before them

古罗马的科林斯式立柱　　组合式立柱　　托斯卡纳式立柱

我们经常很难分辨出，一种立柱究竟属于科林斯式还是属于组合式。在组合式立柱上，那种爱奥尼亚式柱顶，通常都要比科林斯式立柱的柱顶大，区别仅在于此。古罗马人还对多利克式立柱进行了改动，他们给这种立柱加了一个基座，并且省去了柱身上的压槽，以及柱顶上的碟形部分。古罗马人修建的这种立柱，叫作伊特鲁里亚的多利克式立柱，或者称托斯卡纳式立柱。

在建筑风格上，古罗马人还做出了其他的一些改变，有的人可能会说，这些改变是朝着差的方向发展了。为了让立柱看上去比实际的更高，他们经常会在每根立柱底下加上一个方方正正的基座或者底座。他们将劈开的半截柱子，顶在墙上。这种顶在墙上的半截柱子，叫作“附墙柱”。他们还用其他的柱子水平地顶在墙上，从而使得它们看起来方方正正的。这种水平的柱子，叫作“半露柱”。根据“灰泥”（plaster）这个词，你们就可以记住“半露柱”（pilaster）这个词，因为后者只是在p和l之间加了一个字母i构成的。

或许，古罗马人在建筑方面最伟大的一种成就，就是使用拱门了。大家都知道，亚述人发明了拱门，可用得极少，因为他们那里可用于建造拱门的石块很少。而他们之前的古希腊人和其他一些建筑师，则只是将一块长石搭在两根柱子之上。

古罗马式的拱形，加尔桥，现存于法国
（摄影：加里·威肯）

placed a single stone across from column to column. But a single slab of stone could not reach very far, so the spaces between columns were never very great and never could be very great. The Romans were the first to make arches from column to column instead of using straight slabs of stone.

The Romans also found a very interesting use for the column-arch. They built a riverbed on the top and used this waterway, called an *aqueduct*, to carry water, the key to life, great distances to dry lands. I will tell you more about aqueducts later.

The Romans also made barrel vaults and domes that, you remember, were arched ceilings built on the same principle as the arch. By using the dome and the vault, they were able to roof over much larger spaces than ever could have been roofed over with single slabs of stone or with wooden roofs. Furthermore, a vaulted or domed roof of stone was fireproof, whereas a wooden roof, of course, was not. This way, the Romans could build huge buildings for very large crowds. One example is a famous temple in Rome

不过，一块石板不可能很长，因此两根柱子之间的间距都不大，也不可能很大。古罗马人则是率先在两根柱子之间建造拱门，而不再是用平直石板的人。

古罗马人还发现了一种非常有意思的方法来利用拱柱。他们在拱柱顶上修建了一条水沟，然后利用这种叫作“高架渠”的水沟，远距离地把对生命极其重要的水运送到干旱之地。我在后面还会给你们多介绍一点儿关于高架渠的情况的。

古罗马人还修建了许多的桶形穹顶。你们都还记得吧，桶形穹顶就是那种拱形的屋顶，是根据与拱门相同的原理修建的。利用拱顶和穹顶，与只用单块长石或者木质屋顶相比，屋顶就能覆盖更大的面积了。此外，用石头建成的拱顶或穹顶还能防火，而木质屋顶自然是防不了火的。这样一来，古罗马人就可以建造能够容纳很多人的大型建筑了。罗马有一座非常著名的神庙，叫作“万神殿”，就是一个例子，我们将在下一章再来介绍它的情况。如今，万神殿是世界上许多国家都进行过

万神殿，现存于罗马
（摄影：约翰·帕特森）

called the Pantheon, which we will talk about in the next chapter. The Pantheon is one of the buildings copied in many countries today because it is both useful and beautiful.

Another great thing the Romans did for building was to use concrete. Concrete is a mixture of cement with water, sand, and pebbles. This mixture turns into stone when it dries. The Romans used cement between the stones of their arches, and they made their domes and vaults of concrete. Now, an arch or a dome or a vault, if properly put together, needs no cement, for the stones push against one another so tightly that they can't slip through and down. But, as I have told you, an arch does need heavy walls at the side so that the stone in the arch will not push against the walls on either side, for the weight of each stone pushes and shoves sideways.

The Romans found a way out of this difficulty. They made their vaults and domes with cement or concrete to hold the stones together so that the vault or dome became a single solid stone. Such a concrete dome pushes downward but doesn't push sideways, so that

仿制的建筑之一呢，因为这座神庙既实用，又非常美观。

古罗马人在建筑方面还有一项伟大的成就，那就是利用混凝土。所谓的混凝土，就是用水、沙子和小石子混合而成的一种胶结剂。这种混合物干了之后，就会变得像石头一样坚硬。古罗马人在建造拱门时，会将混凝土加到石头之间，从而建造出了混凝土制的拱顶和穹顶。注意，一道拱门，或者拱顶、穹顶，倘若正确组装的话，是不需要混凝土的，因为所有的石头都会紧紧地相互挤压在一起，不可能滑动或者掉落下去。不过，我在前面已经跟你们说过，一道拱门两侧需要两堵厚重的墙壁才行，目的是不让拱门上的石头将两侧的墙壁挤开，因为拱门上每块石头的重量，都是使得它们向两侧挤压的。

古罗马人找到了一种可以克服这一困难的办法。他们用胶结剂或者混凝土将石头紧紧胶结起来，建造拱顶和穹顶，从而使得拱顶或穹顶变成一个坚如磐石的整

heavy side walls are not really necessary.

You can rest a car on blocks or bricks and it will not fall. But if the blocks or bricks are pushed sideways the least bit, the load they carry will fall. Have you ever stood up a row of blocks or bricks and tried to walk across them? Try it. If you press straight down as you step on them, they will not fall, but if you shove them sideways the least little bit, over they go! Well, it's the same with a load on a column or a wall.

As I have explained, if the load presses straight down, a small column or small wall will hold the load perfectly well, but the separate stones in an arch do not push straight down. They push sideways and the wall must be made very heavy to keep from being pushed over by an arch. When, however, you have a row of arches on columns, each arch pushes against the next arch and the next arch pushes back so that there is no side push on the columns.

Arches push and shove. You may not see it, but they do. Try pushing against someone your size who is pushing against you. Imagine leaning together like the sides of a letter A. If one suddenly stops pushing or jumps aside, down goes the other. That's the way one arch pushes against another. Knock away one arch, and down the other goes.

体。这种用了混凝土的穹顶只会向下压，而不会挤压两侧，从而使得两侧根本无须再建什么厚重的墙壁了。

你们可以把玩具汽车停放在一堆积木或者砖块上，车子并不会掉下来。可是，只要在侧面轻轻推一下积木或砖块，积木或砖块上的东西就会掉下来。你们有没有试过，站在一排积木或者砖块上面，想要从上面走过去呢？试一试吧。假如你们踩上去的时候力量是垂直向下的，那么它们就不会倒塌；可只要你们向侧面稍稍用一点儿力，积木或砖块就会翻倒！知道了吧，一根立柱或者一堵墙壁承重的情况，正是这样的。

正如我已经说明过的那样，倘若承受的重量是垂直下压，那么一小根立柱或者一小堵墙壁，便能很好地承受住上面的重量；可用于建造拱门的石头，重量却不是垂直下压的，它们会向两侧挤压，因此墙壁必须建造得又厚又重，才能不被拱门挤倒。然而，倘若建有一排用立柱支撑的拱门的话，那么每道拱门便会挤压相邻的那道拱门，而相邻的拱门又会反过来挤压前一道拱门，因此两道拱门之间的立柱，就不会受到侧面力量的挤压了。

拱门会向两侧挤压。虽说你们可能看不到，但它们确实如此。试着推推一个与自己体型相若的人，同时让对方也推你吧。然后试着像字母A的两侧那样，相互斜推。如果一个人突然停止推对方，或者突然跳开去的话，另一个人就会摔倒。拱门两个支柱之间相互挤压的情况，正是这样。假如敲掉拱门一侧的支柱，那么另一侧的支柱也会倒掉。

Chapter 7 Rome Was Not Built in a Day

Many people wear imitation or costume jewelry because man-made pearls or diamonds are less expensive than real pearls or diamonds. Some people build houses of concrete blocks to imitate stone, construct wood columns painted with the edge of a feather to imitate marble, or erect plaster walls with paper to imitate tile. Such imitations that pretend to be something they are not are called faux, meaning false.

The Greeks never used faux decoration techniques, but the Romans did often. The Romans built buildings of concrete or brick and covered the outsides with thin pieces of marble. It was far less expensive, faster, and gave the same effect as solid expensive materials, at least at first glance.

For a few hundred years, the Romans built many great buildings, and more different types of buildings than had ever been built before. They built them not only in Rome and Italy, but also in other countries that the Romans had conquered. They built roads to connect all these countries, and many of these roads still work, as they were made so well.

Although the Romans built many great buildings, none of them quite equaled those the Greeks built. The reason was that the Romans were less artists than engineers. The Greeks were very religious and built temples while the Romans were great governors and respected everything that concerned governing.

第7章 罗马不是一天建成的

许多人都佩戴着仿制或者人造的珠宝，因为人造的珍珠或钻石，比真正的珍珠或钻石要便宜。有些人则会用仿石制的混凝土砖块建造房屋，用绘有羽毛纹饰的、仿大理石的木质立柱，或者给建造的墙壁贴上仿瓷砖的墙纸。将某种东西伪装成另一种东西，这些仿制品就称为赝品，意思就是假的。

古希腊人从来没有运用过虚假的装饰技术，可古罗马人却经常这样干呢。古罗马人经常用混凝土或者砖块建筑房屋，然后再将房屋外部贴上薄薄的大理石板。这样干，成本要低得多，施工速度也要快得多，而效果也与用牢固、昂贵的材料建成的房屋相同。至少来说，乍一看去，效果是没什么两样的。

在数百年间，古罗马人修建了许多了不起的建筑，而种类也大大超过了以往所建造的建筑。他们可不只是在罗马和意大利国内修建，还在古罗马征服的其他国家内修建了许多这样的建筑。他们修筑了许多的道路，将那些国家全都连通起来，而由于修建得极其完善，因此如今许多道路都还在使用呢。

尽管古罗马人修建了许多伟大的建筑，可它们当中却无一能够与古希腊人所建造的相媲美。原因在于，古罗马人在艺术方面的才能，不如他们在工程方面的才能。古希腊人都非常虔诚，因而修建了许多神庙；而古罗马人则是伟大的统治者，因而凡是与治国理政方面相关的东西，他们都崇拜得很。

The Greeks loved nature, and put buildings in beautiful, natural places with panoramic views. Since the Romans loved governing, they preferred to control nature, to govern it. If they wanted to build where there was a hill, they bulldozed it and flattened out the ground. If they wanted to build where there was a swamp, they drained it and filled it in, and so on.

While the Greeks used their eyes to design buildings, the Romans used instruments. In a Roman building, every line that was supposed to be vertical was vertical. Every line that was supposed to be horizontal was horizontal. Every line that was supposed to be straight was straight. It was as if they had drawn a picture with a ruler, square, and compass instead of freehand.

In the same way, Roman buildings look mechanical. We like them as we like an engine. They are strong and powerful, but some may think they lack the beauty of a handmade picture.

How many kinds of buildings do you think there are where you live? Try to count them. Count houses, of course, but how many others — churches, banks, stores, courthouses, libraries, schools, and so on — can you count?

The Greeks had only a few kinds of buildings, but the Romans built many kinds — not only tombs and temples, houses and palaces, but

⊙ theaters and amphitheaters,
⊙ great baths, bathhouses for crowds of people,

古希腊人热爱自然，因而他们的建筑都位于漂亮、自然且具有全景式景观的地方。由于古罗马人热爱治国理政，因而他们更喜欢掌控自然、统治自然。倘若想要在一座小丘上修建什么东西，他们就会将小丘推倒，把地面整平。倘若想要在某个沼泽里修建什么东西，他们就会把沼泽排干，填上土石，诸如此类。

古希腊人用自己的眼力来设计建筑，而古罗马人却是用仪器设备来进行设计的。在古罗马人建造的一栋房屋里，凡是应该垂直的线条，都会是垂直的。凡是应当水平的线条，都会是水平的。而凡是应该笔直的线条，也都会是笔直的。他们仿佛是用直尺、三角板和圆规绘图，而不是全然徒手绘制一样。

同样，古罗马人的建筑看上去也很符合工程力学的特点。我们喜欢这些建筑，就像喜欢一台机器那样。它们都很牢固、很威武，可是，有些人却觉得，这些建筑缺乏手绘图画的那种美感。

你们都想一想，你们家所在的地方，究竟有多少种建筑呢？试着去数上一数吧。首先当然是数一数房屋，可还要数一数其他的建筑，比如教堂、银行、商店、法院大楼、图书馆、学校，等等；你们能数出多少来呢？

古希腊人只修建过几种类型的建筑，可古罗马人的建筑种类却很多，非但有陵墓和神庙、房屋和宫殿，而且还有

⊙ 剧院和竞技场
⊙ 大型的浴室，供许多人用的公共浴池

⊙ bridges,
⊙ arches and aqueducts to carry water from town to town, and
⊙ courthouses and halls.

Some buildings were artificial, or faux, but not all. Some were magnificent and imposing. Most of the Roman buildings are now in ruins, but one building — a temple built to all the gods — is still standing and in use today. It is called the *Pantheon*, which means "all the gods." It has a porch in front with Corinthian columns, and behind the porch a circular building with a huge dome made like a bowl turned upside down, of concrete.

Have you ever seen a circular building in real life? The circular walls that support the Pantheon's dome are twenty feet thick, and the only window is a large circular opening in the top of the dome to let the smoke out from the days when people built a sacred fire inside. There is no glass in the opening so it is open to the sky, but it is so high above the floor that even a heavy rain barely wets the floor beneath.

I have been inside the Pantheon during a thunderstorm and looked straight up to see the rain pouring in, but fanning out like a funnel, then turning into mist before it reached us far below. I have even seen the Sun

卡累尔神庙，现存于法国的尼姆
（摄影：加里・威肯）

⊙ 桥梁
⊙ 拱门和将用水从一个城镇输送到另一个城镇的高架渠，以及
⊙ 法院大楼和会堂

其中，有些建筑属于用人工装饰或者虚假装饰技术修建的，但并非所有建筑都是这样。有些建筑非常宏伟辉煌，威风壮观。虽说古罗马人修建的绝大多数建筑如今都已变成废墟，可有一栋建筑，即一座供奉众神的神庙，如今却仍然屹立着，并且仍在使用中哩。这座神庙，叫作"万神殿"，它的意思，就是"供奉所有神灵"的庙宇。神庙前部是一道长廊，里面全都是科林斯式的立柱；而长廊后面，则是一栋圆形的建筑，它有一个用混凝土建造的巨大穹顶，就像一个倒扣着的碗。

在现实生活中，你们有没有见过一栋圆形的建筑呢？支撑万神殿的那些圆形围墙，都有二十英尺厚。而整座神庙里唯一的窗户，就是穹顶上有一个圆形的开口，目的是当人们在神庙里点燃圣火的时候，能够把烟排出去，这个开口并没有安装玻璃，是直接通到空中的，可由于庙顶离地面实在太高，因此哪怕是下大雨，下面的地板也几乎不会被打湿。

有一次下大雷雨的时候，我正在万神殿里，抬头看去，大雨倾盆而下，可雨水一过那个开口后，就像漏斗一样散了开来，然后就变得像薄雾似的，落到下方人群的身上。也就在同一次，我甚至还看到阳光从那个开口透进来，在神庙里面形成了

stream in at the very same time and create a beautiful rainbow right inside.

The Square House is another fine Roman building with engaged Corinthian columns as well as free-standing columns. It is not in Rome, however, but in France. When the Square House was built, France was a part of the Roman Empire, and the Romans built it in the capital city of Nimes. In France they call it the Maison Carrée, which means Square House.

The theaters the Romans built had no roofs. Actors put on plays here. The seats were of stone and were arranged in a half circle that sloped upward. In France, at a town called Orange, is a Roman theater in which plays are still presented.

Nero was one of the worst rulers Rome ever had and, at the very same time, he was one of the worst builders. There is a legend about him that tells us how, during a great fire that burned much of Rome, Nero did nothing but play the fiddle, or violin, while he watched. He believed himself to be so important and powerful, he built a colossal

圆形剧场，现存于法国的奥朗日
（摄影：加里·威肯）

圆形斗兽场，现存于罗马
（摄影：约翰·帕特森）

一道美丽的彩虹呢。

方形大殿是古罗马的另一座精美建筑，其中既有承重的科林斯式立柱，也有随意散立的柱子。然而，这座建筑却不在罗马，而是在法国。方形殿建造的时候，法国还属于古罗马帝国的一部分，而古罗马人就将它修建在当时这一地区的首都尼姆。在法国，人们将它称为“卡累尔神庙”，也就是“方形大殿”的意思。

古罗马人修建的圆形剧场，都是没有屋顶的。这里是演员们演戏的地方。剧院里的座位都是石制的，并且排列成一个半圆形，向前倾斜而下。在法国一个叫作奥朗日的城市里，就有一座古罗马人建造的剧院，如今那里仍然有戏可看呢。

尼禄是古罗马历史上最坏的君主之一，并且，他也是那个时代最糟糕的建造者之一。有一个传说，说罗马有一次发生大火，把罗马城的许多地方都夷为了平地，可尼禄却什么也没干，而是一边看着大火肆虐，一边演奏着小提琴。由于他自以为非常重要、非常有权势，因此还给自己建造了一尊巨型的雕像，有些史学家曾称，这尊雕像竟然高达一百二十英尺呢。如今，这尊雕像只剩下一个基座了。

statue of himself that some writers say was 120 feet high. Only its base still exists.

Nero also built himself an enormous palace surrounded by parks and lakes. It was called the Golden House. Later rulers destroyed his palace.

Near where the colossal statue of Nero stood, a huge amphitheater was built called the Colosseum. An *amphitheater* is something like a football stadium. In ancient Rome, however, instead of games, there were fights held among men, or between men and wild animals. The Colosseum had stone seats arranged in an oval shape. The outside walls were four stories high while the lower three stories were rows of arches. Between the arches on the first or ground floor were engaged Doric columns. Between the arches of the second story were engaged Ionic columns. Between those of the third floor were engaged Corinthian, and on the fourth-story wall were composite pilasters.

The Colosseum is now a partial ruin, with a great part of it still standing. The amphitheater held as many people as a large stadium does today; in fact, our stadiums are really just copies of the Colosseum. But there was a still larger amphithcater called the Circus Maximus, which held over 170,000

圆形斗兽场内景，现存于罗马
（摄影：约翰·帕特森）

古罗马的浴室，现存于英国的巴斯
（摄影：约翰·帕特森）

尼禄还给自己修建了一座巨大的皇宫，周围环绕着花园、湖泊。这座皇宫，叫作“金色大殿”。可这座皇宫，也被后来的统治者毁掉了。

在距尼禄那座巨型雕像不远的地方，古罗马人还修建了一座巨大的竞技场，叫作“圆形斗兽场”。这座竞技场，有点儿像是如今的橄榄球场。然而，在古罗马，这里进行的却不是体育比赛，而是人与人之间，或者人与野兽之间的格斗。圆形斗兽场里的石制座位，呈椭圆形排列。斗兽场的外墙很高，分为四层，下面三层都由一排排拱门构成。第一层的拱门之间，都是承重的多利克式立柱。第二层的拱门之间，是承重所用的爱奥尼亚式立柱。第三层的拱门之间，是承重的科林斯式立柱。而第四层的墙面上，则全都是组合式的半露方柱。

圆形斗兽场如今有一部分已经变成废墟了，但还有一大部分仍然屹立在那里。这个露天竞技场能够容纳的人数，堪比如今的大型体育场哩。事实上，我们如今的体育场，就是仿照圆形斗兽场修建起来的。不过，还有一个更大的露天竞技场，叫

people and, some reports say, as many as 250,000. It was much larger than any stadium today. Circus in this case doesn't mean a circus as we know it. It means a ring, and Circus *Maximus* meant the Largest Ring.

Most of the huge Circus Maximus has completely disappeared, but some of its foundations still remain and can be seen from one of the famous seven hills of ancient Rome to this day.

The Romans built public bathhouses, for the common people had no baths at all in their homes. These baths were huge buildings with arched or vaulted rooms in which a thousand or more people could bathe at one time. There were not only hot, cold, and warm baths; but gymnasiums; game rooms; lounging rooms; and so on. They were public places for amusement and recreation. Our large swimming pools, spas, and athletic complexes are much like the Roman baths.

The Roman baths were so popular that when Julius Caesar moved north through Europe and crossed the English Channel into Great Britain, Roman baths were established near natural mineral springs there. Perhaps the most famous is in a town in England that today is called Bath. The Roman bath for which the town is named is a place you can visit if you like.

The Romans built large victory arches, separate from buildings, just for their rulers who had won great battles. The rulers then marched through the arches with their soldiers. Such victory arches were actually called *triumphal arches*. One, called the Arch of Titus, was built to celebrate Titus' conquest and destruction of the city of Jerusalem. The Arch

作大竞技场，它能够容纳十七万人，还有些报道称，它甚至容纳得下二十五万人。这么说来，它可比如今的任何体育场都要大呢。在这里，“circus”这个词可不是我们所知的“马戏团”的意思了。它是指“圆形”，所以Circus Maximus的意思就是“最大的圆形竞技场”。

这个巨型的大竞技场，虽说如今绝大部分都已经完全不复存在了，可其地基还有一部分仍然存在，从古罗马那著名的七座山丘中的一座上，至今仍可以看到哩。

古罗马人还修建了许多的公共浴室，因为普通百姓家里根本就没有浴室。这些浴室，都是一些有着拱顶或穹顶房间的巨型建筑，一次性可以容纳一千人或者更多人洗澡。其中既有热水、冷水和温水浴室，而且还有健身房、游戏室、休息室，等等。它们都是供公众娱乐和休息的场所。我们如今那些大型的游泳池、温泉浴场和综合性运动场馆，跟古罗马的这些浴室都很相似呢。

古罗马的浴室非常受人欢迎，因此，待裘力斯·恺撒穿过整个欧洲向北挺进，并且横渡英吉利海峡进入大不列颠之后，古罗马人还在大不列颠一些天然矿泉的附近修建了公共浴室呢。其中最著名的一座，就在如今英国一个叫作巴斯的小镇上。如果你们愿意，让这个小镇由此而得名的、由古罗马人修建的那座浴池，倒真是值得你们去看一看的一个地方呢。

古罗马人还修建了许多大型的得胜拱门，它们都与其他建筑不相连，只是为赢得了重大战斗的君主而修建的。胜利班师之后，君主便会率领手下的士兵，浩浩荡荡地穿过这些得胜拱门。这些得胜拱门，实际上叫作“凯旋门”。其中有一座，叫

of Titus has one large single arch, and on the inner walls you can see relief carvings of the goods stolen from Jerusalem, including a large Jewish ceremonial candleholder called a *menorah*.

Another arch, the Arch of Constantine, was built to honor the first emperor of Rome to become a Christian. The Arch of Constantine has one large arch and two smaller ones at each side.

The bridges the Romans built were among the strongest and most substantial structures they made. As I told you before, some of these bridges were built not for people to walk across, but for water to run through. On the top of such a bridge was a trough. Water flowed through this from its source to the city. It was like a river held up by a bridge. Remember that such a bridge of arches carrying water was called an aqueduct. The word actually means water pipe or water carrier.

Today, water is brought to a city from

提图斯凯旋门，现存于罗马

君士坦丁凯旋门，现存于罗马
（摄影：加里·威肯）

作“提图斯凯旋门”，它是为了庆祝提图斯征服并摧毁了耶路撒冷城而修建的。提图斯凯旋门是一个大型的单拱门，在其内壁上，你们还可以看到很多的浮雕，它们描绘了古罗马人从耶路撒冷劫掠而来的东西，其中包括了一个犹太教徒用于宗教仪式的大烛台，叫作“七扦枝大烛台”。

还有一座凯旋门，即君士坦丁凯旋门，是为了纪念古罗马第一位皇帝皈依基督教而修建的。君士坦丁凯旋门不但有一个大型拱门，而且其两侧还各有一个较小的拱门。

古罗马人建造的桥梁，属于他们修建得最坚固、最结实的建筑种类之一。我在前面已经跟你们说过，这些桥梁当中，有一些并非是为了让人行走，而是为了输水才修建起来的。这种桥梁的顶部，是一道水槽。水流从源头起，经由这道水槽输往城市。因此，它就像是一条用桥梁架起来了的小河。记住，这种用于输水的拱形桥梁，被称为“高架渠”。而“高架渠”这个词，本义指的就是水管或者水渠。

如今，城市用水是通过那种能够埋在地下或者翻山越岭的大型管道，从河流、

a river or lake or reservoir through large pipes that may run underground and up and downhill. But the Romans built aqueducts instead of pipes to carry water to a city, and these aqueducts — some of them over fifty miles long — sloped just enough so that the water was always running downhill.

The Romans made one other kind of building from which later Christian churches were copied. These buildings were courthouses or public halls and were called *basilicas*. A basilica is a long building with rows of columns on the inside that hold up the roof. There is a center aisle and two side aisles. The roof over the center aisle is higher than the roof over the side aisles, as is the case in most of our churches today. In a later chapter I'll tell you a lot more about basilicas.

湖泊或者水库输送到城市里去的。可古罗马人却是通过修建高架渠，而不是用管道，将用水输送到城市里来的。而这些高架渠的坡度也设计得很恰当，使得水总是向山下流，有的甚至长达五十英里呢。

古罗马人还修建了另一种建筑，后来的基督教堂就是仿照这种建筑的样式修建起来的。这种建筑，就是法院大楼或者公共会堂，当时被称为“长方形廊柱大厅”。这种长方形廊柱大厅，就是一栋长长的建筑，内部有一排排的立柱，支撑着屋顶。建筑里面，还有一条中央过道和两条侧道。中央过道上面的屋顶，要比侧道上面的屋顶高，而如今，我们的绝大多数教堂也正是如此。在后面的章节中，我还会再给你们多说一说长方形廊柱大厅的情况的。

Chapter 8 Trimmings

Men wear ties and women wear necklaces. Buildings wear decorations, too, in order to keep them from looking too plain and unfinished. These trimmings on buildings we call *moldings* and *borders*. The Greek and Roman builders used moldings and borders of certain shapes and designs, and builders today use many of the same moldings and borders.

Perhaps you have never closely examined the panels of a door, the edges of a doorway or window, or other trimmings around the outside of a building. If you do, however, you may be surprised to see that most of them are not just flat strips. They have different shapes. The different shapes of these moldings have names just as the boys and girls you know have names, so you can become acquainted with them.

I'll introduce them to you. And when I do, imagine that each of them is a piece of a puzzle. Look at the different puzzle pieces and plan what you would do with them if you were an architect and could build your own building. What would you build? How would it look? Let's begin to discover the different puzzle pieces from which we can chose.

There is a molding that is square as seen from the edge, and so simple that you might think a name unnecessary. It is called a *fillet*, which means a ribbon or band. In the past, women — and men, too — wore a fillet around their heads, to keep their hair in place and

第8章 装饰

如今，男士会打领结，女士则会佩戴项链。建筑物上，也有各种装饰品，目的是让建筑看上去不至于太过简单和不加修整。建筑物上的这些小装饰，我们称之为“花饰”和“边饰”。古希腊和古罗马的建筑师们用过的某种形状、图案的花饰和边饰，如今的建筑师们仍旧在用。

或许，你们从来没有仔细地观察过一扇门上的门板，从来没有仔细观察过门或者窗户的边缘，也没有仔细观察过环绕在一栋建筑外部的其他小装饰。然而，假如观察过的话，那你们就会感到惊讶，其中绝大多数部位竟然都不只是简单的条条带带。它们的形状都各不相同。这些形状各异的花饰都有名字，就像你们认识的小朋友们全都有名字，因而你们可以与他们变得很熟悉一样。

我来给你们介绍介绍吧。而在我介绍的时候，你们不妨把其中的每一种都想象成一片拼图。然后再看一看这些不同的拼图片，并且设计设计，假如你们都是建筑设计师，能够修建自家房子的话，打算如何处理这些拼图。你们会修建一栋什么样的建筑呢？这栋建筑会是个什么样子呢？现在，就让我们开始去发现这些能够供你们挑选的不同拼图吧。

有一种花饰，从边缘来看是方形的，由于它非常简单，因此你们可能会觉得，根本就没有必要给它命名呢。这种装饰线条，叫作“木折”，意思就是条板或条纹。在过去，女士头上都会围着一条

as a decoration. Today buildings often wear fillets just as an ornament. A fillet, as seen from the edge, is like the following drawing.

When a fillet is sunken in, like a square groove, it is called simply a *sunken fillet*. It is like this drawing.

Here is a molding that is half round as seen from the edge. Architects call it a *toms*, but to carpenters it is a *half-round*.

Here is the torus, or half-round, sunk in, forming a round hollow or groove. Its correct name is *cavetto*, which means "a little cave," but carpenters call it a *groove*.

Here is a molding that, seen from the edge, looks like the curve of an egg. Architects call it an *ovolo*, which means egg-shaped, but carpenters just say egg *molding*.

Here is a molding that is hollowed out with the same egg-shaped curve. It is called a *scotia*.

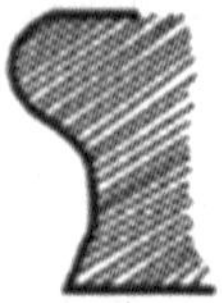

Here is a molding with a curve like an S. The hollow is at the bottom. It is called an *ogee* — just like the exclamation "Oh, gee!"

Here is a molding also with an S curve, and the hollow at the top. It is called a *cyma*, which means a wave.

Do you think you can recognize these moldings when you see them and call them by name? They are in couples — four of them. One of each couple is raised and one is hollow; one fits

带子，既能束头发，又能做装饰，过去的男士也是这样呢。如今的建筑物，常常也带有装饰性的木折。从边缘来看，装饰性的木折就像是上图所示。

倘若装饰性木折是凹进去而非凸出来的，就像一个方方正正的凹槽的话，那么它就被简单地称为“凹木折”，如左图所示。

有一种花饰，从边缘来看是个半圆形。建筑师们将其称为“座盘饰”，而木匠则称之为“半圆饰”。

还有一种座盘饰或者半圆饰是向内凹陷的，形成一个半圆形的空洞或者凹槽。这种边饰的准确名字是“凹槽饰”，指的就是“小凹陷”，可木匠却只称之为“凹槽”。

还有一种边饰，从其边缘来看，呈现出鸡蛋那样的弧度。建筑师们称之为“馒形饰”，可木匠却只是称之为“蛋形花饰”。

还有一种边饰，是用与馒形饰相同的蛋形弧度挖空而成的。这种边饰，叫作“凹弧饰”。

还有一种边饰，其边缘呈S形弧度。挖空的部分位于边饰底部。这种边饰，称为“葱形饰”。“葱形饰”（ogee）这个词，在英语里听上去就像是“噢，哎呀！”（Oh，gee！）这样的一声惊叹呢。

还有一种边饰，也呈S形弧度，只是挖空的部分位于边饰顶部。这种边饰，叫作“波状饰”，意思就是像波浪一样。

你们觉得，在看到这些边饰的时候，你们能够辨认出来并说出它们的名称吗？它们都是成对出现的，总共有四种。其中每一对里，一种是向外凸出，而另一种则向内凹陷，也就是说，两种边饰

into the other.

- ⊙ Mr. and Mrs. Fillet
- ⊙ Mr. Torus and Ms. Cavetto
- ⊙ Mr. Ovolo and Ms. Scotia
- ⊙ Mr. Ogee and Ms. Cyma

Usually, instead of just one simple molding, two or more of these moldings are used, one alongside the other. There are several beautiful moldings made by these combinations.

In most of the combinations, the square fillet is used between the curved moldings. This arrangement of square and curve makes the curved moldings stand out more sharply, as seen here.

Before you begin to draw your own building with all the puzzle pieces, why not go on a scavenger hunt and see how many of these moldings you can find in buildings you visit. Now that you have all those pieces set aside, ready to go, we have a new set of pieces to discover. There are also several kinds of borders. The simplest is the *zigzag*, which is also called *chevron*.

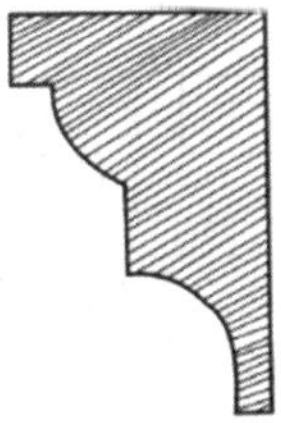

是相互铆合的。你们不妨这样来记：

- ⊙ 木折先生和木折夫人
- ⊙ 座盘饰先生和凹槽饰夫人
- ⊙ 馒形饰先生和凹弧饰夫人
- ⊙ 葱形饰先生和波状饰夫人

通常来说，建筑物上不会只运用一种边饰，而是会成对或者更多地、一种挨着另一种地运用这些边饰。用这些边饰进行组合，可以形成数种漂亮的新边饰。

而在绝大多数组合里，方头的木折通常都是用在弧形边饰之间。将方形与弧形边饰作如此排列，可使弧形边饰显得更加突出和明显，如下图所示。

在你们用这些拼图块开始设计自己的建筑之前，不妨先去找找，看你们究竟能够在看到的建筑物上找出多少种这样的边饰来。既然你们都将这些拼图块放到了一边，准备动身了，那我们就再来看一看一系列新的边饰吧。建筑物上，还有好几种边纹。其中最简单的，就是锯齿纹，也称为波浪饰。

The next simplest is the *scallop*. It is called that because it is like the edge of the scallop shell. It's like this.

第二种最简单的，就是扇形纹。之所以得名如此，是因为这种边纹就像是扇贝壳的边缘。这种边纹，样子就像是这样：

Or it can be upside down like this.

或者，它也可以倒过来，像是这样：

The *embattled* is like this.

而雉堞纹则像是这样的：

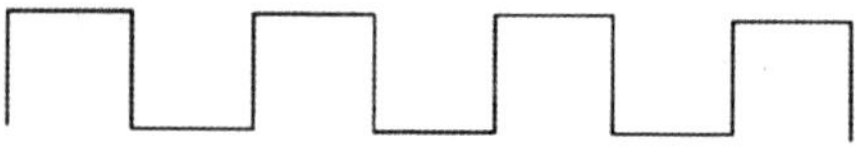

The embattled border is sometimes called the *Wall of Troy*, because Troy had a wall around it, with spaces through which the soldiers could shoot their arrows, and pieces of wall behind which they could jump.

雉堞形边纹，有时也被人们称为“特洛伊城墙纹”。这是因为，特洛伊四周都有城墙，墙上还有一些空隙，士兵们可以从这些空隙里向外射箭，而且还有一些城墙垛，士兵们可以躲在后面跑动。

The *meander* is like this.

曲形波纹边饰则像这样：

The Meander was a river in Asia Minor that flowed in this very crooked way. If you go to school walking in a line that makes a design like this, we say you are meandering.

曲形波纹边饰是根据小亚细亚地区的敏德河命名的，因为那条河流与曲形波纹边饰一样，蜿蜒曲折得很。倘若你们在上学时所走的路线也像这样的话，那我们也会说你走的路线迂回曲折呢。

The *fret* or key is like this.

回形纹或者钥形纹，就像是这样：

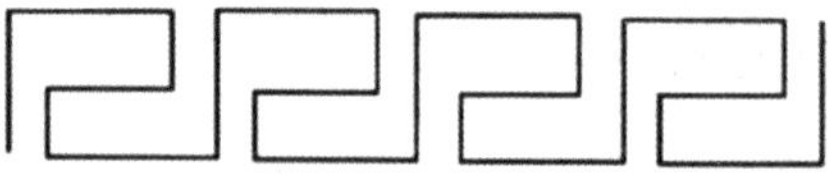

It looks something like a row of keys.

它的样子，有点儿像是一串钥匙。

The *dentil* is like this.

齿形纹像是这样：

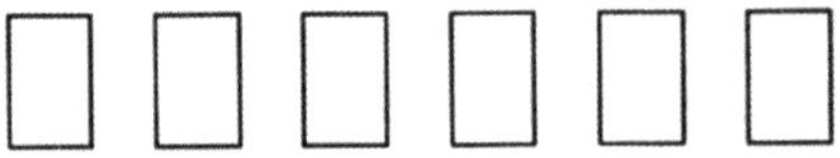

Dentil means tooth and it was supposed to look like a row of teeth. It looks something like a row of piano keys, too.

“齿形”指的就是牙齿的样子，因此这种边纹应当就像是一排牙齿。不过，它也有点儿像是一排钢琴琴键呢。

The *wave* is like this, something like an S lying down with a curl or scroll in one end. Of course you can see why it is called this if you have ever seen waves breaking on the shore.

波形纹如下图所示；它有点儿像是一个横放着的S，并且末端有一个卷状饰。当然，假如见过海浪拍打岸边的情形，你们就会明白，这种边纹为什么会叫这个名称了。

The *running* scroll is like this.

滚波纹就像是这样：

One wave is up and one is down. This is one of the prettiest borders, in my view.

一个波浪在上，一个波浪在下。在我看来，这是最漂亮的边纹之一呢。

The *astragal* is like this.

串珠纹就像是这样：

Astragals were really little bones, but the astragal border looks to me like a string of beads — long beads with two round beads between them.

串珠上的珠子，本来都是小颗小颗的骨头，可在我看来，串珠纹却像是一串念珠，是在两颗长念珠之间，夹着两颗圆念珠呢。

The *chain* is like this.

链形纹如下图所示：

The *cable* or *rope* is like this.

缆状纹或者绳状纹就像是这样：

The *egg* and *dart* is like this.

蛋镖纹就像是这样：

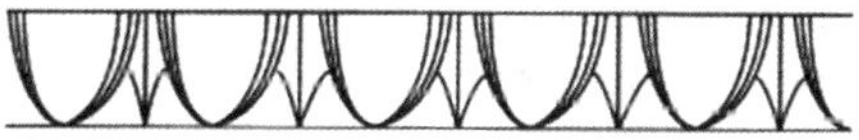

The egg was supposed to represent birth; the dart, death — birth and death, birth and death. Every person is born and dies. Their children are born and die. Generation after generation is born and dies, forever and ever. The astragal — remember, little bones — was always used below the egg and dart border.

其中的蛋形应当象征着生，而镖形则象征着死，合起来就是象征着生而死、死而生，循环往复。每个人都得经历生和死。每个人的孩子，也都得经历生和死。一代又一代人，全都得经历生和死，并且永远循环往复下去。串珠纹（都还记得吧，上面都是一颗颗小骨珠）总是用在蛋镖纹之下。

The *Lesbian leaf* is like this.

蕾丝叶形纹如下图所示：

The *anthemion* is like this.

花状平纹就像是这样：

Leaves are arranged in a heart shape.
这种边纹是一个心形，其中排列着叶状花纹。

The *Greek lily* is like this.
希腊百合纹就像是这样：

The anthemion was often used with the Greek lily alternating.

These are called *classic borders* because the Greeks and Romans used them. Anything Greek and Roman is called classic. These borders have been used time and again by so many other civilizations that admired the classical period of Greece and Rome.

Why not take a list of these decorations along with you the next time you visit a building that looks like it could have been in Greece or Rome. Capitol buildings, courthouses, local government buildings, and some libraries are a good place to start. Play a game to see how many of these decorations from long ago are used today, too. Then you will be ready to begin your work as an imaginary architect designing your very own building for all to see.

Perhaps the next time you draw or mount a picture, try making a border for it in one of these classic designs. It's fun. They have to be done very carefully to look just right — one part exactly like every other, evenly spaced and in line.

花状平纹经常与希腊百合纹一起出现，交错使用。

这些边纹，都称为“经典边饰”，因为它们都是古希腊人和古罗马人运用过的。凡是与古希腊和古罗马相关的东西，都被人们称为“经典”。其他仰慕古希腊和古罗马经典时期的许多文明社会，都曾一遍又一遍地反复运用这些边饰呢。

下次你们再去参观一栋看上去似乎是古希腊和古罗马风格的建筑时，何不随身带上一份记有这些装饰种类的名单呢？议会大厦、法院大楼、地方政府大楼和一些图书馆，都是你们开始熟悉这些装饰的好地方呢。也可以进行一场比赛，看你们能够找出人们如今还在运用的多少种古代装饰来。这样的话，你们就会做好充分的准备，开始一个假想的建筑师的工作，设计出你们自己的建筑，让大家来看一看了。

或许，在你们下次画画的时候，不妨试着用这些经典图案中的某一种，给画儿配上边纹。这样做，会很有意思呢。当然，边纹必须仔细绘制，看上去合适才行，也就是说，边纹的每个部分都得一模一样，间距相等，并且上下对齐，呈一直线才行。

Chapter 9 Early Christian

In architecture, the phrase "early Christian" does not mean Christians who might get up early in the day; instead, it means early in the history of Christians. Some of our finest buildings today are Christian churches, but once upon a time the only Christian churches were holes in the ground.

These holes were called *catacombs*. They were tunnels that were dug underground in Rome because the Christians were persecuted. That means they were punished just for being Christians, so they had to live in hiding. They hid in the dark secret passages of the catacombs. In the catacombs were rooms where Christians could "go to church." There were rooms there, too, where dead Christians were buried.

You can imagine how glad the Christians who lived in the catacombs must have been when a Roman emperor himself became a Christian. His name was Constantine. When Constantine became a Christian, naturally the Christians could come up out of the catacombs and worship God above ground.

The Christians found the best kind of buildings above ground for their church services were the basilicas. Do you remember that I told you that the Romans built basilicas for courthouses? In these courthouses the judge would sit at one end of the building, in the middle, with his back against the wall. In front of the judge there was a long aisle with columns on each side leading to the front door. On each side of the main or central aisle

第9章 早期的基督徒

在建筑领域里，“早期的基督徒”并不是指那些白天起床很早的基督徒，而是指基督教历史的早期阶段。如今，我们一些最精美的建筑都是基督教堂，可是，曾经有过一段时间，仅有的那些基督教堂，却全都是地下的一个个洞穴呢。

那些洞穴，叫作“地下墓穴”。它们是在罗马城下面掘出的一条条地道，因为那时的基督徒都会被当局处死。也就是说，他们仅仅因为自己是基督教徒，就会受到惩处，因此他们只能躲着生活。他们都躲在“地下墓穴”那些黑暗而隐秘的地道里。“地下墓穴”里，有很多的小房间，基督徒可以在这些小房间里“做礼拜”。其中也有一些房间，埋葬着那些死去的基督徒。

你们可以想见，当古罗马一位皇帝本人也皈依了基督教之后，那些生活在“地下墓穴”里的基督徒该有多么高兴。这位皇帝，名叫君士坦丁。君士坦丁皈依基督教后，所有基督徒自然就能走出“地下墓穴”，到地上来礼拜上帝了。

基督教徒发现，地上最适合于他们去做礼拜的建筑，就是那种长方形的廊柱大厅。你们还记不记得，我曾经告诉过你们，古罗马人建造了长方形廊柱大厅来做法院大楼呢？在这些法院大楼里，法官会坐在大厅一头的正中央，背靠着墙壁。法官的前面，是一条长长的过道，两边都有立柱，一直通到大厅前门。而主过道或者中央过道的两侧，还各有一条过道。下图便是长方形廊柱大厅的平面图，这种平面

was another aisle. Here is a plan or kind of map of a basilica. Make believe you are looking straight down from an airplane at the basilica and that the basilica has its roof taken off. The lines are the walls and the dots are the columns. The place where the judge sat is the half circle at the top of the plan.

You can have some fun with paper and pencil, making a plan of your own house. If you imagine everything above the first story taken off the house, you can make a plan of the first floor. If your house has two or three floors, you might make a plan for each of the floors. When I was a boy, I liked to draw plans of make-believe houses, and in my make-believe plans, generally I had a swimming pool, a gym, and a snack bar with all my favorite foods.

But let's get back to the basilica. The Christians used the judge's half-circle in their basilica church for an altar, the place where the minister or priest preached. This part of the building had latticework railings in front of it called *cancelli* by the Romans. That's why some churches still call the minister's end of the church the chancel. The people who came to worship in the basilica sat on benches facing the chancel — just as they do in some churches today. The main central part of a church is called a *nave* because it has the shape of a long naval ship. The

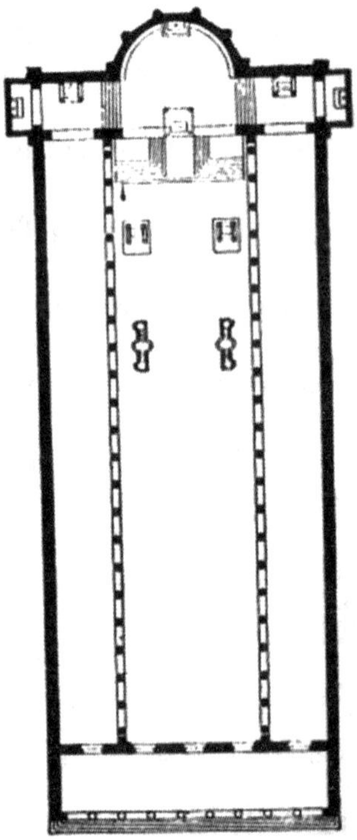

圣母大教堂长方形廊柱大厅的平面图，现存于罗马
（由波士顿的大学印刷协会提供）

图，也算是一种地图哩。假设你们坐在一架飞机上，垂直往下俯瞰一座长方形廊柱大厅，而廊柱大厅的屋顶也早已拆除。其中的实线代表墙壁，而虚线则代表立柱。法官所坐的地方，就是平面图顶端的那个半圆形区域。

你们可以用纸和铅笔绘制出一幅自家的平面图来，那会是很有意思的一件事情呢。假设你家第一层以上的所有东西全都拆走了，那么你们就可以绘制出第一层的平面图来。要是你家的房子有两层或者三层，那你们就可以给每一层都绘制出一幅平面图。小的时候，我就很喜欢绘制想象中的房子平面图，而在这种想象出来的平面图里，我通常都会画上一座游泳池、一个健身房，还有一个堆满了我爱吃之物的零食柜呢。

不过，现在还是让我们回到长方形廊柱大厅上来吧。在他们修建的那种长方形廊柱教堂里，基督教徒将法官所在的那个半圆形区域当成放置祭坛之所，即牧师或祭司布道的地方。大厅这一部分的前面，设有网格状的围栏，古罗马人称之为“围屏”。这也就是如今一些教堂之所以仍然将教堂牧师所在的那一端称为“圣坛”的原因。来到长方形廊柱大厅里做礼拜的人，都会坐在面向圣坛的长椅上，与如今人们在一些教堂里做礼拜时的情形完全一样。教堂中央的主要区域，被称为“中

chancel and the aisles on the side are not part of the nave.

The nave was higher than the side aisles, so the roof of the center part was higher than the side- aisle roofs. The nave was really two stories high but the side aisles were only one story high. The windows were in the second story of the nave, way up near the roof. This part with the windows was called the *clerestory*, which means clear story. I think you can guess why it is called that.

From the outside, some of these basilicas weren't much to look at. A good many of them looked more like big barns than anything else. But inside they were magnificently decorated. The columns were beautiful marble ones taken from old Roman buildings. The walls had mosaic pictures of religious stories made of little pieces of stone or of colored glass and gold that shone like jewels. The floors and lower walls were covered with fine slabs of marble.

After the catacombs, the basilicas must have seemed all the more magnificent to the early Christians.

The largest of these early Christian basilicas is the church of St. Paul outside the Walls. It got its name because the church was built by the side of the road that led from Rome to a nearby town, Ostia. It has a nave and

城外圣保罗大教堂的内景，
现存于罗马的城外圣保罗大教堂
（由波士顿的大学印刷协会提供）

殿”，其形状则像是一条长长的海军军舰。圣坛和两边的过道，都不属于中殿的组成部分。

中殿比两侧的过道都要高，因此中殿的屋顶也比侧廊上方的屋顶要高。中殿实际上有两层楼高，而侧廊只有一层楼高。窗户安放在中殿的第二层上，距屋顶不远。安有窗户的这一部分，叫作天窗，意思就是通风窗。我觉得，你们肯定能够猜出，它为什么会叫这个名字。

从外部来看，有些长方形廊柱大厅实在是没有多少看头。其中，有很多看上去更像是一座座大谷仓，而不像是别的什么场所。可它们的内部，却装饰得非常壮观。其中的立柱，都是仿照古罗马建筑形式建造的、漂亮的大理石柱子。四面墙上，都有根据宗教故事绘制的马赛克图画，或是用小石子铺就，或是用彩色玻璃及黄金制成，都像珠宝一样熠熠生辉。大厅里的地板和下层墙壁上，都贴有精美的大理石板。

在“地下墓穴”里躲藏了那么久的时间之后，对早期的基督徒来说，这种长方形的廊柱大厅，一定就是最辉煌壮观的教堂了。

这些早期的基督教廊柱大厅中，最大的一座就是“城外圣保罗大教堂”。之所以得名如此，是因为这座教堂建在罗马通往附近一个叫作奥斯蒂亚的小镇的路边。这座教堂里，有一个中殿，并且中殿的每一边都有两条侧道，而不是每一边只有一

two aisles on each side instead of one on each side. Here is a picture of the inside looking along the nave toward the chancel.

You can see the clerestory windows very plainly.

St. Paul outside the Walls was built in 380 A.D., and people worshiped there for hundreds of years. Then in 1823 it caught fire and burned down. It was rebuilt to look the way it had before the fire, so you can still visit it as a reconstruction if you go to Rome.

This chapter has four new vocabulary words for builders of churches. See what score you can make without looking back in the book. Each word you can give the right meaning for — out loud — counts as 25. What can you score?

条侧道。上页图所示，便是沿着中殿往圣坛看去时的情景。

你们可以很清楚地看到殿中的天窗呢。

城外圣保罗大教堂修建于公元前380年，此后的数百年里，人们都在这里做礼拜。接下来，1823年的时候，这座教堂失了火，烧成了平地。后来人们进行了重建，使之看起来与失火前一样了。因此，如今你们去罗马的话，还是可以参观一下重建起来的这座教堂呢。

这一章中，出现了修建教堂者所用的四个新名词。看一看，你们在不回过头去查找的情况下，能得多少分吧。每一个你们能够大声说出其正确意思的名词算二十五分。那么，你们能得多少分呢？

plan (in architecture)	☐	（建筑）平面图	☐
nave	☐	中殿	☐
chancel	☐	圣坛	☐
clerestory	☐	天窗	☐
	Score		得分

Chapter 10 Eastern Early Christians

Are you a good detective? Can you tell what part of the country a person comes from, just by hearing him or her talk? Perhaps you can tell the difference between a southerner and a New Englander, or the difference between someone from England and Australia by the sound of the voice and the way words are pronounced.

People from different places not only speak differently but may be unique in other ways, too. They may wear different kinds of clothes, abide by different laws, eat different kinds of food, paint different types of pictures, or build different kinds of buildings.

As you remember, when the Roman emperor Constantine became a Christian, the Christians in Rome came out of the catacombs and built basilicas for churches.

But many subjects of the Roman emperor, citizens of the Roman Empire, lived a long way from Rome. The Roman Empire reached eastward into Mesopotamia. Many people in this eastern part of the empire were Christians, too. Under Constantine they began to build churches just as the Christians in Rome did. Because the Christians of the eastern empire came from a different part of the world, they built their churches in their own way. They didn't care much for basilicas.

Christians in the eastern part of the empire built buildings called *Byzantine* since Byzantium was the most important city in the eastern part of the Roman Empire. The city is still a large and important city, but you won't find Byzantium on the map. Byzantium

第10章　早期的东方基督徒

你们是不是优秀的侦探呢？你们能够仅听一个人说话，就能辨别出这个人来自我国的哪个地区吗？没准，你们都能够通过口音上的差异，以及使用某些词汇的方式，分辨出一个南方人和一个新英格兰地区的人，或者分辨出一个英国人和一个澳大利亚人来呢。

不同地方的人非但口音有差异，在其他方面可能也会很独特。他们可能会穿着不同类型的服装，服从不同的法律法规，吃不同种类的食物，绘制不同类型的画作，或者修建不同种类的建筑。

你们都还记得吧，古罗马皇帝君士坦丁皈依基督教后，罗马的基督徒纷纷从“地下墓穴”里走了出来，并在各个教堂里修建了方形廊柱大厅。

可是，罗马皇帝手下的许多臣民，罗马帝国境内的许多公民，却都生活在离罗马很远的地方。罗马帝国的疆域，向东扩张到了美索不达米亚。在帝国这个东部地区，许多人也都是基督教徒。在君士坦丁治下，他们也像罗马那些基督徒一样，开始修建教堂了。由于罗马帝国东部的基督徒来自世界上一个不同的地区，因此他们便是按照自己的想法来修建教堂的。他们不太喜欢长方形的廊柱大厅。

帝国东部基督徒修建的那些建筑，叫作拜占庭风格的建筑，因为拜占庭是当时罗马帝国东部地区最重要的一座城市。拜占庭如今也仍是一座大型的重要城市，

changed its name not once, but twice. Constantine went to live in Byzantium and made it his capital instead of Rome. When he did this he changed the name of the city to New Rome, but it soon became Constantinople or City of Constantine. But you won't find Constantinople on the modern map, either, for now it is called Istanbul. The old word, *Byzantine*, however, stuck to the architecture that began to be used there and to the Christian Roman Empire that was centered there.

There was one very important difference between this Byzantine architecture and the basilican architecture. A Byzantine church usually had some kind of dome on it. In some churches the dome was small; in some it was covered with a square roof so you could see the dome only from below, on the inside; and in many churches there were several domes.

The Pantheon in Rome has a dome, but the Pantheon is not like the Byzantine style of building. The Pantheon's dome is made of concrete. The domes of Byzantine churches were usually made of bricks or tiles. The Pantheon dome rests on a circular wall. The Byzantine dome covers a square space.

拜占庭式教堂的平面图，
取自罗马的圣彼得大教堂

The plan of most Byzantine churches looks like this.

This kind of cross with all the arms equal is called a *Greek cross*. The central dome was generally right over the square in the center of the cross.

不过你们在地图上可找不到它。拜占庭不止改了一次名，而是改了两次名。君士坦丁后来住到了拜占庭，把这里当成帝国的首都，取代了罗马。同时，他还把这座城市更名为“新罗马”，可不久后又改成了“君士坦丁堡”，意思就是“君士坦丁之城”。可你们在现代地图上，也是找不到君士坦丁堡这座城市的，因为如今这里叫作“伊斯坦布尔”了。然而，这座城市的原名“拜占庭”，却在建筑学里留存了下来，开始用于指这里的建筑，以及以这里为中心的、信奉基督教的罗马帝国的建筑了。

这种拜占庭式的建筑，与廊柱大厅式的教堂建筑之间，有一个重大的差异。拜占庭式的教堂里，通常都建有某种形式的穹顶。有些教堂的穹顶很小。有些教堂的穹顶上还盖有一个方形的屋顶，因此人们只能从下面、从教堂内部才能看到上面的穹顶。还有许多教堂，里面则建有多个穹顶。

虽说罗马的万神殿里有一个穹顶，可万神殿却与拜占庭风格的建筑不同。万神殿里的穹顶，是用混凝土建成的。而拜占庭式教堂里的穹顶，通常却是用砖块或者瓷砖建成的。万神殿里的穹顶，是建在一堵圆形墙壁之上。而拜占庭式的穹顶，覆盖的却是一个方形的空间。

绝大多数拜占庭风格教堂的平面图，看起来都是下面这个样子。

这种四臂长度相等的十字架，称为“希腊十字架”。中央穹顶，通常位于十字架中心那个方形区域的正上方。

All these Byzantine buildings with domes were quite small except for the ones the Emperor Justinian built. Justinian had his architects build the best and finest and biggest building ever built in the Byzantine style. We call it St. Sophia or Santa Sofia, but Sofia was not the name of a saint. Sofia means "divine wisdom," and the real name of Justinian's church is Holy Wisdom. Many people around the world call this famous place Hagia Sophia, which is what we shall call it here.

See if you can understand how Hagia Sophia is built. In the middle is a huge dome. This dome rests on the top of four big arches. Each arch stands on one side of a square. The bottom of the dome rests on top of each *wicket*, or arch.

The spaces between the tops of the arches below the dome are not empty. They are filled in with brick, so the bottom of the dome is resting on something all the way around. These spaces between the tops of the arches look like curved triangles pointing downward. The curved triangles are called *pendentives*.

Pendentives make it possible for a circular shape to sit on top of a square shape. I hope you can remember the word *pendentive*. Perhaps it will help to know that its root word is *pendent*, meaning

圣索菲亚大教堂，现存于伊斯坦布尔
（摄影：约翰·迪安）

所有这些建有穹顶的拜占庭式建筑都很小，只有查士丁尼皇帝所建的教堂除外。查士丁尼役使手下的建筑师，修建了自拜占庭风格出现以来最优秀、最精美和最大型的一座建筑。我们称之为“圣索菲亚大教堂”，尽管索菲亚并不是一位信徒的名字。“索菲亚”的意思，指“神圣的智慧”，因此，查士丁尼所建的那座教堂，本来是叫作“圣智堂”的。世界各地有许多人，都将这处名胜称为“索菲亚圣殿”，而我们在这里，本来也应当用这个名称来称呼它的。

看看你们能不能理解圣索菲亚大教堂的建筑方式吧。教堂中部是一个巨大的穹顶。这个穹顶，建在四个巨大的拱门之上。每个拱门都占据了一个正方形的一面。而穹顶的底部，就坐落在每个侧门（即每座拱门）的顶部之上。

拱门顶部到穹顶底部之间，并不是中空的。其间砌满了砖块，因此穹顶底部是实的。拱门上部各面之间形成的四个区域，看起来都像是倒立的弧形三角。这种弧形三角，叫作斗拱。

这种斗拱，使得一种圆形之物可以稳稳当当地立在一个方形物的上面。我希望，你们都能记住斗拱这个词。或许，告诉你们斗拱（pendentive）这个词的词根是pendent，意思是“悬挂的”，可能有助于你们去记住这个词。由此，你们就能看

hanging. So, you can see that the curved triangles pointing down look like something hanging, or several pendents. Well, it is the use of pendentives that makes Byzantine architecture very different from other kinds. You won't find any pendentives in the Pantheon in Rome, for instance.

In this picture you can see three of the arches under the dome and two of the pendentives between the arches.

Because the dome of Hagia Sophia is made of bricks, the whole dome isn't held together like a saucer or like the concrete Pantheon dome. This means that the dome pushes down on the walls that hold it up and also pushes outward or sideways on the walls. You know how a ladder leaning against the wall of a room will slide out at the bottom when a heavy man climbs the ladder, unless the bottom is braced against something on the floor. Well, the dome pushes out in all directions just as the ladder does in one direction, and so there must be something to brace the walls to keep the dome from pushing them over.

The arches resting on the ground hold the downward push of the dome. The architects of Hagia Sophia took care of the outward push very cleverly. On the outside of two of the arches, opposite each other, they built half-domes on walls reaching to the ground that braced the two arches just like bookends, pushing toward the middle of the building. They were props to hold the arches from falling outward.

Against the legs of the other two arches they built big piles of stone and brick, and these piles kept the arches in place just like bookends, too. These piles were called *buttresses*, and they held the wall in place.

出，这些头朝下的弧形三角，看上去就像是某种悬挂着的东西，或者说是好几个悬饰。注意，正是运用了斗拱，拜占庭风格的建筑与其他种类的建筑才会大不相同。比如说，你们在罗马的万神殿里，就找不到任何斗拱呢。

在下页这幅照片里，你们能看到穹顶之下有三道拱门，而拱门之间则有两个斗拱。

由于圣索菲亚教堂的穹顶是用石头砌成的，因此整个穹顶并未像一个盘子，或者像万神殿的那个混凝土穹顶一样紧紧地结合在一起。这就意味着，穹顶的重量全都压在下面的承重墙上，并且会将承重墙向外或者向侧面挤压。你们都知道，倘若一个胖子去爬斜靠在房间墙壁上的一架梯子，梯子底部就会往外打滑，除非梯子的底部顶着地板上的某种东西。注意，穹顶会向四面八方挤压，就像梯子会朝一个方向滑动那样，因此，四面墙壁必须顶在某种东西上，才能不被穹顶挤倒。

立在地面之上的那四个拱门，支撑住了穹顶向下的重量。而设计圣索菲亚大教堂的建筑师们，还很巧妙地解决了穹顶向外挤压的问题。在相对而立的两道拱门的外墙上，他们修建了许多直达地面的半道拱门，一起向整栋建筑的中部推挤，就像书挡那样顶住了两道拱门。它们就是支撑物，使得所有拱门都不至于向外垮塌了。

而在对着其他两道拱门的腿部，他们又修建了两个巨大的砖石堆，这些砖石堆也像书挡一样，将拱门固定到位。这些砖石堆，叫作“扶垛”，它们固定住了墙壁。

And then — after all this care and work — the dome of Hagia Sophia fell down! It collapsed a few years after it was finished, in the mid-sixth century. But we can't blame the builders. An earthquake shook the bricks out of place and down came the dome. The builders couldn't prevent an earthquake.

When the builders put the dome up again, they made an improvement. All around the bottom of the new dome, little windows were made — forty windows in all. This lets in such a band of light that the dome seems to be resting on light when you look up at it from inside, or as if it were hanging from the sky a few feet above the top of the four big arches.

The builders made another improvement. By raising the dome's *pitch*, or steepness, they increased its height another twenty-two feet. This made the dome easier to support since the weight came down more vertically. And, instead of being shallow, like an upside-down saucer, it was deep, like an inverted holy cup or chalice. It became even more impressive to see.

The inside of Hagia Sophia has been called the most magnificent interior in the world. Along each side of the nave run aisles that have second stories or *galleries*. The galleries are supported by many columns.

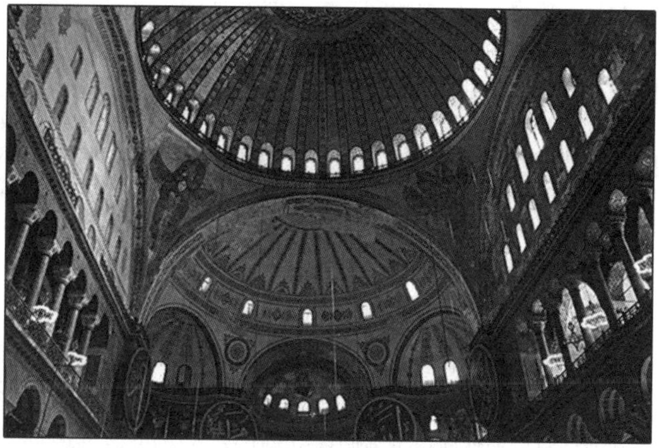

圣索菲亚大教堂内景，现存于伊斯坦布尔
（摄影：约翰·迪安）

可是，尽管如此谨慎、付出了如此巨大的努力，但圣索菲亚大教堂的穹顶后来还是塌了！教堂完工后没过多少年，穹顶就塌了，当时正值十七世纪中叶。但是，我们可不能怪那些建筑师。是因为一场地震将穹顶下方的砖块震松动了，穹顶才掉了下来。建筑师们可没法阻止一场地震呀。

建筑师们重建穹顶的时候，便做出了一项改进。他们在新穹顶的底部四周都开了小窗，总计开了四十扇窗户。这种改进，让阳光透了进来，因而，人们在殿内仰视时，整个穹顶似乎都浮在光线之上，或者说似乎是悬在空中，悬在那四道巨大的拱门顶上几英尺开外的地方哩。

建筑师们还做出了另一项改进。通过增大穹顶的斜度，或者说陡度，他们又将穹顶的高度再次升高了二十二英尺。这使得穹顶更易支撑起来，因为穹顶重量下压的角度更加垂直了。而且，穹顶不再像一个倒扣的盘子那样浅，而是变得很深，就像一个倒扣的圣杯或高脚杯。这让整个穹顶看上去更加令人印象深刻了。

圣索菲亚大教堂的内景，被人们称为是世界上最辉煌、最壮观的内景。沿着中殿两侧，有两道侧廊，而这两道侧廊，建有上下两层，称为长廊。这些长廊，都是用许多的立柱支撑着。

The lower walls are all covered with slabs of beautiful marble, in even more colors than the columns of different-colored marble — some red, some green, some gray or black. Higher up on the walls are mosaic pictures with colored pieces of glass and marble set in gold, like a brilliant picture book laid wide open for everyone to see.

Almost a thousand years after the church of Hagia Sophia was built, Constantinople was captured by the Turks. The Turks were Muslims and worshiped in *mosques* instead of churches. The leader of the Turks rode his horse right into Hagia Sophia and ordered the Christian church to be turned into an Islamic mosque. The Christian mosaics were covered with plaster and whitewash because Islam, the religion of Muslims, prohibits religious imagery.

And then no one was allowed to enter Hagia Sophia without first taking off his shoes. That is the rule for all mosques. No shoes may tread on *Allah's* (God's) holy ground.

Today Hagia Sophia is neither a church nor a mosque. It is a museum, for all to admire.

From the outside of Hagia Sophia looks big, but some people think it not very beautiful. Notice in the picture the great buttresses that stick up on each side of the arch to brace the push of the dome.

What about those towers? The tall narrow spires, or *minarets*, were not part of the church, but were added on by the Turks when the church became a mosque. Every mosque needs minarets, for the *muezzin* (or crier) to climb up and call Muslims to worship five times every day. But as everyone likes decoration, and symmetry, there are four minarets and not just the required one. To imagine Hagia Sophia as a church, just pretend for a

下层的墙壁上，都贴有美丽的大理石板，颜色甚至比那些彩色大理石立柱还要丰富，有些是红色的，有些是绿色的，有些是灰色或者黑色的。而上层墙壁上，则全都是马赛克图画，它们由镶嵌在黄金里的彩色玻璃片和大理石构成，就像一本灿烂无比的图画书籍，打开了供大家观赏似的。

距圣索菲亚大教堂落成差不多一千年后，君士坦丁堡被土耳其人攻陷了。土耳其人都是穆斯林，他们是在清真寺里做礼拜，而不是在教堂里做礼拜。土耳其人的头领，骑着马儿径直来到圣索菲亚大教堂，下令把这座基督教堂改成一座伊斯兰教的清真寺。教堂里那些与基督教相关的马赛克画，都被人们用灰泥和石灰盖住了，因为穆斯林信奉的伊斯兰教是禁止描绘宗教图像的。

然后，每个人只有先脱掉鞋子，才能进入圣索菲亚大教堂了。这也是所有清真寺的规矩。任何人的鞋子，都不准踏上真主安拉（即上帝）的圣地。

如今，圣索菲亚既非天主教堂，也非清真寺了。这里变成了一个博物馆，所有的人都能前来瞻仰。从外面看去，圣索菲亚大教堂看上去非常宏伟，可有些人却觉得它不是很漂亮。注意图片中那些巨大的扶垛，它们支撑着拱门的两侧，以顶住穹顶的推挤之力。

图中那些高塔又怎么样呢？那些又高又窄的尖塔，或称宣礼塔，原本并不是教堂的一部分，而是土耳其人在这座教堂变成清真寺之后加建起来的。每座清真寺都得有宣礼塔，以便宣礼员（或者召唤员）每天爬上去五次，召唤所有的穆斯林来做礼拜。不过，由于大家都喜欢装饰、喜欢对称，因此这里才建有四座宣礼塔，而不

minute that there are no minarets.

You may think it is strange to have a building that was once a church suddenly become a mosque. Actually, it is not strange at all. You see, there are three religions that are very close together in a special way. They share some of the same sacred texts since they all started from the same beginnings.

In the Jewish faith, there are three sets of books called the Torah, the Prophets, and the Writings. Christians call these three sets of books the Old Testament, to which they then add the New Testament, which includes books of stories about and reflections on the teachings of Jesus. The Muslims study one sacred text called the Koran or Qu'ran that "sets the seal on" or validates the teachings of both the Old and New Testament. So, as unusual as it may seem, it is understandable that three faiths can be seen in one beautiful building.

But I don't want you to believe that Hagia Sophia was the only great Byzantine building or that all Byzantine buildings were in Constantinople. The Byzantine style of architecture spread wherever the religion of the Greek Christian Church spread. The churches of Russia, like St. Sophia, were almost

圣索菲亚教堂，现存于俄罗斯的诺夫哥罗德
（摄影：加里·威肯）

是只有必需的一座宣礼塔。要想把圣索菲亚堂想象成一座天主教堂，只需假装那里没有什么宣礼塔就成了。

你们可能会觉得奇怪，一座曾经的基督教堂，怎么会在突然之间就变成了一座清真寺。实际上，这一点都不奇怪。你们都知道，世界上有三种宗教，它们在某个特殊的方面都非常相近。它们拥有同样的神圣经文，因为它们都是从同一种源头开创出来的。

犹太教的经文有三部分，分别叫作“律法书”、“先知书”和“圣著”。基督教徒则将这三部经文合称为《圣经·旧约》，后来他们还加上了《圣经·新约》，它由关于耶稣教义的故事和人们对于这些教义的思考所组成。穆斯林诵读的是另一种圣经，叫作《可兰经》或者《古兰经》，它“认可”或者承认了《圣经·旧约》和《圣经·新约》的教义。因此，尽管看上去罕见得很，但我们在同一栋美丽的建筑中能够看到三种宗教的影子，这一点就是可以理解的了。

不过，我可不希望你们以为圣索菲亚大教堂是唯一一座属于拜占庭风格的伟大建筑，或者以为所有拜占庭风格的建筑全都位于君士坦丁堡。凡是希腊基督教会所到之处，拜占庭风格的建筑也随之而来。俄罗斯的教堂，比如圣索菲亚教堂，几乎

all built in the Byzantine style because the Russians became members of the Orthodox Church instead of members of the Roman Church. Churches in the Byzantine style are still being built in different parts of the world.

Just as famous as Hagia Sophia is another Byzantine church built in Venice, hundreds of years later. Venice was a seaport republic. The city belonged to no country, but was the capital of the Venetian Republic, an independent state. Fleets of ships from Venice sailed east and brought back the beautiful silks and spices of Asia. As a result of this trade, Venice became rich and powerful. Her people learned to love the bright colors of the goods from the East. They put so much lovely color on their Byzantine church that it shone like a beautiful jewel in the Sun. They called their church St. Mark's because it was built over the spot where Saint Mark was supposed to lie buried.

A legend about this says that after Saint Mark, one of the twelve disciples of Jesus, died, he was buried in Alexandria, in Egypt. The Venetians believed that his remains — or *relics* as they were called — should rest in the altar of the basilica in Venice. So, when a Venetian fleet of

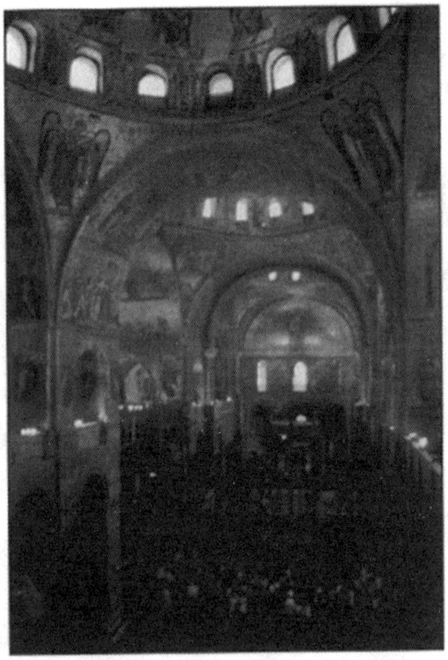

圣马可大教堂内景，现存于威尼斯
（摄影：约翰·帕特森）

全都是按照拜占庭风格建造的，因为俄罗斯人皈依的是东正教，而不是罗马天主教[1]。如今，世界各地还在继续修建拜占庭风格的建筑呢。

与圣索菲亚大教堂齐名的，是数百年后在威尼斯修建的另一座拜占庭风格的教堂。威尼斯当时还是一个海港共和国。该市不隶属于任何国家，而是独立城邦威尼斯共和国的首都。从威尼斯出发的船队向东航行，然后再将亚洲的美丽丝绸和香料带回来。由于此种贸易，威尼斯变得非常富庶和强大了。威尼斯人民开始喜欢上了东方之物的亮丽色彩。因此，他们在这座拜占庭风格的教堂上倾注了许多可爱的色彩，使得它就像是太阳底下一颗璀璨的珍珠。他们将这座教堂命名为“圣马可教堂”，因为这座教堂据说是修建在安葬圣马可的那个地方之上。

在传说中，位列耶稣十二门徒之一的圣马可死后，被安葬在埃及的亚历山大。可威尼斯人却认为，他的遗体，或者说我们所称的“遗骸”，应当安放到威尼斯那座方形廊柱教堂里的祭坛里才是。因此，当一支威尼斯船队前往亚历山大进行贸易

[1] 东正教（Orthodox Church）和罗马天主教（Roman Church），基督教的两大主要派系。罗马皇帝君士坦丁迁都拜占庭，为基督教的分裂埋下了伏笔。公元 1054 年，东正教从罗马教廷中分裂出来，自称正统，不再承认罗马教廷的信仰根基，理由是《圣经》中说“不可崇拜偶像”，而罗马教廷却在崇拜偶像。由于正教的势力范围主要在罗马教廷的势力范围以东，故又称“东正教”、“希腊正教”等，而为了区分这两大派系，罗马教廷则被称为“罗马天主教”。

ships sailed to Alexandria to trade, some of their leaders found the saint's bones, stole them before anyone noticed, and sailed triumphantly back into the Venetian lagoon up to St. Mark's Square to bury the remains in a solemn ceremony, in the altar of the basilica. No one knows if these bones are those of Saint Mark or not. What do you think?

St. Mark's has five domes — a big dome in the center and four smaller domes around it. The domes were not high enough to be seen well on the outside, so the Venetians made a much higher dome over each of the five domes. So each dome is double, like a hat or helmet over each dome. You can see just what I mean when you go to the top of the bell tower near the basilica and look down.

The basilica is covered inside and out with brilliant mosaics and slabs of alabaster brought from far and near. It is probably the most colorful building in the world.

It also has four bronze horses on the roof over the main door. They are almost as famous as the church itself. The horses were taken from a track for chariot races, called the Hippodrome, in Constantinople. Their bad luck did not end there, however. When Napoleon was ruler of France and was taking his army across Europe, he liked these bronze stallions so much that he had them shipped

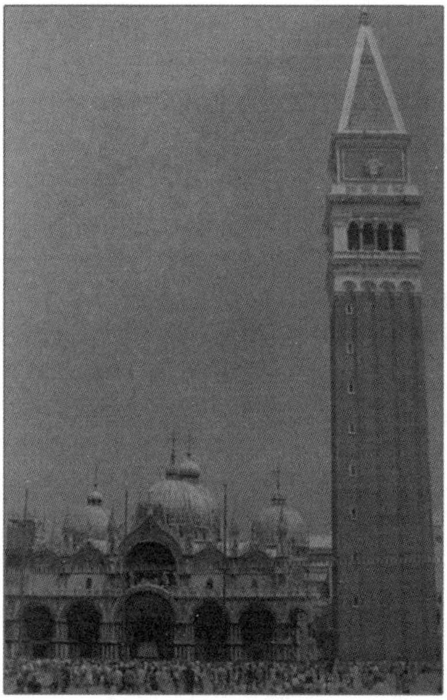

圣马可大教堂，现存于威尼斯
（摄影：约翰·帕特森）

时，船队的一些领头者便找到了这位圣徒的遗骨，在大家不知不觉的时候偷走了遗骨，胜利地带着遗骨回到威尼斯那个通往圣马可广场的潟湖，然后举行了隆重的仪式，将这位圣徒的遗骨埋葬到了圣马可教堂廊柱大厅的祭坛里。没人知道，这些遗骨究竟是不是圣马可的遗骨。你们觉得呢？

圣马可大教堂里有五座穹顶：中央是一座大穹顶，周围则是四个较小的穹顶。这些穹顶都不太高，在外面看得不是很清楚，因此威尼斯人后来又在这五座穹顶之上，分别修建了一座高得多的穹顶。因此，其中的每座穹顶都是双层的，就像每座穹顶上都戴了一顶帽子或者一顶头盔似的。倘若有机会到那座方形廊柱教堂附近的钟楼顶上去俯瞰一番的话，你们就会明白我的意思了。

教堂里的那座方形廊柱大厅，内外都镶有华丽灿烂的马赛克，以及从远近各地运来的汉白玉板。这座教堂，很可能是世界上色彩最为丰富多样的一栋建筑呢。

教堂大门上方的屋顶上，还有四座青铜铸造的马儿雕像。这几匹马儿，与这座教堂本身一样声名赫赫呢。这些马匹雕塑，都是从君士坦丁堡一个叫作“跑马场”的战车比赛场上运过来的。然而，它们的噩运却并没有到此为止。在拿破仑当法国皇帝，并且指挥着手下大军横扫欧洲的时候，他看上了这几尊青铜马儿，因此命人将它们运到了巴黎。直到他在滑铁卢战败后，这些雕像才返回来，而它们的噩运也

to Paris. Only when he was defeated at Waterloo were they returned, and with them came their bad luck.

You see, the Venetian lagoon is surrounded by a crescent of land that seems like two arms embracing the city of islands and canals. Early in the 1900s a city, Mestre, was built up there as an industrial center. There are so many factories that the air became polluted, almost ruining the bronze stallions. They had to be taken inside the basilica to be restored, which is where they are today. A set of four replicas has proudly taken their place for all to see, in the spot where the originals once stood.

Now that we have finished our stories for a while, it's time for one more scorecard. Here are the new names in this chapter. Each counts for 20. Can you spell them correctly and make as good a score as in the last chapter? Try it — out loud, remember.

圣马可教堂的青铜马匹雕像细部，
现存于威尼斯
（摄影：约翰·帕特森）

再次随之而来了。

你们都知道，威尼斯的那个潟湖周围，是一片新月形的陆地，看上去就像是两支胳膊，将威尼斯这座岛屿和运河之城抱在怀里似的。十九世纪早期，这里曾经建起了一座叫作梅斯特雷的城市，是个工业中心。由于那里工厂林立，因此空气受到了污染，几乎把这四尊青铜马匹雕像毁掉了。人们不得不把它们搬到方形廊柱大厅里进行修复，后来就一直放在里面，直到今天。于是，四尊复制品便得意扬扬地取代了它们的位置，立在原作所在的地方，供大家瞻仰了。

既然我们已经暂时结束了本章的故事，那么就该再来替你们打一打分数了。下面就是本章出现的新名词。每个新名词记二十分。你们能不能将它们正确地拼写出来，并且像上一章那样，说出它们的准确意思，得个高分呢？试一试吧，不过要记得大声说出来哟。

Byzantine	☐	拜占庭	☐
Greek cross	☐	希腊十字架	☐
pendentive	☐	斗拱	☐
buttress	☐	扶垛	☐
mosque	☐	清真寺	☐
	____ Score		____ 得分

Chapter 11 Lights in the Dark

"What goes up must come down." The Roman Empire had reached the height of its power. The Romans had conquered, ruled, and civilized almost all of Europe. Then the mighty empire that the Romans had built up came tumbling down.

It began with the split between the eastern and western parts of the empire. When Constantinople became the new capital, naturally Rome, the old capital, lost power. Finally the East and West separated. Constantinople remained the capital of the eastern Roman Empire. Rome was capital of the western Roman Empire. Then there were two Roman Empires and two emperors, but that didn't last long.

Hordes of men from the North began pushing and fighting their way down across France, to Italy. These men were fierce and rough. They had never learned to read or write. We call them Barbarians. The word *barbarian* comes from a Greek word for a person from another country, referring to those who did not speak Greek; however, it has come to mean savage, wild, or uncivilized.

The Barbarians finally overran France, Spain, and Italy. They took Rome itself, and that ended the old Roman Empire in the West. I wonder what the Barbarians thought when they entered Rome and saw the great palaces and theaters, the temples and monuments. Can you imagine what they might have thought?

The Barbarians, who seemed rude and rough and ignorant, were also strong, brave,

第11章 黑暗中的明灯

俗话说得好："三十年河东，三十年河西。"古罗马帝国已经达到了其实力的巅峰。古罗马人已经征服和统治了几乎整个欧洲，并让这一地区进入了文明社会。接下来，古罗马人建立起来的这个强大帝国，便开始走下坡路了。

这一过程，始于罗马帝国分裂成东、西两个部分。君士坦丁堡成为帝国的新都之后，旧都罗马自然就没有了影响力。最后，东、西两部分便分裂开来了。君士坦丁堡仍是东罗马帝国的首都。罗马则是西罗马帝国的首都。这样一来，就有两个罗马帝国和两个罗马皇帝了，不过，这种情况并没有持续多久。

北方的游牧部落开始向南推进，并且一路征伐，经由法国而下，直抵意大利。这些人都非常凶猛、野蛮。他们既不认字，也不会写字。我们称之为"野蛮人"。"野蛮人"这个词，源自希腊语中用于指外国人的那个词，指的就是那些不会说希腊语的人，然而，后来它却逐渐演化成了指野蛮、粗野或者不文明的意思。

这些野蛮人最终征服了法国、西班牙和意大利。他们占领了罗马城，从而终结了古老的西罗马帝国。我不知道，这些野蛮人进入罗马城，看到那些伟大的宫殿、剧院、神庙和纪念碑时，他们心里在想什么。你们能够猜到，他们当时想的都是些什么吗?

这些野蛮人虽说看上去粗鲁、残暴而无知，但同时他们也很强壮、勇敢，并且

and were good fighters. Although it is impossible to know what they thought when they entered Rome itself, we do know what happened after they arrived.

The Barbarians gradually became Christians and learned the languages of the parts of Europe where they settled. All parts of the Roman Empire had once spoken Latin, the language of Rome, but under the rule of the Barbarian tribes, the language of each part of Europe became different. The Latin spoken in France gradually became French. The Latin spoken in Spain became Spanish, and the Latin spoke in Italy and in Rome itself became Italian. No longer could a man from Spain talk with a man from France in his own language. It made things far more confusing than it had been when everyone spoke the same language of Rome, Latin.

But Spain and France and Italy did not become real nations right away. Everywhere there was fighting. One tribe fought with another. One town fought with another town. The old civilized life was upset. Everything became darker and darker for civilization as the Romans had developed it.

The ways of the Romans were forgotten. The old basilican churches were still used, but few new ones were built. Things got so bad that the time from about 500 to 800 A.D. (up to when Charlemagne started schools and brought people back together) is called the Dark Ages. After Charlemagne, and until the rebirth of learning in the Renaissance in Italy during the 1400s, when things were getting a little more of the light of learning, is a period we call the Middle Ages. They were in the middle, between ancient Rome and the Renaissance period.

都骁勇善战。尽管我们不可能知道他们进入罗马城时有些什么感受，可他们到了罗马城之后发生的事情，我们却是知道的。

这些野蛮人逐渐变成了基督徒，并且学会了各自在欧洲定居之地的语言。古罗马帝国的所有地区曾经都是说拉丁语，即罗马人所用的语言，可在这些野蛮民族的统治下，欧洲各地的语言开始产生了差异。法国人所说的拉丁语，逐渐演变成了法语。西班牙人所说的拉丁语，演变成了西班牙语。而意大利人和罗马人所说的拉丁语，则变成了意大利语。一个西班牙人，再也无法用本国的语言与一个法国人进行交谈了。与以前大家都说罗马的语言即拉丁语相比，这种情况要复杂得多了。

但是，西班牙、法国和意大利并没有马上变成真正的国家。各个地方都在打仗。一个部落对付另一个部落。一个城市与另一个城市打仗。原来的文明生活被打乱了。对于古罗马人一点点地培育起来的文明而言，一切都变得越来越黑暗了。

古罗马人的生活方式，被人们忘却了。虽然那些古老的、建有长方形廊柱大厅的教堂仍在使用，但这一时期的人几乎没有修建起几座新的教堂。由于当时的形势变得极其糟糕，因此从公元500年左右到公元800年左右（直到查理曼大帝开始设立学校、将人们重新凝聚起来的时候）这段时期，就被称为“黑暗时代”。而查理曼大帝之后，直到十五世纪意大利“文艺复兴”时期知识获得重生、整个社会开始获得了更多一点儿知识之光的这段时间，我们称之为“中世纪”。这一时期，正好是夹在古罗马时代和“文艺复兴”时期的中间。

现在我们再回到中世纪来。尽管一切在欧洲人看来自然黑暗得很，但其中还是

Now, returning to the Dark Ages, although everything certainly looked black for Europe, there were a few lights to be seen. An early bright spot was the reign of Charlemagne. You may be surprised to learn that Charlemagne was a Barbarian himself. He grew up uneducated and he never learned to write. Can you imagine a ruler today — the president of the United States, for instance — who couldn't write a letter? But Charlemagne had a good mind and he wanted to learn all there was to know. He became King of France, but he wasn't satisfied until he had brought Germany and Italy under his rule, too.

Charlemagne encouraged building. He brought to his court in Aachen, on the border between France and Germany, all the wisest men he could find. He helped get back for the world some of the knowledge and learning that had been lost when the ancient Romans ceased to govern. He was crowned emperor of a new Roman Empire on Christmas Day by the Pope in the Vatican in 800 A.D., and he called his new unified nation the Holy Roman Empire.

Another light flickering in the Dark Ages was kept burning by the Christian monks, who lived in monasteries. A chief monk, called an abbot, ruled a monastery. The monks thought they could live better lives if they worked hard and kept away from all the violence that was going on in the world.

The monks worked hard in the monasteries. They raised vegetables, built churches and houses, taught school, made paintings, wrote histories, and helped the poor and sick who came to them for help. Best of all for you and me, they studied the ancient Roman writings and kept them safe, so that we can know about the ancient Roman ways today.

可以看到几道亮光的。中世纪早期的一大亮点，就是查理曼大帝统治的时期。得知查理曼本人也曾是一个野蛮人，你们可能会觉得很惊讶吧。他在长大成人的过程中，一直没有接受过教育，并且后来始终都没有学会写字。你们能够想象，如今的一位统治者，比如说美国总统，竟然写不了一封信吗？可查理曼很聪明，希望自己能够学到所有应学的知识。他先是当上了法国国王，可他并不满意，最终又将德国和意大利两国也置于自己的统治之下了。

查理曼鼓励臣民大兴土木。他把自己能够找到的、那些最聪明的人，全都集中到了他的朝廷里，当时，他的朝廷位于法、德两国边境上的亚琛。他协助世界找回了自古罗马人不再当权之后就失落了的一些知识和学问。公元800年的圣诞节那天，在梵蒂冈，他由教皇加冕，成了一个新的罗马帝国的皇帝，并把这个新的、统一的国家称为“神圣罗马帝国”。

“黑暗时代”里另一道闪烁的微光，是由那些住在修道院里的基督教修道士们点燃和保持着的。修道士的头领，叫作“院长”，一座修道院，就是由院长管理着。修道士们都认为，假如努力工作并且远离世界正在发生的各种暴力活动，他们就会过上更好的生活。

修道士们都在修道院里辛勤地劳作着。他们种植蔬菜、修建教堂和房屋、给学校上课、绘制画作、记录历史，并且帮助那些前来向他们求助的穷人和病人。而对你我来说，最重要的则是，他们研究了古罗马人的著作，并且将这些著作保存得妥妥当当，从而让我们如今能够了解到古罗马时期的生活方式。

回廊，现存于西西里的蒙雷阿莱大教堂
（摄影：加里·威肯）

The monastery where the monks lived was built around a church, called an *abbey*. On one side of the abbey was a courtyard. Across the courtyard from the church was generally the dining hall, which was called the *refectory*. The church and the refectory were connected along each end of the courtyard by hallways. These hallways were like long porches with columns on the sides facing the courtyard, and were called *cloisters*.

The columns in the cloisters were not like the Greek and Roman columns. They weren't Doric or Ionic or Corinthian or Tuscan or composite, but were of many different shapes, even in the same cloister. Some were twisted in a shape like a screw, or like a wet towel when you try to wring the water out of it. Some were decorated with bands around them or with crisscross stripes. In many cloisters the columns were in pairs, two and two, like animals going into Noah's ark, and these were called *coupled columns*. Not much like the columns on the Parthenon, were they?

修道士们居住的修道院，都修建在教堂附近，称为隐修院。隐修院的一侧，是一个院子。从教堂穿过院子，通常就是餐厅，称为饭堂。教堂和饭堂之间，有一条走廊相连。这种走廊，就像是一条长长的门廊，并且朝着院子的那一侧都建有立柱，称为回廊。

回廊里的这些立柱，可不像古希腊和古罗马时期的那种立柱。它们既非多利克式、爱奥尼亚式、科林斯式，也不是托斯卡纳式或者组合式，哪怕是同一条回廊里，也有各种不同形状的立柱呢。有些立柱是扭转式的，样子就像是一颗螺丝，或者像你们想要拧干水的湿毛巾那样。有些立柱上盘绕着条纹，或者是盘绕着相互交叉的十字形条纹。在许多回廊里，立柱都是成双成对的，两两一组，好像是带到挪亚方舟上去的那些动物一样，因而这种立柱被称为“对柱”。它们都不太像万神殿里的那种立柱，对不对？

Chapter 12 Round Arches

Suppose you thought the world was going to end next year! Most people in Europe thought the world was going to come to an end in 1000 A.D. They weren't sure just how it would happen. Perhaps it was going to burn up, they thought, or fall apart or blow up with earthquakes and volcanoes. But they felt sure from what they read in the Bible that the world was going to end. Important buildings were not built because what was the use? They would be destroyed with the end of the world.

Then 1000 A.D. came and nothing happened to the world. Still the world was there, and so people found they must have been mistaken. More good buildings began to be built. The light in the darkness of the Dark Ages began to get brighter.

And now I'll have to tell you of the new kind of architecture that was used after 1000 A.D. This new kind of architecture is called *Romanesque*. The easiest way for you to tell that a building is Romanesque is to look at the tops of the windows and doors. If all the windows and doors have round arches for tops, then the building is probably Romanesque.

People call it Romanesque because, as you might have guessed already, it was used in the countries that once belonged to Rome. Just as each of these former Roman countries came to have its own language, descended from Latin, so each country came to have its own Romanesque architecture, descended from Roman architecture.

第12章 圆拱

假如你们认为，明年就是世界末日，会怎么样呢？绝大多数欧洲人都曾以为，世界末日会在公元1000年降临。他们并不清楚，世界末日究竟会用一种什么样的方式降临。他们觉得，没准会是一场大火烧掉整个世界，没准是地球会因地震和火山爆发而土崩瓦解，或者发生大爆炸。不过，他们却相当确信自己在《圣经》中看到的预言，确信世界末日终会来临。人们不再修建重要的建筑，因为他们想，修建这些建筑又有什么用呢？反正世界末日一来，它们就会毁掉的。

然后，公元1000年到了，可世界上什么也没有发生。世界一如既往地存在着，因此人们发现，他们一定是搞错了。于是，他们又开始兴建更多优秀的建筑了。“黑暗时代”一片漆黑之中的那道亮光，开始变得更加明亮了。

现在，我就来跟你们介绍介绍公元1000年以后人们所用的那种新建筑风格。这种新的建筑风格，叫作罗马式风格。分辨出一座建筑是不是属于罗马式建筑的最简方法，便是看一看其门窗的顶部。倘若所有门窗的顶部都有圆拱的话，那么十有八九，这栋建筑属于罗马式建筑。

人们之所以把这种建筑叫作罗马式建筑，是因为曾经归属于罗马帝国治下的那些国家都用过这种建筑风格；你们可能已经猜到了这一点吧。就像各国后来一个个都拥有了由拉丁语发展演化而来的本国语言那样，这些曾经属于罗马帝国治下的国家，也开始拥有了从罗马建筑发展演化而来的、各自特有的罗马式建筑风格。

The Romanesque architecture of Italy is most like the old basilican kind, and so I'll tell you first about the most famous Italian Romanesque buildings.

I'm sure you know the tower in this picture. It is the famous Leaning Tower of Pisa. The building next to the bell tower is the *cathedral* and next to the cathedral is a *baptistery*.

Every church isn't a cathedral. A cathedral is a church with a bishop. The chair that the bishop uses in his church is called a cathedra. As the bishop's church always has a *cathedra*, the bishop's church is called a cathedral. This is the cathedral of the Bishop of Pisa.

If you were to look down on a cathedral from the top of the leaning bell tower, you would see it was built in the shape of a cross. But this cross isn't a Greek cross because all the arms are not the same length. A cross with the main stem longer than the other parts is called a *Latin cross*. Most Romanesque churches were built in the form of a Latin cross. The top of the cross was always pointed toward the east so that the altar in that end of the church could be nearer the Holy Land in the East, where Christ was born.

The outside of the cathedral at Pisa is worth looking at, especially if you make believe you are

洗礼堂、大教堂和钟塔（斜塔），现存于意大利的比萨
（摄影：约翰·帕特森）

意大利的罗马式建筑，与原来的那种长方形廊柱大厅式极为相似，因此我会先给你们说一说意大利那些最著名的罗马式建筑。

你们肯定都认识下面照片里的那座钟塔吧。它就是著名的比萨斜塔。紧挨着钟塔的那栋建筑，是一座大教堂，而紧挨着大教堂的，则是一座洗礼堂。

并不是所有的教堂都是大教堂。大教堂是指其中拥有一位主教的教堂。主教在教堂里的座位，叫作主教座位。由于拥有主教的教堂里总是会有一把主教座位，所以拥有主教的教堂便被称为大教堂。这张照片里所示的，就是比萨主教的大教堂。

假如从那座倾斜着的钟塔上俯瞰大教堂的话，你们就会看出，人们是按照十字架的形状来修建这座大教堂的。不过，这种十字架并不是希腊十字架，因为其四臂并不是等长的。主臂比其他各臂都要长的十字架，称为拉丁十字架。绝大多数罗马式风格的教堂，都是按照拉丁十字架的格局建造的。十字架的顶端总是朝着东方，以便位于教堂这一端的祭坛，能够离耶稣基督降生的东方圣地更近一点儿。

比萨大教堂的外部，很值得我们一看。倘若你们假装自己是一名侦探，能够看

a detective and can see things that most people don't notice. The rows of columns with arches over them are called *arcades*. A detective would notice at once that all the arches are round arches, and so he could guess the building is probably Romanesque. There are four of these rows of arches or arcades on the west end of this cathedral.

And here is something I don't believe you'd notice unless you were a very good detective. Each arcade is a different height. The third arcade from the ground has the tallest columns. The next arcade is not quite as tall, the next one is still shorter, and the bottom arcade has the shortest columns of all. A very, very good detective would notice that the middle arch in the two arcades nearest the ground is bigger than the other arches.

Now look even more closely. An extra very good detective would see that the columns in the top two arcades are not always exactly over the columns below them.

All these differences were not accidental. The arcades were built that way on purpose. If all four arcades had been identical, the entire front of the cathedral would have looked monotonous and uninteresting.

Now if you will look at the Leaning Tower, you can see that all the arcades are just alike. For that reason, the tower isn't as beautiful as the cathedral. Many people even call the tower ugly. I don't

从斜塔顶上俯瞰意大利的比萨大教堂
（摄影：约翰·帕特森）

出绝大多数人都注意不到的东西，那就尤其如此了。一排排立柱，连同它们上面的拱门，构成了拱廊。一名侦探马上就会注意到，所有的拱门都属于圆拱，由此，他就可以猜出，这座教堂十有八九属于罗马式建筑风格。这座大教堂的西端，有四条这样的立柱长廊或者拱廊呢。

这里还有一个细节；我觉得，除非你们都是非常优秀的侦探，否则就会注意不到。每条拱廊的高度都不相同。从地面那一层往上数，第三条拱廊的立柱最高。接下来，第二条拱廊的立柱要矮一些，第一条拱廊的立柱更矮，而最下面那条拱廊里的立柱则最矮。一名非常、非常优秀的侦探还会注意到，底下的那两条拱廊里，最中间的那道拱门要比其他拱门都大。

现在，我们不妨更加仔细地来看一看。一位超级优秀的侦探会看到，顶上那两条拱廊里的立柱，并不是始终都位于底下各层立柱的正上方。

所有这些差异，都不是偶然形成的。人们是故意将拱廊建成这样的。如果四条拱廊都完全一样，那么大教堂的整个正面看上去就会单调得很，毫无意思了。

注意，假如再看一看比萨斜塔，那么你们就能看出，斜塔上的所有拱廊都是一模一样的。正因为如此，比萨斜塔才没有大教堂那么漂亮。许多人甚至还说，比萨斜塔丑陋得很哩。虽然我觉得比萨斜塔并不丑，但我当然也没法说它有比萨大教堂

think it is ugly, but I certainly can't say it's as pleasing to look at as the cathedral, though you may find it more interesting because it leans. The Leaning Tower was built later than the cathedral. Maybe by then the architects had forgotten why the cathedral arcades were not built all alike.

The tower started leaning almost as soon as it was begun. Before the first story was finished, the foundations on one side were much lower than on the other, so work on the building was stopped. After several years, another architect managed to get three more stories built before he had to stop because of the slant. Still later another architect finished the tower. But some people have said the tower was meant to lean in the first place, so it would be different from other towers.

It is true that every city in Italy was trying to get ahead of every other city with buildings that would attract attention. But most people now believe the foundations sank in soft ground on one side and that the lean of the tower was an accident. Its top leans about fourteen feet out over the bottom. There are seven bells in the top, and the heaviest bell is kept on the side away from the lean to help balance the tower.

Now, I have a confession to make. I told you that all of the arcades in the Leaning Tower are just alike. That is only partly true. They were intended to be alike, but, if you look closely, you can see that the builders made the columns on the leaning side longer than those on the opposite side to do what they could to straighten up the tower. So, instead of being perfectly straight and leaning over in the direction of the river that flows through Pisa, it actually looks a little like a banana.

那么好看，不过，由于它是斜的，你们可能会觉得它更加有意思呢。比萨斜塔是在比萨大教堂之后修建起来的。没准儿，是因为到了那个时候，建筑设计师们都忘掉大教堂里的拱廊为什么没有建得一模一样的原因了吧。

比萨斜塔几乎是在刚刚动工兴建的时候，就开始倾斜了。第一层还没有完工，一侧的地基就比另一侧低了许多，因此人们只得停工不建了。过了几年后，另一位建筑师又设法建起了三层，可后来也因为塔身倾斜得厉害，而不得不停了下来。后来，又有一位建筑师，终于建完了这座塔。不过，也有些人说，人们一开始就是有意让这座钟塔斜着，目的是让它与其他的塔看上去不一样呢。

的确，意大利的每一座城市，都曾想方设法，希望通过兴建引人注目的建筑，来胜过其他的城市。不过，绝大多数人如今却认为，建在较松软地面上的一侧地基下陷，使得比萨斜塔倾斜，是一种意外事故。这座斜塔的塔顶，比塔底向外倾斜了大约十四英尺。塔顶有七口大钟，而最重的那一口钟则放在与倾斜方向相反的那一边，以便于协助整座斜塔保持平衡。

现在，我要向你们承认一个错误。我曾经跟你们说过，比萨斜塔上的所有拱廊都是一模一样的。这句话，只有部分属于实情。人们本来是打算将它们建得一模一样的，可是，倘若仔细观察的话，你们就能看出，建筑师们将倾斜那一侧的立柱，建得比相反方向的立柱要长一些，目的是尽可能地让整座斜塔站直。因此，这座塔并不是上下笔直、并且向流经比萨的那条河的方向倾斜的，而是有点儿像只香蕉那样弯着的呢。

Sometimes visitors play games with the tower. They stand on the grass next to the cathedral and hold their hands up so it looks like they are holding up the tower from falling over while a friend takes their picture.

Near the cathedral stands a circular building called the Baptistery of Pisa. A baptistery is used to baptize or christen new members of the church. The Baptistery of Pisa was changed a great deal in looks after the Romanesque period was over because later architects thought they could make it look better than it looked at first.

The baptistery is another place in Pisa that has something special about it. You can see that it looks like a scoop of vanilla ice cream. When you enter it, however, it is a dome. It is not a dome that is high above your head, but one that surrounds you on the ground. Inside, if you face the wall and whisper in one direction, and your friend is listening on the far side, it's possible to hear exactly what you just said as clearly as if you were standing next to one another.

I remember one day when I was visiting Pisa and went into the baptistery, a man came inside and closed the door. He said everyone should be silent, and then he began to sing a melody, and then a second one, and then a third and so on. Each melody echoed in the dome and did not stop, so it sounded as if he, just one man, could multiply himself into a whole choir! It was as beautiful as any music I have ever heard.

There is another good example of a Romanesque building I want to tell you about. It is the Cathedral of Angoulême in France. The front, as you can see in the picture, is decorated with sculpture. Notice the round arches that belong to all Romanesque

有的时候，游客还会与这座钟塔玩游戏。他们会站在大教堂旁边的草地上，举起双手，看上去就像是托着这座斜塔，不让它倒下来一样，然后让朋友给他们拍照。

距比萨大教堂不远的地方，有一座圆形的建筑，叫作比萨洗礼堂。所谓的洗礼堂，是用于举行洗礼，或者给新加入教会的人施洗的地方。自罗马式建筑风格那个时期过去之后，比萨洗礼堂的样子已经改变了许多，因为后来的建筑师认为，他们可以让这座洗礼堂看上去比最初的样子更漂亮。

这座洗礼堂，是比萨另一个拥有特别之处的地方。你们都看得出，它有点儿像是一个香草冰淇淋甜筒呢。然而，走进去之后，你们就会发现里面是一个穹顶。可这并不是那种罩在头上的穹顶，而是一个从地面就环绕在你们周围的穹顶。站在里面，如果面对墙壁，朝着一个方向低声说话，而你的朋友站在很远的地方听着的话，他也可以听得很清楚，就像你们挨在一起说话似的呢。

我还记得，有一天我在比萨游玩，进入这座洗礼堂后，有个人走了进来，关上了大门。他要大家都保持安静，然后他开始唱起一首旋律，接着是第二首旋律，第三首旋律，一直唱下去。由于每首旋律都在穹顶之下回响，经久不息，因此听上去就像是他一个人能够分身，组成一个合唱队似的！这与我曾经听过的所有音乐，都同样美妙呢。

我想再向你们介绍一栋建筑，因为它也是罗马式建筑风格的一个典型例子。这就是法国的昂古莱姆大教堂。你们在下图中便可以看出，这座大教堂的正面装饰着

buildings.

In England, the Normans who came over from France with William the Conqueror built many stone churches, cathedrals, and castles. Norman buildings are Romanesque just as much as the French and Italian, but they are usually called Norman buildings instead of Romanesque. Very little of the Norman Romanesque looks now as it did when the Normans built it, because later builders kept adding to it and changing it. Often some parts of an English church are Norman, while later parts of the same church are not Norman style at all.

Germany also has some fine Romanesque cathedrals and churches. And they all have arcades and round arches over the windows and doors. And that's really the main thing to remember about Romanesque buildings — round arches and arcades.

昂古莱姆大教堂，
现存于法国的昂古莱姆
（摄影：加里·威肯）

雕塑作品。请注意其中的那些圆拱，它们都是所有罗马式建筑共有的。

在英国，在征服者威廉[1]的率领下，从法国而来的那些诺曼人[2]，修建了许多用石头建成的教堂、大教堂和城堡。诺曼人修建的这些建筑，与法国人、意大利人兴建的建筑一样，都属于罗马式风格，不过，它们通常都被称为“诺曼式建筑”，而不是称为罗马式建筑。诺曼人的这些罗马式建筑当中，如今几乎没有几座保留着诺曼人最初将它们修建起来时的模样了，因为后来的建筑师们不断地给它们添砖加瓦，并且不断地改变着它们。一座英国教堂里，通常都会有一些部位属于诺曼风格，而同一座教堂里，后建的部分则可能完全不再属于诺曼风格了。

德国也有一些精美的、属于罗马式风格的大教堂和教堂。而且，它们全都建有拱廊，门窗之上也都建有圆拱。因此，关于罗马式建筑，你们真正需要记住的一个要点，就是圆拱和拱廊。

[1] 征服者威廉（William the Conqueror，1027—1087），即英国国王威廉一世（1066—1087在位）。他本来是法国的诺曼底公爵，后来率军渡海入侵英国，打败英王哈罗德后自立为王。他是欧洲中世纪最具影响力的君主之一，其影响包括统治者的改变、对英语的改革、社会和教会上层等级的变化等，并且他还采用了一些欧洲大陆上关于教会改革的观点。

[2] 诺曼人（Norman），指居住在法国北部的维京人及其后裔。

Chapter 13 Castles

Once upon a time there lived a very wicked monster. He lived in a strong castle set on the top of a hill, and whenever any traveler was unlucky enough to pass along the road below the castle, down would come the monster and carry the traveler off to his dungeon tower.

That sounds like the beginning of a fairy tale, and that is just what it is. But there is more truth than you might think in a fairy tale. In the Middle Ages, when people believed in fairies and ogres, there were many real castles — most of them built on the top of a hill. And although there were no real ogres, there were, I'm sorry to say, bad knights living in some of these castles who would lock up anyone from whom they thought they could get money. Although not all knights who lived in the castles were bad, most of them were warlike and fierce, and all the old castles had dungeon cells for prisoners.

These castles were built because of the feudal system, which worked like this. The king or prince who conquered a country would divide the country up among several of his lords. These lords would then divide their land among other lords, and these would divide their share again among the knights. Each lord and knight had to promise that he would help the lord from whom he got the land whenever the lord needed him. Then each lord and knight built himself a strong castle to protect his part of the land from anyone who might try to take it away from him. There were no policemen in those days to keep

第13章 城堡

很久以前，有一个特别邪恶的怪物。它住在山顶一座坚固的城堡里，任何时候，只要城堡之下的山路上出现倒霉的过客，这个怪物便会从城堡里下来，把过客掳到塔上的地牢里关起来。

这听起来有点儿像是一个神话故事的开头，而事实上也是如此。不过，一个神话故事里包含的事实，可能比你们所想的更多呢。在人们还相信神话故事和吃人怪物的中世纪，确实有着许多真正的城堡，并且其中绝大多数也都修建在山顶上。而且，尽管那时并没有真正的食人怪物，但我不得不遗憾地告诉你们，当时确实有一些很坏的骑士，居住在这些城堡里，凡是他们觉得可以榨出钱财的人，都会被他们掳去关起来。虽然并不是所有居住在这些城堡里的骑士都很坏，但他们中的绝大多数却都是既好斗、又凶狠，而所有古老的城堡里，也都有关押犯人的地牢呢。

之所以修建这些城堡，是因为当时实行的是封建制度。所谓的封建制度，是这样的：征服了某个国家的国王或者王子，会将这个国家分封给手下的几个领主。接下来，这些领主又会将自己的土地分封给其他的贵族，而那些贵族再把自己获得的土地分封给手下的骑士。每位贵族和骑士，都得向分封给他们土地的那位领主宣誓，无论后者何时需要，他们都得前去支援。然后，每个贵族和骑士便会给自己修建一座强大的城堡，以便保护自己的土地，不让其他人把土地从他们的手中夺走。

one man from trying to steal another man's land, and so each knight had to have his own soldiers and his own castle to protect his rights.

Near each castle was a village where the common people — who were not lords or nobles — lived. These people were not very well cared for. They lived in miserable little huts. Most of them had to give part of all the food they raised to the lord of the castle, and all the men had to serve the lord as soldiers whenever he needed them. In return, the lord of the castle protected the poor people from enemies.

The castle was built with great, thick stonewalls all around it. Outside of the wall was a deep ditch of water called a moat. The only way to get into the castle was across a drawbridge over the moat. The drawbridge could be drawn up from inside the castle so that an enemy could not enter. If the enemy reached the drawbridge before it was drawn up, he found his way blocked by a huge latticework gate called a *portcullis* that was dropped across the gateway of the castle.

The castle had huge stone towers at the gateway and along the wall, with very narrow slits for windows. Archers could shoot arrows out of these slits, but the slits were hard to shoot through from the outside.

卡尔卡松城堡，现存于法国
（摄影：加里·威肯）

那时还没有什么警察，没法防止一个人去抢走另一个人的土地，因此，每位骑士只有组建自己的军队、修建自己的城堡，才能保护好自己的权利。

每座城堡的附近，都会有一个村庄，普通百姓，即那些既非领主、又非贵族的人，就生活在这里。这些百姓并没有得到很好的照顾。他们都住在肮脏的小棚里。绝大多数百姓都得将自己辛辛苦苦耕种出来的粮食收成中的一部分交给城堡里的领主，并且无论领主什么时候需要，所有男子便都得为领主去服兵役。作为回报，城堡里的领主则保护穷人，让他们不受到敌人的袭扰。

城堡的四周，都建有又大又厚的石头城墙。城墙之外，是一道里面全都是水的深沟，称为“护城河”。进入城堡的唯一道路，便是经由横跨在护城河之上的一座吊桥。吊桥可以在城堡内部升起，这样城外的敌人就进不来了。倘若不待吊桥升起，敌人就来到了桥上，那么还有一扇巨大的栅格状大门挡住敌人的去路，这扇大门，叫作“吊闸”，横在城堡的入口。

城堡入口和城墙周围，都建有一座座巨大的石塔，上面留有很窄的缝隙，当作窗户。弓箭手可以通过这些缝隙向外射箭，而敌人从城堡外面射来的箭矢，却很难射进来。

Inside the walls there was a courtyard around which were the stables; soldiers' and servants' quarters; kitchens; and a high tower, which was called the *keep*, and was where the lord of the castle lived. There was a large dining hall and often a little church or chapel in the keep. Down below the ground level were the prison cells and torture chambers. In case of an attack, all the people of the village came into the castle, often with their cattle and flocks, and stayed there, so there had to be great stores of food on hand.

Castles were great defensive fortresses where the knights would gather and train, where their horses could be kept and where the royal family could live in safety. Many times, we think of castles only in Europe and only in stories from long ago. But when we do, we are mistaken!

When the settlers moved westward in North America, they built forts that were needed for the same reasons and served the same purpose.

史卡拉城堡，现存于意大利的希尔米内

皮埃尔丰城堡，现存于法国

城墙里面，是一个大院子，院子四周则是畜舍、士兵和仆人的住地、厨房，以及一座高高的、叫作“主堡”的塔楼，主堡就是城堡领主居住的地方。城堡里有一座巨大的饭堂，而主堡里通常还有一个小型的教堂或者礼拜堂。城堡的地下，则是囚室和审讯室。在遭到敌人攻打时，村庄里的所有人都会进入城堡，并且通常还会带上他们所养的牛羊牲口，然后留在城堡里，所以，城堡里必须储存大量的食物才行。

城堡是一种大型的防御要塞：骑士们可以在此聚集和进行训练，他们的战马可以在此饲养，而王室成员也可以在这里安全地生活。我们经常以为，只有欧洲、只有很久以前的故事传说里才有城堡。可要是我们真的这样想的话，那就大错特错了！

北美洲的殖民者向西迁徙的时候，出于同样的需要、为了达到同样的目的，他们也曾经修建了许多的要塞。有些要塞是用石头建成的，就像城堡一样，可还有许

大阪城堡，现存于日本

Some forts were built of stone like castles, but many were built of wood, just like the early castles in Europe were.

In many lands around the world, like China and Japan, there were castles, too. Are you wondering why? Well, people the world over all have the same needs for food, clothing, shelter, and protection. And for just that reason, even without communicating with each other, and no matter how far apart they were or how many years separated them, often they would discover the very same solution to the very same problems.

多是用木头建成的，就像欧洲早期的那些城堡一样。

世界上的许多国家，比如中国和日本，也都建有城堡。你们想知道这是什么原因吗？好吧，全世界的人对于食物、衣服、住所和保护，都有着同样的需要。正是由于同一个原因，所以他们甚至无须彼此交流，并且无论相距多远、无论生活的时代相隔多少年，对于同样的问题，他们都会想出同样的解决办法来。

Chapter 14 Pointing Toward Heaven

Now I'm going to tell you about a kind of architecture named for a group of people called the Goths, who never had any architecture. All they ever built were huts. Yet the kind of buildings named for these people is one of the greatest styles of architecture in the world. It is called Gothic architecture.

That certainly seems strange, doesn't it? Why in the world is it called Gothic architecture, if the Goths didn't have anything to do with it?

The reason is strange. Today we think that Gothic architecture is very beautiful, but, strange as it may seem, there were people of the time who despised these beautiful buildings. They thought any architecture that didn't come from Greece or Rome was no good. They thought it was crude and uncivilized.

The crudest, roughest, and most uncivilized people that the admirers of classic style could think of were the Goths who had conquered Rome, and so they called this architecture *Gothic*. They did this not only to show how crude they thought it was, but because they thought the Goths had begun it. Like most bad nicknames, it stuck.

Gothic architecture grew out of the Romanesque architecture. The builders kept trying to make stone ceilings over the naves of the churches because stone was safer from fire than wood was. At first the stone ceiling was a barrel vault, shaped like the side of a

第14章 直指天堂

现在，我打算给你们介绍一种建筑，它是用一个叫作“哥特人”的民族来命名的，可这个民族，却从来没有修建过什么建筑。他们修建过的，充其量不过都是些小棚子罢了。然而，用这个民族命名的这种建筑，却属于世界上最伟大的建筑风格之一哩。这种建筑，就叫哥特式建筑。

这一点，看上去当然奇怪得很，不是吗？要是这种建筑风格与哥特人毫无关联的话，那么究竟又是因为什么，而要将它们称为哥特式建筑呢？

原因也很古怪。如今我们都认为哥特式建筑非常漂亮，可尽管看上去奇怪得很，当时却有些人对这些漂亮的建筑不屑一顾呢。他们觉得，任何不是源自古希腊或者古罗马时期的建筑，都是不好的。他们认为，这种建筑都是粗俗的、不文明的。

由于这些崇尚经典风格的人能够想到的最粗鲁、最野蛮和最不文明的民族，就是曾经征服了罗马的哥特人，因此他们便把这种建筑风格称为哥特式。他们之所以这样做，非但是为了表明他们觉得这种建筑有多粗俗，而且是由于他们以为，哥特人才是这种建筑风格的始作俑者。于是，就像绝大多数不雅的绰号一样，这个名称也一直存续下来了。

哥特式的建筑风格，是从罗马式建筑风格中发展出来的。建筑师们一直都在试图给教堂的中殿建造石制屋顶，因为石头比木材更能防火。起初，他们修建的石制

barrel. The barrel vault took a great deal of wooden centering to build, because the vault was quite long, and each part had to be held up by the centering until all the stones were in place. The centering took so much wood that it was a great discovery when someone found a way of building vaults with very little centering.

Then another discovery was made — that a pointed arch was better sometimes than a round one. It wasn't really a new discovery, for the people in the Middle East had used pointed arches for many years. The knights brought the idea back to Europe when they returned from their crusades in the Holy Land.

You might not think that such a little thing as making an arch pointed on top instead of round would be important. But important it was, and this is why a round arch has to be just as high as it is wide. The wider the opening it has to cover, the higher the round arch has to be. But a pointed arch is different. You can build a pointed arch as high as you want or as low as you want, no matter how wide the opening it must stretch across.

If you put your fingertips together so they form an arch, you can prove this. If you keep your hands the same distance apart you can only form one round arch with your fingers. But you can form pointed arches of several different sizes by curving your fingers and keeping your hands still.

The builders of the stone cathedrals found it much easier to build vaults over a wide nave with pointed arches instead of round ones. Of course these stone vaults pushed down on the walls and also pushed sideways. So the walls had to be very thick and well braced with buttresses. But the builders found that when they used ribbed vaults instead of plain

屋顶是一种桶形穹顶，样子就像是一只水桶的侧面。桶形穹顶需要大量的木制拱架才能建起，因为这种穹顶相当长，而每个部位都得用拱架支撑，直到所有石头都安放就位才行。由于拱架所需木材太多，因此，等有人找到了一种只需极少拱架便可建造穹顶的方法之后，人们便都认为那是一种非常伟大的发现了。

接下来，人们又有了一个发现，那就是：有的时候，尖拱比圆拱更好。实际上，这并不是一种新发现，因为中东地区的人早已利用尖拱多年了。参加向圣地进行“十字军东征”的骑士们回师时，便将这个办法带回了欧洲。

你们可能会认为，将拱形换成尖顶、不再使用圆顶这样的小事，不会有什么重要性。可是，这一点的确重要，而圆拱的高度必须与圆拱的宽度相当的原因，也在这里，穹顶覆盖的面积越大，圆拱就必须建得越高。可尖拱却不同。无论尖拱必须覆盖多大的范围，人们都可以将尖拱想建多高就建多高，想建多矮就建多矮。

倘若你们将双手的指尖顶在一起，形成一个拱形，就能证明这一点了。如果双手之间的距离保持不变，那么你们只能用手指形成一个圆拱。但是，在双手不动的情况下，你们却能通过弯曲手指，形成多个大小不同的尖拱呢。

那些用石头修建大教堂的建筑师发现，利用尖拱而不是圆拱，在一个很宽的中殿上面建造穹顶要容易得多。当然，这些石制穹顶既会向下重压墙壁，也会对侧面构成挤压。因此，下面的墙壁必须建得非常厚重，并且须用扶垛妥善支撑才行。但是，建筑师们又发现，他们用的是肋架拱顶而不是普通的桶形穹顶时，绝大部分侧推力都来自于肋架末端。他们发现，假如在肋架末端修建厚重的扶垛，那么墙壁的

barrel vaults, most of the side push came just at the ends of the ribs. They found that if they put heavy buttresses at the ends of the ribs, the rest of the wall could be made very thin. The walls between the buttresses finally became so unnecessary for holding up the roof that they were made of glass. The walls became walls of glass between buttresses of stone.

This may be difficult to imagine unless you can feel what it's like for yourself. Try this. Stand up and, standing a full step away from the wall you are facing, put your hands above your head and lean forward until your hands are flat against a wall. Where is the pressure? All over? No, I didn't think so. Running from your hands down your arms and sides and legs to your feet? That's just what I thought.

Now imagine you are doing just that, being a flying buttress holding up a wall that is leaning out because it is holding up a very heavy roof. Now you can feel how it works.

As builders made improvements, the walls got lighter, and the buttresses changed. You couldn't really say the buttresses learned to fly, but they are called *flying buttresses* just the same, because they "flew away" from the building. A flying buttress is one that leans against the wall like a prop. It would be like a man pushing against a wall with a stick. Flying buttresses press against the top of the walls and keep the walls from being pushed over by the weight of the vault and the roof.

Here is the picture of flying buttresses on a cathedral in Paris famous for its flying buttresses. Do you recognize it? It is called Notre Dame, and is one of the most famous buildings of all.

其他部分就可以修得很薄了。最终，由于扶垛之间根本无须什么墙壁再来支撑屋顶的重量，因此人们便可以用玻璃来做这种墙壁了。于是，这种墙壁便变成了石制扶垛间的玻璃幕墙。

除非你们能够亲自感受到那是怎么回事，否则你们是难以理解这一点的。不妨试试下面这种方法。站起来，走到距墙壁一大步远的地方，面朝墙壁，将双手举过头顶，身体前倾，直到双掌平贴墙面。压力在哪里呢？全身都是？不，我觉得不是这样的。从你们的双手往下，经由双臂、身体两侧、双腿，直到双脚？我觉得正是这样的。

现在，假设你们正像上面所说的那样做，假设你们是一道飞扶垛，正在支撑一堵因为所承屋顶太重而向外倾斜的墙壁。那样，你们就能感受到飞扶垛的工作原理了。

随着建筑师的不断改进，墙壁变得越来越轻，而扶垛也发生了变化。你们可不能真的认为扶垛学会了飞行，但称它们为“飞扶垛”也无妨，因为它们的确是“飞离”了整栋建筑。飞扶垛就是斜撑着一堵墙壁、像是支柱的那种东西。它就像是一个人，正在用木棍顶住一堵墙那样。飞扶垛抵着墙壁的顶部，从而让墙壁不会被穹顶和屋顶的重量压塌。

下图便是法国一座大教堂里的飞扶垛，这座教堂，正是因为拥有这些飞扶垛而远近闻名呢。你们认出来了吗？这座大教堂，叫作“巴黎圣母院”，是世界上最著名的一座建筑呢。

巴黎圣母院的飞扶垛细部，
现存于巴黎
（摄影：约翰·帕特森）

巴黎圣母院，现存于法国的巴黎
（摄影：约翰·帕特森）

These three discoveries — the ribbed vault, the walls mostly of glass between buttresses, and flying buttresses — are the three most important things to remember when learning about the Gothic style. When these three things had been discovered, there finally came that beautiful and marvelous kind of architecture known as Gothic — but not because the Goths had anything to do with it, remember.

Gothic architecture was as different from the Greek and Roman as it could be.

The Greek and Roman buildings were solidly set on the ground. Almost all the weight pushed straight down. But a Gothic cathedral was a balance of all sorts of thrusts and pushes and forces. Where there was a side push, there was a buttress to push against it.

In the Greek and Roman temples, most of the lines ran lengthwise. They were horizontal buildings. In contrast, the Gothic cathedrals climbed into the air as though

肋架拱顶、扶垛间几乎全为玻璃的墙壁以及飞扶垛这三大发现，就是我们在了解哥特式建筑风格时应当记住的三大要点。有了这三大发现之后，最终才出现了众所周知的哥特式这种美丽而神奇的建筑风格，但你们可要记住，哥特人与这种建筑风格没有什么关系。

哥特式建筑在诸多方面都尽可能地与古希腊和古罗马的建筑不同。

古希腊和古罗马时期的建筑，都是稳固地建立在地面之上。建筑差不多所有的重量，都是垂直下压的。可是，一座哥特式大教堂却是所有推力、压力和力量的平衡。哪个地方有侧向压力，就会有扶垛来顶住。

古希腊和古罗马时期的神庙，里面的绝大多数线条都是纵向的。也就是说，它们都是水平的建筑。相比而言，哥特式的大教堂却都是直指空中，仿佛要伸入天堂似的。其中的绝大部分线条，似乎都是吸引着我们的目光从地面向上而去。教堂的

reaching up toward heaven. Most of their lines seem to carry the eye upward from the ground. Every part of the building helped to do this. Think of the pointed arch, for one thing. In many towns throughout Europe, when you see the skyline come into view, it is the cathedral that rises up above all else. It was the town's center, the gathering place for all in the town and those around. In fact, if you are lost, searching for the downtown of most any European town, just look for the cathedral, and you'll get there! And remember, its front door always faces west.

每一个部分，都是这样。首先，我们可以想一想这种教堂的尖拱。在欧洲的许多城镇里，只要地平线映入眼帘，就可以看到比其他建筑都要高耸的大教堂。这里一般都是市镇的中心，是所有市民和四周乡民聚集的地方。事实上，如果你们在绝大多数欧洲市镇里迷路了，找不到市中心的话，那么只要找到市镇的大教堂，也就找到了市镇的中心区域！并且还要记住，大教堂的正门，始终都是朝着西方的。

Chapter 15 In Praise of Mary

Big buildings today take only months to build. Big Gothic buildings often took hundreds of years to build. One Gothic building, Cologne Cathedral, took more than 600 years. You can see its famous spires rising above the city of Cologne, in Germany, where it rests on the banks of the Rhine River.

When "Gothic" is mentioned, most people think of France, for France has the finest Gothic cathedrals in the world.

The Gothic cathedrals were built with loving care. Everyone in the village and the surrounding country did his bit for the cathedral. The stones were shaped and set in place by the members of the *guilds*, or clubs of workmen in the same trade. The guild would not let any work pass that was not good enough. There was nothing "fake" about a cathedral. The stone carvings all the way up in the roof were just as carefully made as if people could get near enough to examine them.

Perhaps this is why the Gothic cathedrals rate next to the Greek buildings as the world's most wonderful examples of architecture. The men who built the Greek temples and the men who built the Gothic cathedrals left behind them very different kinds of architecture. But the buildings are alike in their fine workmanship.

Most of the French Gothic cathedrals were built to the glory of Mary, the mother of Christ, who in French was called *Notre Dame* or, in English, Our Lady. There were so

第15章 颂扬马利亚

如今，一些大型建筑只需要几个月就可以建成。可是，一些大型的哥特式建筑，却经常是花了几百年时间才建成的哩。有一栋哥特式的建筑，即科隆大教堂，甚至经过了六百多年才建成。在德国的科隆，你们可以看到，这座大教堂那些闻名遐迩的尖顶高高地耸立在城市之上，而这座教堂，就建在莱茵河岸边。

一提到“哥特式”，绝大多数人都会想到法国，这是因为，世界上最精美的一些哥特式大教堂，全都位于法国。

这些哥特式的大教堂，都是人们怀着满腔的热情修建起来的。整个村庄和附近乡村里的人，全都会为修建大教堂出一分力。同业公会里的人，即从事同一行业的工人，会将石头打磨成形并安放到位。同业公会不会让任何一项工作干得马马虎虎、差强人意。在大教堂里，没有任何东西属于“假冒伪劣”呢。教堂屋顶一路往上的那些石雕，全都是精雕细刻，好像人们可以靠得很近，仔细地去欣赏它们似的。

或许，这就是哥特式大教堂之所以被人们认为是仅次于古希腊建筑的、世界最精美的建筑风格范例的原因吧。那些修建古希腊神庙的人，和那些修建哥特式大教堂的人，留下的是两种风格迥异的建筑式样。不过，建筑本身的精美工艺，却是毫无二致的。

法国的绝大多数哥特式大教堂，都是为了颂扬基督之母马利亚的荣光而修建

many cathedrals of Notre Dame built that we generally call the cathedral simply by the name of the town it is in, such as Chartres or Reims. But if someone speaks of just the Cathedral of Notre Dame, he usually means Notre Dame of Paris, the one I showed you, because of its famous flying buttresses.

Notre Dame of Paris has on the west end — remember, the end opposite the altar — two large towers. Beneath the towers and in the center are the doorways, one to the nave and one to each side aisle. The doorways are covered with rows of statues of prophets and saints, with the head of one statue below the feet of another. Above each doorway is a row of very large statues of kings. Above the kings is a huge round window called a *wheel window or a rose window*. The rose window is stained glass, filled with brilliant colored pieces of glass that cast a soft purplish glow inside the church.

科隆大教堂尖顶的细部，
现存于德国的科隆
（摄影：约翰·帕特森）

的；马利亚在法语里被称为“圣母”，而在英语中则称为“我们的夫人”。由于各地修建的圣母大教堂太多，因此我们通常都只是用教堂所在的市镇名称来称呼它们，比如沙特尔大教堂，或者兰斯大教堂。不过，倘若有人只是说“圣母大教堂”的话，那么他通常指的就是巴黎圣母院了，我在前面已经让你们看过这座教堂的照片，让你们看过其中那些著名的飞扶垛了。

巴黎圣母院的玫瑰形窗细部，现存于巴黎
（摄影：加里·威肯）

巴黎圣母院的西端（记住，也就是与祭坛相对的那一端）有两座大型的塔楼。这两座塔楼的下方以及中央，是两条门廊，一条通向中殿，另一条则通向两条侧道。门廊上，贴有上下两排先知雕像和圣徒雕像，下面雕像的头顶着上面雕像的脚。每条门廊的上方，还有一排巨型的国王雕像。而这些国王雕像的上方，则是一扇巨大的圆形窗户，叫作“轮形扇窗”或者“玫瑰形窗”。玫瑰形窗用彩色玻璃镶嵌而成，上面全都是一块块色彩鲜艳的彩色玻璃，将一种柔和的紫色光芒投入教堂内部。

As most Gothic churches are, this cathedral in Paris is in the form of a Latin cross, with the horizontal arms shorter than the vertical bar. The arms of the cross are called the *transepts* of the cathedral. The place where the transepts cross the nave is called the *crossing*. Over the crossing is a tall slender spire. You could see this spire and the shape of a cross from the roof if you were brave enough to climb to the very top!

The front of a building, like the front of Notre Dame that you see in the picture, is called the *façade*. Facade means about the same thing as face. Now, Notre Dame of Paris is supposed to have the finest façade of any Gothic cathedral in the world. In fact, each of the great cathedrals of France has a part that someone considers the best in the world. What a building it would make if the best of each cathedral were taken and put together to make one best cathedral! But perhaps such a building wouldn't be as interesting, after all, as the separate cathedrals.

巴黎圣母院耳堂，现存于巴黎
（摄影：约翰·帕特森）

The towers with their square tops on the cathedral of Paris were meant to have tall spires on them. But by

巴黎圣母院正面，现存于巴黎
（摄影：加里·威肯）

跟绝大多数哥特式教堂一样，巴黎这座大教堂的格局也是拉丁十字架形，横向两臂的长度比竖向臂短。十字架形的横向两臂，被称为大教堂的“耳堂”。耳堂与中殿交叉的地方，则被称为“交叉口”。交叉口的上方，是一座又高又细的尖塔。如果你们很勇敢，敢爬到屋顶上去的话，那你们就能看见这座尖塔以及十字架的形状了！

一栋建筑物的前面，比如你们在下面这幅照片中看到的巴黎圣母院的前面，叫作“正面”。“正面”的意思，其实和“表面”差不多。如今，人们认为巴黎圣母院的正面，是世界上所有哥特式大教堂中最为精美的。要是把每座大教堂里最优秀的部分都拿出来，放到一起，建成一座最精美的大教堂的话，那该是一栋什么样的建筑啊！不过，或许这样组合而成的一栋建筑，终究不会像分成各个大教堂那样有意思呢。

巴黎圣母院那些带有方顶的塔楼上，原本都是应当有高耸的尖塔的。不过，到了这座大教堂可以修建尖塔的时候，却已经过去了许多年，使得这些尖塔再也没

the time the cathedral was ready for the spires, so many years had gone by that the spires were never built. On some cathedrals one tower was built but the other never finished. On one very fine cathedral the spires were put on at different times, so they are not alike.

沙特尔大教堂，现存于法国的沙特尔
（摄影：约翰·帕特森）

This is the famous Cathedral of Chartres.

Chartres is a little city about sixty miles from Paris. The Cathedral of Chartres is noted not only for its two spires but for the wonderful stained-glass windows in its walls. Do you remember I told you that Gothic churches had walls of glass? This stained glass was made with brilliant color to show pictures that helped remind people of the stories in the Bible. The sunlight streaming through the colored glass has a marvelously beautiful effect on the interior.

You remember how cathedrals usually rise above the whole town and can be seen easily from anywhere, don't you? Now I'm going to tell you about an almost hidden surprise chapel right in the center of Paris. It is called the Sainte Chapelle. It is very near Notre Dame on

沙特尔大教堂远景，现存于法国的沙特尔
（摄影：约翰·迪安）

有修建起来了。有些大教堂里，甚至在修建了一座塔楼之后，其余塔楼再也没有修建起来呢。还有一座非常精美的大教堂，其中的尖塔都是不同时期修建的，因此样子都很不相同。

这座大教堂，就是举世闻名的沙特尔大教堂。

沙特尔是一座小城，距巴黎大约六十英里。沙特尔大教堂为世人所称道的，并非仅仅在于它有两座尖塔，还在于教堂墙壁上那些精美绝伦的彩色玻璃窗户。你们还记得我曾经跟你们说过，一些哥特式教堂里还有玻璃墙壁吗？这种彩色玻璃，颜色都非常亮丽鲜艳，上面绘有图画，以帮助人们记起《圣经》中的那些故事。阳光从彩色玻璃中流淌进来，在教堂内部形成了一种美轮美奂的效果。

你们都还记得，这些大教堂通常都是高高耸立于整座市镇之上，在任何地方都很容易看到，对吧？现在，我打算给你们来说一说一座隐藏在巴黎市中心、令人惊讶的礼拜堂。它叫圣礼拜堂。这座礼拜堂，位于流经巴黎中心地带的塞纳河中央两座小岛

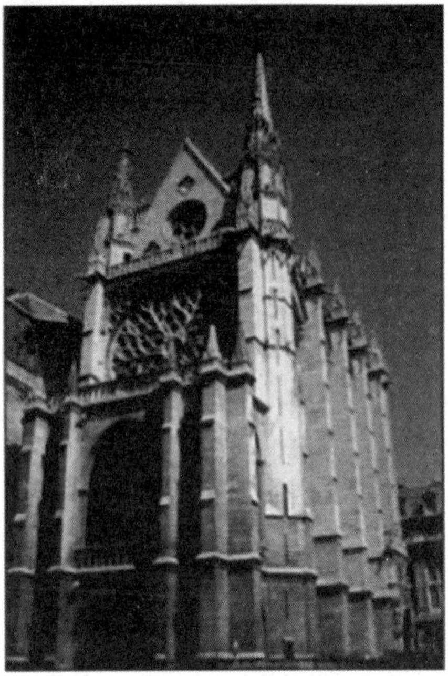

圣礼拜堂，现存于巴黎
（摄影：加里·威肯）

one of two islands in the middle of the Seine River in the heart of Paris.

To find the chapel, you must enter through an iron gate, cross a courtyard with cobblestones so anyone can hear you coming, then go inside a small entrance hall. You then begin to climb up an almost completely dark spiral staircase that seems to go up and up and up as you turn and turn and turn. Then, suddenly you are back in the light again, but it is a light more beautiful than anything you have seen before. Every wall is made up of stained-glass windows. And every window panel is made up of different geometric shapes. When people enter, they cannot say anything at all, and find it very difficult to leave even if they have been there for quite awhile.

The glass is held by stone framework in the windows, and the separate pieces of glass are kept in place with strips of lead. The stone

圣礼拜堂内景，现存于巴黎
（摄影：加里·威肯）

中的一座上，离巴黎圣母院不远。

要想找到这座礼拜堂，你们必须从一道铁门进去，穿过一个地上铺有鹅卵石的院子（这样大家都能听到你们进来时的声音），然后走进一座小小的门廊。接下来，你们就会开始爬上一条几乎漆黑一片的螺旋式楼梯，这座楼梯，似乎在一直往上、往上、往上，而你们呢，则似乎在不停地转弯、转弯、转弯。然后，突然之间，你们会再次回到光明之中，可这种光明，却要比你们见过的任何东西都漂亮。那里的每一堵墙壁，都由彩色的玻璃窗户所组成。而每一扇窗格，又是由不同的几何图形构成的。人们进来后，都会惊讶得目瞪口呆，哪怕只在里面待上一小会儿，他们就会觉得，自己再也不忍离去了呢。

礼拜堂窗户上的玻璃，都是镶嵌在石制的框架里；而那一块块的玻璃，也用铅条焊合得稳稳当当。窗户上支撑玻璃的那

framework holding the glass in the windows is called *tracery*.

As new Gothic cathedrals were built, the tracery was made in different shapes. Often you can tell in what period the cathedral was built by looking at the different shapes of the tracery.

Reims Cathedral is thought to have the best *portals*, or doorways. It also is famous for its proportion, or shape as a whole building. And many of the carved stone statues that are all over the building are famous. Unfortunately this beautiful cathedral was in a battle area during World War I and seriously damaged by German shells. After the war, the damage was repaired as carefully as possible, so that Reims looks almost the same as before.

Fortunately Reims could be repaired. The wonderful Parthenon, by the way, had its roof blown off by an explosion during a war.

The best Gothic nave is thought by many to be the nave of the cathedral at Amiens. So now let's see what we have best from these cathedrals.

⊙ the *façade* of Paris
⊙ the nave of Amiens
⊙ the doorways of Reims
⊙ the statues of Reims
⊙ the spires and glass of Chartres

些石制框架，叫作花饰窗格。

随着新的哥特式大教堂越建越多，花饰窗格的形状也变得越来越多。通过观察花饰窗格的不同形状，人们通常能够说出一座大教堂是在哪个时期修建的。

人们认为，兰斯大教堂拥有最为精美的大门，或者说入口。它还因为比例协调而著称，即整座教堂的外形非常优美。而遍布教堂上下的那些石雕，也很有名。可惜的是，这座美丽的大教堂由于在第一次世界大战期间处于交战地带，因此在德军的炮火下受到了严重的损毁。战争结束后，人们尽可能仔细地修复了那些损毁之处，因此如今的兰斯大教堂，看上去几乎与战前一模一样了。

兰斯大教堂可以进行修复，这是件好事。顺便说一句，那座奇妙无比的万神殿，殿顶却在战争期间的一次爆炸中完全炸坏了。

许多人都觉得，哥特式教堂里最优秀的中殿，当属亚眠大教堂里的那座中殿。因此，现在就让我们来看一看，这些大教堂里最精美的部分都是哪些吧。

⊙ 巴黎圣母院的正门
⊙ 亚眠大教堂的中殿
⊙ 兰斯大教堂的门廊
⊙ 兰斯大教堂的雕塑
⊙ 沙特尔大教堂的尖塔和玻璃

And let's add to our list the surprise of Saint Chapelle.

Northern France has many Gothic buildings. Almost every town has its Gothic church or cathedral. The cathedrals were built to the glory of God, and all the people added what they could to the glory of the church. All the art of the Middle Ages was found there. Paintings and stained glass, sculpture and architecture, music and tapestry, jewels and precious metals for the altar — all were part of these great buildings or of the religious services held in them.

Soaring Gothic style is so suited for a church that even today, many people think that no style of building is better for modern churches. Have you visited a Gothic church or cathedral? If so, do you remember the façade, the nave, the doorways, the statues, the spires, and the glass?

我们不妨再在其中加上：圣礼拜堂给人们带来的惊喜。

法国北部有许多的哥特式建筑。在这一地区，几乎每座城镇都建有哥特式的教堂或者大教堂。这些大教堂，都是为了颂扬神的荣光而修建的，因此所有的人都曾不遗余力地为这些教堂增光添彩。中世纪的所有艺术成就，在这一地区都可以看到。油画作品和彩色玻璃、雕塑和建筑、音乐和织锦、珠宝和建造祭坛的贵重金属，都是这些伟大建筑的组成部分，也属于在这些建筑里举行的宗教仪式的一部分。

高耸入云的哥特式风格极其适合于教堂，因此即便是到了今天，还是有许多人认为，没有别的风格比哥特式风格更适合于修建现代教堂了呢。你们有没有参观过一座哥特式的教堂或者大教堂呢？要是参观过的话，那你们还记不记得教堂的正面、中殿、门廊、雕塑、尖塔和玻璃呢？

Chapter 16 Country Cathedrals

Did you notice in the pictures in the last chapter that all the cathedrals seem to be in cities? Almost all the French Gothic cathedrals are in cities or towns. They have very little open ground around them. Dwelling houses and shops are crowded about them so close that it is often hard to get a good view of the outside of a French cathedral.

Many English Gothic cathedrals are just the opposite. They were generally built out in the country, so most of the English cathedrals have plenty of open space around them — lawns and trees instead of stores and crowded streets. They stand in beautiful settings that make the buildings themselves look even more beautiful.

Here is a question for you. Why would cathedrals be in the cities in France and in the country in England?

Well, in France the people of the towns built the cathedrals. Cathedrals were used much more often than a church is used now. The French cathedrals were the schools, the theaters, the public meeting places of the people, besides being houses for prayer and worship. They had to be in the center of things because they were so important in the lives of the people of the towns.

But in England the cathedrals were usually built by the monks for their own use. The villagers had parish churches where they could worship. Of course ordinary people could worship in the cathedrals, but the cathedrals were built chiefly for the monks. Because

第16章　乡间教堂

你们有没有注意到，上一章的图片里所示的那些大教堂，好像全都位于城市里面呢？法国的那些哥特式大教堂，差不多全都修建在城市或者市镇里。它们的四周，很少有什么空地。它们的周围，都是林立的住宅和商店，并且相互挨得很近，因此我们通常都很难好好地欣赏到一座法国教堂的外部。

而英国的许多哥特式大教堂，却正好与此相反。它们通常都修建在乡间，因此英国的绝大多数大教堂周围，都有大片大片的开阔空间，都是草坪呀、树木呀，而不是商店和拥堵的街道。它们屹立在美丽的背景之中，从而使得这些教堂本身看上去也更漂亮了。

问你们一个问题。为什么法国的大教堂都修建在城市里，而英国的大教堂却都修建在乡间呢？

好吧，在法国，是住在城镇里的人来修建大教堂。过去，人们对大教堂的利用频率，要比现今我们对小教堂的利用频率更高。法国的这些大教堂，除了是人们做祷告、做礼拜的地方，同时也是学校、剧院和公共会堂。由于它们对城市居民的生活极其重要，因此必须修建在中心位置才行。

但在英国，大教堂通常却是修道士们修建起来供自己使用的。村民们都有教区教堂，可以去教区教堂做礼拜。当然，普通百姓也可以去大教堂里做礼拜；可这

monks wanted to get away from the outside world, monasteries were more often built in the countryside. And of course the monastery or abbey church was built in the country, too.

English cathedrals are also much longer than French cathedrals. An English cathedral looks long and narrow, while a French cathedral looks short and wide. The eastern ends of the English cathedral, where the monks worshiped, had to be much longer because there were so many monks. The French cathedrals with their crowds of people who came to listen to their priest, needed a wider and shorter space so all the people could hear him. Each country shaped its cathedrals to fit the uses to which the cathedrals were put.

Here is another difference. Most of the French cathedrals have doors at their western ends opening into the nave and aisles. Most of the English cathedrals have doors at the side, as well as at the end, with little porches to keep out the wind and rain.

And here is yet another difference. Most of the French Gothic cathedrals have two towers on their western ends above the doors. But many of the English Gothic cathedrals have their main tower over the crossing of the transept and nave, and sometimes no towers at all on the western end.

An important thing to remember about Gothic cathedrals is that few cathedrals were built all at one time. In many cases the cathedral was begun as a Romanesque building and finished as a Gothic building

达勒姆大教堂，现存于英国

些大教堂，主要还是为修道士们修建的。由于修道士们都希望远离外面的尘世，因此修道院通常都是修建在乡间。所以，修道院教堂自然也是建在乡间了。

英国的大教堂，也要比法国的大教堂长得多。英国的大教堂看上去又长又窄，而法国的大教堂看上去则是又短又宽。英国的大教堂里，修道士们做礼拜的东端必须建得很长才是，因为修道士的人数实在是太多了。而法国的大教堂由于有众多民众前来聆听牧师布道，因此需要一个较短但较宽的空间，才能让所有的人都听得到牧师的声音。每个国家，都会根据大教堂的用途，来确定本国大教堂的建筑格局。

还有一个不同之处。法国的绝大多数大教堂里，西端都开有通往中殿和侧廊的大门。而英国的绝大多数大教堂里，除了西端，侧面也开有大门，并且还有小巧的、能够挡风避雨的走廊。

此外，两国的教堂还有一种差异。法国的绝大多数哥特式教堂里，西端的大门之上都建有两座塔楼。可在英国的许多哥特式教堂里，主塔却建在耳堂和中殿的交叉口上方，有的时候教堂西端根本就没有修建塔楼。

关于哥特式教堂，我们要记住的重要一点，就是很少有大教堂是一次性修建起来的。在许多情况下，教堂在动工的时候是罗马式建筑，而数年之后完工时，却变成

years later. The great Durham Cathedral, which was built in England as a church as well as a fort against the Scottish, has a Norman nave but Gothic towers. Durham is plainer and less decorated on the outside than other cathedrals, and for this reason it looks strong and solid and is very dignified.

As time went on, the Gothic style changed in England. There are really four kinds of Gothic there, corresponding to four different periods of time. Sometimes it took so long to build a cathedral that all four periods of architecture can be found in one building.

In the thirteenth century, churches were built in *Early English Gothic*. Salisbury Cathedral, with the tallest spire in England, is Early English.

Studying the shapes of the tracery is often a good way to tell in what period the cathedral was built.

In the fourteenth century

索尔兹伯里大教堂，现存于英国
（摄影：约翰·帕特森）

林肯大教堂，现存于英国
（由波士顿的大学印刷协会提供）

哥特式建筑了。英国那座杰出的达勒姆大教堂，既是一座教堂，也是一座防御苏格兰人的要塞；其中的中殿是诺曼式的，而塔楼却是哥特式的。达勒姆大教堂的外部，比其他大教堂都要朴素，没有那么多的装饰；正是由于这个原因，所以它看上去既坚固、牢靠，又很威严。

随着岁月的流逝，英国的哥特式建筑风格发生了变化。那里实际上形成了四种哥特式风格，对应四个不同的历史时期。有的时候，由于一座大教堂修建的时间太久，因此这四个时期的建筑风格，从一栋建筑上就能看出来。

十三世纪修建的教堂，属于早期英国哥特式风格。索尔兹伯里大教堂的尖塔，是全英国最高的，这座教堂就属于早期英国哥特式风格。

研究研究花饰窗格，往往是分辨一座教堂究竟修建于哪个时期的好办法。

十四世纪的建筑风格，变成了盛饰哥特式。林肯大教堂的中殿和东端，就属于

坎特伯雷大教堂，现存于英国
（摄影：约翰·帕特森）

威斯敏斯特大教堂，现存于伦敦
（由波士顿的大学印刷协会提供）

the style was *Decorated Gothic*. The nave and east end of Lincoln Cathedral is in the Decorated style.

In the fifteenth century the style was *Perpendicular Gothic*. *Perpendicular* is a long word, meaning straight up and down. The towers of Canterbury Cathedral are Perpendicular Gothic.

And last came the Tudor period. The famous chapel of Henry VII in Westminster Abbey is Tudor. Westminster Abbey itself is more like French cathedrals than most English buildings, perhaps partly because it is in a city — London. It is famous as the burial place of many of England's royalty, nobility, and famous writers.

盛饰哥特式风格。

到了十五世纪，又变成了垂直哥特式风格。“垂直”（perpendicular）是个很长的单词，它指的就是上下笔直。坎特伯雷大教堂的塔楼，就属于垂直哥特式风格。

最后，便出现了都铎王朝式风格时期。威斯敏斯特教堂里的亨利七世礼拜堂，便属于都铎王朝式风格。至于威斯敏斯特教堂本身，它与英国的绝大多数教堂相比，更像是法国的大教堂；之所以这样说，或许部分原因在于它是修建在伦敦这座城市里吧。这座教堂，以英国有许多皇室成员、贵族和著名作家葬在这里而著称。

Chapter 17 Here and There

I knew a man who spent one summer on a bicycle trip from one place in Europe to another, seeing the sights. As a young American architect, he wanted to see as many famous Gothic buildings as he could and get some exercise at the same time. He traveled 1,100 miles on his bicycle. But when the summer was almost over, he found there were certain buildings he very much wanted to see that he hadn't had time to reach, especially as they were all in different parts of Europe. So he sold his bicycle and, instead, decided to fly to these places.

First he flew to Cologne, Germany. Cologne sounds like a perfume, but it is a big city famous for its huge Gothic cathedral that I mentioned earlier. Cologne Cathedral is the largest Gothic church of northern Europe. The spires are 500 feet high — as high as ten three-story houses all stacked up. It is famous for its tall spires made of stone that look like lace, but it is also famous for something inside, a large gold triple tomb that many believe contains the bones of the three Wise Men who visited Jesus when he was first born.

Cologne Cathedral was begun in 1248 and took a very long time to build. It wasn't finished until 1880, more than 600 years later. But that was better than many cathedrals that were not finished at all and never will be now. During World War II, the whole city

第17章 欧洲各地的建筑

我认识一个人，他曾经花了整整一个夏天，骑着自行车在欧洲各地旅行、观光。他是一名年轻的美国建筑师，希望自己能够看到尽可能多的、著名的哥特式建筑，同时也可以借此锻炼锻炼身体。他骑着自行车，旅行了一千一百英里。不过，到了夏季差不多快要结束的时候，他却发现，还有一些建筑，虽说他非常想看一看，却没有时间去了；尤其是，这些建筑都分处于欧洲的不同地区。于是，他卖掉了自行车，决定坐飞机前往这些地方。

他首先飞到了德国的科隆。“科隆”听上去似乎是一种香水的牌子[1]，可实际上它却是一座大城市；我在前面已经提到过，这座城市因为拥有巨大的哥特式教堂而著称。科隆大教堂是欧洲北部最大的哥特式教堂。它的尖塔高达五百英尺，有十栋三层楼房叠起来那么高呢。虽说这座教堂以其高耸的、像是蕾丝的石制尖塔而著称，但内部还有一个地方也声名赫赫：那就是一座巨大的金色三角形陵墓。许多人都相信，其中葬有耶稣刚一出生时就来看望过他的那三位智者的尸骨哩。

科隆大教堂于1248年动工兴建，经过了很长一段时间才建成。它直到1880年，也就是六百多年之后，才彻底完工。不过，与许多根本就没有完工、而如今也不会

[1] 指著名的“古龙香水”（Cologne）。它是一种含有龙涎香与2%~3%的精油的清淡香水，最先于1709年由德国科隆人约翰•玛丽•法里纳派到意大利，推出了这款以水果和药草为原材料的淡香型香水，因而得名。

of Cologne was bombed so extensively, at the end of the war, it looked like a great fire had razed the entire city to the ground. The cathedral was badly damaged, but the spires remained, as did many other parts of the cathedral. Master craftsmen set to work to restore the mighty cathedral on the banks of the Rhine River. Today, you can see it just as it was in 1880, with a few exceptions. The stained-glass windows were replaced in a contemporary style rather than exactly the way they had once been.

You remember that some cathedrals were not completed for centuries. Part of the reason is that so much of the work had been done by hand. Another reason is that many things can happen to such a large and important building, including natural disasters or wars. A cathedral, however, was a place treasured by the people of the town and country, so often it was the very first place to be restored.

科隆大教堂，现存于科隆

Cologne Cathedral is so wide that many people do not think it as beautiful as the French cathedrals. Its twin western towers, with their tall spires, are so big and bulky at the bottom that they make the rest of the building look smaller than it is.

The proportions of one part of the building compared with another are not as fine as they might be. This means the

再有完工那一天的教堂相比，科隆大教堂还算是好的了。在第二次世界大战期间，整个科隆城都遭到了密集的轰炸，因此到了战争结束的时候，整座城市就像是被一场大火夷为了平地似的。这座大教堂也遭到了严重的损毁；可其中的尖塔，以及教堂的许多其他部位，却都幸存下来了。于是，一些工艺大师开始动工，修复这座位于莱茵河畔的、威风凛凛的大教堂。如今，你们看到的这座教堂，就是1880年时的样子，只有少数地方例外。其中的彩色玻璃窗户换成了当代的风格，而不再与曾经的风格一模一样。

你们都还记得吧，有些教堂经历了几百年都没有建成。之所以如此，部分原因在于，有很多的工作都只能通过人力来完成。而另一个原因就是，对于一座如此大型而重要的建筑来说，可能发生很多的意外事件，比如自然灾害或者战争。然而，大教堂是全市乃至全国人民都非常珍视的地方，因此，意外过后，这里往往也是人们最先进行修复的地方。

科隆大教堂非常宽阔，因此许多人都觉得它不如法国的大教堂那么漂亮。教堂西面那两座双子塔楼，连同它们上方那高耸的尖塔，都非常巨大，底部也很臃肿，从而使得教堂的其他地方看上去都比实际尺寸要小。

整座教堂各个部分的比例，并不像它们可能做到的那样精美。也就是说，教堂

building doesn't look just right as a whole, although each part by itself may be correctly and splendidly made.

Of course my young architect friend knew these faults, but he could forget the cathedral's imperfections as he gazed with awe at the thousands of carved stone figures, the *pinnacles*, towers, and flying buttresses that make this building one of the best known in the world. It is magnificent, huge, and impressive.

From Cologne my friend flew to Antwerp, Belgium. There he went to see the most impressive church in Belgium — Antwerp Cathedral. This cathedral has a place for two towers on its western front, but only one tower is there. The other one was never built. A little steeple stands where the tower might have been built.

Its one tower rises high in the air and becomes narrower at the top, like a spire. It has so much stone carving on it that, like the spires of Cologne Cathedral, it looks like lacework made of stone. The tower is graceful, but today some may think the lacy look seems a little too fancy. Antwerp Cathedral may really look better for having only one tower. Two towers might have made the building seem more towers than cathedral, like Cologne Cathedral.

This is just one of the many beautiful towers in Belgium. Many of them are not on churches at all but stand by themselves. They are often called singing towers because the bells inside ring out beautiful music. Singing towers were often useful as well as beautiful. The peal of the bells called the people together, spread an alarm in time of danger, and rang out in triumph to announce good news. Belgium can be proud of her beautiful Gothic

整体看上去并不是很协调，尽管每个部分本身修建得比例恰当、华丽优美。

我那位年轻的建筑师朋友，自然是了解这些瑕疵的；不过，当他敬畏地凝视着成千上万座石制雕像，凝视着那些小尖顶、塔楼以及飞扶壁的时候，他可能就把这座大教堂的不完美之处忘得一干二净了；正是这些地方，才令科隆大教堂成了全世界最负盛名的建筑之一。这座教堂，既富丽堂皇、硕大无比，又令人印象深刻。

随后，我的这位朋友又从科隆飞到了比利时的安特卫普。到了那里后，他便去参观比利时最引人瞩目的一座教堂，即安特卫普大教堂。这座教堂的西端，原本打算修建两座塔楼，可如今那里却只有一座塔楼。另一座塔楼，一直都没有建起来。而原本该是修建这座塔楼的地方，如今却立着一个小小的尖顶。

这座教堂的塔楼，高高地耸立在空中，顶部收窄，就像一座尖顶似的。由于这座塔楼上有许多的石雕，与科隆大教堂的尖塔一样，因此看上去就像是石制的蕾丝花边。塔楼非常优美，可如今有些人却有可能觉得，它那种花边状的样子似乎有点儿太过花哨。实际上，安特卫普大教堂只有一座塔楼，可能会比有两座塔楼更好看呢。因为两座塔楼可能会让整栋建筑看起来塔楼似乎比教堂更多，就像科隆大教堂似的。

这还只是比利时境内众多美丽塔楼中的一座。有许多的塔楼，根本就不是建在教堂顶上，而是自成一体。它们经常被称为“歌塔”，因为塔内的大钟会敲出美妙的音乐。除了漂亮，歌塔通常也很实用。钟声既可以将人们召集拢来，在危险临近的时候可以发出警报，还可以发出得胜之声，来宣布好消息。比利时完全可以为拥

安特卫普大教堂，
现存于比利时的安特卫普
（由波士顿的大学印刷协会提供）

towers.

Besides the singing towers, there are many other Gothic buildings in Belgium that aren't churches. Remember, Gothic architecture suits churches well because it seems to be trying to reach up to heaven. The most beautiful Gothic buildings are churches, but many of the other Belgian Gothic buildings are beautiful, too.

Naturally, these buildings would not be shaped like a cross. Some of then have towers and spires like churches and some do not. Some were built as town halls, where public business was carried on. Some were built as meeting halls or headquarters, for guilds.

You may recall me mentioning guilds. Each kind of trade or business had its own guild, or band of skilled workers. There were guilds of stonemasons, goldsmiths, ship captains, merchants, butchers, bakers, and candlestick makers. Of course each guild wanted its own meeting hall. Some of the Belgian guild houses show very beautiful Gothic architecture.

市政厅和市政广场，现存于布鲁塞尔
（摄影：约翰·帕特森）

有这些漂亮的哥特式塔楼而感到自豪。

除了歌塔，比利时境内，还有其他许多并非教堂的哥特式建筑。要记住，哥特式建筑风格之所以很适合于教堂，是因为这种风格的建筑，看起来都是在努力向上，想要直抵天堂。虽说最漂亮的哥特式建筑都是教堂，但比利时许多其他的哥特式建筑，也很漂亮呢。

当然，这些建筑可不会修建成十字架的格局。其中有些建筑也像教堂一样，建有塔楼和尖顶，有些建筑却没有这种东西。有些被建成了处理公共事务的市政厅。有些则建成了会堂或者同业公会的总部。

你们可能还记得，我在前面提到过同业公会。各行各业都有自己的同业公会，也就是由一群技术熟练工所组成的行会。石匠、金匠、船长、商人、屠夫、面包师以及蜡烛制造商，都有同业公会。而每个同业公会，自然也想拥有自己的会议厅。比利时的一些同业公所，都呈现出了非常漂亮的哥特式建筑风格。

The first time I ever visited Brussels, before I entered the town square with its town hall and guildhalls, I was told it was the "jewel box" of Europe. When I saw it at last, I could see why. Can you?

Many of the Gothic town halls and guildhalls had steep roofs with rows of dormer windows. A dormer window is the kind that sticks out of a sloping roof.

Let's return to my architect friend.

"From Belgium," he told me, "I flew to Spain. I wanted to see the largest Gothic cathedral in the world. It is in the little Spanish town of Burgos. The twin towers with their tall spires reminded me a little of the towers of Cologne. There is a big eight-sided tower in the middle, besides the two spires at the end. Around the cathedral at Burgos are cloisters, chapels, and an archbishop's palace."

Burgos is in the northern part of Spain and is more like French and German cathedrals than the Spanish churches farther south. The Moors from Arabia had long ruled the south of Spain, and the Gothic cathedrals there have many details that were suggested to the Spanish

布尔戈斯大教堂，
现存于西班牙的布尔戈斯

我第一次访问布鲁塞尔期间，还没等进入建有市政厅和同业公所的市政广场，就有人告诉我说，这里是整个欧洲的“珠宝盒”。而最终看到这里之后，我就明白他们为什么会那样说了。你们能明白吗？

许多哥特式风格的市政厅和同业公所，都有陡峭的屋顶和一排排的顶窗。所谓的顶窗，就是那种伸出斜面屋顶的窗户。

我们还是再来说一说我的那位建筑师朋友吧。

“从比利时，”他告诉我说，“我飞到了西班牙。我希望看一看世界上那座最大的哥特式教堂。它位于西班牙的布尔戈斯小镇上。这座教堂双子塔楼上那两个高耸的尖顶，让我有点儿想起了科隆大教堂的塔楼。除了西端的两座尖顶，教堂中央还建有一座巨大的八边形塔楼。布尔戈斯大教堂的周围，修建有回廊、礼拜堂，以及一座大主教的宅邸。”

布尔戈斯位于西班牙的北部，因此与再往南去的那些西班牙教堂相比，布尔戈斯大教堂更像是法国和德国的大教堂。来自阿拉伯半岛的摩尔人[1]，长期以来都统治着西班牙南部，因此据说那里的哥特式大教堂，有很多细节都是西班牙建筑师们从摩尔人的建筑中借鉴过来的。在本书的后面，我还会另用一章，来向你们介绍这

[1] 摩尔人（Moor），指居住在非洲西北部的、阿拉伯人与柏柏尔人的混血后代。

builders by the Moorish buildings. In another chapter I'll tell you about these Moorish buildings.

My architect friend then took a quick trip across the Pyrenees Mountains, which divide Spain from France. He flew across France and then across the Alps, to Italy. My friend knew what he wanted to see there — the Gothic buildings of Venice.

On the Square of St. Mark stands the Cathedral of St. Mark with its five domes and Byzantine architecture. Next to St. Mark's stands a long building four stories high. It is called the Doge's Palace. The Doge was the duke and ruler of Venice. The palace of the doges is Gothic (notice the pointed arches), but it is quite different from all other Gothic buildings. The two lower stories have long rows of pointed arches on columns. Rows of arches like these, you remember, are called arcades. The arcades form covered porches around the Doge's Palace.

The upper hall of the Doge's Palace has flat walls of pink and white marble in a pattern. The flat upper half of the walls makes the fancier lower half look better in just the way an old car makes a new one look even newer. If more of the Doge's Palace were like the upper part, it would be too plain. As it is, the whole building makes a beautiful part of the beautiful Square of St. Mark.

Other smaller palaces and houses in the Gothic style can be found in

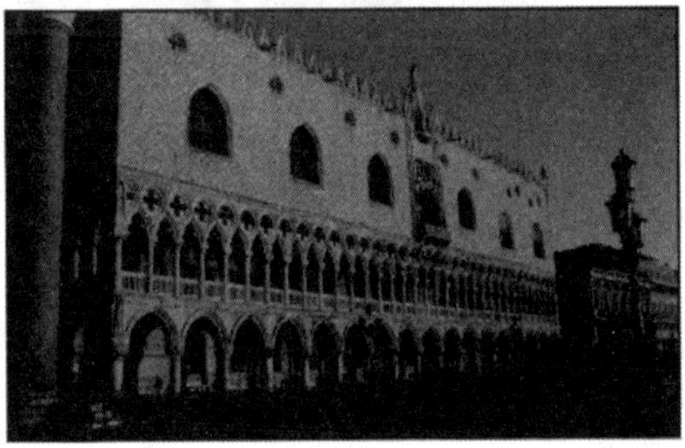

总督府，现存于威尼斯
（摄影：加里・威肯）

些摩尔式建筑的情况。

我的那位建筑师朋友，接下来迅速越过了比利牛斯山脉；这条山脉，就是法国和西班牙的国界。他飞越了整个法国，然后又越过阿尔卑斯山，抵达了意大利。我的这位朋友很清楚，自己希望在那里看到什么；那就是威尼斯的哥特式建筑。

在圣马可广场上，是有着五个穹顶、具有拜占庭建筑风格的圣马可大教堂。紧挨着圣马可大教堂的，是一栋长长的、有四层楼高的建筑。这座建筑，被称为“总督府”。总督就是威尼斯的公爵和君主。虽说总督府是哥特式的（请注意其中的尖拱），但它与其他所有的哥特式建筑都大不相同。下面两层的立柱上方，建有数排长长的尖拱。你们都还记得吧，这种长排的拱形，叫作拱廊。这些拱廊，构成了总督府四周的有顶游廊。

总督府上层大厅里的墙壁很单调，是用粉色和白色的大理石按照一定的方式搭配砌成的。墙壁上半部的单调，使得较为花哨的下半部看起来感觉更好了，就像是在一辆旧车的衬托下，一辆新车显得更新似的。如果总督府有更多的部位都像上半部一样，那就太过单调了。实际上，整座总督府构成了美丽的圣马可广场上一个美丽的组成部分。

在威尼斯，我们还可以看到其他一些较小的、属于哥特式风格的宫殿和房屋。

威尼斯的贡多拉，现存于威尼斯
（摄影：约翰·帕特森）

Venice. You have to take a boat to see them, for most of them are on streets that are made of water. A boat can take you right up to the steps leading to the front door. That's what my architect friend did. He took one of the small, private boats Venice is famous for, called a *gondola*.

Once he was home, he looked at the pictures he had taken and was very happy to show me all he had seen, such as his favorite pictures of these sights.

不过，你们必须乘坐一种船只才能看到，因为它们中的绝大多数，都修建在由水路形成的街道上。小船可以把你们直接送到通往这些建筑前门的台阶上。我的那位建筑师朋友正是这样干的。他乘坐的，就是一种威尼斯以此而著称、名叫“贡多拉”的小型私家船只。

回到家里后，他看着自己拍摄的那些照片，很高兴地向我介绍了他的所见所闻；并且还说，他最喜欢下述景点的照片。

⊙ Cologne Cathedral	⊙ 科隆大教堂
⊙ Antwerp Cathedral	⊙ 安特卫普大教堂
⊙ a singing tower of Belgium	⊙ 比利时的一座歌塔
⊙ a Gothic guildhall	⊙ 一座哥特式的同业公所
⊙ the cathedral at Burgos	⊙ 布尔戈斯大教堂
⊙ the Doge's Palace	⊙ 总督府
⊙ some small Venetian palaces	⊙ 威尼斯一些小型的宫殿
⊙ a gondola	⊙ 一艘“贡多拉”

Chapter 18 Open Sesame

Ali Baba came to the cave of the forty thieves. The door in the rock was shut. "Open sesame," said Ali Baba, and the door swung open.

Ali Baba was a Muslim, of the faith called Islam. So were Sinbad the Sailor, Prince Agib, and all the rest of those fascinating people in the *Arabian Nights*.

"Open sesame." Let's see if the magic words will open the door of this chapter to show the treasures of Islamic architecture.

You will recall that Muslims study one sacred text called the Koran or Qu'ran, which "sets the seal on" or validates the teachings of the Hebrew Bible and New Testament. Now, the Qu'ran forbids any Muslim to make a picture or a likeness of God. So you can easily guess that a Muslim place of worship, which remember is called a mosque, must be very different from a Gothic cathedral that is covered with hundreds of statues of religious figures.

Another difference you would probably notice at once if you were in Istanbul, or any other Muslim city, would be the number of domes. These domes are generally oblong instead of round, more like half an egg or an onion. They often have points on the tops, like the end of a fat turnip or beet. But not all mosques have domes, for an Islamic dome used to be the sign of a tomb, and a dome was built only when it served as a tomb.

第18章 芝麻开门

阿里巴巴来到了四十大盗所住的那个洞穴边上。岩石里面的门是关着的。“芝麻开门，”阿里巴巴说，那道门便应声打开了。

阿里巴巴是个穆斯林，信仰的是伊斯兰教。水手辛巴达、阿吉布王子以及《一千零一夜》里其他所有令人神往的人物，全都是穆斯林。

“芝麻开门。”我们不妨来看一看，这句咒语会不会打开本章的大门，会不会让你们看到门里的伊斯兰建筑宝藏吧。

你们肯定都还记得，穆斯林诵读一种圣经，叫作《可兰经》或《古兰经》，它“认可”，或者说“确认”了希伯来《圣经》和《圣经・新约》中的教义。注意，《古兰经》禁止所有穆斯林绘制上帝的画作或者肖像。因此，你们很容易就能想到，穆斯林做礼拜的地方（都还记得吧，这个地方叫作清真寺），一定与一座镶有成百上千尊宗教人物雕像的哥特式大教堂很不一样呢。

一旦来到伊斯坦布尔，或者来到其他任何一座穆斯林城市，你们很可能还会注意到另一种不同之处，那就是穹顶的数量。这些地方的穹顶通常都是椭圆形，而不是圆形的，更像是半个鸡蛋或者洋葱。它们通常有一个尖顶，像是一个胖胖的萝卜头或者甜菜头。但是，并非所有的清真寺都有穹顶，因为伊斯兰教的穹顶以前往往是坟墓的标志；因此，只有一栋建筑用作陵墓时，才会修建穹顶。

倘若走近一栋伊斯兰风格的建筑细看，你们就会注意到，修建这些建筑的人，

When you get close to an Islamic building, you notice that the builders must have been good carvers of stone and marble, even if their religion does not allow carving religious statues. Their carving is a pattern, a seemingly endless repeating pattern, of straight lines and curves, squares and circles, diamond shapes and star shapes, zigzags, and crisscrosses. Some of the carving is so fine that it forms a network that looks like stone lace.

Inside, the carvings and decorations become even richer than those outside. The designs are called *arabesques* because the first Muslims were Arabs, and the Arabs built many mosques decorated in this way. Sometimes the arabesques are writings from the Koran. And beautiful writing, called *calligraphy*, does the same thing as pictures and sculpture in Christian churches. The Arabian letters are graceful and make beautiful decorations. In fact, sometimes the words are impossible to read, even for a person who knows Arabic, because the words are so ornate. Still, they inspire the person praying. After all, the stained-glass pictures high up in a Gothic cathedral are hard to see in detail, as is the sculpture high up on the Parthenon. Still they inspire everyone who enters. Holy words are like holy images.

Inside these Islamic buildings we are apt to find still another form of decoration that other buildings do not have. The vaults under the domes (the ceilings of the rooms) often have a curious carved work that looks like hundreds of little stone icicles hanging down from the roof.

Remember that in every mosque is at least one minaret or tower for the muezzin, a man

必定都是一些石雕高手，尽管他们信仰的宗教并不允许他们去雕刻宗教塑像。他们雕刻的都是一种图案，一种似乎永无休止地重复着的图案，由直线和曲线、方形和圆圈、菱形和星形、锯齿形和十字形构成。其中有些雕刻作品非常精美，因此形成了一种网状，看上去就像是石制的蕾丝花边似的。

而在建筑里面，雕刻作品和装饰品甚至比建筑物外部还要丰富。其中的图案，叫作阿拉伯式花纹[1]，因为最初的穆斯林都是阿拉伯人，而阿拉伯人修建的许多清真寺，也都是用这种花纹做装饰的。有的时候，阿拉伯式花纹实际上就是源自《古兰经》上的经文。而那种叫作“书法”的漂亮笔迹，也可以起到与基督教堂里的绘画和雕塑作品相同的作用呢。阿拉伯字母都很优美，因而可以做漂亮的装饰品。事实上，有的时候，甚至是一个懂阿拉伯语的人，也不可能认出其中的文字来，因为这些文字都装饰得非常华丽。尽管如此，它们还是会给祷告的人带来启发。毕竟，一座哥特式大教堂里那些高高在上的彩色玻璃图画是很难看清的，就像万神殿里那些高高在上的雕塑作品一样。可尽管如此，它们也会给走进万神殿里的每一个人带来震撼。神圣的文字与神圣的图像是一样的。

在伊斯兰建筑的内部，我们往往能够看到其他风格的建筑所没有的另一种装饰形式。拱顶之下的穹隆（即下面房间的天花板）上，经常会有一种古怪的雕刻作品，看上去就像是成百上千根小石柱从屋顶上垂了下来似的。

记住，每座清真寺里至少会有一座宣礼塔或尖塔，宣礼员每天都会爬上去五次，

---

[1] 阿拉伯式花纹（arabesque），亦称“蔓藤花纹”。

who climbs up five times a day to call the people to prayer. Some of the mosques have a minaret at each corner.

"Come to prayer, come to prayer. There is no God but Allah and Mohammed is his prophet," sings the muezzin, and then all observant Muslims face toward the sacred city of Mecca and kneel in prayer. Mecca is the sacred city because Mohammed himself was born and lived there. Each mosque has a niche or hollow in the wall pointing toward Mecca, to show worshippers which way to face in prayer. There are no seats in a mosque, just many rugs placed side by side, and, as you have already read, people take off their shoes before they walk in to sit on the rugs and face Mecca.

Islam spread quickly from Arabia where it started, for the Arabs were great conquerors. Eastward it spread, farther and farther, through Persia and across India. Baghdad became the capital city of these eastern Muslims.

The Arabs pushed westward across Egypt and northern Africa until they came to the Strait of Gibraltar, which separates

阿尔罕布拉宫[1]的阿拉伯式花纹细部，
现存于西班牙的格拉纳达

召唤人们做祷告。有些清真寺里，四个角上都各有一座宣礼塔。

“来做祷告，来做祷告。真主安拉，就是上帝；穆罕默德，就是先知。”宣礼员会如此颂唱，然后所有虔诚的穆斯林便会脸朝麦加圣城的方向，跪下来做祷告。麦加之所以被称为圣城，是因为穆罕默德本人正是在麦加出生的，并且在那里生活。每座清真寺里都有一个壁龛，也就是墙壁上有个洞，朝着麦加那个方向，用以表明信徒应当脸朝哪个方向做祷告。清真寺里没有设置座位，只是地上并排铺着许多小地毯；并且，像你们在前面已经看到的那样，人们会脱下鞋子再进去，然后脸朝麦加的方向坐在地毯上。

伊斯兰教从阿拉伯半岛发源后，便迅速传播开来，因为阿拉伯人都是些了不起的征服者。这种宗教向东扩张，传播的距离越来越远，并且经由波斯，席卷了印度。于是，巴格达便成了这些东方穆斯林地区的首都。

阿拉伯人还向西推进，横跨了埃及和整个北非，最终到达了直布罗陀海峡；这条海峡，将西班牙和北非隔了开来。但是，这条海峡并没有阻挡住阿拉伯人的脚

[1] 阿尔罕布拉宫（Alhambra），摩尔人建于十三世纪至十四世纪期间的一座皇宫，位于西班牙的格拉纳达，全称为 Alhambra Palace。

northern Africa from Spain. This did not stop them. They built boats and sailed across to Spain. All of Europe might have become Muslim if the French had not stopped the Arabs in a battle fought at the town of Poitiers, France.

But much of Spain did become Muslim. The Arabs in Spain were called Moors. The Moors set up a capital at Cordova for all the western Muslims, just as Baghdad was the eastern capital, just as the Roman Empire had once had an eastern and western capital — Rome and Constantinople. For over 700 years the Moors ruled in Spain until they were finally driven out about the time of Columbus.

In Cordova the Moors built a huge mosque that is still standing. You remember how the Muslims turned the Christian church of St. Sophia in Constantinople into a mosque. Well, in Cordova just the opposite happened. For when the Moors were finally driven out of Spain, the Christians turned the Muslim mosque into a church. And a church it still is.

When visiting the famous cathedral, you can see how clever the architects were because they found ways to build a church inside a mosque and keep the

科尔多瓦大教堂内景细部，
现存于西班牙的科尔多瓦

步。他们建造起船只，然后渡海进入了西班牙。要不是法国人在普瓦捷市的一场战斗中挡住了阿拉伯人的话，那么整个欧洲可能早已变成伊斯兰国家了呢。

不过，西班牙的很多地方的确皈依了伊斯兰教。西班牙的那些阿拉伯人被称为摩尔人。在科尔多瓦，摩尔人为所有的西方穆斯林兴建了一个首都，就像巴格达是东方穆斯林的首都，就像古罗马帝国曾经也有罗马和君士坦丁堡一西一东两座都城那样。摩尔人统治了西班牙达七百年之久，直到哥伦布航海那个时期，他们才最终被赶出了西班牙。

在科尔多瓦，摩尔人修建了一座巨型的清真寺；如今，这座清真寺仍然屹立在那里。你们都还记得，穆斯林是怎样把君士坦丁堡的那座圣索菲亚基督教堂改成了清真寺的吧。好了，在科尔多瓦，情况却恰好相反。这是因为，摩尔人被赶出西班牙后，西班牙的基督徒便将这座清真寺改成了一座教堂。如今，这里仍然是一座基督教堂呢。

科尔多瓦大教堂里的拱廊细部，
现存于西班牙的科尔多瓦
（摄影：约翰·帕特森）

在参观这座著名的大教堂时，你们就可以看出，设计建造这座大教堂的那些建

阿尔罕布拉宫里的狮子院，
现存于西班牙的格拉纳达

best parts of each.

But by far the most famous Muslim building in Spain is the Alhambra. The Alhambra was built by the Moorish kings of Granada in Spain as a kind of fortress palace. The Alhambra is on a tall hill of rock with steep cliffs that helped keep back enemies. Inside the different buildings are guardrooms and halls, gardens and courts, all decorated with thousands of arabesques.

The Court of Lions is one part of the Alhambra that you may have heard of. It looks something like a cloister, for around its four sides are arcades. A big marble basin, held on the backs of twelve lions, is used as a fountain and stands in the middle of the room.

And now I'm sure you are going to ask a trick question. It's tricky because so many people don't get the answer. "How could the Moors have marble lions if they were not supposed to carve statues?"

筑师有多聪明了；因为他们既找到了在一座清真寺内修建一座教堂的办法，同时又保留下了清真寺和基督教堂各自的精华。

不过，迄今为止，西班牙国内最著名的穆斯林建筑，还是阿尔罕布拉宫。阿尔罕布拉宫是西班牙格拉纳达的摩尔人国王修建的，本来是一座城堡宫殿。阿尔罕布拉宫建在一座高耸的石山上，那里崖壁峭立，有助于抵御敌人的进攻。城堡内部，有卫兵室和大厅、花园和庭院等各式建筑，全都装饰着成千上万种阿拉伯式花纹。

“狮子院”是阿尔罕布拉宫的一部分，你们可能都听说过这个地方吧。这个院子，看上去有点儿像是一座修道院，因为它的四面都有拱廊。院子中央十二头狮子背上驮着的那个巨型大理石盆，其实是喷泉呢。

现在，我敢肯定，你们正打算提出一个捉弄人的问题吧。之所以说它捉弄人，是因为许多人都不知道答案。这个问题就是：“假如不让摩尔人制作雕像的话，那么他们又怎么可能有石狮子呢？”

The answer is that the Moors could carve statues or paint pictures, as long as the subjects were not *religious*. Look at the picture of the lions and the arcade. Do you see any arabesques?

Now I'm going to take you far from Spain in the West, to India in the East. In Agra, India, lived a Muslim ruler who erected a building in honor of his wife. You will be surprised to hear what kind of building it was. It was a tomb! And yet his wife was still alive when he built it.

That seems strange to us, but it was the custom there. It was a sensible custom, at that, for the ruler and his wife used the tomb as a kind of reception hall where visitors were received and parties were held. Then when the rulers died they were buried there.

This tomb is called the Taj Mahal. Because it was a tomb, it was crowned with a dome. Many travelers have called it the most beautiful building in the world. They have even placed it ahead of the Parthenon. The Taj Mahal is built all of marble, with semiprecious jewels laid into the stone in some places as decoration. It shines in the Sun like a beautiful white jewel with colored designs in it. Around the building are gardens, trees, lawns, and fountains. Directly in front of it is a long rectangular pool of water that reflects the trees and the Taj Mahal, too.

And with the Taj Mahal we will end our story of Islamic buildings, saying as Ali Baba might say to close the chapter, "Shut sesame."

答案就是，摩尔人还是可以制作雕像和绘制画作的，只要雕塑或绘画的对象与宗教无关就行了。看一看图片中的石狮子和拱廊吧。你们看得见其中的阿拉伯式花纹吗？

现在，我打算将你们带得远远的，从西方的西班牙带到东方的印度去。在印度的阿格拉，曾经有一位穆斯林君主；他修建了一座建筑，来向自己的妻子致敬。你们得知那是一种什么样的建筑之后，肯定会大吃一惊的。它竟然是一座陵墓！而且，在修建这座陵墓的时候，他的妻子仍然健在呢。

虽说在我们看来，这种做法很奇怪，可那里的风俗就是这样。而且，这也是一种合情合理的风俗，因为那位国王和他的妻子曾经也把这座陵墓当成过会客室，在这里接待客人、举办宴会呢。然后，待国王夫妇去世后，他们就葬在这里了。

这座陵墓，叫作泰姬陵。正因为那是一座陵墓，因此上面才是一个穹顶。许多游客都称，它是世界上最漂亮的一座建筑。他们甚至还把泰姬陵排在万神殿的前面哩。泰姬陵完全用大理石建成，有些部位的石头上，还嵌有次等宝石作为装饰。在阳光之下，它熠熠生辉，宛如一颗美丽的、绘有彩色图案的白珍珠。泰姬陵的周围，建有花园、树木、草坪和喷泉。它的正前方，则是一个长长的、呈长方形的水池，水中倒映着周围的树木，还有泰姬陵的美丽倩影。

我们就用泰姬陵来结束关于伊斯兰风格建筑的这个故事，并且用阿里巴巴的那句咒语："芝麻关门"，来结束这一章吧。

Chapter 19 Dome Trouble

Once upon a time a cathedral was being built in Florence, Italy. The cathedral was almost finished except for a huge dome on top. Then one day the workmen had to stop work and leave the cathedral unfinished. The architect, the only person who knew how to build a dome big enough for this cathedral, had died. He had left no drawings or plans to guide the builders. He had told no one how he thought the dome should be built.

So for over 100 years, the cathedral at Florence stood there with a big hole in the crossing where the dome should have been. Can you imagine how that must have looked? Finally it was decided to hold a competition and see if anyone could be found who could build the dome and thus finish the cathedral.

In the competition many plans were suggested. One man said he was sure he could build the dome, but there would need to be a big column underneath the center to hold it up. Another man said he could build it, but he would have to have the help of a big pile of earth.

"If," said this one, "we mix gold coins with the earth and put this earth in a huge pile where the dome is to be, then we can build the dome around the pile. When the dome is completed, invite the people to carry off the earth to look for the coins. When all the earth is carried away, there will stand our dome."

It would have been like looking for a needle in a haystack.

第19章 穹顶的麻烦

很久以前，意大利的佛罗伦萨正在修建一座大教堂。除了最上面的那个巨型穹顶，这座大教堂差不多算完工了。接下来有一天，工人们却不得不停了下来，让整座大教堂都处于未完工的状态了。这是因为，唯一知道给这座大教堂修建那么大一座穹顶的那位建筑师去世了。他既没有留下图样，也没有留下设计图来指导工人们继续修建穹顶。他也没有跟任何人说起过，他认为这座穹顶应当如何来修建。

因此，在一百多年的时间里，佛罗伦萨的这座大教堂便一直矗立在那里；而本该是穹顶的那个交叉口，也一直都是一个大窟窿。你们想象得出那是一种什么样子吗？最终，人们决定举办一场比赛，看能不能找到一个有本事修建穹顶的人，来建完这座大教堂。

在比赛中，人们提出了很多的设计方案。有人说，他确定自己能够修建这座穹顶，只是穹顶下方中央需要有一根巨大的立柱来支撑才行。还有人说，他能够修建穹顶，但需要借助一个大土堆才能完成。

"如果，"这个人说，"我们把金币与泥土混合起来，在修建穹顶的地方堆起一座巨型土堆的话，那我们就可以绕着这个土堆来修建穹顶了。而当穹顶完工后，我们又可以邀请人们来寻找土堆里的金币，从而将土运走。所有泥土都运走之后，我们的穹顶就会屹立在那里了。"

这一过程，真像是在大海里捞针啊。

The man who won the competition and got the job was named Brunelleschi. He had studied the ancient Roman buildings in Rome. He had worked as a sculptor, and he was also a very good architect. Brunelleschi said he could build the dome, and that he could construct it without the wooden centering that would use up so much timber. But in spite of Brunelleschi's confidence, the men in the charge didn't feel quite so sure. So they also named Ghiberti as an architect for the dome.

Now, Ghiberti was a fine sculptor — his Gates of Paradise prove that — but he really had no idea how to build the dome. Therefore, he did no work on it, although he was getting as much pay for the jobs as Brunelleschi, who did all the planning.

Of course this didn't please Brunelleschi at all. So Brunelleschi made believe he was sick and stayed home in bed. Then the workmen had to stop work, for Ghiberti didn't know what to tell them to do next. As long as Brunelleschi stayed in bed, the work waited.

In spite of this, Ghiberti was not taken from the job, so Brunelleschi had to try another way of getting rid of him. He told the men in charge that he thought it best to divide the work between the two architects.

"There are two difficult things to be done," said Brunelleschi, "the bridges upon which the masons must stand and the chain that is to bind together the eight sides of the dome. Let Ghiberti take one of them, and I will take the other, that no more time be lost."

This did the trick. Ghiberti chose the chain but couldn't make it work. He was soon taken off the job, and Brunelleschi could go ahead alone.

Brunelleschi finished the dome successfully. It is a different kind of dome from that of

最终，赢得比赛并且接受了这一任务的那个人，名叫布鲁内莱斯基。他在罗马研究过古罗马时期的建筑。他曾经做过雕塑家，可同时也是一位非常杰出的建筑师。布鲁内莱斯基说，他不但可以修建穹顶，同时还无须搭建那种颇耗木材的木质拱架。不过，尽管布鲁内莱斯基信心满满，可主管这事的那些人却觉得很没有把握。因此，他们后来又指定吉贝尔蒂为修建这座穹顶的建筑师。

注意，虽说吉贝尔蒂是一位优秀的雕塑家（他的作品“天堂之门”就证明了这一点），可实际上他却根本不知道如何去修建这座穹顶。因此，他完全没有出力；可他拿的报酬，却跟一手设计这座穹顶的布鲁内莱斯基一样多！

自然，这让布鲁内莱斯基觉得很是恼火。于是，布鲁内莱斯基便假装生了病，躺在自家床上不起来。这样一来，工人们不得不停工，因为吉贝尔蒂不知道吩咐工人们接下来应当如何干。布鲁内莱斯基在床上躺了多久，工程就停了多久。

尽管如此，吉贝尔蒂还是没有调走；于是，布鲁内莱斯基不得不另想办法，来赶走吉贝尔蒂。他对管事的人说，最好还是让两位建筑师分工，各干一部分活儿。

“有两大难题需要解决，” 布鲁内莱斯基说，“一是泥瓦匠们所站的架子，二是将穹顶八个面联成一体的链子。让吉贝尔蒂选一个吧，剩下的那个由我来解决，这样就再也不会浪费时间了。”

这个主意成功了。吉贝尔蒂选择了链子的问题，可他无法解决。他很快便被解雇，而布鲁内莱斯基就可以一个人继续干下去了。

布鲁内莱斯基成功地建成了这座穹顶。它不但与罗马万神殿里的穹顶不属于

the Roman Pantheon, and it is different from the dome of Hagia Sophia. The dome is of brick, with ribs of stone running down from the top. These ribs divide the dome into eight parts or sides, so it isn't smoothly round like most domes. For another thing, this dome has a little *cupola* or tower on top. This is known as a *lantern* although there is no light burning inside.

佛罗伦萨大教堂穹顶细部，
现存于佛罗伦萨
（摄影：约翰·帕特森）

Just how Brunelleschi managed to build the dome without using centering remains a mystery. But he did build it — and built it well. Today it still rises above the roofs of Florence to be seen from far and near, one of the great domes of the world. It gives to the cathedral its name, the Duomo. If you go to Florence, you will see a statue of Brunelleschi near the Duomo. He is shown seated, looking up at the dome, with plans on his lap.

There is still another reason for telling you about Brunelleschi. He was the first architect of a new kind of architecture known as Renaissance.

As I have told you, the Renaissance was a rebirth of interest in worldly life — in writing, painting, sculpture, and architecture. It was

同一类型，而且与圣索菲亚大教堂里的穹顶也大不一样。这座穹顶是用砖头砌成的，从上到下还有多条石制肋拱。这些肋拱，将整个穹顶分成了八个部分，或者说分成了八个面；因此，它并不像绝大多数穹顶那样浑圆一体。而另一方面，在这座穹顶上头，还建有一座小小的顶篷，或者说一座小塔。这座小塔被称为“灯塔”，尽管里面并没有点灯。

布鲁内莱斯基究竟是如何在不用拱架的情况下建起了这座穹顶，迄今仍然是一个谜。可他的确建成了，并且修建得非常好。如今，这座穹顶依然耸立在佛罗伦萨其他建筑的屋顶之上，很远就能看到，属于世界上最了不起的穹顶之一。那座大教堂的名称也由此而来，叫作杜莫主教堂[1]。要是你们去佛罗伦萨的话，就会看到，杜莫主教堂附近屹立着一尊布鲁内莱斯基的雕像。雕像中的布鲁内莱斯基坐在那里，仰头看着那座穹顶，而膝盖上则放着穹顶的设计图。

之所以跟你们介绍布鲁内莱斯基的情况，还有另一个原因。他是一种新的、叫作“文艺复兴式”建筑风格时期的第一位建筑师。

我在前面已经跟你们说过，“文艺复兴”运动，是人们重新燃起对世俗生活，

[1] “杜莫”（Duomo）是“穹顶”（dome）一词在意大利语里的拼法。如今，它专用于指大教堂或者中央教堂。

especially a rebirth of interest in everything left by the ancient Greeks and Romans. I have told you that Brunelleschi studied the ancient Roman ruins. He had measured them, drawn pictures of them, and learned all he could about them. So when Brunelleschi designed buildings, he used the kinds of columns, decorations, vaults, and plans that he admired from studying the Roman ruins. I don't mean he built copies of Roman buildings. He just used them to go by. And so did all the Italian architects after Brunelleschi.

The Italians didn't care for Gothic architecture much, anyway. There was too much sunlight in Italy for churches with walls of glass. The Italians liked their buildings dark and cool inside, instead of full of sunlight, even if the sunlight did come through the marvelous stained-glass windows of a Gothic cathedral. Perhaps that is because Gothic architecture built in the north, where it is cooler and darker, needed more light, while Renaissance architecture built in the south, where it is hotter and brighter, needed more shade.

This new Renaissance architecture was good in many ways, but in some ways it was not so good. The Gothic buildings had always been built so that every part of the building had its own special job to do. The buttresses were to push against the walls. The decorations carved on top of the

佛罗伦萨大教堂的穹顶和钟楼，
现存于佛罗伦萨
（摄影：加里·威肯）

比如对文学、对绘画、对雕塑和建筑的兴趣的过程。它尤其是人们对古希腊人和古罗马人所留下的一切重新燃起兴趣的过程。我已经告诉过你们，布鲁内莱斯基曾经研究过古罗马的废墟。他给这些废墟进行过测量、绘制过图画，尽可能地了解过它们的情况。因此，布鲁内莱斯基在设计建筑的时候，便运用了他在研究古罗马废墟过程中所崇拜的那种立柱、装饰、拱顶和设计方案。我可不是说，他修建的都是古罗马建筑的仿制品。他只是按照古罗马建筑的风格来进行设计罢了。而布鲁内莱斯基之后，意大利的所有建筑师也都这样干过呢。

总之，意大利人都不太喜欢哥特式的建筑风格。意大利阳光充足，不太适合修建带有玻璃墙壁的教堂。意大利人都喜欢让他们的建筑内部保持阴暗、凉爽，而不是充满阳光；哪怕阳光只是从一座哥特式大教堂里那些奇妙的彩色玻璃窗户中透射进来，他们也不喜欢。或许原因就在于，北部地区凉爽、阴天多，需要更多的光线，因此修建哥特式建筑；而南部地区炎热、晴朗，需要更多阴凉，因而多修建“文艺复兴”风格的建筑。

虽说这种新的“文艺复兴”式建筑风格许多方面都是不错的，但也有一些方面不是那么好。修建哥特式建筑时，建筑的每个部分始终都有自己特定的用途。扶壁是用来顶住墙壁的。扶壁顶部的装饰性雕刻，是为了增加扶壁的重量，使之能够更

buttresses were to give them more weight so they could hold more solidly. The stained-glass windows and the statues were to tell the Bible stories to people who couldn't read. There was scarcely any part of a Gothic building that was not honest or useful.

But the Renaissance buildings weren't always made up of so many useful parts. Often they were designed just to look good. Columns and pilasters were put on for decoration, without really helping to hold up anything, as columns should. An ornament, many would agree, should look like an ornament, not like a column that should be a hardworking, load-bearing support.

Sometimes a Renaissance architect would cover a Gothic building with Renaissance ornament, to make it look like a Renaissance building.

The best artists of the Renaissance became architects and designed buildings. New Gothic cathedrals ceased to be built. Indeed, there were almost enough churches already, and so most of the Renaissance buildings were palaces or government buildings or libraries.

加稳固地支撑墙壁。教堂里的彩色玻璃窗户和雕像，是为了给那些不识字的人描述《圣经》故事的。一栋哥特式风格的建筑里，几乎没有哪个部位不是实打实或者有用途的。

可“文艺复兴”风格的建筑，却并非始终都是由那么多实用性部位所组成的。在设计它们的时候，通常都只是为了美观。修建立柱和半露方柱，都是为了起装饰作用，而不是像立柱本来的作用那样，真正有助于支撑什么东西。其实，许多人都会同意说，一件装饰品看上去就该像是一件装饰品，而不能像是一根原本就该辛辛苦苦、支撑重量的立柱。

有的时候，“文艺复兴”风格的建筑师还会在一栋哥特式的建筑上，添加“文艺复兴”风格的装饰，以便使之看上去像是一栋“文艺复兴”风格的建筑。

“文艺复兴”时期那些最杰出的画家，后来都成了建筑师，都设计过建筑。人们不再新建哥特式的大教堂了。事实上，由于当时已经有了足够多的教堂，因此绝大多数属于“文艺复兴”风格的建筑，都是宫殿、政府大楼或者图书馆了。

Chapter 20 Backward and Forward

In 1492 Columbus arrived in America. Everyone knows that date. And so it is easy to remember when Renaissance architecture began in Italy because it was about the same time. Some of the earliest Renaissance buildings of the 1400s are the best. The Riccardi Palace in Florence is one example. It looks more like a fort than a palace, and that is what it really was on the outside — a fort.

There was so much fighting going on that these palaces in Florence had to be built like forts. There are iron bars on the lower windows. There are heavy rough stones in the lower story. That kind of stonework is called *rusticated*. The stones bulge out from the joints between them. This makes the building look strong and solid.

A ledge that sticks out all around the wall crowns the top of the building. This type of ledge is called a cornice. The cornice keeps the building from looking like a plain box. The cornice finishes off the top of a building just the way a capital finished off the top of a column. The windows have round arches, not pointed ones like Gothic windows.

The building is even more like a palace inside than outside. In the middle of the inside is an open courtyard with balconies around it. There is a big banqueting hall, a library, and other finely furnished rooms. This Renaissance building is called the Riccardi Palace because Riccardi was the name of the family who bought it from the Medici family, who

第20章 回顾与前行

1492年，哥伦布抵达了美洲。大家都熟悉这个年份。因此，你们也不难记住意大利开创“文艺复兴”式建筑风格的时间，因为这个时间也正是1492年左右。十五世纪一些最早的“文艺复兴”式建筑，都曾是最杰出的建筑。佛罗伦萨的里卡迪宫，就是一个例子。它看上去更像是一座要塞，不像是一座宫殿；而从它的外部来看，实际上也正是如此：它就是一座要塞。

当时，由于到处都在打仗，因此佛罗伦萨的这些宫殿都不得不建得像要塞一样。下层窗户上，都焊有铁条。宫殿底层，则是用又厚又粗的石头砌成的。那种石墙，叫作粗琢墙。墙上的石头，都从接缝处向外凸起。这使得整座宫殿看上去既牢固又结实。

宫殿顶上，是沿着四周墙壁向外突出的壁架。这种壁架，叫作“飞檐”。飞檐使得整栋建筑不至于看起来像是一个简简单单的盒子。用飞檐给一栋建筑封顶，就像是用柱头给一根立柱封顶那样。宫殿里的窗户上都有圆拱，而不是哥特式窗户上的那种尖拱。

整栋建筑的内部，比外部更像是一座宫殿。宫殿内部的中央，有一个露天的院子，周围都建有阳台。里面有一座大型的宴会厅、一座图书馆，还有其他一些装修精美的房间。这栋“文艺复兴”风格的建筑之所以称为里卡迪宫，是因为那个从美第奇家族手中购得这座建筑的人姓里卡迪，而这座宫殿本来是美第奇家族修建起

built it and first lived there.

Now is a good time to notice a great big difference between Gothic and Renaissance buildings. In Gothic buildings most of the lines are up and down, so the eye is carried from the ground straight up to the top of the building. But in Renaissance buildings most of the lines are horizontal. In the Riccardi Palace, your eye notices the horizontal lines of stones, the windows all in line, the horizontal ledges under the windows, and the long, straight cornice.

Now take a moment and think back to the last chapter, where I told you about Brunelleschi. Several famous Renaissance architects followed Brunelleschi. One named Bramante planned for a great cathedral to be built in Rome for the Pope. It was to be the largest church in the world and was to be called St. Peter's. But Bramante died before much work had been done. Several other architects worked on this big building, until it was finally given into the care of the mighty Michelangelo, who was the greatest Renaissance sculptor as well as a great painter, poet, and wonderful architect. Michelangelo's plan was to have the church built in the form of a Greek cross, with its four arms of equal length, with a magnificent dome over the middle. Michelangelo was an old man, but he

里卡迪宫，现存于佛罗伦萨
（由缅因州桑福德的大学印刷协会提供）

来，用于居住的。

现在，我们就能注意到哥特式建筑和“文艺复兴”风格的建筑之间，存在一种极其重大的差异了。在哥特式的建筑里，绝大部分线条都是上下纵向的，因此会让人们的目光从地面一直往上，直到建筑物的顶部。但在“文艺复兴”风格的建筑里，绝大多数线条却都是横向的。在里卡迪宫里，你们会看到石头上的水平线条、排成横排的窗户、窗户下方水平的壁架，以及又长又直的飞檐。

现在，请停下来回想一下上一章；在上一章里，我曾经给你们介绍过布鲁内莱斯基的故事。布鲁内莱斯基之后，又出现了好几位“文艺复兴”风格的著名建筑师。其中有一位叫伯拉孟特，他设计了一座杰出的大教堂。这座大教堂，原本是要为教皇在罗马修建的。它本来会是世界上最大的一座教堂，并且本来应当叫作“圣彼得大教堂”的。可是，还没干多久，伯拉孟特就去世了。之后，其他好几位建筑师都接手修建过这座大型建筑，而最终这一任务则落到了伟大的米开朗琪罗头上；他是“文艺复兴”时期最伟大的雕塑家，同时也是一位杰出的画家、诗人和一位了不起的建筑师。米开朗琪罗计划将这座教堂建成希腊十字架结构，即四臂等长的十字架结构，并在中央部位修建一座壮观的穹顶。虽说当时的米开朗琪罗已经年老体

pushed the work forward on St. Peter's so that it was almost finished at his death.

Michelangelo made everything about St. Peter's so large that the cathedral doesn't look as large as it really is. That sounds funny, I know. You'd think the bigger a thing was, the bigger it would look. That isn't always so.

It depends on something called scale. If you take a photograph of a tree, you can't tell from the photograph how big the tree is unless there is a man or a dog or a house or something near the tree to give you some way of measuring. (It is the same with a map. You can't tell whether a town is 30 miles away or 300 miles unless there is a scale by which to measure.)

The windows of St. Peter's are about four times as tall as a man. So unless you see a man near them, you would naturally think they were about four times as small as they are, since most windows are about as tall as *one*

罗马圣彼得大教堂前面的广场
（摄影：约翰·帕特森）

圣彼得大教堂的穹顶细部，现存于罗马
（摄影：约翰·帕特森）

衰，可他还是尽力推进圣彼得大教堂的修建工作，因此到他去世的时候，这座教堂基本上完工了。

由于米开朗琪罗把圣彼得大教堂的各个部位都设计得非常庞大，因此这座大教堂看上去似乎没有实际的那么大。我知道，这一点听起来是很不可思议的。你们可能会想，东西的尺寸越大，看上去也会越大啊。可实际上，情况却并非始终如此。

这一点，取决于一种叫作“比例”的东西。如果你们拍了一张照片，上面是一棵树的话，那么，除非照片中这棵树的附近有个人、有条狗、有栋房子或者其他什么东西，能够让你们进行参照测量，否则你们就无法仅凭照片，说出这棵树究竟有多大。（地图也是一样。除非地图上标明了进行测量的比例尺，否则你们就没法判断出一座城镇究竟是在三十英里外呢，还是在三百英里以外。）

圣彼得大教堂里的窗户，每一扇都有差不多四个人高。因此，除非你们看到窗户附近有个人，否则的话，你们自然就会觉得，它们都只有实际的四分之一那样大，因为绝大多数窗户看上去，都跟一个人的身高差不多。这就是圣彼得大教堂存

man. That is the great trouble with St. Peter's. It lacks scale, so even when you are there, you cannot even imagine the size and proportion of things unless you can see people as a comparison.

罗马圣彼得大教堂平面图
（由波士顿的大学印刷协会提供）

From the bottom rim of the great dome, for example, you can look down at the canopy under which the pope leads services. Leading to the floor below is a double staircase that goes down to the burial places of the popes. Perhaps in this picture, you can see the people far below and begin to see how high the bottom of the dome really is.

Long after Michelangelo had died, another architect added a new front to the cathedral, and this cut off the front view of Michelangelo's wonderful dome. This architect also made the church a Latin cross by extending the front. Then still later another artist named Bernini added two *colonnades*, or rows of columns, to the front. These rows of columns are built around two sides of a great circular open space out in front of the cathedral. They look like big arms, welcoming you.

The colonnades by Bernini are beautiful, but they

罗马圣彼得大教堂内景
（摄影：加里·威青）

在的一个严重问题。它缺乏参照比例，因此就算你们来到教堂里，也无法判断出东西的大小和比例来，除非看得见别人，用别人来当参照物。

比方说，从那座大穹顶的底圈，你们可以俯瞰到一座天篷；教皇就是在这座天篷下面，率领信徒做礼拜的。一条双层楼梯通往天篷之下的地面，并且一直向下，通到了历任教皇下葬的地方。或许，在这张照片中，你们能够看到远处于下方的那些人，就能看出穹顶底部究竟有多高了。

米开朗琪罗去世很久之后，另一位建筑师又给这座大教堂添上了一座新的正门，从而让人们从大教堂的正面，再也看不到米开朗琪罗修建的那座杰出的穹顶了。这位建筑师还延长了大教堂的前部，使得整个教堂变成了拉丁十字架格局。再后来，又有一位名叫贝尔尼尼的建筑师，给教堂的前部增添了两条由一排排立柱所组成的柱廊。这几排立柱，都矗立在大教堂前部外面一块巨大的圆形露天空地两侧。它们就像是两支巨臂，伸开来欢迎你们呢。

贝尔尼尼修建的这两条柱廊非常漂亮，但它们同样缺少参照比例，就跟大教堂

lack scale, just as the cathedral itself does. Look very closely at the picture, and you will see some people in the square. When you measure the cathedral by them, you get some idea of how big it really is.

Look at the plan of St. Peter's, showing the cathedral itself. At the top of the plan, you will see the arrangement of the Bernini colonnades.

圣彼得大教堂的柱廊，现存于罗马
（摄影：约翰·帕特森）

Gothic columns were never really very much like Roman columns. But the Renaissance architects used the Roman capitals on the columns of their buildings. Sometimes they even pulled down Roman buildings and used the columns for new Renaissance buildings. Notice, too, the columns, which are like Roman columns.

There are two secret places in St. Peter's Square. The double row of columns is so perfectly lined up that you cannot see the second behind the first when you stand in just the right place. It is fun to walk toward this special place because,

圣彼得大教堂柱廊里的立柱细部，
现存于罗马
（摄影：约翰·帕特森）

本身的情况一样。仔细观看这张照片，你们就会看到，广场里有一些人。倘若把这些人物当成大教堂的参照物，那你们就能看出这座教堂究竟有多大了。

再来看一看显示了教堂主体的那幅圣彼得大教堂平面图。在平面图的最上方，你们就会看到贝尔尼尼所建柱廊的格局。

哥特式的立柱，事实上一直都不太像古罗马式的立柱。不过，“文艺复兴”风格的建筑师，却在他们所建的立柱上，利用了古罗马式的柱头。有的时候，他们甚至还会推倒古罗马式的建筑，将原来的立柱用于新建的、属于“文艺复兴”风格的建筑呢。还要注意，他们所用的立柱，也与古罗马式的立柱很相似。

在圣彼得广场上，有两个隐秘的地方。由于柱廊里的那两排立柱排列得非常完美，因此，倘若正好站在合适的位置，那么你们就只能看到一根立柱，而看不到后面的第二根。朝着这个特定的位置走过去，是一件很有意思的事情；因为随着你们向前走，除了你们正前方的那一排之外，所

圆厅别墅，现存于意大利的维琴察

as you do, all those columns slowly disappear, leaving only the row in front for you to see.

You probably know that Michelangelo did many things with perfection as a painter, a sculptor, and an architect. Did you know that he also designed clothing? The uniform of the Swiss Guard with its ribboned sleeves and pantaloons have one color on the outside and another on the inside. Can you imagine anything Michelangelo could not do well?

There were many famous Renaissance architects in Italy, and they have left many famous buildings. A man named Palladio was famous for his special use of columns. The columns ran from the ground up past two or three stories. This is called the Palladian style because Palladio wrote a book about it that architects in Italy and other countries found very useful.

His book is still in print and used so widely that it has made Palladio the most copied architect of all. Today buildings from Russia to the United Kingdom to the United States have buildings based on designs from his famous book.

有立柱便会慢慢地在你们的眼前消失。

你们很可能都知道，米开朗琪罗创作出了许多完美的作品，因为他既是画家、雕塑家，也是建筑师。可你们知不知道，他也设计过服装呢？他给罗马教皇手下的瑞士侍卫兵设计的制服，上衣衣袖上饰有缎带，下身是马裤，并且制服外面是一种颜色，里面又是一种颜色呢。你们想象得出，米开朗琪罗还有什么事情做不好吗？

意大利还有许多著名的、属于“文艺复兴”式风格的建筑师，他们也留下了许多著名的建筑作品。有位名叫帕拉迪奥的建筑师，就以特别擅长于利用立柱而著称。他修建的立柱，从地面一直往上，有两三层楼高。这种风格之所以被称为帕拉迪奥风格，是因为他曾经写过一本书来介绍这种风格；后来，意大利和其他各国的建筑师也都发现，这种建筑风格非常实用呢。

如今，他的这本著作仍在出版，并且得到了广泛应用，从而使得帕拉迪奥成了人们最喜欢仿效的一位建筑师。如今，从俄罗斯到英国，再到美国，到处都有根据他这本名著中的设计方案而修建起来的建筑呢。

When you look at Palladio's buildings, you can see that he knew the history of architecture of Greece and Rome so well. He used many parts over and over again with great success. Look at this house in the country on a farm, called a *villa*. You can see parts of so many buildings I have told you about, that the villa may look familiar to you even though you have not seen it before.

All styles of architecture grow out of earlier styles. Renaissance architecture grew by looking backward toward Rome, but its use came at a time when the world was looking forward to greater things. Explorers, scientists, and thinkers were showing the way to modern times, though they were getting some of their ideas from studying ancient ways. They were looking backward but moving forward. Renaissance architecture spread from Italy to other countries and has been used ever since.

在欣赏帕拉迪奥的建筑时，你们就可以看出，对古希腊和古罗马的建筑史，他简直可以说了如指掌。很多地方他都重复运用了一遍又一遍，可每次都运用得极为成功。看看下面这栋位于乡间农场上的房子吧；这种房子，叫作“别墅”。从图片中，你们可以看出我向你们介绍过的诸多建筑部位来；因此，即便你们以前没有看见过，这种别墅可能也会让你们看上去觉得很熟悉呢。

所有的建筑风格，其实都是由早期的风格发展演化而来的。“文艺复兴”式的建筑风格，是在回顾古罗马时期建筑风格的基础上发展起来的；而应用这种风格的，却是世界正在期待着做出更大成就的一个时期。探险家、科学家和思想家，全都在指出让世界通往现代的道路；可他们的一些思想，其实是在研究古人生活方式的过程中产生出来的。他们虽说是在向后看，其实是在向前迈进。“文艺复兴”式的建筑风格，从意大利传播到了其他国家，然后被人们一直沿用到了今天。

Chapter 21 The Homes of England

Have you ever been locked up? I knew a boy who was locked up by mistake. He hadn't done anything bad, and he wasn't locked up in jail.

The boy had gone to a big museum to see the paintings. He walked and walked through gallery after gallery, until his feet hurt and he felt very tired. When he saw a comfortable sofa in one of the rooms, he sat down to rest. The sofa was so comfortable that the boy fell fast asleep.

When he woke up, everything was dark. Of course, he was a little frightened. Who wouldn't be! Great stone statues of Egyptian kings looked black all around him. He hurried to the door, but the door was locked!

He called and yelled and pounded on the door, but the museum had been closed for the night and no one heard him. There was nothing for the poor boy to do but stay there all night. When the doors were unlocked the next morning, you can imagine how surprised the guards were to find a very scared and very hungry boy waiting to get out.

A museum isn't a comfortable place to live, even for just one night. The boy who got locked up found that out. And almost all the buildings you have read about in this book would make very poor homes. Who would want to live in the Parthenon, or St. Sophia, or the Leaning Tower of Pisa, or Reims Cathedral? Even the castles and palaces of the

第21章 英国的住宅

你们有没有被人关起来过呢？我认识一个小男孩，他就曾经被无意中关起来过。当然，他并没有干什么坏事，也不是被关到了监狱里。

当时，这个小男孩到一座大型博物馆里去看画展。他不停地走，从一个画廊走到另一个画廊，最后脚都走疼了，觉得非常累。于是，当他看到一个房间里有张舒适的沙发后，便决定坐上去休息休息。由于那张沙发非常舒适，因此这个小男孩便在上面熟睡过去了。

他醒来后，发现到处都黑乎乎的。当然，他有一点点害怕。谁都会害怕呢！他的周围，全是一尊尊古希腊国王的巨石雕像，看上去都黑黝黝的。他赶紧向门口跑去，可大门却锁上了！

他大声叫喊，用手锤门；但是，由于博物馆夜间闭馆，因此没人听到他的喊声。这个可怜的小男孩什么办法也没有，只能整夜都待在博物馆里了。你们完全想象得出，第二天上午博物馆开门，保安发现这个吓得不轻、又饿又累、等着出去的小男孩时，会是多么吃惊呀。

博物馆可不是一个适合居住的好地方，哪怕只住一个晚上也不行。那个被关在博物馆里的小男孩，已经明白了这一点。而你们在本书中业已了解到的差不多所有建筑，也都是不适合居住的。谁会希望自己住在万神殿、圣索菲亚大教堂、比萨斜塔或者兰斯大教堂里呢？即便是那些“文艺复兴”式风格的城堡和宫殿，要是没有

Renaissance would be inconvenient as homes without a great number of servants to keep them in order.

Yet from the very earliest times people have lived in houses. Why haven't these houses been more important in the story of architecture?

One reason is that the houses people live in are not generally built to last as long as a great temple or cathedral. Houses were often built of wood that gradually decayed. Houses wore out just as shoes or shirts or ships do. Old houses were torn down to make room for new ones. Many burned down. So a dwelling as old as a Greek temple would be very hard to find.

Houses that people live in, however, are often more truly interesting than the great celebrated buildings. For instance, I like the everyday houses of England more than I like the big, handsome, famous public buildings built since the English Gothic cathedrals. I think you may like them more, too. I'll tell you about them.

Gothic architecture in England had been slowly changing, until the later Gothic buildings looked quite different from the early Gothic buildings. By the time Queen Elizabeth began to rule in 1558, English Gothic architecture had changed so much that it could hardly be called Gothic anymore, so it was give a special name.

The English rulers at this time belonged to the Tudor family, and the architecture was called Tudor. Tudor architecture was between Gothic and Renaissance architecture. It came after the true Gothic had died out and before the true Renaissance architecture had

一大群仆人来清洁、整理的话，住在里面也是很不方便的哩。

可是，从很古老的时代起，人们就是住在房屋里了。那么，为什么住宅在建筑史上，却没有显得比其他建筑更加重要呢？

其中的一个原因就是，人们居住的房子，通常建造得都不像大型神庙或者大教堂那样牢固和经久耐用。住宅常常都是木质建筑，一般都会腐朽。与鞋子、衣服或者船只一样，住宅也会磨损。人们会将老旧的住宅推倒，给新住宅腾出地方来。许多住宅还被火灾焚毁了。因此，像一座古希腊神庙那样历史悠久的住宅，我们是很难看到的。

然而，人们居住的住宅，其实往往要比那些声名赫赫的建筑更有意思。比如说，与那些自英国哥特式大教堂以来修建的大型、漂亮而著名的公共建筑相比，我就更喜欢英国那些普通的住宅。我觉得，你们可能也会更喜欢这些住宅呢。下面，我就来跟你们说一说这些住宅。

英国的哥特式建筑风格，一直都在缓慢地改变着；最终，后来的哥特式建筑变得与早期的哥特式建筑大相径庭了。到1558年伊丽莎白女王登基的时候，英国哥特式建筑的风格已经有了巨大的变化，以至它们都难以再称为哥特式了，于是人们便给这种风格专门起了一个名称。

由于这一时期英国的君主都属于都铎王室，因此这种建筑风格便称为都铎王朝式风格。都铎王朝式建筑风格，属于从哥特式过渡到“文艺复兴”式建筑风格的中间阶段。它是在真正的哥特式建筑风格消失之后，真正的“文艺复兴”风格进入英国之前出现的。都铎王朝式建筑风格，属于所有英国建筑中最具有英国特色的一种

哈登庄园，现存于英国的德比郡
（由波士顿的大学印刷协会提供）

come to England. Tudor architecture is the most English of all English architecture.

Manor houses took the place of the medieval castles. A manor house is not a castle or a palace, but is the main house — that is often very grand — for the owners of a very large farm called an estate. Several of the old manor houses of this Tudor period are still standing. They have big bay windows that stick out from the walls, sometimes three stories high. The Tudor windows often had flat tops instead of pointed arch tops like the Gothic, but most of them still had stone tracery in them like the Gothic.

The windows were not arranged in even rows like the windows of the Riccardi Palace in Italy. Wherever a room needed a window, there a window would be put. In the same way, the chimneys were put wherever a fireplace was needed, and not just so they would look good from the outside. Often the chimneys were round like columns, instead of square, and some were twisted like corkscrews.

风格。

此时，庄园式的宅邸取代了中世纪的那种城堡。庄园宅邸并不是一座城堡或者宫殿，而是一个拥有一座巨型农场（叫作庄园）的人所住的正房。有好几座都铎王朝式风格时期修建起来的古老庄园式宅邸，如今依然存在呢。它们都有着一扇扇巨大的、从墙体上向外凸出的飘窗；有时，这种飘窗甚至还有三层楼高。都铎王朝式风格的窗户之上，通常都是平顶，而不是哥特式建筑上的那种尖拱；不过，其中绝大多数窗户上，却仍然有与哥特式相似的那种石制花窗格。

而这些窗户，也与意大利里卡迪宫的窗户不一样；它们并不是一排一排，整齐地排列着。只要哪个房间需要窗户，就会开上一个窗户。同样，无论什么地方需要安装壁炉，那么就会在壁炉上方修建烟囱，而不是仅仅为了外观漂亮才修建烟囱。烟囱通常都是圆形的，像立柱一样，而不是方形的；有些烟囱，甚至还是螺旋形的呢。

都铎王朝式风格的住宅都非常实用，而不仅仅具有装饰作用；因此，我们称之

莎士比亚故居，现存于英国埃文河畔的斯特拉特福
（摄影：约翰·帕特森）

The Tudor houses were so useful, not just decorative, that we say they are *honest architecture*. They were built to be comfortable and useful homes, not for show with all the beauty on the outside. That is one thing that makes them so pleasant and homelike to look at. They were built of whatever materials could be found in the neighborhood — sometimes stone, sometimes brick, sometimes partly wood and plaster. They seemed to fit into the landscape as if they had grown there.

Now here's a paragraph you'll probably have to read twice because there are so many insides and outsides to it. As a Tudor house was built for a home, the inside was considered more important than the outside. The outside was not put on the way Italian Renaissance outsides were, to make a pretty picture. The outside was really just the outside of the inside. But a Renaissance building was built for the outside effect. The Renaissance inside was just the inside of the outside. That is really a big difference when you think of

为“诚实的建筑”。它们都被建成了舒适、实用的住宅，而不是大肆炫耀其外部的美观。它们之所以都是一些赏心悦目、亲切如家的建筑，原因之一就在这里。附近地区有什么材料，人们就会使用什么材料来建造房屋；有的时候是石头，有的时候是砖块，有的时候是部分用木材、部分用灰泥。它们看上去都融入了山水之间，好像是从山水中自然生长出来的。

注意，这一段你们很可能得看上两遍才行，因为其中出现了许多的“内部”和“外部”。由于都铎王朝式风格的房子都是为住家而修建的，因此人们认为房子的内部比外部更加重要。它们的外部，修建方式与意大利“文艺复兴”式风格的建筑外部不同，不会把外部变成一幅漂亮的图画。也就是说，建筑外部实际上是服从于建筑内部需要的外部。可一栋“文艺复兴”式风格的建筑，却很讲究外部效果。“文艺复兴”式风格的建筑内部，却是服从于其外部需要的内部。仔细想一想这个，你们就会看出，这确实是一种重大的差异呢。上面的话，把你们搞糊涂了吧？

安妮·海瑟威的小木屋，现存于英国的休特利
（摄影：约翰·帕特森）

it. Does all that mix you up? Then read it once more and probably you can get straightened out.

Indoors on the first floor of a Tudor manor house was the great hall. On the second floor there was often a long gallery, or hall, running the length of the building. This long gallery connected the rooms of the second story and was also often used as a place to hang the family portraits.

Besides the manor houses, there are many smaller houses of this period still left in England. These often have the first story built of brick and stone and the higher stories of oak timbers as a framework. The spaces between the timbers are filled in with brick and plaster. The dark timbers against the white plaster make a very striking effect. One little girl always calls them zebra houses because of the stripes, but their proper name is *half-timbered houses*.

Many of the jolly-looking little old inns and taverns of England are in half-timbered

要是这样的话，那就再看一遍，然后你们很可能就会理解了。

一栋都铎王朝式风格的房子里，第一层往往是一个巨大的厅堂。第二层上，通常都有一条与建筑等长的长廊，或者走廊。这条长廊，将二楼上的各个房间连通起来，并且通常还用于悬挂家人的画像。

除了庄园宅邸，这一时期英国还有许多较小的住宅，如今也依然保留着。这些房屋，第一层通常都是用砖头、石块修建的，而上面各层则是橡木结构。而木头之间的空隙，也全都用砖头和灰泥填满了。黑色的木头和白色的灰泥，形成了一种非常醒目的效果。有个小姑娘，曾经因为那种黑白条纹而总是把这种房屋称为“斑马房子”；可它们的正式名称，却是“半木结构建筑”。

英国有许多看上去令人觉得非常愉快的、古老的小酒馆和小客栈，它们都是半

style. Here the stagecoaches used to stop, and travelers would find the inns cozy and warm after a long day's journey. Some of these old inns have memorable names like the Fighting Cocks, or the Fox and the Hounds, the Six Bells, the Dolphin, the Feathers, or the Eagle and Child.

Two small half-timbered houses have become so famous that you may have seen pictures of them. They are famous as homes. One was the home of the Shakespeare family, and in it William Shakespeare was born. The other was the home of Anne Hathaway, the woman whom Shakespeare married. Here is a picture of the birthplace of Shakespeare in Stratford-on-Avon.

Honest, picturesque, comfortable — don't you like these homes of England?

木结构的。过去的驿站马车，都会在这些酒馆和客栈停留；而旅人在经历了一整天的长途跋涉之后，也会发现这些客栈非常舒适、温馨。这些古老的客栈中，有一些的名字令人过目难忘，比如“斗鸡酒馆”、“狐狸和猎犬客栈”、“六只铃铛”、“海豚旅舍”、“羽毛酒馆”或者“老鹰与儿童客栈”等。

有两座半木结构的小房子举世闻名，因此你们可能都已经看见过它们的照片了。它们都是著名的住宅。其中一座，便是莎士比亚家族的住宅，威廉·莎士比亚便出生在那里。另一座则是安妮·海瑟威的家，她后来嫁给了莎士比亚。上面的照片中，有一张便是莎士比亚在埃文河畔斯特拉特福的出生地。

朴实、别致，而且舒适；你们喜欢英国的这些住宅吗？

Chapter 22 Trademarks

You have heard of a fireproof building. But have you ever heard of a fireproof animal? A little animal that looks like a lizard and is called a salamander was always supposed to be fireproof. The people of the sixteenth century thought that if they put a salamander in the fire, the salamander wouldn't mind it a bit. In fact, the hotter the fire, the more he'd like it.

In those days of the sixteenth century, there reigned in France a king named Francis I whose badge was a salamander. Francis I also used a capital letter F as a badge. The salamander and the letter F were like trademarks, and this king had them put on all the many buildings he built during his reign.

Francis I was a powerful monarch with plenty of money to spend. He delighted in spending money on the works of the best painters, goldsmiths, sculptors, and architects. Many of the painters, goldsmiths, and sculptors were Italians who came to work for Francis I. The architects were mostly Frenchmen.

The buildings of these French Renaissance architects were different from the Italian Renaissance buildings. Most of the French Renaissance buildings were still Gothic in shape. The lines still ran vertically up from the ground as they did in the Gothic style. You remember the horizontal lines of some of the Italian Renaissance buildings. This difference was because the Renaissance in France changed from Gothic little by little,

第22章 “商标”

你们都听说过能够防火的建筑吧。可你们有没有听说过能够防火的动物呢？有一种样子像是蜥蜴的小动物，叫作“火蛇”，人们一直都认为它能够防火呢。十六世纪的人认为，如果把一条火蛇放进火中的话，火蛇根本就不会被烧死。事实上，火烧得越旺，火蛇就越喜欢呢。

在十六世纪的时候，法国有位国王，叫作弗朗西斯一世；他所用的徽章上的标志，就是一条火蛇。弗朗西斯一世还把大写字母F也当成自己的徽章标志。他用的火蛇和大写字母F，就像是两个商标；因为这位国王，曾经把自己在位时修建的许多建筑，全都打上了这两个商标呢。

弗朗西斯一世是一位强大的君主，有花不完的钱。他喜欢花巨资，收购那些最优秀的画家、金匠、雕塑家和建筑师的作品。许多画家、金匠和雕塑家都是意大利人，他们纷纷前来为弗朗西斯一世效力。而建筑师呢，绝大多数却是法国人。

这些属于“文艺复兴”式风格的法国建筑师修建的建筑，与意大利“文艺复兴”式风格的建筑都不一样。法国绝大多数“文艺复兴”式风格的建筑，在外形上仍属于哥特式风格。建筑的线条仍然像哥特式风格一样，是从地面垂直向上的。你们都还记得意大利一些“文艺复兴”式风格的建筑里的横向线条吧。之所以存在此种差别，是因为法国的“文艺复兴”式风格是从哥特式风格一点一点地演变而来

while in Italy the Renaissance was not a slow change, but a sudden break from the Gothic. After all, the Italians had ancient buildings scattered all around their country, to remind them of Classical architecture, so they revived that style first.

In Italy many of the Renaissance buildings were churches. In France there were already plenty of fine Gothic churches. Most of the French Renaissance buildings, therefore, were palaces and castles, called *chateaux*. So many of these chateaux were built along the Loire River in France that the valley of this river is known as the chateau country.

A very famous chateau still stands at Blois in the chateau country. Parts of the Chateau of Blois were built in the Gothic style before the Renaissance reached France, but one whole section was built by Francis I in the Renaissance style. This section is called the Wing of Francis I.

There is a celebrated spiral staircase attached to the outside wall of the building in an open tower — something like a fire escape. The staircase tower is stone and marble, like the rest of the building. The salamander and the letter F are carved again and again on the staircase. The salamanders are royal salamanders, and each has a crown above him. Little flames of fire seem to be flying all around the salamanders. These "trademarks" of Francis I are on other parts of the building, as you can see in the picture.

布洛瓦城堡的“弗朗西斯一世之翼”，现存于法国的布洛瓦
（由波士顿的大学印刷协会提供）

的；可意大利进入“文艺复兴”式风格，却不是一个缓慢的过程，而是突然摆脱了哥特式风格之后出现的。毕竟，古代建筑散布于意大利全国各地，使得意大利人想起了经典的建筑风格，从而率先重新采用了那种风格。

在意大利，许多属于“文艺复兴”式风格的建筑，都是教堂。而在法国，当时已经有了大量建筑精美的哥特式教堂。因此，法国绝大部分属于“文艺复兴”式风格的建筑，都是宫殿和城堡；这些城堡，在法语里称为“沙托”。由于许多城堡都是沿着法国的卢瓦尔河而建，因此卢瓦尔河河谷还被人们称为“城堡之乡”。

有座非常著名的城堡，如今仍然屹立在这个“城堡之乡”的布洛瓦。布洛瓦城堡的许多部位，都是“文艺复兴”式风格进入法国之前，用哥特式风格修建的；可其中有一整段，却是由弗朗西斯一世用“文艺复兴”式风格修建起来的。因此，这一段便称为“弗朗西斯一世之翼”。

这座城堡的外墙上，有一条著名的螺旋形楼梯；它修建在一座露天塔楼里，有点儿像是消防通道呢。这座楼梯塔，与城堡的其他部位一样，都是用石块和大理石建成的。楼梯上，到处都雕有火蛇和大写字母F的图案。这种火蛇图案，属于皇室专用图案；因此，其中每条火蛇的头上，都戴有一顶皇冠。城堡里的其他部位，也都带有弗朗西斯一世的这种“商标”，你们在图中就能看出来。

Notice that the building is still Gothic enough to have Gothic gargoyles sticking out from the staircase and the roof.

If you walked down the staircase at the Chateau of Blois and someone else started to walk up at the same time, you two would meet on the stairs. But there is another staircase in France where persons going down never meet persons going up at the same time. It sounds mysterious, but it really happens just that way. The pass-without- meeting staircase is in the central tower of a large chateau at Chambord, and is the part every visitor wants to see before leaving.

Any student who likes to read of knights and ladies in the days of chivalry will get a thrill at seeing the Chateau of Chambord. It is a huge castle, partly fortified and once protected by a moat, or ditch of water that surrounds the castle. It has towers, steep roofs, tall chimneys, and thick stone walls. With its towers and chimneys pointing toward the sky, it really looks more Gothic than Renaissance.

The pass-without-meeting staircase is in the tallest tower and works the way it does because there are two sets of steps which corkscrew up the tower together, one set above the other. The Statue of Liberty in New York has an iron staircase inside it built the same way as the stone staircase

布洛瓦城堡的"弗朗西斯一世之翼"及楼梯，现存于法国的布洛瓦
（由波士顿的大学印刷协会提供）

注意，这座城堡仍然呈现出了众多的哥特式风格，因而楼梯和屋顶上都修建了许多向外凸出的雨漏。

假如你们沿着布洛瓦城堡的这座楼梯而下，而另一个人同时沿楼梯而上的话，那你们两人就会在楼梯上相遇。可法国还有一座楼梯，下楼梯的人与同时上楼梯的人永远都不会相遇。这听起来很神秘，可实际情况就是如此。这座"对面不相逢"的楼梯，位于尚博尔一座大型城堡的中央塔楼里；每位游客倘若没有看到这座楼梯，都是不会离去的。

每个喜欢阅读关于骑士时代里的骑士和贵妇故事的学生，在看到尚博尔城堡时，都是会激动不已的。这是一座巨大的城堡，部分地方修建有防御工事，曾经还有一条护城河加以保护；所谓的护城河，就是环绕着城堡的一条水沟。城堡里有许多的塔楼，有陡峭的屋顶、高耸的烟囱和厚厚的石墙。由于塔楼和烟囱都直指苍穹，因此城堡实际上看起来更像是哥特式风格，而不是"文艺复兴"式风格哩。

那座"对面不相逢"的楼梯，位于城堡最高的那座塔楼里；而它之所以"对面不相逢"，是因为有两条楼梯一起沿着塔楼旋转而上，其中一条楼梯在上，一条在下。纽约的"自由女神像"内部也有一座铁楼梯，其建造方法与尚博尔城堡里的这

at Chambord. That should come as no surprise since the Statue of Liberty was made in France as a gift for America.

Francis I liked to stay at Chambord when he wanted a change from city life. He liked to stay at Blois, too. But he liked best of all the palace of Fontainebleau, which is noted for its beautiful gardens, terraces, and lakes, and for its rich interiors. The outside of the palace buildings aren't as interesting as Chambord and Blois, so we'll hurry on to still another palace of Francis I. This is the Louvre in Paris.

"But I thought the Louvre was a museum!" you say. So it is now, the second biggest art museum in the world — after the Hermitage Museum in St. Petersburg in Russia — but it wasn't built as a museum. Kings of France built it for their use as a palace — just as the Hermitage Museum once was as well.

The Louvre is so big that just one gallery is a quarter of a mile long. It would take you hours and hours just to walk all through it. Perhaps you can see that it is large enough that the king, as the story goes, could have earth brought in and laid down on the floor, then trees in boxes brought in to make the palace look like a garden or forest.

For entertainment, the king and nobility would ride ponies to hunt foxes let loose in the palace. Of course, such a palace could not be built all at one time. Francis I built

尚博尔城堡，现存于法国的卢瓦尔河谷

座石制楼梯是一样的。由于“自由女神像”是法国建造并送给美国的一件礼物，所以这一点就不足为奇了。

弗朗西斯一世厌倦了城市生活，想要换换环境的时候，是很喜欢待在尚博尔城堡里的。他也喜欢去布洛瓦城堡。不过，他最喜欢去的，还是枫丹白露宫；那里以拥有美丽的花园、阳台、湖泊以及内部装饰奢华而著称。这座宫殿的外部，并不像尚博尔城堡和布洛瓦城堡那样有意思，因此我们还是赶紧去看一看弗朗西斯一世的另一座宫殿吧。那座宫殿，就是巴黎的卢浮宫。

“可是，我还以为卢浮宫是一座博物馆呢！”你们没准会说。如今，卢浮宫确实是一座博物馆，并且仅次于俄罗斯圣彼得堡的冬宫博物馆，属于世界上第二大艺术博物馆了；不过，最初修建的时候，它却并非是一座博物馆。法国国王修建卢浮宫，是将它用作皇宫，供自己使用的；而俄罗斯的冬宫博物馆，起初也是这样呢。

卢浮宫极其庞大，一条走廊就达四分之一英里长呢。光是走遍其中的所有区域，就得花上好几个小时。由此，或许你们就能看出，正如传说的那样，由于卢浮宫实在是太大了，因此法国国王肯定是命人将土运过来铺在地上，然后再用箱子把树一棵棵地运进来种上，才让整个皇宫看上去就像是一座花园或者森林。

作为消遣，国王和贵族们还会骑上小马，在这座宫殿里随心所欲地猎狐呢。当然，这样一座宫殿是不可能一次建成的。弗朗西斯一世修建了其中的一部分。然

part of it. Then other kings added other parts. It wasn't finished until late in the nineteenth century. So the Louvre is a good building to study for a complete history of Renaissance architecture in France, from the earliest to the latest styles.

The Louvre is so big that a photograph doesn't do it justice. In a photograph you can only see one part of it at a time, and as each main part looks quite different from its other parts, you really have to be in Paris and see it for yourself to get a good view of it.

Two of the most important of the many architects of the Louvre were Pierre Lescot and Claude Perrault. Lescot was the architect for Francis I. Perrault's work came a century later. Perrault did the famous east facade with its long row of coupled Corinthian columns. The strange fact is that Perrault was the king's doctor, not an architect at all, but he managed to do a very good job on the east facade of the Louvre.

The Louvre was used as the king's palace until the French Revolution, although the last several kings of France preferred to live outside Paris in the Palace of Versailles. After the revolution, the Louvre was made into a national art museum, and it has been one ever since.

You remember that I have told you famous buildings do not stop changing just because they have become famous. Well, that is the case with the Louvre as well. The palace museum had a C-shaped cobblestone courtyard that surrounded the entrance. For many years, it was difficult for the museum to find the best way to greet visitors and help them find the sections they most wanted to visit, so a plan was devised. A famous modem architect named I. M. Pei, a Chinese American, was asked to solve the problem. Can you

后，其他历任国王又增建了其他的部位。直到十九世纪晚期，这座宫殿才全部完工。因此，卢浮宫极适合于我们去研究法国“文艺复兴”式建筑从最早期直到最晚期风格的完整历史。

由于卢浮宫极其庞大，因此一张照片可呈现不了它的全貌。拍一张照片，你们一次只能看到卢浮宫的一个部位；而由于每个主要部位看上去都与其他地方风格迥异，因此你们实际上只有直接去巴黎，亲眼去看一看，才能充分了解这座建筑。

在设计修建卢浮宫的诸多建筑师当中，最重要的两位就是皮埃尔·莱斯科与克劳德·佩劳。莱斯科就是曾经为弗朗西斯一世效力的那位建筑师。佩劳则比他晚了一个世纪。佩劳修建了卢浮宫著名的东向正面，那里建有一长排科林斯式对柱。奇怪的是，佩劳本是国王的御医，根本就不是建筑师，可他最终竟然将卢浮宫的东面设计建造得非常出色。

直到法国大革命之前，卢浮宫都是国王的皇宫；但法国的最后几任国王，却都更愿意住到巴黎郊外的凡尔赛宫去。法国大革命后，卢浮宫变成了一座国家艺术博物馆，并且此后便一直如此了。

你们都还记得吧，我曾经跟你们说过，著名的建筑正是因为它们声名远播，因而一直都在发生变化。好吧，这种情况也适用于卢浮宫。这座宫殿式博物馆的入口周围，是一个呈C字形的、用卵石铺成的院子。多年来，博物馆都找不到一种欢迎游客并且帮助游客找到他们最希望参观区域的最佳办法；于是，人们便想出了一个计划。著名的现代建筑设计师、美籍华人贝聿明被请来解决这一问题。你们猜得出他

imagine what he did?

Pei thought about ancient Egypt and the pyramids, and then decided to take the courtyard apart and build an entrance hall for visitors where the earth had once been. What do you suppose he did to cover the enormous new hole in the courtyard grounds? He put a very large glass pyramid on top so you could see where to go, but, at the same time, the new structure would not block the view of the original palace.

When his workmen were digging, they found many layers of building underneath the palace that told story beneath story about the buildings that once stood there long before the Louvre. So, today, if you visit the Louvre, you can see not only the palace with its collection of art, but take a walk through the history of Paris beneath a new glass pyramid!

Let us return to our original story now. Although Francis I was showy and spent too much money in building, there was a later French king who was even more showy and spent even more money in building even more magnificent palaces. This king was Louis XIV, whose architect built the tremendous palace of Versailles.

Later kings added to the palace of Versailles until France became a republic. It is now owned and cared for by the French Government. Its beautifully laid-out grounds add to the magnificence of the palace. The

卢浮宫，现存于巴黎
（摄影：约翰·帕特森）

的解决办法是什么吗？

贝聿明想到了古埃及和金字塔，便决定将那个院子分开来，并且在原来的泥土地面上修建一个游客接待大厅。你们觉得，他会如何来盖住院中那个新划出来的巨大空间呢？告诉你们吧，他在大厅顶上修建了一座巨大的玻璃金字塔；这样一来，既能让游客知道自己要去哪儿，同时这个新建的结构又不会挡住人们的视线，使游客可以欣赏到宫殿的原貌了。

就在他所率的工人向下挖掘的过程中，他们发现宫殿下方还有多层建筑，从而说明了修建卢浮宫之前，这里曾经有过那一层又一层建筑物的情况。因此，如今去参观卢浮宫的时候，你们不但可以欣赏到这座宫殿本身和其中收藏的艺术品，还可以在一座新建的玻璃金字塔之下，徒步穿越整个巴黎的历史了！

现在，还是让我们回到原先的主题上来吧。尽管弗朗西斯一世喜欢炫耀，花了很多的钱修建建筑，可后来还有一位法国国王，甚至比他还要喜欢炫耀，比他还花了更多的钱，来修建更加金碧辉煌的宫殿呢。这位国王，就是路易十四；而他手下的建筑师，则设计修建了那座巨大的凡尔赛宫。

后来的历任国王都曾扩充过凡尔赛宫，直到法国变成一个共和国为止。现在，凡尔赛宫归法国政府所有，归法国政府管理了。它那一座座布局精美的庭院，让整座宫殿更显壮观。宫殿各个部分本身都非常相似，都是又长又很规则。其中最著名

buildings themselves are very much alike, for they are long and regular. The most famous part is the Hall of Mirrors, a gigantic room with mirrors along the walls. The peace treaty that ended World War I was signed in the Hall of Mirrors. That treaty led to the formation of a union of countries that wanted peace. Its original name was the League of Nations, but it was later to be called the United Nations.

凡尔赛宫里的镜厅，现存于法国的凡尔赛
（摄影：约翰·帕特森）

At Versailles, not very far from the big palace, are other, smaller places where the royal family lived with more quiet than the grand palace allowed. There is a pink palace, a smaller golden palace, and a village as if it was in the countryside — all places built by Louis XV that became the favorite residences of Marie Antoinette, his queen, who was later beheaded in the French Revolution.

The French Revolution brings us almost up to the nineteenth century. During the nineteenth century

小特里亚农宫，现存于法国的凡尔赛
（由波士顿的大学印刷协会提供）

的部分就是镜厅，是墙壁上全都挂着镜子的一个巨大的房间。结束了第一次世界大战的那份和约[1]，就是在这个镜厅里签署的。那份和约，促成了一个希望和平的国家联盟的成立。这个联盟，起初叫作国际联盟，后来又改名叫作联合国了。

在凡尔赛，离这座大型皇宫不远的地方，还有一些较小的宫殿；皇室成员们住在这里，可以享受到比那座大型皇宫更多的宁静。这里有一座粉色的宫殿、一座较小的金色宫殿，还有一个小村庄，好像这里是乡间似的；所有这些宫殿，全都是路易十五修建的，后来成了他的王后玛丽–安托瓦内特[2]最喜欢住的地方，而在随后的法国大革命中，玛丽–安托瓦内特却被砍掉了脑袋。

法国大革命差不多把我们直接带入了十九世纪。在十九世纪，法国人又修建了数栋后来变得举世闻名的建筑。其中一座，便是荣军院的穹顶；这是路易十四命人

[1] 即《凡尔赛和约》，全称《协约国和参战各国对德和约》。它是第一次世界大战后，战胜国（协约国）与战败国（同盟国）缔结的一份和约，主要目的就是惩罚和削弱德国。亦称《凡尔赛条约》。

[2] 玛丽–安托瓦内特（Marie Antoinette，1755—1793），法国大革命前的王后，以生活奢侈著称。此处似乎有误，因为她应是路易十六而非路易十五的王后。

the French erected several buildings that have become famous. One of these is the Dome of the Hôtel des Invalides, a building constructed by Louis XIV as a hotel or kind of hospital to care for wounded soldiers. It is now a place of honor to Frenchmen because it contains the tomb of Napoleon. In it you can see Napoleon's badge or trademark — a capital letter N.

The French Pantheon has a somewhat similar dome, with a circle of slim columns around the base. The Pantheon is used as a church and is a shrine to the memory of St. Genevieve, the patron saint of Paris. It contains the celebrated mural paintings of scenes from the life of Saint Genevieve, but that is not the only reason it is famous.

The Pantheon is the center of the most famous university in France, the Sorbonne. The Sorbonne is situated in the part of Paris known as the Left Bank. It is so

荣军院，现存于巴黎
（摄影：约翰·帕特森）

拿破仑墓，现存于巴黎
（摄影：约翰·帕特森）

先贤祠，现存于巴黎
（由波士顿的大学印刷协会提供）

修建起来的，当成旅馆或者照料受伤军人的医院。如今，这里成了法国人的骄傲，因为拿破仑的墓地就在其中。在这里，你们可以看到拿破仑的徽章标志，或者说“商标”：一个大写的字母N。

法国的先贤祠里，建有一个与之有点儿类似的穹顶；但这座建筑的底座周围，还立有一圈修长的立柱。这座先贤祠既是教堂，也是纪念圣日内维耶的一座祠堂；圣日内维耶就是巴黎的主保圣人。先贤祠里，有许多根据圣日内维耶生平所绘的著名壁画；不过，这可不是先贤祠举世闻名的唯一原因。

先贤祠还是法国最著名的一座大学，即索邦神学院[1]的中心。索邦神学院坐落于巴黎市内叫作左岸的那个地区。之所以得名如此，是因为如果面向西边

[1] 索邦神学院（Sorbonne），现泛指巴黎大学。

索邦神学院，现存于巴黎

马德莱娜教堂，现存于巴黎

凯旋门，现存于巴黎

埃菲尔铁塔，
现存于巴黎

巴黎歌剧院，现存于巴黎

named because it is on the left side of the Seine River if you are facing west toward the Atlantic. Another equally famous name for the Left Bank is the Latin Quarter. It got its name because when the Sorbonne was founded, students from across Europe gathered to study there. They spoke different languages but came together to learn from the ancient Greeks and Romans, so their readings, lectures, and discussions were in Latin. The people of Paris, entering the Left Bank heard only Latin being spoken, as if they had returned to ancient Rome, so they nicknamed the neighborhood of the Sorbonne the Latin Quarter.

I wish I could tell you about all the handsome buildings in France, and especially in Paris. But I'm sure this chapter has given you enough new names of places you would like to visit. Your memory will be kept busy. If you can't name all the places without looking back, you'll know why I'm not going even to mention the Madeleine, which looks like the Parthenon; the Arc de Triomphe; the Eiffel Tower, which shows how structural steel opened the way for skyscrapers; or the Opera, which took the design of theaters to new places entirely. What! I've already mentioned them? So I have.

大西洋那个方向的话，这一地区就是位于塞纳河的左岸。左岸地区还有一个同样著名的名称，即“拉丁区”。之所以叫这个名称，是因为索邦神学院成立后，欧洲各地的学生纷纷汇集，到这里来求学。虽然他们说着不同的语言，但他们都是到这里来学习古希腊和古罗马著作的，因此在阅读、讲座和讨论的时候，他们用的都是拉丁语。巴黎人来到左岸地区后，听到的全都是拉丁语，好像回到了古罗马时代似的；因此，他们便给索邦神学院附近的地区起了个绰号，叫作拉丁区。

我真希望自己能够将法国，尤其是巴黎所有的漂亮建筑全都介绍给你们听。不过我确定，这一章已经让你们了解到了许多的新地名，你们可能都希望到这些地方去看一看呢。你们或许一直都在忙着记住这些地名。如果你们不回过头去看前面的内容，就无法说出这些地名的话，那你们就会明白，我为什么甚至不打算给你们提及样子看上去与先贤祠很相似的马德莱娜教堂、凯旋门、用钢结构建成并且直指苍穹的埃菲尔铁塔，或者完全将剧院设计提升到了一个新高度的巴黎歌剧院的原因了。什么！我已经提到这些地方了？确实这样呢。

Chapter 23 Breaking Rules

Have you ever gotten tired of being good? Have you ever felt like throwing chalk at the blackboard at school, or standing on your head when your teacher asked you a question in math? Have you ever wanted to whistle out loud just because everything was so quiet and serious and you knew you shouldn't?

The trouble with doing any of these things is that afterward you generally wish you hadn't. It's not much fun being punished. I found that out, myself, almost every time I tried not being good.

The architects of Italy seemed tired of being good after about 200 years of Renaissance buildings. They seemed tired of obeying all the rules for beautiful Renaissance buildings. The rules "cramped their style." In the strict Renaissance architecture almost every part of the building had to be based on some idea from the ancient Romans. Well, a new kind of architecture grew out of the Renaissance architecture.

I can't tell you for sure how the word *Baroque* started, but people say it came from a Portuguese word for an irregular-shaped pearl. Baroque architecture has been punished by being held up as a bad example ever since.

It has really been punished too much, for some Baroque buildings are very fine and very beautiful, but the worst Baroque buildings are terrible. In these buildings, the Baroque architects broke too many rules, like a bully in school.

第23章 打破规则

你们有没有过厌烦得很、不想再做个好学生的时候呢？你们有没有过这样的经历：在学校里，当老师提算术问题的时候，你们很想拿起粉笔砸向黑板，或者是来个倒立呢？你们有没有过只是因为一切都太过安静、太过严肃，就想要大声吹下口哨，可你们明知不该那样做的时候呢？

做这种事情的麻烦之处就在于，事后你们通常都希望自己没有那样做。接受惩罚可不是件好玩的事情。几乎每次想要不做一个好学生的时候，我都有亲身体会呢。

经过“文艺复兴”式风格的建筑风靡了差不多二百年之后，意大利的建筑设计师们似乎正是厌倦了再当一个“好学生”。他们似乎已经厌倦得很，不想再遵循漂亮的“文艺复兴”式建筑的所有规则了。那些规则，“束缚了它们的风格。”根据严格的“文艺复兴”式建筑风格，建筑的每个部位，都必须建立在古罗马时期的某种理念基础之上。于是，从“文艺复兴”式的建筑风格中，便演化出了一种新的建筑风格。

我没法确切地告诉你们，“巴洛克”这个词是怎么来的；可人们却说，它源自葡萄牙语里的一个词，用于指一种形状不规则的珍珠呢。自那以后，巴洛克风格的建筑便受到了惩罚，一直被人们用来做不好的榜样了。

实际上，这种惩罚太重了，因为有些巴洛克风格的建筑，其实非常精美、非常漂亮；不过，最糟糕的巴洛克式建筑，也的确令人生厌哩。在这些巴洛克风格的建

But the best Baroque buildings are really good. They broke just enough rules to be interesting. Buildings in the Baroque style are generally very well planned. They fit the place where they are built and seem to go well with the scenery around them. The trouble with them is that they look too proud, too crowded with decoration, as if they were trying to show off. They are covered, inside and out, with columns, statues, scrolls, twists, and fancy marble slabs. They make you think of a very fancy birthday cake with icing frills and curlicues all over it.

Baroque architecture began in Italy and became the chief architecture of the seventeenth century in that country. And in Italy stands one of the most beautiful of all Baroque buildings. It is a church beside the Grand Canal in Venice, built for a very special reason. A frightful disease called the plague had killed about a third of all the people in Venice. Sixty thousand people had died.

Then the plague stopped. The people who were left alive were so thankful for being spared, that they built the beautiful Baroque church as a monument of thanksgiving. They named it the church of St. Mary of Good Health. Everybody, of course, calls it by its Italian name, so you will have to try to learn Saint Mary of Good Health in Italian — Santa Maria della Salute.

Santa Maria della Salute is in the form of a Greek cross, with its four parts being the same length. It has a big dome over the central part and a small dome over the *chancel*. A chancel is the space around an altar for the clergy and sometimes the choir, often enclosed by a lattice or railing. The buttresses supporting the dome are shaped like rolls of ribbon.

筑上，建筑设计师们打破了太多的规则，就像学校里一个调皮捣蛋的孩子一样。

但是，那些最优秀的巴洛克式建筑，却的确优秀得很。它们只会打破一定的规则，使建筑看起来更有意思。属于巴洛克风格的建筑物，通常都经过了精心的设计。它们与修建地点非常协调，并且与周围的景色似乎也相得益彰。问题在于，它们看上去都高傲得很，装饰得也太过分，仿佛有意要炫耀似的。这种风格的建筑，不论内外，全都饰有立柱、雕塑、卷饰、扭纹饰和花哨的大理石板。它们常常会令人想起一个极为花哨、上面遍布糖衣饰边和花饰的生日蛋糕呢。

巴洛克式的建筑风格始于意大利，并且变成了十七世纪意大利的主要建筑风格。因此，所有巴洛克风格的建筑中最漂亮的一座，就位于意大利境内。那是坐落在威尼斯大运河畔的一座教堂，而修建这座教堂的原因也很特别。当时，一种叫作瘟疫的可怕疾病，杀死了威尼斯大约三分之一的人口，总共死了六万人。

接下来，瘟疫结束了。幸存下来的人，都对他们能够幸免于难非常感激，因此便修建了这座漂亮的巴洛克式教堂，以此来纪念他们的感恩之心。他们将这座教堂命名为“健康圣母教堂”。当然，大家都是用意大利语来称呼它的，因此你们也必须记住意大利语里“健康圣母”这个词才行，即“安康圣母”。

安康圣母教堂的格局呈希腊十字架形，即十字架形的四臂等长。其中心区域上方，有一座巨大的穹顶，而圣坛之上又有一个小穹顶。所谓的“圣坛”，就是祭坛周围供牧师所用的空间，有时也供唱诗班站立，并且通常有格栅或者栏杆隔离开来。支撑穹顶的那些扶壁，样子就像是一卷一卷的缎带。

Notice how crowded with statues and with these rolls the church seems to be. But also notice the beautiful flight of steps that leads down toward the canal. The church makes one of the most beautiful sights in Venice as you look at it across the water.

This fancy Baroque architecture spread all over Italy and into Spain and Portugal. In Spain a few of the Baroque churches are crowded with decoration. Other Spanish Baroque buildings are quite beautiful, although they might not look as good in a country where the sunlight wasn't so bright. The brighter the light, the more decoration a building seems to be able to stand.

Now that we have reached Spain, we come to the people who used Baroque architecture all over the world. In the Roman Catholic Church, a body of men, similar to the monks of the Middle Ages, was formed to spread the Catholicism. The men who belonged to this body were called Jesuits. The Jesuits built churches wherever they went, and these churches were usually in the Baroque style.

In the seventeenth century, the kingdom of Spain was very powerful. The Spaniards had gone exploring and took, in the name of their king, most of South American and a great deal of North America, too. Wherever the Spanish explorers went, the Jesuits soon followed, preaching Christianity to the Native Americans, founding schools for them, and building churches for the communities they found. Soon there were

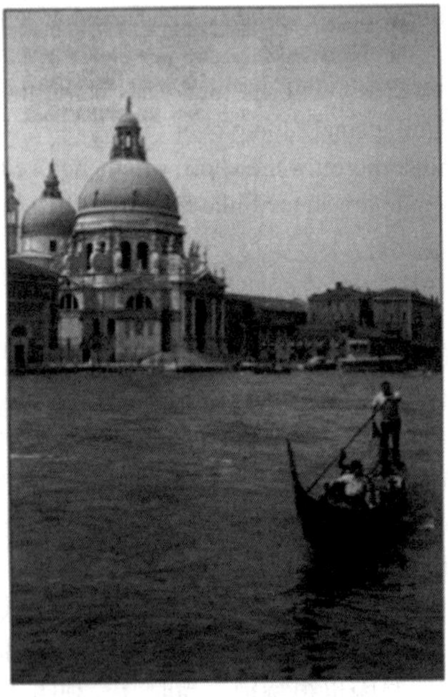

安康圣母教堂，现存于威尼斯
（摄影：约翰·帕特森）

请注意，整座教堂里，似乎到处都是雕像和这种卷状装饰。不过，我们还要注意那条向下通往运河的漂亮台阶。倘若从运河对岸看去，这座教堂就是威尼斯最漂亮的景色之一呢。

这种花哨的巴洛克式建筑风格，先是席卷了整个意大利，然后又传播到了西班牙和葡萄牙。在西班牙，只有少数巴洛克风格的教堂装饰得很繁复。西班牙其他的巴洛克式建筑都非常漂亮；但在阳光不太明亮的乡间，它们可能却不是很好看。光线越明亮，一栋建筑上的装饰似乎就可以越繁复。

既然来到了西班牙，那我们就再说一说在世界各地运用巴洛克式建筑风格的人吧。古罗马的天主教会里，有一群与中世纪的修道士相类似的人，他们的任务就是传播天主教。隶属于这个组织的人，被称为耶稣会会士。凡是所到之处，耶稣会会士们都修建了教堂；而这些教堂，通常都属于巴洛克风格。

在十七世纪的时候，西班牙王国的实力非常强大。西班牙人到处探险，并且以西班牙国王的名义，占领了南美洲的绝大部分，以及北美洲的许多地区。凡是西班牙探险者所到之处，耶稣会会士很快便会接踵而至，向美洲的土著印第安人传播基

more Baroque churches in the Americas than in all of Spain.

These Jesuit churches were so well built that most of them are still standing in spite of earthquakes, revolutions, and neglect.

You can imagine what a hard job the Jesuits had. First they had to learn the native language or teach the Native Americans Spanish. They had to show the Native Americans how to build the stone buildings, often in the hottest climates. And before the buildings could be built, the land had to be cleared and the stones dug out of the quarries.

The picture shows you the great cathedral at Mexico City. It doesn't look much like the Santa Maria della Salute, does it? But it, too, is Baroque in style. You can see how much decoration there is on it.

Baroque architecture was used also in Germany. One of the best examples in Germany can be found on a tiny side street in the heart of the Bavarian city of Munich.

Two brothers from the Asam family created a masterpiece. They paid for this now-famous church that was connected to their own residence, so it is called the Asam church or, in German, Asamkirche. They brought together architecture, painting, and sculpture,

国家大教堂，现存于墨西哥城
（由波士顿的大学印刷协会提供）

督教教义，为印第安人兴建学校，并且在他们成立的社区里修建教堂。不久之后，南、北美洲巴洛克式教堂的数量，就超过了整个西班牙。

这些耶稣会教堂都修建得非常牢固，因此不管地震也好，革命也好，疏于管理也罢，绝大多数教堂如今仍然保存着。

你们完全可以想见，那些耶稣会会士的工作有多辛苦。首先，他们必须学会当地的语言，或者教会印第安人说西班牙语。然后，他们必须告诉美洲的印第安人如何去修建石结构的建筑，并且通常是在最炎热的气候条件下去修建。而在修建教堂之前，还得清理场地，从采石场里将石头开采出来才行哩。

上图所示的，就是墨西哥城里那座了不起的大教堂。它看上去与安康圣母教堂不太相像，对不对？可它也属于巴洛克风格。你们可以看出，教堂上面的装饰也很繁复呢。

巴洛克式的建筑风格，在德国也得到了运用。我们在慕尼黑巴伐利亚市中心的一条小巷子里，就可以看到德国巴洛克风格建筑的一个最佳范例。

阿萨姆家族的两兄弟，曾经创造了一件杰作。由于是他们出钱，修建了这座如今非常著名的、与他们家连接起来的教堂，因此这座教堂便被称为“阿萨姆家的教堂”，在德语里就是“阿萨姆教堂”。他们在这座教堂上综合了建筑、绘画和雕塑

covering what seems to be every tiny bit of the interior with decorations that make a straight line seem impossible to find. There are cherubs, lavish gilded accents, silver, and stones of every kind and color. Some people may think going in is like eating several desserts all at the same time, but for the brothers Asam, it was the most beautiful church they could imagine, and it was just around the corner.

Some of Baroque came to France, but very little was ever used in England. If you will remember the seventeenth century, Spain and Portugal and their colonies, and Italy and Germany, you will have in your mind the time and places where this decorative Baroque style that broke the rules of classical taste was most frequently used.

三种艺术。在教堂内部，哪怕是非常细小的地方，也都进行了装饰；并且，这些装饰都形成了一条肉眼似乎难以发现的直线。教堂里有小天使、奢华的镀金经文、银器，以及各种各样、颜色各异的石子。有的人可能会觉得，走进这座教堂，就好像是一次品尝好几道甜点；可对于阿萨姆兄弟来说，这却是他们能够想象出来的、最漂亮的一座教堂，并且非常近便呢。

有一部分巴洛克风格传到了法国，可英国却几乎没有修建过这种风格的建筑。假如你们记住十七世纪、西班牙和葡萄牙及其殖民地、意大利和德国这几个方面，那你们就会记住人们最经常运用这种装饰华丽、打破了经典风格规则的巴洛克风格的时间和地点了。

Chapter 24 The English Renaissance

Do you have a bicycle? Where I lived as a child, most of the children in the neighborhood had bikes. We used to ride them out to a field where we could play baseball. One afternoon one of the boys was late getting there. But when he did come, he had left his old bicycle — the one just like ours — at home and was riding one we had never seen before. When we arrived, he said he had just gotten it for his birthday.

Every one of us wanted a new bike, just like the one he had. When we got home, however, our parents did not seem to agree! And that is just like what happened 300 years ago in England. An architect named Inigo Jones went to study architecture in Italy. He saw the Italian Renaissance buildings there. He studied the ancient Roman buildings, and when he got back to England he began designing Renaissance buildings. They were new to Englishmen, just as the new bike was new to us, and everyone wanted a Renaissance building.

Renaissance architecture was late in reaching England, just as the boy with the new bike was late in reaching the ball game, but when it finally did get there, nothing else would do.

Soon a great palace for the king, called the Palace of Whitehall, was designed in the Renaissance style. But the only part of the design that was built was the banqueting hall.

第24章 英国的“文艺复兴”

你们都有自行车吗？我小的时候，附近地区的绝大多数孩子都有自行车。我们还经常骑着自行车到田野上去打棒球呢。有天下午，一个小男孩迟到了。待他来了之后，我们却发现，他骑着一辆我们从未见过的新自行车，而把原来那辆旧自行车（与我们的一样）留在家里了。我们到达那里后，他告诉我们说，那辆新车是他刚刚收到的生日礼物。

我们都想要一辆新的、就像他那辆一样的自行车。然而，待我们回到家里后，父母却似乎都没有答应！那种情形，正像三百年前英国的情况。一位名叫伊尼戈·琼斯的建筑师，曾经跑到意大利去学习建筑。在那里，他看到了意大利那些“文艺复兴”式风格的建筑。他研究了古罗马时期的建筑，而当他回到英国后，便开始设计“文艺复兴”式风格的建筑了。对于英国人来说，这些建筑非常新颖，就像我们觉得那辆新自行车的模样很新颖似的；于是，大家便都想拥有一座“文艺复兴”式风格的建筑了。

这种“文艺复兴”式的建筑风格，很晚才传到英国，就像那个得到了一辆新自行车的男孩很晚才来到球场那样；可最终传到英国之后，却没有什么可以盖过此种建筑的风头了。

不久，人们便用“文艺复兴”式风格为英国国王设计出了一座大型的王宫，叫作白厅宫。不过，唯一按照这种设计风格建造起来的部位，就是其中的宴会厅。这

This was Inigo Jones' best-known piece of architecture. The Banqueting Hall of Whitehall became a famous building. It looks something like the Petit Trianon at Versailles. It was the first of many English buildings based on the Roman and Italian designs.

Do you remember that paragraph about insides and outsides, in Chapter 21? The Banqueting Hall is a good example of the outside not being the outside of the inside. The outside looks like a building with two stories, but there is only one story inside — just one big room with a balcony around the walls.

The Banqueting Hall is, however, a beautiful building both inside and out. Notice the Roman columns and the rusticated stonework at the street level, just like the Italian Renaissance buildings. The Banqueting Hall is still called by that name, although it was used as a chapel for many years and finally turned into a museum.

The next great architect in England after Inigo Jones wasn't an architect at all, at least, not at first. He was an astronomer and a college professor. He was Sir Christopher Wren.

Sir Christopher Wren became famous as an architect because of a fire. It was one of the biggest fires in the history of the world and happened in 1666. A fire started in London and quickly

白厅宫里的宴会厅，现存于伦敦
（由波士顿的大学印刷协会提供）

就是伊尼戈·琼斯最著名的一件建筑作品。白厅宫里的这座宴会厅，变成了一座著名的建筑。它的样子，有点儿像是凡尔赛宫里的小特里亚农宫。虽说英国拥有众多根据古罗马风格和意大利设计而建造起来的建筑，可这个宴会厅，却是其中的第一座。

你们都还记得第二十一章里面关于“内部”和“外部”的那一段吗？这座宴会厅，就是说明建筑物外部并非简单地适应内部这一原则的合适范例。宴会厅的外部，看上去像是一栋两层的建筑；可实际上，内部却只有一层，其中只有一个大房间，四面都是阳台。

然而，不论是从内部来看还是从外部来看，这个宴会厅都是一栋漂亮的建筑。请注意那些古罗马风格的立柱，以及那些与街道水平的粗琢石雕；它们完全类似于意大利那些属于“文艺复兴”式风格的建筑。如今，这座宴会厅还是叫这个名字，尽管它后来多年被用作礼拜堂，并且最终变成了一座博物馆。

伊尼戈·琼斯之后，英国下一位伟大的建筑师，其实根本就不是一位建筑师，至少起初不是。他本是一位天文学家，还是一名大学教授。他就是克里斯多夫·雷恩爵士。

克里斯多夫·雷恩爵士是因为一场火灾，才变成一位著名建筑师的。这是世界历史上最大的一场火灾之一，发生在1666年。伦敦的一栋房子燃起了大火，然后迅

spread to other buildings. It could not be stopped since most of the city of London was built of wood and straw thatch instead of stone or brick.

Soon a large part of London was burning down. Besides London Bridge and thousands of other buildings, over fifty churches were burned. The biggest of these was old St. Paul's Cathedral. After the fire, Sir Christopher Wren was given the job of making new designs both for St. Paul's and for the other churches.

Wren thought Gothic was a poor kind of architecture. He liked the Renaissance style, so he built the new St. Paul's Cathedral as a Renaissance building.

Like the Gothic cathedrals, St. Paul's is in the form of a Latin cross, with its cross bar shorter than the vertical bar. Over the crossing, Sir Christopher erected a very large dome with a stone lantern on top. Really it is a three-in-one dome, that is, an outside dome, an inside dome for a ceiling, and a brick dome between the other two. This brick dome between the other two was made to hold up the heavy stone lanterns or cupolas. Wren used the clever idea of having a lightweight, larger dome to see from the outside, and a heavier smaller dome to see from the inside.

The outside of St. Paul's has two orders of columns, one above the other like the Banqueting Hall. This makes St. Paul's look better than St. Peter's in Rome, because the two orders give a better scale than the one order of huge columns on St. Peter's.

Unfortunately, St. Paul's wasn't very carefully built. The walls were filled with poor materials, and in time the building became unsafe. As a result, it was closed while workmen strengthened the foundations and the supports. Now it is again open and strong

速蔓延到了其他的建筑。由于当时伦敦城里的绝大多数房子都是木结构和茅草房顶，而不是砖石结构，因此人们根本就不可能阻断这场大火。

很快，伦敦的大部分地方就被烧成了平地。除了伦敦桥和数千座其他的建筑，还有五十多座教堂被焚毁了。其中最大的一座，就是老圣保罗大教堂。火灾过后，克里斯多夫·雷恩爵士便接受命令，为圣保罗大教堂和其他教堂设计新的建筑方案。

雷恩爵士认为，哥特式风格是一种很差劲的建筑风格。他喜欢“文艺复兴”式风格，因此便将圣保罗大教堂建成了一座属于“文艺复兴”式风格的建筑。

与哥特式大教堂一样，圣保罗大教堂是拉丁十字架格局，即横向比竖向窄。在交叉口的上方，克里斯多夫爵士修建了一座巨大的穹顶，顶部还有一个石制的灯塔。实际上，这是个三合一式的穹顶；也就是说，它有一个外层穹顶、一个当作天花板的内层穹顶，以及它们中间的一个砖制穹顶。之所以修建这个砖制穹顶，是为了支撑顶上那座沉重的石制灯塔。雷恩爵士想出的主意很聪明，让人们从外部可以看到一个重量轻、尺寸大的穹顶，而从内部看到的则是一个重量较大、尺寸却较小的穹顶。

圣保罗大教堂的外部有两种立柱，其中一种位于另一种的上方，就像白厅宫里的宴会厅那样。这使得圣保罗大教堂比罗马的圣彼得大教堂更好看，因为与圣彼得大教堂只有一种巨型立柱相比，两种立柱提供了更好的参照比例。

可惜的是，圣保罗大教堂在修建的时候，建得却不是很仔细。墙壁之间填充的，全都是些劣质材料；因此随着时间的推移，这座教堂变得很不安全了。结果，

圣保罗大教堂，现存于伦敦
（摄影：约翰·帕特森）

enough not to collapse. This is not an unusual story about famous buildings that need great help as they get older. Perhaps they are more like people than we first imagined!

Sir Christopher Wren himself is buried in St. Paul's. On his tomb, in Latin, is carved, "If you would see my monument, look around you." St. Paul's is indeed his monument, the great landmark of London and the largest cathedral in England.

As for Sir Christopher Wren's other churches, no two, of the more than fifty, are alike. Some are noted for the outside design, many for their beautiful interiors, and many more for their graceful steeples. In fact, Sir Christopher Wren is famous for his Renaissance steeples. People liked them so well that even in the American colonies, churches were built with steeples that look like his designs.

大教堂不得不关门，请工人来对地基和承重结构进行加固。如今，这座大教堂再次开放了，并且已经变得很牢固，不会再坍塌了。对于一些著名的建筑来说，由于历史变得悠久而需要加以修缮加固，可不是一件罕见的事情。或许，它们比我们最初所想的更像人类呢！

克里斯多夫·雷恩爵士去世后，就安葬在圣保罗大教堂里。他的墓碑上刻着一行拉丁文："若想看到我的纪念碑，就请看看您的四周吧。"圣保罗大教堂的确就是他的纪念碑；它既是伦敦一座了不起的地标，也是英国最大的一座大教堂。

至于克里斯多夫·雷恩爵士设计修建的其他教堂，可以说在那五十多座重建的教堂里，没有哪两座是相同的。有些教堂以其外部设计而著称，许多教堂以其内部精美而闻名，还有更多则是以其优雅的尖塔而享誉。事实上，克里斯多夫·雷恩爵士就是因为他设计的那些"文艺复兴"式风格的尖塔而闻名遐迩的。人们都很喜欢这些尖塔，因此即便是在美洲的殖民地里，人们也会按照他设计出来的样子，给教堂修建尖塔呢。

圣保罗大教堂，现存于伦敦
（摄影：加里·威肯）

At the time of Sir Christopher Wren, books were being published giving the rules and designs for Renaissance architecture, and many buildings were constructed from designs and descriptions in these books. Palladio's book on architecture, which I have mentioned, was translated into English and was used by architects in both England and America.

Renaissance architecture was used for many years in England after Sir Christopher Wren's death. Under Kings George I, George II, and George III, the English Renaissance architecture had reached a style all its own. This is named after them all, so it is called the Georgian style. I'll tell you more about the Georgian style when we come to American architecture.

在克里斯多夫·雷恩爵士那个时代，人们已经出版了一些论述“文艺复兴”式建筑风格的规则和设计的书籍，因此许多建筑都是按照这些书籍里的设计方案和描述修建起来的。前面我已经提到过的、帕拉迪奥那部论述建筑的著作，也已经翻译成了英语，为英国和美洲的建筑师们所利用了。

克里斯多夫·雷恩爵士去世后，“文艺复兴”式建筑风格还在英国流行了多年。在英王乔治一世、乔治二世和乔治三世统治时期，英国的“文艺复兴”式建筑形成了自己特有的风格。这种风格，便以这三位乔治国王的名字命名，叫作“乔治式风格”。后面谈到美洲的建筑风格时，我还会给你们介绍乔治式风格的更多情况的。

Chapter 25 From Huts to Houses

Suppose you had to go to a wild, unexplored land and live there the rest of your life. What kind of house would you build? Probably you would build a log cabin if you had an ax and could find plenty of trees. But if you had never heard of a log cabin, the chances are you would build some other kind of shelter that you had heard of — a cave perhaps.

The first English settlers who landed in America had never seen a log cabin. What they thought of first were the little huts of the charcoal burners that they had seen in the woods in England. These huts were made of branches and twigs woven together, somewhat as a wicker chair is woven. The early settlers built their shelters like the charcoal huts and put steep-pointed thatched roofs on them. Do you know what a *thatched roof* is? It's a roof made of straw. When these huts were finished, they must have looked very much like the wigwams of the Native Americans.

But what about log cabins? Surely the early settlers used them? Yes, they did use them as soon as the Swedes had settled in Delaware. The Swedes had lived in log cabins in Sweden, and when they came to America, where logs were easy to get, they built log cabins there also. Pioneers and settlers built log cabins as they pushed west away from the seacoast, for trees were plentiful.

At least one log cabin has become famous. It is the one Abraham Lincoln was born

第25章 从茅屋到住宅

假设你们要到一个人迹罕至的荒郊野外去，并在那里度过余生。那么，你们会建造一种什么样的住宅呢？十有八九，倘若有一把斧头，并且找得到足够多的木材，那么你们都会建造一所小木屋。不过，倘若连小木屋是什么都没听说过，那么，你们很可能就会建造一座自己听说过的其他种类的住宅，没准还会是一个洞穴呢。

最先到达美洲的那些殖民者，就从来没有见过小木屋。他们最先考虑的，就是像他们在英国森林里看到过的、那些烧制木炭的人搭建的小棚子。那些茅棚，都是用棍子和树枝织在一起搭建而成，方法有点儿像是编织藤椅。因此，早期殖民者所建的住房，都是像木炭烧制者搭建的那种棚子，上面还有一个尖尖的茅草屋顶。你们知道茅草屋顶是什么吗？就是用茅草搭成的屋顶啊。这些茅棚完工后，样子一定与土著印第安人的篷屋很相似呢。

可是，小木屋呢？早期的殖民者一定也修建过小木屋吧？是的，瑞典殖民者来到特拉华州之后，的确搭建过小木屋。瑞典殖民者在国内住的本来都是小木屋，因此来到木材资源丰富且极易获得的美洲之后，他们搭建的自然也是小木屋了。在拓荒者和殖民者从沿海地区向西部推进的过程中，他们修建的也都是小木屋，因为一路上木材很丰富。

至少有一栋小木屋，后来变得举世闻名了。它就是亚伯拉罕·林肯出生的那座

in. Now the whole cabin is kept in Hodgenville, Kentucky, in a big marble building built especially to hold it and protect it.

Some of the early buildings that the settlers from England built were Gothic in style. At Jamestown in Virginia, the settlers built a simple little brick Gothic church that has since fallen to pieces. But another little early church called St. Luke's is still standing. St. Luke's has the pointed windows and steep roof of the Gothic, and this seems strange because the Renaissance had reached England some years before America was settled by Englishmen, and the Gothic style had gone out of style in England.

In both New England and Virginia some of the early houses were Gothic as well. They were built of wood and had windows called *casement windows* opening at the side on hinges (the way a door opens), with many small panes of glass in each window. Generally the second story of these houses stuck out a foot or so beyond the first story so that there was an overhang in front. Several of these old Gothic houses are still standing.

After a while, books about architecture began to find their way into the American colonies. These books came from England, where Renaissance architecture was in full swing. The books had plans and diagrams or drawings in them that American carpenters found very handy guides for making houses.

King George was reigning in England — first King George I, then George II, then George III, and so the English Renaissance architecture was called Georgian architecture, as I have told you already. And after the first few Gothic buildings, early American architecture was Georgian, too. We call it now Georgian Colonial — or sometimes it's just

小木屋。如今，这座小木屋被整体保存在肯塔基州的霍金维尔，存放在一栋专门为容纳并保存它而修建起来的巨型大理石建筑里。

英国殖民者早期修建的一些建筑，都属于哥特式风格。在弗吉尼亚州的詹姆斯敦，殖民者还修建了一座简单的砖结构哥特式小教堂，只是这座教堂早已倒塌了。不过，还有一座早期的小教堂，即圣路加教堂，却一直保存到了今天。圣路加教堂拥有哥特式风格的尖顶窗户和陡峭的屋顶；这似乎有点儿奇怪，因为待英国人来到美洲殖民时，“文艺复兴”式风格已经进入英国多年，而哥特式风格在英国也早已过时了。

在新英格兰地区和弗吉尼亚，一些早期的住宅同样属于哥特式风格。这些房屋都是木结构，窗户都是用合页从一侧打开的平开窗（就像开门一样），并且每扇窗户上都有多块小型的玻璃窗格。这些房屋的第二层，通常都会在第一层的基础上向外凸出一英尺左右，从而在房屋正面形成一种飞檐。这些历史悠久的哥特式房屋中，有些至今还保留着呢。

过了一段时间之后，建筑方面的书籍开始进入美洲这些殖民地了。这些书籍都来自英国；当时，“文艺复兴”式的建筑风格正在英国大行其道。这些书籍中，有平面图、图解或绘画，从而让美洲的木匠有了一种建造房屋的、非常便利的指南。

此时，统治英国的一直都是乔治国王，首先是乔治一世，然后是乔治二世，接下来又是乔治三世；因此，英国的“文艺复兴”式建筑风格又称为“乔治式风格”，这一点我在前面已经跟你们介绍过了。所以，除了最初为数不多的哥特式建筑，美洲早期的建筑风格也成了乔治式风格。如今，我们将这种风格叫作“乔治

called Colonial.

Most of the Georgian Colonial houses were made of wood in the North and of brick in the South, but in Pennsylvania, between the North and South, stone was used. The houses weren't built by regular architects, but by the master carpenters who used the books sent from England to guide them. The houses were so suited to this country that architects today still often use this Georgian Colonial style for houses.

乔治式风格的宅邸，
现存于亚拉巴马州的蒙哥马利

Besides Georgian Colonial, there was Dutch Colonial, much liked by the Dutch settlers in New York. The Dutch Colonial houses generally had a roof that sloped down beyond the front of the house to cover the porch. The Dutch Colonial style has also been used again in modem houses in America.

The Colonial houses were generally plain and simple. They were never decorated much, like Baroque buildings

乔治式风格的扇形窗
（摄影：约翰·帕特森）

殖民时期风格”，有时也只是简称殖民时期风格。

属于乔治殖民时期风格的绝大多数房屋，在北方地区多为木结构，在南方地区则多为砖结构；不过，夹在南北之间的宾夕法尼亚，房屋却是石结构的。这些房屋，都不是由正规的建筑师设计修建，而是由那些技艺精湛、用英国传来的书籍做指南的木匠修建的。由于这些房屋与美国这个国度非常和谐协调，因此如今的建筑设计师，仍然经常运用这种乔治殖民时期的风格来修建房屋呢。

除了乔治殖民时期风格，还有一种“荷兰殖民时期风格”，纽约的荷兰殖民者非常喜欢。用荷兰殖民时期风格修建的房屋，屋顶通常都是倾斜向下，在房屋正面伸出去一截，遮住走廊。荷兰殖民时期风格，在美国的现代住宅中也再次得到了应用。

殖民时期的房屋，通常都很朴素、很简单。它们决不会像属于巴洛克风格的建筑那样装饰华丽，而这也是我们觉得它们非常有魅力的原因之一。其中的绝大多数

were, and that is one reason they seem so charming to us. Most of the decoration was carved in wood on the doorways, the mantelpieces, the stairways, and the ceilings. Sometimes there were wooden pilasters or half columns or columns in the Roman style at each side of the door. Often there was a *transom window* over the front door. This would be decorated with carved wooden tracery sometimes in the shape of a fan, called a *fanlight*.

Many of these old houses of colonial times are still standing. Most of them, of course, are in the eastern United States, which were settled first. Some are famous for other reasons than architecture — Mount Vernon, for instance, is famous because it was the home of George Washington. Mount Vernon on the Potomac is visited every year by thousands of people who come to see where the "Father of his Country" lived.

Independence Hall in Philadelphia is famous as the building where the American Declaration of Independence was signed. That is how it got its name. Designed by a lawyer, Independence Hall is a fine example of Georgian Colonial architecture in brick. The tower reminds us of one of Sir Christopher Wren's steeples in London. In Independence Hall is the famous Liberty Bell that rang so hard it cracked.

The man who wrote the Declaration of Independence was Thomas Jefferson, later

独立大厅，现存于费城
（由波士顿的大学印刷协会提供）

装饰，都是门口、壁炉台上、楼梯和天花板上的木雕。有的时候，门口两边还有属于古罗马风格的木制壁柱、半露方柱或者立柱。前门的上方，通常都会有一扇气窗。气窗上会饰有木质窗格；有时，窗格会呈扇形，因此这种气窗就叫扇形窗。

殖民时期的这种古老房屋，仍有很多一直保存到了今天。当然，其中绝大多数都位于美国的东部地区，因为人们最先在那里殖民。其中有一些房屋，还因为别的原因（不是建筑艺术）而变得举世闻名了；比如弗农山庄之所以著名，是因为那是乔治·华盛顿的故居。每年都有成千上万人来到波托马克河边的弗农山庄，去参观这位“国父”生活过的地方呢。

再比如，费城的独立大厅之所以著名，是因为美国的《独立宣言》就是在这栋建筑里面签署的。而这一点，也是让这座建筑得名“独立大厅”的原因。独立大厅由一位律师设计建造，是乔治殖民时期风格砖结构建筑的典范。其中的塔楼，让我们想起了克里斯多夫·雷恩爵士在伦敦修建的那种塔楼。在独立大厅里，本来还有一口著名的“自由之钟”；可由于敲得太厉害，这口钟竟然被敲裂了。

起草《独立宣言》的，就是后来曾任美国总统的托马斯·杰斐逊。得知托马斯·杰斐逊也是当时最优秀的建筑设计师之一，你们可能会觉得很惊讶吧。不过，

president of the United States. You may be surprised to learn that Thomas Jefferson was one of the best architects of his time. Architecture was not his business, but his hobby. He was a great believer in ancient Roman architecture, and he designed many buildings that were Roman in style. One of these is Monticello, Jefferson's own home, which you can see on the backs of some U.S. nickels.

Monticello looks a great deal like the Rotunda, the main building of the University of Virginia. Both buildings look like the Pantheon in Rome, giving you an idea of how much Jefferson appreciated the architecture of ancient Rome.

The buildings of the University of Virginia are arranged around the sides of a big square lawn or campus he called the Academical Village. The white columns against the dark red brick of the buildings are very attractive.

There is a row of buildings on each of the two long sides of an open green Jefferson called the Lawn. On one narrow side is the Rotunda, and on the other the view is open to the mountains. These side buildings are examples of classical architecture — columns of all kinds, and replicas of ancient temples and so on — so that the professors could lead their students around the Lawn and teach them about the famous buildings by showing them examples instead of pictures in books.

Jefferson's work in architecture was mostly done after the American Revolution. We can hardly call it Colonial, because the country was no longer part of Great Britain's colonies. A better name would be Early Republican.

Then came a time when almost all buildings were made with Greek details — Greek

建筑可不是他的主业，而是他的业余爱好。他极其推崇古罗马时期的建筑风格，因此设计了许多属于古罗马风格的建筑。其中一座便是蒙蒂塞洛，它是杰斐逊的家；在美国的一些五分硬币背面，你们还可以看到这座建筑呢。

蒙蒂塞洛的样子，与弗吉尼亚大学的主楼“圆形大厅”非常相似。而这两座建筑的外形，又都像是罗马的万神殿，从而让你们可以看出，杰斐逊是多么欣赏古罗马时期的建筑风格。

弗吉尼亚大学里的房屋，全都沿着一块巨大的方形草地（或称校园草坪）而建，杰斐逊称之为“学术村”。白色的立柱，映衬着深红色的砖墙，使得这些建筑看上去非常迷人。

在一片空旷的长绿地两侧，各有一排房屋；杰斐逊将这片绿地称为“草地”。其中较窄的一侧就是圆形大厅，而另一侧则可以看到群山。两侧的这些建筑，都是经典风格的建筑典范，其中有各式各样的立柱、古代神庙的仿制建筑，等等；因此，大学里的教授便可以领着自己的学生，绕着草地转上一圈，用实例而不是书本上的图片，来将这些著名建筑的知识教给学生了。

杰斐逊设计的建筑，大多是在美国革命之后修建的。我们很难说他的作品属于殖民时期的风格，因为那时美国已经不再是英国的殖民地了。更恰当的名称，应当是“共和国早期风格”才是。

接下来，就出现了一个几乎所有建筑都具有古希腊装饰风格、具有古希腊式立柱和造型的时期。一个名叫罗伯特·米尔斯的建筑师，曾经给位于华盛顿特区的财

华盛顿纪念碑，
现存于马里兰州的巴尔的摩
（由波士顿的大学印刷协会提供）

华盛顿纪念碑，
现存于华盛顿特区

columns and shapes. An architect named Robert Mills made a Greek facade of columns for the Treasury Building in Washington, D.C.

Mills also made the first monument to George Washington — a huge Doric column with Washington's statue on top, which stands in Baltimore. It was the same Robert Mills who designed the tallest building in the world at that time, the Washington Monument in Washington, D.C.

The Washington Monument is a huge obelisk that was not finished for many years after it was begun, and you can see that for yourself if you look closely enough. The Washington Monument is really two colors, one on the lower part and a different one on the upper part, which was added when there was enough money to complete it. Do you remember the Egyptian obelisks, like Cleopatra's Needle?

政部大楼设计修建了一个古希腊式的立柱正面。

米尔斯还修建了乔治·华盛顿的第一座纪念碑；那是一根巨大的多利克式圆柱，顶上坐落着华盛顿的雕像，位于巴尔的摩。也是这位罗伯特·米尔斯，设计了当时世界上最高的建筑，即位于华盛顿特区的华盛顿纪念碑。

华盛顿特区的这座纪念碑，是一座巨大的方尖碑，开工之后过了许多年才完工；这一点，倘若仔细观察，你们自己就能看出来。实际上，这座华盛顿纪念碑上有两种颜色，下部是一种颜色，上部又是另外一种颜色，因为上部是后来资金凑足了才加上去完工的。你们还记得古埃及的那种方尖碑，比如“克里奥帕特拉之针”吗？

But while the United States was being born in the East, what about the western side of America?

Well, in the Southwest and far West most buildings were Spanish. Mexico had been settled by people from Spain. The Jesuit priests built churches in Mexico, and what today is Texas and New Mexico, in the Baroque style. These buildings are called *Spanish Colonial* because they were built in Spanish colonies.

About the time of the American Revolution, some Spanish monks called Franciscans pushed into California from Mexico. In California the Franciscans built churches and other buildings. Their settlements were called *missions*. They were built along the coast, a day's journey apart, on a road called the King's Highway. A mission was very much like a monastery of the Middle Ages. Each mission had a church connected by cloisters with other buildings around a courtyard. The buildings were made usually of Sun-dried brick, or *adobe*.

传教修道院和教堂，
现存于加利福尼亚的圣巴巴拉
（由波士顿的大学印刷协会提供）

This Mission style has been used by present-day architects too, just as the Georgian and Dutch Colonial

陶斯印第安村，现存于新墨西哥州的陶斯

但是，正当美国在东部地区诞生之时，美国以西的那些地区，又是个什么情况呢?

注意，在美国的西南方和遥远的西边，绝大多数建筑都属于西班牙风格。因为到墨西哥殖民的，就是西班牙人。耶稣会的牧师，在墨西哥以及如今得克萨斯州和新墨西哥州所在的地区，修建了许多巴洛克风格的教堂。这些教堂被称为“西班牙殖民风格”的建筑，因为它们都是修建在西班牙的殖民地中。

差不多就在美国革命期间，一些称为“方济各会修士”的西班牙修道士，纷纷从墨西哥进入了加利福尼亚。这些方济各会修士，在加利福尼亚修建了许多教堂和其他的建筑。他们定居的地方，称为“传教院”。这些传教院都修建在沿海地区，相距不过一天的行程，都建在一条叫作“国王大道”的路上。这种传教院，很像是中世纪的修道院。每个传教院里，都有一座教堂，由回廊与院子周围的其他建筑相连。这些建筑通常都是用晒干的砖块，或者说土砖建成的。

如今的建筑设计师，也仍然在使用传教院式的建筑风格，就像如今的人仍然在

法国区的住宅，现存于新奥尔良

styles have been used. The Spanish Colonial seems suited to the warm climate of California and the Southwest better than any other kind of architecture. In California many of the old missions may still be seen. Some are in ruins while others have been carefully preserved.

Another kind of Spanish Colonial architecture grew out of the architecture of the Native Americans — houses built of adobe. Called pueblos, these were really apartment houses because they had rooms for many families. Since so little rain falls in this region, pueblos had flat roofs because sloping roofs weren't necessary. These houses were often several stories high and had ladders outside, instead of stairs inside, to get from one story to another.

The Spanish colonists who settled in New Mexico copied this pueblo style from the Native Americans. You can always tell houses in pueblo style because the flat roofs are on logs whose ends stick out from the top of the walls. The very old Governor's Palace in

使用乔治式风格和荷兰殖民时期风格一样。西班牙殖民风格，似乎比其他建筑风格更适合于加利福尼亚的炎热气候。在加利福尼亚，如今仍然可以看到许多古老的传教院呢。虽说有一些已成废墟，但其他一些传教院却得到了精心的保护。

还有一种西班牙殖民风格，是从土著印第安人的建筑，即土砖建造的房子发展演化而成的。这些房子，叫作“普韦布洛”，实际上都是公寓式的住宅；因为其中有很多房间，可供多家居住。由于这一地区很少下雨，因此普韦布洛都是平顶，根本就无须坡顶。这些房子通常都有好几层高，连接楼层之间的楼梯都建在外部，而不是建在里面。

在新墨西哥安顿下来的那些西班牙殖民者，从土著印第安人那里学会了这种普韦布洛式的建筑风格。我们始终都能分辨出那些属于普韦布洛风格的房子来，因为它们的平顶都是建在圆木之上，而圆木的两端也会在墙头上露出来。圣达非那座非常古老的总督府，就是用这种普韦布洛风格建造起来的，不过它只有一层楼高。你

Santa Fe is built in this pueblo style although it is only one story high. You can see that is was built based on the traditional pueblo designs of the Native Americans.

New Orleans, settled by the French, introduced from France a style of architecture with long French windows and iron balconies. The old section of New Orleans is called the French Quarter. Today, it is not unusual to hear a dialect of French called Cajun spoken in the heart of New Orleans.

So you see that in its early days America used many different kinds of architecture. I'll make a list of them for you, so you can remember them better. If you want to test yourself, see if you can name one fact about each kind. Here is the list:

⊙ log cabins
⊙ Gothic Colonial
⊙ Georgian Colonial
⊙ Dutch Colonial
⊙ Early Republican
⊙ Spanish Mission
⊙ Spanish Indian (pueblo)
⊙ French Colonial

们可以看出，这座建筑就是根据土著印第安人传统的普韦布洛风格修建起来的。

法国人殖民的新奥尔良，则采用了从法国传来的一种建筑风格；这种建筑，都有长长的法式窗户和铁制阳台。新奥尔良历史最悠久的那个地区，叫作法国区。如今，在新奥尔良的中心城区里，我们经常还会听到有人说一种叫作“卡真”的法语方言呢。

这样，你们就可以看出，美国早期拥有多种不同的建筑风格。我会把它们一一列举出来，从而让你们更好地记住这些风格。假如你们想要考考自己，那就看一看你们能不能给每一种风格举出一个特点来吧。这些风格列举如下：

⊙ 小木屋
⊙ 哥特式殖民风格
⊙ 乔治殖民时期风格
⊙ 荷兰殖民风格
⊙ 共和国早期风格
⊙ 西班牙传教院风格
⊙ 西属印第安人风格（普韦布洛）
⊙ 法国殖民风格

Chapter 26 AL and OL

Just like a person, each country has a head — a chief, a president, a king, a prime minister, or a dictator. And where the chief ruler rules is generally the capital city. Remember that *capital* comes from a word meaning "head."

After the American Revolution, the new republic of the United States had to have a capital. After trying out both New York and Philadelphia, the new country decided to build an entirely new city as a new capital for the new nation.

A place on the Potomac River was chosen, a place of fields and forests. It was named Washington. Frenchmen had helped the Americans in the Revolution and now a Frenchman helped them plan the new city. He was Major Pierre L'Enfant, who drew a plan for Washington with wide avenues and streets and parks. With L'Enfant's plan to go by, the new city was started. But Washington wasn't much of a city at first — just a few houses in the woods, with "streets" of mud connecting them.

A capital city, of course, needs a capitol building. You might think that the name of the city and the building would have the same spelling. But al refers to the city, and ol refers to the building.

A big competition was held to get the best design for a capitol. Many good designs

第26章 首都和国会大厦

跟一个人一样，每个国家都有一个领头人，比如元首、总统、国王、首相或者执政官。而元首治理国家的地方，往往就是该国的首都。记住，"首都"正是由一个用于指"头部"的词发展而来的。

美国革命后，新的合众国必须设立一个首都才行了。新的共和国在尝试过用纽约和费城来做首都之后，决定兴建一座全新的城市，来做这个新国家的首都。

当局选定了波托马克河上的一个地方，那里放眼都是田野和森林。后来，这里被命名为华盛顿。法国人曾经帮助美国人进行革命，如今又有一位法国人来帮他们设计这座新的城市了。这位法国人，就是皮埃尔·朗方上校；他设计了一张图纸，把华盛顿这座城市设计得街道宽广、公园林立。于是，人们便按照朗方上校的图纸，开始动工兴建这座新的城市了。不过，起初华盛顿可不太像是一座城市哩，只是树林中有为数不多的房屋，其间有泥土"街道"相连罢了。

一个首都，自然还需要一座国会大厦。你们可能会以为，"首都"这个名称，与国会大厦这座建筑的称呼是一样的。不过，al指的是首都，而ol则指国会大厦这座建筑[1]。

为了获得国会大厦的最佳设计方案，美国还举行过一场大规模的比赛呢。人们

[1] 在英语中，"首都"是capital，而"国会大厦"则是capitol。作者是为了防止学生混淆，因此才这样说。

came in, but the one by Dr. William Thornton was chosen. Both George Washington and Thomas Jefferson said they liked the Thornton design very much, and so the Capitol was begun.

If there was to be a capitol, there certainly ought to be a special house for the president. So a president's house was begun the same year as the Capitol. For the first twenty years or so the president's house was always called just that — the President's House. But suddenly the name changed and became the White House. Do you know why?

It was because a fire. Some British soldiers who attacked Washington during the War of 1812 also burned both the new Capitol and the President's House. After the fire the President's House still had the walls standing, but the stones were blackened and scorched. The building was repaired and the walls were painted white to hide the fire stains, and ever since, the President's House has been called the White House.

Luckily, the Capitol had not yet been finished when it was burned. It, too, was rebuilt after the fire, but it wasn't finished for years and years.

At first the Capitol had a low flat dome over the central part. When more space was needed, an addition was built on each end of the building. These new ends are called *wings* — the Senate wing at one end and the wing for the House of Representatives at the other. When the new wings were added, a larger dome was designed for the center.

During the Civil War President Lincoln kept work going on this dome even though workmen were scarce. He felt the dome stood for the union of the states and that people on the Northern side would be encouraged by seeing this dome grow day-by-day.

提交了许多不错的设计方案，可最终却只选定了威廉·桑顿博士的方案。乔治·华盛顿和托马斯·杰斐逊两个人都说，他们非常喜欢桑顿的设计方案，于是国会大厦便开始兴建了。

既然有了一座国会大厦，那么美国总统当然也应当有一座专门的官邸才行。于是，在国会大厦动工的同一年，一座总统府也开始动工了。在后来的二十来年里，总统的这座官邸一直都是直接称呼，即总统府。不过，突然之间，这个名称便变成了“白宫”。你们知道这是什么原因吗?

这是由于一场火灾。在1812年战争中，一些进攻华盛顿的英军士兵放了一把火，把国会大厦和总统府都烧了。大火过后，虽说总统府的墙壁仍然屹立着，可砌墙所用的石块却被烧黑了，全是焦痕了。人们修复了总统府，其中的墙壁则被刷成了白色，以掩盖大火留下的焦痕；所以，从此以后，总统府便被人们称为“白宫”了。

幸好，在燃起大火的时候，国会大厦还没有完工。火灾过后，这里也进行了重建，可后来又过了多年才修建完成。

起初，国会大厦的中央上方，是一个矮平的穹顶。后来，由于需要的空间增加了，因此人们又对大厦两端进行了扩建。扩建后的两端叫作“侧翼”，即一端是参议院之翼，另一端则是众议院之翼。扩建出这两个新的侧翼之后，人们便为大厦中心区域设计出了一个更大的穹顶。

在美国内战期间，虽说工人短缺，林肯总统还是坚持继续修建这座穹顶。他觉得，这座穹顶象征着各州的统一，觉得北方人民看到这座穹顶一天一天修建起来之

The new dome was almost as big across as the dome of St. Peter's in Rome. It was made of a new building material — not wood or brick or stone, but iron.

To keep iron from rusting, it must be kept painted. Try to think how many buckets of paint 43,000 pounds of paint would make. That is more than twenty-one tons, but that's the quantity of paint it takes each time the dome of the Capitol is painted!

One room in the Capitol is called Statuary Hall. That is where each of the fifty states is invited to put two statues of famous citizens from that state. It's not safe to tell a secret in Statuary Hall, for your whisper can be heard all the way across the room if you whisper from a certain spot that's marked by a metal star in the floor.

You may remember the story of the whisper dome in the Baptistery of Pisa, where a whisper or melody is carried from one side of the dome to the other. That's how many domes work.

Strange to say, the star was not put there for the whisper, but to show where the desk of John Quincy Adams used to stand when he was a member of Congress after being president. The whisper is heard across the room because the waves of sound from that spot all seem to be reflected off the walls and ceiling so as to meet at another spot on the other side of the room.

The Capitol is full of interesting things. One of these is a subway.

国会大厦，现存于华盛顿特区
（由缅因州桑福德的大学印刷协会提供）

后，就会深受鼓舞。

这座新的穹顶，直径几乎与罗马圣彼得大教堂的穹顶一样大。而且，它也是用一种新的材料建成的，既非木结构、砖结构，也非石结构，而是用钢铁修建起来的。

为了不让钢铁生锈，穹顶必须刷上油漆才行。想象一下，四万三千磅油漆有多少桶吧。这些油漆重量超过了二十一吨；可这仅仅是给国会大厦的穹顶刷上一次所需的油漆量！

国会大厦里，有个房间叫作雕像厅。美国五十个州里，每个州都会为该州最著名的两位公民制作两尊雕像，送过来放到这个房间里。在雕像厅里跟人说什么秘密可不安全，因为如果站在房间地板上有个金属星形标志的地方，你们的窃窃私语，甚至在房间那头都听得清呢。

你们可能都还记得吧，比萨洗礼堂里有个私语穹顶，轻声说出的话或者哼出的旋律，会从穹顶一边传到另一边去。许多穹顶都是这样呢。

说来也怪，设置那个星形标志，可不是为了让人说悄悄话的，而是为了标示约翰·昆西·亚当斯在卸任美国总统后担任国会议员期间，其办公桌所在的地方。你们低声说话时，之所以在房间的那一头都听得清，是因为从那个地方发出来的声波，似乎全都被墙壁和屋顶反射出去，然后在房间另一头的一个地方集中起来了。

国会大厦里，到处都是很有意思的东西。其中之一，便是里面竟然还有一条地

The trains run from the Capitol to the Library of Congress, the Senate Office Building, and the House Office Building. These three building aren't very far from each other, but the subway trains save the members of Congress time.

The more you see of the Capitol, the more seems left to see. It has sometimes been called the most stately government building in the world. Yet it is important in architecture for another reason. It has been such a good building for a capitol that many of the fifty state capitols have been modeled from it, only smaller. It is a building to proud of, and it is pleasant to think that the cornerstone was laid by the first president of the United States.

Among the many other splendid buildings in Washington is the Lincoln Memorial. It is built in the Greek style, yet it is American. It uses the old Greek forms of columns and other details but uses them in a new way to fit the kind of building it is. You will notice it has no pediment, or triangular space, above the columns as a Greek temple has.

New buildings in Washington are always built according to Major L'Enfant's plan for the streets and avenues. This makes Washington one of the most planned cities in the world. Its design as a city and its architecture make references to so many countries and cities and buildings that have come before it. So, in many ways, while it is the capital of one nation, it is a city of the nations of the world, too.

林肯纪念堂，现存于华盛顿特区

铁。地铁从国会大厦开往国会图书馆、参议院办公大楼和众议院办公大楼。虽说这三座建筑彼此相距不远，但这条地铁还是能够节约国会议员们的时间。

你们在国会大厦里看到的东西越多，似乎就会有越多的东西没有看完。有的时候，人们还会说，这是世界上最庄严宏伟的一座政府大楼呢。不过，还有另一个原因，使得国会大厦在建筑艺术上占有重要的地位。由于这是一座极其漂亮的国会大厦，因此美国五十个州中，有许多州都仿照这座建筑的样式，修建了州议会大厦，只是没有那么大规模罢了。这是值得美国人引以为傲的一座建筑；而一想到它的奠基石是由美国第一任总统安放的，就令人愉快得很呢。

在华盛顿其他诸多杰出的建筑中，有一座就是林肯纪念堂。这座纪念堂属于古希腊风格，然而同时又具有美国特色。它运用了古希腊的立柱和其他装饰细节，但用的是一种适合于此种建筑本身的新方式。你们会注意到，纪念堂与古希腊的神庙不同，立柱顶上并没有人字墙，即那种小三角墙。

如今，华盛顿的新兴建筑，始终都是按照朗方上校对于街道的设计图来修建的。这使得华盛顿成了世界上规划最为完善的一座城市。整座城市的设计图纸和建筑工艺，都参照了历史上的许多国家、许多城市和许多建筑。因此，从诸多方面来看，它既是一个国家的首都，同时也是结合了世界各国特色的一座城市。

Chapter 27 Rainbows and Grapevines

"Now who will stand on either hand,
And keep the bridge with me?"

When I was a boy, my favorite poem was "Horatius at the Bridge." What a thrill I got whenever my father read aloud the story of the brave Roman and his two companions who held back a whole army while the bridge was being cut down to save the city! I even knew parts of the poem by heart, without trying at all to memorize them.

"Horatius at the Bridge": even if you know the story of Horatius, you may not know the story of the bridge.

It was the first bridge in Rome, and when "the dauntless three" stood there with flashing swords, mocking all 90,000 men of the invading army, it was the only bridge in Rome. It was a wooden bridge, one that could be cut down with axes, and it was so important to Rome that priests were in charge of it.

Have you ever heard the Pope spoken of as the Supreme Pontiff? Supreme Pontiff is one of his titles. Would you ever guess that this title of the Pope came from the ancient bridge that Horatius defended? The chief priest in ancient Rome was called the Pontifex Maximus. In English this means the Greatest Bridge Builder. He was called this because

第27章　彩虹和葡萄藤

"现在，谁会伴我左右，
托起这座桥梁？"[1]

小的时候，我最喜欢的一首诗歌就是《桥上的贺雷修斯》。无论什么时候，只要父亲一朗读这个故事，我就会激动不已；那位勇敢的罗马人，与他的两个战友抵挡住了一整支军队，而当时为了挽救罗马城，他们身后的桥梁还被砍断了！我甚至还记住了这首诗的部分诗句，尽管我根本没有想要去记忆。

上面的诗句，就是选自《桥上的贺雷修斯》；但即便知道贺雷修斯的故事，你们可能也不知道那座桥本身的故事呢。

那是罗马的第一座桥梁，而当那"无畏的三人"站在桥上，手持寒光闪闪的利剑，蔑视着入侵的九万大军时，这还是罗马唯一的一座桥呢。这是一座木桥，可以用斧头劈断；而由于它对罗马至关重要，因此是由祭司们掌管着。

你们有没有听到过，人们在谈到教皇时，会把他称为"至高教宗"呢？"至高教宗"是他的称号之一。那你们猜不猜想得到，教皇的这个头衔，竟然是源自贺雷修斯所捍卫的那座古桥呢？古罗马的首席大祭司，称为"最高祭司"。但在英语里，这个称呼指的却是"伟大的造桥者"。而大祭司之所以叫这个名称，是因为他

[1] 引自十九世纪英国诗人托马斯•巴宾顿•麦考莱（Thomas Babington Macaulay）的诗作《桥上的贺雷修斯》。

he was chief of those in charge of the bridge. So *pontifex*, or *pontiff*, came to mean priest, and that is why the Supreme *Pontiff* or Bridge Builder is one of the Pope's titles.

The pont part of pontiff turns up in another unexpected use. Try to imagine what Horatius would have thought if he had suddenly seen a seaplane flying overhead, its propeller roaring, its pontoons glistening in the Sun. A *pontoon* is a kind of boat used to hold up a bridge. A bridge across boats is called a *pontoon bridge*. And so the pontoons that hold a seaplane upon the water got their name because they are like the boats that hold up a pontoon bridge.

And now I'd better tell you what kinds of bridges there are. There aren't as many different kinds as you might think. Really there are only five kinds, and that's a good thing, because you can easily learn those five, and then you can name any kind of bridge you see.

Here they are.

⊙ Number one is the *simple beam* bridge. A log across a stream is the simplest kind of a simple beam bridge.

⊙ Number two is the *arch*. A rainbow would make a beautiful arch bridge, if only you could walk across it. The Chinese have some beautiful arch bridges.

⊙ Number three is the *suspension bridge*. A wild grapevine stem that hangs from one tree to another is a good suspension bridge — for a monkey.

是掌管这座桥的祭司头领。因此，“大祭司”一词后来便用于指教士，而教皇之所以有“至高教宗”或者“造桥者”的头衔，原因也在于此。

不过，“大祭司”（pontiff）一词中的pont这个部分，后来竟然演化出了另一种料想不到的意思。想象一下，倘若贺雷修斯突然看到一架水上飞机从头顶呼啸而过，飞机的螺旋桨轰鸣着，机身下方的浮筒在阳光下闪烁着光芒，他的心里会有什么感受呢？“浮筒”（pontoon）本来是一种船，用来支撑桥梁的。由船只架成的桥梁，就被称为“浮桥”。用于在水上支撑一架飞机的浮筒，正是由此得名的，因为它们与支撑浮桥的那些船只很相似。

现在，我该告诉你们，世界上都有些什么样的桥梁了。桥梁的种类，并没有你们可能想象的那样多。实际上，世界上只有五种桥梁；这可是件好事情，因为你们可以轻而易举地熟悉这五种桥梁，然后就可以说出自己看到的任何一种桥梁的名称了。

这五种桥梁就是：

⊙ 第一种，是简支梁桥。架在小溪上的一根圆木，就是最简单的一种简支梁桥。

⊙ 第二种，是拱桥。一道彩虹，样子就是一座漂亮的拱桥，只是你们可没法在上面走呢。中国就修建了一些非常漂亮的拱桥。

⊙ 第三种，是吊桥。悬挂在两棵树之间的一根野生葡萄藤，就是一座不错的吊桥；当然，这是对猴子而言。

⊙ Number four has the hardest name to remember. It is the *cantilever bridge*. A cantilever is a simple beam supported at one end, something like a diving board. Often the bridge has a cantilever coming from both banks of a stream and meeting in the middle.

⊙ Number five is the *truss bridge*. A truss bridge has its beams strengthened by a stiff framework of different parts fastened together. The framework may either rise above the roadway of the bridge or be beneath it. The frame of a bicycle is something like a truss. Cantilever bridges are often built with trusses. Most truss bridges are built of wood or iron or steel.

These are the five kinds of bridges. What about pontoon bridges? Pontoon bridges are just-simple beam bridges with the beams resting on boats instead of on posts or piers.

The earliest bridges were, naturally, beam bridges. Xerxes of Persia, a great king, built a pontoon bridge across the Hellespont when he came to fight the Greeks in 480 B.C.

The Greeks were not bridge builders, preferring to travel by boat rather than by road. Then too, the rivers of Greece are generally small enough to be crossed without a bridge, though the Greeks probably got their feet wet in crossing.

But let's return to the Romans, the greatest bridge builders until modem

加尔桥，现存于法国
（摄影：加里·威肯）

⊙ 第四种，它的名称最难记忆。它就是悬臂桥。所谓悬臂，就是一端固定的一根单梁，它有点儿像是一块跳水板。整座桥通常都是由一根悬臂从河的两岸伸出，然后在中间汇合。

⊙ 第五种，就是桁架桥。桁架桥的梁桁，通常都由一个绷紧的、不同部位固定在一起的框架进行加固。这个桁架，既可以突出于桥面上方，也可以设在桥面之下。一辆自行车的车架子，就有点儿像是桁架。悬臂桥上，往往建有桁架。而绝大多数桁架桥都是木桥、铁桥或者钢桥。

这就是五种桥梁。怎么没有浮桥呢？其实，浮桥就是一种简支梁桥，只不过桥梁不是架在木桩或者桥墩上，而是架在船只上罢了。

世界上最早的桥梁，自然都是简支梁桥。公元前480年，波斯的薛西斯这位伟大的国王，就曾在达达尼尔海峡上架起一座浮桥，率军前去与古希腊人作战。

古希腊人并不擅长造桥；相比于陆路，他们更喜欢坐船出行。再则，希腊的河流通常都不大，不用架桥也可过河，尽管希腊人在过河的时候很可能会弄湿脚。

不过，还是让我们再来说说罗马人吧，他们可是现代以前最了不起的桥梁建造师呢。条条大路通罗马，而这些大路上，也有许多的桥梁。除了意大利，在西班

times. All roads led to Rome, and the roads had many bridges. Not only in Italy but in Spain and France, in England and in Austria, the fine Roman bridges are still standing, and are still in use after 2,000 years of service. Some were of wood, which disappeared long ago. Most, however, were built of stones, fit together so well that often no mortar was needed.

You may be surprised to learn that the biggest Roman bridges were not meant to carry people. They were bridges to carry water. Do you remember learning about these?

Now, if you had wanted to take a bath in ancient Greece, you would have had to carry the water in jars from the stream or well or else use the stream for a bathtub.

But in a Roman city many of the houses had running water. And remember, there were also public bathhouses, where you could bathe in beautiful indoor swimming pools full of fresh, clear water.

All this water was brought to town by long aqueducts, which I have mentioned a couple times. You can think of an aqueduct as a stone bridge with a trough on top. The aqueducts went across country for miles from the mountain streams to the city.

When an aqueduct came to a valley, it didn't go dipping down into the valley and then up on the other side. It went straight across — as a very high bridge indeed. The Romans couldn't make water pipes very well, and so if the aqueducts had gone downhill and then up again, the water would have spilled out at the bottom of the dip. The best- known aqueduct is now the famous ruin called the Pont du Gard over the river Gard near Nimes, in the south of France.

牙、法国、英国、奥地利等国家里，罗马人修建的许多精美桥梁如今依然存在，并且在历经了两千年的风雨之后，如今依然还在使用呢。其中有些桥梁是木桥，它们早已不复存在了。然而，绝大多数桥梁却是用石头修建而成的；由于石头之间拼合紧密，因此经常连灰浆都用不着呢。

倘若我告诉你们说，古罗马最大的那些桥梁，并不是让人们来过河的，你们可能会觉得很惊讶吧。事实上，它们都是一些用于引水的桥梁。你们还记不记得，前面我们已经了解过这些桥梁的情况了呢?

注意，在古希腊，如果你们想洗个澡的话，就得用罐子从河里、井里打水回来，或者干脆就到河里去洗。

可在古罗马的城市里，许多家庭却都用上了自来水。并且还要记住，那里也有公共浴室；你们可以到公共浴室去，在那些漂亮的、盛满新鲜而清澈的水的室内游泳池里，痛痛快快地洗澡哩。

所有的用水，都是通过长长的高架渠引入市镇里来的；我在前面已经两次提到过这种高架渠了。你们可以把高架渠想象成是一座顶上有条水渠的石桥。这些高架渠，在乡间横跨数英里之远，将山间的溪水引到城市里面去。

高架渠穿过山谷时，并不是顺着山谷一侧而下，然后再沿着山谷另一侧升上去。水渠是径直架在山谷之上，因而实际上就是一座高架桥。古罗马人不太擅长于修建水管；而且，假如高架渠上下起伏的话，水就会在底部溢出去。如今，最著名的一座高架渠，也是一处著名的遗迹，叫作加尔桥，位于法国南部距尼姆不远的加尔河上。

After the fall of the Roman Empire, bridge building had a fall, too. For years and years during the Dark Ages, very few bridges were built. Then in the twelfth century A.D. a strange thing happened. Bridges throughout Europe went back to the care of priests, this time Christian priests. They formed a society called the Brothers of the Bridge.

At first the Brothers of the Bridge just kept little inns at river crossings, where travelers might stop. But soon they built their own bridges at these places. Often the Brothers made the roadway over the bridge so narrow at the middle of the bridge that only one horseman could cross at a time. This was to make it hard for robbers and soldiers to dash across and attack travelers. Of course such bridges weren't much good for wagons, but the roads weren't much good for wagons, either. Many of these bridges were strongly fortified with huge stone towers at each end, so robber bands or even armies could be stopped from crossing.

Probably the most famous bridge of the Middle Ages was the old London Bridge over the River Thames. It had houses built on it, some of them four and five stories high, but its foundations weren't very solid and so it was always needing repairs. Parts of it even fell down at various times. Do you remember the song "London Bridge Is Falling Down"?

The London Bridge lasted, however, with many repairs, from 1209 to 1831, when it was

伦敦桥，现存于伦敦

古罗马帝国衰落后，桥梁建造工作也开始走下坡路了。在那段漫长的“黑暗时代”里，几乎没有新建几座桥梁。接下来，十二世纪却发生了一件奇怪的事情。欧洲所有的桥梁，重新回到了教士的掌管之下；但这一次，它们却是由基督教牧师来掌管了。他们组建了一个社团，叫作“桥梁兄弟会”。

起初，“桥梁兄弟会”只是在河流的渡口开设一些小酒馆，供旅人歇歇脚。可不久之后，他们便在这些地方修建起了自己的桥梁。“桥梁兄弟会”通常会把桥梁中间的桥面修得非常狭窄，一次仅能供一人一马通过。这样做，是为了防止强盗和士兵冲过桥梁去袭击旅行者。这种桥梁，自然不太适合马车通行；而当时的道路，其实也不太适合马车通行啊。许多桥梁两端都建有巨大的石制塔楼，具有强大的防御性，从而使得强盗、甚至军队都难以通过哩。

很可能，中世纪最著名的一座桥梁，就是泰晤士河上的老伦敦桥了。这座桥上，还修建了房屋，其中有些房屋甚至有四五层楼高；可它的桥墩却不是非常牢固，因此时时需要维护。桥身的有些部位，甚至在不同时代垮塌过多次呢。你们还记得《伦敦桥要倒了》这首童谣吗？

然而，经过一次又一次的修缮，伦敦桥还是保存下来了，从1209年到1831年；

torn down to make way for the new London Bridge. That bridge has now been taken down and moved to the desert of Arizona, and another new London Bridge is in its place.

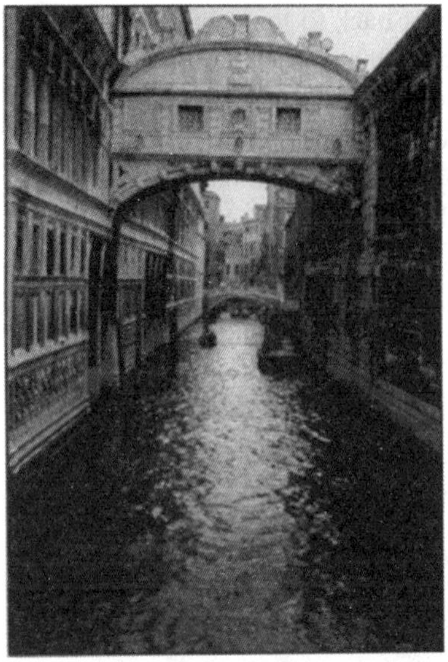

叹息桥，现存于威尼斯
（摄影：约翰·帕特森）

As you know, after the Middle Ages came the Renaissance, when many famous bridges were built. I'd like to tell you about some of them if I had more space — about one of the most photographed bridge in the world, the Bridge of Sighs in Venice; and about the Ponte Vecchio in Florence; and about the oldest bridge in Paris, that is still called the Ponte Neuf or the New Bridge. All these are stone bridges — and each of them has a story to tell.

Let me tell you just a little about each. It was said the Bridge of Sighs got its name because those found guilty in the courts held in the Doge's Palace would cross the bridge, which was over a canal. The prisoners could look through the stone- lace window to the sky for one last time and sigh as they made their way into a very dark and terrible dungeon.

老桥，现存于意大利的佛罗伦萨
（摄影：约翰·帕特森）

1831年，人们才将它拆掉，并在原址修建了一座新的伦敦大桥。如今，后建的那座桥也已拆掉，并运到了亚利桑那州的沙漠里，而原址上则又修建了一座新的伦敦大桥。

你们都知道，中世纪过后，便是“文艺复兴”时期了；在这一时期，人们兴建了许多著名的桥梁。要是篇幅允许的话，我倒是很愿意跟你们说一说其中的一些桥梁，比如世界上被人们拍照留念最多的、威尼斯的“叹息桥”，比如佛罗伦萨的“老桥”，比如巴黎虽属最古老、如今却仍被人们称为“新桥”的那座桥。这些桥梁，全都是石桥，并且每座桥都有自己的故事呢。

我还是给你们稍稍介绍一下上述每座桥梁的情况吧。据说，“叹息桥”之所以得名如此，是因为以前那些被判有罪、被关押到总督府里的人，都会经过横跨在一条运河之上的这座桥。在这座桥上，囚犯们可以透过那扇石格窗户，叹息着，最后看一眼蓝天，然后再被关进一间暗无天日、可怕的地牢里去。

The Ponti Vecchio, which simply means "old bridge," was a bridge where the cattle from the hills of Tuscany that surrounded Florence were slaughtered and sold for meat. The Medici family that ruled Florence found this to cause such a terrible scene, they forbid the butchers to use it anymore and told the fine gold and silversmiths to move their jewelry shops there where they remain today.

The Ponte Neuf, meaning New Bridge, is the bridge that marked the end of the Middle Ages in France. King Henry II planned it, but it was not until his son Henry III laid the first stone years later in 1578 that building began. Many city leaders could not see what advantage there would be in a bridge linking the two sides of the Seine from the Louvre Palace to the Sorbonne in the Latin Quarter of the Left Bank. However, once it was finished and no houses were permitted to be built on it to make it narrow and take away the view of the river, all of Paris celebrated its opening.

Modern bridge building began with the railroads, about 1830. At that time iron bridges were built. I should note the first iron bridge was built in 1779 in Shropshire, England.

Modern bridge building continued with steel bridges, and finally concrete and reinforced concrete bridges. Reinforced concrete bridges have iron bars inside the concrete to make them stronger. Many handsome

新桥，现存于巴黎
（摄影：加里・威肯）

顾名思义，“老桥”指的就是一座古老的桥；这座桥，曾是佛罗伦萨周围托斯卡纳山区的牛羊被屠宰，以及屠夫们售卖牛羊肉的地方。后来，统治佛罗伦萨的美第奇家族发现了这座桥上是一片如此可怕的场景之后，便禁止屠夫们再使用这座桥，并下令全城的金匠和银匠都把各自的珠宝首饰店搬到了桥上。如今，这里依然珠宝首饰商店林立。

“新桥”，就是指新建的桥；它是法国标志着中世纪结束的一座桥梁。这座桥，是法国国王亨利二世设计的；可直到许多年之后的1578年，待他的儿子亨利三世砌上第一块石头后，这座桥才开始动工修建。当时许多的城市领导人都看不出，修建一座横跨塞纳河两岸的桥，来连接卢浮宫和位于左岸拉丁区的索邦神学院，究竟有什么好处。然而，这座桥一旦完工，并且禁止在桥上修建房屋，以免使桥面变窄并破坏河上景观之后，全巴黎的人便都因为建造了这样一座桥而欢欣鼓舞了。

现代的桥梁建造，大约始于1830年的铁路修建。当时修建的都是铁桥。你们应当记住，世界上的第一座铁桥，是1779年在英国的什罗普郡修建的。

现代桥梁接下来变成了钢桥，最终又变成了混凝土桥梁以及加固混凝土桥梁。加固混凝土桥是在混凝土里加入钢筋修建而成的，从而使得桥梁更加坚固。近年，

布鲁克林大桥，现存于纽约
（摄影：尤因·加洛维）

reinforced concrete bridges have been built in recent years. Generally, they are arch bridges — sometimes with one arch and sometimes with many. In the United States they are the favorite road bridges.

The iron and steel bridges are often truss bridges. In fact, truss bridges are altogether modem.

Some of the earliest bridges in Asia and South America, by the way, were suspension bridges. These were hung from cables of rope or vine and were pretty shaky. Some of them are still in use. When you cross one you can't help hoping you'll get over alive. Really they are quite strong in spite of being so shaky. But I'd hate to try to cross one on an elephant — or in a car.

Modem suspension bridges are hung from steel cables. Most of them are very large and cost millions of dollars to build. The Brooklyn Bridge is one of the most famous suspension bridges because it was the longest — 3,460 feet — when it was built. And

人们修建了许多美观的加固混凝土桥。它们通常都是拱桥，有的时候只有一拱，有的时候则具有多拱。在美国，这种桥是人们最喜欢的道路桥梁。

铁桥和钢桥通常都属于桁架桥。事实上，桁架桥完全属于现代桥梁。

顺便说一句，亚洲和南美洲最早的桥梁中，有一些属于吊桥。它们都由绳索或者藤蔓悬吊而成，似乎很不稳当。可其中有些吊桥，如今却仍在使用呢。过这种吊桥的时候，你们会情不自禁地求菩萨保佑，希望自己能活着走过去。实际上，尽管摇晃得厉害，它们却牢固得很。不过，我还是不会想要骑着大象，或者开着车子去过这种桥的。

现代的吊桥，则是用钢索悬吊的了。其中绝大多数都属于大型桥梁，成本动辄数百万美元。布鲁克林大桥就是世界上最著名的吊桥之一，因为它长达三千四百六十英尺，建成后是当时世界上最长的一座拉索桥。而这座桥，也始终是人类历史上的第一

it will always be the first suspension bridge to use steel cables. It spans the East River in New York City. Bigger ones have been built since, but this grandfather of modern suspension bridges is still considered one of the finest to look at.

Perhaps you have heard of other famous suspension bridges, too. The Golden Gate Bridge leads into San Francisco and, in 1937, set a record for the length of a suspension bridge. It was built even though fog from the Pacific Ocean so often makes it invisible, and even though the tides and earthquakes might threaten it.

The longest and tallest suspension bridge of all spans 12,831 feet has towers that are like skyscrapers, rising 928 feet above the water. This modern bridge, the Akashi Kaikyo Bridge in Kobe, Japan, can thank the iron bridge in England that started it all.

When you go for a trip next time, keep your eyes open for bridges. Many of the finest bridges in the world are in the United States. Some travelers play games with bridges as they travel along. In one game a suspension bridge counts twenty points, a cantilever bridge fifteen points, an arch bridge ten points, a truss bridge five points, and a simple beam bridge two points. Sometimes when you go over a bridge you can't see what kind of bridge it is. All you can see are the rails and the road. That would count only one point. Whoever sees the bridge first, gets the points.

座钢索悬拉桥。它横跨在纽约市的东河上。虽说自那以后，人们又修建了许多更大的桥梁，可如今人们却依然认为，这座属于现代吊桥始祖的布鲁克林大桥，是其中最好看的一座呢。

没准，你们还听说过其他著名的吊桥。建于1937年、通往旧金山的金门大桥，创造了吊桥长度的纪录。尽管经常消失在太平洋上涌起的雾气之中，尽管海潮和地震可能会威胁到它的安全，可这座大桥终究还是修建起来了。

而世界上最长、最高的一座吊桥，跨度达一万二千八百三十一英尺，桥上修建的塔楼有如摩天大楼，桥体距水面高达九百二十八英尺。这座现代桥梁，就是位于日本神户的明石海峡大桥；能够修建这样一座宏伟的跨海大桥，可要归功于开创了钢铁桥梁历史的英国铁桥哩。

下次你们出去旅行的时候，不妨瞪大眼睛，去观察观察各地的桥梁吧。世界上最优秀的桥梁中，许多都位于美国。有些游客在旅游的时候，还会用桥梁做游戏呢。比如这样一个游戏：一座吊桥算二十分，一座悬臂桥算十五分，一座拱桥算十分，一座桁架桥算五分，而一座简支梁桥算两分。有的时候，你们在过桥的时候，是看不出那座桥属于哪一种类型的。你们只能看到桥上的栏杆和路面。这种情况只能算上一分。谁先看到并说出桥梁的种类，谁就能得到相应的分数。完了再比一比，看谁的得分最高吧。

Chapter 28 The Scrapers of the Sky

How high is "up"? For a mountain, "up" may be several miles. For an airplane, "up" is far higher than the highest mountain and well above the clouds. For a building, "up" is a little over 1,00.0 feet. Not nearly so high as the mountain top, not nearly as high as the airplane can fly, but the 1,000 feet "up" of the building seems to me as wonderful as mountain heights or airplane flights.

Very tall buildings, as you know, are called *skyscrapers*. They are an American invention but now are seen around the world. Most American cities have skyscrapers, but the place where they make the finest showing is New York City, and in the city where they first began, Chicago.

One might say that New York, with its landscape of skyscrapers, has become a manmade mountain range — not of stone but of steel and glass.

The era of skyscrapers began in Chicago in 1885, when the Home Insurance Building made the company look very solid in its Chicago office building that stood 138 feet above the street.

Gothic cathedrals have tall towers and lofty spires, but next to the tall skyscrapers the Gothic cathedrals do not look high at all. How can men, you wonder, possibly build so far above the ground? But there you are, so high above the ground, and people and cars on the

第28章 摩天大楼

多高才算"高"呢？对于一座大山来说，它的"高度"可能达几英里。对于一架飞机而方，它的"高度"可能比最高的大山还要高得多，比云层也要高得多呢。不过，对一栋建筑来说，它的"高度"却只有一千英尺多一点儿。尽管根本不像山顶那样高，尽管根本比不上飞机的飞行高度，但在我看来，一栋建筑那一千英尺的"高度"，却与山峰的高度、飞机的飞行高度一样令人惊叹哩。

你们都知道，那些很高、很高的建筑，叫作"摩天大楼"。这是美国人发明出来的，可如今世界各地都有摩天大楼了。美国绝大多数城市里，都建有摩天大楼；可最能呈现出摩天大楼风采的地方，却还是纽约市，以及最先修建这种大楼的芝加哥市。

有的人可能会说，纽约有那么多的摩天大楼，使得这座城市如今已经变成一条人造的山脉了；只是这条山脉并不是土石堆成，而是用钢铁和玻璃筑成的。

摩天大楼的时代，是从1885年的芝加哥开始的；当时，"家庭保险公司"在芝加哥的总部修建了一栋"家庭保险大厦"，高达一百三十八英尺高，屹立在街面上，使得这家公司看上去资金非常雄厚。

虽说哥特式大教堂都建有高耸入云的塔楼和尖顶，可倘若旁边有座高耸的摩天大楼，那么哥特式大教堂看上去就一点儿也不高了。你们可能会感到奇怪，人类怎么可能将楼房建得距地面如此之高呢？可人们的确修建了这些高楼大厦，而当

streets below look like moving black specks. You pinch yourself and it hurts, so you must be awake and not dreaming. The building is real, after all. What a long time it must have taken to build it!

Perhaps you are asking yourself, how did it happen in the first place that people wanted to make buildings that did not stay close to the ground, but went toward the clouds instead? Think about this as you read.

You might be surprised to know it takes a very short time to build a skyscraper. The Gothic cathedrals, you remember, took hundreds of years to build. The Empire State Building in New York City took only fourteen months to complete. And yet it has 102 stories. Magic!

Here is more magic. A skyscraper rises in the air according to schedule. Each steel girder, each piece of stone, and each section of pipe rolls into the building on a truck at just the right time. If the wrong piece arrives first, it cannot be used at once. There would be no place to put it on the streets below because there is no extra space. It would just get in the way, and traffic would be blocked on the street. The whole building would have to wait.

You can easily see, then, that a very important part of building a skyscraper has to be done

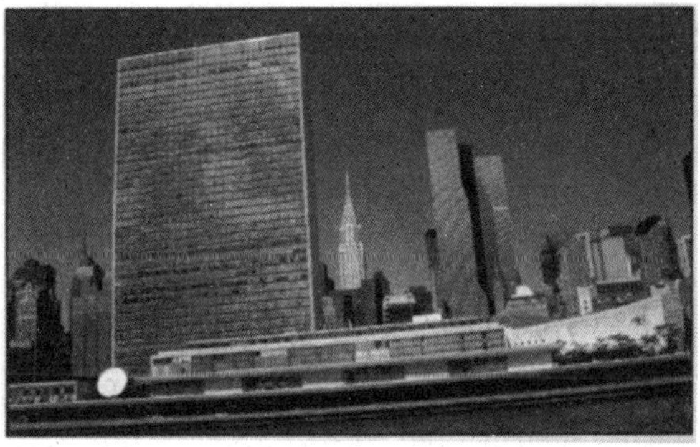

纽约的摩天大楼
（摄影：加里・威肯）

你们爬到距地面如此之高的楼顶后，下面街道上的行人和车辆，看上去就会像是一个个移动的小黑点呢。你们掐一掐自己，感觉到了疼痛，便知道自己很清醒，并不是在做梦。毕竟来说，大楼实实在在，就在自己的脚下。建起这样的一座大楼，得花多久的时间啊！

或许你们正在心中自问，人们起初为什么想要修建这种离地面不近、又高耸入云的建筑呢？在阅读后续内容的过程中，想一想这个问题吧。

修建一栋摩天大楼，只需要很短的时间；听到这个，你们可能会觉得很惊讶。你们都还记得吧，有些哥特式大教堂，竟然花了几百年的时间才建起来。可纽约市里的“帝国大厦”，却只花了十四个月就建起来了。这座大厦，可有一百零二层呢。真是不可思议啊！

还有更加不可思议的呢。有座摩天大楼，正在如期地耸立起来。每一根钢梁、每一块石头、每一段管道，都在恰到好处的时候，用一辆辆卡车运送到了建筑物的内部。如果材料运送的顺序不对，那么先到的材料就没法立即使用。下方的街道上没有多余的空地，因此根本就没有地方存放这些材料。这样，材料就会挡住道路，街上的交通就会受阻。而整个工程，也就只能停下来等待了。

这样一来，你们就不难看出，在修建摩天大楼的时候，先期准备工作是一个至

beforehand. The plans of the architect and engineer have to be very carefully made and checked. All the material has to be ordered and made ready for use so that it will arrive at just the right time — neither too soon nor too late. And that is one reason why the whole huge, wonderful structure can be put together so quickly and without even blocking the streets around it.

A skyscraper is made differently from the older kinds of buildings. It has a steel framework. Each story is a kind of steel cage, and on the cage are fastened the outside walls. These walls don't help at all to hold up the building. The steel cages do all the holding up. The walls are like the walls of a tent — to protect the inside from the weather, not to help support the weight. You would be surprised if you found the outside walls of your house were not resting on the ground, but the outside walls of a skyscraper do not rest on the ground. They hang on the steel cages stacked on top of each other. Sometimes you can even see a crack between the sidewalk and the walls of a skyscraper where the walls aren't even touching the ground!

Of course no one would want to walk up to the top floor of a skyscraper. It would take too long. If you tried it, you would find you were so tired out when you reached the top that you probably couldn't walk down again. So skyscrapers wouldn't be any good without elevators. There are locals and expresses, as with trains, so that you can reach the top stories quickly without stopping at each floor all the way up. The elevators on the latest skyscrapers are arranged so that a passenger never has to wait for one for more than a minute.

The first skyscrapers were built in the last years of the nineteenth century, like the one

关重要的组成部分。建筑师和工程师设计的图纸，必须制作得非常仔细，并且经过精心核对才行。所有的材料都得预先订购好，随时可用，才能在恰当的时间抵达施工现场，既不能过早，也不能太迟。整栋巨大而令人惊叹的建筑之所以能够如此迅速地修建起来，甚至不用堵塞周围街道的交通，原因之一就在于此。

摩天大楼的建筑方法，与以前的所有建筑种类都不相同。摩天大楼都属于钢结构。每一层都会先修建起一种钢罩，而外墙就是固定在这个钢罩上。但是，那些外墙对于支撑整栋建筑来说，根本就不起作用。支撑整栋建筑的，就是每层的钢罩。因此，这些外墙的作用，就跟帐篷一样，只是为了保护内部不受风吹雨打，而不是为了支撑建筑物的重量。假如你们看到自家的外墙并不是直接建在地面上，肯定会大吃一惊呢；而一栋摩天大楼的外墙，也不是直接修建在地面之上的。它们都是悬挂在上下堆砌起来的钢罩上。有的时候，你们甚至看得见人行道和摩天大楼那些根本没有与地面接触的外墙之间，还留有缝隙呢。

当然，没有哪个人会想要步行爬上一栋摩天大楼的顶层去。爬上去可要花很久的时间呢。假如试一试的话，你们很可能就会发现，爬到顶楼之后自己已经累得个半死，十有八九再也没有力气下楼了呢。因此，倘若没有电梯，摩天大楼就一点儿也不好了。摩天大楼通常都既有普通电梯，也有直达电梯，就像火车有慢车和快车之分那样，从而让人们可以迅速到达顶层，不用每层都停下来了。在一些最新式的摩天大楼里，电梯还安排得非常合理，绝不会让人等上一分钟甚至更久呢。

第一批摩天大楼，是在十九世纪的最后几年里建成的；比如，前面我已经向你

I told you about in Chicago. These early skyscrapers were shaped like tall shoeboxes standing on end. After many of these box buildings were built, people found that they cut off the light from the streets below and from buildings next door. And so cities made rules about how skyscrapers should be built. The rules said that skyscrapers could no longer be built with a shape like a shoe box. The higher the building rose in the air, the rules said, the narrower it had to be.

The lower part of a skyscraper, for instance, might cover an entire city block. But after the building had risen a certain number of stories, the other stories above had to be set back from the edge of the streets so as not to cut off the light. The tower of the building might be built as high as the sky, as long as its base didn't cover more than one quarter of the base of the first floor of the skyscraper.

These set-back rules made the new skyscrapers look quite different from the older ones. The older skyscrapers also look different because architects had tried to make them in the style of some architecture of the past. Some had Greek columns at the base, although the columns carried no weight and weren't used for anything except show. Some had huge cornices at the top that were copied from the Renaissance buildings, but were just as useless and ornamental as the columns.

The new skyscrapers are not made to imitate some style of the past. Some people call them *stripped architecture*. The architects tried to make their shapes beautiful without sticking old- fashioned decorations on the outside. Color began to be used. Several skyscrapers have the outside walls made of black brick trimmed at the top of the building

们介绍过的芝加哥的那座摩天大楼。这些早期的摩天大楼，样子都像是一个个高耸的、直立的鞋盒子。待修建了许多这样的鞋盒子大楼之后，人们发现它们挡住了下方街道以及隔壁建筑的光线。因此，各大城市都制定了关于修建摩天大楼的法律法规。它们规定，不应当再把摩天大楼的外形建成鞋盒子状。它们还规定，大楼建得越高，就必须建得越窄才是。

比方说，一栋摩天大楼的下部，可能会有整个城市街区那样宽。不过，待大楼向上建到一定数量的楼层之后，上面各层就必须从垂直于街道边缘的地方向内收缩，以不致挡住街道的光线。而大楼顶上的塔楼，却可以建得高耸入云；只要塔楼的基座面积，不超过摩天大楼底层地基面积的四分之一就行。

这种向内收缩的规定，使得新建的摩天大楼看上去与原来的那些摩天大楼大相径庭了。而原有的那些摩天大楼，样子也有了改变，因为建筑师已经尽力用过去的某些建筑风格，对它们进行了改造。有些大楼的底座，建有古希腊风格的立柱；但这些立柱并不承重，只是用作装饰。有些大楼的顶部，建有仿“文艺复兴”式建筑的那种巨型飞檐；但它们与底座上的立柱一样，根本没有实际用途，只具有装饰作用。

而新建的摩天大楼，却不会刻意模仿过去的某种建筑风格。有些人称它们是“纯粹的建筑”。建筑师们都尽力在不固守对外部进行老式装饰的情况下，将摩天大楼的样子建得漂亮、美观。他们开始使用色彩。有几座摩天大楼的外墙，都是用黑色砖块建成，而整栋建筑顶部则饰有金色。还有一些摩天大楼的下层用的是深红

with gold. Other skyscrapers have dark red bricks at the lower stories, with the color growing lighter and lighter toward the upper stories. The Chrysler Building and the Empire State Building use the bright nickel-color of stainless steel on the outside.

The hundreds of windows in a skyscraper are no longer just holes in the wall. They are used to add to the beauty of the building. In some skyscrapers, the windows look like stripes running from the ground to the top. They seem to carry the eye upward like the lines of a Gothic cathedral. Others have the windows arranged in rows that make stripes across the building instead of up and down. Other skyscrapers are made like blocks, small blocks on top of larger blocks.

Although I haven't yet told you what skyscrapers are used for, you probably know already. Some are used as offices where people work. Some are used as apartments where people live. Above all, skyscrapers must be useful. It costs millions and millions of dollars to build a real skyscraper, and the buildings have to make money after they are built.

Skyscrapers make money by having their rooms rented for offices or apartments. In an office skyscraper, there is often a bank or a store or even a theater on the first floor. Some office buildings have tens of thousands of people working in them, and when all these people start going home between 5 and 6 p.m., they jam the sidewalks and fill the streets with traffic.

帝国大厦，现存于纽约
（摄影：加里·威肯）

色的砖块，并且越往上，颜色就越淡。“克莱斯勒大厦”和“帝国大厦”的外墙，用的就都是鲜艳的镍色不锈钢呢。

摩天大楼里成百上千的窗户，也不再只是墙面上开出的一个个孔洞。如今，它们都被用于增添整栋建筑的美观了。有些摩天大楼的窗户，就像是从地面一直通到楼顶的一道道斑纹。它们就像是哥特式大教堂的线条那样，带着我们的目光一路向上望去。有些摩天大楼的窗户则是一排一排的，像是一道道横向而非竖向的斑纹。还有些摩天大楼建得则像积木一样，看上去就像是小积木搭在大积木之上呢。

尽管我还没有告诉你们，摩天大楼是用来做什么的，但你们很可能都已经明白了。有些是人们工作的办公大楼。有些是人们居住的公寓大楼。而最重要的是，摩天大楼必定是有某种用途的。修建一座真正的摩天大楼，成本需要数百万美元；因此，大楼建成之后，必须能够赚钱才行。

摩天大楼的赚钱之道，可以是将其中的房间当成办公室或者公寓出租。一栋办公大楼的一层，通常都有一家银行或者一家商店，甚至还会有一座剧院。一些办公大楼里，会有好几万人在里面上班哩；而当这些人全都在下午五点到六点钟之间开始下班回家时，他们就会将人行道和整个街道都挤得满满当当，引起交通拥堵呢。

Skyscrapers seem wonderful at a distance, they seem wonderful near at hand, and the more one learns about them the more wonderful they seem.

If you've never seen a high skyscraper, this will give you an idea of how very high one is. When skyscrapers were built in the first half of the twentieth century, the mail chutes had to be made with parts in them to slow up the letters dropping down from the top, for otherwise the letters would go so fast they would be scorched!

Now, you may wonder, how high can a skyscraper be? No one knows yet. The race to the sky started in 1885 and continues to this very day. The race began in New York between the builders of the Empire State Building and the Chrysler Building.

The builders for each structure knew the plan well, because they had seen the blueprints that showed exactly how to build the skyscraper. The builders of the Empire State Building knew they would win because they could see the plans guaranteed their building would be taller. Little did they know there was a part of the plan they had not seen.

When the Chrysler Building was nearing completion, the architect added an arch to the steel dome, and to finish it, added a 27-ton steel tip or spike called a *vertex*. The building gained 186 feet right away. The Chrysler builders knew they had

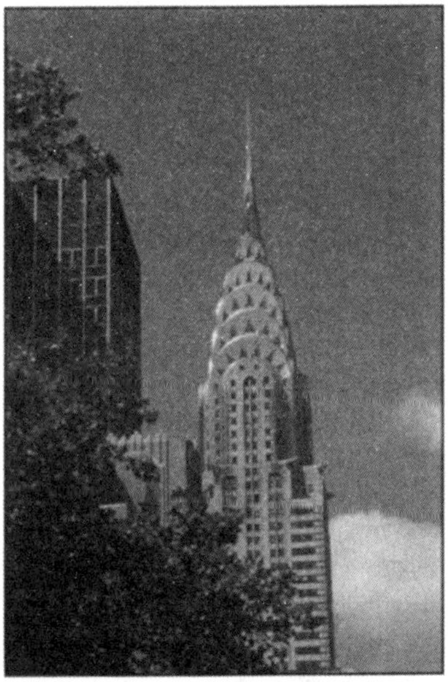

克莱斯勒大厦，现存于纽约

不管是远望还是近观，摩天大楼都令人惊叹；而我们对摩天大楼了解得越多，它们似乎就越令人觉得神奇。

倘若你们从来没有见过一栋高耸入云的摩天大楼，那么下面这一点，就会让你们对摩天大楼的高度有个概念了。在二十世纪上半叶修建的一些摩天大楼里，那种用于发送信件的邮道里必须装上某种部件，以减缓信件从顶层下落的速度才行；否则的话，由于下落速度太快，信件上就会留下摩擦过热时烧焦的痕迹哩！

那么，你们可能很想知道，一座摩天大楼究竟能够建到多高呢？迄今为止，可还没人说得清哩。向空中迸发的这种比赛，始于1885年，并且一直持续到了今天。而纽约的这种比赛，则是在“帝国大厦”和“克莱斯勒大厦”的建造者们之间开始的。

每栋建筑的建造者，都对建造规划了如指掌，因为他们已经看到过准确说明如何修建摩天大楼的设计图。“帝国大厦”的建造者们很清楚自己会赢，因为他们明白，自己的设计能让“帝国大厦”建得更高。可他们并不清楚的，是在整个设计图里，还有个部分他们并没有看到。

“克莱斯勒大厦”快要完工的时候，建筑师们在大楼的钢制穹顶上添加了一个拱顶；为了完成这座拱顶，建筑师们增加了二十七吨钢铁，建成了被称为“顶点”

won and had created the tallest building in the world. But they did not know what was coming next.

Suddenly, it was announced that the Empire State Building would be 202 feet taller than the Chrysler Building. Everyone wondered how this would be possible until they saw the trick. A mooring mast for *zeppelins*, sometimes called *blimps*, topped the building. Zeppelins are gas- filled airships. The fact that it would be impossible for any such blimp to land at 1,250 feet up in the air because of the crosswinds made no difference to the builders — they had their mast and won their race!

That very race has continued ever since. In New York, the famous twin towers of the World Trade Center rose side-by-side, one reaching 1,364 feet and the other reaching 1,368 feet until they were destroyed on September 11, 2001. The World Trade Center Memorial is intended to reach 1,776 feet, even taller than the skyscrapers in such places as Kuala Lumpur in Malaysia, and Shanghai in the People's Republic of China. So, you can see, the dream to reach the sky continues to come true.

的那个尖顶或者尖突。这栋建筑的高度马上就增加了一百八十六英尺。“克莱斯勒大厦”的建造者们以为自己赢了，并且建成了世界上最高的一座大楼。不过，他们并不知道接下来会发生的情况。

突然之间，有人宣称，“帝国大厦”会比“克莱斯勒大厦”高二百零二英尺。大家都不知道这是怎么可能做到的，直到最后才明白后者的花招。原来，“帝国大厦”的楼顶安装了一座齐柏林式飞艇的系泊塔；齐柏林式飞艇，有时也称为小飞艇，就是那种充气的飞艇。事实上，任何一艘这样的飞艇，都是不可能在空中一千二百五十英尺高的地方着陆的；不过，空中的侧风与建筑师们可没有什么关系。这就是说，他们只是因为修建了这样一座系泊塔，便赢得了这场高度比赛！

自那以后，这场比赛一直都没有停下来。在纽约，举世闻名的世贸中心双子塔肩并肩地耸立着，一座高达一千三百六十四英尺，另一座高一千三百六十八英尺；可最终，它们都在2001年的“9·11”事件中毁掉了。后来，美国人还打算将世贸中心纪念碑建到一千七百七十六英尺的高度，甚至超过了马来西亚的吉隆坡、中华人民共和国的上海这些地方的摩天大楼呢。由此，你们就可以看出，人类向天空拓展的梦想还会持续下去，并且变成现实。

Chapter 29 New Ideas

Have you ever seen a blue house? Blue all over, I mean — blue roof, blue walls, blue chimney. I've never seen a house like that, but I'm sure it would be unusual.

Have you ever seen a house all made of steel and glass? Such a house might seem unusual at first, but it would be a different type of variation from the blue house. The blue house might have no good reason for being blue; but a steel and glass house might have a very good reason for being made all of steel and glass.

After you became used to the steel and glass house, you might like it very much and find it more pleasant to live in than an ordinary house. But the blue house — well, I can't see what advantage you would get from a blue house, no matter how used to it you became.

A blue house and a steel and glass house have no ancestors. But most styles in architecture do have ancestors, long lines of ancestors.

Just as

⊙ the Roman style developed from the Greek,
⊙ the Romanesque style developed from the Roman,
⊙ the Gothic style developed from the Romanesque,

第29章　新的思想

你们有没有看见过蓝色的房子呢？我是说，房子上下里外都是蓝色的：蓝色的屋顶、蓝色的墙壁、蓝色的烟囱。虽说我从来没有见过这样的房子，但我敢肯定，这样的房子会是很不寻常的。

你们有没有见过一座全部用钢铁和玻璃建成的房子呢？这样的一座房子，乍一看去可能会很不寻常；但这种不寻常，却与蓝色房子给人的感受不一样。房子刷成蓝色，可能根本就没有什么合理的原因；而一栋钢铁玻璃的房子全由钢铁和玻璃建成，可能却会有很好的理由呢。

习惯了钢铁玻璃的房子之后，你们可能就会非常喜欢，并且发现住在这种房子里，比住在普通的房屋里更舒适。可蓝色的房子呢，我却看不出你们住在一座蓝色的房子里面会有什么好处，无论你们多么习惯这座房子。

蓝色的房子和钢铁玻璃房子都是没有原型的。不过，绝大多数建筑风格却是有原型的，并且有着一长串的原型呢。

比如：

⊙ 古罗马时期的风格，演变自古希腊时期的风格；
⊙ 诺曼式风格，演变自古罗马时期的风格；
⊙ 哥特式风格，演变自诺曼式风格。

so most new styles have grown from past styles in architecture.

And most buildings put up today make use of the styles that have been found good or beautiful (or both) in the past.

This modem use of past styles seems quite right as long as the modern buildings have the same uses as the buildings of the past. But many modern buildings have entirely new uses not even imagined by the architects of past styles. And so it seems to some architects that these buildings should be just as free from past styles as the uses of the buildings are. Why design a modern building in Gothic style when there is no connection between what you are building now and any building built when Gothic architecture was in its glory? Why have Roman columns on a gas station when the Romans had never heard of gas stations?

Many architects, therefore, find it better to design their buildings in a manner that they think suited to the modern use of the building. They think it better to have the style of the building show the purpose of the building than to have its use concealed in the forms of the past. This very modem style of architecture is sometimes called *functional* because it shows the use or function of the building.

You can see what I mean very well in the history of skyscrapers. As I mentioned, the early skyscrapers generally had huge Renaissance cornices. Often they had Greek or Roman columns at the main entrance. Later it was thought that the Gothic style was most suitable for skyscrapers, as in the Woolworth Building in New York City, because of the

因此，绝大多数新的建筑风格，都是从过去的建筑风格中发展演化而来的。

而且，如今修建的绝大多数建筑，利用的都是人们一直认为非常优秀或者漂亮（或者兼而有之）的、过去的风格。

只要现代建筑的用途与过去建筑的用途一样，那么现代人运用过去的建筑风格，就是很合理的一件事情。不过，许多现代建筑却有着全新的用途，运用过去风格的那些建筑师，可能想都没有想过哩。因此，在一些建筑师看来，这些建筑也应当像建筑的用途一样，完全摆脱过去的风格才是。既然人们正在修建的东西，与哥特式风格鼎盛时期修建的任何建筑都毫无关系，那么为什么还要用哥特式风格来设计一栋现代建筑呢？既然古罗马人连加油站都没有听说过，那么为什么修建一座加油站时，要用古罗马风格的立柱呢？

因此，许多建筑师都发现，最好是用他们自己觉得适合于现代建筑用途的方式来设计建筑。他们都觉得，最好是让建筑的风格体现出建筑的用途，而不要让过去的形式掩盖住建筑的用途。这种非常现代的建筑风格，有的时候被称为“实用风格”，因为它表明了建筑的用途或者功能。

从摩天大楼的发展历史中，你们就能很清楚地明白我的意思。正如我已经提到过的那样，早期的摩天大楼通常都建有属于“文艺复兴”式风格的巨型飞檐。它们的主入口，通常有古希腊或者古罗马风格的立柱。后来，人们认为，由于摩天大楼和哥特式大教堂都强调线条的垂直性，因此哥特式风格最适合于摩天大楼；比如，纽约市里的“伍尔沃斯大厦”，用的就是这种风格。不过，更多现代的摩天大楼在

vertical emphasis in both skyscraper and Gothic cathedral. But more recent skyscrapers are designed to look like what they are, steel skeletons covered with a protecting material.

A good example of such a skyscraper is the office building of the United Nations in New York City. It is a tall flat-sided building shaped like a thin closed book standing upright. It looks so thin that you think perhaps a very large pair of bookends might help it from blowing over. But no bookends are needed, for, like all skyscrapers, this building is anchored deep in the ground by strong steel girders. It is a beautiful building because it is so plain and simple. It has no fancy decorations, no gargoyles, no cornices, no sculptured figures. It has no curved lines; all its lines are straight up- and-down or straight across from side-to-side. The many windows of the United Nations building keep it from being too plain and simple. The windows also make it seem not only well lit but light in weight.

And what a lot of windows this building has! It takes someone several hours to wash all the windows in just one house. Think what a big job it is to wash all the windows in the United Nations building. It is supposed to have about five acres of windows.

Even dwellings have been designed to match their present purpose instead of using styles of the past. An American architect named Frank Lloyd Wright was one of the first to design houses in a functional style. He built houses in such new ways that they have become museums, for people to visit and study.

In Europe there has grown up a style of architecture that, like the house of glass and steel, has no ancestors. In Holland and Germany this functional style has been very much

设计上却更强调建筑的本来面貌，只是在钢铁结构之外，盖上了一层保护性的材料罢了。

这种摩天大楼的一个典范，就是纽约联合国总部的办公大楼。这是一座高高的、扁平的建筑，样子就像是一本薄薄的、合起来并直立着的书本。它看上去非常单薄，因此你们会觉得，要是有一对巨型书挡把它夹起来的话，可能就不会让风把它吹倒了。但是，其实它并不需要什么书挡，因为就像所有的摩天大楼一样，这座建筑也被深埋在地下的钢梁牢牢地固定着。这是一座非常漂亮的建筑，既朴素，又简单。整座大楼没有花哨的装饰，没有怪兽雨漏，没有飞檐，也没有雕像。大楼没有弧形的线条；所有线条都是笔直的纵向上下，或者左右水平的。联合国总部办公大楼上的许多窗户，使得整栋建筑不至于显得太过朴素和简单。这些窗户，也使得整座建筑看上去非但光线充足，而且显得其重量减轻了。

这座大楼上，有多少扇窗户啊！就算只是清洁一座住宅的所有窗户，一个人也得花上好几个小时。想想看，将联合国总部办公大楼的窗户全都清洁一遍，得是一件多么浩大的工程啊。据说，大楼所有窗户加起来，面积达到了五英亩左右呢。

连房屋的设计，也已经变成了适合房屋目前的用途，而不再用过去的建筑风格了。一位叫作弗兰克·劳埃德·赖特的美国建筑师，属于率先按照实用风格设计房屋的建筑师之一。他修建的房屋，风格非常新颖，因此这些房屋都成了博物馆，供人们前去参观和学习了。

在欧洲，也崛起了一种建筑风格；这种风格，就像玻璃钢铁房屋一样，也属于没有先例可循的原创风格。这种实用风格，已经在荷兰和德国广泛地应用到了住宅

used for dwellings. They are constructed of steel and glass, brick and concrete, and they seem to use these materials better than any past style could. For instance, they generally have flat roofs instead of sloping roofs, because the use of steel has made the roofs strong enough to stand any weight of snow that might fall upon them. These flat roofs are very convenient for sun porches.

You might think these very modern houses in Holland would spoil the looks of the quaint old Dutch brick houses with their high, steep roofs. But the new-style houses are generally built in groups. One little functional house in a whole street of old Dutch houses would look out of place. But when all the new houses are grouped together the effect is pleasant. They look tidy and shipshape with their smooth concrete and glass sides.

In America, dwellings have not generally been built in this style as much as in Europe. The United States has, however, been building more and more factories and warehouses and stores and office buildings in functional styles, and you can see examples in most of our big cities.

Of course you won't find much decoration on a functional factory. Such a building has smooth clean-cut lines and a good shape to make it attractive.

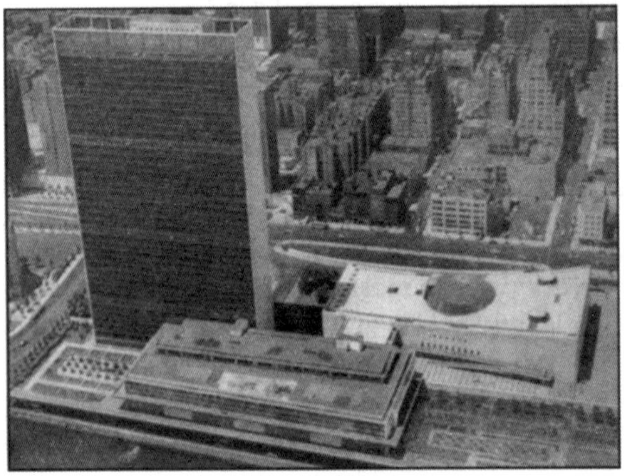

联合国总部大厦，现存于纽约
（由波士顿的大学印刷协会提供）

的设计上。这种住宅都是用钢铁和玻璃、砖块和混凝土建成的；而在这些住宅上，上述材料似乎也比在过去任何一种风格的建筑上应用得更加得心应手呢。比如说，这种住宅通常都是平顶，而不是坡顶；这是因为用了钢筋，使屋顶变得非常牢固，不管下多大多久的雪，屋顶都承受得住。而这种平顶，又非常适于建阳光浴室哩。

你们可能会认为，荷兰这些非常现代的房屋，会破坏荷兰那些精巧而古朴、有着高耸陡峭屋顶的砖结构房屋的原貌。不过，这些新式房屋通常都是集中修建的。倘若整条街上都是古老的荷兰式房屋，其中却有一栋属于实用风格的小房子，那么这座小房子就会显得不合适。但是，倘若所有新风格的房子都集中在一处，效果就会好得多了。它们的混凝土和玻璃外墙，会令它们看上去非常整齐，井然有序。

在美国，住宅通常都不像欧洲那样广泛使用这种风格来建造。然而，美国一直都在兴建越来越多的、属于实用风格的工厂、仓库、商店和办公大楼；因此，在我国的绝大多数大城市里，你们都可以看到这种风格的例子。

当然，在一座属于实用风格的工厂大楼里，你们是看不到很多装饰的。这种建筑都有光滑、轮廓鲜明的线条和漂亮的外形，使得它们看上去都很吸引人。要看现代装饰的话，那就得去看后来修建的那些摩天大楼了。许多新建的公共建筑，比如

The later skyscrapers are the buildings to look at for modern decoration. So also are many of the new public buildings such as libraries, railroad stations, and airports.

A building should be the right building for the place where it stands. A building may be very beautiful and still not be suitable for a certain place. A Greek temple would look out of place among skyscrapers. A modern glass and steel building would look wrong at a university where all the other buildings were in Gothic style.

A building also should be designed for its time in history. Each important period in the history of the world has had its own style of buildings quite different from the buildings that came earlier. Gothic style buildings are still being built, but the important buildings of our time will not be Gothic, or Romanesque, or Greek in style. They will have their own style, a new style unlike styles of earlier periods.

And so when you look at a building, especially a new building, you might ask a question or two. Does the building belong to the time when it was built? Is it the right design for its location? You might ask the building these questions. The building won't answer you in words, of course, but it will give you the answer if you look carefully.

In the future, perhaps buildings will actually answer your questions in words. It isn't too hard to imagine a talking building. You press a button on the wall and from an electric speaker in the building might come a voice saying, "I am a building made of steel, glass, and plastics. My architect was John Jones. I was erected in 1992. I don't want to boast, but I think I'm just the right building for this location. I hope you think so, too."

图书馆、火车站和机场，也是这样。

一座建筑，应当与建筑所在地的环境相协调才是。一栋建筑可能虽然漂亮得很，却仍然与某个地方格格不入。一座古希腊风格的神庙，倘若置身于一群摩天大楼之间，就会显得不合适。一座用玻璃钢铁建成的现代建筑，倘若位于一所其他建筑全属于哥特式风格的大学里，也会显得不合时宜呀。

一座建筑，还应当设计得与它所处的历史时代相符才行。世界历史上的每一个重要时期，都有属于该时期的建筑风格，会与以前的建筑风格大相径庭。虽说如今人们仍然还在修建属于哥特式风格的建筑，但属于我们这个时代的重要建筑，却既不会是哥特式风格、诺曼式风格，也不会是古希腊风格。它们会拥有自己的风格，一种与以前各个时期都不相同的独特风格。

因此，你们在观察一栋建筑，尤其是一栋新的建筑时，不妨问上一两个问题。这座建筑属于它修建时的那个时代吗？它的设计风格与所在地点相协调吗？你们可以对着那座建筑，问一问这些问题。当然，建筑是不会用话语来回答你们的；但如果你们仔细观察的话，建筑就会给出答案。

将来的建筑，没准真的会用话语来回答你们的问题呢。想象出一种会说话的建筑，并不是太难。只要按下墙上的一个按钮，建筑内部的一部电动扬声器里就会传来一个声音，说："我是一栋用钢铁、玻璃和塑料建成的大楼。我的建筑设计师是约翰·琼斯。我建造于1992年。我并不想自夸，但我觉得自己与这个地方非常协调。我希望您也这样认为。"

克里姆林宫，现存于莫斯科

How many different dreams did builders imagine and then show us? They seem to have no end at all.

There are building complexes that are so large, they became a city within a city, in one continual series of connected buildings, like the Kremlin in Moscow, the Forbidden City in Beijing, or the Grand Palace in Bangkok.

There are great parks in great cities, like Central Park in New York and Hyde Park in London.

There are tunnels that go underwater like the Channel Tunnel — nicknamed the "Chunnel" — that lets travelers go between Paris and London without having to leave their original train seat to board a boat to cross the English Channel. Other tunnels go through mountains, such as the Gotthard and the Simplon tunnels through the Alps.

建筑师们怀揣过多少不同的梦想，然后又将这些梦想呈现在我们面前啊。这些梦想，似乎永无止境呢。

有些复合式建筑，由于非常庞大，从而变成了城中城；其中，相互连通的建筑一栋接一栋，连绵不断。比如，莫斯科的克里姆林宫、北京的紫禁城或者曼谷的大皇宫，就是这样。

一些伟大的城市里，还建有许多了不起的公园；比如，纽约的中央公园和伦敦的海德公园。

还有许多水下隧道，比如英吉利海峡隧道（人们给它起了个绰号，叫作“通道”），它让旅客无须离开起初所乘的列车，再换乘船只横渡英吉利海峡，便可以在巴黎和伦敦之间来去。其他一些隧道则是山间隧道，比如穿越阿尔卑斯山的圣哥达隧道和辛普朗隧道。

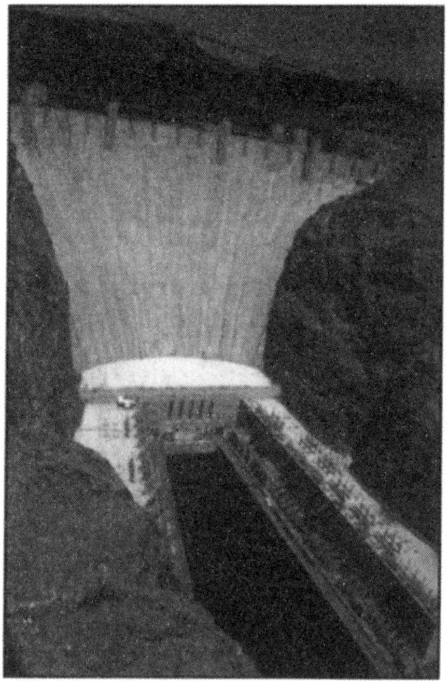

胡佛大坝，
现存于亚利桑那州与内华达州交界处

Imagine dams that hold great rivers back, such as Hoover Dam, or dykes that hold back the sea in the Netherlands so that the Dutch can reclaim land for farming that was once the floor of the sea.

Imagine canals that cut through a whole country to link oceans, such as the Panama Canal. Other dreams have become whole cities, such as Venice, which is made up of islands in a lagoon to keep residents safe from attack by land. St. Petersburg, in Russia, is also made up of islands that were built in a marsh to give Russia a port to the Atlantic Ocean.

And how did these inventions all begin? They began with builders of dreams who were master builders and master dreamers, too.

想一想那些扼住大江大河的水坝吧，比如胡佛大坝；再想一想荷兰那些阻住海浪的防波堤吧，它们让荷兰人可以将曾经是海床的那些地方改成农田。

再想一想那些穿越了整个国家、与海洋连通起来的运河，比如巴拿马运河吧。还有一些梦想，已经变成了整座整座的城市，比如威尼斯；这座城市，是由一个潟湖里的数个岛屿组成的，可以让那里居民免遭来自陆地上的攻击。俄罗斯的圣彼得堡，也是由许多岛屿组成的；该市修建在一片沼泽地里，从而让俄罗斯有了一座通往大西洋的港口。

这些发明创造，又是怎样开始的呢？它们始于那些拥有梦想的建造者；而这些建造者，既是建筑大师，也是梦想大师。